GUINNESS WORLD RECORDS 2016

CONTENTS

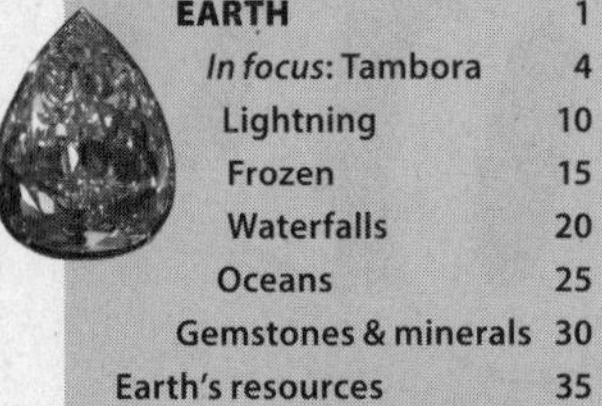

Tallest and shortest living men

On 13 Nov 2014, for the first time ever, Sultan Kösen (TUR), the world's tallest living man, met with Chandra Bahadur Dangi (NPL), the shortest living man. The historical encounter was organized as part of the 2014 Guinness World Records Day celebrations and took place at St Thomas' Hospital in London, UK. With a height difference of 196.4 cm (6 ft 5.5 in), their extreme sizes have made life challenging for both men – and given them much in common, too. Indeed, they got on so well that Sultan invited Chandra to visit him in Turkey. Find out more about these remarkable record holders on pp.113–117.

Published by
Guinness World Records Ltd,
184-192 Drummond Street, London, NW1 3HP

www.guinnessworldrecords.com

Accreditation

Guinness World Records has a very thorough accreditation system for records verification. However, while every effort is made to ensure accuracy, Guinness World Records Limited cannot be held responsible for any errors contained in this work. Feedback from our readers on any point of accuracy is always welcomed.

Abbreviations & Measurements

Guinness World Records Limited uses both metric and imperial measurements. The sole exceptions are for some scientific data where metric measurements only are universally accepted, and for some sports data. Where a specific date is given, the exchange rate is calculated according to the currency values that were in operation at the tie. Where only a year date is given, the exchange rate is calculated from 31 Dec of that year. "One billion" is taken to mean one thousand million.

General Warning

Appropriate advice should always be taken when attempting to break or set records. Participants undertake records entirely at their own risk. Guinness World Records Limited has complete discretion over whether or not to include any particular record attempts in any of its publications. Being a Guinness World Records record holder does not guarantee you a place in any Guinness World Records publication.

For permissions credits please see p. 587

British Library Cataloguing-in-Publication Data

A catalogue record for this book is available on request from the British Library

ISBN 978-1-910561-15-7

Design: Dan Prescott at Couper Street Type Co.
Special thanks: Ben Hollingum

Printed in Germany by GGP Media

5

6

7

8

BONUS CONTENT

Our picture editor, Michael, and videographer, Matt, have travelled the globe to secure amazing new images and footage. By visiting www.guinnessworldrecords.com/bonus, you can gain exclusive access to unseen content, which portrays the stories behind some of the fantastic records in both the *GWR* book and the *Gamer's Edition*. Plus, you'll get a unique behind-the-scenes insight into the world of Guinness World Records.

The content is exclusive, so you'll need to solve the clues on the site. Find the answers in the book, in order to access the content.

GAIN ACCESS TO EXCLUSIVE:

BONUS IMAGE GALLERIES

BEHIND-THE-SCENES VIDEO FOOTAGE

RECORD HOLDER INTERVIEWS

WWW.GUINNESSWORLDRECORDS.COM/BONUS

BE A RECORD-BREAKER

Are you Officially Amazing?

You don't have to be an Olympic athlete or Hollywood star to earn your place in history – record-breaking is free and open to absolutely anybody who wants to make an attempt. And you don't even need to do it at an official event or on TV… you can set a GWR record from the comfort of your own home.

However you choose to attempt your record, there are some basic steps we ask you to follow:

1 APPLY ONLINE

Your first task is to tell our Records Managers as much as you can about your record-breaking idea. The best way to do this is at **www.guinnessworldrecords.com/set-a-record**

Give us as much information as you can: what the record is, plus where, when and how you plan to make the attempt.

2 GET THE GUIDELINES

If you're planning on attempting an existing record, we'll email you the official guidelines that everyone must follow.

If it's a new idea, our Records Managers will discuss it and decide if it's something that qualifies as a Guinness World Records challenge. If approved, we'll write and send you the guidelines.

3 ATTEMPT YOUR RECORD

Once you have your guidelines, you're ready to attempt the record.

Be prepared to gather all the evidence you need to prove your claims, as outlined in the guidelines. Typically, we'll ask for things such as independent witness statements, log books, photographs, video footage and GPS readings.

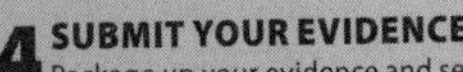

4 SUBMIT YOUR EVIDENCE

Package up your evidence and send it to us for approval. This can take a few weeks, so if you're in a rush, you can take advantage of our premium fast-track services.

If there are any queries, your assigned Records Manager will get in touch. If your claim is approved, you'll receive your official certificate in the post! Good luck!

...ON TELEVISION

Guinness World Records TV is filmed and broadcast all around the world. Every year, records are set and broken in front of a global audience numbering in the millions – could you be our next TV star?

Our talent scouts are always on the look-out for spectacular record ideas for our worldwide TV shows. When it comes to TV, the more dramatic and perilous the attempt the better!

If you're making a new application, let us know whether you think your record will work well in front of a TV audience. And if you're an existing record holder, you might get a call from our talent team asking you to be on a show.

Shown below are just two of the hundreds of record-breakers who enjoyed success on our TV shows...

Heaviest vehicle pulled using a hook through the nose and mouth

On 21 Mar 2012, on the Italian TV show *Lo Show dei Record* (above), filmed in Rome, Ryan Stock (CAN) pulled a 725-kg (1,598-lb) car using a metal hook running into his nostril, through his nasal cavity and out of his mouth! He went on to break his own record in 2013.

Fastest time to blow up and burst a hot-water bottle by a female

Strongwoman Shobha S Tipnis (IND) demonstrated her incredible lung power on our TV show *Guinness World Records – Ab India Todega* in Mumbai, India, on 17 Mar 2011. It took the aerobics coach just 41.2 sec to inflate and pop a rubber hot-water bottle... using only her breath.

...ONLINE

Log into the "Challengers" area of the GWR website for the chance to choose from hundreds of fun, accessible record attempts that you can try at home.

Challengers lets you enjoy the Guinness World Records experience in an instant. Select from five categories of record-breaking – Food and Drink, Household Items, Toys and Games, Sports and Fitness or Videogames – and choose a challenge to attempt. Then just read the guidelines and upload your video. Our judges will log in and adjudicate remotely.

If you're a wannabe record holder, try it now!
www.guinnessworldrecords.com/challengers

Highest score on Level 1-1 of "Poached Eggs" on Angry Birds for Chrome

The UK's "Sizzlin' Steve" Kish logged on to the Challengers site to show us how he amassed a record 37,510 points on *Angry Birds*. Kish is a Challengers regular, and among his numerous records are **fastest time to build a pyramid using 36 dice** (17.23 sec), **most coins stacked into a tower in 30 seconds** (51) and **most envelopes torn in half in 30 seconds** (46).

Most clothes pegs clipped to the face in one minute

Another Challengers fanatic is Italy's Silvio Sabba, who's pictured here successfully clipping 51 clothes pegs to his face in 60 sec. Ouch! Silvio's other records include **most coins balanced on the face in one minute** (57) and **most upright bottles walked across in one minute** (358).

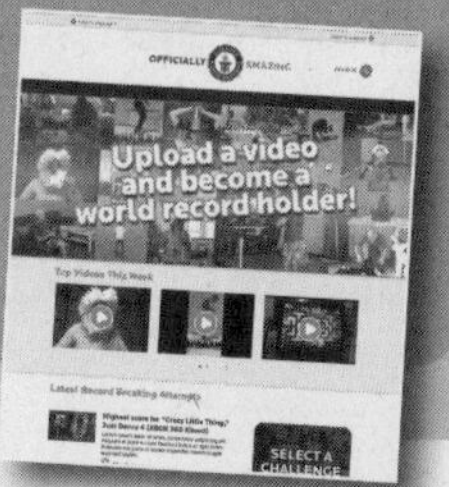

...LIVE!

Guinness World Records Live! venues are the only places you can turn up, select from a menu of records and make your attempt there and then, in front of an adjudicator.

The GWR Live! experience is available at two permanent locations in the USA – the Guinness World Records Museums in Hollywood, California, and San Antonio, Texas – and there are a variety of travelling roadshows and events in different countries around the world. Last year we visited the UK, Japan, Spain, Greece, the UAE and Canada.

Most coins balanced upright in 30 seconds (team of two)

Aaron Kingslien and Ashton Woerz (both USA) walked into the Guinness World Records Museum in Hollywood, California, USA, on 19 Feb 2015 as regular members of the public... and walked out as record holders! The dynamic duo beat the previous record by just one coin, balancing 20 coins on edge, but it was enough to earn them their official GWR certificates.

Most aerobic step-ups in 30 seconds

Jack Picton (UK) really stepped up to the challenge at Butlins in Skegness, UK, on 25 Apr 2015. Among the many records on offer at the holiday camp was a fitness challenge involving aerobic step-ups, and nimble-footed Jack achieved an impressive 40 in 30 sec.

EDITOR'S LETTER

In the past year, GWR processed **more than 100 record claims** every day!

Welcome to the latest, fully updated edition of the world's best-selling annual book. This edition provides a snapshot of the past year in record-breaking, plus a selection of classic superlatives from our archives. And as ever, the pages are packed with all-new illustrations and hundreds of never-before-seen photos.

We've had a remarkable 12 months here at Guinness World Records, celebrating the 60th anniversary of our first edition. It's been an honour to meet the record-breaking legends that have graced the pages of our book over the past six decades – you'll find a selection of them dotted throughout the book – and every one of them has delighted in receiving their special 60th anniversary certificates and medals. I'd like to say a personal thank you to them and to everyone who helped to make this past year so special.

There are now more ways of becoming a record-breaker than ever before, thanks to our book, website, TV shows, live events and museums (see pp.viii–xi), and it's clear that there's no let-up in interest from the public for record-breaking achievements. This year, our Editorial and Records Management Teams have processed 39,740 applications, 4,281 of which were ratified as official Guinness World Records titles.

GWR at the movies – *Paul Blart: Mall Cop 2*

At the *Mall Cop 2* premiere on 11 Apr 2015, actor Kevin James and 108 security guards from NYC participated in the **largest Segway riding lesson**, then set a second record for the **most people performing 360° spins on Segways simultaneously.** James and director Andy Fickman were awarded GWR certificates on the red carpet by adjudicator Alex Angert.

FACT

On receiving his certificate, Kevin said: "Meryl Streep has been nominated for 19 Academy Awards, winning three. I hold two GWR titles on a Segway. So, we're both doing well!"

RECORD APPLICATIONS IN NUMBERS

39,740 total applications received by GWR from 1 May 2014 to 30 Apr 2015

12,393 applications from the USA – the number one country for record claims and approvals

6,892 from the UK

3,253 from India

1,904 from Australia

1,576 from Canada

GWR Day on NBC's *Today*

He could barely speak by the end of it, but, after 34 hr on air at the NBC Studios in New York City, Al Roker of NBC's *Today* had completed the #Rokerthon: the **longest uninterrupted live TV weather report** (12–14 Nov 2014).

A second record awarded on *Today* to celebrate GWR Day was for the **largest high-heeled shoe** – Jill Martin and Kenneth Cole's design for this amazing shoe towered 6 ft 5 in (1.95 m); if you want to see it for yourself, walk on over to "Big Stuff" on p.203.

Most "liked" people on Facebook

On 20 Apr 2015, Colombian singer Shakira (b. Shakira Mebarak Ripoll) shared a photograph of herself on social media with her GWR certificates for the **most "liked" person on Facebook** (87,042,153 "likes" as of 25 Apr 2014) and the **first person to reach 100 million "likes"** (on 18 Jul 2014).

By 6 May 2015, however, as we went to press, Real Madrid soccer star Cristiano Ronaldo (PRT) had taken the most "liked" title, with 102,782,302 "likes". Shakira remains, though, the **most "liked" female on Facebook**.

MTV's Break the Record Week

Todrick Hall (CAN, pictured left with certificate) danced continuously to Beyoncé's biggest hits on MTV's #Beyoncéthon for 24 hr 9 min 8 sec on 9–10 Mar 2015, *bey*-coming the new record holder for the **longest dance marathon relay.** A second record for **most contributors to a time capsule in 24 hours** (1,016) was also set during the five-day live and online event, on 12–13 Mar.

Of these new and updated titles, just over 3,000 were supplied by our team of external consultants and advisors. These are the (usually unsung) heroes behind the records, and this year we wanted to introduce them and put some faces to names.

You can find out more about the people who unearth the records on pp.578–82. They really are an eclectic bunch, ranging from archaeologists and cosmologists to gerontologists and zoologists. Our Founding Editors, Norris and Ross McWhirter, always described their role as coaxing "the -ests from the -ists", and this job is as relevant today as it was 61 years ago.

A SENSE OF SCALE

You won't be surprised to learn that we're a little obsessed by measurements and metrics here at GWR. For this year's hardback edition, we decided to run a regular feature across the bottom of each page that gave

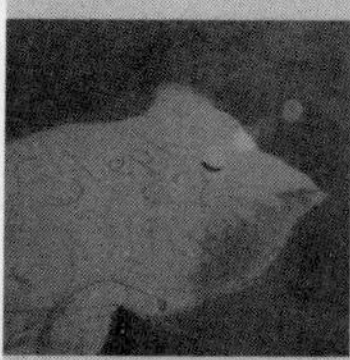

Largest tyre track image

When 12-year-old Stephanie wanted to send a message to her astronaut father on the *International Space Station*, she enlisted the help of Hyundai Motor Company (KOR) to create a 59,808,480.26-sq-ft (5,556,389.63-m2) image at Delamar Dry Lake in the Nevada desert on 18 Jan 2015.

It took 11 Hyundai Genesis vehicles, moving in unison, to recreate the handwritten message, which was roughly one-and-a-half times the size of Central Park in New York. Months of planning paid off, and Stephanie's father immediately saw it from space.

First person to swim from Cuba to Florida without a shark cage or fins

From 31 Aug to 2 Sep 2013, Diana Nyad swam from Havana in Cuba to Key West, Florida, in 52 hr 54 min 18.6 sec. Diana had attempted the 103-mi (166-km) swim four times before her successful, unassisted crossing. Afterwards she was honoured with a commemorative 60th anniversary GWR certificate and medal for her historic achievement.

the measurements of everything from the diameter of the smallest subatomic particle to the width of the observable universe. For this paperback edition, with space on each page at a premium, we've moved this feature to the end of the book (pp. 612–15), where we present a selection of our favourite entries from the list. An explanation of the concept behind this feature, and some more information our peculiar obsession, can be found on p. xx.

As well as looking in depth at scale, we've opened each chapter with a more detailed exploration of a single record. We've called these "In Focus" features, as they examine in detail the workings behind the superlatives, whether it's the

GWR at Super Bowl XLIX

At Super Bowl 49 (see pp.574–77), Tom Brady and Bill Belichick cemented their legacy while NBC's broadcast and Katy Perry's halftime show attracted record-breaking audiences. In the weeks and days leading up to Super Bowl Sunday, other records were set in Arizona.

The record-breaking started on 14 Jan 2015, two weeks prior to the New England Patriots' victory over the Seattle Seahawks. The Arizona Super Bowl Host Committee, in conjunction with Playworks and UnitedHealthcare, achieved the **largest game of red light/green light** with 1,136 participants from 18 schools across Phoenix.

Then some of the NFL's stars stepped up. On the Tuesday of Super Bowl week, NBC Sports teamed up with the Arizona Cardinals' All-Pro cornerback Patrick Peterson to attempt the **most selfies taken in one hour**. The Pro Bowler snapped 1,449 selfies with students and faculty from Deer Valley High School (below), proving himself one of the greatest selfie-taking talents.

Lastly, on the Thursday before the Super Bowl, electrifying New York Giants receiver Odell Beckham Jr and future Hall of Famer Drew Brees of the New Orleans Saints set a brand new record title on the set of ESPN's *NFL Live*, for the **most one-handed football catches in one minute** (33, above). The feat instantly became a viral sensation, with receivers all over the country attempting to break the record using a camcorder. But as of press time, no one had officially done so.

Guinness World Records has sold more than **134 million copies** to date!

Academy of Country Music Awards

A turn-out of 70,252 fans on 19 Apr 2015 made the 2015 ACM Awards the **highest-attended live music awards show.**

Among the superstars to receive GWR certificates, Miranda Lambert (right) achieved the **most consecutive wins of the ACM Female Vocalist of the Year** (six); Brad Paisley (left) the **most consecutive wins of the ACM Male Vocalist of the Year** (five); and Rascal Flatts (above left) the **most wins** (and **most consecutive wins**) **of the ACM Vocal Group of the Year**.

deadliest volcano (Tambora, pp.4–9), the **largest animal** (the blue whale, pp.44–49), the **fastest sport stacking** (pp.140–45) or the workings of the **largest particle accelerator** (the Large Hadron Collider, pp.326–31). We also turn our attention to the **heaviest weight lifted by a human** (pp.476–81) – a classic superlative that was for years

Most live concerts in 24 hours (multiple cities)

Starting in New York City on ABC's *Good Morning America* and performing in six states, country music star Hunter Hayes packed 10 shows and a tour's worth of energy into one day on 9–10 May 2014. The tour celebrated the launch of his album *Storyline* and was a fund-raiser for the charity Feeding America.

obscured by misinformation, falsehoods and inconsistencies, but this year we finally put the record straight.

What this weight-lifting record shows is that there are still many superlatives yet to be set or fully ratified. This has been the story of Guinness World Records since day one: there's no end to record-breaking. And there are new technologies emerging all the time, which means that our adjudicators and researchers will always be busy establishing the extremes.

NEW TOPICS

Nowhere is this novelty more exciting and fast-moving than in the digital realm. As well as the usual exploration of web records (pp.374–79), look out this year for

#EverySimpsonsEver

From 21 Aug to 1 Sep 2014, FXX aired every *Simpsons* episode for the **longest uninterrupted broadcast of a TV franchise** (205 hr 50 min 4 sec). To promote this attempt at the 2014 San Diego Comic-Con International, FXX also set the record for **most contributions to a painting by numbers** (2,263).

IN NUMBERS

256
Nobel Prize laureates from the USA – the **most Nobel winners by country**

163 m
Facebook users in the USA – the **most Facebook users by country**

53,364
People aged 100 years old or more in the USA – the **most centenarians by country**

412
Billionaires in the USA – the **most billionaires by country**

Congratulations James and Ann!

Pictured here are James Foley and his friend Ann, who were the lucky winners of a contest we ran in the USA with United Airlines for a trip for two to New York.

James and Ann spent three days in the Big Apple enjoying visits to record-breaking locations, as well as going to watch the **longest-running musical on Broadway** – *The Phantom of the Opera*.

Largest sports tournament bracket

This year, the National Collegiate Athletic Association (NCAA) gave new meaning to the idea of March Madness by unveiling a 43,480.8-sq-ft (4,040-m2) bracket on the side of the J W Marriott hotel in Indianapolis, Indiana, where the 2015 Final Four and Championship game was won by the Duke Blue Devils. GWR presented their certificate on the court at Lucas Oil Field, Indianapolis, on Final Four Friday, 3 Apr 2015 (left).

new categories for podcasting (pp.403–07), Netflix (p.411), YouTube (pp.413–17) and apps (pp.418–21). Other new topics this year include twins (pp.128–32), pirates (pp.247–51), balloons – both hot-air (pp.463–67) and modelling (pp.204–08) – and videogame favourite *Minecraft* (pp.319–22).

Finally, another new feature this year is the Profile Panel, which you'll find running down the right-hand side of most subject spreads. Here, we take the chance to delve a little deeper into one particular topic, and in some cases we've been able to bring you

Most bottles played in a musical performance

On 19 Mar 2015, a grand total of 1,100 bottles were played by 172 musicians at the Jim Pattison Group "Partners in Pride" Executive Conference in Surrey, British Columbia, Canada. Participants played "Happy Birthday" to celebrate the 100th anniversary of the founding of the Overwaitea Food Group, western Canada's largest food store chain.

exclusive Q&As. Look out for interviews with record holders such as golfer Rory McIlroy, Everest guide Apa Sherpa, graphic novelist Alan Moore, explorer Sir Ranulph Fiennes and entrepreneur and kite-surfer Sir Richard Branson.

As these record holders confirm, every superlative tells a story, and this year's book is packed with thousands of them, each one more impressive than the next. I hope you enjoy them all…

Craig Glenday
Editor-in-Chief

Tallest teenager

On 30 Apr 2015 at Pediatric Associates in Doral, Florida, Kevin Bradford (b. 27 Oct 1998) measured in at 7 ft 1 in (2.16 m). Aged 16 years 185 days, he was officially the world's tallest teenager. Like many boys his age, Bradford, of Virginia Gardens, Florida, is an avid gamer and basketball player.

Jimmy Kimmel Live!

Back in 2008, Guillermo Díaz Rodriguez of ABC's *Jimmy Kimmel Live!* set the inaugural record for the most underpants worn at one time (100 pairs). It was broken later that year and has been surpassed another nine times since then! For nearly seven years, we eagerly waited to see how Guillermo would follow up his record.

Well, we are thrilled to welcome him back into the *Guinness World Records* book again, with the parking-lot security guard turned TV personality adding two more Guinness World Records titles to his name in the past year.

To get into the holiday spirit on 16 Dec 2014, Guillermo wrapped himself up warm in the **most sweaters worn simultaneously**, a total of 25 on the set of *Jimmy Kimmel Live!* The sweaters, which were all of the distinctive Christmas variety, were so tight that they restricted the mobility of Guillermo's arms, and GWR adjudicator Philip Robertson had to hang his certificate over his neck (above).

As many record-breakers know, however, one title is never enough, and Guillermo and Jimmy Kimmel were back a few months later for another attempt at making history. This time, at the South by Southwest Festival in Austin, Texas, Guillermo set another inaugural record live on air, for the **most lanyards worn simultaneously**, with 300 wrapped around his neck – and, indeed, well up to his ears (below).

Guinness World Records is excited to see what record Jimmy comes up with for Guillermo next… Hey Jimmy, Guillermo's old record for the **most underpants worn at one time** now stands at a mere 266 and is ready to be challenged!

A SENSE OF SCALE

The **largest named number** is the **googolplex**: a 1 followed by 10^{100} zeroes!

How many biscuits are in a "family pack"? What is a "generous portion"? And precisely how much milk is a "glass and a half" in Cadbury chocolate? As an introduction to *Guinness World Records 2016*, we present a handy guide to measurement units and understanding scale.

The informal measurement values mentioned above may convey a sense of the amounts on offer, but they are simply too vague to be of much use outside the world of advertising – after all, would you trust a dentist who measured out anaesthetic in "generous portions"?

Our quest to find accurate ways of measuring and describing the world stretches all the way back to ancient times, when the demands of fair trade saw the first attempts at standardization. Some of the earliest of these standard measures were based on the weight and volume of grains and seeds – the term "carat", for example, which is still used by the jewellery trade, dates back to the use of carob seeds as a means of checking weight, the word "carat" being a corruption of "carob".

Length measurements were based on the tools that were closest to hand, such as… well, the hand (and don't forget the arm and the fingers). Five thousand years ago, it would have been a common sight to see people measuring out anything from cloth to capital cities using the "cubit", which is the distance between the elbow and the outstretched middle finger. Shorter lengths were measured using hands or fingers – one

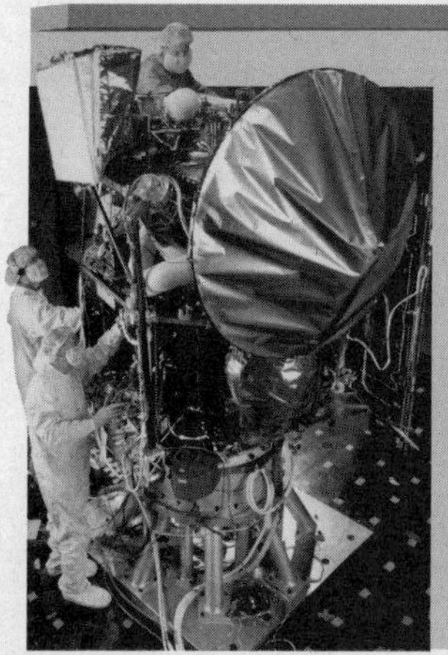

Costliest metric-imperial conversion error

On 23 Sep 1999, NASA's *Mars Climate Orbiter* probe passed behind the planet Mars – and disintegrated in the Martian atmosphere. The cause? Human error involving a measurement conversion. The on-board software had been written using metric units of thrust, but imperial units had been used to enter course correction commands from Ground Control. The mission had cost $327.6 m (£200.5 m).

FACT

The Pirahã tribe in the Amazon region of Brazil has no concept of counting (other than "more than" and "less than"), making them the **culture with the fewest numbers**.

definition of the "inch", for example, was based on the width of the thumb (and another based on the distance between the final joint to the tip); the height of horses is still often measured out in "hands" (see *Vitruvian Man* on p.xxiii).

Our association with horses, of course, gave us the term "horsepower", which remains as a measure of the power of an engine, although it's no longer a vague term: one horsepower is precisely 745.699872 watts.

Improvements in accuracy of all forms of measurement grew out of necessity. As we moved gradually from building mud huts to crafting international space stations, the need for standardization saw a consensus emerge and today, with only three exceptions – Liberia, Myanmar and the USA – every country in the world has adopted, at least officially, the metric system.

This is why we can now say, with absolute confidence, that a "glass and a half" of milk – the slogan once used to describe Cadbury chocolate – is equal to precisely 426 ml (14.4 US fl oz) for every 227 g (8 oz) of chocolate.

All about that base: the SI units

The SI base units (from Le Système International d'Unités) are seven universal fixed measurements defined by the International Bureau of Weights and Measures and agreed in 1960. Certain base units have an interdependency (illustrated below): the metre, for example, is defined by the speed of light so is therefore determined by the definition of the second.

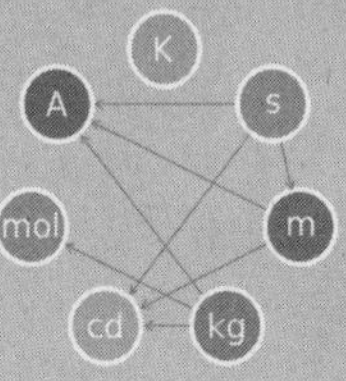

Length: metre
Distance travelled by light in a vacuum in 1/299,792,458th of a second

Mass: kilogram
Mass of the physical "prototype" kilogram

Time: second
9,192,631,770 periods of radiation corresponding to the transition between two levels of the ground state of an atom of caesium-133

Electric current: ampere
Current that, in two parallel conductors placed 1 m apart, would produce a force equal to 2×10^{-7} newton per m

Temperature: kelvin
1/273.16 of the thermodynamic temperature of the triple point of water

Amount of substance: mole
Quantity that contains as many elementary entities as there are atoms in 0.012 kg of carbon-12

Brightness: candela
Luminous intensity of a source that emits radiation of frequency 540×10^{12} hertz and a radiant intensity of 1/683 watts per steradian

Kardashian
Unit of time used to measure the length of a marriage; based on the 72-day union of Kim Kardashian and Kris Humphries, so one year of marriage is equal to 5.07 Kardashians

New York second
Arguably the shortest possible unit of time in the entire universe; corresponds to the period between traffic lights turning green and the driver behind you honking their horn

Milli-Helen
Based on Helen of Troy (the "face that launched a thousand ships"), a milli-Helen is the beauty required to launch just one ship

Warhol
A measure of fame based on artist Andy Warhol, who claimed that "everyone will be world-famous for 15 minutes"; by extension, one kilo-Warhol is equal to 15,000 minutes (or 10.42 days) in the spotlight, while one mega-Warhol equates roughly to a career's worth of fame (28.5 years).

Units of fun

It could be argued that a metre is only a metre because a committee of very important people have agreed on a definition. But why must we restrict ourselves to sensible measures? Why not use Warhols or Kardashians? Here, we trawl the internet for some alternatives to the SI units.

FACT

Road signs in the USA are almost universally given in imperial units, although metric distances are permitted and often included on the same sign (typically on roads nearer Canada and Mexico).

c. 30,000 BC
Earliest known use of tally sticks (bones into which quantities are carved in vertical groups)

c. 3000 BC
Egyptian cubit (distance from elbow to tip of the middle finger) becomes the **first standardized measure**

c. 2600 BC
Carob seeds (above) and grains of wheat – among other things – are adopted as standard weights in the Indus valley

c. 2540 BC
The Great Pyramid at Giza is completed using the royal cubit; the sides are accurate to within 0.05% of each other

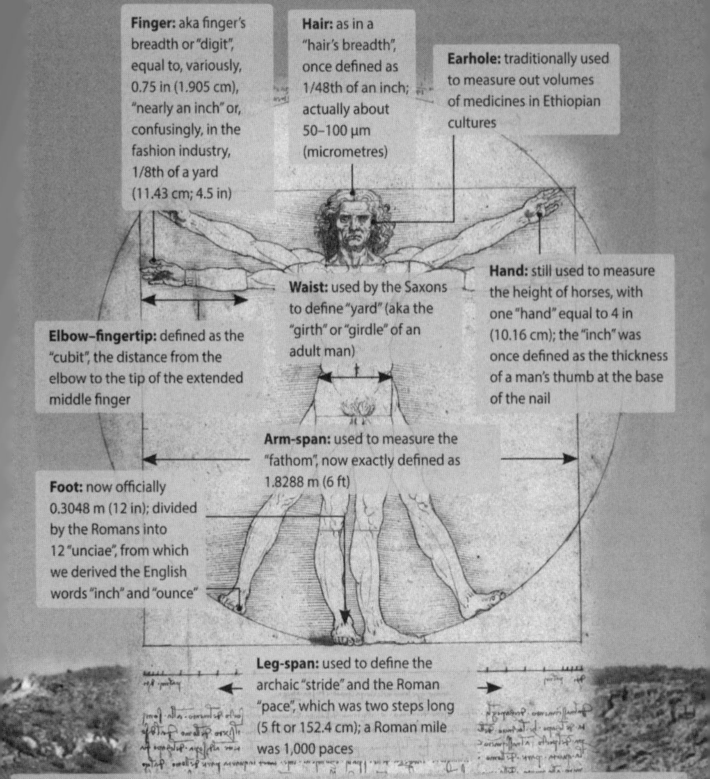

Finger: aka finger's breadth or "digit", equal to, variously, 0.75 in (1.905 cm), "nearly an inch" or, confusingly, in the fashion industry, 1/8th of a yard (11.43 cm; 4.5 in)

Hair: as in a "hair's breadth", once defined as 1/48th of an inch; actually about 50–100 μm (micrometres)

Earhole: traditionally used to measure out volumes of medicines in Ethiopian cultures

Hand: still used to measure the height of horses, with one "hand" equal to 4 in (10.16 cm); the "inch" was once defined as the thickness of a man's thumb at the base of the nail

Waist: used by the Saxons to define "yard" (aka the "girth" or "girdle" of an adult man)

Elbow–fingertip: defined as the "cubit", the distance from the elbow to the tip of the extended middle finger

Arm-span: used to measure the "fathom", now exactly defined as 1.8288 m (6 ft)

Foot: now officially 0.3048 m (12 in); divided by the Romans into 12 "unciae", from which we derived the English words "inch" and "ounce"

Leg-span: used to define the archaic "stride" and the Roman "pace", which was two steps long (5 ft or 152.4 cm); a Roman mile was 1,000 paces

Human scale

Pictured above is the *Vitruvian Man*, a drawing by Italian polymath Leonardo da Vinci (c. 1490). It takes its inspiration from the writings of the Roman architect Vitruvius (1st century BC), who documented the proportions of the human body in relation to architecture, and the use of body parts in standardizing units of measurement.

As Vitruvius explained, the human body is indeed the oldest measuring device. The foot, for example, has been used throughout history as a standard, as have many other body parts such as the arm or finger. Over time, these regional, informal measurements were formally standardized and realized in physical prototypes – such as the royal cubit – to avoid differences in body sizes.

c. 1650 BC
The "mina" emerges as a form of currency and the first widely used standard weight; invented by the Babylonians, the unit (estimated today at somewhere between 640 and 978 g) is adopted by Hittites, Phoenicians, Assyrians, Egyptians, Hebrews and Greeks

1215
In England, the Magna Carta sets out standard measures for, among other things, wine and beer

1586
Flemish mathematician and engineer Simon Stevin – who had introduced decimal fractions to Europe – suggests a measurement system based on decimals, laying the foundation for what would eventually become the metric system

1799
France becomes the **first country to adopt the metric system**; pictured is a metre rod in Paris, placed for public use

1960
Seven SI base units are agreed and (almost) universally adopted (see panel on p.xxi)

Is this why America isn't metric?

On 17 Jan 1794, French scientist Joseph Dombey set sail for the USA to present Congress with solid copper prototypes of the newly named metre and kilogram. They were to be used to help the USA reform the system of weights and measures it had inherited from Britain. Alas, Dombey never reached American soil.

In March, his ship was caught up in a storm so violent that it was blown south to the Antilles, forcing Dombey to shelter at Pointe-à-Pitre on Guadeloupe. On landing, he was promptly arrested and imprisoned by the governor, a French royalist opposed to the new regime in France. By the time he was released and set on his way again, Dombey had picked up a terrible fever.

Matters then took a turn for the even worse when, barely out of harbour, Dombey's ship was attacked by a gang of scurvy-ridden English pirates. The pirates stole the copper metre and kilogram and kidnapped Dombey, taking him to the island of Montserrat, where they held him for ransom.

In April, while still held by the pirates, Dombey died of his fever. His metre and kilogram prototypes were lost forever and the USA missed out on an opportunity to embrace the metric system, remaining to this day one of only three countries in the world that doesn't use it.

EARTH

Oldest national park

Yellowstone National Park – situated primarily in the state of Wyoming, USA – was designated on 1 Mar 1872 by President Ulysses S Grant. The park is home to more than 10,000 geothermal features, such as springs, mudpots and fumaroles (openings in the ground that vent steam and natural gases). Pictured overleaf is the Grand Prismatic Spring – the USA's largest hot spring. As beautiful as they are, it's worth bearing in mind that all these phenomena are fuelled by a supervolcano lurking underground, which, after 640,000 years of dormancy, is overdue an eruption…

According to UNESCO, Yellowstone plays host to the **largest concentration of geysers**, with more than 300, including "Old Faithful" (above). This amounts to two-thirds of the global geyser total.

CONTENTS

FACT

The Grand Prismatic Spring gains its intense colouration of red, orange, yellow, green and blue rings from several colonies of bacteria, which thrive at various temperatures in the mineral-rich water.

IN FOCUS
TAMBORA

The Tambora eruption killed approximately 71,000 people, making it the **deadliest in recorded history**

Mount Tambora, on the Indonesian island of Sumbawa, was thought to be an extinct volcano when first discovered by Europeans. On 5 Apr 1815, however, this sleeping giant awoke and began to erupt.

Beneath the mountain, the pressure inside its magma chamber had been increasing and the weight of the stratovolcano above was no longer sufficient to contain it. Explosions like distant gun fire were heard 1,400 km (870 mi) away, and the next day a light ash was falling all over the region. But this was just a precursor.

On 10 Apr, Tambora literally blew its top. Three distinct columns of fire shot lava and ash into the sky before merging into one and then becoming a terrifying plume reaching 43 km (26 mi) high.

Explosion equivalent to 800 megatons of TNT throws ejecta up to 43 km (26 mi) high
Grey ash thrown for kilometres across Sumbawa
Plumes of flame issue for three hours
Initial eruption heard 1,400 km (870 mi) away on Indonesian island of Ternate
Secondary vents
Magma rises through central vent
Settlements
Magma chamber: underground pool of liquid rock at a pre-eruption pressure of 4–5,000 bars (1 bar = atmospheric pressure)

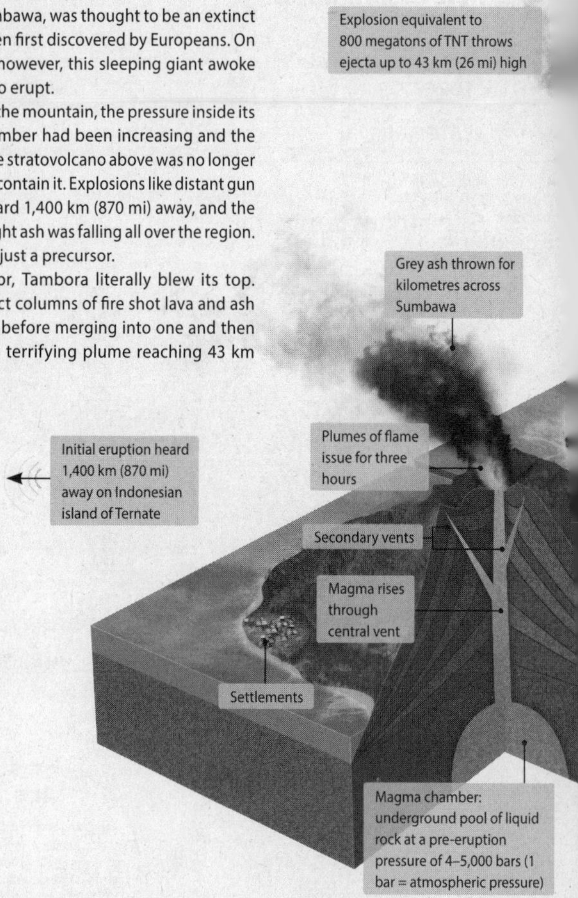

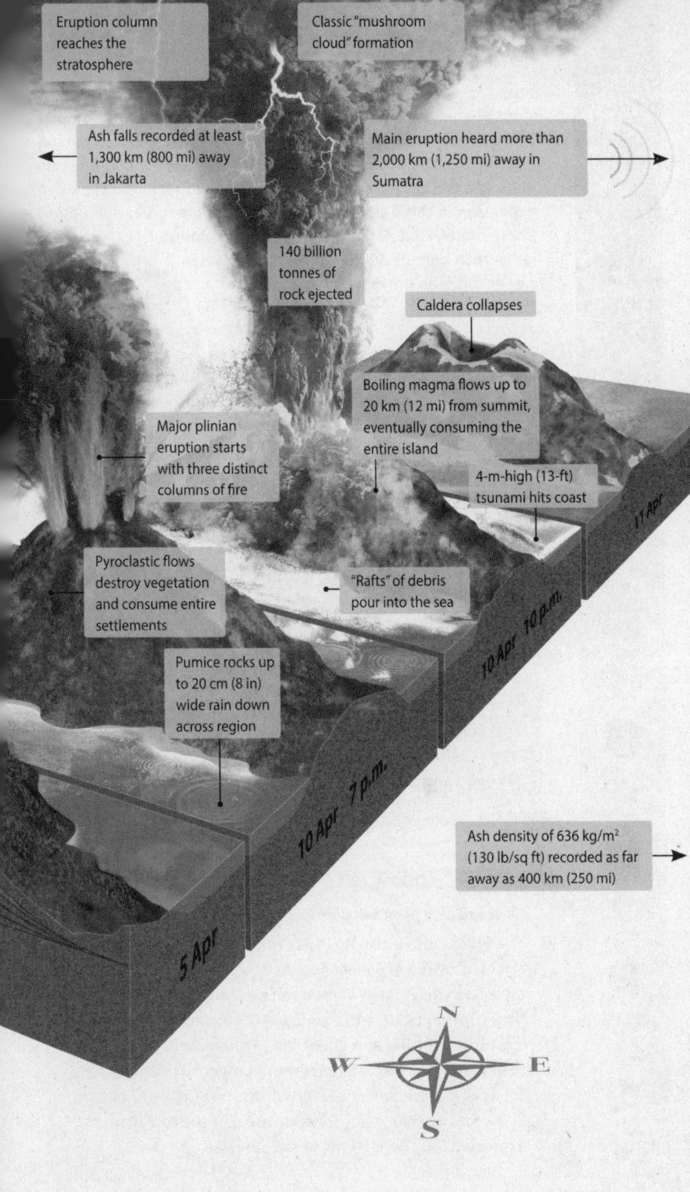

Eruption column reaches the stratosphere
Classic "mushroom cloud" formation
Ash falls recorded at least 1,300 km (800 mi) away in Jakarta
Main eruption heard more than 2,000 km (1,250 mi) away in Sumatra
140 billion tonnes of rock ejected
Caldera collapses
Boiling magma flows up to 20 km (12 mi) from summit, eventually consuming the entire island
Major plinian eruption starts with three distinct columns of fire
4-m-high (13-ft) tsunami hits coast
11 Apr
Pyroclastic flows destroy vegetation and consume entire settlements
"Rafts" of debris pour into the sea
10 Apr 10 p.m.
Pumice rocks up to 20 cm (8 in) wide rain down across region
10 Apr 7 p.m.
Ash density of 636 kg/m² (130 lb/sq ft) recorded as far away as 400 km (250 mi)
5 Apr
N
W
E
S

1
Tambora
Indonesia 1815
VEI 7

2
Paektu (Changbai)
China/Korea AD 1000
VEI 7

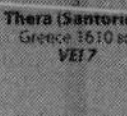

3
Thera (Santorini)
Greece 1610 BC
VEI 7

4
Hatepe
New Zealand AD 180
VEI 7

5
Samalas
Indonesia 1257–58
VEI 7

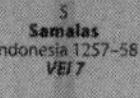

6
Ambrym
Vanuatu AD 50
VEI 6+

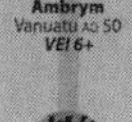

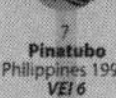

7
Pinatubo
Philippines 1991
VEI 6

8
Novarupta
Alaska, USA 1912
VEI 6

9
Santa Maria
Guatemala 1902
VEI 6

10
Krakatoa
Indonesia 1883
VEI 6

As a liquid, magma holds dissolved gases, just like a bottle of soda contains CO_2, and under sufficient pressure these gases remain dissolved. But as the magma reached the surface, the pressure was gone and the gas formed bubbles in the liquid rock. The explosive expansion of these bubbles made the Tambora "plinian" eruption phase more akin to an ongoing nuclear explosion, rather than a gentle outpouring of syrupy lava as we see today on the Hawaiian Islands.

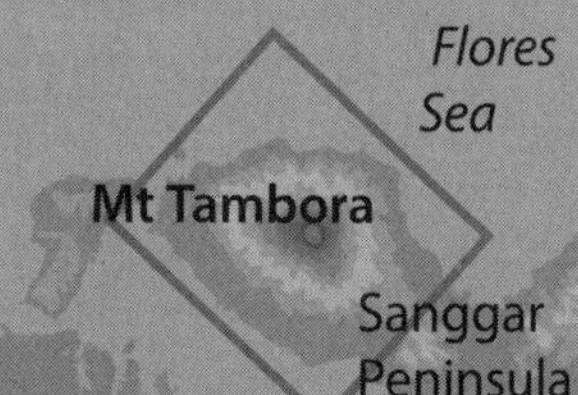

Locator

Tambora (-8.25°S, 118°E) is a stratovolcano found on the island of Sumbawa in Indonesia. It forms the 60-km-wide (37-mi) Sanggar Peninsula to the north of the island.

Volcanic Explosivity Index

The Volcanic Explosivity Index (VEI) is a measure of the magnitude of a volcano. The scale – from 0 to 8 – is based on the volume of material ejected, the height of the eruption cloud and a series of other variables. It's a logarithmic scale, so a VEI of 8 is *10 times* more powerful than a VEI of 7, and *100 times* more powerful than a VEI of 6. Luckily, there hasn't been an eruption with a VEI of 8 in the last 10,000 years. Here we present the top 10 most explosive eruptions of the past 2,000 years.

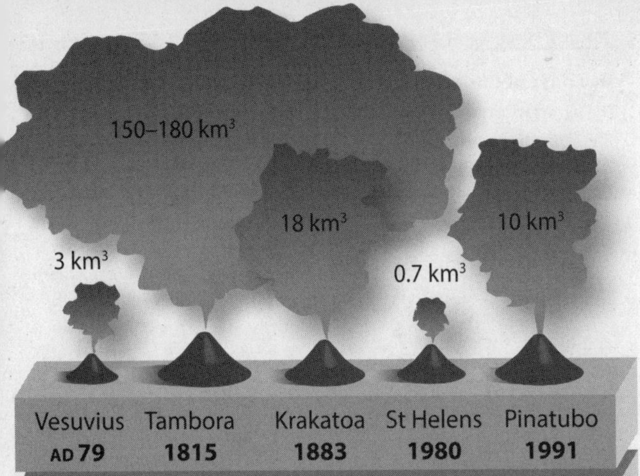

150–180 km^3

3 km^3

18 km^3

0.7 km^3

10 km^3

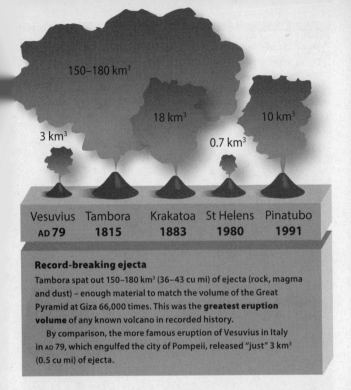

Vesuvius	Tambora	Krakatoa	St Helens	Pinatubo
AD 79	1815	1883	1980	1991

Record-breaking ejecta

Tambora spat out 150–180 km^3 (36–43 cu mi) of ejecta (rock, magma and dust) – enough material to match the volume of the Great Pyramid at Giza 66,000 times. This was the **greatest eruption volume** of any known volcano in recorded history.

By comparison, the more famous eruption of Vesuvius in Italy in AD 79, which engulfed the city of Pompeii, released "just" 3 km^3 (0.5 cu mi) of ejecta.

This phase of the eruption lasted around an hour and unleashed the deadliest of volcanic hazards: pyroclastic flows. These currents of ash rushed down the sides of the volcano at speeds of up to 725 km/h (450 mph). Anything in their path was destroyed by the seething mass of gas and rock at around 1,000°C (1,830°F). All vegetation on the peninsula was incinerated, and villages were buried under ash and rock around 1.5 m (5 ft) deep.

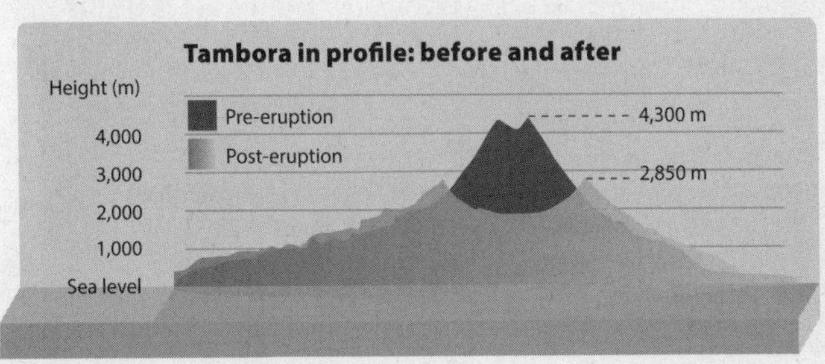

Tambora in profile: before and after

Two days of darkness

The pyroclastic plume that exploded from Tambora was driven west, covering neighbouring islands in ash 50 cm (20 in) deep. After the eruption, the area around Tambora – up to 600 km (370 mi) away – was plunged into two days of pitch darkness. The ash cloud, which reached the stratosphere, soon dispersed across the entire northern hemisphere, with the USA and the UK both reporting abnormal weather effects as a result (see "The year without summer", opposite).

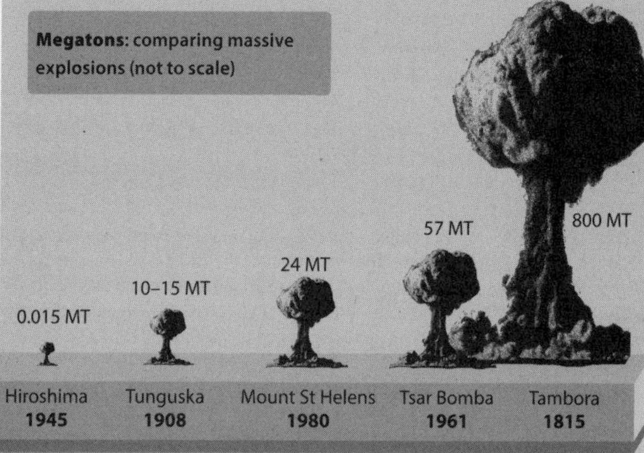

What is a megaton?

Large explosions are measured in megatons (MT), with 1 MT equal to the energy released in 1 million tonnes of the explosive TNT, aka trinitrotoluene. (The "mega-" prefix indicates a million.) Just 1 MT is enough to power a typical Western home for *c.* 120,000 years.

FACT

In just 24 hours, the Tambora ash cloud was the size of Australia. Within two weeks, an aerosol of sulphuric acid – an estimated 100 million tonnes of it – had spread around the world.

By 15 Apr, the explosions had ceased but the volcano continued to erupt clouds of ash for the next week. As these cleared, the volcano revealed its new shape; the cone had collapsed in on itself, filling the void left by the depleted magma chamber below. A vast caldera 6–7 km (3.5–4.5 mi) across and up to 700 m (2,300 ft) deep had replaced the peak, and the volcano itself had lost a third of its height.

The toll on human life was devastating: up to 12,000 people were believed to have died in Tambora's initial eruption, with a further 59,000 killed in the aftermath of the event, as crops failed and the entire region succumbed to famine.

FACT

Tambora exploded with a release of energy equivalent to 14 times that of the *Tsar Bomba*, the **most powerful nuclear explosive tested** (detonated in the former USSR on 30 Oct 1961).

The year without summer

- The ash and sulphur aerosols injected into the atmosphere by Tambora caused global temperatures to drop by 0.4–0.7°C (0.7–1.2°F), triggering the "year without summer". The bleak weather of 1816 can be seen in paintings from the time, such as John Constable's *Weymouth Bay* (below), which depicts blustery conditions despite it being a summer's day.
- Many countries experienced widespread crop failures and famine. Other repercussions included the disruption of the Indian monsoon and outbreaks of cholera and typhus. In Germany, where farmers lost many horses because of the famine, a civil servant named Baron Karl von Drais invented an alternative form of transport: the velocipede (above), which was the **first form of bicycle**.
- The gloom certainly had an impact on the young Mary Shelley; forced to spend much of her summer indoors, the 18-year-old took to reading horror stories, and penned one of her own: the classic *Frankenstein*.

LIGHTNING

The **scientific study** of lightning is known as **fulminology**

Most common lightning

Caused by regions of positive and negative charge that build up within layers of a cumulonimbus cloud, intracloud lightning (see below) accounts for up to 90% of lightning flashes. Other rarer types include cloud-to-cloud, cloud-to-ground and cloud-to-air lightning.

Greatest distance between co-ordinated lightning

Ever since the dawn of the Space Age, astronauts orbiting Earth had noted that lightning in thunderstorms appeared to trigger lightning in other storms at least 100 km (62 mi) apart. Dubbed "sympathetic lightning" by US astronaut Edward Gibson, there is as yet no explanation for this phenomenon, although it has been suggested that electromagnetic radiation may bounce off the Earth's surface and cause a flash in a distant storm.

Most rockets launched by lightning

A stormy night is not the best time to launch a rocket, but on 9 Jun 1987, NASA didn't have much

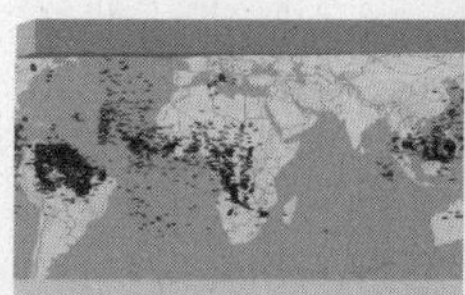

Largest lightning sensor network

With more than 800 detectors in 40-plus countries, the Earth Networks Total Lightning Network (ENTLN) is the world's biggest lightning detection system. The broad-frequency sensors can detect both IC and cloud-to-ground strikes.

Longest type of lightning

While lightning is nature's way of restoring an imbalance of electric charge, it can manifest itself in many forms. In 1956, a flash of intracloud (IC) lightning – like that pictured above right – was recorded by radar covering a distance of 149 km (93 mi). Often referred to as sheet lightning, IC lightning occurs within a cloud and does not reach the ground.

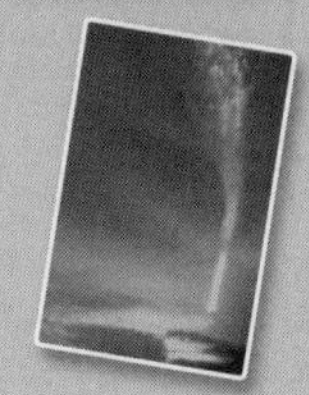

The tallest lightning, in contrast, is known as a "gigantic jet" (below right). A supersized version of a "blue jet", this vertical lightning can measure as much as 90 km (56 mi) high.

Highest lightning death toll

An aviation nightmare became a tragic reality on Christmas Eve 1971, when LANSA Flight 508 was brought down by lightning while flying over the Amazon. Of the 92 people on board, only one survived: 17-year-old Juliane Koepcke (DEU; pictured above). Incredibly, not only did she walk away from the crash with no more than a broken collarbone and a few cuts, but she also endured the perils of the rainforest for 10 days before she was discovered.

say in the matter as *three* of its unmanned rockets took off from the Wallops Flight Facility in Virginia, USA, having been ignited by lightning. Two began following their planned trajectories, while the third careered ignominiously into the ocean around 90 m (300 ft) from the launch pad. Ironically, the third rocket had been designed to study storms.

Highest concentration of lightning

At the point where the Catatumbo River spills into Lake Maracaibo in Venezuela, you can expect to see lightning some 300 nights of the year, in epic storms that can last for nine hours! In fact, this region receives close to 250 lightning strikes per square kilometre every year. This relentless tempest is the result of clashing warm and cold air currents, which become trapped by a chain of mountains bordering the lake.

Negatively charged cloud base

GLOSSARY

Stepped leader: While it appears that a cloud-to-ground lightning strike occurs in one step, the downward path it takes is, in fact, a series of staggered channels of negatively charged air, each about 50 m (164 ft) long, called "leaders".

Upward streamer: A "streamer" (typically a positively charged channel) emanates upwards from high points on the ground – including buildings and people – attracted towards the negative electric field of the leader.

Return stroke: When a stepped leader and upward streamer meet, the circuit completes, resulting in a bright flash. The burst of energy first rushes towards the ground before the current reverses, surging back up towards the cloud; it is this "return stroke" that we perceive as lightning in the sky.

Rapid air expansion around lightning results in thunder
Air particles are superheated up to 30,000°C (54,032°F)
Average diameter of lightning bolt is 2.5 cm (1 in)
Stepped leader
Current flows through the ionized air
Return stroke
Structures on ground carry a positive charge

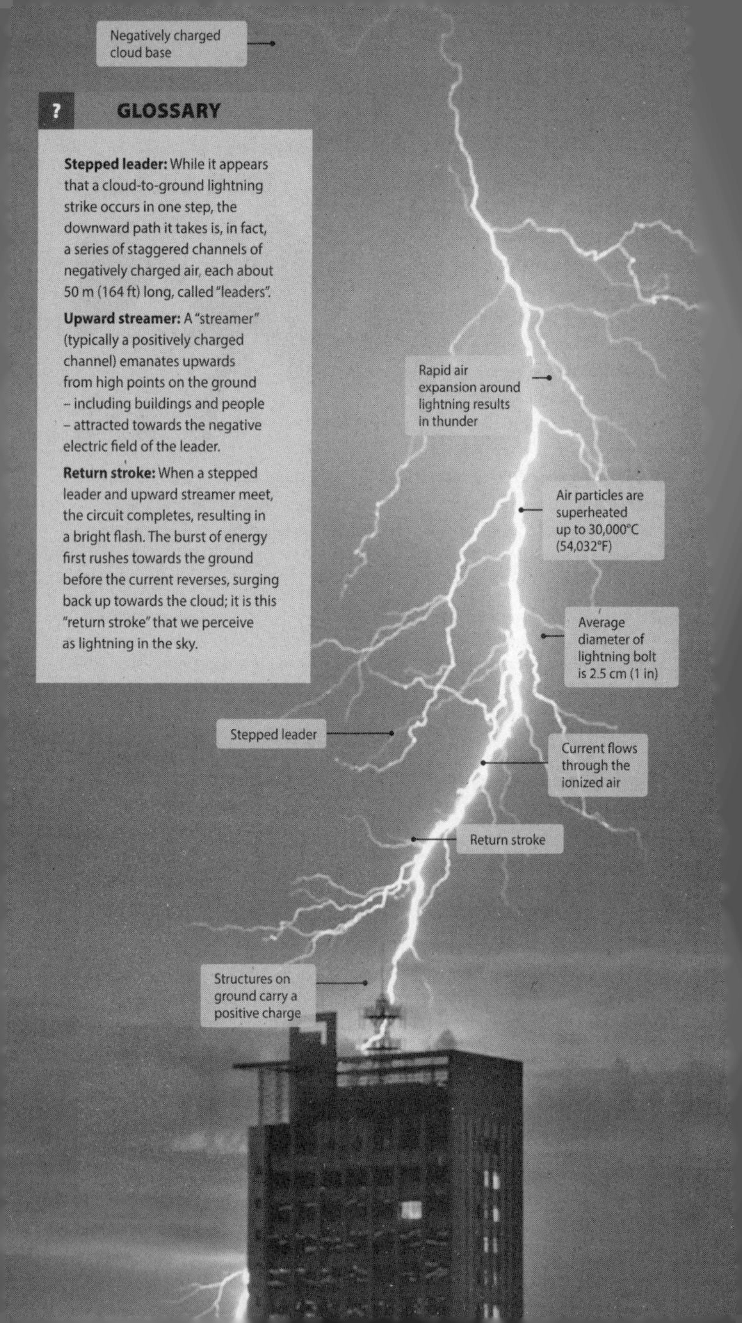

Longest fulgurite

Formed when lightning strikes certain minerals such as silica or even soil, fulgurites are glass-like tubes that capture the movement of electricity as it passes through the ground. In 1996, geologists discovered a spectacular specimen in Florida, USA, with one branch that extended as deep as 5.2 m (17 ft) below the surface.

Longest man-made lightning

Rumoured to have been born during a storm, Croatian scientist and engineer Nikola Tesla – probably best known for inventing the AC induction motor – created a 40-m-long (130-ft) bolt of electricity in 1899 at his laboratory in Colorado Springs, Colorado, USA. It was reported that the ensuing thunderclap was heard up to 35 km (22 mi) away.

Hottest natural temperature on Earth

You might think that this title would go to a desert or even to our planet's molten core, but the reality is that everything else is positively polar in comparison to the temperatures generated by lightning. While it may only be for a few milliseconds, the air through which lightning travels can reach 30,000°C (54,032°F) – that's around five times hotter than the Sun's surface. We see air particles glowing white owing to this intense heat.

The most likely lightning to attain such searing temperatures is "positive lightning", the **most powerful lightning**, occurring when the net transfer of charge from cloud to ground is positive, rather than the much more common negative. Originating in the higher levels of thunderclouds, these strikes can generate a much stronger electric field and a rock-shattering 1 billion volts.

IN NUMBERS

26
Deaths caused by lightning in the USA in 2014

100+
Lightning strikes that hit Earth every second

120 dB
Sound produced by a thunderclap

10%
Fatality rate for people struck by lightning; 70% suffer serious long-term effects

200 milliseconds
Duration of the average lightning strike

16 km
Distance away from the storm that lightning can strike (10 mi)

1 billion
Maximum voltage of lightning

25
Lightning bolts that strike the Empire State Building every year on average; in one storm it received eight hits in 24 min!

Strike it *un*lucky

Thankfully, not many of us can say we've been struck by lightning...

Based on data from the USA's National Oceanic and Atmospheric Administration (NOAA), the odds of being hit are 12,000 to one, rising to 1,000,000 to one in a given year. So the extraordinary case of Roy Sullivan (above) from Virginia, USA, who holds the record for most lightning strikes survived – no less than seven – is enough to baffle any statistician (see pp.468–72 for other unlikely survivors).

A ranger based at Shenandoah National Park in the Blue Ridge Mountains, his first electrifying encounter took place in Apr 1942. While fleeing from a watchtower that had been set ablaze during a thunderstorm, Sullivan's right leg received a direct bolt of several million volts, leaving a scorch mark and obliterating the nail on his big toe.

Little did he know that this was just the beginning of an ongoing battle with Mother Nature. Over the next 35 years, six further strikes left their mark (similar to the scars, right). These would come to earn Roy the nickname "Spark Ranger":

Jul 1969: Eyebrows burned and wristwatch destroyed while driving

Jul 1970: Left shoulder seared while in his garden

Apr 1972: Hair set on fire while in a guardhouse at work

Aug 1973: Hair set on fire again and legs seared while in his vehicle

Jun 1976: Ankle injured while walking

Jun 1977: Chest and stomach burned while fishing on a boat

Tragically, Roy died from a self-inflicted gunshot wound in 1983, aged 71.

First lightning detector

Created in 1742 by British inventor Andrew Gordon at the University of Erfurt, Germany, the lightning bell converted electrical energy into movement, reverberating a clapper between two oppositely charged bells. Built to warn of approaching storms, these instruments came to be called "electric chimes" owing to the melodious sound they produced. A few years later, in 1749, came the **first lightning rod**, invented by Benjamin Franklin (USA). These metal poles, running from the top of buildings to the ground, provide a safer pathway for lightning to follow, protecting the structure.

First rocket-triggered lightning

Lightning's unpredictable and short-lived nature makes it very difficult for scientists to study. One solution is to fire a small rocket into a thundercloud trailing a wire made of steel or copper, to create a path of least resistance for potential strikes. After a number of failed attempts, this was successfully achieved in 1977 in Gansu, China, by the Chinese Academy of Sciences.

FACT

Some scientists think that lightning could have sparked life on Earth. Experiments have shown that applying a bolt of electricity to inorganic compounds has resulted in organic amino acids.

FROZEN

Around 715 million years ago, **Earth** was almost **fully covered in ice**

Coldest desert

It may not look like the archetypal desert, but the McMurdo Dry Valleys in Antarctica receive less than 100 mm (4 in) of precipitation per year, which means the region more than qualifies for desert status.

The annual mean temperature of -20°C (-4°F) is actually quite mild for Antarctica, and the 4,800-km^2 (1,850-sq-mi) region the Valleys cover represents the largest ice-free area on the frozen continent.

First brinicle formation caught on camera

Brinicles are pipes of ice that form beneath sea ice when super-cold, super-saline water sinks and freezes. If a brinicle reaches the ocean floor, in shallow conditions, the super-cold water can spread across the seabed, freezing and killing any lifeforms in its path. The process was first filmed by the BBC for their series *Frozen Planet* in 2011 in Antarctica's McMurdo Sound.

Largest glacier

The Lambert Glacier in Antarctica covers 1 million km^2 (386,100 sq mi), and with a length of 400 km (250 mi) it is also the **longest glacier**. Every year, it delivers some 33 billion tonnes (36 billion US tons) of ice from the East Antarctic Ice Sheet to the Southern Ocean.

Largest wild reindeer herd

The George River population of reindeer (*Rangifer tarandus caribou*) in northern Canada contained some 50,000 deer in 2011. However, this was down significantly from more than 800,000 in 1992.

Largest ice-dome igloo

On 19 Feb 2011, zip-lining company ZipZag.ca (CAN) built an igloo out of 2,500 ice blocks (right and inset). It had an internal diameter of 9.2 m (30 ft 5.5 in) and a floor-to-ceiling height of 5.3 m (17 ft 4 in).

The **largest snow-dome igloo** was made by the TV crew of Pro 7 Galileo (DEU) on 7 Feb 2011. It had an internal diameter of 12.1 m (39 ft 8 in) and inner height of 8.1 m (26 ft 6.5 in).

Largest ice structure

Rebuilt every year from blocks of ice hewn from the River Torne, the ICEHOTEL in Jukkasjärvi, Sweden, covers an area of up to 5,500 m^2 (59,200 sq ft). In 2015, the 25th iteration of the ICEHOTEL featured an ice bar, an ice church and many bespoke bedrooms featuring everything from a London Tube carriage to a pole-dancing polar bear, all made from ice.

Largest ice shelf

First sighted by British naval officer Captain James Clark Ross in 1841, the 472,000-km^2 (182,240-sq-mi) Ross Ice Shelf on the western edge of Antarctica is one of the largest pieces of floating ice on Earth. The edge of the ice shelf presents a near-vertical face towards the sea, up to 15 m (49 ft) high.

Longest ice road

Built in 1982, Canada's Tibbitt to Contwoyto Winter Road is a key supply route to the mines in the Northwest Territories and Nunavut. Rebuilt each year, the road is 568 km (353 mi) long, 495 km (308 mi) of which crosses frozen lakes.

Longest ice runway

At 10,000 ft (3,050 m) long and about 219 ft (67 m) wide, this record is shared by two temporary air strips that are annually carved out of the sea ice near McMurdo Station in Antarctica.

Largest ice-lantern display

In recent years, carving ice lanterns has become something of a winter tradition in Vuollerim, Sweden. On 5 Feb 2013, the local population outdid itself by creating 2,651 lanterns and placing them around their Lapland village.

First artificial snow

Snow was first made using a machine in the 1940s by Dr Ray Ringer (CAN) and colleagues.

Their discovery came by accident, while researching the formation of ice on jet engines. They sprayed water into a chilled wind tunnel in front of a jet engine, which proceeded to produce snow out of its rear end. Ringer published his results, which later inspired the development of the first "snow cannon" in 1954.

Earliest documented snowman

Book of Hours, a prayer book produced by monks c. 1380, includes a doodle in the margin that resembles a snowman. Today, the tome is kept at the Koninklijke Bibliotheek in The Hague, Netherlands.

Most snowmen built in one hour

Organized by the TV show *Unhandy Handyman* (JPN), 1,406 people helped to make 2,036 snowmen in Akabira, Hokkaido, Japan, on 28 Feb 2015. All snowmen were required to have carrots for noses, coal for eyes and twigs for arms.

Tallest snowman

Ask the residents of Bethel in Maine, USA, if they want to build a snowman, and the answer will be a resounding "Yes!". Over a period of a month, people from Bethel and nearby towns made a "snow-woman" that towered 37.21 m (122 ft 1 in) tall. It was completed on 26 Feb 2008.

ICEHOTEL IN NUMBERS

100
Approximate number of people who help to build the hotel

1,000 tonnes
Amount of ice used in its construction (2.2 million lb)

30,000 tonnes
Amount of "snice" (a snow/ice mix that acts like mortar) used in the construction of the hotel (66 million lb)

200 km
Distance north of the Arctic Circle that the ICEHOTEL is located (124 mi)

50,000
Average number of annual visitors to the ICEHOTEL

Largest snow maze
Measured on 15 Feb 2015, a 1,696-m^2 (18,255.59-sq-ft) snow maze was built by the Fort William Historical Park (CAN, above) as part of the 13th Voyageur Winter Carnival.

The **largest ice maze** – partly shaped as a buffalo – was created by the Arctic Glacier Ice Maze (USA) in Buffalo, New York, USA; it covered an area of 1,194.33 m^2 (12,855.68 sq ft), as measured on 26 Feb 2010.

Fastest time to carve 60 ice sculptures

Award-winning ice sculptor Richard Daly (USA) carved 60 artworks in 2 hr 52 min 12 sec in Lakeville, Pennsylvania, USA, on 20 Oct 2013. Daly's sculptures were based on various subjects, including food, buildings and, owing to the date, Halloween.

Most northerly...

• **Hotel:** The highest-latitude hotel in the northern hemisphere is the Radisson Blu Polar Hotel Spitsbergen in Longyearbyen, on the Norwegian archipelago of Svalbard. Ranging from 74° to 81° North, the island group is the most northerly point in Europe; around 60% of it is covered in glaciers.

• **Restaurant:** Also found in Longyearbyen is the mobile kebab shop known as "The Red Polar Bear". Owned by Kazem Ariaiwand (IRN), it is a culinary hit with the 2,000 or so local residents.

• **Royal territory:** Located 83°40'N, Kaffeklubben ("Coffee Club") Island, off northern Greenland, is the most northerly land ruled by a monarchy. Greenland became a Danish colony in 1814 and part of the realm of Denmark in 1953. Although Greenland was granted home rule in 1979, the country remains part of the Kingdom of Denmark to this day.

• **Inhabited place:** Around 800 km (500 mi) from the Geographic North Pole at 82°30'N, 62°W lies the Canadian Forces Station Alert on Ellesmere Island. Alert is nearer Stockholm, Sweden, than the nearest Canadian city: Edmonton in Alberta.

FACT

Italian art historian Giorgio Vasari noted that in 1494, celebrated Renaissance artist Michelangelo (ITA) was commissioned to build a "snow statue" after a cold winter in Florence, Italy.

Longest full-body contact with ice

Claiming back a record that he previously held in 2011, Jin Songhao (CHN) spent a chilly 1 hr 53 min 10 sec buried in ice on the set of *CCTV-Guinness World Records Special* in Fujian, China, on 4 Sep 2014. He beat the existing record by 8 sec.

Exploring the Antarctic

Established in 1962 to coordinate research on the frozen continent, the British Antarctic Survey (BAS) was initially headed up by British explorer Sir Vivian Fuchs. GWR asked Professor David Vaughan (UK, above), director of science at BAS, about their vital work.

What kind of research do you do?

We study the interactions of solar particles with the Earth's magnetic field, which cause aurorae in the high atmosphere and can threaten power supplies, communications and satellites.

We work on unravelling the history of climate and life on the planet that is locked in Antarctic ice and rocks, as well as predicting future climate and how this will change the size of the ice sheet and alter global sea level.

Nowadays, we work in Antarctica and the Arctic, and increasingly wherever our polar expertise can be applied.

What are the practical challenges of working in Antarctica?

The cold is a problem, but actually the immense distances and the isolation are even bigger issues. The months of darkness each winter are psychologically difficult to deal with too.

What discoveries have you made?

We first identified the Antarctic ozone hole in the 1980s (left). By analysing ice cores, we have made notable progress in identifying changes in the climate and how it is controlled by greenhouse gases.

WATERFALLS

On first seeing the **spectacular Iguazu Falls** in South America, First Lady Eleanor Roosevelt exclaimed, **"Poor Niagara!"**

Tallest coastal waterfall

The Hawaiian island of Molokai is home to the world's **highest sea cliffs**. Cascading from the top is Olo'upena Falls, which drops some 900 m (2,953 ft) to the Pacific Ocean. With a width of around 12 m (39 ft) when in full flow, Olo'upena is the world's fourth-tallest waterfall.

Tallest underwater waterfall

Under the Denmark Strait, which separates Greenland and Iceland, an underwater waterfall has formed where cold, denser water drops from the Greenland Sea into the slightly warmer Irminger Sea. The cold water falls more than 3.5 km (2 mi), at least three times the height of Angel Falls.

Discovered in 1989 and known as the Denmark Strait Cataract, this submarine waterfall carries around 5,000,000 m³ (176,573,000 cu ft) of water per second, making it the **largest waterfall** in terms of volume.

TOP 10 TALLEST WATERFALLS

These measurements are for waterfall heights "from top to bottom, regardless of whether it drops straight down or cascades down a mountain at an angle".

Rank	Name of falls	Height	Location
1	Angel	979 m	Bolívar, Venezuela
2	Tugela	948 m	KwaZulu Natal, South Africa
3	Three Sisters	914 m	Junín, Peru
4	Olo'upena	900 m	Hawaii, USA
5	Yumbilla	896 m	Amazonas, Peru
6	Vinnufallet	865 m	Møre og Romsdal, Norway
7	Skorga	864 m	Møre og Romsdal, Norway
=8	Pu'uka'oku	840 m	Hawaii, USA
=8	James Bruce	840 m	British Columbia, Canada
10	Browne	836 m	South Island, New Zealand

Source: World Waterfall Database

Largest waterfall ever

Around 18,000 years ago, towards the end of the last Ice Age, a huge lake was formed in North America, near the present-day city of Missoula in Montana, USA. The lake appeared when a huge advancing glacier dammed a river, resulting in a trapped body of water around 500 cu mi (2,000 km^3) in volume.

Eventually, the water broke through the ice dam created by the glacier and the lake, known as Glacial Lake Missoula, emptied in a catastrophic flood. As the water drained away, some flowed over cliffs, now called Dry Falls, in a spectacular waterfall some 3.5 mi (5.6 km) wide and 380 ft (115 m) tall. By comparison, modern Niagara Falls (see p.23) is about 1 mi (1.6 km) wide and 165 ft (50 m) tall.

Largest plunge pool

Plunge pools are lakes or depressions formed at the base of waterfalls created by the erosive action of the water. The largest is Perth Canyon, off Western Australia, which is around 300 m (984 ft) deep and 2 x 6 km (1.2 x 3.7 mi) in area. It was created in prehistoric times by a waterfall when the region was above sea level.

Greatest waterfall annual flow

The Inga Falls on the Congo River in the Democratic Republic of the Congo has a discharge rate of 910,000 cu ft/sec (25,768 m^3/sec), with a recorded maximum flow of 2.5 million cu ft/sec (70,793 m^3/sec). According to the World Waterfall Database, which monitors the tallest and most voluminous waterfalls, the falls are 315 ft (96 m) tall, with a run of 50,000 ft (15,240 m), a maximum width of 13,200 ft (4,023 m) and a tallest single drop of 70 ft (21 m).

Waterfall with the most natural bridges

Discovered in 1952, the "Cave of the Three Bridges" in Tannourine,

Longest waterfall descent by kayak

On 21 Apr 2009, extreme kayaker Tyler Bradt (USA, inset) descended 186 ft (57 m) on the Palouse Falls in Washington, USA, in a free-fall lasting some four seconds. He emerged with a sprained wrist and broken paddle from this bold feat, which beat the previous record by 59 ft (18 m).

IN NUMBERS

47
Drops in the Angel Falls (see p.24)

275
Drops in the Iguazu Falls, ranging along 2.7 km (1.7 mi) of the Iguazu River on the Brazil-Argentina border

165 m
Height of the **tallest man-made waterfall** (541 ft), the Cascate delle Marmore, near Terni in Italy, created by the Romans c. 270 BC

1,115 ft
Height of Nohkalikai Falls, the tallest plunge waterfall in India (340 m)

1,500,000
Annual number of visitors to the 268-ft-tall (82-m) Snoqualmie Falls in Washington, USA – as seen in the TV series *Twin Peaks*

2,755 ft
Height of James Bruce Falls in Canada – tallest waterfall in North America (840 m)

Lebanon, contains a waterfall that plunges 255 m (738 ft) past three natural stone bridges as it cuts through 160-million-year-old Jurassic limestone.

Widest waterfall

The Khône Falls on the Mekong River in southern Laos has a total width of 10.78 km (6.8 mi). It is 15–21 m (50–70 ft) tall, with a flood flow of 42,500 m^3/sec (1,500,000 cu ft/sec).

Longest waterfall descent by kayak (female)

On 10 May 2009, Christie Glissmeyer (USA) plummeted 82 ft (25 m) on the Metlako Falls in Eagle Creek, Oregon, USA. The descent was twice that of any waterfall she had previously run.

Highest waterfall dive

On 5 Oct 2008, Di Huanran (CHN) dived 12.19 m (40 ft) down the Diaoshuilou Falls of Jingbo Lake in Mudanjiang City, China. Professional surveying equipment was used to measure the exact extent of the drop.

Tallest indoor waterfall

The eight-storey atrium that spans the full height of the International Center in Detroit, Michigan, USA, is graced with a masterpiece of a water feature measuring 114 ft (34.75 m). The water ripples down soaring rectangles of marble, 9,000 sq ft (840 m^2) in all, and shimmers in natural light falling from above.

Most visited waterfall

Niagara Falls, on the border between Canada and the USA, receives 22,500,000 visitors a year, so it is not only the most visited waterfall but also the fifth most popular tourist attraction in the world, ahead of all the Disneylands, Notre-Dame Cathedral and the Great Wall of China.

It comprises three waterfalls: American, Bridal Veil and Horseshoe/Canadian Falls. While there are about 500 taller waterfalls in the world, Niagara is more accessible than most, just a short flight or drive for millions of regional visitors.

Tallest multi-tiered waterfall

The Tugela Falls descend 948 m (3,110 ft) in a series of five steps in the Drakensberg (Dragon's Mountains), Royal Natal National Park in KwaZulu Natal Province, South Africa. Tugela Falls is also the second tallest waterfall overall.

20%
Proportion of the USA's drinking water that comes via Niagara Falls

72
Falls that spill into Switzerland's Lauterbrunnen valley

90%
Proportion of fish that survive the "swim" over Niagara Falls

50 m
Height of "The Fang", an ice pillar in Colorado, USA, that forms from a waterfall in very cold winters (164 ft)

8 m
Largest recorded circumference of Japan's Taroshi Falls, an ice pillar in winter (26 ft 3 in); this measurement, taken annually, is thought to relate to the quality of the rice harvest

FACT

During his high-risk descent of the Palouse Falls (see p.21), Tyler Bradt kept close to the curtain of water, and aimed for the heart of the torrent so that the aerated water would cushion his landing.

Largest waterfall by vertical area

At 1,708 m (5,604 ft) wide and 108 m (354 ft) tall, the Victoria Falls (above), on the Zambezi River between Zimbabwe and Zambia, creates a sheet of falling water with an area of around 184,400 m^2 (2,017,400 sq ft). David Livingstone (UK, 1813–73) named it after Queen Victoria, but locals know it as Mosi-oa-Tunya ("Smoke that Thunders"). The mist it creates can be seen more than 20 km (12 mi) away.

Tallest single drop in a waterfall

Salto Ángel or Angel Falls (right) in Bolívar, Venezuela, has an uninterrupted sheer drop of 807 m (2,648 ft). After falling this distance, the water forms a column of fine mist. Salto Ángel is also the **tallest waterfall**, combining the single drop with sloped cascades to attain a height of 979 m (3,212 ft). It was named after the American pilot Jimmie Angel, who recorded it in his logbook on 16 Nov 1933.

To date, we have explored **less than 5%** of the world's oceans

Warmest average global ocean surface temperature

According to the USA's National Oceanic and Atmospheric Administration (NOAA), the period from Jan to Sep 2014 saw the highest-ever recorded global ocean surface temperatures. Values were 0.66°C (1.19°F) above the average measured for the 20th and 21st centuries so far. These results were published in the online report *State of the Climate: Global Analysis September 2014*, by NOAA's National Climatic Data Center.

According to the same source, Jan to Sep 1911 saw the **coolest average global ocean surface temperature** for the 20th and 21st centuries recorded to date: -0.49°C (-0.88°F).

Deepest marine biome

The bottom part of the pelagic zone (open sea, away from the coastline or sea floor) is known as the hadal zone. It covers deep ocean trenches, beginning at a depth of 6,000 m (19,680 ft) and continuing to the ocean floor. This region is characterized by a total lack of sunlight and pressure levels up to 986.9 atmospheres (1.01 tonnes per cm²/14,503 psi). Most

Deepest blue hole

Blue holes are found at or just below sea level, and were once dry caves or shafts that filled with seawater as the ice-caps melted and the water levels rose following the last ice age, which ended around 12,000 years ago. Dean's Blue Hole is a 76-m-wide (250-ft) vertical shaft that sinks for 202 m (663 ft) at Turtle Cove near Clarence Town, on the Atlantic edge of The Bahamas. Lying just off shore, it contains 1.1 million m³ (38.8 million cu ft) of water.

animals at this depth are colourless, and use bioluminescence as a light source. This biome includes hydrothermal vents, whose heat and chemical nutrients have allowed bizarre varieties of life to exist, including the scaly-foot snail, which has iron-sulphide armour plating on its foot.

Fastest ocean acidification

The world's oceans absorb up to 30% of emitted carbon dioxide, by reacting with it chemically and forming carbonic acid. Approximately 20 million tonnes (22 million US tons) per day are "scrubbed" from the atmosphere in this way. As a consequence, the oceans are becoming more and more acidic over time, with an increase of around 30% since the beginning of the Industrial Revolution in the 18th century. While the pH levels of the oceans varies regionally, the current rate of change globally is around 100 times faster than at any point in the last 20 million years.

Tallest internal waves

Internal waves occur in parts of the ocean where the water is stratified – in other words, made up of different layers. The waves occur at the boundary between layers of water of different salinity and density, rather than at the ocean's surface. The largest discovered to date occur in the South China Sea, where internal waves of up to 170 m (560 ft) move at the rate of just a few centimetres per second. This discovery was revealed by scientists at the Massachusetts Institute of Technology (USA) on 8 Jan 2014.

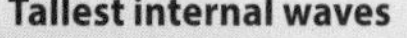

Tallest sea stack

Located in the Pacific Ocean to the south-east of Australia's Lord Howe Island, Ball's Pyramid is 561 m (1,843 ft) tall, although it has a base axis of just 200 m (660 ft). By way of comparison, it is slightly more than six times the height of the Statue of Liberty, including its pedestal.

This outcrop was once considerably taller, however. Ball's Pyramid is the 7-million-year-old remnant of a massive volcano, and represents only 0.5% of the original size.

Clearest sea

On 13 Oct 1986, scientists from the Alfred Wegener Institute in Bremerhaven, Germany, measured the clarity of the Weddell Sea, off Antarctica. To do so, they lowered a black-and-white, 30-cm-wide (1-ft) disc, known as a Secchi disc, into the water until it could no longer be seen. The disc was visible down to a depth of 80 m (262 ft) – a clarity similar to that of distilled water.

LARGEST...

Area of sea ice

According to NASA, on 20 Sep 2014 the sea ice surrounding Antarctica reached its maximum ever recorded extent of 20.15 million km^2 (7.78 million sq mi). The data came from the US National Snow & Ice Data Center, which has monitored global sea ice levels since 1979.

Subsurface body of water

On 12 Jun 2014, US scientists revealed their discovery of water trapped within a layer of the mineral ringwoodite around 700 km (435 mi) deep in the Earth's mantle, between the crust and the core. It was discovered by analysing seismic waves from earthquakes, which slowed down while passing through this layer, indicating the presence of water. So far, this layer of ringwoodite and water has only been discovered under the continental USA and it is believed to contain around 4 billion km^3 (960 million cu mi) of water, some three times the volume of all the Earth's oceans.

IN NUMBERS

4 km
Average depth of the Earth's oceans (2.5 mi)

70%
Proportion of the oxygen we breathe that is produced by oceans

90%
Proportion of volcanic activity on Earth that takes place in the ocean

1,000 years
Time it would take 1 m^3 (35.3 cu ft) of sea water to travel around the world

65,000 km
Length of the **longest submarine mountain range** (40,000 mi), the Mid-Ocean Ridge, running between the Atlantic and Arctic oceans

9.4 million km2
Area of the Arctic Ocean, the **smallest ocean** (3.6 million sq mi)

166.2 million km^2
Area of the **largest ocean**, the Pacific Ocean (64.1 million sq mi)

Largest glacier calving filmed

On 16 Nov 2012, the documentary film *Chasing Ice* was released in the USA. Directed by Jeff Orlowski, the film follows photographer James Balog and his EIS team as they collect evidence of anthropogenic (human-caused) climate change in Greenland, Iceland and Alaska. During filming, the team spent several weeks camping at the Jakobshavn (Ilulissat) Glacier in Greenland, where they witnessed a calving event that lasted 75 min, resulting in around 4 km^3 (1.7 cu mi) of ice falling into the ocean (above). This is also the **longest-duration glacier calving ever filmed.**

Manganese nodule deposit

Manganese nodules are roughly spherical concretions of manganese hydroxides and iron around a core of oceanic debris. They arise naturally on the ocean floor, owing to the precipitation of metals and other chemical processes, and can take millions of years to form. They range in size from microscopic to around 20 cm (8 in) across. The largest deposit occurs in the Clarion-Clipperton Zone, which covers approximately 9 million km^2 (3.4 million sq mi) of the Pacific Ocean's floor. This region is estimated to contain around 21 billion tonnes (23 billion US tons) of manganese nodules.

Greatest ocean pollutant

According to the UN Environment Programme, plastic bags make up more than 50% of all marine litter, with 46,000 pieces of plastic for every square mile of ocean. In parts of the Pacific Ocean, for every 1 kg (2 lb 3 oz) of biomass there are 6 kg (13 lb 3 oz) of plastic. The Blue Ocean Society for Marine Conservation estimates that more than 1 million birds and 100,000 marine mammals die each year from choking on, or becoming entangled in, plastic.

Largest area of glowing sea

In 1995, scientists at the US Naval Research Laboratory detected luminous sea in the Indian Ocean, off the coast of Somalia, via satellite. The patch of water was more than 250 km (155 mi) long, with an area of around 14,000 km² (5,400 sq mi). Bioluminescent bacteria are believed to have caused the unusual glow.

FACT

As waves batter the base of cliffs over time, cracks develop, then caves. If this occurs on either side of a headland, the caves form an arch. Further erosion removes the top, creating a pillar, or stack.

Captain Donald Walsh

On 23 Jan 1960, Dr Jacques Piccard (CHE, below right) and Donald Walsh (USA, right and below left, then a lieutenant) performed the deepest manned ocean descent: 10,911 m (35,797 ft), in the US Navy bathyscaphe Trieste. The location? The Challenger Deep section of the Mariana Trench, the deepest point on Earth (see p.354). Captain Walsh kindly reflected on that historic day for GWR.

What was it like inside the bathyscaphe?
After all our equipment was installed, the interior of the sphere was quite small. Our two-person crew had about the same space as a large household refrigerator; the temperature inside was about the same!

Could you explain how the descent was made and how long it took?
This dive took nine hours. About five hours going down, 20 minutes on the bottom and the balance returning to the surface. Going down, the speed was much slower, to ensure we didn't encounter an unknown obstruction.

How would you sum up the legacy of your dive?
Well, there was the general excitement of conquering one of the last geographic frontiers in the world. It's impossible to measure how what we did may have excited young people to become ocean explorers, scientists or engineers.

More specifically, our "fingerprints" and "DNA" can be found in most undersea vehicle systems today. It's great to be at a trade show seeing equipment on a new submersible and thinking, "Yeah, we made the first one of those 50 years ago."

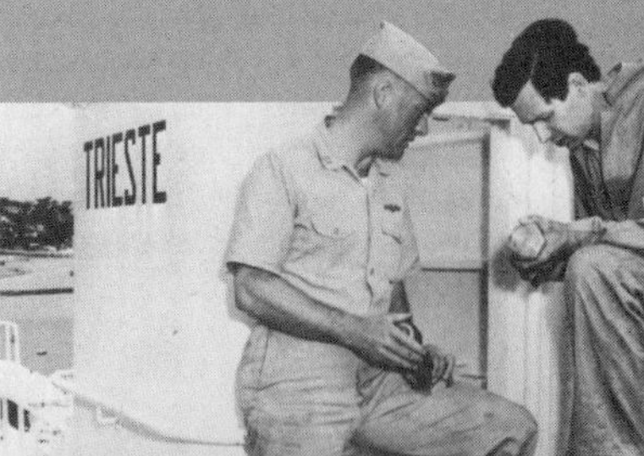

GEMSTONES & MINERALS

There are about **35 different minerals in a TV set**. And about **15 in a car**

Oldest use of diamonds as tools

Researchers at Harvard University in Cambridge, Massachusetts, USA, have shown that the ancient Chinese used diamonds to grind and polish ceremonial stone burial axes some 6,000 years ago. The level of skill with which they were crafted is difficult to match, even with modern polishing techniques. Ranging from 13 to 22 cm (5.1–8.6 in), the axes date to the Sanxingcun culture of 4000–3800 BC and the Liangzhu culture, dating to c. 2500 BC. The finding was reported in the Feb 2005 issue of the journal *Archaeometry*.

The diamond, an allotrope of carbon (C), has a value of 10 on the Mohs hardness scale, making it the **hardest element**. Diamonds have been mined principally in India, Brazil, South Africa and Russia.

Talc is the **softest mineral** on Earth. The Mohs hardness scale uses talc as its starting point, with a value of 1.00. Talc

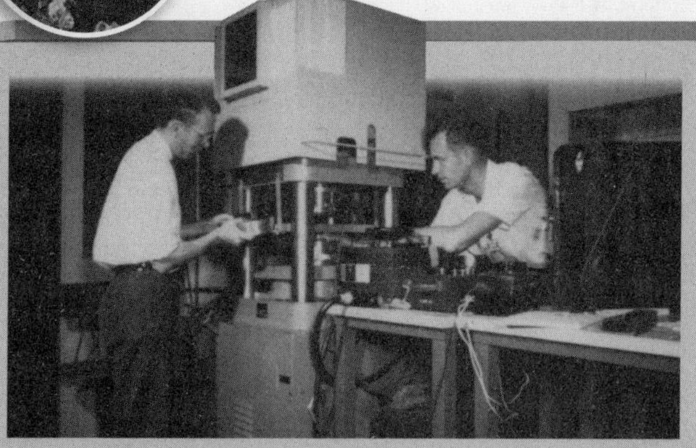

First man-made diamond

In Feb 1955, scientists at GE's lab in Schenectady, New York, USA, unveiled an ultra-high-pressure apparatus: the "Diamond Press". A small chamber surrounded by pistons, it could produce some 1.5 million lb/sq ft (1 billion kgf/m^2) of pressure and temperatures of 5,000°F (2,760°C). Metal and carbon were melted together with an electrical current, then cooled for 10–20 min. Result: perfect man-made diamonds weighing up to 1/10th of a carat.

is a silicate, like many of Earth's most important minerals, and contains silica, magnesium and a trace of the elements of water.

Largest diamond deposit

Located in Sakha (Yakutia), Russia, the Yubileyny open-pit diamond mine sits on the largest known deposit of diamonds. Also known as the Jubilee mine, it contained more than 153 million carats (Mct) of recoverable diamonds, including 51 Mct of probable underground reserves, as of Jan 2013. It has been owned and operated since 1986 by the Aikhal mining and processing division of Russia's state-owned diamond company Alrosa.

Largest producer of lead

Lead is a metal that has been mined and used by humans for millennia. It is easily extracted from lead ore and highly malleable. In 2014, China was the top lead producer, with 2,950,000 tonnes (3,251,818 US tons), accounting for around half of global production.

Earliest use of obsidian

Obsidian – a rock formed when felsic lava from a volcanic eruption cools quickly – is given its dark-brown-to-black colour by magnesium and iron. When worked, obsidian develops sharp edges, which made it invaluable to early humans, who used it for cutting. The oldest evidence of it being used by humans has been found at the Kariandusi prehistoric site in Kenya, dating back some 700,000 years to the Lower Palaeolithic Era.

LARGEST...

Abalone pearl

A 718.50-carat baroque abalone pearl measuring 14 x 8 x 4 cm (5.51 x 3.14 x 1.57 in) was found by Dat Vi Truong (USA) in Mendocino, California, USA, on 31 May 2010. Abalone pearls cannot be manufactured, so all of them are natural in origin. The abalone (*Haliotis* spp.) mollusc inhabits mid-temperature oceans and is fairly common, although it rarely produces pearls. When it does, the result is an irregularly shaped gemstone with iridescent colours including reds, greens, blues and yellows.

Agate

On 25 Oct 2009, an agate weighing 61,090.2 kg (134,680 lb 13 oz) was verified at an event organized by the Development and Reform Commission of Fuxin Municipal Government in Fuxin City, Liaoning Province, China.

Most abundant mineral in Earth's crust

Feldspar (right) is a mineral that crystallizes in magma and has the formula KAlSi3O8 - NaAlSi3O8 - CaAl2Si2O8. Along with quartz and mica, it is one of the main constituents of the rock granite. Feldspar has numerous varieties including plagioclase, orthoclase, albite and anorthite, making up around 60% of all rocks in Earth's crust.

The **most abundant minerals on Earth** are the silicates (formed with silicon and oxygen) – including feldspar – which account for about 95% of the planet's crust. This explains why oxygen forms such a large part – around 46% – of the mass of the crust. Shown left is a lump of crystalline silicon.

Amber chunk

The House of Amber and the Copenhagen Amber Museum (both DNK) own a piece of amber that weighs 47.56 kg (104 lb 13 oz). It was measured at Kanneworffs House in Copenhagen, Denmark, on 31 Mar 2015. This unique object, discovered in 2014 in the Dharmasraya region of West Sumatra in Indonesia, is most likely 15–25 million years old.

Largest rose quartz ball

Owned by Yoshiyuki Nishiyama of Machida, Tokyo, Japan, the largest rose quartz ball measures 96.6 cm (3 ft 2.03 in) in diameter. Its size was certified on 21 May 2013. The colossal streaked-pink gemstone weighs 1,220 kg (2,689 lb 10 oz) and originally came from Brazil.

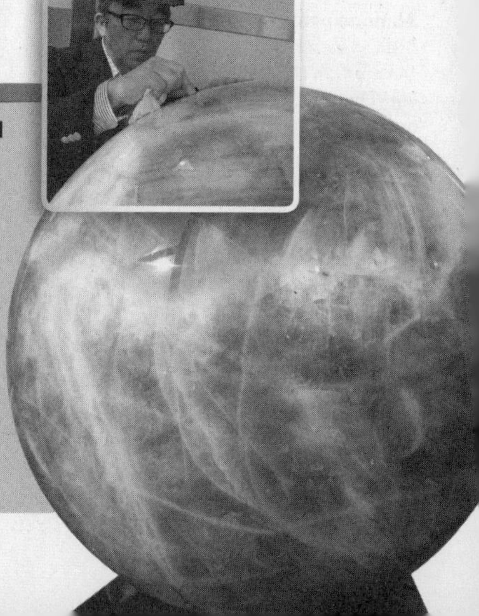

Most expensive diamond

On 16 Nov 2010, at Sotheby's Geneva in Switzerland, the Graff Pink, a 24.78-carat Fancy Intense Pink diamond, fetched 45,442,500 Swiss Francs ($46,158,674; £28,757,507). It is also the **most expensive piece of jewellery sold at auction.** Pictured left is the **most expensive Fancy Orange diamond sold at auction.** It fetched 32.6 m Swiss francs ($35.5 m, £22 m) at Christie's Geneva in Switzerland on 12 Nov 2013.

Amethyst geode

Displayed in Shandong Tianyu Museum of Natural History in Shandong, China, the largest amethyst geode measures 3 m (9 ft 10 in) long, 1.8 m (5 ft 10 in) wide and 2.2 m (7 ft 2 in) high, and weighs 13 tonnes (28,660 lb).

Largest gypsum crystal

The Cave of Crystals, located below Naica mountain in the Chihuahuan Desert, Mexico, was first discovered in 2000. It contains translucent single crystals of gypsum, the largest of which measure about 11 m (36 ft) long and weigh an estimated 55 tonnes (121,254 lb).

THE BRITISH CROWN JEWELS IN NUMBERS

2.23 kg
Weight of St Edward's Crown, with which new British sovereigns are crowned (4 lb 14 oz)

530.2 carats
Weight of the First Star of Africa, mounted on top of the Sovereign's Sceptre; it is the **largest flawless cut diamond** (106.04 g)

3,000
Gems in the Imperial State Crown, with which King George VI (the present Queen's father) was crowned

317 carats
Weight of the Second Star of Africa, set in the Imperial State Crown (63.4 g)

3,106 carats
Weight of the Cullinan, the **largest diamond** ever found (621.2 g), from which the First and Second Stars of Africa were cut

6,000
Diamonds, rubies and emeralds in the Imperial Crown of India, worn once, in 1911, by King George V at a ceremony in Delhi

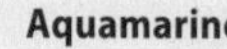

The heist that never was

Over the Easter Bank Holiday weekend in Apr 2015, thieves raided 70 deposit boxes in London's Hatton Garden jewellery district, escaping with some £200 m ($380 m) in gems. A sizeable fortune, but it would have been easily topped by the haul from the largest jewel heist that *never* happened...

In 2000, London's Millennium Dome (below) was hosting an exhibition of stones from De Beers, the pre-eminent diamond company. One of the prize exhibits, a flawless 203-carat gem named the "Millennium Star" (above), was worth £200 m ($285 m) alone. A gang of thieves hatched a plot to ram-raid the exhibition using a JCB backhoe, snatch 12 diamonds worth around £350 m ($500 m) and flee by speedboat on the River Thames.

It was not to be. Two of the gang, both known to the police, were caught on camera reconnoitring the exhibition two months before the attempted raid. Police switched the diamonds for crystal fakes on 6 Nov 2000 – the day the gang had intended to make the raid, though unfavourable conditions on the Thames made them postpone for 24 hours. The next day, they smashed into the exhibition, under cover of smoke bombs and wearing masks (inset right, top), and broke into the display case (inset left, bottom), but were swiftly overwhelmed by police.

As one gang member mused ruefully afterwards, "We would have got away with it but for the fact there were 140 police waiting for us."

Aquamarine

A huge 520,000-carat aquamarine ($Al_2Be_3[Si_6O_{18}]$) was discovered near Marambaia in Brazil in 1910. It yielded more than 200,000 carats of gem-quality stones.

Black opal

Measuring 2,450 x 1,460 x 527 mm (96.45 x 57.48 x 20.74 in) and weighing 11,340.95 carats (2.268 kg), the largest black opal is owned by Dallas, Judith, Shannon, Jeffery and Ken Westbrook (all AUS). It was found in Lightning Ridge, New South Wales, Australia.

Carved sapphire

A blue-gold-grey polished carved sapphire weighing 80,500 carats (16.1 kg) was displayed at the Unifour Gem, Mineral, Bead, Fossil & Jewelry Show at the Hickory Metro Convention Center in North Carolina, USA, on 19 Mar 2005. The owner spent three years whittling it with diamonds.

Gold nugget

The Holtermann Nugget was found on 19 Oct 1872 in the Beyers & Holtermann Star of Hope Mine at Hill End (then known as Bald Hill) in New South Wales, Australia. It contained some 82.11 kg (2,896.35 oz) of gold within a 235.14-kg (8,294.3-oz) slab of slate.

Our oceans contain around **eight times the quantity of gold** that has ever been mined

Deepest undersea drilling

In Sep 2009, the Deepwater Horizon rig, owned by Transocean (USA), drilled the deepest oil well in history at a measured depth of 35,055 ft (10,685 m). That's greater than the height of the **tallest mountain**, Mauna Kea, in Hawaii, USA, which extends 33,480 ft (10,205 m) from seabed to peak. The drill took place in the Tiber field at Keathley Canyon Block 102, some 250 mi (400 km) south-east of Houston, Texas, USA, in 4,132 ft (1,259 m) of water.

First country to mine gas hydrates

Sometimes known as "flammable ice", gas hydrates take the form of a solid resembling water ice that contains methane gas trapped in its crystalline structure. They occur beneath sediments on the ocean floor. In Mar 2013, Japan announced that it had extracted methane gas from hydrate deposits in the Nankai Trough, some 50 km (31 mi) offshore from Japan's main island. As of Feb 2015, however, commercial mining had not yet begun at the site.

Largest oil tanker

Four TI-class ultra-large crude carriers were built in 2002–03 by Daewoo Shipbuilding & Marine Engineering (KOR). They are 379 m (1,243 ft) long and 68 m (223 ft) wide, with a displacement of 517,659 tonnes (570,621 US tons) when full. Named *TI Europe*, *TI Oceania* (both owned by Euronav NV), *TI Africa* and *TI Asia*, they are the largest ships built since the *Jahre Viking* (aka *Seawise Giant* and *Knock Nevis*). In 2010, two of them became floating oil-storage vessels.

Highest gas pipeline

> **FACT**
>
> Below the Earth's surface are layers of shale – a type of rock that can trap natural gas. This is a good source of energy, but environmentalists are concerned at the damage that extracting it may cause.

Managed by Peru LNG SLR and Techint SAC (both PER), the highest gas pipeline stood at an altitude of 4,900 m (16,077 ft) when measured on 16 Aug 2009. It runs for more than 400 km (250 mi) across Peru, from Chiquintirca in Ayacucho to Pampa Melchorita.

The **longest offshore gas pipeline** is the Nord Stream, a pair of pipes running parallel for 1,222 km (759 mi) under the Baltic Sea. On 8 Oct 2012, they became active, linking Vyborg in Russia to Greifswald in Germany. The pipes can carry 55 billion m³ (1.9 trillion cu ft) of natural gas from Russia to Europe per year: enough to supply more than 26 million European houses.

Largest deposits of shale gas

In 2013, the US Energy Information Administration (EIA) published an analysis of global shale-gas reserves. China has the largest deposits – some 31.57 trillion m³ (1,100 trillion cu ft) of shale gas, which is recoverable with today's technologies. Second is Argentina, with 22.71 trillion m³ (800 trillion cu ft) of reserves.

By way of comparison, China's shale-gas reserves are the equivalent in volume of approximately 12.6 billion Olympic-sized swimming pools.

Largest natural-gas field

Discovered in 1971, the South Pars/North Dome Field gas field straddles the Iran-Qatar border and covers an underground area of 9,700 km^2 (3,745 sq mi). Its reserves have been estimated at an area the size of Cyprus – or 360 billion barrels of oil.

Deepest mine

The TauTona gold mine near Carletonville in South Africa is owned by AngloGold Ashanti. It opened in 1962 and, by 2008, had reached a depth of 3.9 km (2.4 mi).

Largest lapis lazuli mine

Prized for its intense, deep-blue colour, lapis lazuli is a semi-precious stone. An estimated 9,000 kg (19.8 million lb) per year is recovered from the Sary-Sang deposit in the Kokcha valley in Badakhshan Province, Afghanistan.

Heaviest offshore oil platform

The Hibernia oil platform is in the Atlantic off the coast of Newfoundland, Canada. It consists of a 37,000-tonne (81.5 million-lb) production facility atop a 600,000-tonne (661,387-US-ton) base that can store 1.3 million barrels of crude oil. The base also houses some 450,000 tonnes (992 million lb) of solid ballast, which secures the platform to the seabed. Crewed by 280 workers, the surface facility is designed to withstand impacts from Arctic icebergs.

First oil wells

The earliest known oil wells were dug in China during the 4th century AD. The first of these wells were simply bamboo poles hammered a few metres into oil-bearing soil, but by AD 347 workers were using basic drilling bits to reach depths of 240 m (785 ft). A modern recreation of the latter procedure is pictured right.

Deepest open pit mine

Bingham Canyon mine, owned by Rio Tinto Kennecott (USA), is around 4 km (2.4 mi) wide and 1.2 km (0.7 mi) deep. Located in Salt Lake City, Utah, USA, it has been in operation since 1906. In 2012, it produced around 179,317 tonnes (395.3 million lb) of copper, plus gold and other metals.

Longest continuously burning oil spill

Elastec/American Marine, Inc. (USA) deliberately started an oil-spill burn that lasted for 11 hr 48 min continuously, to remove oil spilled after an explosion on board the Deepwater Horizon oil drilling rig in the Gulf of Mexico, USA. The burn occurred on 19 May 2010.

Largest consumer of coal

China used 3.61 billion tonnes (3.98 billion US tons) of coal in 2013, according to the country's National Bureau of Statistics. The USA is the **largest consumer of natural gas**. Some 730 billion m^3 (26.1 trillion cu ft) was used in 2013, according to the US Energy Information Administration.

First country to ban fracking

Hydraulic fracturing, aka "fracking", is a technique to extract hydrocarbons using a high-pressure mixture of water, sand and chemicals. The potential risks – such as pollution to groundwater and perhaps even earthquakes – have made the process controversial. On 30 Jun 2011, the French parliament voted to ban it completely in France.

IN NUMBERS

1.5 kg
Weight of fossil fuels required to make just one 32-MB microchip (3 lb 8 oz)

28%
Amount of energy derived from coal in developed countries; for natural gas, the figure is 20%, while oil is the main source of energy, at 40%

60
Approximate number of chemical elements in a mobile phone

75 lb
Weight of gold that can be extracted from every 1 million recycled mobile phones (34 kg)

19 billion
Barrels of oil used daily in the USA

60 billion tonnes
Weight of raw materials extracted worldwide each year (66.1 billion US tons); that's more than the weight of 40,000 Empire State Buildings

Mine craft

Modern humans emerged about 200,000 years ago. Archaeologists estimate that the oldest mine – the chert (silica) mine at Nazlet Sabaha in Ga[illegible], Egypt – was first used just 100,000 years later, in the Middle Palaeolithic era. Our ancestors used silica to make tools, and to produce fires. Since then, we've been digging ever deeper in search of precious metals, energy supplies and useful minerals.

Grasberg mine (above left) in Papua, Indonesia, is the **largest gold mine** and sits on the single **largest gold deposit**. As of 31 Dec 2012, the total known reserves of gold here were estimated at 202,172.6 kg (445,714 lb). Grasberg also produces a range of other metals and ranks as the third-largest copper mine in the world.

The McArthur River uranium mine in northern Saskatchewan, Canada, owned mostly (69.8%) by Cameco (CAN), is the **most productive uranium mine**. In 2013, it produced 7,744 tonnes (17,072,597 lb) of uranium, which at that time constituted 13% of global uranium production. Carajás mine (above right) in Pará, northern Brazil, is the **largest iron-ore mine** and contained around 7.27 billion tonnes (8 billion US tons) of iron ore as of Dec 2012. That year, it produced 106.7 million tonnes (117.6 million US tons) of iron ore. The presence of rich iron-ore deposits was discovered accidentally in the 1960s by surveyors, who landed on a hill in the area to refuel their helicopter and took samples upon noticing how barren the land was. Like Grasberg, Carajás mine also produces other metals including gold, copper and tin.

Largest oil-producing company

Saudi Arabian Oil Co. (aka Saudi Aramco) controls 303,285 billion barrels' worth of oil reserves.

The **largest manufacturer of offshore rigs** is Keppel FELS (SGP), which delivered 21 offshore rigs from 1 Jan to 31 Dec 2013.

Most northerly oil terminal operational year-round

The Varandey offshore facility is located at 69°03'11"N 58°09'07"E, 22 km (13.7 mi) off the coast of Varandey in Nenets Autonomous Okrug, Russia. Owned by LUKOIL (RUS), it opened on 9 Jun 2008.

FACT

The Bingham Canyon mine (see p.38) is about four times the height of the Eiffel Tower in Paris. And it's about as broad as the island of Manhattan in New York City, USA, which is 3.7 km (2.3 mi) at its widest.

ANIMALS

Largest predatory fish

Adult specimens of the great white shark *(Carcharodon carcharias)* average 14–15 ft (4.3–4.6 m) long and weigh around 1,980 lb (900 kg). There are many claims of huge specimens reaching 33 ft (10 m) in length, and there is plenty of circumstantial evidence to suggest that some individuals exceed 20 ft (6 m) in length.

This extraordinary shot of a female great white was captured on 22 Aug 2014 by shark enthusiast and school teacher Amanda Brewer from New Jersey, USA, who was volunteering with the charity White Shark Africa in Mossel Bay, South Africa. She photographed the great white with her new GoPro camera while cage-diving off the coast of Seal Island; the image quickly went viral when posted on Twitter on 5 Oct.

CONTENTS

FACT

Shark fin soup is considered a delicacy in many parts of Asia, and an estimated 100 million sharks are killed each year because of the commercial trade in shark fins.

IN FOCUS
BLUE WHALE

Scientists can determine the **age of a whale** by counting the **layers of wax** that build up in its ear

A blue whale has a total lung capacity of 5,000 litres (1,320 US gal) – enough to inflate an estimated 2,000 party balloons

The vertical movement of the spine and digit-like bones in the fins hint at the whale's evolution from land mammals

On coming up for air, the blue whale can shoot a spout of steam/water up to 10 m (33 ft) from its blowhole

The brain is relatively small, weighing in at 6 kg (15 lb); a human's is 1.4 kg (3 lb)

Each upper jaw features about 400 baleen plates

Proportionally tiny, the eye is about the size of a grapefruit

Heart

Fine bristles (baleen) are used to sift out krill and small fish from water. They are made of keratin – the same material that forms our hair and fingernails

Weighing 4 tonnes (8,800 lb), the blue whale's tongue is the heaviest tongue – large enough to accommodate 50 people

Around 60 grooves run down the throat, enabling the gullet to stretch when gulping in water to feed

FACT

A blue whale calf can consume over 190 litres (50 US gal) of 40–50% fat milk daily for its first few months. After a year, it will put on about 32,850 kg (72,420 lb) in body weight!

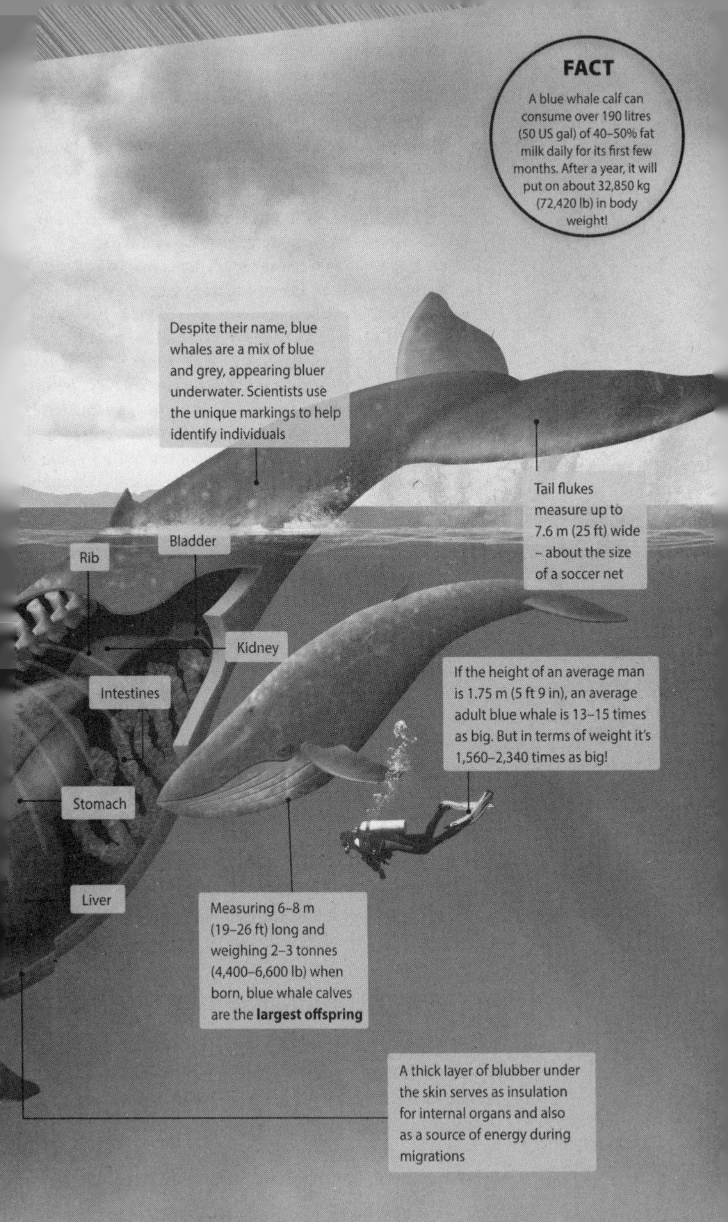

Despite their name, blue whales are a mix of blue and grey, appearing bluer underwater. Scientists use the unique markings to help identify individuals

Tail flukes measure up to 7.6 m (25 ft) wide – about the size of a soccer net

Rib

Bladder

Kidney

Intestines

Stomach

Liver

If the height of an average man is 1.75 m (5 ft 9 in), an average adult blue whale is 13–15 times as big. But in terms of weight it's 1,560–2,340 times as big!

Measuring 6–8 m (19–26 ft) long and weighing 2–3 tonnes (4,400–6,600 lb) when born, blue whale calves are the **largest offspring**

A thick layer of blubber under the skin serves as insulation for internal organs and also as a source of energy during migrations

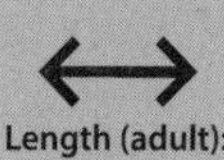

Length (adult):
Up to 30 m (100 ft)

Weight (adult):
Up to 200 tonnes (440,000 lb)

Average life span:
80–90 years

Gestation:
10–12 months

Speed:
Up to 50 km/h (31 mph)

Global population:
10,000–25,000

Maximum diving depth:
500 m (1,640 ft)

It comes as a surprise to many people that Earth's biggest ever creature wasn't a dinosaur. In fact, the **largest mammal ever**, and indeed the **largest animal ever**, is very much alive and kicking today, or at least alive and flipping.

The blue whale (*Balaenoptera musculus*) can measure some 30 m (100 ft) long and weigh 200 tonnes (440,000 lb), though on average they tend to fall within 23–27 m (70–90 ft) and 100–150 tonnes (200,000–300,000 lb). For a better grasp of their size, see the infographic on the previous page.

In comparison with dinosaurs, this upper weight limit is 28 times that of the *T. rex*, and around three times the estimated weight of the largest sauropod dinosaurs found to date.

So what exactly has enabled this creature to outscale anything that has lived before it? It all comes down to its environment. While dinosaurs and other land animals had to compete with gravity, the natural buoyancy in water counters this downward force. While terrestrial beasts could grow to huge sizes, there was always a biological cut-off point, because the proportional skeleton and muscles that are needed to support such bulk and also allow effective movement only work up to a limit.

If this is the case, you might reasonably ask: why aren't blue whales even bigger? Well, their anatomy has its limitations too. As a whale grows, so must all its component parts; vital organs such as the lungs and heart can only cope with so much body mass. Then there's the issue of being able to locate enough food to fuel that huge body. So the blue whale's size record seems fairly safe for the foreseeable future.

With 10,000–25,000 blue whales left in the wild today, they are classed as endangered by the International Union for Conservation of Nature. This may sound like quite a lot, but it's only 3–11% of the population in 1911. This massive decrease is mainly the result of intensive commercial whaling in the early 20th century.

Since being classed as a protected species in 1966, numbers have seen a steady rise, so the future is looking brighter for these gentle giants.

Big whale, big numbers

Whichever way you look at it, the blue whale is big. No animal has ever weighed more, several of its organs are record-breakers and even blue whale babies outsize many fully grown animals. We explore its supersized anatomy in the cutaway diagram on p.44.

A big-hearted beast

To maintain such a big body, the blue whale needs an equally big heart – the **largest heart** in the world, in fact. It weighs 680 kg (1,500 lb) – more than 2,226 times that of a human's – and is about the size of a VW Beetle car. The aorta is big enough for a human to crawl through (right).

There is a correlation between heart rate and longevity – see graph below for a comparison with us and other animals. Blue whales have the **slowest heartbeat in a mammal**, beating four to eight times per minute, and they live to 80–90 years.

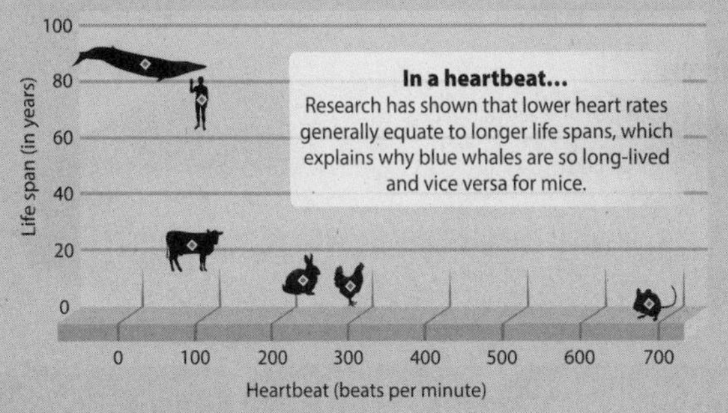

In a heartbeat...

Research has shown that lower heart rates generally equate to longer life spans, which explains why blue whales are so long-lived and vice versa for mice.

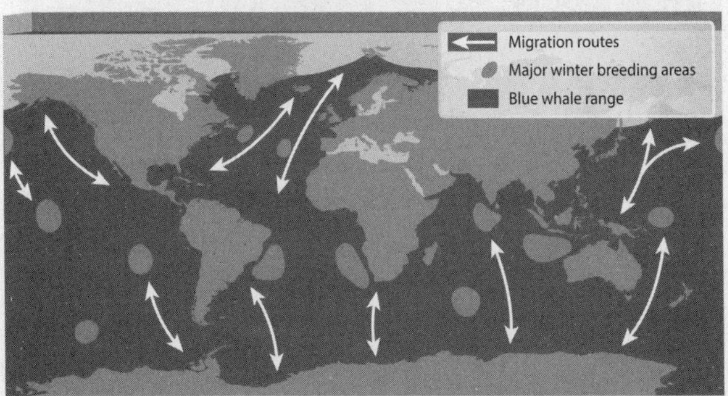

Blue whales live in all of Earth's oceans except polar waters. They generally spend the winter in the tropics to breed, moving to higher latitudes to feed in the summer months; this makes the blue whale the world's **largest migrant**.

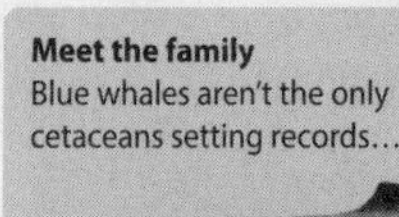

Meet the family
Blue whales aren't the only cetaceans setting records…

Humpback whale

Travelling up to 8,200 km (5,000 mi) each way, the humpback lays claim to the **longest mammal migration**.

Killer whale

Actually a dolphin, in spite of its name, the orca is the **fastest marine mammal**, reaching speeds of 55.5 km/h (34.5 mph).

How long?

How heavy?

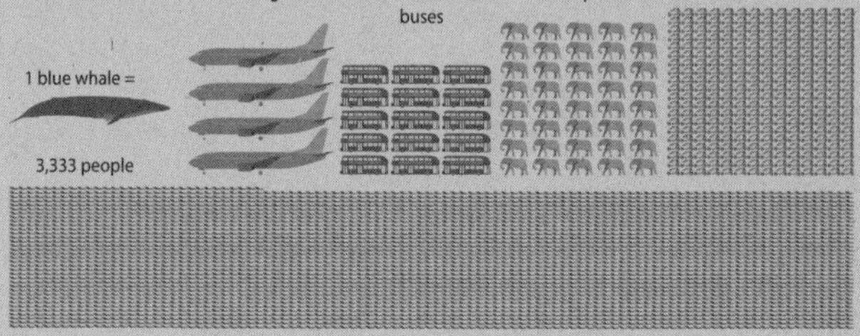

1 blue whale =

4 Boeing 737s

15 double-decker buses

40 elephants

270 Smart cars

3,333 people

Based on maximum size (rather than average)

Cuvier's beaked whale

A 2013 study tracked these whales reaching depths of 2,992 m (9,816 ft) – the **deepest dive by a mammal**.

Sperm whale

The sperm whale's brain tips the scales at 9 kg (19 lb 13 oz) – the **heaviest brain**.

Vaquita

With fewer than a hundred in the wild, and restricted to the Gulf of California, the world's **smallest porpoise** is also deemed the **rarest cetacean** by the IUCN.

Food for thought

The blue whale's diet is composed, for the most part, of crustaceans called krill (below), which are no more than a few centimetres in length; this extreme size gap represents the **greatest difference between predator and prey** in nature.

To feed, they open their cavernous mouth and gulp in huge quantities of krill-filled seawater. The world's **heaviest tongue** (see p.44) then comes into play, rising to the roof of the mouth to push out the water. The krill's escape is impeded by the long strands of baleen that hang from the whale's upper jaw. Here, they become entangled before being swallowed.

BATS

Bats are the **only mammals** capable of **true flight**, by beating their wings

Largest bat family

Vespertilionidae, the vesper bats, currently house over 300 species, with new ones described every year. They include pipistrelles, serotines, tube-nosed bats, mouse-eared bats and barbastelles. The **smallest bat family** is Craseonycteridae, which contains just a single species: *Craseonycteris thonglongyai*, aka Kitti's hog-nosed bat or bumblebee bat (see opposite).

Largest bat colonies

From March to October each year, up to 20 million females and offspring of the Mexican free-tailed bat species (*Tadarida brasiliensis*) populate Bracken Cave in San Antonio, Texas, USA. Their spiralling sorties for food each night can be picked up on local airport radar.

The same migratory species forms the **largest urban bat colony** at the Ann W Richards Congress Avenue Bridge in Austin, Texas, USA. In summer, 750,000–1.5 million bats hang out below the bridge's deck, roosting in gaps between the component structures.

Rarest bat

Exact numbers of the ghost bat (*Macroderma gigas*) are unknown, but there are probably no more than 1,500. They were formerly found across northern Australia, but the largest colony is now in the Mount Etna Caves in Queensland, Australia. In 1966,

Largest bat

Flying foxes or fruit bats (family Pteropodidae) are considered megabats. Several species in the genus *Pteropus* have a head–body length up to 45 cm (17.75 in), a wing-span of 1.7 m (5 ft 7 in) and weigh in at 1.6 kg (3 lb 12 oz). Largest of all are the large flying fox (*P. vampyrus*) and the gigantic or Indian flying fox (*P. giganteus*). Unlike other bats, flying foxes do not have echolocation for catching insects, but feed on nectar, flowers, pollen and fruit in the tropical forests of Asia.

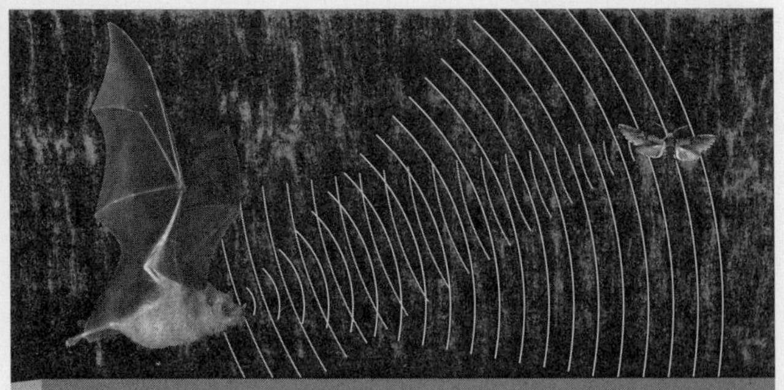

Most acute hearing of any non-aquatic animal

Bats use ultrasonic echolocation to find prey and communicate. They send out sound waves with their mouth or nose, and when the sound hits an object, an echo comes back. Most species use frequencies of 20–80 kHz, though some can hear frequencies as high as 120–250 kHz, the human limit being just under 20 kHz. Their echolocation system is so accurate that they can detect insects as tiny as gnats.

before open-cast limestone quarrying began, there were 450 bats inhabiting the caves, but, despite having full protection, today there are fewer than 150.

Newest mammal in Europe

Endemic to the island of Cyprus and formally described in 2007, the Cypriot soprano pipistrelle (*Pipistrellus pygmaeus cyprius*) is the latest mammal to be discovered in Europe. Its echolocation call is 55 kHz, 10 kHz higher than that of the closely related common pipistrelle (*P. Pipistrellus*).

Smallest mammal

The tiny Kitti's hog-nosed bat (*Craseonycteris thonglongyai*) has a body no bigger than a large bumblebee. Its head–body length is only 2.9–3.3 cm (1.14–1.30 in), its average wing-span is 13–14.5 cm (5.1–5.7 in) and it weighs just 1.7–2 g (0.06–0.07 oz).

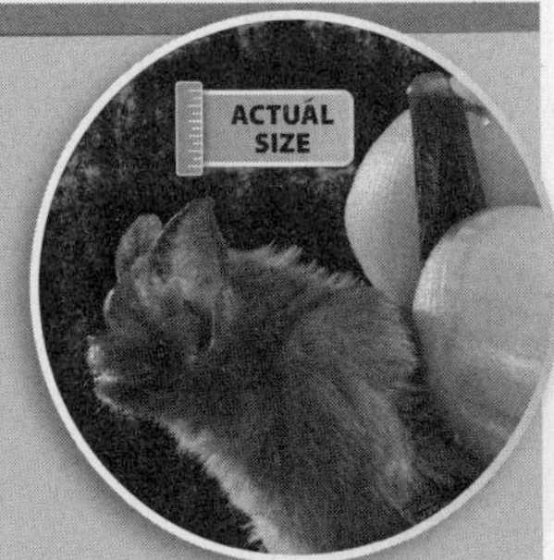

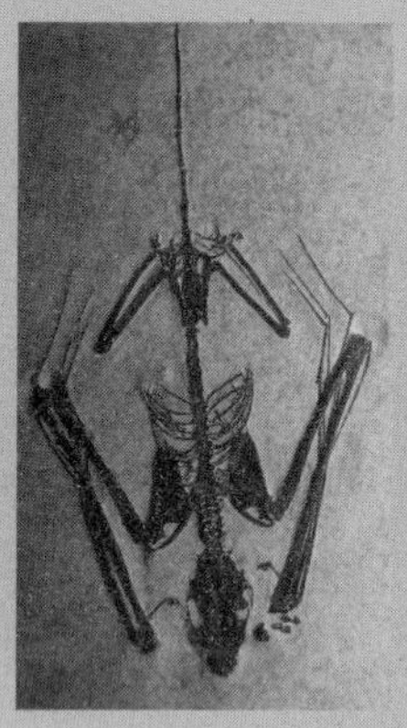

First bat species

Officially named and described in 1966, the earliest confirmed species of bat is *Icaronycteris index*, dating from the early Eocene epoch (53.5–48.5 million years ago).

It is known from four exceptionally well-preserved fossil skeletons discovered in the Green River Formation of Wyoming, USA, and belongs to the micro-bat (microchiropteran) suborder. The fossils reveal that it was approximately 5.5 in (14 cm) long, and sported a wing-span of 14.5 in (37 cm).

Most northerly bat species

The northern bat (*Eptesicus nilssonii*) is a widely distributed Eurasian species found inside the Arctic Circle in Norway, with one specimen documented from Austertana in Norway, at 70°N 25°E.

Longest distance flown by a bat

A specimen of the European noctule (*Nyctalus noctula*) achieved the astounding distance of 2,347 km (1,458 mi). The animal was originally ringed in Aug 1957 at Voronezh, Russia,

Largest carnivorous bat

The sharp-fanged spectral bat (*Vampyrum spectrum*) of Mexico, Central America and northern South America flaps away with this prize, as well as being the **largest bat in the New World.** Its wing-span can just exceed 100 cm (39 in) and its head–body length is 12.5–13.5 cm (5–5.3 in). It is a species of false vampire bat, a group that was once wrongly believed to feed on blood. It preys on small mammals (including other bats), birds, small reptiles, amphibians and insects.

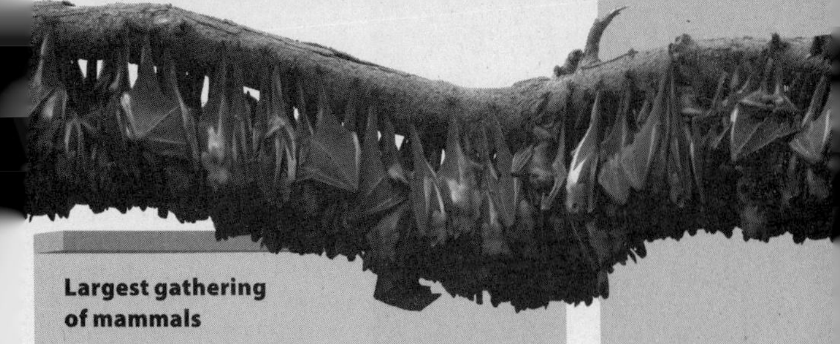

Largest gathering of mammals

Every October, 5–10 million straw-coloured fruit bats (*Eidolon helvum*) converge from all over Africa on 1 ha (2.5 acres) of swamp forest in Kasanka National Park in Zambia. During their six-week stay, they make nocturnal excursions to feed on wild fruit. By day, they sleep upside-down in the trees, which often break under their massed weight!

by Russian bat specialist Dr Petr P Strelkov, and was recorded again in Jan 1961 in southern Bulgaria.

The award for the **greatest weight carried by a bat in flight** goes to the adult female eastern red bat (*Lasiurus borealis*). This impressively strong flier, which weighs 9.5–14 g (0.34–0.5 oz) on average, is able to fly with two or even three infants clinging to her thick fur, their combined weight readily exceeding her own.

Longest gestation period for a bat

The common vampire bat (*Desmodus rotundus*; see panel, p.54) has a very prolonged gestation period of seven to eight months, compared with nine months in humans. The newborn then

IN NUMBERS

225
Bat species in Indonesia, the **most bat species by country**

1,240
Living bat species, approximately, known to science; new species are added each year

300,000
Bats in the **most populated artificial bat roost**, at the University of Florida, USA

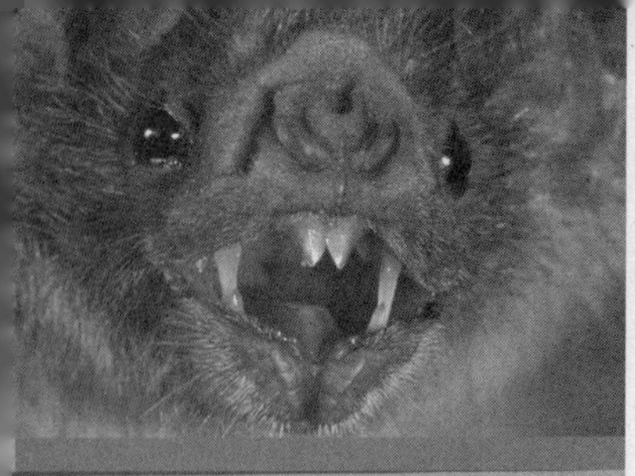

Feasting on blood

Bram Stoker's classic Gothic novel *Dracula* has inspired horror films such as *Nosferatu the Vampyre* (inset below) – and given us a very dark view of vampire bats. The truth is rather less frightening – but just as fascinating.

The common vampire bat (*D. rotundus*, above) has only 20 teeth in total, making it the **bat species with the fewest teeth**. The upper incisors and upper canines, used for slicing through skin to inflict bleeding wounds, are large, but the other teeth are tiny. The three species of vampire bat live in Central and South America.

Vampire bats quickly starve without regular meals of around 1 oz (28.4 ml) of blood. A colony of 100 bats can drink the equivalent of 25 cows' worth of blood in a year, but the bats themselves are only just larger than an adult human's thumb.

Vampire bats prefer the blood of pigs, chickens, cows or horses to humans'. They inflict bite wounds with their incisor teeth, then lick rather than suck the blood flow with their groove-shaped tongues (below). An anticoagulant in the bat's saliva – named Draculin – prevents the blood from clotting. Their victims don't die, but may get infections from their uninvited guests.

suckles its mother for nine months, sometimes even longer.

Largest litter by a bat species

Most species give birth to a single young or pup, but several species of the genus *Lasiurus*, including the eastern red bat (*L. borealis*), the hoary bat (*L. cinereus*) and the northern yellow bat (*L. intermedius*), produce litters of up to four pups.

Bats with the longest ears (proportionate to body)

The spotted bat (*Euderma maculatum*) of south-western Canada, the western USA and northern Mexico has translucent pink ears, each up to 5 cm (2 in) long. Its entire head–body length is only 6–7.7 cm (2.3–3 in) long.

Longest mammalian tongue (proportionate)

The nectar bat (*Anoura fistulata*) of the Ecuadorian Andes has a tongue with a reach of 8.49 cm (3.34 in): 150% of its body length. When not in use, it is stored inside its ribcage. Discovered and first described in 2005 by Dr Nathan Muchhala of the University of Miami in Florida, USA, the nectar bat is the sole pollinator of *Centropogon nigricans*, which has tubular flowers measuring 8–9 cm (3.14–3.54 in) long.

FACT

At birth, a bat pup weighs up to 25% of its mother's weight. This equates to a woman giving birth to a 14-kg (31-lb) baby – the same weight as the average three-year-old child!

BEARS

The **grizzly** was named after its white- or grey-tipped (**"grizzled"**) outer hairs

Most common bear species

The American black bear (*U. americanus*) numbers an estimated 600,000–800,000 individuals, or twice the total number of all the world's other seven bear species. It inhabits much of the continent's forests.

The **bear with most subspecies** is the brown bear (*U. arctos*), native to Eurasia and North America. It heads up a family tree of 15 surviving subspecies including the red-furred Himalayan isabelline bear (*U. a. isabellinus*), the Tibetan blue bear (*U. a. pruinosus*), the common grizzly (*U. a. horribilis*, see below) and the Kodiak bear (*U. a. middendorffi*).

Newest giant panda

For the first time, in 2005, the Qinling giant panda (*Ailuropoda melanoleuca qinlingensis*) was formally recognized as a separate subspecies. It differs from the familiar giant panda in having dark brown and light brown fur, a rounder, smaller head and longer teeth. It is thought that 200–300 individuals inhabit the Qinling Mountains in southern China.

Largest litter of bears born in captivity

Tiny, furry and helpless, quintuplet brown bears (*Ursus arctos*) were born on 6 Jan 2002 in Zoo Košice, Košice-Kavečany, Slovakia. The three males and two females were named Miso, Tapik, Dazzle, Bubu and Cindy. This was a particularly impressive result both for parents and zoo, as most bears usually have just one or two cubs at a time.

Smallest bear

With the adult male measuring 1.4 m (4 ft 6 in) long, the Malayan sun bear (*U. malayanus*) scoops the diminutive prize. Named after the golden crescent on their chest, sun bears are agile tree climbers, using their long tongue and 15-cm (6-in) claws to forage for fruit, honey and grubs.

Most varied diet for a bear

South America's only bear and largest land mammal carnivore, the spectacled bear (*Tremarctos ornatus*) eats more than 80 different items. Its diet includes the vicuña (a species related to llamas), rabbits, deer, birds, 32 species of fruit, 11 species of cactus, 22 species of bromeliad and various moss and orchid bulbs. Its hefty jaw muscles and sharp teeth allow it to tear and chew the toughest plants.

The **smallest species of giant panda** was the now-extinct dwarf or pygmy giant panda (*A. microta*), which evolved 2–2.4 million years ago. Around 1 m (3 ft 3 in) long, it resembled a fat domestic dog and lived in lowland tropical bamboo forests in China.

Bear with the longest tail

Most bear species have very short or insignificant tails (unlike their early ancestors) and the Asian sloth bear (*Melursus ursinus*) has the longest of all, at 15–18 cm (6–7 in).

BRUISING BRUINS ON PARADE – COMPARING BEARS FROM LARGE TO LITTLE

Evolutionists believe that bears' tails became shorter because they served no useful purpose. In dogs, close relatives of bears, the tail plays a very important role in communication, and so has remained long and prominent. During display behaviour, however, bears tend to confront or pose face-on, and the tail is not in view.

Fastest bear (sustained)

Bears are not generally noted for quick movement. The fastest reliably recorded speed is 56 km/h (35 mph), achieved by a polar bear (*U. maritimus*) running along a road in Churchill, Manitoba, Canada, on 16 Dec 2011.

The polar bear has the **most efficient insulation of any bear species**. Even when the external temperature drops as

Largest bear ever

The tyrant polar bear (*U. m. tyrannus*; likely appearance shown below far left) of the mid-Pleistocene epoch (250,000–100,000 years ago) would have towered over, if not tyrannized, all other bears yet to come. Standing 1.83 m (6 ft) at the shoulder and measuring 3.7 m (12 ft 2 in) long, it weighed on average at least 1 tonne (2,200 lb). This fossil subspecies was also the very **first polar bear**, and the **largest terrestrial mammalian carnivore**.

Next in line, the modern polar bear is the **largest bear** (see overleaf), with the male reaching 2.4–2.6 m (7 ft 11 in–8 ft 6 in) long, nose to tail. At 1.5–2.5 m (5–8 ft), its neighbour, the grizzly (*U. a. horribilis*), still easily dwarfs a human. The giant panda (*A. melanoleuca*) may attain a less prodigious 1.9 m (6 ft 9 in) but looks bulky alongside *U. malayanus*, the smallest bear (see opposite).

IN NUMBERS

30,000 km^2
Home range of the polar bear, the **largest range of any land mammal** (11,583 sq mi)

15
Number of hours per day a panda spends eating

8
Bear species alive today

200,000
Estimated population of brown bears living in the wild in Eurasia and North America

82°C
Temperature a black bear's fur can reach in direct sunshine (179.6°F)

50
Age of Andreas, the **oldest brown bear in captivity**, who died on 24 May 2013 in Greece

5,300,000
Years ago that several lineages of the genus *Ursus* appeared, of which the sloth bear is a survivor

25 years
Average lifespan of a grizzly in the wild; bears can live twice this long in captivity

Largest carnivore on land

Adult male polar bears (*U. maritimus*) typically weigh 400–600 kg (880–1,320 lb) and have a stomach capacity of c. 70 kg (150 lb). Their digestive system is more adapted to a meat than a vegetarian diet, and they are known to kill walruses (500 kg; 1,100 lb) and beluga whales (600 kg; 1,320 lb) – the **largest prey** of any animal.

In the open sea, they paddle with their massive forepaws, and have been known to swim 3,000 mi (4,800 km) to hunt seals.

low as -37°C (-34.6°F), its body temperature and metabolism remain normal owing to a layer of pelage (fur) and blubber up to 10 cm (4 in) thick.

Equipped with the **most sensitive nose for a land mammal**, the polar bear can detect prey, such as seals, over 30 km (18 mi) away and even below the ice. One bear was recorded walking in a direct line for 32 km (20 mi) to reach food.

Rarest bear

A controversial species, MacFarlane's bear (aka the patriarchal bear or unexpected bear), consists of one specimen: a large, yellow-furred individual killed on 24 Jun 1864 by two hunters in Canada's Barren Grounds region.

It was originally assumed to be a grizzly, but in 1918 renowned American naturalist Prof C Hart Merriam examined its skull and pelt. He considered the bear to be so different from all others that he made it a new species, *Vetularctos inopinatus*. Recent researchers, however, have suggested it might have been an unusual grizzly or a grizzly-polar bear hybrid – a pizzly.

FACT

American black bears (see p.55) range in colour from black through shades of brown to white. These variations aid camouflage and heat control, since lighter fur reflects sunlight more than darker fur.

The bear necessities

This giant panda (*A. melanoleuca*) has long been a symbol of animal conservation. This real-life teddy bear has many unique facts to its name.

Origins: The panda diverged from all other bears 18–25 million years ago and has its own subfamily, Ailuropodinae, making it the **most primitive species of living bear**.

Habitat: Indigenous to China, pandas live in mountain forests with a dense growth of bamboo, which makes up 99% of their diet. The Sichuan Giant Panda Sanctuaries in the Qionglai and Jiajin Mountains represent the **largest contiguous panda habitat**. More than 30% of the world's panda population lives in this 9,245-km^2 (3,569-sq-mi) network of nature reserves and scenic parks.

Breeding and young: Solitary pandas only associate when a female is ready to mate, which she indicates by a system of distinct calls. One or two tiny cubs are born nearly naked and just 15 cm (6 in) long. At just 1/900th the size of its mother, the panda cub is the **smallest placental mammal baby relative to adult body size**.

In captivity: All pandas in captivity are owned by China. Four zoos in the USA each pay the Chinese government an annual leasing fee of $1 m (£0.66 m) per pair of pandas. A one-off payment of $600,000 (£394,000) is also due for any cub born. With upkeep expenses, such as bamboo production and security, this makes the panda the **most expensive zoo species**.

BEES, WASPS & HORNETS

To produce 1 kg of honey, a hive of bees will fly **145,000 km** – that's more than **three times around the Earth**!

Largest bumblebee species

The giant bumblebee (*Bombus dahlbomii*) is the only native bumblebee in South America's temperate forests; the ginger-furred queens of this species measure up to 4 cm (1.5 in) long. Giant bumblebees once ranged across thousands of kilometres in Patagonia, in southernmost South America, but in recent years they have become rare and experts fear that they face extinction in the near future.

Lightest wasp

Caraphractus cinctus is a tiny species of parasitic chalcid wasp, commonly known as a fairyfly, that can weigh as little as 0.005 mg. It would take 5,670,000 of these wasps together to make just a single ounce (about the weight of a pencil). The fairyfly is an aquatic freshwater species, widely distributed through Europe. It parasitizes the eggs of water beetles, and uses its wings as paddles to swim around.

Unsurprisingly, the fairyfly also produces the **lightest eggs laid by a wasp**. Each egg weighs just 0.0002 mg, so it would take an astonishing 141,750,000 of these eggs to weigh an ounce.

Oldest hymenopterans

The most ancient members of this order belong to the family Xyelidae, and consist of prehistoric sawflies dating back to the Triassic Period,

Largest wasps' nest

In Apr 1963, a wasps' nest discovered on a farm at Waimauku in New Zealand measured 3.7 m (12 ft 2 in) long, with a diameter of 1.75 m (5 ft 9 in) and a circumference of 5.5 m (18 ft).

Shown inset is a wasps' nest photographed in an abandoned home on the Spanish island of La Gomera in 2013; although it was never accurately measured, police estimates put its length at 6.6 m (21 ft 9 in).

245–208 million years ago. They have been discovered variously in central Asia, South Africa and Australia. The first such species to be discovered was *Archexyela crosbyi*, represented by two specimens found in the Mount Crosby Formation near Ipswich in Queensland, Australia; it was officially named and described in 1955. A second species, represented by a single specimen found in the same formation, was described in 2005 and was named *A. ipswichensis*.

FACT

Hornets, like this Asian giant hornet, are "true wasps", belonging to the family Vespidae. Several other wasp families are not true wasps – including Pompilidae, the spider wasps (see p.63)

Largest hornet and largest true wasp

The Asian giant hornet (*Vespa mandarinia*, also pictured on p.61) is native to the mountains of Japan and can grow to 2.2 in (5.5 cm) in length, with a wing-span of approximately 3 in (7.6 cm). Its sting is about 0.25 in (0.6 cm) long and can inject a venom so powerful that it dissolves human tissue.

It is both the largest hornet and the **largest true wasp** (see Fact on p.61). The common wasps that we see in summer are also true wasps.

Largest bee

Females of the king bee (*Megachile pluto*) are 4.5 cm (1.7 in) long, including mandibles. Males are a relatively modest 2.4 cm (0.9 in). The king bee occurs only in the Moluccas (Maluku) Islands of Indonesia, and was discovered in 1859 by British naturalist Alfred Russel Wallace.

Longest hymenopteran eggs

The order Hymenoptera includes bees, wasps, ants and sawflies. Some eggs laid by *Xylocopa auripennis*, a species of Sri Lankan carpenter bee – so named as they build their nests in burrows in dead wood or timbers – measure up to 1.65 cm (0.6 in) long, though only about 0.3 cm (0.1 in) wide.

FACT

About 40 people die each year after being stung by an Asian giant hornet (*Vespa mandarinia japonica*, see opposite). Medical treatment is typically required after as few as 10 stings.

Largest wasp

The giant tarantula hawk wasp (*Pepsis heros*) preys on the goliath bird-eating spider and other tarantula species. The largest recorded specimen is a female that was obtained in Peru's Yanachaga-Chemillén National Park and is currently in a collection at the Universidad Nacional Mayor de San Marcos in Peru's capital city, Lima. The specimen has a curved body length of 6.2 cm (2.25 in) and a total wing-span of 12.15 cm (4.75 in) – the **largest wing-span for a hymenopteran.**

The males, which are considerably smaller than the females, do not hunt spiders. They feed on flowering vegetation.

ACTUAL SIZE

IN NUMBERS

25,000+
Bee species

7
True honey bee species

20+
Hornet species

200
Wingbeats per second for a flying bee

1 oz
Weight of honey that would be needed to fuel a bee's flight around the world

3–6,000
Wasps in an average nest

12–22
Average life-span in days of a worker wasp

The ultimate buzz

"Bee bearding" is a carnival act thought to date back to the 19th century. Performers place a queen bee on their bodies, attracting thousands of insects. Current king of the bearders is Ruan Liangming (CHN), who achieved the heaviest mantle of bees and longest duration with head covered by bees.

What did your family think when you began "bee bearding"?
I started beekeeping in 1995 and became involved with bee bearding in 2000, aged 24. My family supports me very much. My brothers help load the bees in the car when I do outdoor honey collection and help carry bee boxes on record attempts.

Do you get used to bee stings?
I was stung in the learning stage, but rarely now that I'm getting to know bees' habits.

What did you think about for those 53 min 34 sec when your head was covered by bees?
At first, only half of my face was covered. I kept thinking, "How can I make them cover my whole face?" When they were fully over my face, the adjudicator announced the beginning of the attempt.

The challenger must keep calm when dealing with bees. Bees will die once they sting you, so they usually avoid stinging unless they think you're threatening them. If you notice bees are in an "unsteady" mood, you need to figure out the reason quickly or stop the record attempt.

LARGEST...

Honeycomb

Honey bees secrete wax in order to build hexagonal cells – honeycombs – in their nests, which they use for the storage of larvae, honey and pollen. On 30 Aug 2007, a honeycomb weighing 10.4 kg (22 lb 14 oz) was removed from a beehive owned by Argirios Koskos (GRC).

Hornets' nest sculpture

Sculptor Yoshikuni Shiozawa (JPN) has created a composite hornets' nest in the shape of Mount Fuji, composed of 160 genuine hornets' nests joined together. It measures 4.8 m (15 ft 9 in) wide at its base, stands 3.7 m (12 ft 4 in) high, and contains an estimated 160,000 Japanese yellow hornets (*Vespa simillima xanthoptera*).

As it houses living hornets, the sculpture also qualifies as the **largest hornets' nest**.

Bee house

On 18 Jun 2011, London Wildlife Trust (UK) completed a bee house measuring 13.04 x 1.27 x 0.36 m (42 ft 9 in x 4 ft 2 in x 1 ft 2 in) at Barking Riverside in the London Borough of Barking and Dagenham, UK. The house was built from more than 20,000 pieces of bamboo, and was designed specifically to attract solitary bees, which make up 90% of the UK bee population but which do not form colonies of their own.

FACT

In the 1950s, Brazilian scientists bred bees from southern Africa with local bees to try to produce a hyrid adaptable to Brazil's tropical climate. The Africanized honey bee (right) was the result.

Smallest bee

Native to the south-western USA, *Perdita minima* is a minute solitary bee just under 0.2 cm (0.07 in) long and weighing only 0.333 mg (or 85 to the ounce). It constructs a tiny nest in sandy soils, and feeds upon the nectar and pollen of spurge flowers.

Most dangerous bee

The Africanized honey bee (*Apis mellifera scutellata*) will generally only attack when provoked, but is persistent in pursuit. It is very aggressive and fiercely protective of territories of up to a half-mile radius (0.8 km). It attacks in swarms, so although its venom is no more potent than that of other bees, its victims can easily be killed owing to the number of stings received.

BUTTERFLIES & MOTHS

Butterflies **"taste" plants** through receptors on **their feet**

Earliest lepidopteran

A small, primitive moth-like insect, *Archaeolepis mane*, formally named and described in 1985, is the earliest known species of fossil lepidopteran. Found in Dorset, UK, it is about 190 million years old, from the Lower Jurassic Period.

The **oldest moth whose colouration is known** is an unnamed fossil species around 47 million years old, from the mid-Eocene Epoch. In Nov 2011, scientists from Yale University used electron microscopy on some well-preserved fossils to deduce, from anatomical detail in their scales, that the dorsal forewings had a very vivid, "psychedelic" yellow-green hue with blue tips. Colouration usually becomes lost during the process of fossilization.

Largest family of butterflies

Nymphalidae, the brush-footed butterflies, currently contains around 6,000 species and has a worldwide distribution. It includes some of the best-known and most beautiful species, such as the monarchs, fritillaries, tortoiseshells, browns (satyrids), passion-flower butterflies, morphos and admirals. Nymphalids are known as brush-footed butterflies because their small forelegs are very hairy and brush-like.

All male and most female Nymphalids have the **fewest functional legs in a butterfly**. Of the usual six legs, the first pair (the forelegs) are reduced in size, as they lack limb portions.

Most venomous caterpillar

Giant silkworm moths in the genus *Lonomia* carry a potent anticoagulant in their dense covering of hairs. This can cause massive internal haemorrhaging, renal failure and even death.

Lowest temperature endured by insects

The woolly bear caterpillar of the Greenland tiger moth (*Gynaephora groenlandica*), native to the high Arctic, can survive up to 10 months of the year frozen solid at temperatures as low as -50°C (-58°F).

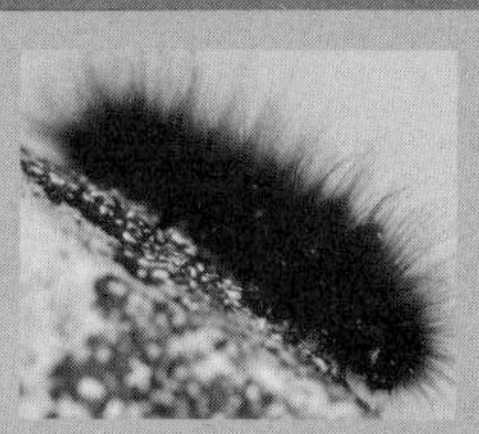

Most acute sense of smell

The male emperor moth (*Eudia pavonia*) can detect the sex attractant of the virgin female at a range of 11 km (6.8 mi). The female carries less than 0.0001 mg of scent, but sensitive chemoreceptors on the male moth's antennae can detect just a single molecule of this.

The Noctuidae or owlet moths are the **largest family of moths**, with more than 35,000 species known to science worldwide. Many have cryptic (well-camouflaged) upper forewing colouration and patterning, making them difficult to spot, so there may be numerous other species (possibly up to 65,000 or so) still awaiting formal discovery.

Greatest wing-span for a moth

The white witch or great owlet moth (*Thysania agrippina*) usually has a wing-span of around 28 cm (11 in), but one exceptional specimen from 1934 sported a wing-span of 30.8 cm (12.1 in). Great owlets are native to South America, Central America and Mexico, but sometimes stray asfar north as Texas, USA.

Largest moth

The atlas moth (*Attacus atlas*, right), found natively in south-east Asia, is the giant of them all in terms of wing-span – 30 cm (12 in) – so it is often mistaken for a bird. It has no mouth, and only lives for about four days, subsisting on fat stored at earlier stages in its cycle.

The female hercules moth (*Coscinocera hercules*) of Australia and New Guinea has a wing-span of 28 cm (11 in) with a surface area of up to 300 cm2 (46 sq in), and therefore is the largest moth by wing-span surface area.

IN NUMBERS

174,250
Estimated number of butterfly and moth species

4,000
Muscles in certain caterpillars (more than six times the number in humans)

6 mm
Forewing length of the grass blue (*Zizula hylax*), the **smallest butterfly by forewing length** (0.2 in)

2 mm
Wing-span of the **smallest moth** (0.07 in): *Stigmella ridiculosa*

31.2 g
Weight of the **heaviest moth specimen** (1.1 oz): a female giant wood moth (*Endoxyla cinereus*)

5
Beats per sec, the **slowest wing beat by an insect**, for the European swallowtail butterfly (*Papilio machaon*)

2–4 weeks
Life span of a butterfly; some overwintering species live up to nine months

13°C
Ambient temperature below which butterflies cannot fly (55.4°F)

Largest skipper

Housed in their own superfamily, skippers are separate from so-called true butterflies in having certain features more reminiscent of moths than butterflies. More than 4,000 skipper species worldwide are recognized.

The largest species is the bear giant-skipper (*Megathymus ursus*), native to the southern states of the USA, including Texas, Arizona and New Mexico. It has a wing-span of 6.3–7.6 cm (2.5–3 in).

Highest whistle by a caterpillar

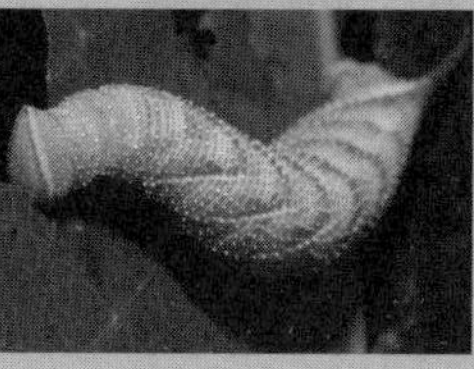

If attacked, the caterpillar of the walnut sphinx (*Amorpha juglandis*), a North American hawk moth, sharply expels air from a pair of respiratory holes, making a high-pitched whistle that can hit frequencies of 22 kHz.

Largest appetite relative to weight in an animal

The caterpillar of the North American silk moth (*Antheraea polyphemus*) lives on the leaves of oak, birch, willow and maple trees. In the first 56 days of its life, it consumes an amount equal to 86,000 times its own weight. In human terms, this would equate to a 3.17-kg (7-lb) baby taking in 273 tonnes (601,861 lb) of nourishment over the same period.

Fastest caterpillar

When threatened, the larva of the mother-of-pearl moth (*Pleuroptya ruralis*) can travel 38.1 cm (15 in) in one second (1.37 km/h; 0.8 mph). It does this by turning into a "wheel" and rolling out of danger. In 2011, this form of "ballistic rolling" inspired roboticists researching locomotion to create "GoQBot": a soft-bodied rolling robot.

Largest butterfly

Female specimens of Queen Alexandra's birdwing (*Ornithoptera alexandrae*), native to Papua New Guinea, can have a wing-span in excess of 28 cm (11 in) and weigh over 25 g (0.9 oz). They are larger than the males (inset), whose wing-span is 16–20 cm (6–8 in). This is a poisonous species, since the caterpillars live off the toxic pipevine plant.

Smallest butterfly by wing-span

The male dwarf blue (*Oraidium*, formerly *Brephidium*, *barberae*) of South Africa has a 1.4-cm (0.55-in) wing-span and weighs under 10 mg (0.00035 oz). Its name refers to the subfamily of blues to which it belongs, rather than its colouring.

From grub to beauty

Strange as it may seem, the grub-like caterpillar is as much a butterfly or moth as the fragile creature hovering over a flower. Its life cycle of changes from egg to winged beauty is one of the wonders of the natural world.

Take one egg...

A butterfly starts out as one of many tiny eggs laid on a leaf by the female. They may be round, oval or cylindrical, and with some, such as the monarch, it is possible to see the caterpillar inside.

The mother lays her eggs on the kind of leaf the caterpillars will like. When the eggs hatch, they must eat voraciously to grow. Their skin cannot stretch, so they shed it several times as they expand.

When a caterpillar has reached its full length and weight, it stops eating and becomes a pupa or chrysalis. Inside a dry outer casing, the body changes completely to form the tissue, limbs and wings of the butterfly.

When the fully formed adult emerges, it pumps blood into its crumpled wings to distend and strengthen them. Once it has mastered the art of flying, which takes about 3–4 hours, it is off to find a mate.

Migrating species

Not all butterflies have a brief life. Some are migratory, such as the monarch of North America (inset right, bottom), which flies south in October to winter in California and New Mexico. They make the longest journey of any butterfly – around 3,000 mi (4,828 km). Only adults that emerge in late summer make the round trip, and they do so just once. Several generations intervene before the next migration, yet those new adults will know exactly when and where to go.

The monarch's journey also represents the longest insect migration, outflying its nearest rival, the desert locust *Schistocerca gregaria*, which has been recorded travelling 2,800 mi (4,500 km).

Most acute hearing in an insect

The greater wax moth (*Galleria mellonella*), native to Europe and Asia, can detect sound frequencies of up to 300 kHz. This is 15 times higher than the highest frequency – around 20 kHz – that humans can hear. It is believed to have evolved such exceptional hearing to avoid bats, its major predators, many of which communicate via sonar using ultrasonic squeaks (see p.51).

Longest insect tongue

Morgan's sphinx moth (*Xanthopan morganii praedicta*), a large hawk moth native to Madagascar, has a tongue, or proboscis, measuring 30–35 cm (12–14 in). This is more than twice the length of the moth itself, enabling it to reach the nectar stored deep inside the star-shaped flowers of the comet orchid. In the process, the moth benefits the flower by pollinating it.

FACT

Unlike his larger partner, the male Queen Alexandra's birdwing (below) has dramatic green and black patterning and slightly pointed wings – key differences known as sexual dimorphism.

DOLPHINS

A dolphin mother **constantly whistles** to her newborn calf for several days so it will **recognize her sound**

Largest dolphin genus

Six species of worldwide distribution are housed in the genus *Lagenorhynchus*. They are the Atlantic white-sided dolphin (*L. acutus*), the white-beaked dolphin (*L. albirostris*), Peale's dolphin (*L. australis*), the hourglass dolphin (*L. cruciger*), the Pacific white-sided dolphin (*L. obliquidens*) and the dusky dolphin (*L. obscurus*).

Smallest dolphin species

The petite and extremely rare Hector's dolphin (*Cephalorhynchus hectori*) is confined to the waters off New Zealand. Mature adult specimens have a total length of 1.2–1.6 m (3 ft 11 in–5 ft 2.8 in) and weigh 40–60 kg (88–132 lb).

First hybrid marine mammal species

The clymene dolphin (*Stenella clymene*), a small, sleek inhabitant of the Atlantic Ocean, is the first documented instance of a marine mammal species originating from the natural hybridization of two other species. A molecular analysis published in Jan 2014 revealed it to be the product of hybridization between the spinner dolphin (*S. longirostris*) and striped dolphin (*S. coeruleoalba*), and now a valid species in its own right. The creation of a new species via natural hybridization is common in plants but very rare in animals.

Newest freshwater cetacean

The Araguaian river dolphin or Araguaian boto (*Inia araguaiaensis*) was scientifically recognized in Jan 2014. Native to the Araguaia River basin in Brazil, it is the first discovery of a new species for almost a century. It

Highest jump by a dolphin

The bottlenose dolphin (Tursiops truncatus) – named for its stubby beak – can make leaps as high as 26 ft (8 m) above the surface of the water. The reason that dolphins jump in the wild is debated but may be to do with saving energy, cleaning themselves, locating prey, communicating with their pod or even just for fun.

? GLOSSARY

Blubber: The thick layer of fat beneath a dolphin's skin that allows it to regulate its temperature.

Melon: The fatty structure in a dolphin's forehead that focuses the clicking sounds (click trains) whereby the animal locates food or obstacles underwater. When the clicks hit an object, the echo returns to the dolphin via its jaw and inner ear, giving information on size, distance and so on.

joined with two other South American species to make Iniidae, the **largest family of freshwater dolphins**. Its fellow species are the Amazon river dolphin (*I. geoffrensis*) and Bolivian river dolphin (*I. boliviensis*).

First dolphin to become extinct in modern times

Formerly native to China's Yangtze River, the baiji or Chinese river dolphin (*Lipotes vexillifer*) was officially declared extinct in Dec 2006. From that time, there have been no confirmed sightings documented.

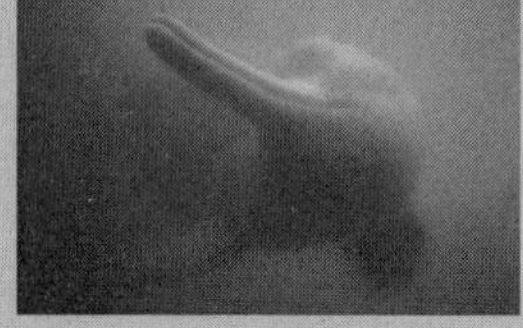

First scientific description of a killer whale

The Swiss naturalist Conrad Gesner was the first to describe *Orcinus orca*, in 1558, including it in the fish volume of his classic multi-volume animal encyclopaedia *Historiae Animalium* (1551–58). He based his description on a dead killer whale stranded in the Bay of Greifswald, off the shores of Germany in the south-western Baltic Sea, which understandably fascinated the local populace.

As if in celebration of this historic event, four centuries later a bull killer whale measuring around 20–25 ft (6.1–7.6 m) long,

Largest species of river dolphin

The boto or Amazon river dolphin (*I. geoffrensis*, pictured below) can attain 2.6 m (8 ft 6 in) in length. Found in the Amazon and Orinoco rivers of South America, it is a flexible swimmer with free-floating neck vertebrae that allow it to bend its neck at a 90° angle to its body. It is also the only dolphin with hair, making it technically the hairiest dolphin. The stiff bristles on its long, slender beak are thought to help it feel for prey as it probes the mud of the riverbed.

sped off with the record for **fastest marine mammal**. On 12 Oct 1958, he was timed to be travelling at 34.5 mph (55.5 km/h) in the north-eastern Pacific. Similar speeds, although in short bursts, have also been reported for Dall's porpoise (*Phocoenoides dalli*).

Orca records continue with the adult male's possession of the **tallest dorsal fin of a cetacean**. This can measure a total vertical height of 5 ft 11 in (1.8 m), as tall as an adult man.

Dolphin with fewest teeth

The little-known Risso's dolphin (*Grampus griseus*), an inhabitant of tropical, subtropical, temperate and subantarctic waters, typically possesses up to seven pairs of teeth in its lower jaw, specifically in the front region, but can have as few as two pairs. It usually has no teeth at all in its upper jaw. Unlike other dolphins, it has almost no beak and its rounded head resembles that of a pilot whale. It feeds primarily on squid, along with a variety of fish.

In contrast, the long-beaked common dolphin (*Delphinus capensis*) possesses 47–67 pairs of small conical teeth in each jaw, used for grasping slippery prey, which makes it the **dolphin with most teeth**.

Dolphin with the smallest degree of vision

The Ganges river dolphin (*Platanista gangetica*), a freshwater species inhabiting the Ganges and Indus rivers of Asia, is the only dolphin lacking a crystalline lens in its eyes. Indeed, the optic opening of each eye is so tiny – no more than a pinhole in diameter – that virtually no light can enter the eyes, rendering the dolphin's vision almost non-existent.

Most brightly coloured dolphin

The adult Chinese pink dolphin (*Sousa chinensis chinensis*) has a pink-coloured skin owing to blood vessels just below the surface that dilate to cool its body temperature. At birth it is black, turning grey then pink as it matures.

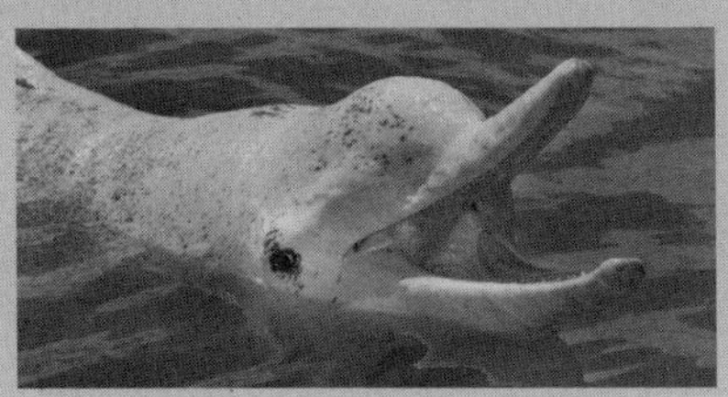

IN NUMBERS

2
Stomachs in a dolphin

30 min
Longest time for which a dolphin can hold its breath

43
Dolphin species in total, of which seven are freshwater

3
Main types of sounds made by a dolphin: whistles, pulsed sounds (grunts or squawks) and clicks

700
Ultrasonic clicks per second emitted by a dolphin during echolocation

Most aerial spins by a dolphin

The highly acrobatic spinner dolphin (*Stenella longirostris*) can spin round as many as seven times in a single leap. A slender, muscular 1.3–2 m (4 ft 3 in–6 ft 6 in) long and 45–47 kg (99–103 lb) in weight, this gregarious inhabitant of tropical waters may spin to rid itself of parasites or as an echolocation exercise, courtship display or expression of emotion, but as with all dolphin leaps (see p.71), the true reason or reasons remain unknown.

Largest dolphin species

Despite its name, the killer whale or orca (*Orcinus orca*) belongs to the dolphin family Delphinidae and is the largest of them all. The male is 6–8 m (19 ft 8 in–26 ft 2 in) long and weighs c. 6 tonnes (13,220 lb).

FACT

Dolphins breathe through a blowhole on their heads and regularly rise to the surface for air. When a dolphin sleeps, one half of its brain stays awake to ensure it keeps breathing – otherwise it would drown!

A helping flipper

Intelligent and sociable, few aquatic animals have interacted with humans as much as the dolphin. Legends of benevolent dolphins even appear in ancient Greek and Roman literature, with the historian Plutarch describing the creature as "a friend to all men [that] has often given them great aid".

Dolphins still lend a helping flipper to this day. In 2007, as surfer Todd Endris was being attacked by a great white off California, USA, a pod of bottlenose dolphins intervened to form a barrier between him and the shark, enabling him to make a getaway.

In 2013, Australian policewoman Lynn Gitsham insisted that dolphins saved not only her but also her cocker spaniel, Ramsay, from drowning by "forming a horseshoe" when she and her dog became trapped in rough surf and pushing them towards the shore.

These marine mammals make for industrious workers, too. Fishermen in the city of Laguna, Brazil, have teamed up with the local dolphins to help catch their haul (below), with the mammals corralling mullet towards the shore into awaiting nets. The helpers are happy to receive payment in the form of fish.

In 1970–71 during the Vietnam War, five bottlenose dolphins trained by the US Navy were sent to Cam Ranh Bay, Vietnam, to defend US military boats from enemy swimmers – the **first use of marine mammals in defence**. The US Navy began training dolphins to detect mines in 1960, and there is currently a squad of about 80 animals on active service (pictured above). The Navy insists that the dolphins are not at risk, and that they have been trained to remain at a safe distance from any mines they find.

ELEPHANTS

Elephants often employ a **system of look-outs** while a group is **bathing**

Largest mammal on land

The adult male African bush elephant (*Loxodonta africana*) is 3–3.7 m (9 ft 10 in–12 ft 1 in) at the shoulder and weighs 4–7 tonnes (8,800–15,400 lb). The combined weight of 146 adult men equates approximately to the weight of the heaviest known specimen, around 12.24 tonnes (26,984 lb). It has the **heaviest brain of any land mammal**, up to 5.4 kg (11 lb 14 oz) – only those of the biggest whales are heavier among mammals.

Earliest elephant

Elephants belong to the taxonomic order Proboscidea, of which the earliest known species is *Eritherium azzouzorum*. The first recorded specimen, dating from 60 million years ago, was found in Morocco and formally described in 2009 from skull and jaw fragments.

Early proboscidean relatives of today's true elephants were the mastodons of North America. They had relatively short legs, long skulls, shaggy fur and distinctive teeth, with nipple-shaped cusps – their

name means "nipple tooth". The **most recent mastodon** is the American mastodon (*Mammut americanum*) that became extinct 10,500–11,500 years ago.

The **first true elephants** were *Primelephas gomphotheroides* and *P. korotorensis*, which lived in Africa during the Miocene and Pliocene epochs, 23.03–2.58 million years ago. They are believed to have given rise not only to today's African and Asian elephants, but also to the now-extinct woolly mammoth (see panel on p.80).

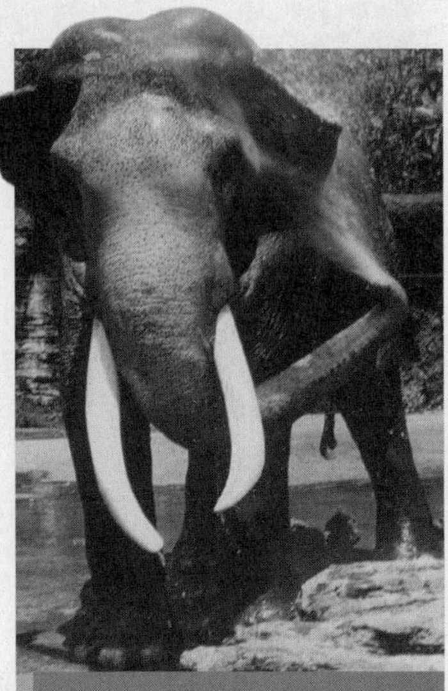

Oldest elephant

The average elephant life span is 60, but Lin Wang, an Asian elephant (*Elephas maximus*), died in Taipei Zoo on 26 Feb 2003 at the age of 86 years. "Grandpa Lin" carried supplies through the jungles of Burma for the Japanese army during World War II, until he was captured by the Chinese in 1943. He joined the zoo with a female companion in 1954, and on his death he was widely mourned and honoured.

Most elephant subspecies

Researchers widely agree that the Asian elephant (*E. maximus*) has the most subspecies, four in all: the Borneo pygmy (*E. m. borneensis*, see box p.79); the Indian (*E. m. indicus*); the Sri Lankan (*E. m. maximus*); and the Sumatran (*E. m. sumatrensis*).

The Sri Lankan elephant is the **largest subspecies**. It attains a shoulder height of up to 3.5 m (11 ft 6 in), and a weight of up to 5,500 kg (12,125 lb). Interestingly, historic records and photographs suggest that the average Sri Lankan elephant was once much larger, and that the subspecies' current size is the consequence of decades of hunting, which saw the largest and most impressive specimens weeded out. It is also darker in colour than other Asian elephants, with more patches of decreased skin pigmentation. Unusually, most Sri Lankan specimens have no tusks.

The **rarest subspecies** is the Sumatran elephant, with an estimated 2,400–2,800 individuals in the wild on the island of Sumatra in Indonesia. Its population has declined by about 80% during the past 75 years through hunting and habitat loss.

Longest tail of any land mammal

The tail of the Asian elephant (*E. maximus*) can grow up to 1.5 m (5 ft) long – almost the length of its trunk – and acts as a sizeable fly-swatter. Elephants have been seen running with their tails upright when threatened, perhaps to signal danger to their herd. The smallest Asian subspecies, the Borneo pygmy elephant (*E. m. borneensis*), has such a long tail relative to its size that it sometimes trails on the ground.

Largest prosthetic limb

Motala lost her foot to a landmine in 1999. In Aug 2011, at the Mae Yao National Reserve in Lampang, Thailand, she received a new custom-made prosthesis, capable of bearing 3–5 tonnes (6,500–11,000 lb).

First domestication

The earliest known records of domesticated elephants, which belonged to the Asian species, described tamed elephants being used as beasts of burden at least 4,000 years ago during the Indus Valley civilization (in present-day Pakistan and India).

Smallest true elephant species ever

The Tilo island dwarf elephant (*Palaeoloxodon falconeri*), a species of straight-tusked elephant that inhabited the Mediterranean islands of Sicily and Malta, stood no more than 1 m (3 ft 3 in) at the shoulder. It is a famous example of insular dwarfism, in which normal-sized species isolated on islands often evolve into much smaller forms. It died out 11,700 years ago.

Largest dental caps

Spike, an Asian elephant (*E. maximus*) at Calgary Zoo in Alberta, Canada, is the proud owner of 50-cm-long (19-in), 13-cm-wide (5-in) stainless steel caps weighing 13 kg (28 lb) each. The metal was donated by Corus Steel (CAN) and the caps were fitted over Spike's cracked tusks in a 3-hr 30-min operation on 4 Jul 2002.

Longest gestation period for a mammal

The cow (female) Asian elephant has an average pregnancy of 650 days (more than 21 months) and a maximum of 760 days (more than two years) – over two-and-a-half times that of humans.

At birth, an elephant weighs around 90 kg (200 lb), stands 1 m (3 ft 3 in) tall, and its brain is already well developed.

Smallest Asian elephant

The Borneo pygmy elephant (*E. m. borneensis*) is the "baby" of the family – 30% smaller than its mainland Asian relatives. It was recognized as a separate subspecies in Sep 2003 following DNA research. An adult male measures 1.7–2.6 m (5 ft 6 in–8 ft 6 in) tall and the average weight is about 2,500 kg (5,500 lb). There are approximately 3,500 individuals living on the island of Borneo in southeast Asia.

IN NUMBERS

2
Species of African elephant: the bush elephant and the forest elephant

1
Species of Asian elephant

27
An elephant's pulse rate, compared with 70 for a human and 1,000 for a canary

17 cm
Amount that an elephant's tusks can grow each year (6.7 in)

8–100
Herd size, composed of females and young

12–15
Age in years at which males leave the herd

160 kg
An elephant's approximate daily intake of bark, leaves, branches and grass (350 lb)

A mammoth find

In 2007, the most complete woolly mammoth (*Mammuthus primigenius*) was found near the Yuribei River in Siberia, Russia, by reindeer herder Yuri Khudi and his sons. In May 2014, the 42,000-year-old specimen, an infant, went on display at the Natural History Museum in London, UK (above).

The baby woolly mammoth was called Lyuba, which means "love" in Russian and is also the name of Yuri's wife. Scientists estimate that she died at just one month old. Her size – 85 cm (33 in) tall, 130 cm (51 in) long and weighing 50 kg (110 lb) – makes her slightly larger than a rottweiler dog. Her unusually well-preserved state (even the internal organs were still present) had been made possible by the wet clay and mud in which she was found. The cold climate froze the body in these sediments, and the resulting permafrost created a vacuum, preventing oxygen from decomposing the remains.

It is likely that Lyuba thawed out of her icy resting place during warm spring weather, and her body was later washed up on the banks of the Yuribei. The woolly coat typical of mammoths would have worn away many years ago, and the leathery skin that remained gives Lyuba an even closer resemblance to her modern-day elephant relatives.

Mammoths died out around 5,000 years ago, for reasons that are still unclear – perhaps because of overhunting, climate change, or a combination of the two.

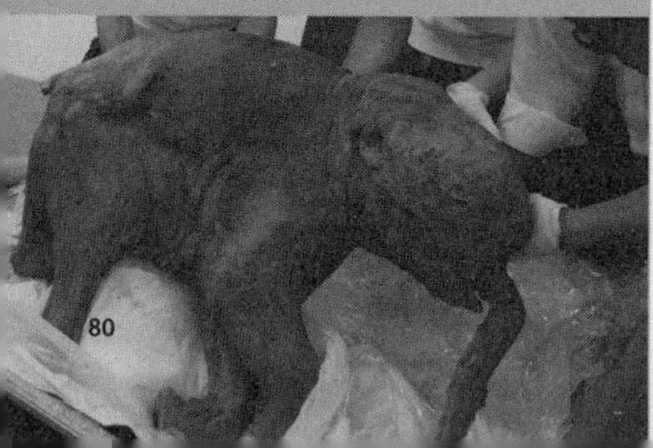

Heaviest nose

The trunk of the African elephant is approximately 2 m (6 ft 6 in) long, weighs 150–200 kg (330–550 lb) and can hold more than 8 litres (2 US gal) of water.

It is believed that the trunk, with its nostrils at the tip, may have developed as a snorkelling device: elephants are the only animals that can remain far below the surface of water with their breathing apparatus above it.

The dexterous outgrowths at the tip allow them to pick up and manipulate objects.

Most nasal musculature

The two African species (the bush or plains elephant, *L. africana*, and the forest elephant, *L. cyclotis*) possess more nasal muscles than any other elephant or any other mammal. Their trunks contain around eight major muscles on each side, along with 150,000 muscle fascicles (portions). They support its many functions, including feeding, drinking, cleaning and gripping.

Largest elephant relocation project

In Aug 1993, the wildlife charity Care for the Wild International transported more than 500 elephants in whole family groups some 250 km (155 mi) across Zimbabwe. They were moved from Gonarezhou National Park to the Save Valley Conservancy to prevent them being culled.

FROGS & TOADS

A **group of frogs** is called an **army**; a **group of toads** is known as a **knot**

Greatest frog/tadpole size difference

Found in Trinidad and parts of the Amazon, the adult in the tree frog genus *Pseudis* actually *shrinks* as it develops from a tadpole. It can reach a length of 16.8 cm (6.6 in) as a tadpole – believed by some scientists to be the specimen pictured above. However, the adult frog measures no more than 6.5 cm (2.5 in) – a length reduction of 10.3 cm (4.1 in).

First frogs and toads

Frogs and toads belong to the taxonomic superorder of amphibians called Salientia. The two earliest-known fossil species from this superorder both date back to the early Triassic Period, approximately 250 million years ago, and are known as "proto-frogs" or "proto-salientians". One of these is *Triadobatrachus massinoti* from Madagascar; the other is *Czatkobatrachus polonicus*, which was discovered in Poland.

First lungless frog

Confirmed by research conducted in 2008, the Bornean flat-headed frog (*Barbourula kalimantanensis*) has no need for lungs to breathe as it obtains all of its oxygen by direct absorption through its skin.

Largest frog ever

Native to Madagascar and dating from the late Cretaceous Period some 70 million years ago, the devil toad (*Beelzebufo ampinga*) – actually a frog – is believed to have exceeded 40 cm (15.7 in) long and had a particularly large head. Visualized above, its first recorded fossil remains were unearthed in 1993.

First living embryo grown from an extinct frog

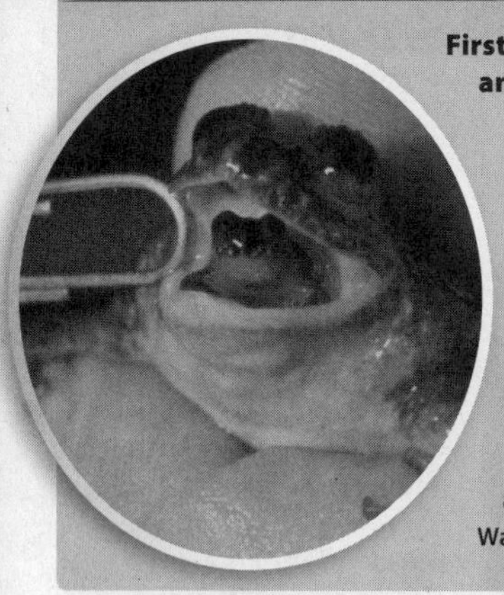

The gastric-brooding frog (*Rheobatrachus silus*), famous for swallowing its eggs and giving birth via the mouth (left), became extinct in 1983. But in 2013, genes from frozen tissue samples were combined with the eggs of a related species to create gastric-brooding frog embryos at the University of New South Wales in Sydney, Australia.

Largest frog

An African goliath frog (*Conraua goliath*) found on the Sanaga River in Cameroon by Andy Koffman (USA) in Apr 1989 had a snout-to-vent length of 36.8 cm (14.5 in) and an overall length of 87.6 cm (34.5 in) with its legs extended. The average length for this species is 30 cm (11.8 in) and they can weigh as much as a newborn baby (up to 3.3 kg; 7 lb 3.2 oz). Pictured holding a goliath frog here is Rod Clarke (UK), a photographer who worked on location for the BBC's *Planet Earth* series.

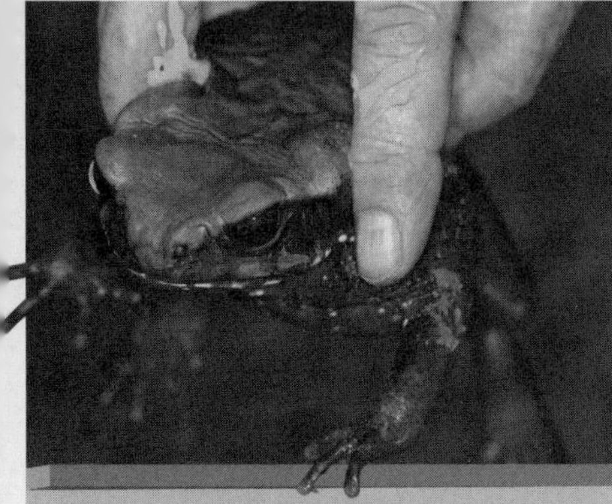

First poison-squirting toad

In several species of toad, a pair of glands known as the parotoid macroglands, located behind the eyes, passively secrete toxins if bitten. However, the Amazonian toad *Rhaebo guttatus*, native to Brazil, is the first toad species that is known to squirt jets of toxin actively and voluntarily from these glands if threatened by potential predators. Only documented in 2011, the defence mechanism allows the toad to fire its toxin as far as 2 m (6.5 ft).

Largest genus of toads

The *Bufo* genus currently contains no less than 205 of the 355 species of toad known to science. Some researchers have removed certain species from this genus and placed them in others, but even in these alternative classifications, *Bufo* is still by far the biggest genus.

This figure is almost doubled by the **largest frog genus**, though. Native to southern Central and northern South America, *Pristimantis* boasts more than 400 species, with new ones being discovered each year.

Widest frog family range

Ranidae, the taxonomic family containing the ranids or true frogs, occurs on every land continent except for Antarctica, plus various islands. The family includes some of the world's best-known frogs, such as the goliath frog, the edible frog, pond frogs and bullfrogs.

IN NUMBERS

355
Toad species currently recognized, though more are being discovered all the time

6,000+
Frog species currently recognized

200 million
Estimated population of cane toads in Australia today

15 km
Longest migration by an amphibian (9.3 mi), made by two species: the pool frog (*Rana lessonae*) and green frog (*Rana esculenta*)

3 m
Distance that goliath frogs can leap (10 ft)

1
Number of known living Rabbs' fringe-limbed tree frogs (*Ecnomiohyla rabborum*) – the **rarest tree frog**

Largest toad

The cane or marine toad (*Bufo marinus*) of tropical South America and Queensland, Australia (introduced), weighs an average of 450 g (1 lb). The biggest ever recorded was a male named "Prinsen" ("The Prince"), owned by Håkan Forsberg (SWE). In 1991, Prinsen measured 38 cm (1 ft 3 in) from snout to vent, exceeding the average length by 15–25 cm (6–10 in). He was 53.9 cm (1 ft 9.25 in) when fully extended. The species is also the **most fecund amphibian**, with females laying up to 35,000 eggs per year.

Smallest toad

At almost 16 times smaller than the **largest toad** (see above), the largest recorded specimen of *Bufo taitanus beiranus* from Africa was just 24 mm (0.94 in) long.

Smelliest frog

If it comes under attack, the aptly named Venezuelan skunk frog (*Aromobates nocturnus*) secretes a vile-smelling liquid through its skin. The secretion contains the same stink-producing compound used by skunks. Although related to poison dart frogs (see panel opposite), this species is not toxic.

Most paternal amphibian

The West European midwife toad (*Alytes obstetricans*) takes its name from its active role in caring for its offspring. After the female lays her eggs, the male fertilizes them and then wraps the string of eggs, which can be 3–4 ft (0.9–1.2 m) long, around his thighs. The male, which is only 3 in (7.6 cm) long, carries the eggs around in this manner for up to four weeks, until they're ready to hatch.

Highest frequency croak

With a call of 128 kHz, the croak of the concave-eared torrent frog (*Odorrana tormota*) is technically ultrasonic, well beyond our range of hearing (humans can't detect sounds above 20 kHz). The reason this frog produces such a high-frequency croak is to compensate for the very loud, low-frequency sound of the waterfalls where the species resides in eastern China, enabling it to communicate with its neighbours.

Most cold-resistant amphibian

Native to the Arctic Circle, where temperatures regularly plummet to well below freezing, the wood frog (*Rana sylvatica*) is the only amphibian able to survive *after* it has been frozen. Glucose in their blood acts as

FACT

In the 1930s, cane toads were introduced to sugar cane plantations in Australia to control insect pests. Although effective, the thriving toads themselves now pose a threat to native species.

Killer Kermit

It may not have big teeth, sharp claws or brute strength – and it might even appear quite cute – but don't be fooled: the golden poison dart frog (*Phyllobates terribilis*, pictured) is not only the most poisonous frog, but also one of the deadiiest of all animals on the planet. In fact, the average individual has enough toxins in its skin to kill 10 humans – or as many as 20,000 mice!

Native to a small area of rainforest on the western coast of Colombia, the golden poison dart frog gained its name from local tribesmen who take the great risk of capturing it to coat the tips of their blow-darts (below), used for hunting game such as monkeys. The frog is particularly prized as it can produce more poison than any of its relatives – mainly because it's the **largest poison dart frog species**, at a length of around 6 cm (2.7 in).

It's now widely accepted that the frog gains its poison from the ants, beetles and other insects that it eats, which themselves acquire toxicity through the plants they consume. The batrachotoxins in the poison paralyse muscles, which can quickly lead to heart failure in any creature that dares venture too close. As a result, poison dart frogs in zoos aren't typically poisonous, because their diet doesn't include toxic insects.

Even a creature as formidable as this has to be vigilant, as it is preyed upon by a species of snake, *Leimadophis epinephelus*, that has developed a resistance to the frog's bio weapon. A much greater threat to the endangered amphibian, however, is deforestation, as agriculture and logging continue to take a toll on their rainforest home.

a kind of antifreeze that concentrates on the frogs' vital organs, protecting them from damage while the rest of the body freezes solid.

They control the rate at which they thaw in the spring, ensuring that they defrost evenly; if the brain thawed before the heart, for example, the frog would suffocate.

Furriest frog

During the mating season, the hind legs of male hairy frogs (*Trichobatrachus robustus*) from West Africa develop hundreds of tiny skin filaments. Scientists believe that the frog uses these as accessory breathing aids, like gills, making up for its poor lungs.

Longest leap by a frog relative to body size

The frog that can jump the farthest in a single bound, relative to body size, is the southern cricket frog (*Acris gryllus*). Native to North America's Atlantic Coast Plain, this frog measures just 2.5 cm (1 in) long, but can jump a distance of more than 60 times its body length.

Frog-jumping contests – inspired by US folk tales, and in particular "The Celebrated Jumping Frog of Calaveras County" (1865) by Mark Twain – are the aggregate of three consecutive leaps. A sharp-nosed frog (*Ptychadena oxyrhynchus*) called "Santjie" achieved the **farthest triple jump by a frog**, covering 10.3 m (33 ft 9 in) at a frog derby at Lurula Natal Spa in Pietersburg, South Africa, on 21 May 1977.

The **most consecutive jumps by a frog** goes to a spring peeper (*Hyla crucifer*) that leapt 120 times in a row on a lawn in eastern USA, as recorded by the herpetologist Stanley Rand (USA) in 1952.

FACT

Generally, goliath frogs eat the same things as other frog species, being adept nocturnal hunters of insects, fish and crustaceans. However, a researcher did find a bat in the stomach of one specimen!

Smallest frog

With some adults reaching just 7 mm (0.27 in) long, *Paedophryne amauensis*, from Papua New Guinea, is also the world's **smallest amphibian**. Easily fitting on a fingernail, or a US dime as shown, the species was only found in 2012 – little wonder considering its diminutive size.

ACTUAL SIZE

LIZARDS

Like **snakes**, lizards smell using their **tongues**

Largest lizard ever

Hainosaurus bernardi was a prehistoric marine lizard known as a mosasaur (see p.92). It lived 70.6–66 million years ago, during the Late Cretaceous Period. Most researchers believe it reached 15 m (49 ft) in length, although one researcher has downgraded this to 12.2 m (40 ft). A related species, *Mosasaurus hoffmannii*, has recently been estimated to have grown to a length of 18 m (59 ft). No lizards other than mosasaurs are known to have attained a length exceeding 8 m (26 ft), however, so whichever of the above two species was the longer, the record for the largest lizard ever is held by a mosasaur.

The **largest terrestrial lizard ever** was the giant monitor lizard (*Megalania prisca*), a huge species native to southern Australia during the Pleistocene Epoch. It vanished 30,000–40,000 years ago and no complete skeleton has so far been uncovered.

The most recent authoritative estimates of its length have been made by Australian reptile fossil specialist Dr Ralph Molnar. In 2004, he proposed a length of 7–7.9 m (22 ft 11 in–25 ft 11 in), depending on body weight and tail size.

Longest legless lizard

The European glass snake (*Pseudopus* [aka *Ophisaurus*] *apodus*) ranges from south-eastern Europe to central Asia, and can grow to a length of 135 cm (4 ft 5 in). Despite its name, some specimens have 2-mm-long (0.07-in) hind legs.

Fastest lizard

Ctenosaura, a spiny-tailed iguana from Central America, reached a speed of 34.9 km/h (21.7 mph) in tests by Raymond Huey (USA) and colleagues at the University of California in Berkeley, USA. The results appeared in 1988, in a paper co-written with Theodore Garland Jr (USA).

Most venomous lizard

Heavily built, and up to 60 cm (24 in) long, Gila monsters (*Heloderma suspectum*) are brightly coloured lizards that live in the arid parts of Mexico and the south-western USA. They have eight well-developed venom glands in their lower jaws and carry enough venom to kill two adult humans. Under normal circumstances, they are relatively harmless – unless provoked.

Largest lizard family

The largest taxonomic family of lizards is Scincidae, the skinks, which contains more than 1,500 species of worldwide distribution, with new ones discovered and described every year. Skinks resemble typical lizards in overall morphology, but they have no noticeable neck and generally have only small or very small limbs. Indeed, some species lack one or even both pairs of limbs.

Largest parthenogenetic lizard

Parthenogenesis, or "virgin birth", is the asexual production of offspring by a female without prior fertilization by a male. Several lizard species have been shown to reproduce parthenogenetically – in fact, some are exclusively parthenogenetic.

The largest species for which parthenogenesis has been confirmed is also the **largest species of living terrestrial lizard**, the Komodo dragon (*Varanus komodoensis*, see p.91), which can grow to a length of 3.1 m (10 ft 2 in).

Most prolific egg-laying lizard

Meller's chameleon (*Trioceros* [aka *Chamaeleo*] *melleri*) is native to the savannahs and interior mountains of East Africa (Malawi, Mozambique and Tanzania). Typically, it lays a single clutch of up to 80 eggs in a year.

T. melleri is a remarkably large species of chameleon, the largest to inhabit mainland Africa. There are larger specimens only on the island of Madagascar.

IN NUMBERS

1.2 m
Distance that some horned lizards (genus *Phrynosoma*) can squirt blood from their eyes (4 ft)

30 ft
Distance that the draco lizard (genus *Draco*) can typically "fly" (9.1 m); it actually glides, using extendable ribs interspersed with folds of skin

50 years
Average life span of a Komodo dragon (*Varanus komodoensis*)

90%
Proportion of its own body weight that a Komodo dragon can eat in one meal

317
Teeth possessed by the common leaf-tailed gecko (*Uroplatus fimbriatus*), the **most teeth in a living land animal**

6,000
Estimated number of lizard species

Smallest lizard

Both *Sphaerodactylus parthenopion* and *S. ariasae* have an average length of only 16 mm (0.6 in). They are the smallest of the 23,000 species of amniote vertebrates. The term "amniote" denotes species in which fertilized eggs are kept in the mother, or laid on land, rather than in the water.

Largest meal eaten by a lizard

The largest fully confirmed single meal eaten by a lizard was a 41-kg (90-lb 6-oz) wild pig, which was consumed in a single sitting by a Komodo dragon (*V. komodoensis*) – pictured opposite. As the lizard only weighed 46 kg (101 lb 6 oz) prior to eating the pig, the gargantuan meal almost doubled its body weight upon consumption.

Largest pre-birth vertebrate infant relative to size of mother

At birth, an Australian stump-tailed skink or bobtail (*Tiliqua rugosa*) can weigh more than a third of its mother's body weight. This is the equivalent of a woman giving birth to a baby the size of an average six-year-old child.

Largest water walker

The South American basilisk lizard, or Jesus Christ lizard (*Basiliscus basiliscus*), can run bipedally at a velocity of 1.5 m/s (5 ft/s) for about 4.5 m (14 ft 9 in) before sinking. It can also "walk on water" on all fours, extending the surface distance that it can travel by some 1.3 m (4 ft 3 in).

Largest living lizard

The Komodo dragon (*Varanus komodoensis*), otherwise known as the Komodo monitor or ora, is found on the Indonesian islands of Komodo, Rinca, Padar and Flores. Males average 2.25 m (7 ft 5 in) in length and weigh about 59 kg (130 lb). The largest accurately measured specimen was 3.1 m (10 ft 2 in) long and weighed 166 kg (365 lb).

Smallest monitor lizard

Native to Asia, Africa and Oceania (and occurring in the New World as invasive species), the monitor lizards, or varanids, include the largest terrestrial lizards. That said, the short-tailed pygmy monitor (*Varanus brevicauda*) of Australia grows to only 25 cm (10 in), and may even be the smallest monitor ever – including fossil species.

Most acute hearing for a lizard

The peace delma (*Delma pax*), a pygopod or Australian legless gecko, can detect a 60-decibel sound with an 11.1-kHz frequency. This is more than an octave above the top note on a standard piano – too high to be picked up by other lizards.

Mosasaur

Top predators with long, fearsome jaws lined with razor-sharp, slanting teeth, mosasaurs patrolled the oceans 66–93 million years ago, towards the end of the Late Cretaceous Period. They have been dubbed the *Tyrannosaurus rex* of the sea.

Propelled by rudder-like tails, they snaked through the water, consuming whatever they came across. No prey was too large or tough for those crushing jaws.

A rich excavation site in Angola has also shown that they ate their own kind: the remains of three mosasaurs were found in the fossilized belly of a fourth, packed into sandstone cliffs at Bentiaba.

As with terrestrial dinosaurs, mosasaurs were wiped out in the great extinction event of 66 million years ago. Their fossils remained hidden in sedimentary rock until the first mosasaur discovery – in the 1770s, on the Meuse river near Maastricht in the Netherlands. This gave rise to their name, which means "Meuse river lizard".

Three main genera (groups) of mosasaur were native to the area corresponding to present-day Manitoba, Canada, where the **largest mosasaur on display** – *Hainosaurus pembinensis* (more familiarly known as "Bruce"), was found. He is shown below in situ at the Canadian Fossil Discovery Centre in Morden, Manitoba, Canada. Bruce swam the Western Interior Seaway, a deep-sea environment that bisected North America, and at 13 m (43 ft) long was larger than the average *T. rex*. The genus *Hainosaurus* featured the **largest mosasaurs**: they grew up to 15 m (49 ft) long.

The animal with the **most acute nocturnal colour vision** is the helmeted gecko (*Tarentola chazaliae*), which is active at night.

Most southerly lizard

The Magellanic iguana (*Liolaemus magellanicus*) inhabits the archipelago of Tierra del Fuego, situated at the southernmost tip of Argentina in South America.

Occurring well into the northern extremes of mainland Norway, high above the Arctic Circle, the **most northerly lizard** is the common (viviparous) lizard (*Lacerta vivipara*).

Most efficient thermoregulating lizard

The lava iguana (*Liolaemus multiformis*) is a black-scaled species native to the Peruvian Andes. After spending just an hour basking in the sun in near-freezing external conditions of only 1.5°C (34.7°F), it can utilize solar radiation to raise its body temperature to 33°C (91.4°F).

FACT

The venom of the Gila monster (see p.88) is not injected, but seeps into the wound created when it bites its victim. A lizard may hang on after it has bitten and chew for several minutes afterwards.

Penguins moult **all their feathers** at once – known as a **"catastrophic moult"**

First penguin

Waimanu manneringi inhabited New Zealand some 62 million years ago, during the Palaeocene Epoch. In common with all subsequent penguin species known to science, it was flightless and probably resembled the modern-day aquatic birds known as loons or divers (genus *Gavia*).

Heaviest penguin ever

Scientists estimate that the Antarctic giant penguin (*Palaeeudyptes klekowskii*) weighed as much as 115 kg (253 lb 8 oz). It lived on Antarctica's Seymour Island some 37 million years ago, during the Late Eocene Epoch, and is represented by the most complete fossil remains ever found for a penguin species in Antarctica.

Not only was it extremely heavy, the Antarctic giant penguin was also exceptionally tall, reaching a height of 2 m (6 ft 6 in). Following its discovery in 2014, it has also taken the record for the **tallest penguin ever**. The previous title holder was the contemporaneous Nordenskjoeld's giant penguin (*Anthropornis nordenskjoeldi*), which stood 1.7 m (5 ft 6 in) tall.

Largest penguin colony

The most populous penguin colony is on Zavodovski Island, part of the South Sandwich Islands in the southern Atlantic Ocean. Some 2 million chinstrap penguins (*Pygoscelis antarctica*) breed on the slopes of the island, which is an active volcano. The name "chinstrap" derives from the thin curved line of black feathers that run under the bird's chin.

Largest auk ever

Native to the coasts of both sides of the North Atlantic, the great auk (*Pinguinus impennis*) reached 85 cm (2 ft 9 in) tall and weighed approximately 5 kg (11 lb). This flightless black-and-white seabird was the original penguin, after which the superficially similar but unrelated flightless birds of the southern hemisphere were named.

Once common, by 1844 the great auk had been hunted to extinction by sailors for food and by museums for specimens.

Largest penguin genus

There are between seven and nine species in the genus *Eudyptes*, depending on which taxonomists you consult. Known as the crested penguins, owing to their distinctive, often golden-coloured crest, they include the macaroni penguin (the **commonest**

Largest living penguin

Native to the frozen southern continent of Antarctica, the emperor penguin (*Aptenodytes forsteri*) is the world's largest extant (living) species of penguin. The two sexes are of similar size, both reaching a height of 4 ft 3 in (1.3 m) and weighing up to 100 lb (45 kg).

penguin, see overleaf) and rockhopper penguin. Crested penguins live on subantarctic and Antarctic islands.

Most broods per year for a penguin

The little blue or fairy penguin (see below) can produce up to three successful broods per year. All other species of penguin produce only a single brood annually.

Lightest egg compared to body weight

Penguins are the birds with the lightest eggs compared to their adult body weight. The lightest eggs of all are those laid by the emperor penguin (*A. forsteri*). The egg of this species normally weighs 1 lb (450 g), just 2.3% of the mother's weight.

Least colonial penguin

Whereas other penguin species nest in (often high-density) colonies, the yellow-eyed penguin (*Megadyptes antipodes*) is the world's least colonial and least social penguin species. It nests alone, out of sight of all other penguins and each with its own separate nesting site, located in forests, scrub or dense flax. It is native to New Zealand and the subantarctic Auckland and Campbell islands.

Most northerly penguin

The Galápagos penguin (*Spheniscus mendiculus*) is native to the Galápagos Islands, situated off Ecuador in South America. The vast majority of individuals inhabit the islands of Fernandina and Isabela. The northern tip of Isabela crosses the equator, jutting into the northern hemisphere,

Smallest penguin

The little blue or fairy penguin (*Eudyptula minor*) is native to southern Australia and New Zealand. It stands no taller than 40 cm (1 ft 3.75 in), weighs no more than 1 kg (2 lb 3 oz), and has an average life span of only six years. Several subspecies have been described, but there is no consensus as to how many of them are valid.

meaning that this is the only penguin that occurs naturally in both the northern and southern hemispheres. All other living species are confined entirely to the southern hemisphere.

Lowest temperature endured by a bird

On the Antarctic sea ice, breeding emperor penguins can survive an average temperature of -20°C (-4°F).

This hardy species also holds the record for the **longest continuous fast by a bird**. One male emperor penguin survived without food for 134 days, utilizing its plentiful reserves of subcutaneous fat, which can be 3–4 cm (1.2–1.6 in) thick.

Fastest bird swimmer

The gentoo penguin (*Pygoscelis papua*) has a maximum burst speed of about 27 km/h (17 mph).

Commonest penguin

There are some 6.3 million breeding pairs of Antarctica's macaroni penguin (*Eudyptes chrysolophus*) alive. The species has seen a notable decline in populations since the 1970s, however, and is now categorized by the IUCN as Vulnerable.

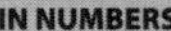

Longest penguin beak

The giant spear-billed penguin (*Icadyptes salasi*) lived in tropical South America 36 million years ago, during the Late Eocene Epoch. Its beak measured 25 cm (10 in) and accounted for almost two-thirds of its skull.

Deepest dive by a bird

The greatest depth accurately measured for any bird is 534 m (1,751 ft) by a 29-kg (63-lb 14-oz) emperor penguin. The dive was recorded in Nov 1993 at Coulman Island in the Ross Sea, Antarctica, by Professor Gerald Kooyman of the Scripps Institution of Oceanography. Kooyman measured almost 16,000 dives by five different birds, the longest of which lasted 15.8 min.

IN NUMBERS

1 in 50,000
Penguins born with brown, rather than black, plumage; they are known as Isabelline penguins

3–4 weeks
Time it takes penguins to moult

50–70%
Additional body weight penguins gain prior to moulting

2 m
Distance above the water's surface that penguins can propel themselves when swimming at speed, an activity known as "porpoising" (6 ft 6 in)

15–20
Heartbeats per minute for a penguin during a long dive

30
Fish that an adult penguin can collect in one dive

38°C
Normal body temperature for a penguin (100°F)

80%
Proportion of their lives that penguins spend in the water

20 million
Breeding pairs of penguins in Antarctica

Avian rescue

On 23 Jun 2000, a disastrous oil spill polluted the South African coast, leading to the world's largest penguin rescue. Dyan deNapoli was part of the rehabilitation team on the ground.

What was the situation when you arrived?

My team arrived one week after the oil spill, and systems were still being put into place. A massive rescue centre had just been constructed to house the still-arriving stream of oiled birds. Within a few days, nearly 20,000 oiled penguins, mostly from Robben Island, were delivered. The day after we arrived, the oil spill hit Dassen Island, necessitating the evacuation of another 20,000 clean penguins to prevent them getting oiled. These birds were transported up the coast to Port Elizabeth, and released into the unpolluted waters to make the long swim home.

How do you clean an oily penguin?

It's very important to let the animal adjust for 24–48 hours before attempting to wash it, because the washing process is very stressful. Once ready, the penguin is first sprayed with a degreaser, which stays on for about half an hour and starts to break down the heavier oil. The penguin is then dipped into a succession of tubs of hot soapy water, which is agitated through its feathers until all the oil is removed and the water runs clear. Then, high-pressure hoses are used to remove all of the residual soap from the feathers and the birds are placed under heat lamps to dry.

FACT

The Robben Island penguin rescue included the **largest penguin airlift**: 15–20,000 birds were flown to safety. This would have been the first time these birds had ever been airborne.

Highest density of feathers

Penguins have the most closely packed feathers. In a study published in 1967, Dr Bernard Stonehouse (UK) noted 11 to 12 feathers per cm² (70–77 per sq in) in fairy, emperor, Adélie and yellow-eyed penguins.

FACT

Muscles at the base of each feather shaft allow the penguin to adapt to different conditions. On land, the feathers stay erect, trapping air for insulation; in water, they flatten to form a watertight barrier.

HUMANS

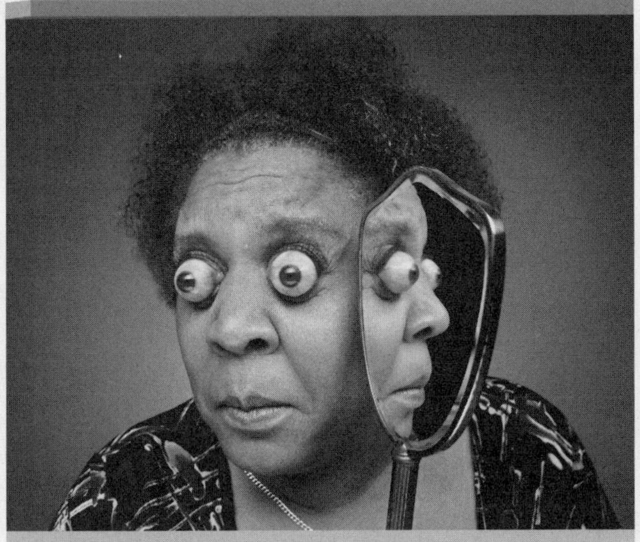

Farthest eyeball pop

Truly eye-popping in more ways than one, Kim Goodman (USA) has a record-making ability to push her eyeballs from their sockets. She popped them out to a distance of 12 mm (0.47 in) in Istanbul, Turkey, on 2 Nov 2007, improving by 1 mm (0.04 in) on her previous best from 1998. Measuring the "pop" is an exact science that has to be done by an optometrist using a device known as a proptometer; an average of three measurements gives the final, eye-watering result.

CONTENTS

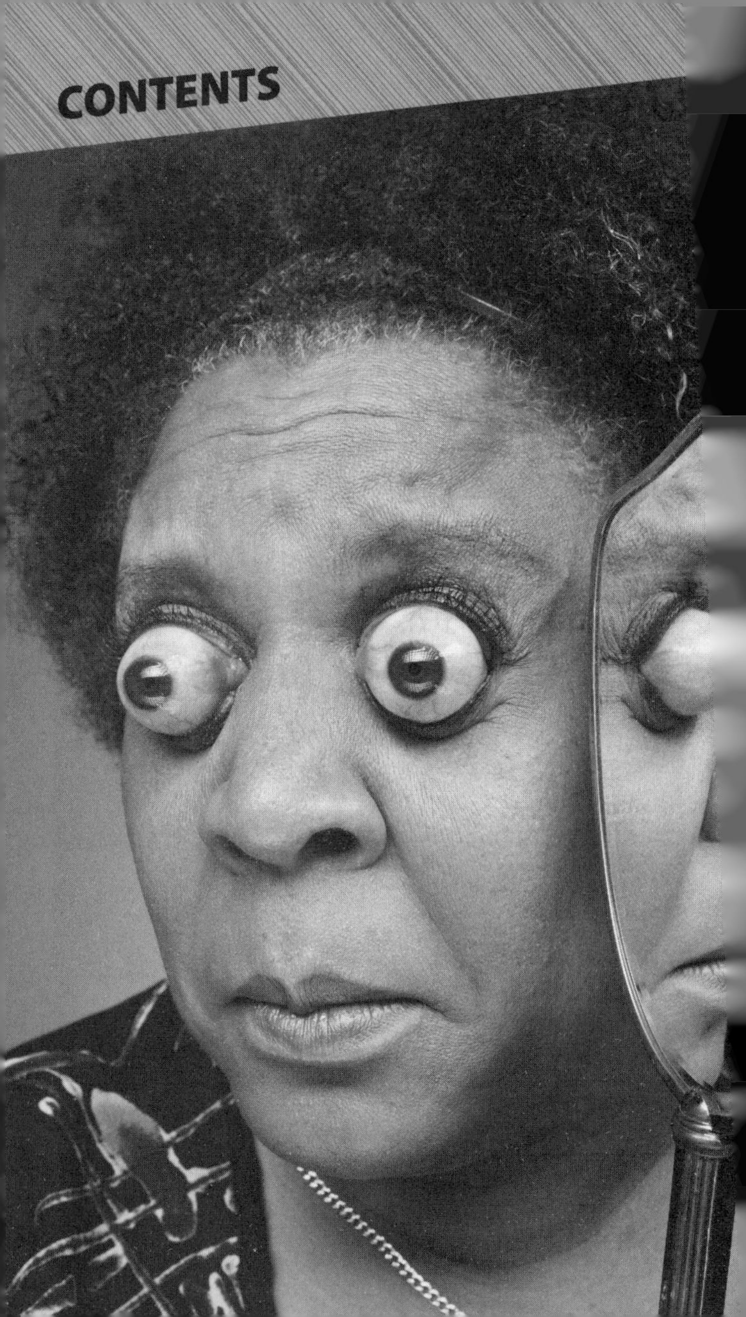

FACT

"Proptosis" is the term for eyeball displacement or bulging eyes. Kim discovered her talent when she was hit on the head by a hockey mask, but can now pop out her eyes on cue.

IN FOCUS AWESOME ANATOMY

Humans **share 95% of their DNA with chimpanzees** and about **50% with bananas**!

Organs

The resolving power of the eye enables us to distinguish objects 100 microns apart from a distance of 25 cm (10 in) – the **smallest visible object**. In Oct 1972, Veronica Seider (BRD) was reported to have a visual acuity 20 times better than average

Whether it's running a marathon, solving a Rubik's Cube or eating the most grapes in a minute, very few records would be possible if it weren't for the incredible machine that is the human body.

Some 10 trillion different cells form the tissues that make up a wide array of muscles, bones and organs. Coordinated by the brain, all of these individual components work together to perform our bodily functions, some of which happen without us even thinking about it.

Although we may not always notice it, the human body is continually in a state of flux – breaking down, renewing, growing, shrinking – whether you're six or 116, such as the world's **oldest person** (more about her on p.108).

In this feature we turn the spotlight inside the body to reveal some of the awesome anatomy we could neither live – nor break records – without.

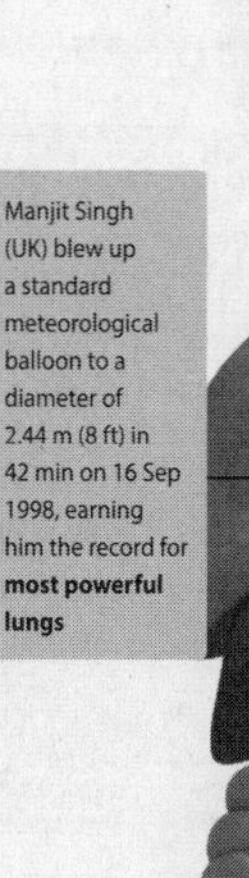

Manjit Singh (UK) blew up a standard meteorological balloon to a diameter of 2.44 m (8 ft) in 42 min on 16 Sep 1998, earning him the record for **most powerful lungs**

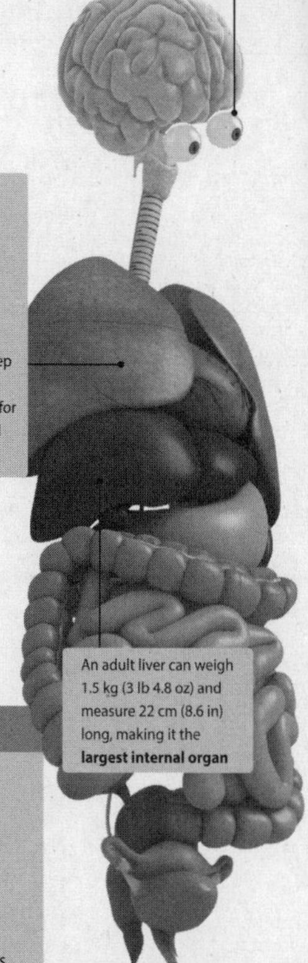

An adult liver can weigh 1.5 kg (3 lb 4.8 oz) and measure 22 cm (8.6 in) long, making it the **largest internal organ**

? GLOSSARY

DNA: The double-helix-shaped molecules in all our cells, deoxyribonucleic acid contains our genetic instructions and dictates how a cell develops, as well as the function(s) it performs.

Ligament: Connective tissue that binds bones together to keep the skeleton stable.

Tendon: Also known as a sinew, this fibrous tissue links bones and muscles, allowing movement.

Skeletal system

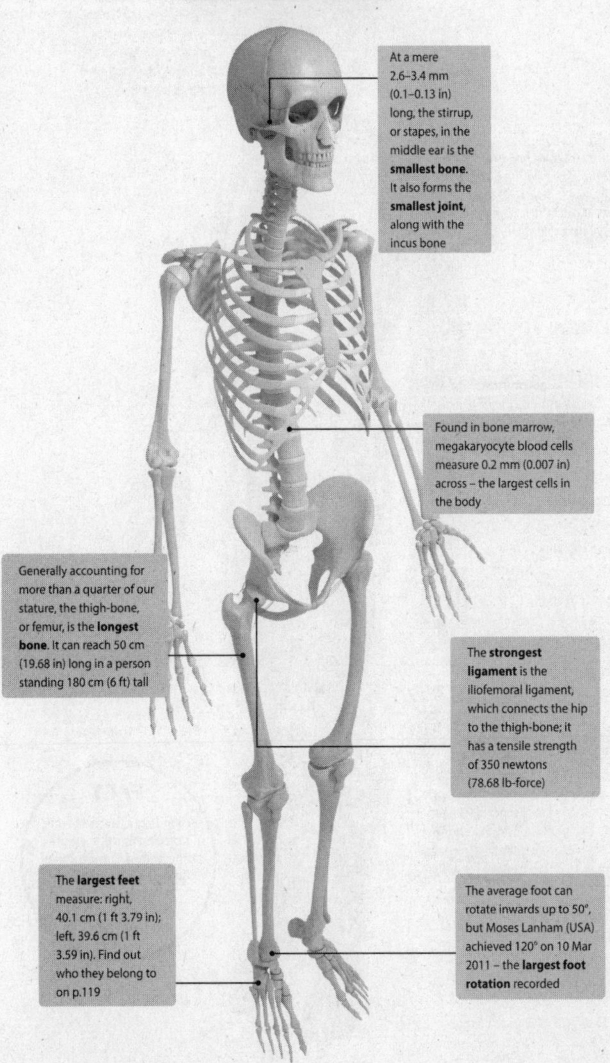

At a mere 2.6–3.4 mm (0.1–0.13 in) long, the stirrup, or stapes, in the middle ear is the **smallest bone**. It also forms the **smallest joint**, along with the incus bone
Found in bone marrow, megakaryocyte blood cells measure 0.2 mm (0.007 in) across – the largest cells in the body
Generally accounting for more than a quarter of our stature, the thigh-bone, or femur, is the **longest bone**. It can reach 50 cm (19.68 in) long in a person standing 180 cm (6 ft) tall
The **strongest ligament** is the iliofemoral ligament, which connects the hip to the thigh-bone; it has a tensile strength of 350 newtons (78.68 lb-force)
The **largest feet** measure: right, 40.1 cm (1 ft 3.79 in); left, 39.6 cm (1 ft 3.59 in). Find out who they belong to on p.119
The average foot can rotate inwards up to 50°, but Moses Lanham (USA) achieved 120° on 10 Mar 2011 – the **largest foot rotation** recorded

Muscular system

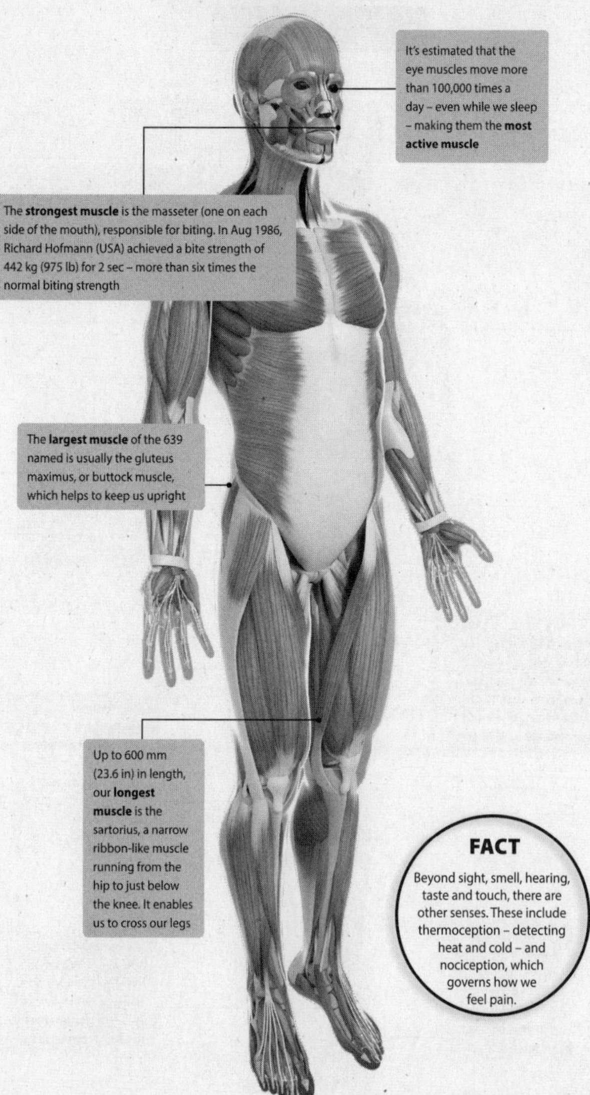

It's estimated that the eye muscles move more than 100,000 times a day – even while we sleep – making them the **most active muscle**
The **strongest muscle** is the masseter (one on each side of the mouth), responsible for biting. In Aug 1986, Richard Hofmann (USA) achieved a bite strength of 442 kg (975 lb) for 2 sec – more than six times the normal biting strength
The **largest muscle** of the 639 named is usually the gluteus maximus, or buttock muscle, which helps to keep us upright
Up to 600 mm (23.6 in) in length, our **longest muscle** is the sartorius, a narrow ribbon-like muscle running from the hip to just below the knee. It enables us to cross our legs

FACT

Beyond sight, smell, hearing, taste and touch, there are other senses. These include thermoception – detecting heat and cold – and nociception, which governs how we feel pain.

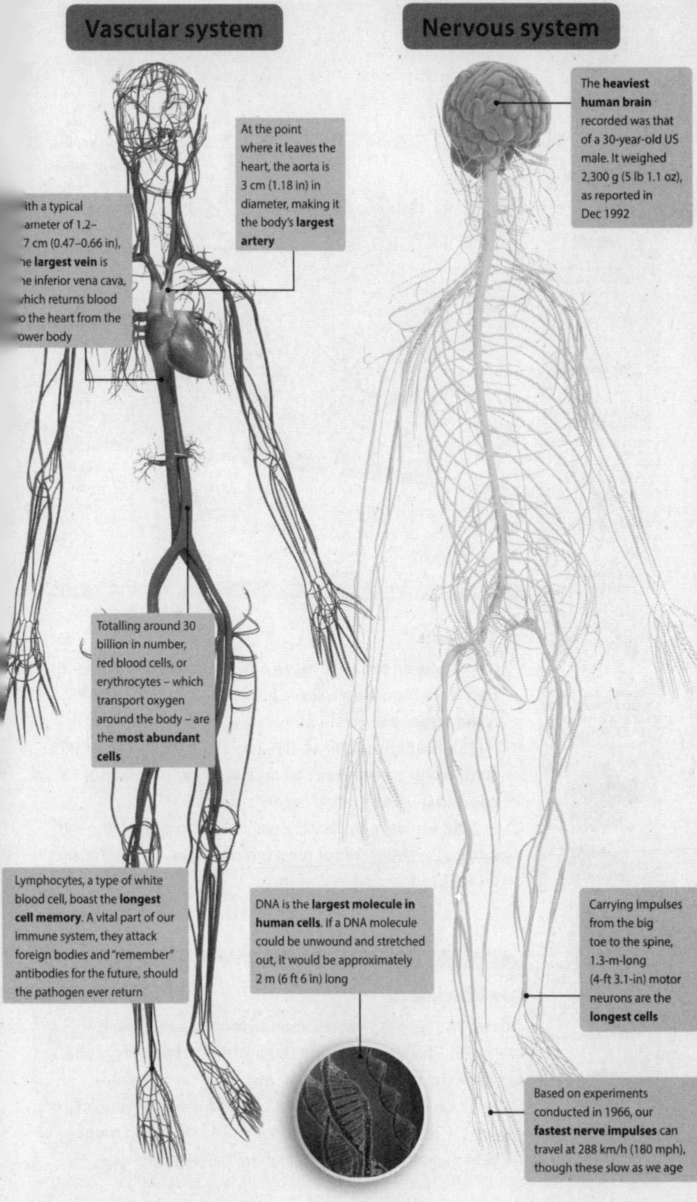
Vascular system
Nervous system
ith a typical
ameter of 1.2–
7 cm (0.47–0.66 in),
e **largest vein** is
e inferior vena cava,
hich returns blood
o the heart from the
ower body
At the point where it leaves the heart, the aorta is 3 cm (1.18 in) in diameter, making it the body's **largest artery**
The **heaviest human brain** recorded was that of a 30-year-old US male. It weighed 2,300 g (5 lb 1.1 oz), as reported in Dec 1992
Totalling around 30 billion in number, red blood cells, or erythrocytes – which transport oxygen around the body – are the **most abundant cells**
Lymphocytes, a type of white blood cell, boast the **longest cell memory**. A vital part of our immune system, they attack foreign bodies and "remember" antibodies for the future, should the pathogen ever return
DNA is the **largest molecule in human cells**. If a DNA molecule could be unwound and stretched out, it would be approximately 2 m (6 ft 6 in) long
Carrying impulses from the big toe to the spine, 1.3-m-long (4-ft 3.1-in) motor neurons are the **longest cells**
Based on experiments conducted in 1966, our **fastest nerve impulses** can travel at 288 km/h (180 mph), though these slow as we age

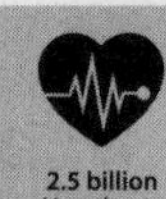
2.5 billion
Heartbeats

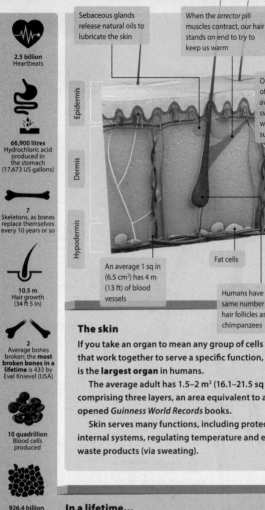

66,900 litres
Hydrochloric acid produced in the stomach (17,673 US gallons)

7
Skeletons, as bones replace themselves every 10 years or so

10.5 m
Hair growth (34 ft 5 in)

2
Average bones broken; the **most broken bones in a lifetime** is 433 by Evel Knievel (USA)

10 quadrillion
Blood cells produced

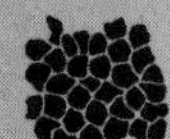
926.4 billion
Skin cells shed, at a rate of about 1,500,000 per hour

494 million
Times we will blink, based on 8 hr of sleep per day

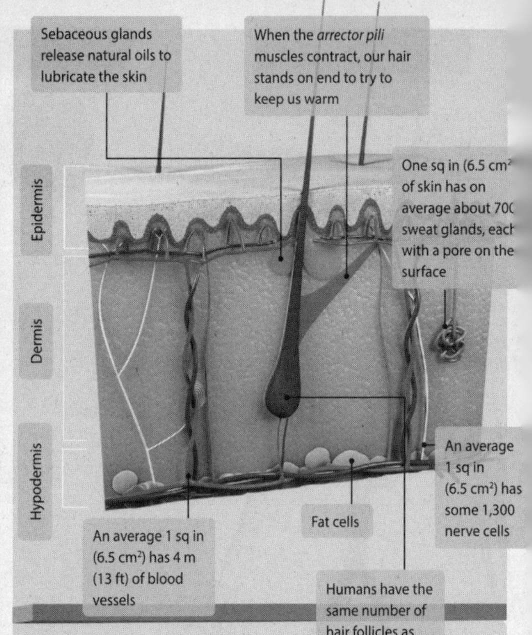
Sebaceous glands release natural oils to lubricate the skin
When the *arrector pili* muscles contract, our hair stands on end to try to keep us warm
One sq in (6.5 cm²) of skin has on average about 700 sweat glands, each with a pore on the surface
Epidermis
Dermis
Hypodermis
An average 1 sq in (6.5 cm²) has some 1,300 nerve cells
Fat cells
An average 1 sq in (6.5 cm²) has 4 m (13 ft) of blood vessels
Humans have the same number of hair follicles as chimpanzees

The skin

If you take an organ to mean any group of cells or tissues that work together to serve a specific function, the skin is the **largest organ** in humans.

The average adult has 1.5–2 m^2 (16.1–21.5 sq ft) of skin comprising three layers, an area equivalent to about 13 opened *Guinness World Records* books.

Skin serves many functions, including protecting our internal systems, regulating temperature and excreting waste products (via sweating).

In a lifetime...

Our body may not seem to change much day to day, but over your life it is constantly transforming. With the global average life expectancy on the rise – the World Health Organization (WHO) puts it at 73 years for women and 68 for men as of 2014 – these numbers are only set to get bigger. All these stats are based on a mean 70.5-year life span.

Recipe of a human

US scientists Robert W Sterner and James J Elser estimated the elemental make-up of the body in their book *Ecological Stoichiometry* (2002). These were their calculations, based on 1 mg of cobalt.

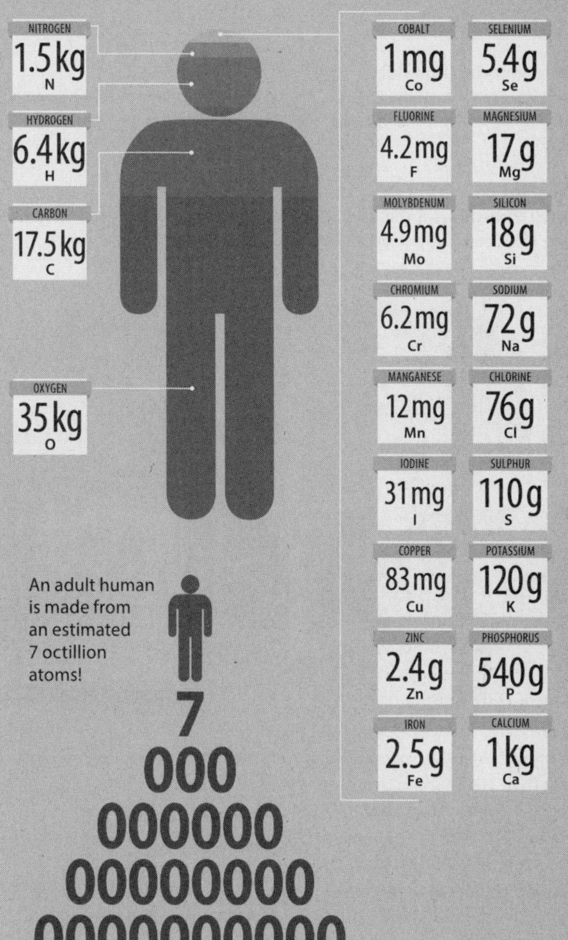

OLDEST PEOPLE

The term **"supercentenarian"** describes anyone **over the age of 110**

OLDEST...

Channel swimmer (female)

The oldest woman to swim the English Channel is Sue Oldham (AUS, b. 24 Nov 1945). Aged 64 years 257 days, she crossed from England to France in 17 hr 11 min on 8 Aug 2010.

Military pilot

On 18 Oct 2012, aged 64 years 305 days, Major Mike Crabtree (UK) flew an AgustaWestland Super Lynx helicopter for the Royal Air Force of Oman at Salalah in Dhofar, Oman.

Oldest living people

Jeralean Talley (USA, b. 23 May 1899) became both the **oldest living woman** and the **oldest living person** following the death of 116-year-old Gertrude Weaver (USA) on 6 Apr 2015. Aged 115 years 349 days as of 7 May 2015, Jeralean lives in Detroit, Michigan, USA, with her daughter, Thelma Holloway, who is herself a septuagenarian.

The world's **oldest living man** is Sakari Momoi, who was born on 5 Feb 1903 in Fukushima, Japan. He was aged 112 years 91 days as of 7 May 2015. His fellow countryman Jiroemon Kimura was the **oldest man ever**: born on 19 Apr 1897, he died on 12 Jun 2013 aged 116 years 54 days.

Oldest tandem parachute jump

Armand Gendreau (CAN, b. 24 Jun 1913) performed his first tandem parachute jump, from a height of 13,500 ft (4,114.81 m), above Notre-Dame-de-Lourdes in Quebec, Canada, on 27 Jun 2014. He was aged 101 years 3 days at the time.

Coach at the FIFA World Cup

Otto Rehhagel (DEU, b. 9 Aug 1938) was 71 years 317 days old when he managed Greece in their final 2010 World Cup group game versus Argentina in Polokwane, South Africa, on 22 Jun 2010.

Hockey player (female)

Aged 79 years 311 days, Australia's Marie Larsen (née Lenon, b. 25 Jul 1934) played for Tuggeranong Vikings Women's Hockey Club against Australian National University Team in the Hockey ACT Women's State League 5 competition in Canberra, Australia, on 1 Jun 2014.

Person to climb Mount Kilimanjaro

On 1 Oct 2012, Martin Kafer (CHE, b. 10 May 1927) scaled Mount Kilimanjaro in Tanzania at the age of 85 years 144 days. Martin made the voyage with his wife, Esther Kafer – at 84 years 161 days old, the **oldest woman to climb Mount Kilimanjaro**.

Videogame actor

The oldest actor to have performed in a videogame is Sir Christopher Lee (UK, b. 27 May 1922), who provided the voice of DiZ/Ansem the Wise in *Kingdom Hearts 358/2 Days* (Square Enix, 2009). He was aged 87 years 125 days at the time of the game's US release on 29 Sep 2009. Lee went on to break his own record when he narrated and played Saruman in *LEGO® The Hobbit* (Traveller's Tales, 2014), aged 91 years 316 days as of its release on 8 Apr 2014.

Highest combined age for a parent and child (living)

As of 21 Apr 2015, Violet Brown (JAM, b. 10 Mar 1900, see table p.111) and her son Harland Fairweather (JAM, b. 15 Apr 1920) had a combined age of 210 years 48 days. Violet, who lives in Duanvale, Trelawny parish, Jamaica, is the last living verified subject of Queen Victoria.

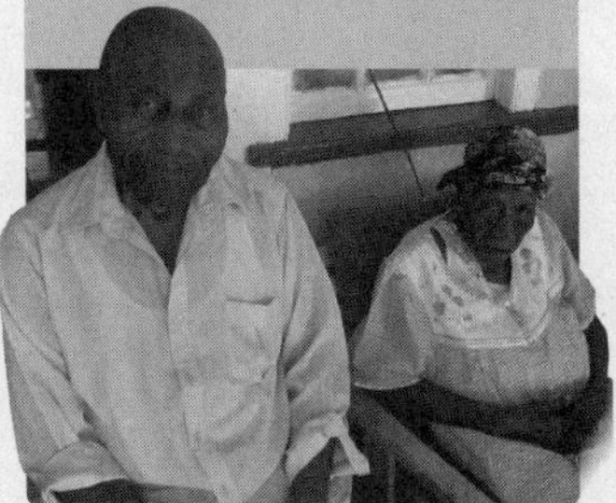

OLDEST...

TV producer

The oldest active TV producer is Fukuko Ishii (JPN, b. 1 Sep 1926), who continued to produce TV shows for Tokyo Broadcasting System Television, Inc. in Tokyo, Japan, at the age of 87 years 341 days as of 8 Aug 2014.

Person to top the UK albums chart

The most elderly act to reach No.1 on the UK albums chart is Dame Vera Lynn (UK, b. Vera Welch, 20 Mar 1917). She was 92 years 183 days old when *The Very Best of Vera Lynn – We'll Meet Again* climbed to No.1 on 19 Sep 2009.

On 14 Feb 2015, Bob Dylan (USA, b. Robert Zimmerman, 24 May 1941) topped the UK albums chart with *Shadows in the Night*, a collection of classic standards originally sung by Frank Sinatra. At the age of 73 years 266 days, this made Dylan the **oldest person to top the UK albums chart (male)**.

Boxing coach

An active boxing coach and trainer since 1935, Abraham "Abe" Pervin (CAN, b. 13 Aug 1919) was aged 94 years 287 days as of 27 May 2014. Pervin was the head coach of the Canadian boxing team for the 1976 Olympic Summer Games and was elected into the Canadian Boxing Hall of Fame on 24 May 1988.

Bungee jumper

Mohr Keet (ZAF, b. 31 Aug 1913) completed a bungee jump when he was 96 years 222 days old at Bloukrans Bridge in Western Cape, South Africa, on 10 Apr 2010. Keet was unaware that he had broken a world record until after the jump.

Conductor

On 23 Feb 2014, at the age of 99 years 311 days, Juan Garcés Queralt (ESP, b. 18 Apr 1914) conducted a concert at the Sala Simfónica of the Auditori i Palau de Congressos de Castelló in Valencia, Spain – his home town.

Teacher

Father Geoffrey Schneider (AUS, b. 23 Dec 1912) retired from full-time teaching on 11 Apr 2014, aged 101 years 109 days. He concluded his 74-year career at

Oldest person to abseil

On 18 May 2014, on her 100th birthday, Doris Cicely Long, MBE (UK, b. 18 May 1914) abseiled down the Spinnaker Tower in Portsmouth, UK. The Spinnaker Tower is 170 m (560 ft) tall, although Mrs Long abseiled from a height of "only" 92.96 m (305 ft).

OLDEST PEOPLE

As of 7 May 2015, there are 50 verified supercentenarians in the world – 48 women and just two men. Currently, the top 10 consists entirely of females, with an average age of 114 years 318 days. *Source: grg.org*

Name	Born	Age
Jeralean Talley (USA)	23 May 1899	115 years 349 days
Susannah Mushatt Jones (USA)	6 Jul 1899	115 years 305 days
Emma Morano-Martinuzzi (ITA)	29 Nov 1899	115 years 159 days
Violet Brown (JAM)	10 Mar 1900	115 years 58 days
Antonia Gerena Rivera (PRI/USA)	19 May 1900	114 years 353 days
Nabi Tajima (JPN)	4 Aug 1900	114 years 276 days
Goldie Steinberg (RUS/USA)	30 Oct 1900	114 years 189 days
Kiyoko Ishiguro (JPN)	4 Mar 1901	114 years 64 days
Dominga Velasco (MEX/USA)	12 May 1901	113 years 360 days
Olympe Amaury (FRA)	19 Jun 1901	113 years 322 days

According to Japan's Ministry of Health, Labour and Welfare, a 115-year-old woman in Tokyo is not only Japan's oldest person, but would also figure in fifth place in the table above. However, the name of the woman, who was born on 15 Mar 1900, was not released at the request of her family.

St Aloysius' College in Milsons Point, New South Wales, Australia, where he had taught Years 3 to 12.

Bride

The oldest bride is Minnie Munro (AUS), who was aged 102 when she married 83-year-old Dudley Reid at Point Clare in New South Wales, Australia, on 31 May 1991. The **oldest bridegroom**, meanwhile, was Harry Stevens (USA), who was aged 103 when he married Thelma Lucas, 84, at the Caravilla Retirement Home in Wisconsin, USA, on 3 Dec 1984.

Competitive sprinter

Hidekichi Miyazaki (JPN, b. 22 Sep 1910) was exactly 104 years old when he competed in the 18th Asia Masters Athletics Championships in Kitakami, Iwate, Japan, on 22 Sep 2014. He ran the 100 m in 34.61 sec.

Person ever

The greatest fully authenticated age to which any human has ever lived is 122 years 164 days, by Jeanne Louise Calment (FRA). Born on 21 Feb 1875, Jeanne died at a nursing home in Arles, southern France, on 4 Aug 1997.

IN NUMBERS

71 years
Average global life expectancy for women in 2013

66 years
Average global life expectancy for men in 2013

48 years
Average global life expectancy in 1955; by 2025, it will be 73 years

50 million
People who live in countries where life expectancy is less than 45 years

2 billion
Projected number of people aged 60 years or over by 2050; in 1950, 205 million people were this age

60
Age that the UN regards as marking the onset of old age

Sources: World Health Organization; United Nations

Turn of the century

Robert Young researches extreme longevity; he is seen below with Besse Cooper (USA), then the oldest living person, on her 116th birthday in 2012.

When did you become involved with the Gerontology Research Group?

I became involved with the organization in June 1999. It's a volunteer group with more than 100 contributors worldwide.

What made you interested in studying people who reach extreme old age?

When I was about five years old, I saw a story on the news about a woman celebrating her 109th birthday. It fascinated me that there could be someone alive more than a hundred years older than me. I surmised that living to extreme age was a huge rarity.

What are the challenges involved in proving someone's age?

The biggest challenge in proving, or disproving, someone's age is to find sufficient evidence covering a period of more than 110 years. Only about 20% of the world's population in 1900 had proper government registration of birth. However, in some cases we may be able to substitute census, baptismal or other early-life documentation, as well as mid- and late-life documents such as marriage records, military enlistment records, pension records, ID cards and death records. It's also important to build a case to show that the person alive today is the same person shown in the original birth documentation. More than 98% of all claims to be age 115 or greater turn out to be false.

FACT

After abseiling down the side of the 170-m Spinnaker tower in Portsmouth, UK (see p.110) Doris Long remarked "I don't know any other people my age who do this sort of thing,"

Oldest best man

Ronald Hornby (UK, b. 5 Oct 1917) served as best man at the marriage of James Beattie – his nephew – and Isobel Coote (both UK, above) in Clogher, County Tyrone, Northern Ireland, UK, on 2 Jan 2014. Ronald was aged 96 years 89 days on the big day, at which his wife, Frankie, also served as matron of honour.

FACT

Armand Gendreau (see p.109) said after his plunge with instructor Richard Lavoie. "I liked it so much, I could jump [again] tomorrow," adding, "It would make a beautiful pastime, no?"

In the French Revolution, a dwarf named Richebourg, **disguised as a baby**, was a **spy** for the aristocracy

Tallest woman ever

Zeng Jinlian (26 Jun 1964–13 Feb 1982), of the Bright Moon Commune in Hunan Province, China, measured 248 cm (8 ft 1.75 in) at her death. This figure allows for a normal spinal curvature, because she suffered from severe scoliosis (curvature of the spine). She began to grow abnormally from four months old and stood 156 cm (5 ft 1.5 in) before her fourth birthday, and 217 cm (7 ft 1.5 in) at age 13.

Tallest woman living

In Dec 2012, Siddiqa Parveen of South Dinajpur, India, was measured by Dr Debasis Saha from Fortis Healthcare and found to be at least 222.25 cm (7 ft 3.5 in) tall. Due to ill health, and Ms Parveen's inability to stand upright, it is impossible to ascertain her exact stature. However, Dr Saha estimated that her standing height must be at least 233.6 cm (7 ft 8 in).

Most variable stature

Adam Rainer (AUT, 1899–1950) is the only person in medical history to have been both a dwarf and a giant. At the age of 21 he measured just 118 cm (3 ft 10.5 in), but suddenly started growing at a rapid rate.

By 1931, he had nearly doubled in height to 218 cm (7 ft 1.75 in). He grew so weak as a result of his intensive growth spurt that he became bedridden and remained so for the rest of his life. At the time of his death, he measured 234 cm (7 ft 8 in).

Shortest woman ever

Pauline Musters (NLD, 1876–95), aka Princess Pauline, was 30 cm (1 ft) tall at birth and 55 cm (1 ft 9.6 in) at the age of nine. On her death in New York City, USA, at 19 years old, she was 61 cm (2 ft).

Shortest woman living

On 16 Dec 2011, her 18th birthday, Jyoti Amge (IND) measured 62.8 cm (2 ft 0.7 in) in Nagpur, India, so replacing her title of **shortest teenager**. She is 8.2 cm (3.2 in) taller than Chandra Dangi, the **shortest man** (see p.115), who she met on the TV show *Lo Show dei Record* in Rome, Italy, in Apr 2012.

Tallest man living

Sultan Kösen (TUR, b. 10 Dec 1982), seen with GWR Records Manager Sam Mason, stood 251 cm (8 ft 3 in) tall in Ankara, Turkey, on 8 Feb 2011.

Sultan's hands, measuring 28.5 cm (11.22 in) from the wrist to the tip of the middle finger, are the **largest hands on a living person.** They span 30.48 cm (12 in) – longer than an American football.

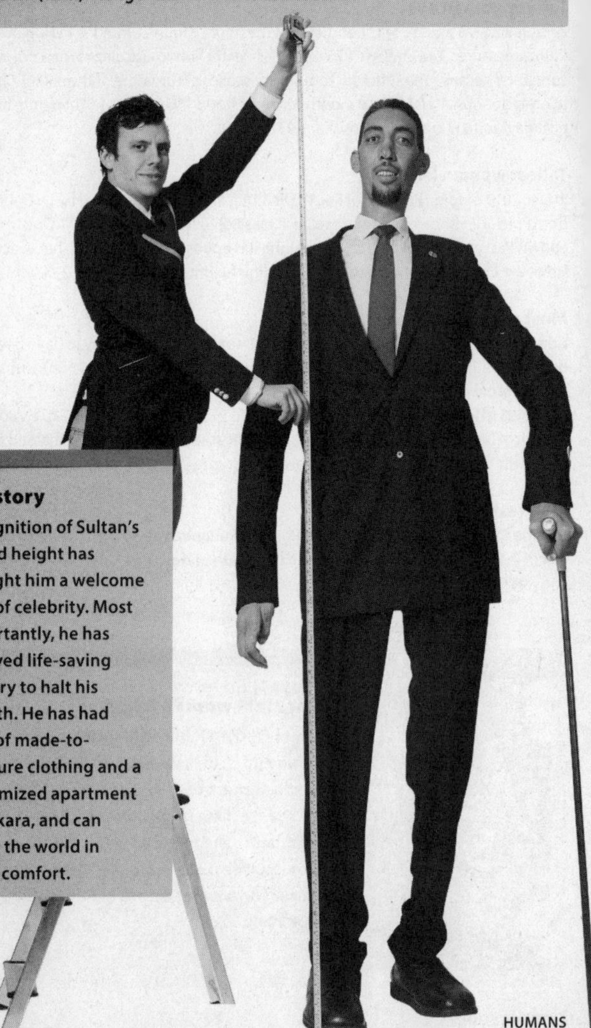

Tall story

Recognition of Sultan's record height has brought him a welcome kind of celebrity. Most importantly, he has received life-saving surgery to halt his growth. He has had gifts of made-to-measure clothing and a customized apartment in Ankara, and can travel the world in some comfort.

TALLEST PEOPLE OVER TIME

The last 10 tallest people date back almost 100 years. No one has yet beaten Wadlow – the **tallest man ever**.

Name (nationality)	Height (cm)	Year
Bernard Coyne (USA)	248	1921
Robert Wadlow (USA)	272	1940
Edward "Ted" Evans (UK)	234	1957
Suleiman Ali Nashnush (LBY)	246	1964
John F Carroll (USA)	263	1966
Don Koehler (USA)	248	1970
Haji Mohammad Alam Channa (PAK)	232	1981
Radhouane Charbib (TUN)	235	1999
Xi Shun (CHN)	236	2005
Sultan Kösen (TUR)	251	2011

Shortest man ever

Chandra Bahadur Dangi (NPL) measures 54.6 cm (1 ft 9.5 in) tall. This was verified at CIWEC Clinic Travel Medicine Center in Lainchaur, Kathmandu, Nepal, on 26 Feb 2012, when his height was taken six times over a 24-hour period, witnessed by GWR Editor-in-Chief Craig Glenday.

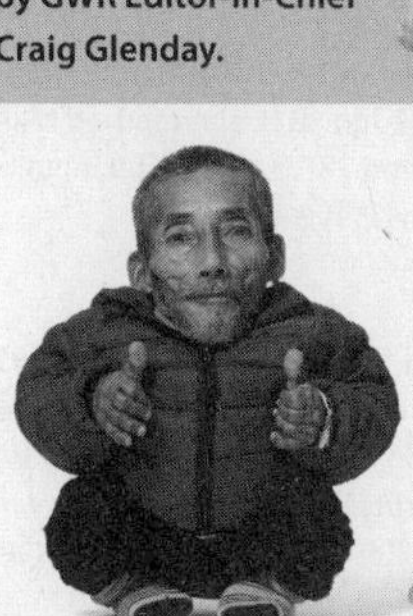

IN NUMBERS

14 in
Longest beard on a woman (36 cm), owned by Janice Deveree (USA), as measured in 1884

90
Instances of human horns found by English dermatologist Sir Erasmus Wilson (1809–84)

302 cm
Largest waist size (119 in): that of Walter Hudson (USA)

132 cm
Longest human legs (51.9 in), belonging to Svetlana Pankratova (RUS)

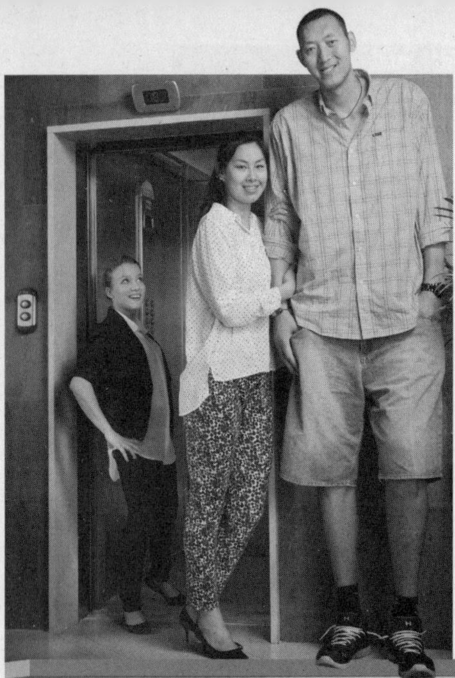

Tallest married couple living

The **tallest basketball player**, Sun Mingming, and handball player Xu Yan (both CHN) were married in Beijing, China, on 4 Aug 2013. They stand 236.17 cm (7 ft 8.98 in) and 187.3 cm (6 ft 1.74 in) tall respectively, as measured in Beijing on 14 Nov 2013. Their heights total 423.47 cm (13 ft 10.72 in), beating the previous record by 4.37 cm (1.72 in).

Tallest married couple ever

At 17 years old, Anna Haining Swan (CAN, 1846–88), the daughter of Scottish immigrants to Nova Scotia, measured 241.3 cm (7 ft 11 in) tall. On 17 Jun 1871, she married Martin van Buren Bates (USA, 1837–1919) in London, UK. He stood 236.22 cm (7 ft 9 in) tall, so the couple had a combined height of a record 477.52 cm (15 ft 8 in).

Heaviest person ever

Jon Brower Minnoch (USA, 1941–83) suffered from obesity from childhood. He was 1.85 m (6 ft 1 in) tall, and by Sep 1976 weighed 442 kg (975 lb; 69 st 9 lb). Just two years later, Minnoch was admitted to University Hospital in Seattle, Washington, suffering from heart and respiratory failure. Here, consultant endocrinologist Dr Robert Schwartz calculated his weight to be more than 635 kg (1,400 lb; 100 st), a great deal of it due to water accumulation.

After nearly two years on a diet of 1,200 calories per day, Minnoch was discharged at 216 kg (476 lb; 34 st). In Oct 1981, however, he was readmitted after gaining around 90 kg (200 lb; 14 st). When he died on 10 Sep 1983, Minnoch weighed more than 362 kg (798 lb; 57 st).

In contrast, Minnoch's wife Jeannette (USA) weighed just 50 kg (110 lb; 8 st) – 585 kg (1,290 lb; 92 st) less than Minnoch at his heaviest, making theirs the **greatest weight differential in a married couple**.

Heaviest woman living

Pauline Potter (USA) weighed (647 lb 6 oz; 46 st 3 lb) 293.6 kg in Jul 2012, making her the heaviest living woman to have had her weight confirmed medically. Although other women have claimed to be heavier, none has been able to submit medical proof.

Almost double the size of Pauline, however, was Rosalie Bradford (USA, 1943–2006), who registered a peak weight of around 1,200 lb (544 kg; 85 st) in Jan 1987, making her the **heaviest woman ever**.

FACT

The most exaggerated height claimed for a giant was 283.2 cm (9 ft 3.5 in) by Finland's Daniel Cajanus (1704–49). His actual height was determined post mortem to be 222.2 cm (7 ft 3 in).

Tallest teenage boy

Just as we were going to press, we heard from the mother of Kevin Bradford – a 16-year-old boy in Miami, Florida, USA, who supposedly measures over 7 ft (213 cm). "Is my son the tallest teenage boy?" she asked...

GWR does indeed monitor categories for tallest male and female teens, but the previous **tallest teenage boy** – Broc Brown (USA, b. 14 Apr 1997) – had since turned 18, meaning that he no longer qualifies for this title. (GWR considers claimants aged 18 or older to be adults.)

Kevin was born on 27 Oct 1998, and to confirm him as the new tallest male under the age of 18, he was measured at Paediatric Associates in Doral, Florida, USA, on 30 Apr 2015. There, doctors in the presence of GWR adjudicators confirmed that Kevin was 215.9 cm (7 ft 1 in) tall – an incredible height given his age of 16 years 186 days.

After assessing X-rays, doctors concluded that Kevin's "growth plates" are not yet closed. Known as epiphyseal plates, these pieces of cartilage are situated at the end of your long bones, and when they "seal", around the time of puberty, you stop growing. In some cases, such as Kevin's, however, the plates do not close, resulting in extreme growth and meaning that Kevin might continue to grow...

On average, a girl's **feet grow** until the **age of 13**, and a boy's until the **age of 15**

Longest tongue

Nick "The Lick" Stoeberl's (USA) tongue measured 10.1 cm (3.9 in) from tip to mid-top lip, as verified on 27 Nov 2012. Nick partly attributes his record to his dad being a fan of rock band KISS – famed for their tongue-wagging antics on stage.

Chanel Tapper (USA) has the **longest female tongue**, with a 9.75-cm (3.8-in) licker, as measured on 29 Sep 2010.

Widest tongue

At its broadest point, the tongue of Byron Schlenker (USA) spans 8.57 cm (3.37 in), as measured on 2 Nov 2014, beating his previous record of 8.3 cm (3.26 in). It's clearly a family trait: on the same day, his daughter Emily (USA) was confirmed to have the **widest tongue (female)**, with a maximum breadth of 7.33 cm (2.89 in).

Longest nose

Mehmet Özyürek's (TUR) nose was 8.8 cm (3.46 in) from the bridge to the tip when checked on *Lo Show dei Record* on 18 Mar 2010. But this might not be the **longest nose ever**: there are reports from the 1770s that English circus act Thomas Wedders had a nose measuring 19 cm (7.5 in).

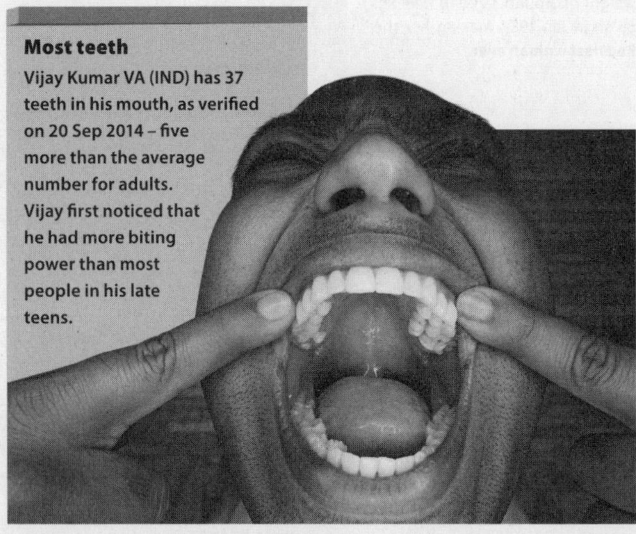

Most teeth

Vijay Kumar VA (IND) has 37 teeth in his mouth, as verified on 20 Sep 2014 – five more than the average number for adults. Vijay first noticed that he had more biting power than most people in his late teens.

Largest hairy family

Comprising 19 members in total, the Ramos Gomez family (all MEX) have a very rare genetic condition known as congenital generalized hypertrichosis (CGH), which causes excessive hair growth. While CGH affects both men and women, it is more noticeable in the male family members, with thick hair covering about 98% of their body, except for their palms and soles.

Largest feet

Jeison Orlando Rodríguez Hernández (VEN, pictured here with his nephew) has to specially order shoes from Germany to fit his huge feet. As of 6 Oct 2014, Jeison's right foot measured 40.1 cm (1 ft 3.8 in) and his left foot 39.6 cm (1 ft 3.6 in).

The **largest feet ever**, however, belonged to the **tallest man ever**, Robert Wadlow (USA, 1918–40), who wore US size 37AA (UK size 36) shoes, which equates to 47 cm (1 ft 6.5 in).

LONGEST HAIR...

On the head

Female: When measured on 8 May 2004, Xie Qiuping's (CHN) hair reached a staggering 5.6 m (18 ft 5.5 in). She began growing her locks in 1973 and now needs an assistant to help her carry them when moving around.

Male: There are reports from 1949 that Indian monk Swami Pandarasannadhi, of the Tirudaduturai monastery in Madras, had 26-ft-long (7.9-m) hair. But this may have been the result of a scalp condition called plica neuropathica, which makes the hair so matted that it can't be untangled.

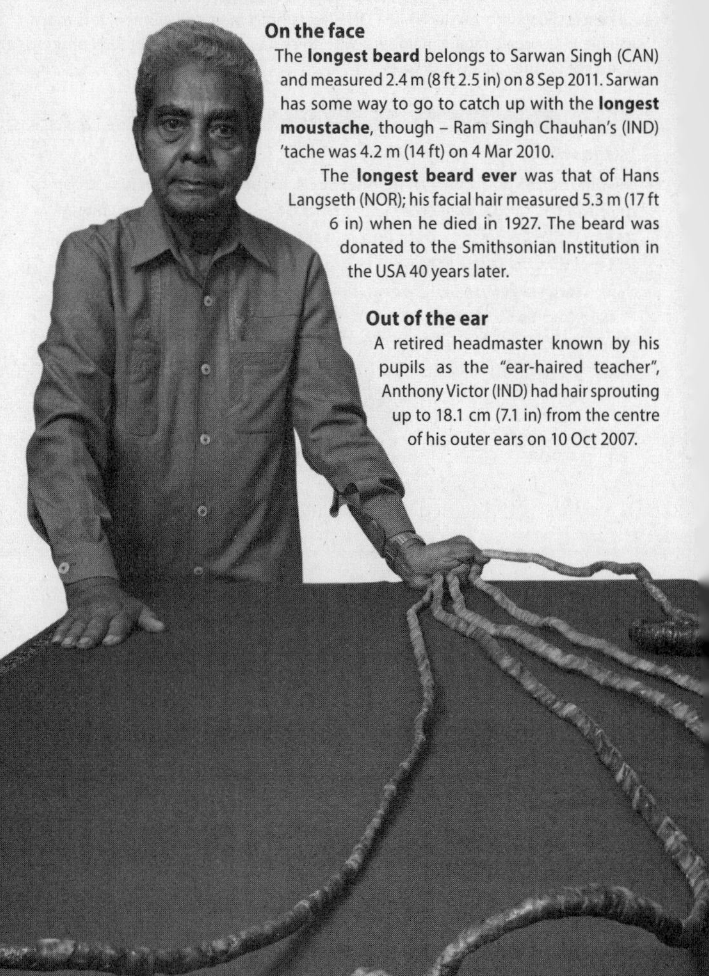

On the face

The **longest beard** belongs to Sarwan Singh (CAN) and measured 2.4 m (8 ft 2.5 in) on 8 Sep 2011. Sarwan has some way to go to catch up with the **longest moustache**, though – Ram Singh Chauhan's (IND) 'tache was 4.2 m (14 ft) on 4 Mar 2010.

The **longest beard ever** was that of Hans Langseth (NOR); his facial hair measured 5.3 m (17 ft 6 in) when he died in 1927. The beard was donated to the Smithsonian Institution in the USA 40 years later.

Out of the ear

A retired headmaster known by his pupils as the "ear-haired teacher", Anthony Victor (IND) had hair sprouting up to 18.1 cm (7.1 in) from the centre of his outer ears on 10 Oct 2007.

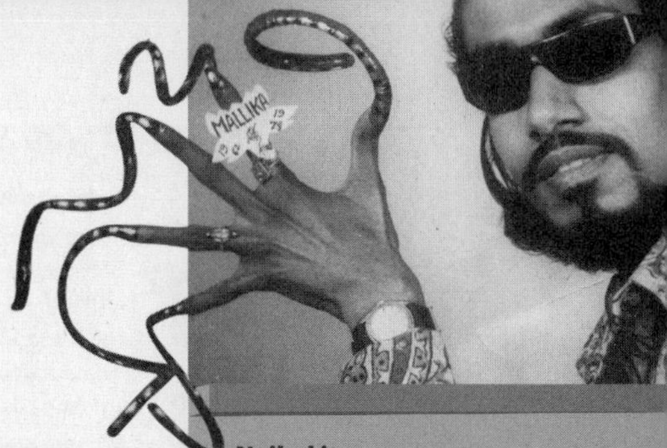

On the chest

The longest chest hair measured 23.5 cm (9.25 in) and belonged to Zhao Jingtao from China, as confirmed on 13 Sep 2014. The **longest nipple hair** was grown by Italian Daniele Tuveri, logged at 17 cm (6.6 in) on 13 Mar 2013.

On the back

As of 9 Nov 2012, Craig Bedford (UK) had a 13-cm-long (5.1-in) hair on his back.

FACT

Shridhar's nails measure: thumb – 6 ft 5.8 in (197.9 cm); index finger – 5 ft 4.7 in (164.5 cm); middle finger – 6 ft 1.4 in (186.6 cm); ring finger – 5 ft 11.5 in (181.6 cm); and little finger – 5 ft 10.5 in (179.1 cm).

Nailed it

Shridhar Chillal (IND, pictured above in 1975 and left in 2014) has the longest fingernails on a single hand. After 52 years of growth, they measured in total 29 ft 10 in (9.09 m). We asked him how his nails have affected his life...

Why did you start growing your nails?

After a friend and I got into trouble at school in 1952, a teacher said we didn't understand the value of the patience needed to grow a nail, so I took up the challenge. My parents opposed my decision initially, but this only spurred me on to grow them. Later, when they saw my determination, they began to support me.

How much work does it take to look after your fingernails?

They're extremely fragile. Even a small touch can break nails of this size, so I apply a layer of [lacquer] to protect them.

Also, I have to take precautions when I sleep, as I can't move much, so every half an hour or so I wake up and move my hand to the other side of the bed.

Do your nails offer any benefits?

Yes, I'm always recognized everywhere I go. Plus, I never have to wait in a queue. Eventually, I would like to donate my nails to a museum for posterity.

And disadvantages?

I've been rejected from many jobs because of my nails. I was also turned down by about 10 girls before my wife agreed to marry me.

IN NUMBERS

20
Average number of milk teeth a child has by the age of three

100,000
Estimated number of hairs on the human head; we lose between 50 and 100 strands every day

2–3 mm
Average rate of fingernail growth per month (0.08–0.12 in)

26
Bones in the human foot – about an eighth of the entire skeleton

10
Most common shoe size for men in the UK, according to a 2014 study by the College of Podiatry – up from size 8 in the 1970s

Most fingers and toes

Born with a condition called polydactylism, Devendra Suthar (IND) has 28 digits: 14 fingers and 14 toes, as verified in Himatnagar, Gujarat, India, on 11 Nov 2014. A carpenter, Devendra says that the extra fingers don't affect his work, though he has to be extra careful when cutting!

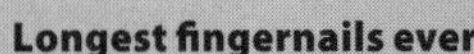

Longest fingernails ever

Male: Melvin Boothe (USA, 1948–2009) had the longest nails on record, with a combined length of 9.85 m (32 ft 3.8 in).

Female: The total length of Lee Redmond's (USA) nails was 8.65 m (28 ft 4.5 in) in 2008, although she sadly lost them in a car accident the next year.

Frozen mummy **Ötzi the Iceman** (c. 3300 BC) has both **stretched ears** and **tattoos**

Most body modifications for a married couple

Husband and wife Victor Hugo Peralta (URU) and Gabriela Peralta (ARG) have a total of 84 different modifications between them, as verified on 7 Jul 2014. These mods comprise 50 piercings, eight microdermals, 14 body implants, five dental implants, four ear expanders, two ear bolts and one forked tongue.

Largest earlobe flesh tunnel

A tattoo and body-mod artist himself, Kalawelo Kaiwi (USA) boasts flesh tunnels spanning 10.5 cm (4.14 in) in each ear, as confirmed at the Hilo Natural Health Clinic in Hawaii, USA, on 14 Apr 2014. About the diameter of a teacup, the tunnels are big enough to fit a clenched fist through. In addition to the flesh tunnels, Kala also sports tattoos, piercings, subdermal horns and a bifurcated (split) tongue.

MOST PIERCINGS...

In a single count

A medical examination of Rolf Buchholz (DEU) on 16 Dec 2012 revealed 481 body piercings. The human pincushion also boasted, among other adornments, two sub-dermal "horn" implants and five magnetic implants in the fingertips of his right hand, taking his total count of mods to 516 and earning him the record for **most body mods (male)**.

The **most body mods (female)** is 49 for Maria Jose Cristerna (MEX), who has transformed her body with tattoos, transdermal implants and piercings in her belly button, ear lobes, eyebrows, lips, nipples, nose and tongue.

The record for the **most piercings in a single count (female)** is held by Elaine Davidson (BRA/UK), who recorded 462 piercings on 4 May 2000. Elaine has also

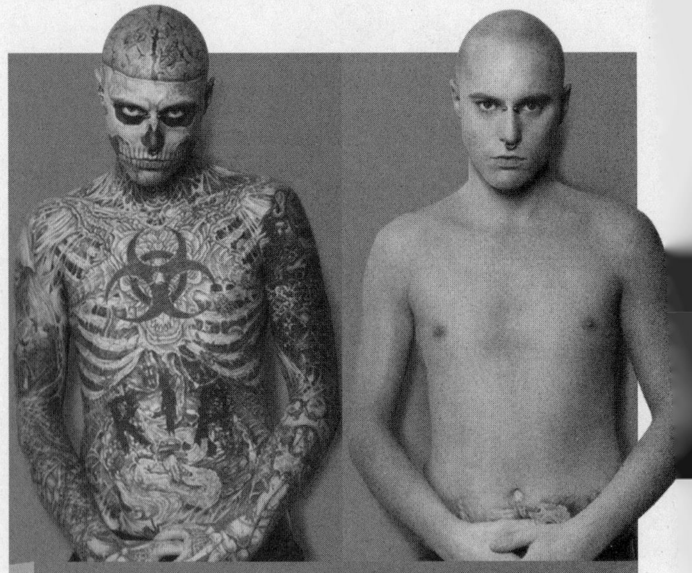

Most tattoos of bones

Horror-movie fan Rick Genest (CAN) has had 139 bones – nearly 70% of the skeleton – inked on to his body. Also known as "Zombie Boy", Rick has spent thousands of dollars on the work and gained fame along the way, even appearing in Lady Gaga's "Born this Way" music video. Continuing his passion for the macabre, Rick also has the **most insect tattoos**, with 176 creepy-crawlies such as millipedes and cockroaches. In the shot above, he is demonstrating the effectiveness of make-up that conceals blemishes by covering up his tattoos.

Largest lip plate

Girls of the Surma tribe in Ethiopia wear lip plates up to 15 cm (6 in) wide to signify that they are ready to marry. Those with the largest plates are considered the most eligible, and plate size is typically equated to the number of cattle expected from a suitor.

Pictured here is 20-year-old Ataye Eligidagne (ETH), whose plate is 59.5 cm (23.4 in) in circumference and 19.5 cm (7.6 in) wide – the largest ever recorded. She was photographed by Australian film-maker Abraham Joffe during a trip to Ethiopia in 2014. Inset, Ataye shows her lip with the plate removed.

amassed the **most piercings in a lifetime**, with a count of 4,225 as of 8 Jun 2006. The number she wears is always fluctuating as jewellery grows out and new additions are made.

On the face

Aiming for a "mask of piercings", Axel Rosales from Argentina had 280 facial studs and hoops on 17 Feb 2012. The final nine were added on the day of the count, as Axel said he wanted a "more rounded" number than 271.

IN NUMBERS

86%
People with a tattoo who do not regret getting one, according to a US Harris Poll

1:5
Estimated ratio of UK and US population with at least one tattoo

35%
Ear piercings that result in complications (77% of these are minor infections)

30–39 years
Age group most likely to have a tattoo in the USA

3,000
Number of times a tattoo gun can pierce the skin in a minute

$12 bn
Amount spent on surgical and non-surgical cosmetic procedures in the USA in 2013 (£7 bn)

Most square tattoos

Check out this record-breaker! With 201 squares on his head alone, the "Human Chequerboard" Matt Gone (USA) has 848 squares tattooed over his body, as counted on 7 Jul 2014. Matt has even tattooed his tongue and the whites of his own eyes, although this isn't medically endorsed owing to the high risk of infection.

TATTOOS

Most tattooed person

Lucky Rich (AUS/NZ) represents the ultimate in tattooing, having endured more than 1,000 hr of inking. New tattoos are inked over old, giving him a coverage estimated at over 200%.

The most tattooed woman is Maria Jose Cristerna (MEX): the "Mexican Vampire

Lady", as she is also known, had a total body coverage of 96% on 8 Feb 2011.

The most tattooed senior citizen (male) is Tom Leppard (UK), with a 99.9% coverage of a leopard print, while the most tattooed senior citizen (female) is Isobel Varley (UK), with a coverage of 93% as of 25 Apr 2009.

Most tattoos of...

Jigsaw pieces: Body-mod-loving entertainer "The Enigma", aka Paul Lawrence (USA), has 2,123 puzzle pieces tattooed over his body, as counted on the set of *Lo Show dei Record* on 13 Apr 2011.

A cartoon character: Few *Simpsons* fans are as dedicated as Lee Weir (NZ). As of 5 Jun 2014, he had 41 tattoos of Homer Simpson in various guises on his left arm, including a baby Homer, an Incredible Hulk Homer and even one of him as a jack-in-the-box. The sleeve took more than 25 hr to complete.

Flags: Between Jul 2009 and Jul 2011, Guinness Rishi (IND) acquired 366 tattoos of world flags. His geography-themed body art doesn't stop at flags either, as he has many more tattoos of country names and maps.

FACT

Extreme body modifications are the equivalent of surgical operations, and should therefore only ever be carried out by qualified and licensed practitioners. Never try body modifying at home!

Tunnel vision

Joel Miggler (DEU) holds the record for most facial flesh tunnels: 11, as of 27 Nov 2014. Find out what drew him to the "holey" grail of body mods...

When did you first become interested in flesh tunnels?

It started when I was 13 years old and I had a flesh tunnel in my earlobe. I really liked it and, step by step, I've come to this!

Do you have any difficulties eating or drinking?

No, I don't have any problems. I can only take small bites, though.

...and how about kissing?

No, not really! My girlfriend also has a big "labret" [a lip piercing], but kissing is only a little bit harder.

Tell us about the process of creating the tunnels in your cheeks.

First, we made a little cut through my cheeks of around 10 mm and pushed the Teflon jewellery in. After three months of healing, we cut it to 18 mm; that took about a month to heal. Then I stretched it again for 1 mm each month until I got to 22 mm, before cutting to 30 mm. Now I'm aiming to stretch to 40 mm [they currently measure 34 mm], which will be my limit. The man who carries out my mods did a medical apprenticeship in the military and has carried out extreme modifications for eight years. I trust him with my whole body. He is highly trained. He needs to be, as it's a very complicated process to cut through the cheeks. It's really dangerous to cut the salivary glands.

How long does the pain tend to last during the healing process?

The cuts are painful for about a week, but they don't hurt after that.

Even **identical twins** do not have **identical fingerprints**

Richest twin

David H Koch (USA) was born on 3 May 1940, with his twin brother William (USA), and has a net worth of $42 bn (£28 bn). He is executive vice-president of Koch Industries, founded by his father, Fred Koch, in 1940. David comes sixth in the Fortune 500 rich list, a rank he shares with his older (non-twin) brother, Charles. William "Bill" Koch is founder and head of the Oxbow Corporation.

Longest interval between birth of twins

A period of 87 days separated the birth of twins Amy Ann and Kate Marie ("Katie") Elliott to Maria Jones-Elliott (IRL). The twins were both born at Waterford Regional Hospital in Ireland. Amy was born prematurely on 1 Jun 2012 and Kate followed on 27 Aug.

Most multiples in the same academic year at one school

Henry James Memorial School in Simsbury, Connecticut, USA, enrolled 20 multiple birth sets in one academic year: 18 sets of twins and two sets of triplets. The figures were verified on 31 May 2012.

Oldest octuplets

The Suleman octuplets were born at the Kaiser Permanente Medical Center in Bellflower, California, USA, and celebrated their sixth birthday on 26 Jan 2015. They were born by in vitro fertilization (IVF) to 33-year-old Nadya Suleman (USA).

FACT

The octuplets arrived nine weeks prematurely and weighed between 0.68 kg and 1.47 kg (1 lb 8 oz–3 lb 3 oz). Babies usually average 3.4 kg (7 lb 8 oz).

Oldest twin Holocaust survivors

Annetta Able and Stephanie "Stepha" Heller (née Heilbrunn) turned 90 on 4 Feb 2015. Born in Subotica, Yugoslavia (now Serbia), they were 18 years old when they were sent to the Terezín (Theresienstadt) work camp in Czechoslovakia. In 1943, aged 19, they were sent to the Auschwitz camp in Poland. They are believed to be the oldest co-twins to have survived the brutal and dehumanizing medical experiments conducted by Dr Josef Mengele. After being evacuated from Auschwitz in 1945 they ended up in German camps, but escaped. Days later they received assistance from US soldiers.

Longest-separated twins

Elizabeth Ann Hamel (née Lamb, USA, left) and Ann Patricia Hunt (née Wilson, UK, right) were born on 28 Feb 1936 in Aldershot, UK. They were reunited in Fullerton, California, USA, on 1 May 2014 after 77 years 289 days apart.

First twins born in different countries

Dylan Fox (UK, left) was born at his grandparents' home in Wooler in Northumberland, England, after his mother, Donna Keenan, went into early labour on 1 Jul 2012. His sister Hannah (right) was not ready to be born, so Donna was taken by ambulance to the Borders General Hospital in Melrose, about 72 km (45 mi) away in Scotland. The trip took an hour. Hannah was born 90 min after her brother.

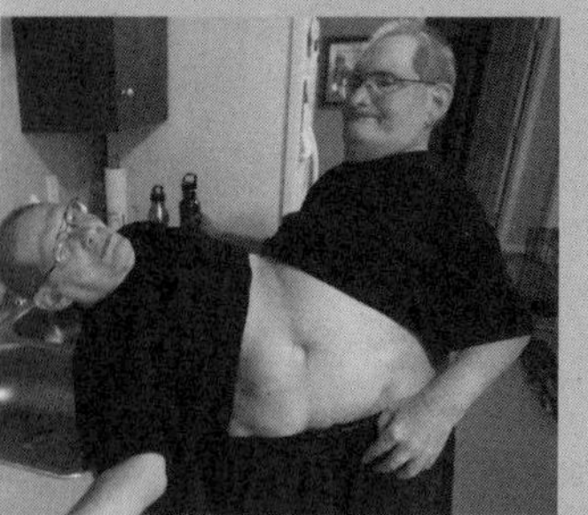

Oldest conjoined twins ever

On 4 Jul 2014, Donnie (far left) and Ronnie Galyon (near left; both USA) were 62 years 252 days old, surpassing their heroes Chang and Eng Bunker (11 May 1811–17 Jan 1874), the world-famous conjoined twins who had lived to the age of 62 years 251 days (see opposite).

Ronnie and Donnie turned 63 on 28 Oct 2014. In doing so, they surpassed the twins previously recognized as the oldest conjoined twins ever, Giacomo and Giovanni Battista Tocci (ITA, b. c. 1875), who were widely reported to have lived for 63 years.

First identical twin astronauts

Scott and Mark Kelly (USA, b. 21 Feb 1964) are the only identical twin astronauts and the only siblings to have flown in space. Scott (left) carried out his first space flight as the pilot of the shuttle *Discovery* on the STS-103 mission from 19 to 27 Dec 1999. Mark (right) made his space debut as pilot of the shuttle *Endeavour* on the STS-108 mission from 5 to 17 Dec 2001.

FIRST...

Twin on the Moon

On 21–23 Apr 1972, US astronaut and identical twin Charles Moss "Charlie" Duke Jr became the first – and, to date, only – twin to walk on the Moon. Charlie, who served as the Lunar Module pilot for Apollo 16, was the 10th and **youngest Moon walker**, and remains one of only 12 people who have ever set foot on the Moon.

Twin heads of state

Polish identical twin brothers Lech Aleksander Kaczyński and Jarosław Aleksander Kaczyński were born on 18 Jun 1949. Lech was elected President of Poland and served from Dec 2005 to Apr 2010. His twin Jarosław was Poland's Prime Minister from Jul 2006 to Nov 2007.

US First Lady to deliver twins

Laura Bush (USA), wife of the 43rd US president George W Bush, is the only US First Lady to have given birth to twins. The two girls, Jenna and Barbara, were born on 25 Nov 1981 in Dallas, Texas, USA.

CONJOINED TWINS

Oldest conjoined twins ever (female)

Masha and Dasha Krivoshlyapova (RUS, b. 3 Jan 1950) were a rare form of conjoined twins – *dicephales tetrabrachius dipus* (two heads, four arms and two legs). They died within 17 hours of each other on 17 Apr 2003, aged 53 years 104 days, in an old people's home in the Russian capital Moscow.

Technically, this record is now held by Lori Lynn and Dori Schappell (USA, b. 18 Sep 1961), who are craniopagus conjoined twins, with partially fused skulls but separate bodies. As of 23 Mar 2015, they were 53 years 186 days old. Although the twins are genetically identical, in 2007 Dori declared that he was transgender, identifying himself as a male named George. This unusual situation qualifies them as the **first conjoined twins to identify as mixed-gender**.

Most children born to unseparated conjoined twins

Chang and Eng Bunker, conjoined twins from Siam (now Thailand), were born in 1811. In 1843, they married sisters Adelaide and Sarah Yates and fathered 21 children in all – Chang and Adelaide had 10 and Eng and Sarah had 11.

First identical twins to perform a transplant for identical twins

In Jan 1999, in Los Angeles, USA, identical twin doctors Rafael and Robert Mendez performed a kidney transplant on identical twins Anna and Petra Martinez (all USA). Identical twins are ideal donors and recipients for one another, owing to their close genetic match. Seen above, from left to right: Rafael, Petra, Anna and Robert.

IN NUMBERS

14 weeks
Age at which twin foetuses start to touch each other in the womb

22%
Proportion of twins that are left-handed; among non-twins, the figure is less than 10%

17 min
Average time between the delivery of the first and second twin

1 in 250
Chances of a birth resulting in identical twins

1 in 200,000
Chances of a birth resulting in conjoined twins; 1 in 200 births of identical twins results in conjoined twins

Dr Nancy Segal

GWR talks with our new twins consultant – shown below with the longest-separated twins (see p.129).

What made you want to study twins?
My interest in twins is closely linked to my being part of a fraternal (non-identical) female twin pair. My sister and I have always looked different and behaved quite differently. I found this intriguing, even as a child. After all, we had the same parents and shared many important experiences.

Is the birth rate of twins rising or falling?
In the USA, the twinning rate has risen from 18.7 in every 1,000 infants in 1980 to 33.7 in every 1,000 infants in 2013. About two-thirds of the increase is due to assisted reproductive technologies (ART) such as IVF, which mostly give rise to fraternal twins. However, ART has also increased the rate of identical twinning, possibly associated with manipulation of the fertilized egg in laboratory settings, ovarian stimulation or other factors.

The other one-third of the increase is due to the fact that some women are delaying motherhood for educational and professional reasons. Older women who conceive are more likely to release two eggs instead of one, increasing the chances of fraternal twinning.

Is there any evidence of psychic connections between identical twins?
The word "psychic" implies extrasensory communications between twins, for which no scientific evidence exists. It is the case, however, that identical twins especially share a very close social relationship, with some pairs finishing each other's sentences, purchasing the same outfits and choosing the same gifts.

Highest natural twinning rate

The term "natural twinning" applies to twins born without the aid of reproductive technology such as IVF. According to Twinning Across the Developing World, an international study and global twins database published in 2011, Benin has the highest natural twinning rate, with 27.9 twins per 1,000 births.

The country with the **lowest natural twinning rate** is Vietnam, with 6.2 per 1,000 births.

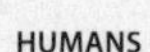

Ernő Rubik (HUN) invented the **Rubik's Cube** in 1974… and it took him **one month** to solve it!

Largest tangram

A tangram (which in Chinese translates as "seven boards of skill") is a tile-based puzzle that involves rearranging seven pieces into a range of shapes and profiles.

The biggest tangram measured 36.28 m^2 (390.53 sq ft) on 6 Sep 2014, created by Jiangsu Sunan Vanke Real Estate Co, Ltd (CHN).

Most crosswords compiled in a lifetime

After 50-plus years of setting crosswords for some 115 publications, Roger F Squires (UK) had published more than 77,854 by Feb 2015, which equates to roughly 2.34 million clues.

Most Rubik's Cubes solved underwater

With a single breath, speedcubing champion Anthony Brooks (USA) completed five Rubik's Cubes in 1 min 18 sec while submerged in a pool of water on 1 Aug 2014.

Brooks isn't the only one putting a twist on this classic puzzle. On 6 Oct 2010, Adrian Leonard from Ireland solved the **most Rubik's Cubes while riding a unicycle**: 28.

Marcin Kowalczyk (POL) couldn't even see during his Rubik's record. In just under an hour, he finished 41 out of 41 cubes – the **most cubes solved wearing a blindfold**.

Most people solving Rubik's Cubes

A crowd of 3,248 people pitted their wits against the coloured cube at the College of Engineering in Pune, Maharashtra, India, on 4 Nov 2012. Only 19 who took part failed to complete their Rubik's Cubes, so these weren't included in the final count.

Longest binary number memorized in five minutes

Binary is the simplest number system, comprising just 1s and 0s. Familiar with crunching numbers for a living, accountant Ben Pridmore (UK) recalled 930 digits from a random sequence, which he had just five minutes to study at the 2008 UK Memory Championships.

Smallest Rubik's Cube

A Rubik's Cube measuring just 10 mm (0.39 in) wide was created by "grigorusha", aka Evgeniy Grigoriev (RUS). The tiny cube – made using a multi-jet modelling 3D printer from frosted plastic – can be turned and solved like a standard Rubik's Cube.

ACTUAL SIZE

IN NUMBERS

20–30 sec
Length of time that our short-term memory can retain seven items

59
Most decks of cards memorized in a single sighting, achieved by Dave Farrow (CAN)

12 days
Recall of African cichlid fish, according to a 2014 study – refuting the "goldfish have short memories" myth

20%
Reduction of nerve cells in the brain's hippocampus by the time we reach our 80s

13 min 7 sec
Fastest time to complete the GWR Hasbro puzzle, by Deepika Ravichandran (USA)

Most cards memorized underwater

Matteo Salvo (ITA) held his breath for 2 min 51 sec while memorizing the order of pre-shuffled playing cards on 16 Dec 2013. After leaving the swimming pool, he used a new deck to sort a total of 52 cards into the same order that he'd observed underwater.

Longest-standing maths problem (current)

First posited in 1742 by Prussian mathematician Christian Goldbach (1690–1764), "Goldbach's Conjecture" is still unresolved 273 years later. The conjecture states that every even positive integer greater than three is the sum of two (not necessarily distinct) primes; as of 2015, no one has proven or disproven it.

Most capitals named in one minute

Boris Konrad (DEU) supplied the capital cities of 56 nations picked by a computer on 24 Jul 2014.

Konrad also memorized the **most three-digit flash numbers** – 15 – on *CCTV-Guinness World Records Special* in China on 7 Sep 2014.

The Great GWR Memory Test

Now you've read about all these amazing mental feats, how about putting your own memory to the test? Below are 100 random objects. Try looking at them for a minute before closing the book and seeing how many you can recall. It'll be great practice for the real challenge, which is available for all to try at **www.guinnessworldrecords.com/memory**. Beat everyone else and you could appear in next year's *GWR* book.

FASTEST TIME TO...

Mentally multiply two five-digit numbers

Aged 16 years old in 2010, Marc Jornet Sanz (ESP) took just 1 min 16 sec to multiply 10 pairs of five-digit numbers, giving an average time of 7.6 sec per sum. All numbers were selected arbitrarily by a computer at the University of Valencia in Spain.

Total recall

Johannes Mallow (DEU) is the current World Memory Champion. Here he takes us on a trip down memory lane...

What techniques do you use to train?

Basically, I always transform any information I have to memorize, whether it's words, names, dates or even numbers, into mental images. With those mental images, I make up creative, funny or scary stories, as these stories are much easier to remember.

Did your memory help you at school?

I used the memory techniques for exams during my studies. It helped me especially with things like definitions and for memorizing complex science processes.

Should people work out their brains as much as their bodies?

Yes! I believe things happen to your body if you don't treat it well, and the same applies to your brain. Regularly working out your brain, especially using your creativity and imagination, will help you in the long run in other parts of your life.

Is there anything you ever forget?

I often forget where I put my keys and USB sticks. And one time I almost forgot to pay in a restaurant!

WORLD MEMORY CHAMPIONS

The World Memory Sports Council oversees the annual World Memory Championships and many regional events.

Discipline	Time	Name	Total
Abstract images	15 min	Johannes Mallow (DEU)	492
Names & faces	15 min	Simon Reinhard (DEU)	186
Historic/future dates	5 min	Johannes Mallow (DEU)	132
Random words	15 min	Simon Reinhard (DEU)	300
Spoken numbers	1-sec intervals	Jonas von Essen (SWE)	380
Speed numbers	5 min	Johannes Mallow (DEU)	501
Long numbers	1 hr	Wang Feng (CHN)	2,660
Long cards	1 hr	Ben Pridmore (UK)	1,456
Speed cards	<5 min	Simon Reinhard (DEU)	21.19 sec
Binary digits	30 min	Ben Pridmore (UK)	4,140

Mentally calculate the square root of a six-digit number

On 2 Sep 2013, at the Memoriad Center in Ankara, Turkey, 12-year-old Granth Rakesh Thakkar (IND) calculated the square roots of 10 six-digit numbers in a total time of 1 min 7.52 sec – that's an average of just 6.75 sec per calculation. Each number was given to a precision of eight significant numbers, without a single error.

Spell 50 words backwards

Electronics engineer Shishir Hathwar (IND) correctly spelt 20 six-letter words, 15 seven-letter words and 15 eight-letter words in just 1 min 22.53 sec at the Press Club of Bangalore in Karnataka, India, on 13 Nov 2010.

Most cards memorized in 30 minutes

Memory athlete Ben Pridmore (UK) recalled 884 cards – or 17 decks (left) – at the Derby Memory Championships held in Derby, UK, in 2008. Pridmore has also recorded the most cards memorized in one hour, recalling 1,456 cards, or 28 full decks, at the 2010 World Memory Championships in China.

HUMANS IN ACTION

Highest-altitude ground-supported tightrope walk

On 20 Mar 2015, daredevil funambulist Freddy Nock (CHE) carried out a death-defying traverse along an inclined tightrope connecting two peaks in the Swiss Alps. He started at an altitude of 3,532 m (11,587 ft 11 in) above sea level and climbed by 50 m (164 ft) – recording an average altitude of 3,557 m (11,669 ft 11 in). During his walk, the multiple record holder faced a maximum drop of c. 1,000 m (3,280 ft 10 in) to the valley below.

Nock's tightrope was 347 m (1,138 ft 5 in) long and just 18 mm (0.7 in) wide. What's more, he made the crossing without any safety harness or ropes – and all in a scant 39 min. Truly a high achiever.

CONTENTS

FACT

Tightrope walking is known as "funambulism", coined in 1793 from the Latin for "funis" (rope) and "ambulare" (to walk). Prior to this, the term "equilibrist" was used, meaning "one who balances".

IN FOCUS

SPORT STACKING

Studies have shown that sport stacking can **improve reaction time and hand-eye coordination** by some 30%

It sounds simple enough. Construct and then deconstruct a pile of plastic cups in a certain order in the quickest time. But when you see sport-stacking champions in action, you quickly realize why this is much more than just a kids' game.

The earliest incarnation of sport stacking is believed to have originated in the USA at a youth recreation programme in the 1980s, in which paper cups were stacked into pyramids.

The sport we're more familiar with today, with specially designed plastic cups being moved in set patterns, emerged later in the decade. But it didn't really come to the public's attention until it featured on US TV's *The Tonight Show Starring Johnny Carson* in 1990.

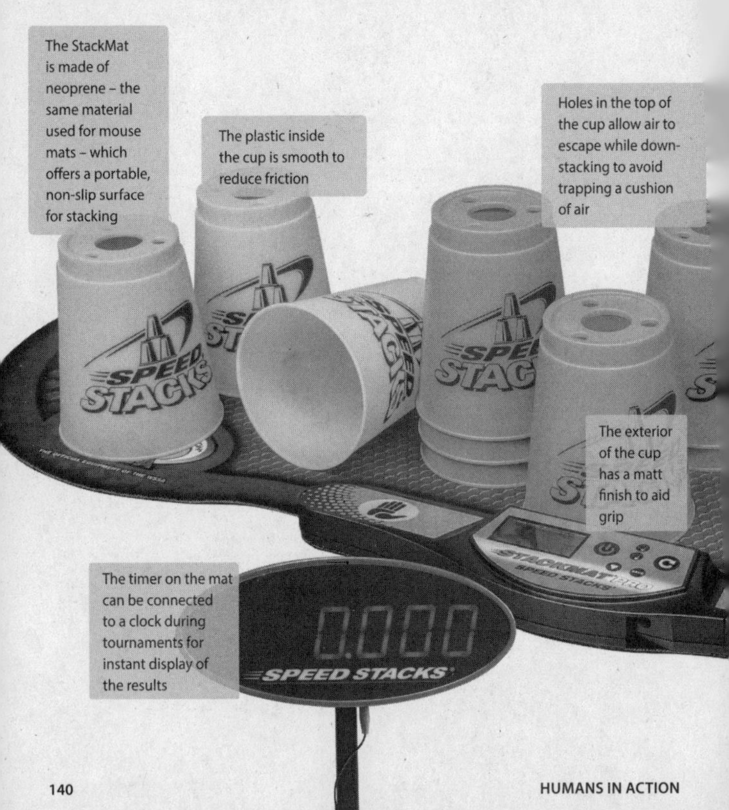

The StackMat is made of neoprene – the same material used for mouse mats – which offers a portable, non-slip surface for stacking
The plastic inside the cup is smooth to reduce friction
Holes in the top of the cup allow air to escape while down-stacking to avoid trapping a cushion of air
SPEED STACKS
The exterior of the cup has a matt finish to aid grip
The timer on the mat can be connected to a clock during tournaments for instant display of the results
0.000
SPEED STACKS

Chu-Chun Yang

Unlike William Orrell (interviewed on p.145), who recently lost his 3–6–3 record, 14-year-old Chu-Chun Yang (Chinese Taipei, right) holds all three individual titles among female stackers: 1.631 sec for the 3–3–3, 2.054 sec for the 3–6–3 and 5.564 sec for the Cycle.

What attracted you to sport stacking?
At 12 years old, I had my first sport-stacking class at school. Sport stacking was so fast, it was just like magic.

Is it more unisex than other sports?
Yes, sport stacking is more unisex and suitable for both the young and old. It can improve your concentration, patience and hand-eye coordination.

How do you celebrate? At the last Asian Championships, I broke three world records. I was very happy. I celebrated with my family, and my mum gave me a new iPhone.

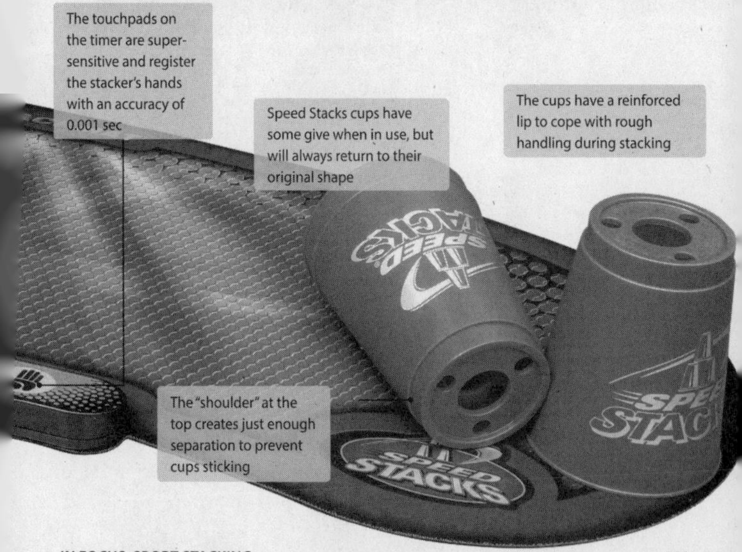

The touchpads on the timer are super-sensitive and register the stacker's hands with an accuracy of 0.001 sec

Speed Stacks cups have some give when in use, but will always return to their original shape

The cups have a reinforced lip to cope with rough handling during stacking

The "shoulder" at the top creates just enough separation to prevent cups sticking

Physical education teacher Bob Fox (USA) took the phenomenon to the next level, founding the World Sport Stacking Association (WSSA) in 2001 to standardize events and stage global competitions.

Fox tells us: "The appeal of sport stacking is truly universal. It's simple to learn but challenging to master, and wanting to get faster is nearly addictive. Teachers and coaches love it as it's great for hand-eye coordination. Stackers love it because it's fun. The future of this sport continues to stack up!"

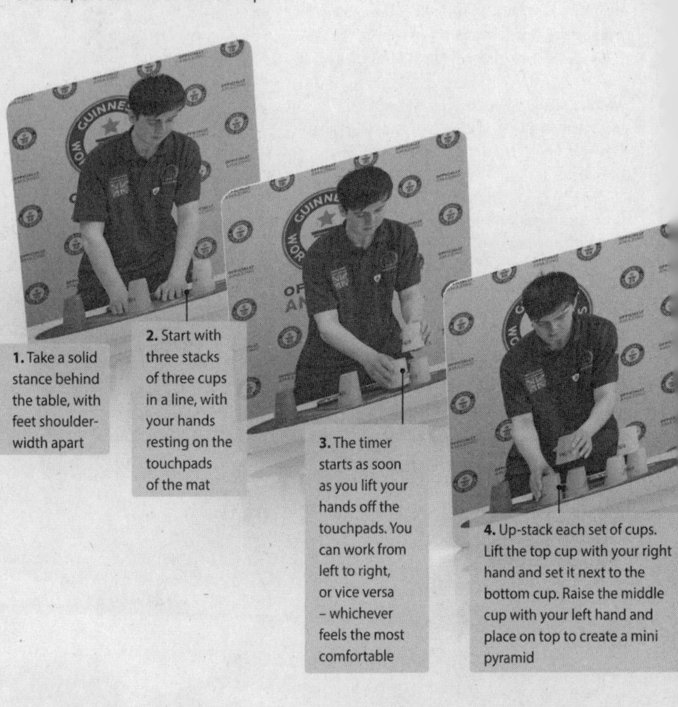

1. Take a solid stance behind the table, with feet shoulder-width apart

2. Start with three stacks of three cups in a line, with your hands resting on the touchpads of the mat

3. The timer starts as soon as you lift your hands off the touchpads. You can work from left to right, or vice versa – whichever feels the most comfortable

4. Up-stack each set of cups. Lift the top cup with your right hand and set it next to the bottom cup. Raise the middle cup with your left hand and place on top to create a mini pyramid

Get involved!

To learn more about sport stacking, including step-by-step guides for each of the competitive stacks, head to www.thewssa.com. You'll also find news about upcoming events and the most up-to-date national and global records.

Go con–figure!

In pro sport stacking, there are three main configurations, or "competitive stacks", for individuals: the 3–3–3 (outlined below), the 3–6–3 (right, top) and the Cycle (right, bottom). This is in addition to doubles competitions, plus timed and head-to-head relays contested by teams of four.

Differentiating these configurations is the number of cups used and the order in which they are moved. In the numbered series below, James Acraman (UK) – a member of the reigning champion British 3–6–3 relay team – guides us through the simplest of the formats: the 3–3–3 stack.

3–6–3 (12 cups)

Cycle

5. Up-stack the final pile of three cups into a pyramid and prepare to move back to the start

6. Now it's time to down-stack. Place your right hand around the side of the top cup, and your left hand around the bottom-left cup

7. Slide the top cup over the bottom-right cup, followed by the cup in your left hand to return to a nested stack of three. Repeat for the other two pyramids

8. As soon as the final pyramid is down-stacked, place your hands back on the touchpads to stop the timer

USA
524,658
stackers

Canada
38,030

Hungary
5,554

Chinese Taipei
4,697

South Korea
3,174

Israel
2,707

Spain
2,522

Mexico
1,493

UK
1,361

Singapore
1,263

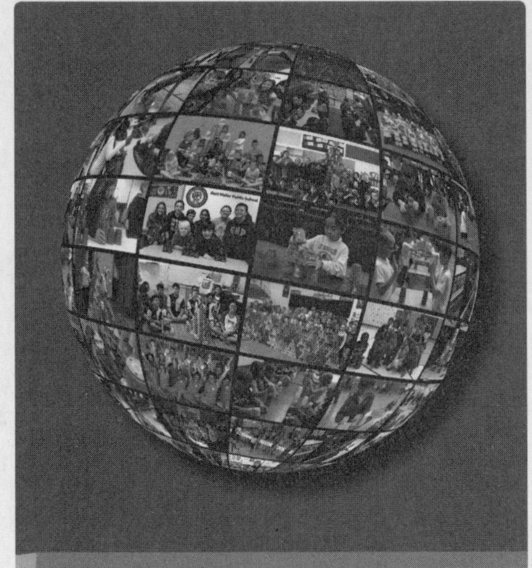

World cups

Since 2006, the WSSA has organized the STACK UP! event, encouraging people to get involved with the sport and each year aiming to set a new record for **most people sport-stacking in multiple venues.** The 2014 meet was no exception, with a phenomenal 592,292 stackers taking part – bettering 2013 by 36,360 (see the top nation turnouts in the sidebar, left). With 2015 ushering in the 10th STACK UP!, could the 600,000 mark be surpassed?

How the world stacks up

At the ninth annual STACK UP! event in 2014, organized by the WSSA, a record 592,292 participants took part (see "World cups" above). Here are the top 10 nations that contributed to the record…

Fastest stacking nations

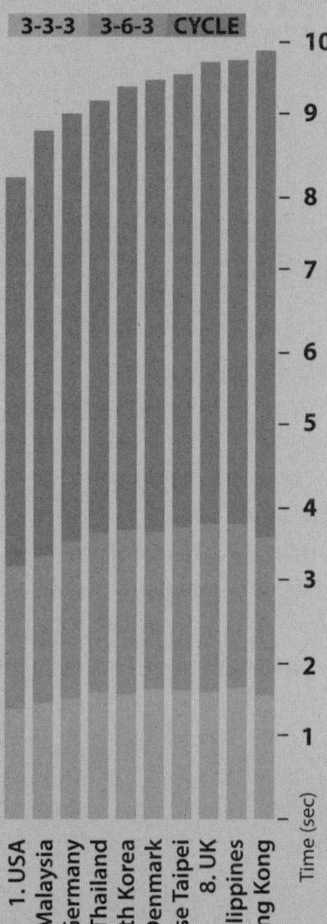

Taking the average times for each WSSA member country's top 3–3–3, 3–6–3 and Cycle attempts, recorded at official events, these are the 10 speediest sport-stacking countries, as of Mar 2015.

William Orrell

Sixteen-year-old William Orrell, from North Carolina, USA, is a sport-stacking tour-de-force. He currently holds the records for fastest individual 3–3–3 (1.418 sec) and fastest individual Cycle (5.000 sec), as well as fastest 3–6–3 relay with Zhewei Wu, Chandler Miller and William Polly (all USA): 12.558 sec.

What attracted you to sport stacking? The speed of the sport attracted me. I was seven years old. It took a few days to learn the stacking patterns.

What are the key differences between individual and team stacking?
A team has to work together and be consistent. An individual doesn't have to be concerned with the fumbles of others. I like individual and team events equally.

Can you share your top three tips?
Practise, don't give up and don't expect to be very fast when you start.

RUNNING

Jim Fixx (USA), who is credited with popularizing jogging, **died of a heart attack… while jogging**

FASTEST…

Mile wearing swim fins

Encumbered by amphibian-style flippers twice the length of his own feet, Zachary Miller (USA) completed a one-mile dash in 5 min 48.86 sec at Brunswick High School in Brunswick, Maine, USA, on 1 Jul 2014.

Mile piggyback race

US students Scott Weiss (runner) and Zack Navabi ("piggy") trained with weights and core exercises before triumphing in the one-mile piggyback race at Karrer Middle School in Dublin, Ohio, USA, on 14 Aug 2013 in 11 min 58 sec.

100-m sack race

Olympic long- and middle-distance champion Mo Farah (UK) turned his hand to sack racing on 14 Jul 2014 at an event organized by Weetabix at the Queen Elizabeth Olympic Park in London. He hopped 100 m in a sack in a record 39.91 sec.

400 m on spring-loaded stilts

Miles McDonald (USA) sprang this one in 1 min 7.49 sec in Stanhope, New Jersey, USA, on 14 Aug 2014, slicing 25.29 sec off the old record.

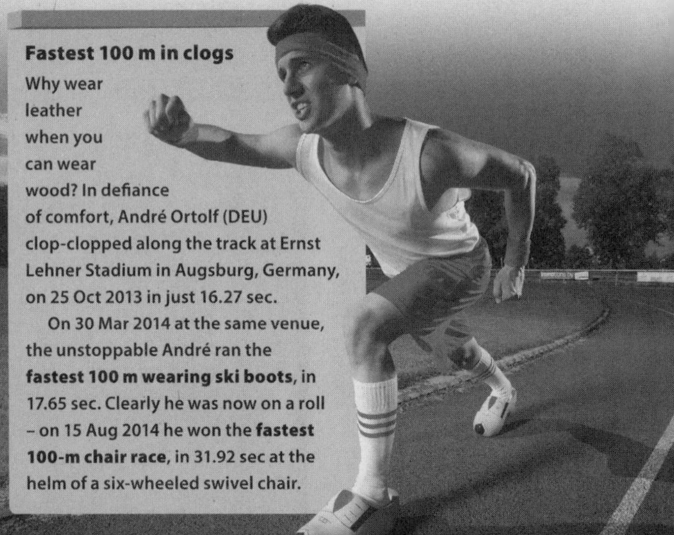

Fastest 100 m in clogs

Why wear leather when you can wear wood? In defiance of comfort, André Ortolf (DEU) clop-clopped along the track at Ernst Lehner Stadium in Augsburg, Germany, on 25 Oct 2013 in just 16.27 sec.

On 30 Mar 2014 at the same venue, the unstoppable André ran the **fastest 100 m wearing ski boots**, in 17.65 sec. Clearly he was now on a roll – on 15 Aug 2014 he won the **fastest 100-m chair race**, in 31.92 sec at the helm of a six-wheeled swivel chair.

Fastest mile in a bomb-disposal suit

Wrapped up in 17 kg (37 lb 5 oz) of highly engineered protective clothing, Zoltán Mészáros (HUN) shaved a precious second from the previous record, setting a new time of 8 min 29 sec on 27 Mar 2014 in Budapest, Hungary. The EOD 9 suit and helmet worn by Zoltán are designed to protect against blast, heat and fragmentation.

Fastest 100 m on all fours

Moving on just hands and feet, Katsumi Tamakoshi (JPN) covered 100 m in 15.86 sec at Setagaya in Tokyo, Japan, on 13 Nov 2014, GWR Day. Katsumi was in the track and field team at his high school.

IN NUMBERS

0
IAAF world records that can be set at the Boston Marathon (because the course drops 140 m)

2,000
Calories needed to run 30 km (18 mi)

30 ft
Distance that a runner's heart, under pressure, could squirt blood (9.14 m)

90 km
Distance of the Comrades Marathon in South Africa, the **oldest** and **largest ultramarathon** (55 mi)

1 hr 14 min 10 sec
Longest time spent running in a film by one character – Italy's Giulio Base in *Cartoline da Roma* (ITA, 2008)

Fastest 100 m on forearm crutches

Balanced in a handstand position on his own crutches, Tameru Zegeye (ETH) covered 100 m in 57 sec on 6 Mar 2014 in Fürth, Germany. Circus performer Tameru was born with deformed feet, and learned to move on his hands in early childhood.

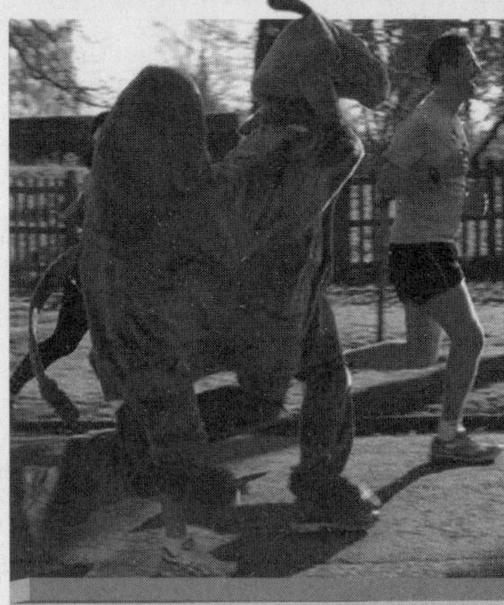

Fastest 5 km in a two-person pantomime costume

A camel in sneakers joined participants in a Saturday morning run at Colchester Castle Park in Colchester, UK, on 5 Apr 2014. Perfectly in step, Robert Saunders and Lorraine Collins (both UK) finished the 5K in a cool 25 min 30 sec – as it happens, well in line with the average speed of a camel jogging across the desert.

JUMPING

Bungee jumping has its origins as a **rite of passage** for boys in Vanuatu

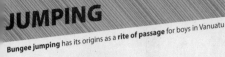

Farthest slam dunk from a trampoline

An airborne Jordan Ramos (UK) landed his shot from 10 m (32 ft 10 in) on the set of *Lo Show dei Record* in Milan, Italy, on 25 Jul 2014, becoming the fourth-time winner of this record. The young gymnast first succeeded as a 13-year-old, even though he had broken his ribs during rehearsals!

HIGHEST...

Jump on a pogo stick

A mighty leap of 2.98 m (9 ft 9 in) was made by Biff Hutchison (USA) on 30 Aug 2014 during the Pogopalooza 2014 High Jump Finals at the Hx 14 Festival in Helsingborg, Sweden.

Beating his own previous record by 2.5 cm, Michael Mena (USA) achieved the **highest forward flip on a pogo stick** on 28 Oct 2014 when he jumped 2.77 m (9 ft 1 in) on the set of *The Queen Latifah Show*.

Most people doing synchronized pogo backflips

On 2 Jul 2014, the world went topsy-turvy as 15 members of Pogopalooza Pittsburgh Athletes (USA) flipped in unison. The record jumped into being at Pogopalooza 2014, the Extreme Pogo World Championship Series (Xpogo) in Pittsburgh, Pennsylvania, USA.

First imported to the USA as a toy some 80 years ago, the pogo stick has made leaps and bounds in technology to become the core of a competitive modern sport.

HIGHEST...

Shallow dive into fire

Veteran record-breaker Professor Splash (aka Darren Taylor, USA) has mastered the art of belly flopping from a height into a shallow pool of water. On 21 Jun 2014, he plunged 8 m (26 ft 3 in) into a pool 25.4 cm (10 in) deep that was ignited just before his dive on the set of NBC's *Show Stopping Sunday Special* in Los Angeles, California, USA.

Another record to admire rather than emulate is the Professor's overall **highest shallow dive**, from 11.56 m (37 ft 11 in) into 30 cm (12 in) of water. He made this splash on the set of *CCTV-Guinness World Records Special* in Xiamen, Fujian, China, on 9 Sep 2014.

Most bungee jumps in 24 hours outdoors (5–10-m cord)

Beau Retallick (AUS, right), in association with Bungy Japan, jumped 158 times from Sarugakyo Bridge in Minakami, Gunma, Japan, on 26–27 Jun 2014.

The **most jumps in 24 hours (20-m cord)** is 151, by Colin Phillips (UK) in association with Gravity Zone in Dubai, UAE, on 21 Mar 2014.

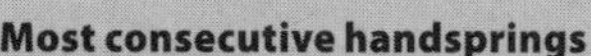

Most consecutive handsprings

Ozell Williams (USA) achieved 57 handsprings at Folsom Field in Boulder, Colorado, USA, on 23 Nov 2013. Ozell belongs to the University of Colorado cheer squad and his attempt took place during the first-quarter break at a Colorado Buffaloes game. The break had a time limit of three minutes, and Ozell's attempt had to be made quickly in order not to interfere with the match.

IN NUMBERS

20
Number of times its own body length a grasshopper can jump

150
Number of times its own body length a tree frog can jump

200
Number of times its own body length a flea can jump

1,000 ft
Estimated height a 6-ft human could leap with a flea's jumping power (300 m)

233 m
Height of the Macau Tower's bungee-jumping platform, in Macau, China (764 ft 5 in)

125 mph
Freefall speed that jumpers off the Macau Tower experience for up to 5 sec (200 km/h)

14.6 m
Distance Mike Powell might have covered if he performed his long jump on the Moon (47 ft 10 in)

PUSHING

Depending on body weight and speed, a **single push-up** can burn **0.5–1 calories**

Farthest distance pushing a car in a day

On 10–11 May 2013, Joey Motsay of Greensboro, North Carolina, USA, celebrated his 50th birthday by pushing a 2014 Fiat 500 car weighing 2,300 lb (1,043 kg) a mile for each year he had lived (80 km).

Proving that four hands are (just) better than two, Matt O'Brien and Dustin Wells (both USA) pushed a Ford Windstar 51.2 mi (82.4 km) on 14–15 Jun 2008 – the **farthest distance to push a car in 24 hr by a team of two**.

Fastest time to push a car one mile

Konda Sahadev (IND) pushed a 2,700-kg (5,952-lb) Tata Winger van 1 mi (1.61 km) in a speedy 11 min 39 sec on 28 Feb 2011.

Most push-ups...

- **In one hour:** Carlton Williams (UK) performed 1,874 push-ups in 60 min in Western Australia on 11 Jan 2014.
- **In 12 hours:** Veteran endurance athlete Paddy Doyle (UK) – Britain's most prolific record-breaker – completed an astonishing 19,325 push-ups in half a day on 1 May 1989.
- **On medicine balls in 1 minute:** Cheered on by a live audience, Gregor Schregle (DEU) managed 47 push-ups with his hands and feet balanced on three 20-cm-wide (8-in) medicine balls during *Wir Holen Den Rekord Nach Deutschland* on 25 Jun 2013.

FACT

According to the American College of Sport Medicine, an adult male in his 20s should be able to achieve 35–44 consecutive push-ups, while a female of the same age should manage 17–33.

Most one-arm push-ups carrying a 40-lb pack in one minute

Having first attempted one-arm push-ups at the age of 15, Hiroyuki Gondou (JPN, below) managed 33 in only 60 sec, despite a 40-lb (18.1-kg) burden, on 10 May 2014. In the same amount of time, Paddy Doyle (UK) achieved 21 push-ups bearing double that weight – the **most one-arm push-ups carrying an 80-lb pack.**

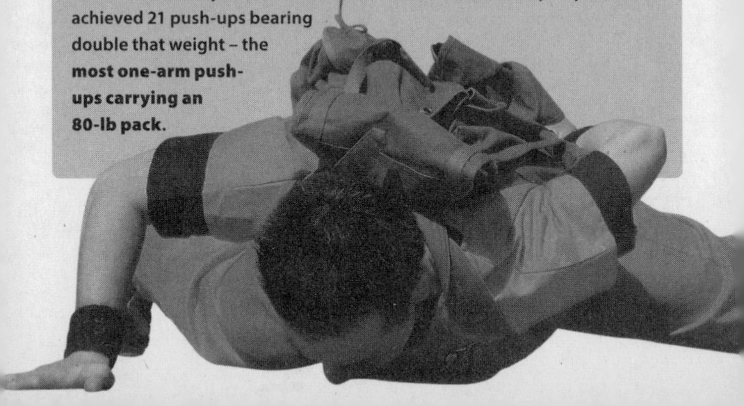

532
Most people performing push-ups simultaneously on 25 May 2014

26.66 km
Farthest distance to push a mini-scooter in one hour, by Harald Hel (AUT) (16.57 mi)

47.7 sec
Fastest time to push a car 50 m using one finger, by Xie Guizhong (CHN)

12
Push-up records held by Paddy Doyle (UK)

14,500 km
Longest journey pushing a wheelbarrow, by Bob Hanley (AUS), starting and finishing in Sydney, Australia (9,000 mi)

Fastest tyre flip over 20 m

Serbian strongman Ervin Katona flipped a tyre 20 m (65 ft) in just 41.18 sec on 5 Sep 2014. He can also boast the record for **longest time to restrain a vehicle on an incline**, holding a 980-kg (2,160-lb) car with passengers on a 45° slope for 1 min 2 sec on 25 Apr 2009.

• **On knuckles in 1 minute:** Completing nearly one press-up per second, Bobby Natoli (USA) achieved 58 press-ups in 1 min at the Pacific Health Club in Liverpool, New York, USA, on 22 Mar 2014.

Bobby is from a record-breaking family: his father Robert holds records for the **most step-ups in one minute with a 40-lb pack** (52), **a 60-lb pack** (47) and **an 80-lb pack** (41), and also the **most weight lifted by dumbbell rows in one minute with one arm** (4,356 lb; 1,975.8 kg), while his brother-in-law David Bourdon (USA) holds the record for the **most pull-ups in one minute** (42).

Fastest half marathon pushing a pram (male)

At the Heroes Half Marathon in Everett, Washington, USA, on 28 Apr 2013, Travis Boyd (USA; left) finished in 1 hr 13 min 50 sec. The **fastest pram-pushing marathon** is 2 hr 42 min 21 sec, run on 6 May 2007 by Michael Wardian (USA).

Fastest 10 km while pushing a pram

Female: Allison Tai (CAN) ran the Squamish Days 10K race in British Columbia, Canada, pushing daughter Amelita (right), in 43 min 7 sec on 5 Aug 2012.

Male: Dougal Thorburn (NZ) ran with his daughter Audrey in an event at the New Balance Hill Free Half Marathon at Dunedin, New Zealand, in a time of 32 min 26 sec on 14 Oct 2012.

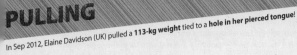

In Sep 2012, Elaine Davidson (UK) pulled a **113-kg weight** tied to a **hole in her pierced tongue**!

HEAVIEST VEHICLE...

Pulled by hair (female)

On 7 Jul 2014, on the set of *Lo Show dei Record*, multiple record holder Asha Rani (IND) tied her hair to a 12,216-kg (26,931-lb) London double-decker bus and hauled it 5 m (16 ft 4.8 in).

Pulled by beard

Muhammad Sadi (PAK) used nothing but his facial hair to tow a 1,740-kg (3,836-lb) vehicle on 17 Jul 2014, beating the existing record by 40 kg (88 lb).

MOST PULL-UPS...

In one minute, clapping

A "clap pull-up" is a little trickier than your average pull-up; midway through a repetition, the person has to let go of the bar, clap their hands and then re-grab the bar, all without feet touching the ground. Ron Cooper (USA) achieved this 21 times in 60 sec on 16 Jun 2014.

Most iron bars bent with the head in one minute

Using his head, Alexander Muromskiy (RUS) buckled 11 iron bars in just 60 sec in Khanty-Mansiysk, Russia, on 17 Oct 2014. This isn't the first time Muromskiy has proven his iron will; he bent 26 bars with his hands on 3 Nov 2012 – the **most iron bars bent in one minute.**

MOST PULL-UPS...

In a day

Endurance athlete Caine Eckstein (AUS) performed 4,210 pull-ups on the *Today* show in New York City, USA, on 6–7 Oct 2014. Eckstein did six pull-ups per minute for 10 hr and then switched to five pull-ups a minute for the next two. He set the record in half the time, also claiming **most pull-ups in 12 hours in the process**. His success came at a cost, however, as he tore one of the tendons in his bicep during the attempt.

Heaviest vehicle pulled in high heels

The founder of organization Up With Women, Lia Grimanis (CAN), hauled a 14,520-lb (6,586-kg) truck 5 m (16 ft 4.8 in) at the Toronto Track and Field Centre in Canada on 11 Jun 2014, wearing boots with a 3-in (7-cm) heel. Grimanis also holds the female record for **heaviest vehicle pulled over 100 feet** (17,820 lb; 8,083 kg). Talking of her motives for attempting these feats, she said: "I wanted to show women who are struggling that we are all stronger than we think we are."

FACT

According to a 2010 study, the taurus scarab – a type of dung beetle – can pull more than 1,140 times its own weight. This equates to a human pulling six double-decker buses full of people!

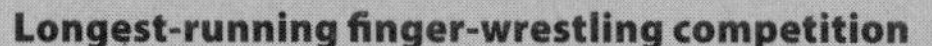

Longest-running finger-wrestling competition

Dating to the 14th century and now continued by the Bavarian Finger Wrestling Championships, the sport of *fingerhakeln* involves competitors hauling their opponent across a table via the lash binding their digits together (see inset).

Most chin-ups in human flag position

"The Flag Man", aka Dominic Lacasse (CAN), pulled off 14 chin-ups while clinging to a pole at a 90° angle on *Lo Show dei Record* on 10 Jul 2014. Lacasse once also laid claim to the **longest duration to maintain a human flag**, although since 15 Aug 2011 that title has been held by Wang Zhonghua (CHN), who hung horizontally for an agonizing 1 min 5.71 sec!

LIFTING

Each fibre in a muscle is **thinner than a human hair** and can lift up to **1,000 times its own weight**

FACT

Scottish strongman Angus MacAskill (1825–63), a star of P T Barnum's circus, was famous for lifting a 2,800-lb (1,270-kg) ship's anchor to his chest. He also performed for Queen Victoria at Windsor Castle, UK.

Fastest power stairs

On 26 Jun 2014, Žydrūnas Savickas (LTU) carried three 225-kg (496-lb) weights separately up five steps (power stairs) in 31.6 sec on the set of *Lo Show dei Record* in Milan, Italy. Žydrūnas competed against strongman/actor "Thor" Björnsson (ISL), whose 29.20-sec attempt was disqualified for a false start.

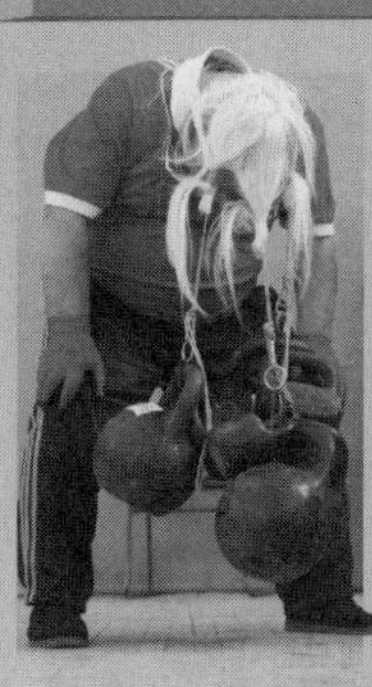

Heaviest weight lifted by the hair

On 16 Nov 2013, 83-year-old Abdurakhman Abdulazizov (RUS) tied 81.5 kg (179 lb 11 oz) of kettlebells to his hair and lifted them off the ground in Zubutli-Miatli, Republic of Dagestan, Russia. He began lifting weights with his hair at the age of 76.

Longest duration holding a 500-kg weight with the shoulders

Derek Boyer (AUS) lifted a metal bar hung with 500 kg (1,102 lb 5 oz) of weights off the ground for a muscle-straining 1 min 9.8 sec in Melbourne, Victoria, Australia, on 26 Mar 2014, beating the previous record by an emphatic 8.4 sec.

Heaviest deadlift in one hour

On 14 Jul 2013, Eamonn Keane (IRL) achieved 824 repetitions on a 140-kg (308-lb 10-oz) barbell at the Louisburgh Gym in Louisburgh, Ireland, hoisting aloft a total of 115,360 kg (254,325 lb 4.5 oz).

HEAVIEST WEIGHT LIFTED...

...and spun with pierced ears

On 19 Jun 2014, sideshow performer "Lizardman", aka Erik Sprague (USA), attached 16 kg (35 lb 4 oz) to his ear piercings, then spun them three times in 360° circles in Milan, Italy.

By the hair (female)

On 18 Jul 2014, Asha Rani (UK) held up 55.6 kg (122.58 lb) with her tresses in Rampur, Punjab, India. She had earlier proved her record-breaking strength in Leicester, UK, on 12 Feb 2014 by achieving the **heaviest weight lifted with both eye sockets (female)** – an eye-watering 15.15 kg (33 lb 6.4 oz).

IN NUMBERS

10
Most people squat-lifted, by Ryan Lapadat (CAN) on 19 Jun 2014

14
Most overhead lifts of a 140-kg quad bike in one minute, by Lithuania's Žydrūnas Savickas

24 kg
Heaviest weight lifted with both eye sockets (male) (52 lb 14.5 oz), by Manjit Singh (UK) in Leicester, Leicestershire, UK, on 15 Nov 2012

2.16 million kg
Greatest weight squat-lifted in 24 hours by a team of 10 (4,780,994 lb) from the St Albans Weightlifting Club and Ware Boys Club in Hertfordshire, UK, on 20–21 Jul 1986

92.5 tonnes
Weight of coal, equal to 227,075 lb, reportedly hewn in a six-hour shift in Aug 1935 by Soviet miner Alexei Stakhanov, the man dubbed the **greatest labourer of all time**

By the neck

On 19 Oct 2013, Eric Todd (USA) lifted 1,000 lb (453.59 kg) using a neck harness and chain in Turney, Missouri, USA. Eric had been encouraged by the previous record holder Frank Ciavattone, whom he surpassed by 192 lb (87 kg).

With a hook through the forehead

On 21 Jul 2014, sideshow performer Burnaby Q Orbax (CAN) of the Monsters of Schlock lifted 4.5 kg (9 lb 14.73 oz) via a hook inserted through the skin of his forehead, on the set of *Lo Show dei Record* in Milan, Italy. On the same occasion, fellow "Monster" Sweet Pepper Klopek (CAN) achieved the **heaviest weight lifted with hooks through the cheeks**: 6 kg (13 lb 3.6 oz).

In one hour by kettlebell jerks

On 15 Jun 2014, Anatoly Ezhov (BLR) lifted 53,424 kg (117,779 lb 12 oz) in Tashkent, Uzbekistan, with 2,226 lifts of a 24-kg (52-lb 14-oz) kettlebell – his sixth successful attempt at this record in 2014.

Longest duration maintaining the crucifix hold

On 3 Aug 2004, Yannick Ollivier (FRA) held a 10-kg (22-lb) dumbbell in each hand, at arm's length and at a 90° angle to his body, for 1 min 18 sec on the set of the summertime TV show *L'été de tous les records* in Bénodet, Brittany, France.

Heaviest tyre deadlift

On 1 Mar 2014, at the Arnold Strongman Classic in Columbus, Ohio, USA, Žydrūnas Savickas (LTU) lifted eight Hummer tyres weighing 524.22 kg (1,155 lb 11 oz), breaking the previous year's record by 12.2 kg (27 lb). Winner of the World's Strongest Man for the fourth time in 2014, Žydrūnas has multiple lifting records (see p.158–159).

THROWING

The **javelin** evolved from the spears used by **early humans** for hunting

Farthest throw and catch of a running chainsaw

On 14 Sep 2012, Chayne Hultgren hurled the deadly machine 4 m (13 ft 1 in) to Gordo Gamsby (both AUS) at London Wonderground, UK.

Farthest throw of a washing machine (individual)

On 17 Jul 2014, Žydrūnas Savickas (LTU, see p.160) tossed a washing machine – with a minimum weight of 100 lb (45.35 kg) – a distance of 4.13 m (13 ft 6.6 in) in Milan, Italy.

Longest darts marathon (singles)

From 13 to 15 Mar 2014, Wayne Mitchell and Mark Dye (both UK) spent 50 hr 50 min 50 sec on the oche in Bromley, Kent, UK – 49 min longer than the previous record.

Most chopsticks thrown at a target in one minute

Champion record-breaker Ashrita Furman (USA, see p.162) pierced an 80-cm-wide (31.5-in) World Archery Federation-approved target with 14 chopsticks in 60 sec in New York, USA, on 29 Jul 2014. Only chopsticks that remain stuck to the target count towards the total.

Farthest basketball shot backwards

On 3 Nov 2014, Corey "Thunder" Law (USA) of the Harlem Globetrotters scored from 25 m (82 ft 2 in) – over his shoulder – at the US Airways Center in Phoenix, Arizona, USA. At the same venue the year before, Thunder also made **the longest basketball shot** forwards: an incredible 33.45 m (109 ft 9 in).

Most plungers thrown and stuck to human targets in one minute

On 14 Sep 2010, on the set of TV Asahi's (JPN) *Torihada Scoop 100 SP #3*, Gerhard Donie (DEU) flung 15 plungers, sticking them to his human targets 10 ft (3.04 m) away. The plungers were the rubber-cup type used for unblocking lavatory systems.

Most custard pies in the face in one minute

On 7 Apr 2010, Bipin Larkin hit Ashrita Furman (both USA) in the face with 56 custard pies. This was the last time that this record was accepted – now, owing to food-wastage concerns, shaving foam must be used… and Ashrita and Bipin hold this new record too with 71 hits on 25 Jun 2013!

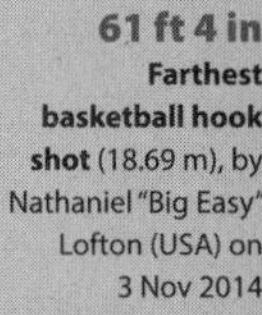

Most caber tosses in three minutes

On 6 Sep 2014, despite wet and slippery conditions, Kevin Fast and Warren Trask (both CAN) made 11 successful caber tosses at the Trenton Scottish Irish Festival in Trenton, Ontario, Canada. Their cabers were 16 ft 6 in (5.03 m) long and weighed 92 lb (41.73 kg).

61 ft 4 in

Farthest basketball hook shot (18.69 m), by Nathaniel "Big Easy" Lofton (USA) on 3 Nov 2014

3.66 m

Highest throw and catch of a person (12.01 ft), by members of the Spelbound gymnastics troupe (UK)

708 BC

Approximate earliest date of discus throwing, as part of the Olympic Games

70 mph

Top speed of a javelin in flight (112.6 km/h)

24

Most throws and catches of a fire sword in 30 seconds, by "Snake Fervor", aka Heidi Bradshaw (UK), on 17 Dec 2013

JUGGLING

During a battle c. 603 BC, **Chinese warrior** Xiong Yiliao **juggled nine balls** before the enemy army, who immediately fled the field

FACT

There are hieroglyphs of female performers "toss juggling" in the mural of an Egyptian prince's tomb built c. 2000–1700 BC. However, the skill is widely believed to precede this era.

Most juggling chainsaw catches

Performing at the Hants County Exhibition in Windsor, Nova Scotia, Canada, on 25 Sep 2011, Ian Stewart (CAN, right) achieved 94 throws and catches with three chainsaws in 37 sec – and, yes, they were running at the time! A stage hypnotist by trade, Ian has since also earned the title for **most juggling catches with a chainsaw and two balls** (158), on 8 Mar 2014.

Aiming for height rather than frequency, Chayne Hultgren (AUS), aka the "Space Cowboy", hurled a chainsaw up to 3.59 m (11 ft 9 in) on 13 Jan 2015 – the **highest chainsaw throw and catch while juggling**.

MOST...

Bowling balls juggled

With an audience of 350 pro jugglers, Milan Roskopf (SVK) kept three 4.5-kg (10-lb) bowling balls aloft for 28.69 sec at the Czech Republic's Juggling Marathon in Prague on 19 Nov 2011. No stranger to the world of heavyweight "power juggling", Milan also holds the title for **longest time to juggle three shot-puts**, at 52.05 sec.

Boomerangs juggled

Danny Luftman (POR) "flash juggled" five tri-blade boomerangs on 29 Dec 2013, with all the boomerangs flying before he caught them one at a time.

Axe juggling catches

Not content with "merely" juggling chainsaws (see opposite), Ian Stewart (CAN) made 580 catches of three axes in Truro, Nova Scotia, Canada, on 21 Aug 2014.

Most soccer balls juggled

Victor Rubilar (ARG) juggled five footballs for more than 10 sec on 4 Nov 2006. Proving his mastery of ball control, he also holds the records for **longest time spinning a football on the forehead** (19.96 sec) and **most football rolls around the face in one minute** (35).

Clubs juggled

Juggling aficionado Anthony Gatto (USA) juggled eight clubs on 30 Aug 2006, ending a long stalemate of seven. Gatto also boasts the **most juggled flaming torches** (7) and **rings** (10); although 11-ring juggles have been reported, there is not sufficient evidence to confirm if they achieved the minimum 22 catches required.

IN NUMBERS

2 hr 50 min 12 sec
Fastest marathon run while juggling three objects, by Michal Kapral (CAN)

5%
Increase in white matter in the brains of participants after juggling, as part of a six-week study

280
Calories burned after an hour of juggling

11
Most balls juggled, by Alex Barron (UK)

6.44 km
Greatest distance juggling on a pogo stick (4 mi), by Ashrita Furman (USA)

4,698
Most consecutive stairs climbed while juggling a football, by Abraham Muñoz (USA)

LONGEST TIME TO JUGGLE...

Five basketballs

Pedro Elis Cinta (ESP) juggled five basketballs for 51.36 sec on *CCTV-Guinness World Records Special* on 8 Sep 2014.

Four diabolos around the leg

Peng Zhan (TPE) juggled four diabolos around his leg for 1 min 21 sec on the set of *Shaonian Zhongguo Qiang* in Beijing, China, on 24 Aug 2014.

Three objects blindfolded

Niels Duinker (NLD) kept a trio of clubs aloft for 6 min 29 sec on 11 Aug 2011 while wearing a blindfold. In doing so, he extended the previous record by a staggering 5 min 42 sec!

Three objects while hanging upside-down

Quinn Spicker from Canada juggled three balls for 12 min 50 sec on 22 Jul 2010 while suspended from a circus trapeze.

The record for **most balls juggled while upside-down** goes to Zdeněk Bradáč (CZE), who defied gravity by juggling four balls in Jablonec nad Nisou, Czech Republic, on 1 Nov 2010, accomplishing 20 catches.

Longest time juggling three objects underwater

SCUBA gear: Kitted out with breathing apparatus, Markus Just (DEU, above) juggled three balls for 1 hr 40 min in Nuremberg, Germany, on 3 Mar 2013. **No SCUBA gear:** With only a diving belt to weigh him down, Nikolay Linder (DEU) juggled three balls for 2 min 48 sec on 1 Apr 2012.

Farthest distance travelled on a unicycle while juggling three objects

While most of us would be happy to be able to juggle or ride a unicycle, Jonathan Oberlerchner (AUT) can perform both at the same time. He covered 4,805 m (15,764 ft) while juggling three balls in Klagenfurt, Austria, on 25 Jul 2013.

SMASHING

In Japan, the martial art of breaking objects is traditionally known as *tameshiwari* or **"trial by wood"**

FASTEST TIME TO...

Break 1,000 pine boards

On 6 Oct 2013, Sung Min Park (KOR) smashed through 1,000 planks of pinewood in 20 min 33 sec.

Break 16 concrete blocks on the body

Male: Australian strongman Neal Hardy (AUS) more than lives up to his name: he endured 16 blocks being sledge-hammered on his body in 7.37 sec by Patrick Bellchambers (AUS) on 15 Jan 2010. **Female:** Circus sideshow entertainer Daniella D'Ville, aka Danielle Martin (UK), had her 16 concrete blocks broken by Johnny Strange (UK) in 30.4 sec at the Doncaster Tattoo Jam in South Yorkshire, UK, on 12 Oct 2013. This daredevil duo are no strangers to dangerous stunts, also laying claim to the title for **most apples held in the mouth and cut in half by chainsaw in one minute** (12).

Smash five glass bottles

Using just his hands, Alberto Delgado (ESP) smashed five glass bottles in just 40.46 sec in Madrid, Spain, on 23 Feb 2008.

Most concrete blocks broken while holding a raw egg

Showing that brute strength and a delicate touch can go hand in hand, Joe Alexander (DEU) smashed 24 concrete blocks (laid out in three stacks), all without cracking an egg that he was clutching throughout the challenge. Proving that he has a sharp eye too, Joe also holds the one- and two-minute records for **most arrows caught by hand** (15 and 43, respectively).

MOST...

Panes of tempered glass sprinted through

For an episode of *CCTV-Guinness World Records Special*, Zhang Jianjun (CHN) ran through 22 sheets of tempered glass. This type of glass is treated with chemicals or heat so that it's tougher than normal glass and therefore harder to break.

MOST EGGS CRUSHED...

23
with the head in the backbend position in one minute, by Casey Martin (USA)

25
with the wrist in 30 seconds, by Balakrishnan Sivasamy (MYS)

70
with the head in 30 seconds, by Tijl Beckand (NLD)

78
with the wrist in two minutes, by Antonio Almijez (ESP)

142
with the head in one minute, by Scott Damerow (USA)

Most baseball bats broken with the back in one minute

Really putting his back into it, Matt Dopson (USA) – who's aptly known as "Timber" – snapped in half 19 baseball bats in 60 sec on the set of *Guinness World Records Unleashed* on 24 Jun 2013.

The **most bats broken by hand in one minute** stands at 55, set by Muhamed Kahrimanovic (DEU) on 17 Nov 2010.

Most drinks cans crushed with the hands in one minute

On 2 Jun 2012, in front of an audience of more than 4.4 million on a live TV show, René "Golem" Richter (CZE) crushed 17 full and unopened drinks cans in 60 sec.

MOST...

Walnuts cracked with the forehead in one minute

At the Punjab Youth Festival in Pakistan on 26 Feb 2014, Muhammed Rashid (PAK) headbutted 150 walnuts.

The **most walnuts crushed by the buttocks in one minute**, meanwhile, is 108 by Cherry Yoshitake (JPN) in Nagoya, Aichi, Japan, on 13 Oct 2014. Cherry also achieved the **most walnuts crushed by the buttocks in 30 seconds**, with 48 on 15 Jan 2013.

Ice blocks broken by a human battering ram

Hurling himself at a wall of ice, Uğur Öztürk (TUR) broke 17 ice blocks on 18 Sep 2014.

Most roof tiles broken in one minute (female)

In 60 sec, Lisa Dennis (UK) smashed her way through a staggering 923 roof tiles (arranged in stacks of 10) on the set of *Lo Show dei Record* in Milan, Italy, on 11 Jul 2014. Amazingly, only two tiles during the record attempt refused to yield to her formidable hand.

On 26 Mar 2014, Lisa also set the female record for **fastest time to break 1,000 roof tiles**, clocking 83.98 sec in Orpington, London, UK.

BALANCING

Our **balance changes with age**, as muscular, sensory and cognitive functions decline

Steepest gradient walked on a tightrope

Accomplished funambulist Aisikaier Wubulikasimu (CHN) traversed a rope with an angle of inclination of 36.24° on 3 Sep 2014 – 0.24° steeper than his previous record. For context, the slope of the Great Pyramid of Giza in Egypt is around 51°. Aisikaier also walked the **fastest 100 m on a tightrope**, with a time of 38.86 sec on 6 Jun 2013.

The **fastest time to walk 100 m on a tightrope backwards** goes to Maurizio Zavatta (ITA), who clocked 1 min 4.57 sec on 20 May 2014. For another tightrope record, see Freddy Nock's (CHE) terrifying crossing on pp.137–39.

Tallest object balanced on the nose

On 10 Jan 2015, Richard Ljungman (SWE) balanced a 14.29-m (46-ft 10.6-in) pole on his nose in China.

LONGEST DURATION...

Balancing a chainsaw on the chin

Ashrita Furman (USA), holder of the **most Guinness World Records titles**, managed to keep a chainsaw on his chin for 1 min 42.47 sec on 15 Sep 2013. It's not the first time that Ashrita has proven his balancing skills. He also holds the titles for **longest duration balancing a ladder on the chin** (4 min 9.22 sec) and **farthest distance walked balancing a baseball bat on the finger** (9 mi; 14.48 km).

Most drinks cans balanced on the head

British strongman John Evans kept a level head to carry 429 cans at once on 5 Jun 2007. They weighed in at 173 kg (381 lb 6 oz), though this fell just short of another of Evans' records: in 1997, he carried 101 bricks, which amounted to 188.7 kg (416 lb) – the **heaviest weight balanced on the head**.

FACT

Comprising a maze of liquid-filled tubes and chambers in our inner ear, the vestibular system governs our sense of balance. Along with visual and muscular cues, these organs help us stay upright.

On a balance board

Silvio Sabba (ITA) stayed on his self-built board for 2 hr 36 min 26 sec in Milan, Italy, on 26 Aug 2011.

Holding the abdominal plank position

Chinese policeman Mao Weidong demonstrated his gravity-defying core strength by maintaining an abdominal plank for a muscle-burning 4 hr 26 min on 26 Sep 2014. This smashed the existing time by an incredible 1 hr 19 min.

Balancing in box splits between two objects

Super-flexible Syed Marij Hussain (PAK) remained in a box splits position for 12 min 44 sec at the Punjab Youth Festival in Lahore, Pakistan, on 28 Feb 2014.

Most consecutive stairs climbed on the head

Li Longlong (CHN) improved on his 2012 record of 34 steps by scaling 36 steps on his head without a break during TV show *CCTV – Guinness World Records Special* in Jiangyin, Jiangsu, China, on 5 Jan 2015.

On an earlier episode, filmed in Xiamen, Fujian, China, on 10 Sep 2014, Tang Tao and Su Zengxian (both CHN) achieved the **most consecutive stairs climbed while balancing a person on the head**, climbing an impressive 25 stairs.

IN NUMBERS

19.23 sec
Longest time to balance on four fingers, by Wang Weibao (CHN)

998
Most people balancing books on their heads, organized by Danielle Di-Masi (AUS)

42.4 kg
Heaviest stack of milk crates on chin (93 lb 7.5 oz), by Ashrita Furman (USA)

Most Thomas flairs on a pommel horse in one minute

A Thomas flair is a gymnastics manoeuvre that comprises a seamless combination of body rotations, some with straddled legs and others with scissored legs. Since 2009, the one-minute record has stood with Louis Smith (UK) at 50 flairs, but this feat was matched by Alberto Busnari (ITA, above) on 10 Jul 2014.

Farthest tightrope in high heels

As if walking on a tightrope wasn't tricky enough, Oxana Seroshtan (RUS) covered 15 m (49 ft) while wearing high-heeled shoes on the set of *Lo Show dei Record* in Milan, Italy, on 10 Jul 2014. Completing two lengths of the 7.5-m (24-ft 7.2-in) rope, Oxana doubled the existing record. As per the rules, she opted to use a fan as a balancing aid during the attempt.

CYCLING

Starting in the 1960s, BMX, aka **Bicycle Moto Cross**, is extreme cycling inspired by **offroad motorcycling**

Most stairs climbed by bike

Male: Scaling the Eureka Tower in Melbourne, Australia, Krystian Herba (POL) ascended a total of 2,755 stairs on 4 Feb 2014.
Female: Monica Guzman Naranjo (COL) cycled up 1,025 steps at the Hotel Riu Plaza Guadalajara in Mexico on 14 May 2014.

Greatest vertical ascent on bicycle in 12 hours

Adrian Ellul (AUS) climbed through a vertical distance of 9,271.8 m (30,419 ft) in Queensland, Australia, on 21 Jun 2014.

Longest dirt-to-dirt bicycle backflip

Extreme biker Cam Zink (USA) leapt 100 ft 3 in (30.56 m) while doing a 360° backflip at Mammoth Mountain's Canyon Lodge in California, USA, on 21 Aug 2014 (above). At the same X Games event, he flew 119 ft 9 in (36.5 m) to achieve the **longest dirt-to-dirt mountain bike jump.** But he's far from resting on his laurels; just after the jump, Zink said, "I think it's just the beginning, as in I'll do – maybe one day – 150 or 200 [feet], who knows?"

IN NUMBERS

2.52 m
Longest bar-to-bar bicycle jump (8 ft 3.12 in), leaping from one horizontal bar to another on the rear wheel, set by Abel Mustieles (ESP)

268 hr 32 min 44 sec
Longest marathon riding a static bike, by Jamie McDonald (UK)

1,016.65
Watt hours; **most electrical energy generated by pedalling on a bicycle in 24 hours (by an individual)**, by Brian Cha (HKG)

1
Number of breaths taken by Homar Leuci to complete his underwater cycling record (see opposite, top)

HIGHEST BICYCLE...

Side hop

At the 2014 Prudential RideLondon cycling event held in London, UK, on 9 Aug 2014, Vincent Hermance (FRA) – who held number one spot in the UCI Trials rankings for the 26-in wheel category in 2014 – side-hopped 1.55 m (5 ft 1 in) on to a platform. He achieved this feat without any run-up or ramps.

Bunny hop

Continuing the success at 2014's Prudential RideLondon, Rick Koekoek (NLD) hopped 1.43 m (4 ft 8.3 in) over a bar, and trials biker Jack Carthy (UK) leapt 1.77 m (5 ft 9.6 in) on to a platform after a short run-up to secure the record for the **highest bicycle forward step-up**.

Fastest 100 m in a pedalo

On 13 Oct 2013, Giuseppe Cianti (ITA) covered 100 m in a pedal-powered boat in just 38.7 sec on the waters of the Marina di Scilla in Italy. Giuseppe used a "Shuttle Bike Kit" in his attempt, an inflatable structure driven by a bicycle affixed to a small metal frame. The craft was invented by engineer Roberto Siviero.

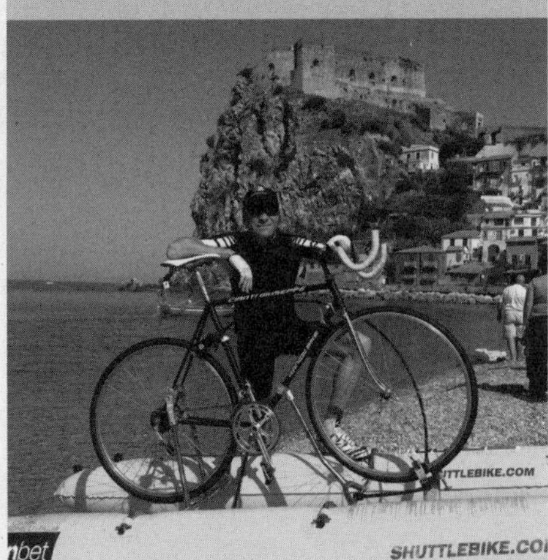

Farthest distance cycling underwater on a static bike

Without any breathing equipment, Homar Leuci (ITA, right) rode 855 m (2,805 ft 1 in) on *Lo Show dei Record* on 25 Jun 2014.

While wearing SCUBA gear, Jens Stötzner (DEU) achieved the **farthest distance cycled underwater**, riding 6,708 m (22,007 ft) on a course at the bottom of a pool on 8 Sep 2013.

Longest bicycle wheelie in one hour

Riding solely on the rear wheel of his bike, Thomas Kaltenegger (AUT, below) covered 24.20 km (15.04 mi) at the Judenburg Stadium in Judenburg, Austria, on 29 Jun 2014, beating the previous record by almost 7 km (4.35 mi).

Going for speed rather than distance on 31 Jan 2001, Bobby Root (USA) claimed **fastest bicycle wheelie** not once but twice, hitting 138.6 km/h (86.1 mph) and 94.6 km/h (58.8 mph) to achieve the **rear wheel** and **front wheel** records respectively.

ROUND-UP

US toymaker **Wham-O** invented the **modern hula hoop**, the **Frisbee** and also the **first Slip 'N Slide**

IN 30 SECONDS...

Most whoopee cushions sat on

There must have been a lot of sniggering on set at *Officially Amazing* (CBBC) on 17 Jul 2014, as multiple record holder "Mr Cherry", aka Cherry Yoshitake from Japan, deflated 52 whoopee cushions at Garden Fields JMI School in St Albans, UK.

Mr Cherry's speed and dexterity have also seen him record the most dried peas moved using a straw (29) and most socks put on one foot (26) – both achieved in 30 sec.

Most backward somersaults on a trampoline

Completing one somersault per second, Shane Connor Smith (USA) flipped heels over head 30 times on his trampoline in Shorewood, Illinois, USA, on 22 Oct 2014, beating the previous record by three.

IN ONE MINUTE...

Most Christmas crackers pulled (team of two)

Regular record-breaking duo Ashrita Furman and Bipin Larkin (both USA) started Christmas celebrations early by pulling 52 crackers in 60 sec in New York City, USA, on 25 Jun 2014.

Most beer bottles opened by chainsaw

Dispensing with the traditional opener, John Nicholson (USA) used a chainsaw to flick the caps off 18 beer bottles in Florida, USA, on 1 Jun 2014.

Most steps climbed wearing an antique diving suit

On 5 Oct 2013, Lloyd Scott (UK) climbed 1,037 steps to the top of the 41-storey "Gherkin" building in London, UK, while wearing a 134-lb (60.7-kg) 1940s deep-sea diving suit complete with a copper helmet. Raising funds for the British Heart Foundation, Lloyd took 2 hr 53 min to finish the climb. It isn't the first time the former firefighter has donned the diving suit for charity, having also completed full-length marathons in the gear, including one along the bottom of Loch Ness in Scotland!

FACT

Feb 2015 saw in the 25th World Championship Hoop Dance Contest at the Heard Museum in Arizona, USA. A form of Native American storytelling, the dance is said to represent the circle of life.

Most hula hoops spun at once

"Marawa the Amazing", aka Marawa Ibrahim (AUS), spun 160 hula hoops simultaneously in New York City, USA, on 7 Apr 2014. The master hooper also led her team of 10 "Majorettes" to glory on 14 Nov 2013 when they earned the record for **most hula hoops spun simultaneously by a team** – 264 hoops (right). Marawa has appeared on many TV shows, including *Lo Show dei Record*, where she went the **longest time on high-heeled roller skates while spinning three hoops**: 2 min 29 sec on 17 Jul 2014.

Linsey Lindberg

The Kansas-born strongwoman, aka "Mama Lou", has been a performer since her teens, when she was a member of a clowning troupe. Aged 25, Linsey turned her attention to feats of strength and has set records for the **most apples crushed with the biceps in one minute** (10) and the **most frying pans rolled in one minute** (6).

Most telephone directories torn in one minute (female)

In 60 sec, US strongwoman Linsey Lindberg (below) tore through five directories at Central Market in Austin, Texas, USA, on 16 Nov 2014.

It's some way off the female record for **most directories torn in three minutes**, though: Tina Shelton (USA) ripped through 21 books on 9 Feb 2007. For both titles, the minimum directory thickness was 1,000 pages.

IN ONE MINUTE...

Most spears caught from a spear gun underwater

Anthony Kelly (AUS) caught 10 spears fired at him from a distance of 2 m (6 ft 6 in) in a swimming pool in New South Wales, Australia, on 13 Nov 2014.

On dry land, Ashrita Furman (USA) caught 13 spears on 17 Jul 2014 – the **most spears caught from a spear gun above water in one minute**. This beat the existing mark by four.

Most iron bars bent with the teeth

Strongman Les Davis (USA) used his teeth to bend 10 iron bars by 90° on 25 Mar 2014. Davis once also held the record for **fastest time to bend an iron bar to fit into a suitcase**, achieving this in 29 sec. But in 2008, this was bettered by Alexander Muromskiy (RUS) with an even faster time of 25 sec.

Fastest mile on roller skis by a linked team

Led by retired World Cup alpine ski racer Chemmy Alcott (UK), "The Arctic V", also comprising Adam Libbey, Max Willcocks, Chris Brooks and Richard Gibbs (all UK), rolled 1 mi (1.6 km) through London's Hyde Park, UK, in 6 min 28 sec on 13 Feb 2015.

Most backflips while swallowing a sword

"Aerial Manx", aka James Loughron (AUS), performed 20 flips while swallowing a 41-cm-long (16.1-in) sword on 2 Jul 2014.

Most martial arts kicks with one leg (male)

In 60 sec, Ahmad Amin Bodla (PAK) performed 355 kicks on 3 Mar 2014. Six days later, he also set a new record for the **most martial arts kicks in one hour** – 6,970.

IN ONE HOUR

Greatest group distance on a Slip 'N Slide

On 5 Jul 2014, at an event organized by Shelby Farms Park Conservancy (USA), 4,072 people slid for a combined distance of 41.4 km (25.7 mi).

Longest distance wakeboarding

Japanese adventurer Osamu Maebashi wakeboarded for 32.5 km (20.19 mi) in the waters of Chuuk State, in the Federated States of Micronesia, on 7 Oct 2014.

IN NUMBERS

12
Most arrows shot simultaneously from a longbow, fired by Hamish Murray (UK) on 27 Jul 2014

2.84 sec
Fastest escape from a straitjacket, by Danilo Audiello (ITA) on 11 Aug 2014

13.24 km
Farthest distance climbed on a ladder in 24 hours (8.23 mi), by Keith Saunders (UK) in Jul 2014

1 hr 11 min 8 sec
Longest duration twerking, by Greg James (UK) on BBC Radio 1on 30 Sep 2014

Most lit candles held in the mouth

With a number of eating records already to his name – see p.191 – Dinesh Shivnath Upadhyaya (IND) opened wide to fit 12 burning candles in his mouth on 10 Jun 2014.

Dinesh is also quite handy, setting a 30-sec record on 16 Feb 2014 for **most dice caught with cupped hands while blindfolded** – 43 – with the help of his brother Manish, who threw them.

IN ONE HOUR

Longest distance moonwalked

Krunoslav Budiselić (HRV) moonwalked 12 laps of the Stadium Mladost in Zagreb, Croatia, on 12 Oct 2009, covering a total distance of 5.7 km (3.5 mi).

Most knuckle push-ups

Military fitness instructor Eva Clarke (AUS) knuckled down to perform 1,206 push-ups in Abu Dhabi, UAE, on 31 Jan 2014. At the same event, Eva also earned the female record for **most knuckle push-ups in 24 hours**, completing 9,241 over the day.

More recently, bodybuilder Eva achieved the **most knuckle push-ups in one minute (female)**, completing 70 on 9 Jan 2015.

Most golf balls hit over 300 yd

Andrew Frakes (USA) whacked 448 golf balls more than 300 yd (274 m) at TPC Craig Ranch in McKinney, Texas, USA, on 7 Aug 2013, also netting $20,000 (£13,000) for charity.

Most full-contact kicks

Individual: The UK's most prolific record-breaker, Paddy Doyle, achieved 5,750 kicks on 8 Nov 2007.

Team: Members of Jayanth Reddy International Taekwondo Academy (IND) performed a staggering 54,127 kicks on 31 May 2014.

Most tennis balls held in the hand

On 8 Sep 2013, Mahadeo Bhujbal (IND) balanced 23 tennis balls in his hand – fittingly, for 23 sec. Mahadeo puts his success down to daily practice and the support of his friends and family.

EXTREME EXPLOITS

Largest hotdog cart

Fast-food vendor Marcus "Hot Dog Man" Daily (USA) and his team serve their hotdogs from a cart measuring 9 ft 3 in (2.81 m) wide, 23 ft 2 in (7.06 m) long and 12 ft 2.75 in (3.72 m) tall from the ground to the handle. The colossal push cart – and yes, it *is* movable – is a scaled-up stainless steel K-D Machine & Tool Model 300 that is three-and-a-half times the size of the original, as verified by a State of Missouri land surveyor. It was measured in the city of Union, Missouri, USA, on 28 Oct 2013.

CONTENTS

FACT

The giant hotdog cart has wheels measuring 6 ft 1.5 in (1.86 m) in diameter, and – per the traditional design – the sides are embossed with diamond-patterned quilted stainless steel.

IN FOCUS

GARDEN GIANTS

At the annual World Championship Punkin Chunkin, teams use **catapults, cannons and more** to **hurl pumpkins** as far as possible

You need more than green fingers to grow a GWR-worthy plant. It takes commitment, patience and a lot of hard work, but as the supersized produce here shows, record-breaking gardeners have all those qualities in spades.

If entering a contest, there's also a strict set of rules to be adhered to before your plant can qualify as a record-breaker, including the soundness of the fruit/veg (e.g. no decay) and no use of prohibited chemicals or additives.

One man who knows all about the challenges of both growing and assessing garden giants is David Stelts of the Great Pumpkin Commonwealth (GPC). Since 1992, this impartial body has monitored the world's largest fruit and vegetables, regulating the arena of competitive growing and encouraging a culture of fairness and sharing knowledge. Competition is fierce – see p.186 to see how often the record for largest pumpkin has changed hands in recent years.

The GPC oversees big veg events all over the globe. One of the most notable in Europe is the UK National Giant Vegetable Championships, currently held at the Malvern Autumn Show in Worcestershire, UK. The contest has ushered in many records over the years, with current titles including **heaviest beetroot** (see p.186) and **heaviest potato** (4.98 kg; 10 lb 14 oz, grown by UK gardener Peter Glazebrook).

What makes these records so special is their inclusivity. It doesn't matter who you are or where you live, *anyone* can grow a garden giant. As David says, "You could grow a world record tomato on the balcony of a Manhattan flat."

To help you get off on the right foot, we've got the GPC's advice on growing big pumpkins on pages 188–89.

FACT

According to the GPC, pumpkin plants require around 1 in (2.5 cm) of rain per week. That equates to some 89 US gallons (336 litres) of water for every 1,000 sq ft of pumpkin patch every day.

Top tomatoes

The **heaviest tomato** was grown by Dan MacCoy (USA, above), and weighed 3.81 kg (8 lb 6.5 oz) on 22 Aug 2014. This beat the existing record by 0.3 kg (10.5 oz).

The **largest tomato plant**, meanwhile, covered an area of 85.46 m² (919.88 sq ft) at Tomato-no-mori in Hokkaido, Japan, as of 10 Nov 2013; it was measured 350 days after the seed was sown.

Heaviest pumpkin

Authenticated by the GPC in Ludwigsburg, Germany, on 12 Oct 2014, this behemoth of a pumpkin weighed in at 1,054.01 kg (2,323 lb 11 oz), beating the existing record by 132.3 kg (292 lb) – see timeline of record-holding pumpkins below. Grown by farmer Beni Meier (CHE, left) on Jucker Farm in Jona, near Zurich in Switzerland, it had a circumference of 5.7 m (18 ft 8.4 in).

Incredibly, Meier entered an even heavier pumpkin in 2013, which tipped the scales at 1,055.9 kg (2,328 lb), but it had to be disqualified as it had a small hole.

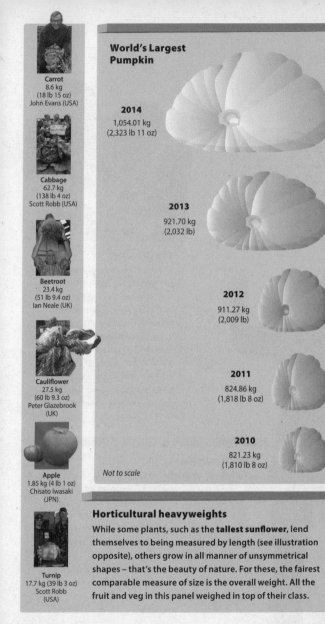

Carrot
8.6 kg
(18 lb 15 oz)
John Evans (USA)

Cabbage
62.7 kg
(138 lb 4 oz)
Scott Robb (USA)

Beetroot
23.4 kg
(51 lb 9.4 oz)
Ian Neale (UK)

Cauliflower
27.5 kg
(60 lb 9.3 oz)
Peter Glazebrook (UK)

Apple
1.85 kg (4 lb 1 oz)
Chisato Iwasaki (JPN)

Turnip
17.7 kg (39 lb 3 oz)
Scott Robb (USA)

World's Largest Pumpkin

2014
1,054.01 kg
(2,323 lb 11 oz)

2013
921.70 kg
(2,032 lb)

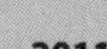

2012
911.27 kg
(2,009 lb)

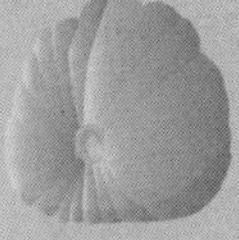

2011
824.86 kg
(1,818 lb 8 oz)

2010
821.23 kg
(1,810 lb 8 oz)

Not to scale

Horticultural heavyweights

While some plants, such as the tallest sunflower, lend themselves to being measured by length (see illustration opposite), others grow in all manner of unsymmetrical shapes – that's the beauty of nature. For these, the fairest comparable measure of size is the overall weight. All the fruit and veg in this panel weighed in top of their class.

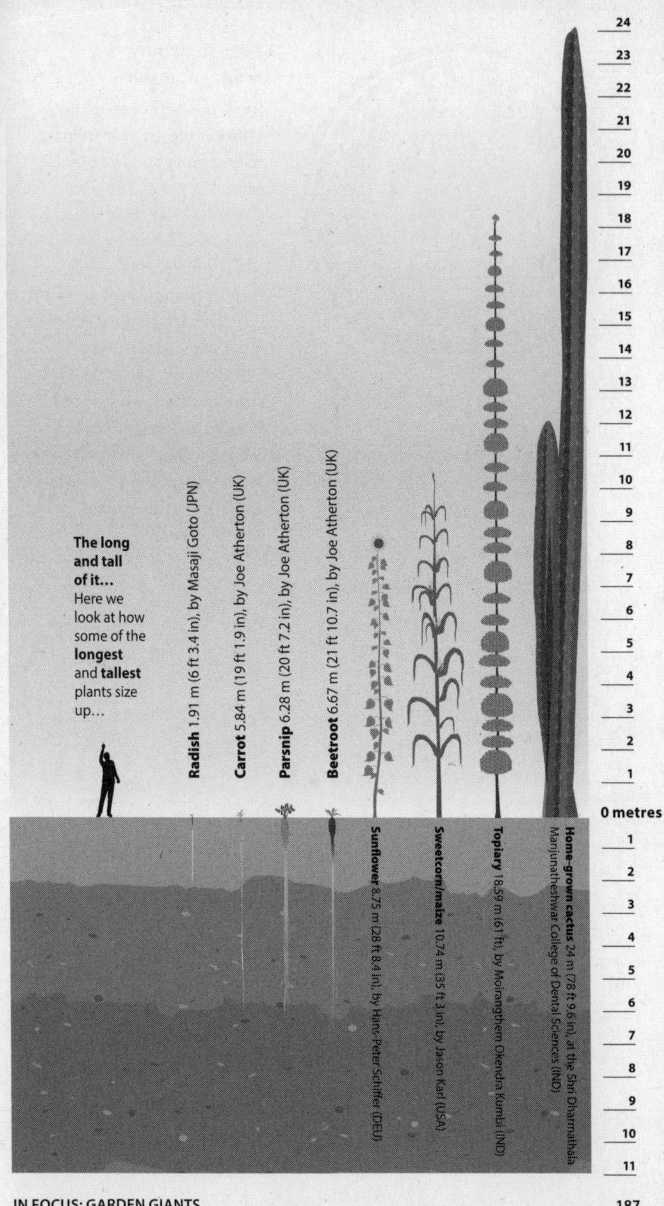

The long and tall of it...
Here we look at how some of the **longest** and **tallest** plants size up...
Radish 1.91 m (6 ft 3.4 in), by Masaji Goto (JPN)
Carrot 5.84 m (19 ft 1.9 in), by Joe Atherton (UK)
Parsnip 6.28 m (20 ft 7.2 in), by Joe Atherton (UK)
Beetroot 6.67 m (21 ft 10.7 in), by Joe Atherton (UK)
Sunflower 8.75 m (28 ft 8.4 in), by Hans-Peter Schiffer (DEU)
Sweetcorn/maize 10.74 m (35 ft 3 in), by Jason Karl (USA)
Topiary 18.59 m (61 ft), by Moirangthem Okendra Kumbi (IND)
Home-grown cactus 24 m (78 ft 9.6 in), at the Shri Dharmathala Manjunatheshwar College of Dental Sciences (IND)
24
23
22
21
20
19
18
17
16
15
14
13
12
11
10
9
8
7
6
5
4
3
2
1
0 metres
1
2
3
4
5
6
7
8
9
10
11

How to grow a mega-pumpkin

Here, the GPC's David Stelts offers a step-by-step guide to growing your own giant pumpkin (times apply to the northern hemisphere), although a lot of the advice will apply to cultivating healthy pumpkins in general.

According to the GPC, the most successful variety is Dill's Atlantic Giant. David stresses *never* to buy seeds from a shop, but to approach other growers who can supply seeds with proven genetics – and usually at no cost whatsoever.

1 Pick a site with good drainage and lots of sunlight. In late March, prepare the soil with natural fertilizers, such as lime and manure. Build a mini-greenhouse to heat up the earth.

FACT

The tradition of carving pumpkins into jack-o'-lanterns at Halloween is believed to have originated from the Gaelic festival of Samhain, although originally turnips would have been used more frequently.

2 In April, lightly rub the edges of your seeds (not the tips) with sandpaper and soak in warm water for 20 min. Plant one seed per pot, and put them somewhere warm to germinate.

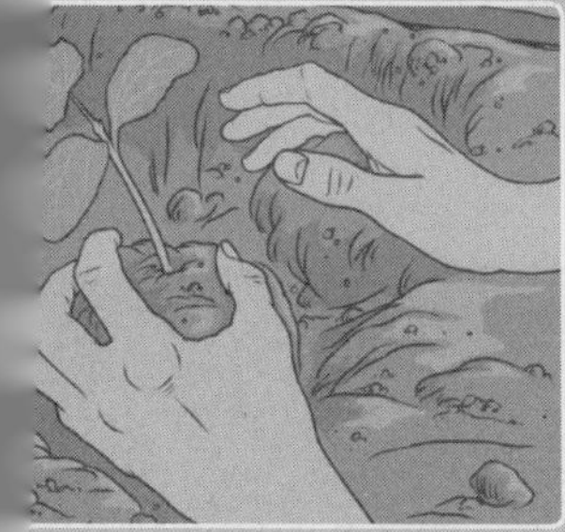

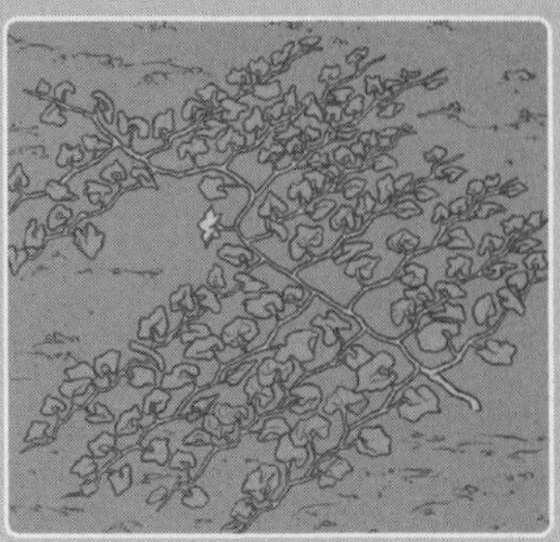

3 Around late April/early May, it's time to transplant. Plant seedlings under the greenhouse in a small mound. Avoid soil compaction by placing boards around the site (see step 1).

4 As the vines start to grow, train them in a branched-out layout. It's best to move shoots in small increments and only at the end of the day, when they're warm and more supple.

5 Each pumpkin plant has both male and female flowers. When it comes to pollination, you have two options: open or closed. Open relies on natural pollinators such as bees, but this is dependent on local insect populations and offers no control over genetics. Self-pollination by hand (i.e., closed) is favoured by the GPC for several reasons: it allows genetics to be tightly regulated, and pollen can be more evenly distributed, plus the specific flowers and dates can be logged, which will help when tracking progress.

6 As fruit appears, measure the most promising-looking specimens with a strong stem (127-cm/50-in circumference after 14 days is a good indicator). By early August, choose one and cull all others. If the stem ever looks strained, carefully adjust the fruit; it's also a good idea to place sand or boards beneath to avoid rot. Set up a mini-tent to protect your pumpkin from intense sunlight. Now all you have to do is let it grow.

FUN WITH FOOD

At 2014's **Tomatina** festival in Spain, **125 tonnes** of tomatoes were thrown

Fastest time to eat 15 Ferrero Rocher

Multi-record-holding speed-eater "Furious Pete", aka Peter Czerwinski from Canada, wolfed down 15 Ferrero Rocher in just 2 min 22 sec at the London office of Guinness World Records on 24 Oct 2014, in celebration of the book's 60th anniversary.

Pete also holds records for the **most Ferrero Rocher eaten in a minute** (9) and the 60-sec titles for **most Creme Eggs** (6) and **most Jaffa Cakes** (17).

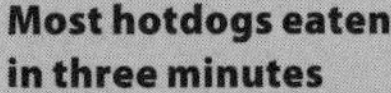

Most hotdogs eaten in three minutes

A competitive eater since the age of 21, Takeru Kobayashi (JPN) ate six hotdogs on 25 Aug 2009, beating the previous total by two dogs.

More recently, on 11 Jul 2014, Takeru ate 12 burgers on the set of *Lo Show dei Record* to claim the **most hamburgers eaten in three minutes.** Each burger weighed 4 oz (113 g) pre-cooked, and he chose mayonnaise for the one condiment allowed by the rules.

Farthest distance to blow a pea

With a single breath, André Ortolf (DEU) blew a pea for a staggering 7.51 m (24 ft 7.6 in) at the Bodyfeeling fitness gym in Augsburg, Bavaria, Germany, on 12 Jul 2014.

It was a bumper year for Ortolf, who also achieved the **fastest 100 m playing tiddlywinks** on 5 Jul (1 min 51.20 sec) and the **fastest mile wearing clogs** on 8 Mar (7 min 26.48 sec); read about it on p.146.

FACT

Widely considered the "father of modern genetics", Augustinian monk Gregor Mendel (AUT, now CZE; 1822–84) developed his theories of heredity by studying the various traits of pea plants.

Most champagne bottles sabered in one minute

Wielding a 15-in-long (38-cm) blade that was made specially for this purpose, Mirko Rainer from South Tyrol, Italy, sliced the necks off 47 bottles on 6 Sep 2014.

Largest mosaic of...

Beans: A portrait of a cow made by the Tokachi–Sekaiichi Project (JPN) in Hokkaido, Japan, used more than 12 million assorted beans and measured in at 430.18 m^2 (4,630.41 sq ft) on 8 Mar 2015.

Sushi: Covering 41.99 m^2 (451.9 sq ft), a mosaic of mackerel and imitation crab meat was created by The Ono Chamber of Commerce & Industry (JPN) in Ono, Fukui, Japan, on 31 Jan 2015.

M&Ms: A candy mosaic of the state of Idaho, USA, created by Jackson McKenzie (USA) on 1 Aug 2014, covered an area of 13.8 m^2 (148.5 sq ft).

Fastest time to peel and eat an orange while blindfolded (team of two)

Both wearing blindfolds, brothers Dinesh and Manish Upadhyaya (both IND) consumed an orange in 17.15 sec on 5 Mar 2014; Manish peeled while Dinesh did the eating. Science teacher Dinesh also holds the record for the **most grapes stuffed in the mouth**, filling his face with 79 grapes in Mumbai, India, on 8 Apr 2012.

IN NUMBERS

91.2 cm
Height of the **tallest stack of pancakes** (35.9 in), built at the Efteling theme park (NLD) on 16 Oct 2014

40 hr
Longest cooking marathon, achieved by Benjamin J Perry (USA)

30.7 sec
Fastest time to eat 10 bhut jolokia chillis, by Amedonuo Kankue (TGO) on 19 Jun 2014

66 m
Farthest distance to throw a haggis (216 ft), hurled by Lorne Coltart (UK)

36
Most cloves of garlic eaten in one minute, by Patrick Bertoletti (USA)

11.41 sec
Fastest time to eat a doughnut with no hands (and without licking lips!), achieved by Philip J Santoro (USA)

Fastest time to crush three watermelons with the thighs

Olga Liashchuk (UKR), whose greatest ambition is to become the world's strongest woman, crushed three watermelons in 14.65 sec on 26 Jun 2014. Asked what drew her to this record, she said, "I thought it may be easier than other strength records… but it turned out to be very hard indeed!"

Longest marathon slicing meat

Noé Bonillo Ramos (ESP) sliced *jamón ibérico* for 72 hr 13 min 8 sec at Les Grands d'Espagne in Paris, France, on 3–6 Feb 2015. Noé sliced off 154.33 kg (340 lb 3 oz) of ham, with each slice being 0.5–1.5 mm (0.02–0.06 in) thick.

Highest jump into marshmallows

It's a sweet tooth's dream… Diving from 8.8 m (28 ft 10.75 in), Brent Steffensen (USA) leapt into a pool of 100,000-plus marshmallows on the set of *Guinness World Records Gone Wild!* on 3 Jul 2012.

Most beer steins carried over 40 m

Male: Oliver Strümpfel (DEU, right) went the distance with 25 steins, all without spilling a drop, on 21 Sep 2014.

Female: Fellow German Anita Schwarz carried 19 steins on 9 Nov 2008, as part of that year's GWR Day celebrations.

Most Mentos and soda fountains

This popular science experiment was taken to a whole new level on 15 Nov 2014 when 4,334 geysers erupted simultaneously at a hot-air balloon festival in León, Mexico. Organized by Chupa Chups Industrial Mexicana and Perfetti Van Melle (both MEX), this explosive feat almost doubled the previous record.

FACT

All potatoes used by the MPWC are (inedible) floor sweepings from a factory or outdated flakes that are no longer saleable. There's no waste, as any leftover mash is fed to local cattle.

Mash master

With four victories under his belt, Steve O'Gratin (aka Steve Barone, USA) holds the record for most wins of the Mashed Potato Wrestling Championships (MPWC)...

How did the MPWC come about?
I'm not sure. When life gives you mashed potatoes, just wrestle in it, I guess! Barnesville [Minnesota] started doing it during their Potato Days Festival in 1999.

Talk us through a few of the rules...
It's a single elimination tournament made up of three two-minute rounds. To win, you must pin an opponent down for three seconds, or the opponent quits. Alliances can be made to team up, but ultimately you will have to turn on that ally, as only one winner is declared. Eating any of the potato is not permitted!

What does it mean to be world champ?
I got to do some local news appearances which was fun. Now, I can't walk down the street in Barnesville without someone asking for an autograph. I did record a video of every competition, so I hope to make a documentary some day. I'd like to age about 15 years and maybe make a comeback.

BIG FOOD

An attempt at creating the **largest sandwich** failed when it was **eaten** before being measured!

LARGEST...

Meal eaten

According to correspondence in the medical journal *The Lancet* (vol. 325, issue 8,432, 6 Apr 1985), the largest documented meal consumed by one person weighed 19 lb (8.6 kg). It comprised 1 lb (453 g) of liver, 2 lb (907 g) of kidneys, 8 oz (226 g) of steak, two eggs, 1 lb (453 g) of cheese, two large slices of bread, 1 lb (453 g) of mushrooms, 2 lb (907 g) of carrots, one cauliflower, 10 peaches, four pears, two apples, four bananas, 2 lb (907 g) of plums, 2 lb (907 g) of grapes and two glasses of milk. It is also noted that the 23-year-old female patient later died following attempts to have the undigested food surgically removed.

Tea bag

Containing enough tea for 100,000 brews, the tea bag, 3 m (9 ft 10 in) wide by 3.7 m (12 ft 1 in) high and weighing 250 kg (551 lb 3 oz), was unveiled by makers Ahmed Mohamed Saleh Baeshen & Co., Rabea Tea, in Jeddah, Saudi Arabia, on 20 Sep 2014.

Bottle of wine

André Vogel (CHE) poured 3,094 litres (817.34 US gal) of red table wine into a 4.17-m-tall (13-ft 8-in) bottle in Lyssach, Switzerland, on 20 Oct 2014.

Most layers in a sandwich

An edible skyscraper containing 40 layers of marshmallow fluff (melted marshmallow), peanut butter and bacon strips was assembled by Sugardale Foods (USA) at the Fabulous Food Show in Cleveland, Ohio, USA, on 15 Nov 2014. Lucky visitors sampled bite-size morsels of the tasty tower.

Serving of doughnuts

In Almaty, Kazakhstan, on 7 Sep 2014, ERA TV's Channel 7 sponsored the making of 856 kg (1,887 lb 2 oz) of traditional square doughnuts known as "baursaks".

Pumpkin pie

New Bremen Giant Pumpkin Growers (USA) cooked up this giant, at 3,699 lb (1,678 kg) and 20 ft (6 m) in diameter, in New Bremen, Ohio, USA, on 25 Sep 2010.

LONGEST...

Skewer of meat

A 121.24-m-long (397-ft 9-in) skewer of meat was made by 623 members of the Oyama Chamber of Commerce and Industry in Tochigi, Japan, on 19 Oct 2014.

The **largest skewer of kebab meat** was made by Zith Catering Equipment Ltd in Pafos, Cyprus, on 31 Dec 2008 and tipped the scales at 4,022 kg (8,866 lb 15 oz) – about the same as a female elephant.

Black pudding

On 19 Jul 2014, butchers in Radomyśl Wielki, Poland, used 85 kg (187 lb) of blood to make a pudding measuring 226.67 m (743 ft 8 in) long – more than three times the length of a jumbo jet. With the addition of barley, pork and fat, the final sausage weighed more than a grand piano!

Largest cup of coffee

Why not take a dip in your iced Americano? For the opening of a roasting factory in Yangju, South Korea, on 17 Jul 2014, coffee chain Caffé Bene poured a very stimulating 14,228.1 litres (3,758.7 US gal) into a cup measuring 3.3 m (10 ft 10 in) tall and 2.62 m (8 ft 7 in) wide.

Brioche

A "golden braid" pastry measuring 117.55 m (385 ft 7 in) long was baked by Minoterie Planchot–Tresse Dorée in St-Paul-en-Pareds, France, on 9 Sep 2012.

Cake roll

A 140.62-m-long (461-ft 4-in) sponge cake – as long as six tennis courts – was created by the Izumigaoka World Record Challenge Project in Sakai, Osaka, Japan, on 8 Nov 2014.

Largest toast mosaic

Graphic designer Ayako Maura (JPN) used slices of bread toasted to varying degrees to create a mosaic at Tokachi Plaza in Obihiro, Hokkaido, Japan, on 7 Jul 2013. The artwork, 14.8 m (48 ft 7 in) long and 11 m (36 ft 1 in) wide, required around 6,500 pieces of toast, made from locally grown wheat. It took three hours to arrange the slices into an area larger than a squash court.

Largest serving of tacos

On 7 Sep 2014, the Municipality of Metepec in Mexico and a team of chefs from the Escuela Culinaria Internacional (International Cookery School) prepared 893 kg (1,968 lb 12 oz) of Tacos de Plaza, a regional speciality. In order to blend together the dish's 30 or so ingredients, the chefs required the world's **largest clay cooking pot**. Made over several months by local artisans, the pot, 2.5 m (8 ft 2 in) wide and 1.27 m (4 ft 2 in) in height, earned Metepec its second GWR certificate.

Largest fruit salad

A serving of strawberries, apples, blueberries and kiwi fruits weighing 8,690 kg (19,158 lb 3 oz) was prepared on 27 Jun 2014 in Vienna, Austria, by the SPAR supermarket group. The salad was later served up to passers-by and local charity groups.

Largest scoop of ice-cream

On 28 Jun 2014, as part of its 100th anniversary festivities, Kemps Dairy LLC (USA) visited the Cedarburg Strawberry Festival in Wisconsin, USA, and sculpted a giant scoop of strawberry ice-cream weighing 3,010 lb (1,365.31 kg). Five nationally ranked snow sculptors worked with 733 containers of ice-cream to create the super-sized scoop, which stood 5 ft 6 in (1.68 m) tall and 6 ft 2 in (1.88 m) wide. As heavy as a family car, the scoop was served up free to the thousands of people visiting the festival.

IN NUMBERS

AD 1040
Founding date of the **oldest working brewery**: Weihenstephan Brewery in Germany

1 billion lb
Total weight of pumpkins grown in the USA annually (453,590,000 kg)

25%
Proportion of air in an apple, which allows it to float in water

11 years
Age of Frank Epperson when he invented the popsicle in 1905

4,700 BC
A likely date for the invention, in Peru, of popcorn

Largest truffle

On 4 Nov 2014, a white truffle (*Tuber magnatum pico*) weighing a record 1.48 kg (3 lb 4.16 oz) was found in the Appennino Woods near Savigno, Bologna, Italy, by a 60-year-old man and his dog Fogy. It was acquired by Luigi and Angelo Dattilo (ITA, above) of Appennino Food SpA, who kindly agreed to an interview.

Was this the largest white truffle you have ever seen?

Yes. And it's even more amazing because it's especially difficult to find the right conditions for white truffles to grow. Then they don't keep more than two weeks. This one was eaten at a charity dinner and raised around 25,000 euros [$29,472; £19,115].

Why are truffles so expensive?

Simply because they are so rare and much prized. It's all up to nature where and if they grow: a combination of humidity, sunshine and soil acidity.

Where do they grow?

A truffle grows underground among tree roots. It absorbs minerals and passes them to the roots, which turn them into sugars. In this case, the interaction just had an extraordinary effect.

How are they found?

Truffles have a strong, special smell, and dogs are trained to sniff them out. A special breed, *Lagotto Romagnolo*, is often used, but any dog with a good nose can go truffle hunting. The relationship between a hunter and his dog is very close, and makes truffle hunting a wonderful experience.

Tallest chocolate sculpture

Patrick Roger (FRA) took one month – and 4,000 kg (8,818 lb) of chocolate – to craft an edible Christmas tree that stood 10 m (32 ft 10 in) tall in Sceaux, France, on 1 Dec 2010.

FACT

In the past, pigs were used to snuffle out truffles, whose intense aroma was very attractive to females. Dogs took over because pigs often ate the truffles before the hunter could get to them!

FACT

Ice-cream variations have existed since ancient times. The Persians ate snow flavoured with grape juice, the Chinese froze a milk and rice mixture, and Emperor Nero liked ice with fruit on top.

The **Statue of Liberty** has 25-ft-long (7.6-m) feet – requiring a **US size 879 shoe**!

Largest Monopoly board

On 27 Jan 2012, SintLucas Eindhovense School (NLD) unveiled a Monopoly board that covered 225 m^2 (2,421.87 sq ft), making it also the **largest board game**. "The planning took a few months," revealed organizer Bas van den Hout. "Preparations such as enlarging and painting took four days and the actual construction took about four hours."

Longest table

A table measuring 1,286.75 m (4,421 ft 7 in) – longer than 11 American football fields – was created by Ölvin, Bistro Cantor and C&D Fastfood in Loviisa, Finland, and unveiled on 20 Aug 2014 as part of a weekend organized to draw in tourists.

By comparison, the **longest foosball table** came in at 101 m (331 ft 4 in) on 25 Jul 2005 and could accommodate 334 players.

After that foosball game, you can kick back on the **longest sofa**. Furniture manufacturer Mnogo Mebeli (RUS) made the 1,006.61-m-long (3,302-ft 6-in) seat to celebrate its fifth anniversary on 25 Jul 2014; it could hold about 2,500 people.

Largest ball-point pen

This ball-point behemoth engraved with scenes from Indian mythology was crafted by Acharya Makunuri Srinivasa (IND). The 9-kg (19-lb 13.5-oz) brass pen measured 5.5 m (18 ft 0.53 in) long – beating the previous record by 1.45 m (4 ft 9 in) – when it was assessed in Hyderabad, India, on 24 Apr 2011. As per the guidelines, the pen "dispenses ink at its tip during use by the rolling action of a small metal sphere".

FACT

Stationery has come a long way since the **first ball-point pen**, invented by newspaperman László Bíró and his brother György (both HUN) in 1938 as a smudge-free alternative to the fountain pen.

Largest whoopee cushion

With a deflated diameter of 6.035 m (19 ft 9.48 in), a giant whoopee cushion commissioned by *What Now* (NZ) in Christchurch, New Zealand, could be considered the ultimate prankster's trick. When inflated on 28 Sep 2014, the fart bag required 15 people pressing down on it to produce the classic comedy noise!

Largest mascot

At 13 m (42 ft 7.8 in) tall, as of 25 Apr 2014, a yeti named "Boro the Great" is the largest of the mythical creatures at the Sol Katmandu Park & Resort in Magaluf, Spain. The 2.2-tonne (4,850-lb) mascot took 58 craftsmen 18 months to build.

Largest ukulele

A ukulele measuring 2.27 m (7.45 ft) long, 0.85 m (2.8 ft) wide and 0.25 m (0.83 ft) deep was made by Xuri Musical Instruments Co Ltd (CHN) on 19 Sep 2014.

The **largest guitar**, meanwhile, is an enormous acoustic instrument that measures 16.75 m (59 ft 11 in) in length and 2.67 m (8 ft 9 in) in depth. The 4-tonne (8,820-lb) creation was first strummed in Porto, Portugal, in Jan 2001.

Largest cowboy boot sculpture

These boots might not be made for walking, but they sure are huge, standing 10.74 m (35 ft 3 in) high, as measured on 4 Nov 2014. This makes them more than four times the size of the **largest cowboy boot** (see p.203). Standing at the entrance of the North Star Mall in San Antonio, Texas, USA, the sculpture was created by local artist Bob Wade (pictured).

Largest trophy

Southland Park Gaming & Racing (USA) created a trophy measuring 10.64 m (34 ft 10.8 in) tall – twice the height of a giraffe! – for the first-prize winner of the Great Steak Cook-Off in Oct 2014.

Largest spade

A garden spade built from recycled materials such as scrap metal and telephone poles was measured at the Garden-Ville garden centre in Creedmoor, Texas, USA, on 17 Jul 2014. The blade was 2.23 m (7 ft 3.8 in) wide and the whole thing stood 12.4 m (40 ft 8.2 in) tall. The gargantuan gardening tool took metal-working artist Chris Anderson (USA) five months to construct; he specializes in recycled art.

Largest greetings card

In honour of Indian Prime Minister Narendra Modi's birthday, Prakash Gurjar (IND) made him a birthday card measuring 14.02 m (45 ft 11.9 in) long and 7.96 m (26 ft 1.3 in) wide.

The **largest greetings card mosaic** was unveiled in Hong Kong, China, by the New World Development Company Limited on 23 Nov 2014; it covered 150.04 m² (1,615 sq ft) and was made of 5,113 cards.

Tallest sandcastle

With a build time of two weeks and requiring a mini-fleet of construction vehicles and seven sculptors to complete, this sandy skyscraper reached 12.59 m (41 ft 3.67 in) when unveiled by Caterpillar Inc. in Rio de Janeiro, Brazil, on 11 Nov 2014. The final structure was made from 730 m³ (25,920 cu ft) – 20 truckloads – of sand.

IN NUMBERS

4.6 km
Length of the **longest wedding veil** (2.9 mi), displayed in Sharjah, UAE, on 6 Mar 2014

7.5 km
Length of eco-leather used in the **longest sofa** (4.6 mi) – see p.199 – by Mnogo Mebeli

Largest T-shirt

In Oct 2014, it took 64 people from Equilibrios Camisetas Promocionais (BRA) a total of 11,000 hours to make a T-shirt measuring 93.2 m (305 ft 9.2 in) long and 62.73 m (205 ft 9.6 in) wide. The pink top was dedicated to breast cancer awareness, in partnership with the Female Network Against Cancer.

Largest disco ball

With a diameter of 10.33 m (33 ft 10 in), this giant glitter ball, covered in 2,500 reflective tiles, added some glitz to the finale of Bestival, the annual music festival held on the Isle of Wight, UK. The theme for 2014, appropriately, was "Desert Island Disco".

Mungo Denison from Newsubstance, the creative agency behind the ball, said: "It's taken the team three months of blood, sweat and mirror tiles to fabricate this beast – it's been a fantastic journey."

Largest fork

Designed by Jean-Pierre Zaugg (CHE) to celebrate the 10th anniversary of Nestlé's Alimentarium museum in Vevey, the 8-m-tall (26-ft 2.4-in) piece of cutlery was first exhibited in the waters of Lake Geneva, Switzerland, in 1995. The stainless-steel fork sculpture was made permanent in 2009.

FACT

Weighing 4,500 kg (9,920 lb), the world's largest T-shirt was made from 50% cotton and 50% recycled PET bottles. It will later be turned into several thousand normal-sized T-shirts!

Killer heels

Jeison Orlando Rodríguez Hernández from Venezuela has to get his shoes specially made to fit the world's largest feet (see pp.119), but even his feet would get lost in this selection of giant footwear...

The **largest high-heeled shoe** (above) measures 1.95 m (6 ft 5 in) long and 1.85 m (6 ft 1 in) tall. Created by Kenneth Cole and Jill Martin (both USA), it was unveiled on NBC's *Today Show* on 10 Nov 2014. The heel alone is 1.06 m (3 ft 5 in) tall!

At 2.50 m (8 ft 2 in) tall, the **largest cowboy boot** was made from five cows' worth of black leather by Belachew Tola Buta (ETH, inset left, top), as of 24 Jan 2008.

Each carved from a block of poplar, the **largest clogs** (inset left, bottom) measured 3.04 m (9 ft 11 in) long on 20 Oct 2012. The wooden shoes were created by Peter de Koning (NLD).

All of these pale in comparison to the **largest shoe**, a supersized Superga 2750 (below), which measured 6.40 m (20 ft 11.97 in) long on 12 Apr 2013. Produced by fashion distributor Electric sekki (Hong Kong), it was big enough to contain more than 11,000 standard-size shoes.

BALLOONATICS

A **hole in a balloon** grows faster than the speed of sound in air, causing a **sonic boom**

Largest balloon Minifigure sculpture

On 30 Nov 2014, at the Brick LEGO® event held in London, UK, a 6-m-tall (19-ft 8-in) LEGO Minifigure – 150 times larger than a standard Minifigure – was completed from 1,985 modelling balloons. A team led by Larry Moss (USA) built it over three days.

FACT

The supersized Minifigure was hollow, and the only support provided was a line from the ceiling to anchor it in place. The entire sculpture, including scaled-up LEGO pieces, used 4,174 balloons.

Fastest time to make a modelling-balloon dog

John Cassidy (USA) twisted a balloon dog in 6.5 sec at the Balloon Saloon store in New York, USA, on 28 Mar 2006. John is a balloon artist with multiple records: the **most modelling-balloon sculptures made in one minute** (13) and **in one hour** (747), plus the **most modelling balloons inflated and tied in one hour** (717). For this last record, balloons must be inflated to 152 cm (60 in) long. There is no such requirement for modelling balloon sculptures – they can be smaller, so more of them can be created in an hour.

Curiously, the record for the **fastest time to make a balloon dog behind the back** is faster than the front-of-body record: "Mago Ciccio", aka Daniele Bottalico (ITA), sculpted a poodle behind his back in 4.54 sec in Cassano delle Murge, Bari, Italy, on 10 Nov 2007.

The **most modelling-balloon sculptures made in 24 hours** is 6,176, by Tim Thurmond (USA) at the Revival Outreach Center International Church in Northville, Michigan, USA, on 16–17 Apr 2004. Contenders for this record must make a minimum of 30 different shapes, and no shape may be repeated consecutively.

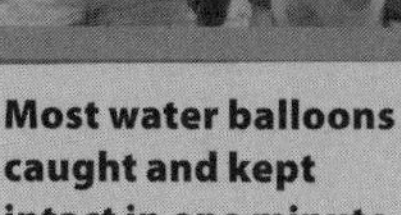

Most water balloons caught and kept intact in one minute

On 2 Aug 2014 in New York City, USA, Ashrita Furman (above left) caught 22 water balloons thrown towards him from a distance of 3 m (9 ft 10 in) by a blindfolded Bipin Larkin (both USA). As per the rules, Ashrita held on to each balloon as he caught them.

LARGEST...

Modelling-balloon sculpture by a team

The side view of a rearing horse was made from 61,107 modelling balloons by Yiwei Chen (TPE) and his team in Hefei, Anhui, China, on 26 Apr 2014. The equine artwork measured 23.95 m (78 ft 6.9 in) long and 19.77 m (64 ft 10.3 in) wide – an area slightly larger than a tennis court – and stood 7.91 m (25 ft 11.4 in) tall.

Largest modelling-balloon sculpture by an individual

This giant spider, 6.76 m (22 ft 2 in) long and 13.77 m (45 ft 2 in) wide, consists of 2,975 modelling balloons and was created by Adam Lee (USA). It was presented and measured at Grand Mound's Great Wolf Lodge in Lacey, Washington, USA, on 6 Oct 2011.

Largest 3D fractal made from modelling balloons

With the help of 11 balloon artists, Caroline Ainslie (UK) of Bubbly Maths created a 3D fractal (a never-ending pattern) from 160Q modelling balloons at the GWR London offices on 24 Feb 2015. The finished sculpture – known as a Sierpinski pyramid – stood 219.1 cm (7 ft 2 in) tall and averaged 264.6 cm (8 ft 8.1 in) along its outer edge.

LARGEST...

Balloon mosaic

A mosaic depicting the Chicago skyline made from 70,884 balloons and measuring 58 x 86 ft (17.6 x 26.21 m) was created by delegates of the International Balloon Arts Convention on 8 Mar 1999 in the lobby of the Hyatt Regency O'Hare hotel in Rosemont, Illinois, USA.

Balloon drop

On 14 Apr 2012, 109,183 balloons were dropped at the *Titanic* Centenary Commemorations held at the Adelaide Convention Centre in South Australia. Organized by 1912 The Event (AUS), the drop was the culmination of the evening and symbolized the sinking of the ill-fated ship.

Water balloon toss (single venue)

On 14 Sep 2014, at the start of the academic year, 902 students, parents and faculty members from Deerfield Academy in Massachusetts, USA, tossed water balloons to raise funds for a youth mentorship scheme.

Water balloon fight

On 27 Aug 2011, a total of 8,957 members of the Christian Student Fellowship at the University of Kentucky (USA) exchanged friendly fire using water balloons. The final count revealed that 175,141 balloons had been lobbed.

Largest balloon sculpture

On 12–15 Mar 2012, Lily Tan (SGP) and her team of fellow balloon artists used a record 79,854 balloons to create the shape of a robot, named "Sentinel", at Marina Square shopping centre in Singapore. The sculpture – 19 m (62 ft 4 in) wide, 23.3 m (76 ft 5 in) long and 11.5 m (37 ft 9 in) high – took the 50-person team 42 hr to create.

FASTEST TIME TO BURST...

20 balloons (individual)

"USA Ray", aka Raymond Butler (USA), popped 20 balloons in 3.94 sec on *Officially Amazing* (CBBC) in Ipswich, Suffolk, UK, on 15 Jul 2014.

20 balloons on a trials bike

Michele Pradelli (ITA) took 1 min 45 sec to pop 20 balloons, spaced at 15-m (49-ft) intervals, on the set of *Lo Show dei Record* in Madrid, Spain, on 23 Feb 2008. Michele burst each one while pulling off a "stoppie" on his motorbike – a trick in which the back wheel is lifted and the bike is ridden on the front wheel.

Three balloons with no hands (blindfolded)

Wearing a blindfold – and a hat with a pin attached – Johnathan Sargent (UK) popped three balloons in 2.97 sec, without using his hands, at the Thomson Family Resorts hotel in Alykanas, Greece, on 31 Jul 2014. He improved upon the previous record by an impressive 2.57 sec.

IN NUMBERS

0.1785 g
Weight of helium per litre (0.006 oz); this is lighter than air, which is why helium balloons float

39,522
Most balloons blown up in one hour by a team, achieved by HUBO in Brussels, Belgium, on 29 Nov 2009

37
Most balloons burst by sitting in 30 seconds, by Ashrita Furman (USA) on 30 Jun 2014

44.49 sec
Fastest time to pop 100 balloons by a dog: Anastasia, owned by Doree Sitterly (USA)

$58.4 m
Most expensive piece of art ever sold at auction by a living artist (£36.8 m): *Balloon Dog*, a mirrored stainless steel sculpture by US artist Jeff Koons

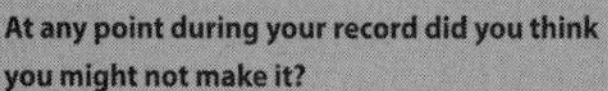

Up, up and away

"Cluster balloonist" Jonathan Trappe (USA) flew over North Carolina, USA, in *The Spirit Cluster* (totalling 57 balloons) on 10–11 Apr 2010. At 13 hr 36 min 57 sec, it is the longest duration flight by helium balloons. Jonathan covered 109 mi (175 km) and reached an altitude of 7,474 ft (2,278 m).

At any point during your record did you think you might not make it?
I launched in the daytime, then stayed aloft all night, something that hadn't been done before. I designed and built the aircraft myself, so I knew it should work and that it was safe. But in the deepest part of the night, I had this feeling that I would fall; it still seemed like there was some magic holding me aloft.

What's different about flying at night?
The biggest difference is that you can't land at night, because you can't see obstacles that would make it dangerous. Also, when the sun goes down, the balloons cool and become smaller. This causes you to lose lift, and you have to drop sand or water to compensate.

What if something goes wrong?
If a single balloon fails, or even if many fail – as happened once when I was flying in Mexico and a rancher shot at them with a rifle – it's not a catastrophic event. I just have to quickly drop a corresponding amount of sand or water.

Any more record attempts in view?
I would like to fly my cluster balloons to extreme altitudes, higher than Mount Everest. I often work with television programmes, and when the show is over I fly away, for as long and as far as I can go, wherever the wind takes me…

Largest object lifted by helium balloons

In Feb and Mar 2011, a house weighing 4,335 lb (1,966 kg) was air-lifted 10,000 ft (3,050 m) above Los Angeles, USA, by the National Geographic Channel (USA). A cluster of 300 balloons 10 storeys high was used, and the event was filmed for the TV series *How Hard Can It Be?*

To find out about hot-air and gas ballooning adventures, float over to pp.463–67

MASS PARTICIPATION

If 30,000 people ran the **Boston Marathon** on a hot day, they would lose around **37,000 gallons (140,000 litres) of sweat**

Largest gathering of Santa's elves

A mass elf-in took place on 25 Nov 2014 to celebrate Christmas and the ninth anniversary of the opening of the Siam Paragon shopping centre in Bangkok, Thailand. After 14 disqualifications for the absence of pointed ears, a total of 1,762 elves grouped together to form the word "SIAM" at the event staged by the Siam Paragon Development Company.

MOST PEOPLE...

Planting flower bulbs

In an event dubbed "Operation Peacebulb", the Stockland Green Community Group (UK), in association with West Midlands police, conducted a mass planting at Brookvale Park in Birmingham, UK, on Remembrance Sunday (9 Nov) 2014 to commemorate World War I. In 15 min, 850 people planted 4,250 daffodil (*narcissus*) bulbs in the memorial garden, an average of five bulbs per person.

Playing in a soccer exhibition match

On 26 Jul 2014, Championat.com (RUS) assembled 1,435 players at the Luzhniki Olympic Complex in Moscow, Russia. The game – played between an Orange Team and a White Team – lasted 13 hr 58 min. The White Team won 56–48.

Largest pillow fight

What better way to hit it off with your fellow students than at the biggest-ever pillow bash? This bonding exercise attracted 4,200 participants just before the fall semester, on 30 Sep 2014 at the University of California, USA.

MOST PEOPLE...

Tasting champagne

Eurostar International (UK) celebrated their 20th anniversary in sparkling style with 515 people at a champagne tasting on a London-to-Paris Eurostar train on 9 Oct 2014. Raymond Blanc OBE introduced the record attempt to the passengers, and Chef-Sommelier Arnaud Goubet led the tasting.

Largest gathering of people dressed as Batman

"Good thinking, bat people" – as our superhero might have said when 542 employees from Nexen Energy (pictured below) donned full Batman outfits, including boots, cape and mask, on 18 Sep 2014 in Calgary, Alberta, Canada.

Soon after, on 2 Oct 2014, Escapade Fancy Dress (UK) organized the **largest gathering of people dressed as Spider-Man** (inset right), with 398 people at the freshers' week event held at Student Central in London, UK.

Sadly, the boy wonder Robin did not count towards the record total...
...and nor did botanical expert and villainess Poison Ivy...
...nor the Joker, lurking with evil intent

Whistling
Event organization Spring Harvest (UK) enabled 853 people to achieve this roof-raising record at the Butlins Resort in Minehead, Somerset, UK, on 11 Apr 2014.

Making paper aircraft (multiple venues)
Deloitte Southeast Asia Ltd (SGP) organized for 803 people to fold paper planes on 31 Oct 2014 at 10 sites in seven countries, with each group of participants starting at the same moment. In 15 min, 3,067 paper aircraft were folded.

Playing Monopoly
Real-estate agents Cushman & Wakefield (UK) organized for 277 people to play the property board game at their office in London, UK, on 23 Oct 2014. The "Cushopoly" benefited the charity LandAid, which received £2,000 ($3,044) for disadvantaged young people in the UK.

Unwrapping a candy
Kinder Surprise (CAN) arranged for 817 people to open their chocolate eggs at the Canadian National Exhibition in Toronto, Ontario, on 30 Aug 2014.

IN NUMBERS

1,033
Participants in the **largest bra fitting,** by Triumph International Japan Ltd (JPN)

895
Largest gathering of Elvis impersonators, by Harrah's Cherokee Casino Resort (USA)

1,093
Most people dressed in *The Wizard of Oz* costumes, by the Judy Garland Museum and Reece Veatch (both USA)

POW! Bat fans should head over to p.398 for more record-breaking comic-book capers (and to p.50 for *actual* bat records!)

REDUCING POVERTY!

nexen
A CNOOC LIMITED COMPANY

LARGEST DANCES...

	Style	People	Location	Date
1	Line dance (multi venue)	25,703	China (multiple venues)	8 Nov 2014
	Hora	13,828	Slatina, Romania	24 Jan 2006
	Bamboo dance	10,736	Aizawl, Mizoram, India	12 Mar 2010
	Time Warp	8,239	West Hollywood, CA, USA	31 Oct 2010
	Kuchipudi	5,794	Hyderabad, India	25 Dec 2012
2	Thai dance	5,255	Udon Thani, Thailand	18 Jan 2014
	Dabke	5,050	Ras el Matn, Lebanon	7 Aug 2011
	Bollywood dance	4,428	Mumbai, India	1 Mar 2012
	Harlem Shake	3,344	Troy, New York, USA	11 Feb 2013
	Twist	3,040	Pearl, Mississippi, USA	23 Aug 2014
	Pentozali	2,705	Crete, Greece	7 Aug 2010
	Kaikottikali	2,639	Dombivli, Thane, India	9 Nov 2012
3	Peruvian folk dance	2,494	Arequipa, Peru	24 Aug 2014
	Bon dance	1,932	Tochigi, Japan	14 Aug 2001
4	Umbrella dance	1,688	Tottori, Japan	14 Aug 2014
	Highland dance	1,453	Nairn Links, UK	22 Jun 2007
	Fandango	1,146	Córdoba, Colombia	30 Nov 2009

1 2 3 4

MOST PEOPLE...

Roasting marshmallows

On 24 Mar 2012, at the Marion County Park and Lake in Kansas, USA, a total of 1,282 people were counted roasting marshmallows. Ten participants were disqualified after their marshmallows failed to reach the qualified degree of "roastedness" or fell off their sticks, bringing the record to 1,272 people.

Largest gathering of mascots

Converging from schools, companies, towns and cities all over Japan, 376 cute characters opened their very own festival on 23 Nov 2013 in Hanyū, Saitama. The occasion was the fourth annual Yuruchara Summit, at which only the regular mascot of each organization takes part, with no duplicates permitted.

The **largest mascot dance** consisted of 134 mascots choreographed by Huis Ten Bosch Co. Ltd (JPN) at Huis Ten Bosch in Sasebo, Nagasaki, Japan, on 27 Jan 2013.

FACT

The small city of Metropolis in Illinois, USA, is the designated home of Superman – even the badges of its police force sport his image. Every June it hosts the Superman Celebration for c. 30,000 fans.

Group efforts

Mass participation claims at GWR – such as the successful attempt on the most people wearing balloon hats (5,911 in Singapore on 31 Dec 2014, above) – are governed by Records Manager Christopher Lynch (below). Here, Chris talks about the process involved in organizing and ratifying a record.

What makes a successful mass participation event?
Dedication, organization and determination. Organizers must be really focused. There are so many variables – for example, events have to take place in specifically coordinated areas and can require stewarding by a small army of independent volunteers. Then they must follow our guidelines step by step – for measuring the record, the venue, the evidence needed… If they have done all that, awarding a new world record should be a straightforward process.

What are the main reasons for claimants failing to break a record?
Witnesses and stewards are our eyes and ears when an adjudicator isn't present. If there aren't enough of them, or if they can't properly oversee the event, their statements often lack vital information. Sadly, many people apply *after* their attempt, and we can rarely approve these.

Which events have you found particularly impressive?
I'm a fan of the "human image" records. This is where a large number of people form a single, recognizable shape and create some amazing imagery. The **largest human logo image**, for example – a Euro 2004 soccer logo formed in Portugal – contained a total of 34,309 people!

STUNTS & DAREDEVILS

Tom Cruise dangled from the world's **tallest building** when filming *Mission: Impossible – Ghost Protocol* (2011)

First professional film stuntman

Ex-US cavalryman Frank Hanaway (USA) secured the first stunt role, in *The Great Train Robbery* (USA, 1903), owing to his ability to fall off a horse without injuring himself.

Trick rider Helen Gibson (USA) became the **first professional film stuntwoman** when she doubled for Helen Holmes in the film serial *The Hazards of Helen* (USA), released in Nov 1914.

FACT

In the 10 takes of the final sinking scene in *Titanic* (USA, 1997), 100 stunt players had to fall on or along the violently tilting stern, while 1,000 extras were attached to the railings by safety harness.

Longest motorcycle ride through a tunnel of fire

Enrico Schoeman and André de Kock (as pillion, both SA) braved the flames for a scorching 120.4 m (395 ft 0.15 in) in Parys, South Africa, on 5 Sep 2014. Riding a motorcycle and sidecar, they beat their own world record by 17.31 m (56 ft 9 in) at South Africa's largest gathering of motorcyclists, the Rhino Rally.

Don't try this at home

Hazardous records are fascinating to read about, but they should only be performed by trained professionals. Any such record attempts are strictly for those with appropriate experience and skills.

Shortest stuntman

Kiran Shah (UK) stands 1 m 26.3 cm (4 ft 1.7 in) tall, and has performed stunts in 31 of the 52 movies he has appeared in since 1976. On 30 Apr 2010, he became the shortest person to wing walk, on a 1940s Boeing biplane, at 984 ft (300 m).

Highest jump without a parachute on film

Doubling for Burt Reynolds in *Hooper* (USA, 1978), A J Bakunas (USA) jumped from 232 ft (70.7 m) on to an air mattress.

The **highest stunt free-fall on film** was by Dar Robinson (USA) in *Highpoint* (CAN, 1982). He leapt 335 m (1,100 ft) from a ledge on the CN Tower in Toronto, Canada, then the tallest free-standing structure. His parachute opened 300 ft (91 m) from the ground after six seconds of free-falling.

Most expensive aerial stunt in a movie

Simon Crane (UK) made a one-off, hazardous transit between two jets at 15,000 ft (4,572 m) for *Cliffhanger* (USA, 1993). The super-high-risk stunt cost $1 million (£568,000).

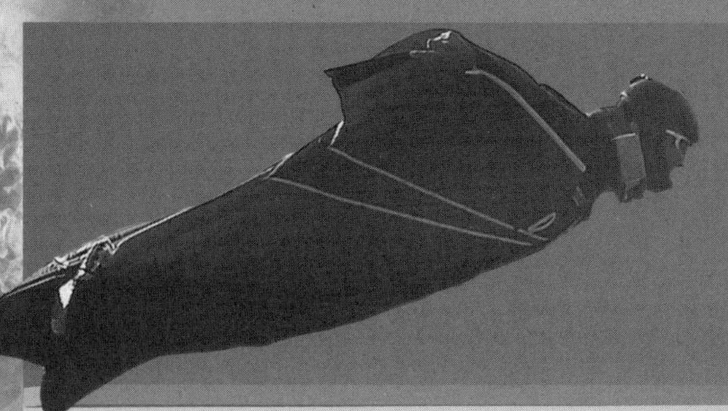

First skydive without a parachute

On 23 May 2012, wing-suited stuntman Gary Connery (UK) jumped from a helicopter at 2,400 ft (732 m) above Oxfordshire, UK, landing safely on a pile of 18,600 cardboard boxes. At the 2012 London Olympic Games, Gary won fame by jumping out of a helicopter dressed as Queen Elizabeth II.

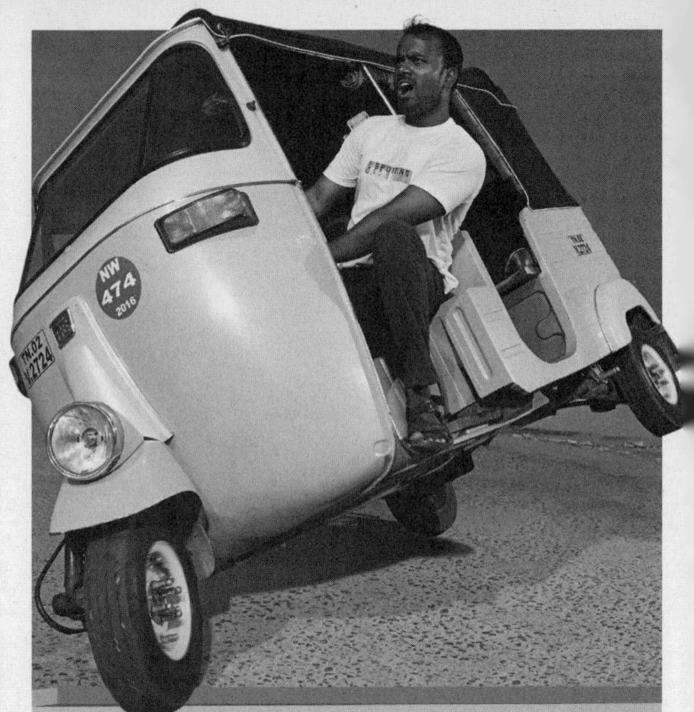

Farthest distance side-wheel driving on a motor tricycle

On 17 Feb 2011, Jagathish M (IND) drove his tilting autorickshaw for 2.2 km (1.4 mi) at the Juhu Aerodrome in Mumbai, India, for the reality TV show *Guinness World Records – Ab India Todega*. Jagathish, 27 years old, is a tuk-tuk driver in Chennai, Tamil Nadu, India.

Largest breakaway glass structure smashed by a car

On 13 Sep 2011, 67-year-old stuntman Rocky Taylor (UK, see p.218) drove through a 23.91-m^2 (257.36-sq-ft) glass structure for Remember A Charity (UK) at The O2 Arena in London, UK.

Most stunts by a living actor

Hong Kong actor, director, writer and producer Jackie Chan is also his own stuntman. He has starred in more than 100 films since 1972, including the *Rush Hour* series (USA, 1998–2007). Along the way he has broken his nose three times, both cheekbones, most of his fingers and his skull.

Longest speedboat jump in a film

In *Live and Let Die* (UK, 1973), Jerry Comeaux (USA), as James Bond, was at the wheel of a 1972 Glastron GT-150 speedboat during a chase through Louisiana's bayou. The 120-ft (36.5-m) jump over a road was rehearsed over 100 times with 26 boats before being filmed.

Most cars driven on two wheels simultaneously

On 26 Nov 2000, a continuous line of 16 cars was driven on two wheels by a team of Renault drivers at Évreux, France. The stunt was filmed for the TV show *L'émission des records*, aired on 23 Dec 2000.

On 14 Nov 2014, in Chongqing, China, Han Yue (CHN) and Zhang Shengjun (TPE), in a Mini five-door Hatch and BMW M4 Coupé, drove the **most donuts (spins) around a car driving on two wheels in one minute**: 10 in all.

First double loop by a car

On 16 Jun 2012, Gary Hoptrough (UK) completed two 8-m-diameter (26-ft) 360° loops on the TV show *Top Gear Live* in Durban, South Africa.

Fastest speed for a car driven blindfolded

On 13 Aug 2014, at Elvington airfield in North Yorkshire, UK, Mike Newman (UK) drove blindfolded at 200.51 mph (322.69 km/h) – the average of two runs in opposite directions. His vehicle was a 1200-bhp Nissan GT-R, modified by Litchfield Motors (UK). Mr Newman followed strict record requirements yet, more amazingly, has been blind since the age of eight.

IN NUMBERS

87
Stuntmen in the Clint Eastwood film *The Rookie* (USA, 1990), which had only 37 actors: the **largest ratio of stuntmen to actors** in a movie

32
Most mounts/dismounts from a moving horse in one minute

65 ft
Motorbike jump (19.8 m), over barbed wire, made by Bud Ekins as Steve McQueen in the movie *The Great Escape* (USA, 1963)

134
Most steps tumbled down in a stunt fall, by Joaquín Ortega (ESP) on 17 Nov 2006

10,000
Blank rounds used in filming the final shoot-out in *The Wild Bunch* (USA, 1969)

Rocky Taylor

Turning 70 years old on 28 Feb 2015, Rocky Taylor (UK, above) has had the longest career as a stuntman. He is also the first stuntman to double for two James Bonds in one year: Roger Moore in *Octopussy* and Sean Connery in *Never Say Never Again* (both USA, 1983).

How did you get into the stunt world?

My father Larry Taylor was a stuntman/actor – so that was one reason. I was a judo black belt at 17, and was asked to teach Cliff Richard some judo throws for *The Young Ones* (UK, 1961). I doubled for him in the film, and that was my debut.

And parts followed on from there?

They did. I worked on the British TV series *The Avengers* for five years, doubling for leading man Patrick Macnee. I doubled for Peter Cook in *Monte Carlo or Bust!* (1969), in which I drove down the Cresta Run – one of my most exciting moments. I've worked on 14 Bond films, including 12 for Sean Connery. I also doubled for Sean in *Indiana Jones and the Last Crusade* (USA, 1989, below).

Have you had any significant injuries?

I've broken about 14 bones. And on *Death Wish 3* (1985), I had a bad accident. I was 40 years old and was out of action for five years. But it didn't make me more worried about doing stunts.

What's most important in your work?

Safety is paramount and I'm known for preparing very carefully. That's why I prefer to be called an action technician than a stuntman. That said, if you don't shake before you start a job, you shouldn't be doing it!

When will you retire?

When the phone stops ringing... I've given my all but I still want to keep on. I'm also writing my autobiography, with Jon Auty. It's called *I Just Fell into It*.

Longest ramp jump by a truck and trailer

On 6 Nov 2014, stuntman Mike Ryan (USA), on behalf of EMC Corp and the Lotus F1 Team, "flew" his hefty transporter 83 ft 7 in (25.48 m) – just more than the width of an Olympic swimming pool – at Bentwaters Park in Suffolk, UK. The truck and trailer jumped from a 5-ft-high (1.5-m) ramp at 70 mph (113 km/h). While the combo was in mid-air, stunt driver Martin Ivanov (RUS) drove a Lotus F1 car underneath.

Actor Tom Hanks collects **vintage typewriters**; actress Demi Moore collects **vintage dolls**

Airline boarding passes

K Ullas Kamath's (IND) collection of boarding passes has truly taken off. He had 3,030 of them by 15 Aug 2014.

Board games

Jeff Bauspies (USA) owned 1,531 different board games as of 19 Aug 2011. He began collecting in 2000.

"Do Not Disturb" signs

Sssh! As of 7 Mar 2014, Rainer Weichert (DEU) had amassed 11,570 "Do Not Disturb" signs.

Duck tape (duct tape)

Stick to your dreams. That's what Selea Nielsen (USA) did. As of 1 Feb 2014, she had 189 rolls of duck tape. Selea even used her tape to make prom outfits for herself and her date!

Batman memorabilia

As of 25 Oct 2013, Kevin Silva of Indianapolis, Indiana, USA, had amassed 2,501 Batman-related items. Kevin has been collecting Batman gear for more than 45 years – his first piece was a Batman lunchbox, bought for him as a child. His favourite item – and probably his most expensive piece – is an outfit modelled on that worn by Adam West in the 1960s *Batman* TV series (pictured).

Harry Potter memorabilia

With seven best-selling books and eight blockbuster movies, it's little wonder that the Boy Wizard has conjured up a wealth of merchandise too. Nobody has collected more of it than Menahem Asher Silva Vargas (MEX), who is even known as Menahem Potter to his friends. As of 5 Nov 2013, he had 3,097 unique items, including figurines, soft toys, cauldrons, wands and even his very own Sorting Hat!

FACT

Menahem's favourite item is a wall plaque with an image of the Chamber of Secrets. It was made out of recycled materials by his mother, who gave it to him as a gift on Children's Day.

Hamburger-related items

As of 20 Sep 2014, "Hamburger Harry" (aka Harry Sperl, DEU) owned 3,724 hamburger-related items, including two burger beds and a burger waterbed.

Scooby Doo memorabilia

Zoinks! As of 31 Aug 2014, Rebecca Findlay (CAN) owned 1,116 Scooby Doo items, including movies, figurines, comics, puzzles, posters, games, fast-food toys and a full-size pinball machine. Her collection was verified in West Vancouver, British Columbia, Canada.

Horseshoes

Moldovan Petru Costin is one lucky man: his collection of horseshoes – traditionally a talisman of good fortune – had reached the 3,200 mark by 21 May 2011.

Keychains

Spain's Josep Andreu Amorós Pérez has no excuse when he loses his keys – as of 1 Apr 2012, he owned 47,200 different keychains.

Masks

Since 1957, Gerold Weschenmoser (DEU) has travelled widely in search of masks; as of 3 Mar 2013, he had 5,600 unique items, displayed in his museum in Starzach, Germany.

Mugs

Bob Thomson (USA) has collected 6,352 different mugs since 1995.

IN NUMBERS

1,500
Largest PlayStation collection, by Jason Dvorak (USA)

2,383
Largest collection of *Tomb Raider* memorabilia, by Rodrigo Martin Santos (ESP)

2,723
Largest collection of *Street Fighter* memorabilia, by Clarence Lim (CAN)

5,441
Largest collection of *Super Mario* memorabilia, by Mitsugu Kikai (JPN)

10,607
Largest videogame collection, by Michael Thomasson (USA)

14,410
Largest collection of *Pokémon* memorabilia, by Lisa Courtney (UK)

17,000
Largest videogame screenshot collection, by Rikardo Granda (COL)

GIANT TOY BOX – THE LARGEST COLLECTION OF...

	Model cars	27,777	Nabil Karam (LBN)	17 Nov 2011
1	**Barbie dolls**	15,000	Bettina Dorfmann (DEU)	10 Oct 2011
2	**Fast-food restaurant toys**	10,000	Percival R Lugue (PHL)	4 Nov 2014
3	**Smurf memorabilia**	6,320	Gerda P Scheuers (USA)	4 Jun 2014
	Rubber ducks	5,631	Charlotte Lee (USA)	10 Apr 2011
	Snowmen	5,127	Karen Schmidt (USA)	19 Mar 2013
	Yo-yos	4,586	John "Lucky" Meisenheimer (USA)	22 Feb 2010
	Trolls	2,990	Sherry Groom (USA)	26 Oct 2012
	Mr Men memorabilia	2,225	Joanne Black (UK)	23 May 2006
	Gnomes and pixies	2,042	Ann Atkin (UK)	25 Mar 2011
	Model motorcycles	1,258	David Correia (USA)	24 May 2012
	Wind-up toys	1,042	William Keuntje (USA)	26 Nov 2011
	Toy soldiers	661	Sergey Valentinovich Spasov (RUS)	3 Aug 2010

1

2

3

Snail shells (single species)

Slowly does it. By 13 Sep 2014, Belgium's Patrick Huyskens (BEL) had amassed 10,368 shells – subdivided by colour, height, markings and size – from the species *Cepaea nemoralis*.

Stickers

Nidhi Bansal (IND) started her sticker collection in 2007 and owned 102,317 by 16 Sep 2013.

Xbox games (PAL region)

Game on! Neil Fenton (UK) had collected 814 PAL-region Xbox games by 16 Jun 2014.

Zebra-related items

Wendy Jarnet (NZ) owned 508 zebra-esque items as of 28 Mar 2014. Her favourite? A plastic wind-up toy that bobs its head, spins its tail and jumps up and down when wound up.

Nintendo paraphernalia

Police officer Ahmed Bin Fahad of Dubai, UAE, had accumulated 2,020 miscellaneous Nintendo items as of 12 Nov 2014. This total comprises 170 consoles and portable devices, 23 games accessories, 591 NES games, 681 Famicom games, 145 GameCube games, 207 DS games, 155 Wii games and 48 Wii U games. The collection hasn't come cheap, though; Bin Fahad estimates that he has spent around 1.5 million dirhams (£270,000; $408,000) on his passion.

FACT

"It is a very expensive hobby," admitted Ahmed, "but I wanted to… give a message to the world that Arabs are not only interested in speeding cars and flashy things."

Collecting GWR

One way into GWR is to collect GWR! Martyn Tovey (UK) holds records for both the largest collection of GWR annuals (353) and the largest collection of GWR memorabilia (2,164). We invited him to our London HQ (above) to find out more…

When did you start your collections?

I received my first *Guinness Book of Records* as a school prize in 1968, and have been given the latest edition as a Christmas present every year since 1971. I started collecting GWR memorabilia about 10 years ago. Guinness World Records toys, games, spin-off publications, novelty items and promotional material have all been produced since the early 1960s.

And what made you start?

I had a childhood obsession with facts and figures. The books gave me a fantastic reference guide, which was updated with the latest data every year.

Which is your favourite piece?

My favourite would have to be a 1960 edition with handwritten corrections by [then editor] Norris McWhirter.

Where do you keep all this stuff?

It used to fill shelves, cupboards and boxes all over the house, but it's now mostly in storage.

Do you have a favourite GWR record?

That would have to be Bob Beamon's world-record long jump at the Mexico Olympics in 1968 [8.90 m; 29 ft 2.5 in – still a current Olympic record]. I can still remember my amazement at such an astonishing feat.

MOST EXPENSIVE...

Worth more than its weight in gold, the spice **saffron** has been used as a dye, a perfume and even as a **cure for melancholy**!

Autographed object

The most expensive signed object is a 1789 custom-bound leather edition of the *Acts of Congress of the United States of America* signed by George Washington. Annotated by the first US president himself, the book contains America's Constitution and Bill of Rights. It was sold by Christie's in New York, USA, on 22 Jun 2012, to Ann Bookout (of the Mount Vernon Ladies' Association), who spent $9,826,500 (£6,269,940) on the volume.

Putting aside specific signed objects and individual sums spent, the most *valuable* autographs are tracked by the 2014 PFC40 – an index that monitors the 40 most sought-after autographs currently traded on the open market. Averaging at £3,750 ($5,874), the **most valuable signed photograph of a living person** is that of Cuba's Fidel Castro, while the **most valuable signed photograph** overall is that of actor James Dean (USA, 1931–55). "Best-quality" examples of Dean's autograph command an average price of £18,000 ($28,200).

Car sold at auction

A 1962 Ferrari 250 GTO Berlinetta two-seater coupé (below) sold for $38,115,000 (£22.8 m), including premium, at Bonhams' Quail Lodge Auction in Carmel, California, USA, on 14 Aug 2014. The sale of the previous record holder was also overseen by Bonhams: a 1954 Mercedes-Benz W196 R F1 Racer that fetched £19,601,500 ($29.6 m) on 12 Jul 2013. Of the 10 most expensive cars ever auctioned, eight of them have been Ferraris.

For those with more modest budgets, the Jaguar XJ13 within the PlayStation 3 game *Gran Turismo 6* (Polyphony Digital, 2013, inset left) is the **most expensive virtual car** – it costs $196 (£119.95) in real-world cash.

FACT

The year 2016 marks the 250th anniversary of the auction house Christie's. It was founded by James Christie (UK) in London. Today it holds 450 auctions every year and has 12 salerooms globally.

Hot dog

Requiring two weeks' notice to prepare, the "Juuni Ban" contains a 12-in (30-cm) smoked cheese bratwurst, Wagyu beef, maitake mushrooms, teriyaki grilled onions, foie gras, shaved black truffle, caviar and Japanese mayonnaise, all served in a brioche bun. This wallet-busting hot dog retails at $169 (£101) and is sold by mobile caterer Tokyo Dog (USA) in Seattle, Washington, USA.

Book

On 26 Nov 2013, a copy of the Bay Psalm Book was sold at Sotheby's in New York City, USA, for $14.2 m (£8.7 m). Dating from 1640, the Bay Psalm Book was the first book ever printed in British North America. Just 1,700 copies were produced by the residents of the Massachusetts Bay Colony. The book sold at Sotheby's was one of 11 surviving copies, and was purchased by US businessman David Rubenstein.

Letter

On 10 Apr 2013, Christie's in New York City, USA, sold a letter written by Francis Crick in 1953 to his son Michael, outlining the revolutionary discovery of the structure and function of DNA, for $6,098,500 (£3,964,025).

Sandwich

As of 29 Oct 2014, the Quintessential Grilled Cheese sold for $214 (£132) at Serendipity 3 in New York City, USA. It comprises two slices of French Pullman bread made with Dom Pérignon champagne and dipped in edible gold flakes.

Painting

- **Ever:** In Feb 2015, *Nafea Faa Ipoipo* (*When Will You Marry?*, 1892) by Paul Gauguin (FRA) reportedly sold in private sale for £197 m ($299.8 m), beating *The Card Players* (1890s) by Paul Cézanne (FRA), which sold in 2011 to Qatar's royal family for $250 m (£158.3 m).
- **At auction:** *Les femmes d'Alger (Version O)* by Pablo Picasso (ESP), dated 14 Feb 1955, sold for $179.3 m (£115 m), including commission of just over 12%, at an auction held by Christie's in New York City, USA, on 11 May 2015.
- **By a living artist (private sale):** *Flag* (1958) by Jasper Johns (USA) was sold to hedge-fund billionaire Steven A Cohen in 2010 for a reported $110 m (then £73 m).
- **By a living artist at auction:** *Abstraktes Bild* (1986) by Gerhard Richter (DEU) sold for £30,389,000 ($46.3 m) at Sotheby's in London, UK, on 10 Feb 2015.
- **By Claude Monet:** *Le Grand Canal* (1908) was sold at Sotheby's in London, UK, on 3 Feb 2015 for £23,669,000 ($35,567,406).

Dalek

The now-defunct UK advertising agency Indeprod paid £36,000 ($61,934) in 2005 for this restored Dalek Supreme. It was first seen on TV in *Doctor Who* (BBC) in the 1970s and made its last appearance in the 1985 story "Revelation of the Daleks".

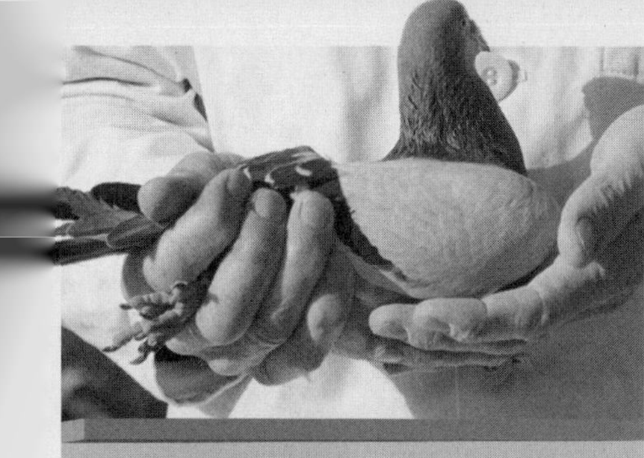

Pigeon

On 18 May 2013, pigeon breeder Leo Heremans (BEL) sold his racing pigeon Bolt (above), named after sprinter Usain Bolt, for €310,000 (£260,000; $400,000) at auction.

The **most expensive duck** (inset right), a Muscovy drake called Big Dave, sold for £1,500 ($2,400) at auction in Oswestry, Shropshire, UK, on 21 Oct 2012. He is seen here with his former owner Graham R Hicks.

- **By Georgia O'Keeffe:** *Jimson Weed: White Flower No. 1* (1932) realized $44.4 m (£28 m) at Sotheby's in New York, USA, on 20 Nov 2014 – the **most expensive painting by a female artist**.
- **By Rembrandt van Rijn:** *Portrait of a Lady, Aged 62* (1632) achieved £19,803,750 ($28,675,830) at Christie's in London, UK, on 13 Dec 2000.
- **By J M W Turner:** *Rome, from Mount Aventine* (1835) sold for £30.3 m ($47.4 m) at Sotheby's in London, UK, on 3 Dec 2014.
- **By Vincent van Gogh:** *Portrait of Doctor Gachet* (1890) achieved $82.5 m (£49 m) at Christie's in New York City, USA, on 15 May 1990.

IN NUMBERS

600
Precious stones inlaid in the **most expensive pen sold at auction**

£1,024
Cost per slice of the **most expensive meat pie** ($1,781)

666-6666
Most expensive mobile phone number; sold in Qatar in 2006 for 10 m QAR (then £1.46 m/$2.75 m)

12 km²
Area of the Palmyra Atoll, south of Hawaii, the **most expensive island** (4.6 sq mi)

467
Pieces in the **most expensive jigsaw puzzle sold at auction**, securing $27,000 (£14,589) in 2005

60 years
Age of the **most expensive spirit**: a malt whisky offered at Fortnum & Mason department store in London, UK, for £11,000 ($15,662)

Time is money

The *Henry Graves Jr Supercomplication* was auctioned by Sotheby's in 2014 and fetched 23.22 m Swiss francs (£15.1 m; $24 m) – to this day the **most expensive watch sold at auction.**

Commissioned from Patek Philippe by US banker and art lover Henry Graves Jr, the watch took seven years to make (1925–32) – hardly surprising, given that it was then the most complicated watch made solely by hand. Master watchmakers, mathematicians and astronomers worked together to create 24 horological "complications" (features that do more than just display the hours and minutes).

They incorporated multiple timekeeping functions, calendar and chronograph (stopwatch) features, four varieties of chime and a celestial chart for the night sky of New York City at 40°41'N Lat. – the exact position of Graves's apartment overlooking Central Park.

Enclosed in a gold case that itself took five years to make, the watch weighed in at 535 g (1 lb 3 oz). Its 920 components included 430 screws, 120 mechanical levers, 110 wheels and 70 jewels.

Graves paid 60,000 Swiss francs (£3,540; $15,000) for this beautifully complex one-off. After his death, it passed to his daughter Gwendolen, who in turn gave it to her son, Reginald Fullerton. In 1969, he sold the *Supercomplication* to Seth Atwood, watch collector and founder of the Time Museum in Rockford, Illinois, USA.

ACTUAL SIZE

Musical instrument

The "Lady Blunt" Stradivarius violin (1721) was sold by Tarisio Auctions for £9,808,000 ($15,875,800) in London, UK, on 20 Jun 2011. The auction was organized online on behalf of the Nippon Music Foundation and the proceeds went to the Northeastern Japan Earthquake and Tsunami Relief Fund. The authenticity of the violin was certified by the firm W E Hill & Sons.

MODERN WORLD

Largest outbreak of Ebola

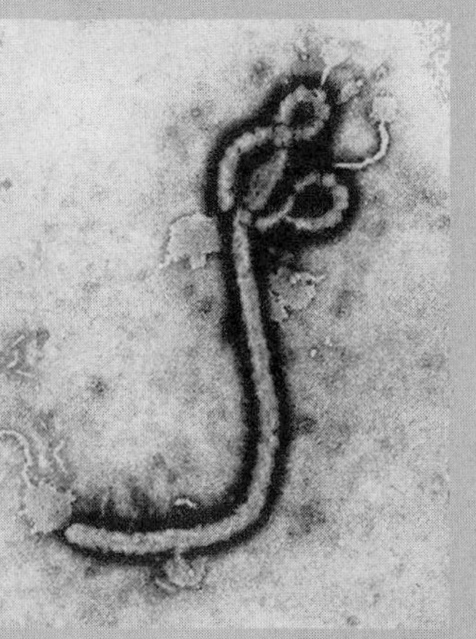

On 23 Mar 2014, the World Health Organization (WHO) announced an outbreak of Ebola virus disease (EVD) in Guinea, Liberia and Sierra Leone in West Africa. As of 15 Apr 2015, the WHO reported that EVD had claimed 10,689 lives and there were 25,791 confirmed and suspected cases. Measures to control the virus (right) include improved burial practices and strict hygiene protocols, as well as the use of full protective equipment. In the picture on the following page, a health worker sprays disinfectant outside a mosque in Bamako, Mali, on 14 Nov 2014, after a Guinean imam, suspected of dying from EVD, had been washed there before burial.

CONTENTS

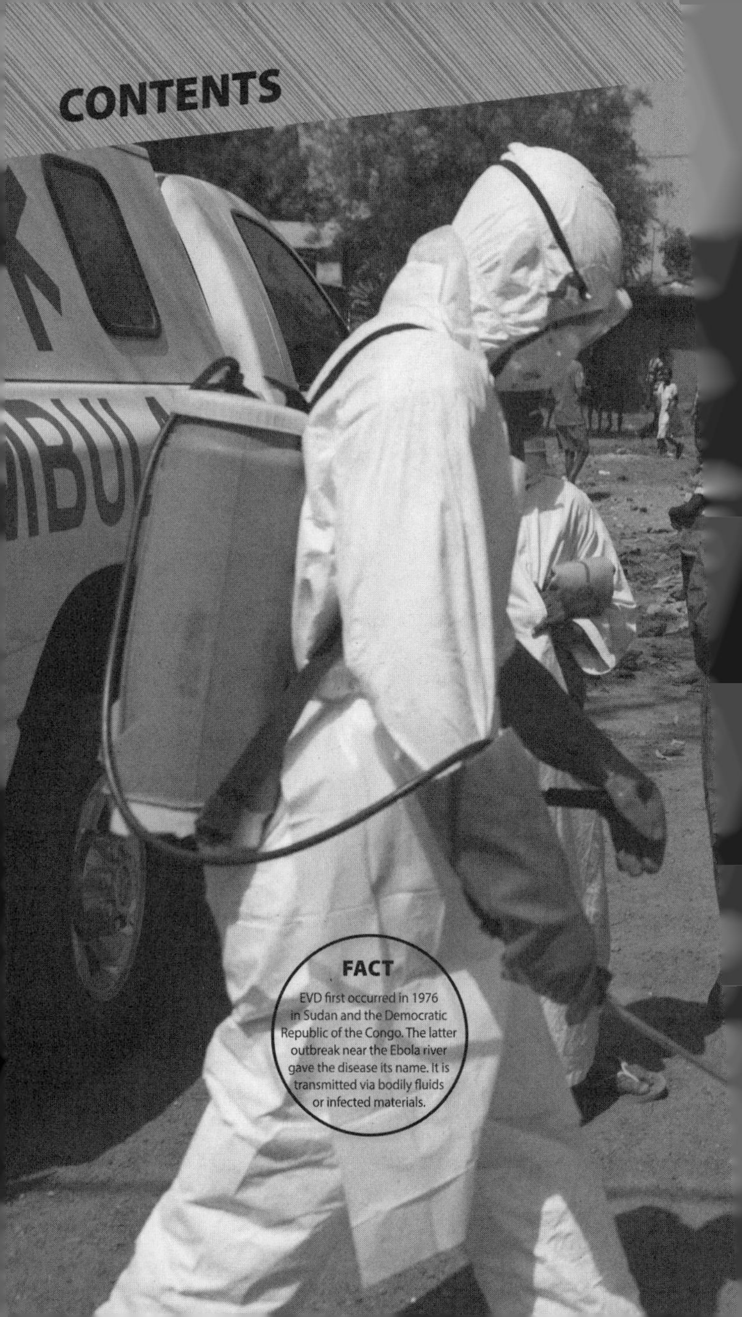

FACT

EVD first occurred in 1976 in Sudan and the Democratic Republic of the Congo. The latter outbreak near the Ebola river gave the disease its name. It is transmitted via bodily fluids or infected materials.

IN FOCUS
HIGHEST EARNERS

In 2014, e-commerce magnate **Jack Ma** made more money than the GDPs of **Iceland and The Bahamas** combined!

The rich get richer; at least that's how the saying goes. And when it comes to the world's wealthiest people, the expression seems to hold true, with just three of the planet's 7-billion population – Bill Gates (USA, see p.237), Carlos Slim Helú (MEX) and Warren Buffett (USA) – vying for the title of **richest person** for the last 20 years.

While net worth is one measure of wealth, an alternative gauge is annual income. This tends to be far more changeable than a person's total assets, where inheritance passes down through the generations and money is generally invested across a range of sectors for damage limitation.

The top earners in a given industry, on the other hand, are more governed by that year's workload or performance – whether that's number of movies made, commercial endorsements signed or tournaments won. The savviest of the world's top earners, though, have taken a leaf out of the realms of commerce and investment, understanding the benefits of diversification.

Super salaries of 2014

Here we pick out some of the year's top earners and their key sources of income…

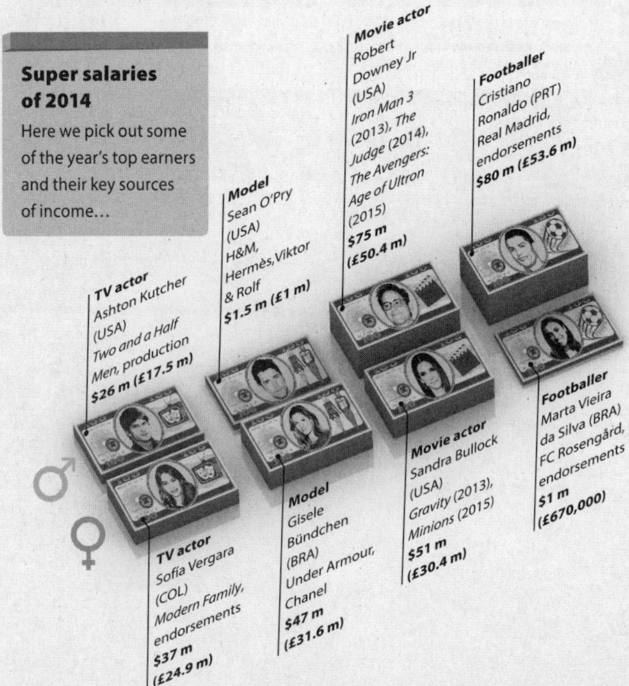

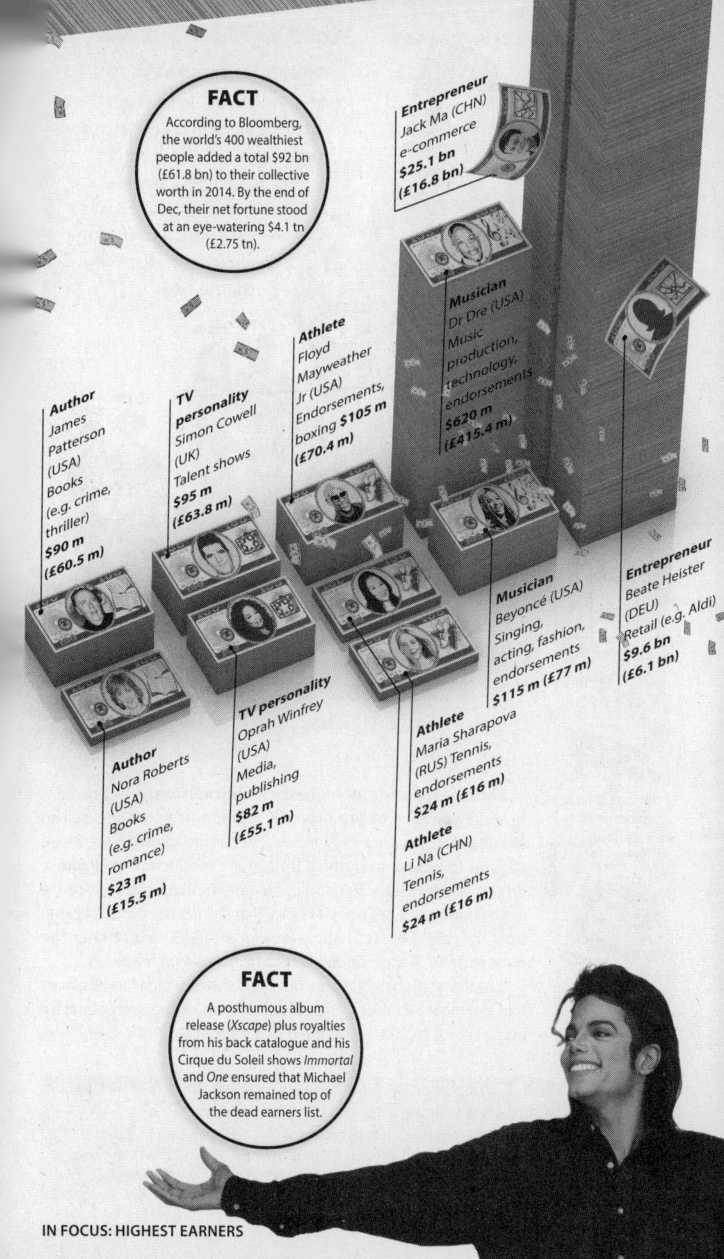
FACT
According to Bloomberg, the world's 400 wealthiest people added a total $92 bn (£61.8 bn) to their collective worth in 2014. By the end of Dec, their net fortune stood at an eye-watering $4.1 tn (£2.75 tn).
Entrepreneur
Jack Ma (CHN)
e-commerce
$25.1 bn
(£16.8 bn)
Musician
Dr Dre (USA)
Music production, technology, endorsements
$620 m
(£415.4 m)
Athlete
Floyd Mayweather Jr (USA)
Endorsements, boxing $105 m
(£70.4 m)
TV personality
Simon Cowell
(UK)
Talent shows
$95 m
(£63.8 m)
Author
James Patterson
(USA)
Books (e.g. crime, thriller)
$90 m
(£60.5 m)
Musician
Beyoncé (USA)
Singing, acting, fashion, endorsements
$115 m (£77 m)
Entrepreneur
Beate Heister
(DEU)
Retail (e.g. Aldi)
$9.6 bn
(£6.1 bn)
TV personality
Oprah Winfrey
(USA)
Media, publishing
$82 m
(£55.1 m)
Athlete
Maria Sharapova
(RUS) Tennis, endorsements
$24 m (£16 m)
Author
Nora Roberts
(USA)
Books (e.g. crime, romance)
$23 m
(£15.5 m)
Athlete
Li Na (CHN)
Tennis, endorsements
$24 m (£16 m)
FACT
A posthumous album release (*Xscape*) plus royalties from his back catalogue and his Cirque du Soleil shows *Immortal* and *One* ensured that Michael Jackson remained top of the dead earners list.

Double your money!

Of course, two A-listers boast twice the earning potential of a single celebrity. These are the top four highest-earning Hollywood couples, based on 2014 data, as well as the proportion each spouse contributed.

34% 66% $175 m

59% 41% $79.8 m

52% 48% $58 m

62% 38% $47 m

1. Beyoncé & Jay Z
2. Gisele Bündchen & Tom Brady
3. Kim Kardashian & Kanye West
4. Angelina Jolie & Brad Pitt

For instance, while the **highest-earning musician** – Dr Dre (USA, b. Andre Young) – made his name in hip-hop, he hasn't released an album of his own since 1999. Instead, he has broadened his revenue streams to include everything from music production to alcoholic drinks, and the Beats Electronics headphones company. Indeed, a large chunk of the $620 m (£415.4 m) that Dre amassed in 2014 came from the sale of Beats to Apple for a reported $3 bn (£1.8 bn) – the most expensive acquisition the tech giant has ever made.

The illustration on the previous page shows which famous faces had the most lucrative 2014. For some context, the average salary in the UK is £26,500, and in the USA it's about $53,900.

Jack Ma's shopping list

King of internet retail in China, Jack Ma (see opposite, top) was 2014's highest earner, seeing his wealth grow by more than $25 bn (£16.8 bn). Here's a few things you could buy with that mind-boggling sum of cash…

17 x Buckingham Palace

62 x Cullinan diamond

190 x Gareth Bale

11,333 x Bugatti Veyron

31.5 million x iPhone 6

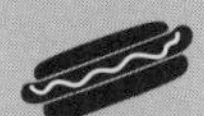

147.9 million x **most expensive hotdog** (see p.225)

850 million x *GWR* book

26.7 billion x 1st-class stamp (UK)

Highest-earning entrepreneur

Jack Ma (CHN) netted $25.1 bn (£16.8 bn) in 2014. He is the founder and executive chairman of the Alibaba Group, which dominates e-commerce in China, owning two of the most-visited websites: Taobao and Tmall (see pp.374–75). As of 8 Apr 2015, he is Asia's richest man, worth $35.4 bn (£23.7 bn), according to Bloomberg.

Pampered pets

Humans aren't the only ones clawing in cash on an epic scale – animals sometimes strike it rich too.

The **wealthiest dog** was a standard poodle called Toby, who received a legacy of $15 m (£10.5 m) from his owner Ella Wendel of New York, USA, in 1931. Adjusted for inflation, that equates to some $233 m (£156.4 m) in today's money. Toby continued to live in Ms Wendel's Fifth Avenue mansion after her death; there, he was looked after by three servants until his own death 18 months later.

The **wealthiest cat**, Blackie, was bequeathed £7 m ($12.5 m) in 1988 by his owner Ben Rea (UK). An antiques dealer, Rea split the lion's share of his fortune between Blackie – the last surviving of 15 cats he lived with – and three feline charities, leaving nothing to his relatives.

Sources: Bloomberg, BusinessInsider.com, Doximity, Finance.yahoo.com, Forbes, IBTimes.com, OECD, Office for National Statistics, Paywizard.org, Spotrac.com, Statista, Unicef

Fictional fortunes

Who are the richest characters from fiction? Here are Forbes' top five in 2013…

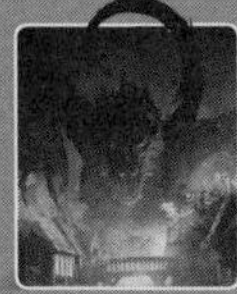

Scrooge McDuck	Smaug	Carlisle Cullen	Tony Stark	Charles Foster Kane
Disney's *DuckTales*	*The Hobbit*	*Twilight*	*Iron Man/The Avengers*	*Citizen Kane*
Treasure hunting	Plundering	Investment	Defence/energy	Media
$65.4 bn (£43.9 bn)	**$54.1 bn (£36.3 bn)**	**$46 bn (£30.9 bn)**	**$12.4 bn (£8.3 bn)**	**$11.2 bn (£7.5 bn)**

DEAD RICH – HIGHEST ANNUAL EARNERS *POST MORTEM* 2014

Name	Profession	Died	Income
Michael Jackson (USA)	Musician	2009	$140 m (£115 m)
Elvis Presley (USA)	Musician	1977	$55 m (£45 m)
Charles M Schulz (USA)	Cartoonist	2000	$40 m (£33 m)
Elizabeth Taylor (UK/USA)	Actress	2011	$25 m (£20 m)
Bob Marley (JAM)	Musician	1981	$20 m (£16 m)
Marilyn Monroe (USA)	Actress	1962	$17 m (£14 m)
John Lennon (UK)	Musician	1980	$12 m (£10 m)
Albert Einstein (DEU/USA)	Scientist	1955	$11 m (£9 m)
Theodor Geisel (USA)	Author	1991	=$9 m (£7 m)
Bruce Lee (HKG/USA)	Actor	1973	=$9 m (£7 m)
Steve McQueen (USA)	Actor	1980	=$9 m (£7 m)
Bettie Page (USA)	Model	2008	=$9 m (£7 m)
James Dean (USA)	Actor	1955	$7 m (£6 m)

Source: Forbes, June 2014

Disposable income mapped

Celebrity incomes are a different ball-game to "normal" salaries. The Organisation for Economic Co-operation and Development (OECD) monitors developed and emerging economies – currently 36 countries, and counting – as part of its Better Life Index. The graphic below represents the top five nations with the highest average household net-adjusted disposable income per capita. For context, the OECD's average annual disposable income is $23,938 (£16,054).

Based on 2014 World Bank data, the **largest GDP** (USA) is **441,265 times** the **smallest GDP** (Tuvalu)

Most followers on LinkedIn

Recognizing the business benefits of maintaining a high profile on social media, British entrepreneur Sir Richard Branson (UK) had a total of 7,481,536 followers as of 16 Feb 2015. Learn about his more unorthodox PR tactics on p.467.

Branson isn't the only mogul getting in on the social media action. Microsoft's Bill Gates was the **most popular entrepreneur on Twitter**, with 20,027,447 followers as of 11 Feb 2015.

Most corrupt country

According to the independent anti-corruption organization Transparency International, in 2014 Somalia and North Korea were the joint holders of this nefarious title.

Based on its clean business and political practices, Denmark was declared to be the **least corrupt country**, closely followed by New Zealand and Finland.

Richest investor

The second richest American in Forbes' Rich List was businessman and CEO of multinational holding company Berkshire Hathaway, Warren Buffett (aka the "Sage of Omaha"), who was aged 84 in Mar 2015. His wealth stood at an estimated $72.7 bn (£47.6 bn).

Richest woman

One of several members of the Walton family to reap Walmart's profits, Christy Walton (USA) was worth $41.7 bn (£27.3 bn), according to Forbes, as of Mar 2015. This put her ahead of L'Oréal owner Liliane Bettencourt (FRA) with $40.1 bn (£26.3 bn).

Richest man

Technology magnate Bill Gates (USA) topped Forbes' Rich List yet again, with an estimated fortune of $79.2 bn (£51.9 bn) by Mar 2015.

He was also 2014's highest donor, according to *The Chronicle of Philanthropy*, giving $9.8 bn (£6.4 bn) to charity.

Largest company by sales

In 2014, retail giant Walmart – partly owned by the **richest woman** (see p.237) – earned a staggering $476.5 bn (£312.1 bn), putting it in front of Royal Dutch Shell, which made "just" $451.4 bn (£295.7 bn) in the same year.

Richest media tycoon

Former Mayor of New York and now owner of the eponymous financial media company, Michael Bloomberg (USA) was worth $35.5 bn (£23.3 bn) in Mar 2015.

LARGEST...

Corporate fine

Two years after the *Deepwater Horizon* oil spill, which released millions of barrels' worth of crude oil into the Gulf of Mexico in 2010, the US Justice Department instructed BP to pay the National Fish and Wildlife Foundation $2.4 bn (£1.5 bn), in addition to a criminal fine of $1.26 bn (£790 m).

FACT

With a $17.6-tn (£11.5-tn) output, China had the **largest economy** in 2014, according to the IMF. Figures are based on purchasing power parity (PPP), which takes regional cost of living into account.

Most expensive office location

A 2014 report by real estate company Cushman & Wakefield revealed that office space in London, UK, costs $271.61 (£164.70) per square foot annually, or $2,923.61 (£1,772.83) per square metre. In second place was Hong Kong at $183.32 (£111.16) per square foot, and Moscow came third at $139.80 (£84.77) per square foot.

First gold-dispensing ATM

Ex Oriente Lux AG (DEU) launched its "GOLD to go" machines in May 2010. Although initially trialled in Germany, the first gold ATM available to the public was installed at the Emirates Palace hotel in Abu Dhabi, UAE. It offers 24-karat bars, weighing 1, 5 or 10 g (0.04, 0.18 or 0.35 oz), as well as gold coins.

The case remains under investigation, however, and as of Dec 2014, BP's fine was still expanding, with the total liability rising to $61 bn (£40 bn) after a judge ruled that BP had been guilty of gross negligence.

Advertising agency

According to the *Financial Times*, British company WPP is the world's biggest advertising agency, with 179,000 staff, 3,000 offices across 111 countries and $11 bn (£6.7 bn) in earnings during 2013. By the third quarter of 2014, WPP had grossed $4.48 bn (£2.76 bn).

Company by assets

In 2014, the US mortgage lender Fannie Mae possessed $3,270.1 bn (£2,147.7 bn) in assets. The Industrial and Commercial Bank of China – the world's **largest bank** – was not far behind, with $3,124.9 bn (£2,052.2 bn) in assets.

HIGHEST...

Economic growth

Based on World Bank data, Paraguay was the fastest-growing country in 2012–13. The South American nation's economy grew by 14.2%, just ahead of South Sudan with an increase of 13.1%. It was an amazing development for South Sudan – the **newest independent country** – which came last in 2011–12.

IN NUMBERS

$107 bn
Brand worth of Google, according to Interbrand's 2014 Best Brands ranking (£70.2 bn)

$82 bn
Brand worth of Coca-Cola, on Interbrand's 2014 Best Brands ranking (£53.7 bn)

164,755,150
Value of Brazilian reais stolen by bank robbers in 2005, the **largest bank heist** $69.8 m/£38.6 m)

142 years
Duration the USA ranked first in the International Monetary Fund's (IMF) GDP rankings, up until 2014 (see Fact, opposite)

$6 bn
Cost of the **most expensive election**, shelled out during the 2012 US elections (£3.75 bn)

24.8 million
US dollar bills delivered by the Bureau of Engraving and Printing per day – amounting to some $560 m (£367 m)

In contrast, the **lowest economic growth** for the 2012–13 period, due to ongoing civil unrest, was experienced by the Central African Republic, with a GDP reduction of 36% over the year.

HIGHEST...

Earnings for a CEO

As of Apr 2014, according to CNN, chief executive officer of software company Oracle, Larry Ellison (USA), was pulling in an annual salary of $78.4 m (£51.5 m). It comprised $1.5 m (£0.99 m) in cash and $76.9 m (£50.5 m) in stock.

Paid bureaucrats

According to a 2012 OECD survey of global civil service salaries, Italy is the highest payer, with some public officials earning as much as $650,000 (£402,000) per year, based on US dollar parity.

Paid public-speaking engagement

Donald Trump (USA) made $1.5 m (£765,650) per speech at the Real Estate Wealth Expos in 2006 and 2007. Trump only had to speak for an hour to earn each fee, which places him some way ahead of the next highest-paid speaker: former British Prime Minister Tony Blair earned an estimated $600,000 (£300,400) per speech in 2007–09.

GNI per capita

Based on 2013 figures from the World Bank, reported in 2014, Norway has a gross national income (GNI) per person of $102,610 (£66,225), pipping Switzerland, with $90,760 (£58,577), to the top spot.

Fastest rising brand

According to Interbrand's 2014 figures, Facebook continues to power up the brand rankings, with a rise of 86%, 10 years after its launch. This takes its estimated worth to around $14 bn (£9.2 bn).

The story of Apple

Apple came top of Interbrand's 2014 Best Brands ranking, making it the most valuable brand in the world, but where did it all begin for this tech giant?

Hard as it is to imagine, the now global corporation, which pulled in almost $183 bn (£120 bn) in 2014's fiscal year, was founded in the garage of Steve Jobs, with friends Steve Wozniak and Ronald Wayne (all USA) back in 1976.

Arguably their key breakthrough would come eight years later with the launch of the Macintosh (below). Offering a graphical user interface (GUI), which let you click on an icon using a mouse to access programs rather than type in instructions, this machine revolutionized computing. Although selling at a premium price, it became the **first commercially successful personal computer with a GUI**.

In the following years, Apple's fortunes would fluctuate and staff would change – Jobs himself resigned in 1985 owing to differences with the CEO – but through all its highs and lows, innovation and high-end products epitomized the brand.

A new era began in 1997, when Steve Jobs – brought back into the fold in 1996 – was made interim CEO. That year, he and designer Jonathan Ive (UK) oversaw the release of the first iMac. Its new sleek look would inspire Apple's hugely popular personal electronics range, including the iPod, iPad and iPhone, which in 2007 became the best-selling smartphone.

Although Jobs died in 2011, his legacy shows no sign of abating, with Tim Cook (USA, above) now at the helm. The iPhone 6 was released in Sep 2014 (left), and in Q4 2014 alone Apple reported sales of 39.2 million.

ODD JOBS

Beauty brands employ **face feelers** to prove that their products make skin feel **smoother**

Fastest time to pluck a turkey

Vincent Pilkington (IRE) plucked a turkey in 1 min 30 sec on RTE TV in Dublin, Ireland, on 17 Nov 1980.

Leading bird spotter

From 1965, Phoebe Snetsinger (USA, 1931–99) spotted 8,040 of the 9,700 known bird species. She had seen more than 82% of the world's species, all of the bird families on the official list and well over 90% of avian genera.

Most characters voiced by an artist in a TV cartoon series

Kara Tritton (UK) voiced 198 parts for 75 episodes of *Blue's Clues* (Nick Jr, UK, 1996–2006), including furniture (Postbox, Paper Recycling Bin), food (Mr Salt and Mrs Pepper), animals (Owl, Hippo), ghosts, planets and people.

Longest distance walked on the spot by a Foley artist

Foley artists record sound effects to synchronize with visual action on screen. The job is named after Jack Foley (USA), who performed this role at Universal Studios from the dawn of the "talkies". His career began with *Show Boat* (USA, 1929), and during his 40-year career he is estimated to have walked 8,000 km (5,000 mi) on the spot, recording footsteps for the likes of actors James Cagney and Marlon Brando.

Most crash tests

By Feb 2015, W R "Rusty" Haight (USA) had endured 998 collisions in cars as a "human crash test dummy", in the course of his work as a traffic-collision reconstructionist. In each collision, Rusty and his vehicle were fitted with an array of sensors to gather data on the crash.

Most tornadoes sighted

As of 15 Aug 2014, professional storm-chaser Roger Hill (USA) had logged at least 582 encounters with tornadoes since 7 Jul 1987, including a staggering 40 sightings on 16–17 Jun 2010. Roger has turned his expertise in predicting tornadoes into a business, offering educational storm-chasing vacations across much of the USA.

Most durable Elvis impersonator

Victor Beasley (BEL) performed as the King for 48 years, from 1955 to 2003, the year he died.

Fastest window cleaner

Terry Burrows (UK) cleaned three standard 45 x 45 in (114.3 x 114.3 cm) office windows with a 30-cm-long (11.75-in) squeegee and 9 litres (2.37 US gal) of water in 9.14 sec at the National Window Cleaning Competition in Blackpool, UK, on 9 Oct 2009.

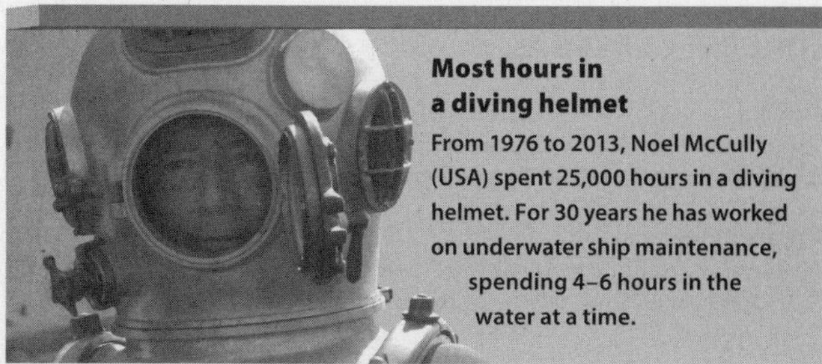

Most hours in a diving helmet

From 1976 to 2013, Noel McCully (USA) spent 25,000 hours in a diving helmet. For 30 years he has worked on underwater ship maintenance, spending 4–6 hours in the water at a time.

Most coffins assembled

Herbert Weber (AUT) assembled a total of 707,335 coffins by hand while working at Moser Holzindustrie GmbH in Salzburg, Austria. He achieved his record over the course of a 30-year career, from 5 Sep 1978 to 5 Sep 2008. During this period he worked for 5,185.5 days in all.

Most feet and armpits sniffed

Madeline Albrecht (USA) was employed at the Hill Top Research laboratories in Cincinnati, Ohio, USA, a testing lab for products by Dr Scholl, for 15 years. During that time, she sniffed approximately 5,600 feet and an indeterminate number of armpits.

Most prolific art forger

At his trial in 1979, Thomas Keating (UK, 1917–84) estimated his output at over 2,000 forged artworks, representing 121 different artists over the course of 25 years.

Most valuable nose

On 19 Mar 2008, Lloyd's reported that Ilja Gort (NLD) had his nose insured for €5 m (£3.9 m; $7.8 m). Gort – the owner of the vineyard Château la Tulipe de la Garde in Bordeaux, France, and producer of Tulipe wines – insured his nose in an attempt to protect his livelihood.

Oldest male stripper

Bernie Barker (USA, 1940–2007) began his career in 2000 at the age of 60 as a way to get in shape after recovering from prostate cancer. He had previously sold real estate. Bernie went on to win more than 40 stripping contests.

LONGEST CAREER AS...

A clown

Charlie Rivel (ESP, b. Josep Andreu Lasserre, 1896–1983) made his public clowning debut aged three. He performed for 82 years, from 1899 to 1981, retiring aged 85.

A gravedigger

In a 50-year career, Johann Heinrich Karl Thieme, sexton of Aldenburg, Germany, dug 23,311 graves. In 1826, his understudy dug *his* grave.

Most claps

It has been estimated that, as of 9 Feb 2015, *Wheel of Fortune* hostess Vanna White (USA) had clapped her hands together 3,721,446 times during 32 seasons of the popular TV game show. She has appeared in all but 10 of the 6,151 episodes in the current syndicated version of the game show since 19 Sep 1983. On average, she has clapped 606 times per show.

Since making her *Wheel of Fortune* debut, Vanna has worn more than 6,000 gowns, and the term "Vannamania" has been coined to describe fans' enduring fascination with her wardrobe.

Longest-serving videogame voice artist

Ed Boon (USA, right, top) co-created the *Mortal Kombat* (Midway Games, 1992) franchise with John Tobias. Technically, Ed is not a voice actor by trade – he's a game developer – but he voiced the character Scorpion (right, bottom) in every version of the game from 1992 to 2011, a period of 18 years 193 days.

The **most prolific videogame voice actor** is Steve Blum (USA), with 354 credited appearances as of 10 Mar 2015, including titles such as *Call of Duty*, *Final Fantasy* and *Star Wars*. The **most prolific gaming voice actress** is Jennifer Hale (CAN), who had voiced a total of 168 games as of 22 Jan 2015.

FACT

Ed Boon and John Tobias have sneaked several references to themselves into the *Mortal Kombat* series. Their surnames – reversed – supply the name of secret character Noob Saibot.

IN NUMBERS

5,000
Golf balls retrieved from water traps on golf courses daily by SCUBA diver Jeffrey Bleim

$35,000
Average starting salary for a crime-scene cleaner (£23,000)

£73,400
Salary Ben Southall (UK) earned as caretaker of an island in the Great Barrier Reef for six months ($111,800)

12,000–15,000
Bicycles dragged from Amsterdam's canals each year by bicycle fishers

$0
Pay for "seat fillers" – attractive people hired to fill empty seats at Hollywood award nights or movie premieres

39 years
Length of time that George Aldrich (USA) has worked as a NASA sniffer; he smells everything that goes into space as – despite filtering – obnoxious odours are not easily diluted in spacecraft

Water-slide tester

Is there really such a job? Indeed there is. Sebastian Smith (UK) rode a record-breaking 186 water slides between 1 May and 31 Oct 2013.

Great job! How did you get it?
I heard about the job through the radio one day when I was writing my dissertation at university. I thought it was too good to be true, but after checking it out online, I discovered it was real.

How do you "test" a water slide?
Fortunately, I was testing the slides for fun factor, not safety. I would write a review of my favourite slide in each water park, considering speed, height, twists and turns.

I'm not too sure I'd have been so keen to take a job as a crash-test dummy, especially when you see the size of some of the slides!

Which slide did you most enjoy?
One of my favourites was *Speed Furious* in Costa Brava. At a height of about 70 ft (21 m), I was locked into a coffin-like cubicle. Looking down at my feet, I couldn't see anything until the trapdoor opened, leaving me free-falling for a second or two until the almost-vertical drop curved gradually to the pool. Definitely the most adrenaline I've ever felt!

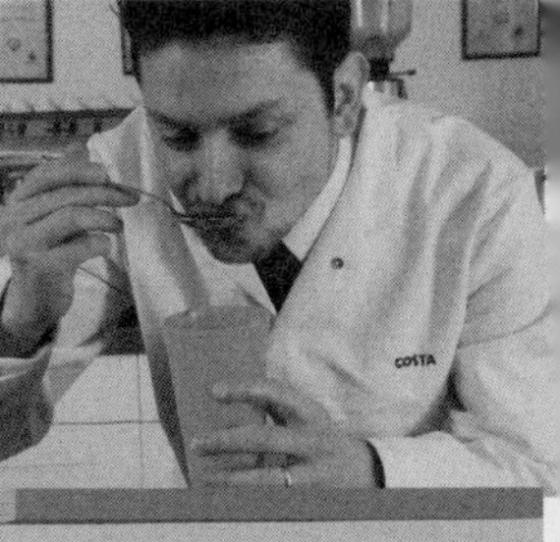

Most valuable tongue

Gennaro Pelliccia (UK) tastes every batch of coffee beans roasted for Costa Coffee (UK) stores. On 9 Mar 2009, insurers Lloyd's reported that his tongue was insured for £10 m ($14 m). "In my profession, my taste buds are crucial," he explains. "My 18 years of experience enable me to distinguish between thousands of flavours."

LONGEST CAREER AS...

An ice-cream man

As of 2014, Allan Ganz (USA, b. 13 Jul 1937) had sold ice-cream for 67 years. He began selling with his father, Louis Ganz, at the age of 10, and since 1977 has sold ice-cream in Peabody, Massachusetts, USA.

Santa Claus

Dayton C Fouts (USA) played Father Christmas every year from 1937 to 1997. He appeared as Santa for 55 years in Harvey, Illinois, USA, and continued the role in Tucson, Arizona, USA.

PIRATES

Not all pirate flags had skulls and crossbones – Bleackbeard's Jolly Roger featured a **skeleton and a bleeding heart**

Largest gathering of pirates

Organized by Roger Crouch (UK), eyepatches and Jolly Rogers abounded when 14,231 buccaneers descended on Pelham Beach in East Sussex, UK, for Hastings Pirate Day on 22 Jul 2012. This claimed back the title from rival pirate town Penzance in Cornwall, UK, by 5,497.

First pirates

Traditional piracy is defined as the act of attempting to board a ship with intent to commit theft or any other crime through force. Piracy has probably existed as long as humans have sailed the oceans, but the first documented account is in Egyptian records from the 14th century BC, when Lukkan pirates from Turkey terrorized ships in the Mediterranean and even raided the island of Cyprus.

First female pirate queen

Queen Teuta was leader of the Ardiaei tribe in Illyria (western Balkan Peninsula) in 231–227 BC. Early in her reign, she granted "letters of marque" – effectively a licence – to privateers to raid and pillage for the state. She attacked Sicily and the Greek colonies, as well as Roman merchant vessels. Later she moved her piratical activities into the Ionian Sea, threatening trade routes between Greece and Italy. As a result, a Roman army was sent against her troops and, after a number of defeats, Queen Teuta surrendered. She continued to rule but was left with only a small area around her capital Scodra (now Shkodër in Albania), and was forced to pay taxes to Rome.

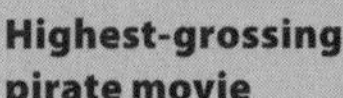

Highest-grossing pirate movie

Of the total $3.7 bn (£2.5 bn) grossed by the swashbuckling *Pirates of the Caribbean* series as of Mar 2015, the second instalment – *Dead Man's Chest* (2006) – had earned the lion's share: $1.06 bn (£711.8 m) in ticket sales.

The fifth adventure following Jack Sparrow, played by Johnny Depp (USA, right) – titled *Dead Men Tell No Tales* – is due for release in Jul 2017.

Largest international anti-piracy force

Set up in 2002, the Combined Maritime Forces (CMF) is a multinational naval partnership now consisting of 30 member nations. The CMF is led by a US Navy Vice Admiral and headquartered in Bahrain in the Persian Gulf. Its purpose is to promote security and stability across international waters, primarily focusing on the major shipping routes between the Horn of Africa and western Pakistan.

First pirate manhunt

Born c. 1653 in Devon, UK, "Long Ben", aka Henry Avery, became a pirate after service in the Royal Navy. In 1695, he attacked 25 ships of the Indian Mughal government, capturing a bounty of precious metals and jewels estimated at £600,000 (around £52.4 m/$78 m today), making him the world's richest pirate at that time and provoking the first recorded worldwide manhunt. A reward of £1,000 (now £87,330/$130,070) was offered for his capture, but he continued to evade arrest. All records of him cease after 1696.

FACT

Seen here, a visit, board, search and seizure (VBSS) team from the guided-missile cruiser USS *Gettysburg* (CG 64) and US Coast Guard Tactical Law Enforcement Team South, Detachment 409 capture suspected pirates in the Gulf of Aden.

IN NUMBERS

15
Countries that accounted for 85% of global piracy incidents between 2000 and 2010, according to the Contemporary Maritime Piracy Database

44%
Reduction in pirate attacks since 2011, according to the International Maritime Bureau's 2014 report

21
Number of vessels successfully hijacked in 2014

£220 m
Estimated loss of annual box-office sales in the UK due to movie piracy, according to the Cinema Exhibitors' Association ($328 m)

Largest tanker-ship hijack

On 15 Nov 2008, pirates off Somalia captured the *Sirius Star* (UAE), a colossal oil tanker measuring 330 m (1,082 ft) long and weighing 162,252 tonnes (178,852 US tons). At the time, it was carrying a load of crude oil bound for the USA valued at $110 m (£77.1 m). It was eventually released on 9 Jan 2009 for a reported ransom of $3 m (£1.95 m).

Youngest pirate

On 9 Nov 1716, John King, aged between eight and 11, and his mother were two passengers on board the ship *Bonetta* when it was captured by English pirate Samuel Bellamy, aka "Black Sam" (see also **most profitable sea pirate**, below). According to a statement by the *Bonetta*'s captain Abijah Savage, King insisted on joining the pirate crew, threatening to kill himself or to harm his mother if his wish was denied. Eventually Black Sam agreed.

In 1984, the wreck of Black Sam's *Whydah* galley ship was discovered. Among other artefacts, a small shoe, a stocking and a leg bone were recovered, later confirmed to be that of a child aged between eight and 11 years old.

Most profitable sea pirate

The most profitable sea pirate during the "Golden Age of Piracy" (1650s–1720s) was Samuel Bellamy, aka "Black Sam", born in England in 1689. Although his career as a pirate was a short one, lasting from just 1715 to 1717, he commandeered 50-plus ships and amassed a fortune that would be worth about £83 m ($123.6 m) today. His most lucrative prize was the *Whydah*, a slave ship that was carrying vast sums of gold and silver. The ship sank on 26 Apr 1717, along with "Black Sam" and all but two of his crew.

Most piracy incidents in a single year

According to the International Maritime Bureau (IMB), which has monitored reported acts of piracy since 1991, there were 469 pirate attacks worldwide in 2000 – a rise of almost 36% over 1999. More than half of those incidents – 242 – occurred around south-east Asia.

Indonesia experiences the **highest incidence of piracy for a country**. In 2003, out of a total 445 actual and attempted attacks globally, 121 occurred in Indonesian waters – accounting for more than a quarter of incidents.

Highest hijack ransom

In Apr 2011, the sum of $13.5 m (£8.3 m) was paid to Somali pirates to secure the release of the Greek ship *Irene SL*. The vessel, a Very Large Crude Carrier (VLCC), and its 25-member crew had been hijacked on 9 Feb 2011 off the coast of Oman.

Most pirated film (current)

The Wolf of Wall Street (2013), directed by Martin Scorsese, was illegally downloaded 30.035 million times in 2014, according to piracy-monitoring company Excipio (DEU).

Frozen (2013) was in second place with 29.919 million illegal downloads – making it 2014's **most pirated animated film**.

FACT

"Walking the plank" was rare but it did occur. An account from 1822 tells of William Smith (UK), captain of the captured Jamaican ship *Blessing*, being "tilted" off a plank on the pirate schooner *Emanuel*.

Blackbeard's rise and fall

Of all the pirates to prowl the seas, few compare to the infamy of Blackbeard. The British seaman – widely thought to go by the name of Edward Thatch or Teach – truly epitomizes the "Golden Age of Piracy".

Blackbeard first came to note working under Benjamin Hornigold (UK), a former privateer, or legal pirate. Rising up the ranks, Thatch became his own captain in 1717 with the capture of *La Concorde*; after renovation, it became his flagship, *Queen Anne's Revenge* (*QAR*).

Under his reign of terror, few ships or ports in the waters of the Americas and the Caribbean could resist his cunning tactics and huge crew. Despite his fearsome reputation and penchant for the theatrical (he's rumoured to have attached burning wicks to his hat to create smoke), there are very few first-hand reports of him killing anyone.

In 1718, the *QAR* ran aground. Thatch and some of his crew escaped to North Carolina, USA, and secured a pardon from the local governor, settling down there. But unable to resist the call of the sea, it wasn't long before they set up a base on Ocracoke Island, in Hyde County, North Carolina, to launch new attacks.

While he had allied with the local establishment, little did Blackbeard know that his demise was being plotted by an official in Virginia. In Aug 1718, a surprise ambush was made on Ocracoke. The pirates put up a good fight, but overconfidence proved Blackbeard's downfall.

Thinking they had taken a ship, Thatch boarded, only to realize that he had been outsmarted as the captain – Lieutenant Maynard – and his men were hiding below decks. Blackbeard may have met his end at Maynard's sword that day, but his legend lives on.

WORLD AT WAR

An estimated **one in two casualties** of war is a **civilian** caught in crossfire

Largest man-made explosion before nuclear weapons

On 6 Dec 1917 during World War I, a Norwegian ship, the SS *Imo*, and the French SS *Mont-Blanc*, carrying a 2,653-tonne (5,848,864-lb) cargo of explosives and inflammables – picric acid, TNT, gun cotton and benzol – collided outside Halifax Harbour in Nova Scotia, Canada. The resulting explosion, later known as the "Halifax Explosion", killed 1,951 identified people, injured 9,000 others and almost wiped out an entire district of the city of Halifax itself.

Largest invasion

The Allied land, air and sea operation against the Normandy coast of France ranks as the largest-ever invading force. For three days from D-Day, 6 Jun 1944, 745 ships in 38 convoys moved in, supported by 4,066 landing craft carrying 185,000 men and 20,000 vehicles, with 347 minesweepers. The air assault comprised 18,000 paratroopers and the 42 divisions were supported by 13,175 aircraft.

Most displaced persons (year)

On World Refugee Day, 20 Jun 2014, the UN Refugee Agency (UNHCR) reported that the number of displaced persons (refugees, asylum seekers and internally displaced people worldwide) had exceeded 50 million for the first time since the end of World War II. As of the end of 2013, there were 51.2 million displaced persons, an increase of 6 million over 2012, attributed to the war in Syria. On 23 Nov 2014, Turkey opened a camp for 35,000 people (inset) near the town of Suruç. Refugees cross the Syrian/Turkish border at this point (below).

Largest importer of arms

For the third year running, in 2013 India was the world's largest buyer of arms, with a spend of $5.58 bn (£3.78 bn). The Stockholm International Peace Research Institute (SIPRI) reported in 2014 that India's weapons imports rose by 111% between the 2004–08 and 2009–13 periods. It accounts for some 14% of the world's arms imports. Above, the Indian Army parades weaponry in New Delhi on 26 Jan 2015.

Largest militarized territorial dispute

The dispute between China, India and Pakistan for the Kashmir region has been ongoing since the end of British rule in India and partition in 1947. India also refuses to recognize Pakistan's ceding of Kashmiri lands to China in 1964. At any one time, up to a million troops confront each other across the Line of Control that separates Indian- and Pakistani-controlled Kashmir.

Most journalists killed in war (current, by country)

In 2014, 17 journalists were killed in Syria, bringing the total since the Syrian conflict began in 2011 – according to the Committee to Protect Journalists (CPJ) – to 80 as of 8 April 2015. The overall death toll for journalists in wars worldwide in 2014 was 61. Right, a Canadian and a Japanese reporter run for cover in Aleppo on 29 Dec 2012.

Largest emergency aid appeal (conflict)

On 8 Dec 2014, the UN's Office for the Coordination of Humanitarian Affairs (OCHA) appealed for $16.4 bn (£11.05 bn) for relief agencies to help at least 57.5 million people in 2015. Over 80% of those in need are located in countries in conflict, such as the Central African Republic (left).

FACT

The Kalma camp for internally displaced people, east of Nyala in Darfur, Sudan, hosts 163,000 residents fleeing the conflict in Darfur, which has killed 300,000 people and displaced 2 million.

Largest evacuation from land by a single ship

During an advance of Communist North Korean forces in the Korean War (1950–53), the US freighter SS *Meredith Victory* evacuated 14,000 civilians from Hungnam in North Korea to Pusan (now Busan) in South Korea between 22 and 25 Dec 1950. She was one of the last ships to leave Hungnam, and US Congress awarded her entire crew the Gallant Ship Unit Citation Bar.

Most nuclear-weapon tests by country

According to the United States Department of Energy's DoE-209 report, the USA carried out some 1,054 nuclear tests between 1945 and 1992, including 24 joint US-UK tests, in which the USA played a significant role.

By comparison, the Soviet Union carried out 715 nuclear tests between 1949 and 1990, according to the *Catalog of Worldwide Nuclear Testing*, edited by Victor Mikhailov. This extensive study covers all 2,049 nuclear tests by the USA, USSR, UK, France and China. The different end dates indicate when the two lead countries stopped nuclear testing.

World Food Programme

The UN World Food Programme (WFP) is the largest humanitarian project. To date it has delivered 68.7 million tonnes (75.7 million US tons) of food to 1.2 billion people in 100 countries, at a total cost of $32 bn (£21.6 bn). GWR spoke to Alexandra Murdoch, WFP's UK outreach coordinator.

When was the WFP established?

It began as an experimental programme that was not due to enter into operation until Jan 1963. But it started earlier, as an earthquake hit Iran, a hurricane swept through Thailand, and newly independent Algeria was overwhelmed by 5 million returning refugees. Food assistance was needed urgently and WFP was tasked with this. It now employs around 14,000 people, 90% of whom work in the field delivering food and monitoring its use.

What are the main causes of hunger?

Poverty, war and displacement, climate change, unstable markets, food waste and lack of investment in agriculture.

Which areas are in the greatest need?

Of the world's 870 million hungry people, over half are in Asia and about a quarter in sub-Saharan Africa [left, Kalma camp in the Sudan, on 6 Nov 2014]. WFP aims to reach 80 million people across 75 countries each year. In 2013, WFP delivered 3.1 million tonnes [3.4 US tons] of food rations.

Support WFP's efforts in building a world with zero hunger: www.wfp.org/donate

IN NUMBERS

254 years
Longest continuous civil war, between seven major state kingdoms in China, 475–221 BC

$1.5 tn
Material cost, as a modern estimate, of World War II, the **costliest war** (£1 tn), far exceeding all of history's other wars combined

56,400,000
Estimated number of people killed in WWII, including battle deaths and civilians – the **highest death toll** in a war

23,000,000
Most landmines in a single country – in Egypt, planted during WWII and the Egypt-Israel wars (1956, 1967 and 1973); Egyptians call the minefields "the Devil's garden"

$640 bn
Highest defence budget (£433.2 bn), that of the USA in 2013, as reported by SIPRI; Oman spends the most as a percentage of GDP (11.3%)

Most assassinated leaders by country

In a study published in 2009 in the American journal *Macroeconomics*, authors Benjamin F Jones and Benjamin A Olken (both USA) looked at a dataset of all assassinations of primary national leaders between 1875 and 2004. Over that period, three countries shared top place: the Dominican Republic, Spain and the USA, with three each. In fact, there was an assassination of a world leader in nearly two out of every three years from 1950.

Most well-funded UN response plan (current)

According to the UN's Financial Tracking Service (FTS), the Syrian Regional Refugee response plan secured the most humanitarian funding in 2014. By 23 Jan 2015, it had received $2.32 bn (£1.57 bn) out of a pledged $3.74 bn (£2.53 bn) – 62% of the total.

The FTS also indicated that the **most underfunded UN Response Plan** by 23 Jan 2015 was the Libya Humanitarian Appeal, which had requested $35 m (£23.6 m) but received just 16% of that sum – $5.5 m (£3.7 m).

First state sanctions as a result of a cyber-attack

On 24 Nov 2014, Sony Pictures Entertainment suffered a cyber-attack that US intelligence blamed on North Korea – a presumed reaction to Sony's film *The Interview* (above), featuring a plot to assassinate its leader, Kim Jong-un (below right). US President Barack Obama (below left) then sanctioned 10 North Korean officials and three state organizations, so they cannot do business with US firms.

SURVEILLANCE

During the 2nd century, an **ancient Roman "secret service"** of informers arose, known as ***frumentarii***

Highest CCTV penetration (country)

Global figures for closed-circuit television use are scant, but data extrapolated from a two-year study of CCTV use in Cheshire, UK, suggests that, as of 2011, there were 1,853,681 cameras nationwide. Factoring in urban and rural differences, this equals one camera for every 32 UK citizens.

First political "hacktivism"

"Hacktivism" is the term used to describe protests using computer networks in line with a political goal. The first recorded instance of this occurred in Oct 1989, when computers worldwide owned by NASA and the US Department of Energy were penetrated by the Worms Against Nuclear Killers worm. This attack is believed to have originated in Australia and occurred just days before the *Galileo* spacecraft carrying nuclear-powered radioisotope thermoelectric generators was due to be launched by the US space shuttle *Atlantis*.

Most wanted hacker

In 2015, the FBI's "most wanted" list of hackers is led by Nicolae Popescu (ROM), indicted for crimes including conspiracy to commit wire fraud, money laundering and passport fraud. Popescu has a $1-m (£650,000) price on his head.

First stealth satellite

When the space shuttle *Atlantis* launched on 28 Feb 1990, it carried into orbit a classified payload for the US Department of Defense. Two days later, *Atlantis* deployed what is believed to be the first of America's "Misty" satellites. These spy satellites allegedly use an inflatable outer shell that can be pointed at Earth to greatly reduce their visibility to radar.

Largest spy satellite

In Dec 2013, the US Defense Advanced Research Projects Agency (DARPA) gave out details of a programme, now in its second and final phase, to create the largest surveillance satellite yet seen. Called the Membrane Optical Imager for Real-Time Exploitation (MOIRE), it will have a 68-ft (20-m) lens capable of covering about 40% of the Earth's surface from an orbit approximately 22,000 mi (35,400 km) above the planet, and able to beam back real-time, high-resolution video and images from anywhere in the world at any time.

The landmark technology uses polymer membrane optics about the thickness of household plastic wrap rather than glass mirrors, which are much thicker and heavier, thus allowing larger, more effective surveillance satellites to get off the ground.

Largest intelligence agency

The US National Security Agency (NSA) is the biggest and most secretive institution of its kind. Its mission is to gather information in the international economic, diplomatic and military spheres. Although accurate figures are impossible to confirm, it is understood that approximately 38,000 people work at its headquarters in Fort Meade, Maryland, USA.

Largest space surveillance network

Through its Joint Functional Component Command for Space at Vandenberg Air Force Base in Lompoc, California, USA, the US Strategic Command is ultimately responsible for the Space Surveillance Network (SSN) of the US Army, Navy and Air Force. The SSN manages ground-based radars and optical sensors at 30 sites worldwide dedicated to monitoring all artificial objects orbiting Earth, such as satellites, as well as potential natural threats such as asteroids.

Largest communications surveillance network

Echelon, the electronic eavesdropping network run by the USA, UK, Australia, New Zealand and Canada, among others, was founded in 1947 (pictured below is Bad Aibling Station in Germany). Some analysts estimate that Echelon is now capable of intercepting 90% of all internet traffic, plus global telephone and satellite communications.

Smallest robotic spaceplane

Built by Boeing's Phantom Works division, the unmanned, reusable US shuttle *X-37B* is 8.9 m (29 ft 2.2 in) long with a wing-span of 4.5 m (14 ft 9.1 in). Launched from Cape Canaveral, USA, in 2010, it landed at Vandenberg Air Force Base in California seven months later. Mission details were classified, but experts believe the goal may have been to develop combat support systems in space.

Largest ATM fraud

In May 2013, it was reported that the largest ever ATM fraud had been broken up by investigators. Cyber-criminals are alleged to have stolen $45 m (£29 m) in just a few hours by hacking into a database of prepaid credit cards in a scheme called "cashout" or "PIN cashing".

They are accused of eliminating withdrawal limits, creating access codes and using associates to spread the information globally (via the internet) to leaders of "cashing crews", who could drain cash machines around the world.

Longest prison sentence for computer hacking

On 25 Mar 2010, Albert Gonzalez (USA) was sentenced to 20 years in federal prison for computer hacking. He was found guilty of masterminding a gang of cyber-criminals who stole in excess of 170 million ATM, credit and debit card numbers from a number of retailers. Gonzalez was also fined $25,000 (£16,500).

IN NUMBERS

8,000
Cameras in the transit system of Madrid, Spain

$38 bn
Estimated worth of the video surveillance market in 2015, according to Electronics.ca (£25 bn)

6,000
Estimated number of years since the **first census** in ancient Babylon, proving that we've been monitoring the masses for millennia

30 cm
Size of objects which the *WorldView-3* satellite, launched in 2014, can see from its 380-mi (612-km) orbit (11.8 in)

400,000
Items of classified data released by WikiLeaks in 2010 – the **largest illegal release of classified documents**

48%
Percentage of CEOs concerned about cyber-crime, according to the Global Economic Crime Survey in 2014

Longest-running hacker convention

Dating back to 1993, DEF CON is the oldest annual hacker convention, with DEF CON 23 taking place on 6–9 Aug 2015 in Las Vegas, Nevada, USA. The event is expected to attract crowds of 5,000–7,000, with tickets only available for purchase at the convention in cash to avoid attempts by police to track attendees via their credit card details.

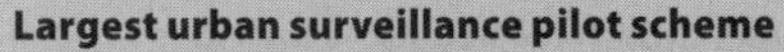

Largest urban surveillance pilot scheme

On 8 May 2014, the UK's London Metropolitan Police Service launched an 18-month pilot project of body-worn surveillance cameras. The 1,000 battery-operated cameras can be attached to uniform or headgear to record a wide-angle view, in colour, of the officer's visual field.

Largest CCTV camera

On 10 Jul 2011, Darwin Lestari Tan and TelView Technology (both IDN) unveiled a scaled-up ST 205 CCTV camera in Bandung, Indonesia. It measures 4.56 m (14 ft 11 in) long, 1.7 m (5 ft 6 in) wide and 1.6 m (5 ft 2 in) tall and has a sensitivity of 0.01 lux.

I spy...

***Pssst*! For millennia, states have used covert surveillance to investigate their enemies – as well as to test the loyalty of their allies and citizens. Here, GWR offers a glimpse into the secretive history of spying.**

500 BC: *The Art of War*, by Chinese general Sun Tzu (above), devotes a full chapter to the importance of spying in both military and civilian contexts
70–44 BC: Julius Caesar appoints spies to flush out intrigues against him. He also develops a secret code, known today as the "Caesar cipher", for secret military communications
1478–1834: The Spanish Inquisition establishes a spy network to identify and interrogate suspected heretics on behalf of the Roman Catholic Church
1793: "Committees of surveillance" (each with 12 members) are set up across France to ruthlessly track down supposed enemies of the French Revolution
1940s–50s: An assortment of former Cambridge University academics pass British secrets to the Soviet Union while variously employed by MI5, MI6, the Foreign Office and the War Ministry. One of them, Anthony Blunt, serves as art adviser to the Crown
1950–c. 1985: East Germany's Stasi intelligence agency carries out secret mass surveillance of ordinary citizens in an attempt to stamp out subversion
2013: Edward Snowden (USA, below), a computer analyst formerly employed by the US National Security Agency, reveals details of the agency's widespread phone and internet surveillance

RUBBISH & RECYCLING

The **plastic** we throw away each year could **circle the Earth four times**

First book printed on recycled paper

The second edition of *Historical Account of the Substances Which Have Been Used to Describe Events, and to Convey Ideas from the Earliest Date to the Invention of Paper*, by Matthias Koops, based in London, UK, was published in 1801. The first edition, in 1800, had been printed on paper made from straw, but part of the second was – as Koops noted – on pages "Re-Made from Old Printed and Written Paper."

Largest population living within 10 km of a dump site

According to D-Waste (see p.266), the rubbish tip that has the highest number of people living within its proximity is Olusosun in Lagos, Nigeria. In all, 5,620,000 people live within 10 km (6.2 mi) of the site. This figure is roughly equal to the population of Denmark, or more than twice the population of the city of Chicago in the USA.

FACT

The Olusosun site covers 0.427 km² (0.16 sq mi), about the size of Vatican City. It houses 17.15–24.5 million tonnes (18.9–27 million US tons) of waste – some 10 times the weight of the *Titanic*.

Most shoes collected for recycling

It took Students Run LA (USA) nearly a year to collect 18,302 shoes, which were then donated to SA Recycling, in Los Angeles, USA. The shoes were counted on 9 Aug 2014 at Belvedere Middle School in East Los Angeles. Students Run LA trains students to run in the ASICS LA Marathon as a way of encouraging goal-setting skills, a healthy lifestyle and character development.

Most paper collected in 24 hours

A total of 194,590 kg (428,998 lb) of paper was collected by San Diego County Credit Union, Shred-it and Clear Channel Media + Entertainment (all USA) in San Diego, California, USA, on 26 Jul 2014.

Highest glass-recycling rate (country)

In 2011, Belgium recycled 98.65% of container glass (i.e., glass bottles and jars). In the same year, the EU average container-glass-recycling rate stood at 70.28%.

Longest underwater clean-up

Astro (MYS) organized a submarine clean-up operation lasting 168 hr 39 min in Tunku Abdul Rahman Marine Park near Kota Kinabalu in Sabah, Malaysia, on 13 Apr 2013. In all, 139 volunteer divers from various countries performed 1,120 dives in the park, recovering waste with a drained weight of 3,098.76 kg (6,831 lb 9 oz).

Largest dump site

Reque, located in Peru, covers an area of 2.35 km^2 (0.9 sq mi), some 324 times the size of the soccer pitch in Wembley Stadium in London, UK.

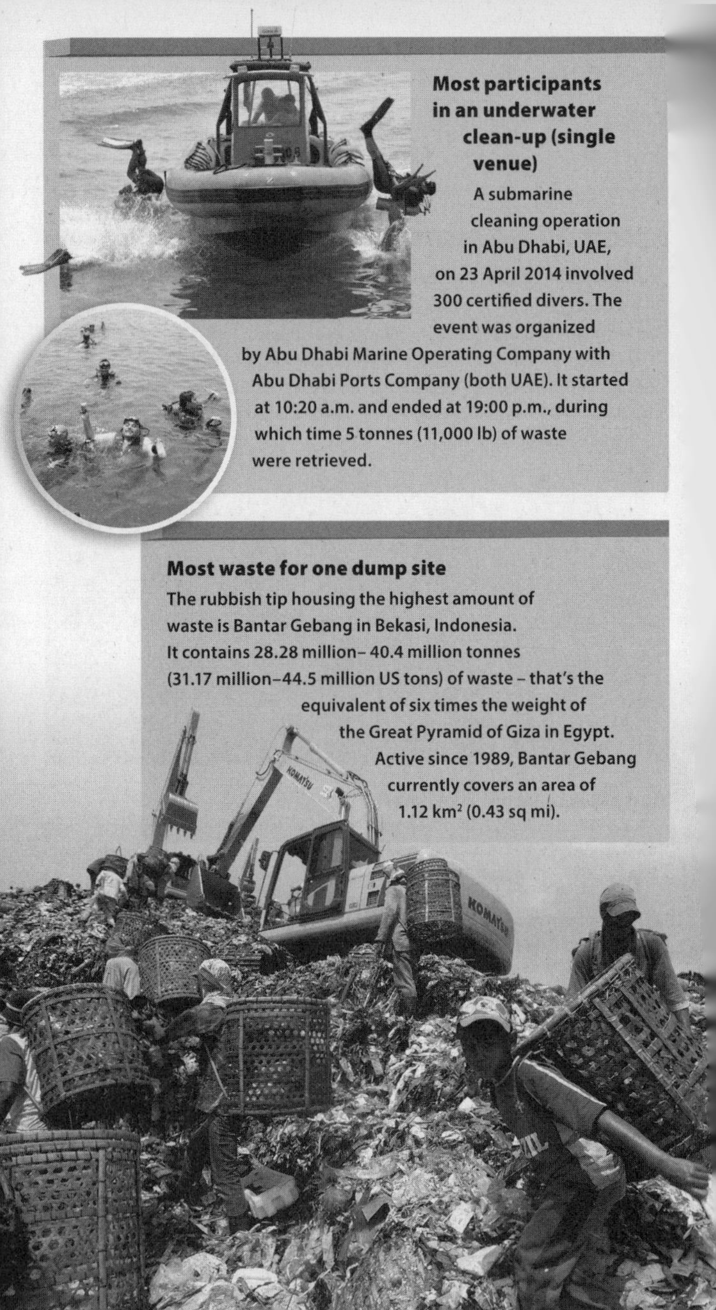

Most participants in an underwater clean-up (single venue)

A submarine cleaning operation in Abu Dhabi, UAE, on 23 April 2014 involved 300 certified divers. The event was organized by Abu Dhabi Marine Operating Company with Abu Dhabi Ports Company (both UAE). It started at 10:20 a.m. and ended at 19:00 p.m., during which time 5 tonnes (11,000 lb) of waste were retrieved.

Most waste for one dump site

The rubbish tip housing the highest amount of waste is Bantar Gebang in Bekasi, Indonesia. It contains 28.28 million– 40.4 million tonnes (31.17 million–44.5 million US tons) of waste – that's the equivalent of six times the weight of the Great Pyramid of Giza in Egypt. Active since 1989, Bantar Gebang currently covers an area of 1.12 km^2 (0.43 sq mi).

Largest clear-up on Everest

Since 2008, the Nepali Eco Everest Expeditions have organized annual trips to the world's highest mountain to clear away rubbish from previous climbs. A record 6,000 kg (13,227 lb) of rubbish was cleared in 2009. More than 14,250 kg (31,416 lb) of ropes, tents, food packaging, oxygen bottles, gas canisters and sundry mountaineering gear has been collected to date.

First waste-to-energy (WtE) plant

A WtE plant – in the form of an incinerator – was designed by Stephen Fryer and built in Nottingham, UK, in 1874. Such incinerators were dubbed "destructors". Some destructors generated electricity as a by-product of burning, but the process was not efficient owing to the level of pollution caused.

Highest WtE production (country)

Germany has the greatest energy production from waste-to-energy plants. In 2013, it generated 18,000 GWh of electricity and 10,000 GWh of heat. This would be enough to run about 32 million 100-watt light bulbs for a year.

The **country with the highest number of WtE plants**, however, is France, with a total of 126 plants as of 2013.

Highest waste-recycling rate (country)

According to D-Waste (see p.266), Singapore currently recycles 59% of its total waste.

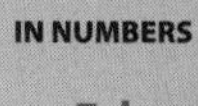

IN NUMBERS

7 days
Time it takes to recycle an old newspaper into a new one

60 days
Time it takes for a recycled aluminium can to return to the shelf as a new can

80 billion
Aluminium cans used every year worldwide

100%
Degree to which glass and aluminium are recyclable; both can be re-used endlessly

15 million
Plastic bottles used in the UK each day

50 million tonnes
Weight of electronic waste thrown away each year (55 million US tons)

80 million tonnes
Weight of plastic produced each year (88.1 million US tons); in 1950, the figure was under 5 million tonnes (5.5 million US tons)

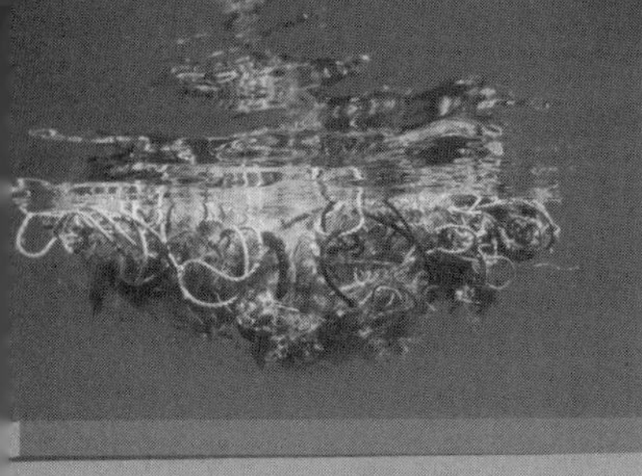

Toxic Pacific

A vast mass of waste – the size of Turkey, Texas or Afghanistan, according to environmental agency Greenpeace – is floating in the North Pacific Ocean.

Gathered in two huge groups (one to the east of Japan, the other to the west of North America), the Great Pacific Garbage Patch is made up largely of non-biodegradable debris, much of it plastic.

Ocean currents carry rubbish around the Pacific in a clockwise direction. But the area in the centre of this vortex is still – a perfect place for waste to settle (see below). Turtles mistake plastic bags for jellyfish and eat them, while fish and seabirds eat smaller pieces of plastic, which they can choke on, or which can harm their internal organs. Larger debris can harm sea life (the photo above shows a mass of rope and fishing nets that traps wildlife such as sharks or sea lions), but most of the plastic exists in microscopic pieces that block out light. This has disastrous repercussions for tiny plankton and algae – vital parts of the marine food chain. The plastic also releases harmful pollutants as it breaks down.

Of the estimated 100 million tonnes (110 million US tons) of plastic produced each year, 10 million tonnes (11 million US tons) ends up in the sea. Cleaning up this huge marine wasteland is beyond the capability of any one country. The solution may lie in a fundamental change in humanity's habits. By giving up our addiction to plastic, and switching to biodegradable (or reusable) materials that decompose safely, we may help to shrink the Great Pacific Garbage Patch over time.

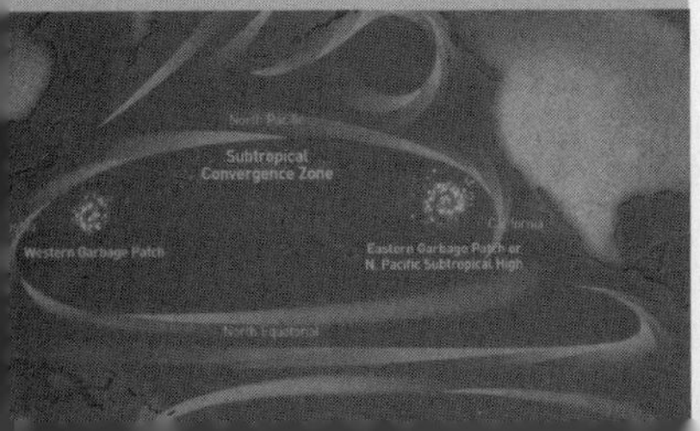

Lowest waste generation per capita (country)

Kenya generates the least waste with 109.5 kg (241 lb 6 oz) generated per person per year.

Mullaitivu in Sri Lanka is the **city with the lowest waste generation per capita**. It generates only 7.3 kg (16 lb) of rubbish per person per year.

Bahrain is the **country with the highest waste generation per capita**, at 906.7 kg (1,998 lb 14 oz) of rubbish per person per year.

Al Ain in the United Arab Emirates is the **city with the highest waste generation per capita**. It registered 2,305.7 kg (5,083 lb 3 oz) of refuse generated per person per year.

D-Waste

The source for many of the records on this spread is D-Waste, a global organization of waste-management consultants. Established 20 years ago, D-Waste works with a variety of clients to provide advice and products that will help them to deal effectively with waste.

ON THE FARM

Pigs are considered the **fifth-most intelligent animal**, after humans, chimpanzees, dolphins and elephants

Most prolific chicken

The highest authenticated rate of egg-laying is 371 in 364 days, laid by a white leghorn (No.2988) in an official test conducted in 1979 by Professor Harold V Biellier at the College of Agriculture at the University of Missouri, USA.

Largest breed of dairy cattle

Most familiar in their black-and-white colouration, Friesians (known as Holsteins in the USA) originated in the Netherlands. An adult reaches an average height of 1.47 m (4 ft 9 in) at the shoulder and weighs 580 kg (1,278 lb). Solid black, solid white and red-and-black varieties also occur, and in all, Friesians make up around 90% of all commercial dairy animals.

Most wool sheared from a sheep in a single shearing

On 25 Jan 2014, 28.9 kg (63 lb 11 oz) of wool was sheared from Big Ben (pictured), owned by Michael Lindsay (NZ) in Twizel, New Zealand.

The **fastest time to shear a mature sheep** is 39.31 sec, by Hilton Barrett (AUS) in Wellington, Australia, on 1 May 2010.

Largest goat

By the time of his death in 1977, aged four, a British Saanen named Mostyn Moorcock, owned by Pat Robinson (UK), had grown to a shoulder height of 3 ft 8 in (1.11 m) and a length of 5 ft 6 in (1.67 m). He weighed 400 lb (181.4 kg).

Largest sheep

In Mar 1991, a Suffolk ram named Stratford Whisper 23H was confirmed as 1.09 m (3 ft 7 in) tall. It was owned by Joseph and Susan Schallberger of Boring, Oregon, USA.

Tallest donkey

Romulus, an American Mammoth Jackstock, measured 1.72 m (5 ft 8 in) tall on 8 Feb 2013. He is owned by Cara and Phil Yellott of Red Oak in Texas, USA. The minimum height for the big breed is 1.47 m (4 ft 10 in).

Greatest milk yield by a cow

The highest recorded lifetime yield of milk from a single cow is 216,891 kg (478,163 lb) – almost one million 8-oz (236-ml) glasses – by Smurf, a Holstein cow owned by La Ferme Gillette Inc. dairy farm in Embrun, Ontario, Canada. The record was verified from the production certificate dated 27 Feb 2012.

The **greatest milk yield by a cow in one day** is 241 lb (109.5 kg) – four times the typical daily production – by a cow named Ubre Blanca ("White Udder") in Cuba on 23 Jun 1982. The prolific zebu-Holstein cross became a Communist symbol of good breeding, and after her death in 1985 she was stuffed, mounted and put on display at the country's National Cattle Health Center.

Highest butterfat yield by a dairy cattle breed

The Jersey cow, native to the island of Jersey in the Channel Islands off France, yields a record 4.84% butterfat – and 3.95% protein – in its milk. It may be small in size, but the Jersey cow is claimed by farmers to be the most intelligent and inquisitive of all cattle breeds, and is second only to the Friesian cattle breed in terms of popularity.

Longest steer horns (living)

In Oct 2013, the horns of Texas longhorn Big Red 907 from El Coyote Ranch in Kingsville, Texas, USA, were measured at 2.92 m (9 ft 7 in) from tip to tip (straight across), beating the previous record from 2011 of 2.77 m (9 ft 1 in).

Shortly before going to press, however, a new claimant emerged. LazyJ's Bluegrass (inset) from Greenleaf, Kansas, USA, boasts horns stretching 2.97 m (9 ft 8.9 in), beating Big Red's horns by 5 cm (1.9 in).

FACT

The **longest horns ever** for a Texas longhorn were those of the red steer Gibraltar at 3.16 m (10 ft 4 in). Born in Mar 1992, Gibraltar was bred and owned by Dickinson Cattle of Ohio, Texas, USA.

Shortest donkey

KneeHi, a brown jack (male) registered miniature Mediterranean donkey, measured 64.2 cm (2 ft 1.29 in) to the top of the withers (the highest part of the back) at Best Friends Farm in Gainesville, Florida, USA, on 26 Jul 2011. His owners are James, Frankie (above) and Ryan Lee (all USA).

Shortest living horse (male)

In Apr 2012, Charly, a miniature Arabian horse owned by Bartolomeo Messina (ITA), measured 63.5 cm (2 ft 1 in) to the withers on the set of *Lo Show dei Record* in Rome, Italy.

Thumbelina, a miniature sorrel brown mare, is the **shortest living horse (female)**: 44.5 cm (1 ft 5.5 in). She lives on Goose Creek Farms in St Louis, Missouri, USA, with Kay and Paul Goessling.

Oldest...

- **Donkey:** A donkey named Suzy had reached the age of 54 years at her death in 2002. Her owner was Beth Augusta Menczer of Glenwood, New Mexico, USA.
- **Goat:** McGinty the goat was aged 22 years 5 months at her death in Nov 2003. Her owner was Doris C Long (UK).
- **Goose:** A gander named George, owned by Florence Hull (UK), died on 16 Dec 1976 at the grand age of 49 years 8 months. George had been hatched in Apr 1927.

Smallest breed of...

- **Dairy cattle:** Adult Jersey cows average 1.2 m (3 ft 11 in) tall, and weigh on average 400–500 kg (800–1,100 lb). They are excellent grazers and exceptionally heat-tolerant, able to breed in even the hottest regions of Brazil.

IN NUMBERS

3,812
Largest display of scarecrows, by National Forest Adventure Farm in Burton-upon-Trent, Staffordshire, UK, on 7 Aug 2014

115 dB
Sound level that a pig's squeal can reach – equivalent to a chainsaw from 3 ft (91 cm) away

200
Approximate number of noises chickens use to communicate

5 mi
Distance over which a cow can detect smells (8 km)

35 US gal
Daily amount of water that a cow drinks – enough to fill a bathtub (136 litres)

4.6 tonnes
Average amount of manure produced by a 1,000-lb (454-kg) cow each year (10,141 lb)

Tallest cow

Blosom, a Holstein cow, measured 1.9 m (6 ft 2.8 in) from hoof to withers at Memory Lane Farm in Orangeville, Illinois, USA, on 24 May 2014. She is seen above with her owner, Patricia Meads-Hanson (USA). Blosom is an official "ambassador" at the farm, which is also a craft retreat, and has her own Facebook page.

FACT

The four compartments in a cow's stomach allow it to digest otherwise indigestible grasses and grains. Cows spend eight hours a day repeatedly chewing regurgitated food, known as the "cud".

Smallest breed of...

- **Domestic goat:** According to both the American Goat Society and the American Dairy Goat Association, bucks (adult males) of the Nigerian dwarf goat should be less than 60 cm (1 ft 11 in) at the withers, and does (adult females) less than 57 cm (1 ft 10 in).
- **Sheep:** The Ouessant comes from the Île d'Ouessant (aka Ushant), a small island off the coast of Brittany, France.

Shortest bull

Chegs HHAR Golden Boy measured 71.6 cm (2 ft 4.2 in) from hoof to withers on 1 Mar 2014. He is owned by Hearts & Hands Animal Rescue (USA) in Ramona, California, USA.

It weighs in at just 13–16 kg (29–35 lb) and stands 45–50 cm (1 ft 6 in–1 ft 8 in) tall at the withers. Believed by some to have descended from a Viking breed of sheep, the species was saved from extinction by breeding programmes in the 20th century.

- **Domestic turkey:** The smallest standard variety of domestic turkey is the midget white. Adult males (called toms) weigh approximately 6 kg (13 lb), and females weigh around 3.5–4.5 kg (7 lb 11 oz–9 lb 14 oz), making them little larger than the largest breeds of domestic chicken.

Short story

GWR travelled to Kerala, India, to visit mini Manikyam, the shortest cow, owned by Akshay N V (IND, above left). Manikyam measured just 61.1 cm (2 ft) from the hoof to the withers on 21 Jun 2014. We asked local veterinarian Dr E M Muhammed for the lowdown on this diminutive bovine.

When did you first hear about Manikyam?
About two years ago, we became aware that this animal was much shorter than ordinary cows. Manikyam was about four years old at the time, but even when she was only nine or 10 months old we could tell there was something different about her. We monitored her closely from the age of two. By the age of four she was around 64 cm (2 ft 1 in) tall.

How does Manikyam compare to a conventionally sized cow?
Usually, our local cows are about 150 cm (4 ft 11 in) in height. Manikyam is a Vechur breed, well known for producing dwarf cows. Vechurs tend to grow to a maximum height of around 90 cm (2 ft 11 in).

Why do you think the area produces such short cows?
We think it may be to do with the unusual climatic conditions of our state. It is hot and particularly humid here, and we believe this has an effect on the height of our cattle. If Vechur cattle are taken elsewhere in the country, over time they increase in height. It's only in Kerala that they maintain their dwarf stature. Really interesting!

We've been working in this field for the past 10 years. It seems that Vechur cattle have what is known in the scientific community as "thermometer genes", which allow them to survive in hot, humid conditions. And they are highly resistant to infection too – they can even withstand foot-and-mouth disease.

A pair of tortoises were the **first animals to circle the Moon**, in a Soviet spacecraft in 1968

Earliest records of domestic goldfish

The Prussian or gibel carp (*Carassius gibelio*) of Asia has silver scales in its wild state. The golden-scaled variant (*C. auratus*), a random mutation, originated in China during the Jin Dynasty (AD 265–419). It gave rise to the domestic goldfish that were first bred in China.

The **earliest historical records of twintail goldfish** also come from China, in approximately 1600. This species has two separate tails, also due to a mutant gene. It has been selectively bred for centuries to create a number of true-breeding twintail varieties.

Fastest 5 m on front paws by a dog

A papillon-chihuahua mix named Konjo covered 5 m (16 ft 4 in) on her front paws in 2.39 sec at Tustin Sports Park in California, USA, on 22 Dec 2014. Konjo averaged a speed of nearly 8 km/h (4.7 mph) and outpaced previous holder, Jiff (USA), by more than 5 sec.

Oldest pig ever

Ernestine was aged 23 years 76 days when she passed away peacefully on 1 Oct 2014. The Vietnamese pot-bellied pig spent a full and happy life with her owners Jude and Dan King in Calgary, Alberta, Canada, and had been a much-loved member of the family since she was three months old.

First canine star

Blair, a collie owned by British film producer-director Cecil M Hepworth, was an early star of the silver screen. His most famous role was in *Rescued by Rover* (1905), the first film to feature a canine star.

Jean the Vitagraph Dog, a female border collie owned by Larry Trimble of New York City, USA, was the **first canine star of self-titled films**. Between 1906 and 1910, Trimble directed her in such films as *Jean Goes Fishing*.

Fastest 100 m on a skateboard by a dog

On 16 Sep 2013, Jumpy (USA) boarded 100 m in 19.65 sec on the set of *Officially Amazing* (CBBC) in Los Angeles, California, USA.

On the same show, on 5 Jul 2014, Norman the Scooter Dog set a 55.41-sec record for the **fastest 30 m on a bicycle by a dog**.

Most dogs attending a music concert

On 5 Jun 2010, musician Laurie Anderson (USA) debuted her composition "Music for Dogs" at the Sydney Opera House, Australia, before an audience of around 1,000 dogs and their owners.

Fastest 10 m travelled on a Swiss ball by a dog

On 31 Jan 2015, Purin the beagle, owned by Makoto Kumagai of Chiba, Japan, rolled 10 m (32 ft 9 in) on top of an inflatable Swiss ball in just 11.9 sec. Two months later, on 22 Mar 2015, the nine-year-old pooch also set a record for the **most balls caught by a dog with the paws in one minute** (below left) – she "saved" 14 mini soccer balls, thrown at her one at a time, by owner Makoto.

Largest dog-grooming lesson

On 21 Sep 2014, in Alliston, Ontario, Canada, Golden Rescue held a grooming lesson with 364 canine models, who also set a record for the **most dogs wearing bandanas**.

Most-travelled sea cat

Siamese cat Princess Truman Tao-Tai covered 2.4 million km (1.49 million mi) in her 16-year life. In 1959, as a kitten, she joined the crew of the British iron-ore carrier *Sagamire*, after which she was never allowed on shore for quarantine reasons.

Longest fur on a rabbit

On 17 Aug 2014, in San Martin, California, USA, 10 strands of fur on Franchesca, a one-year-old English Angora rabbit, were found to be an average of 36.5 cm (14.37 in) long. Franchesca's proud owner is Dr Betty Chu (USA); she's an expert on the English Angora, which is often mistaken for a Pekingese dog and needs a great deal of care… and a lot of grooming of that dense, silky fur.

Oldest living cat

Tiffany Two of San Diego, California, USA, born on 13 Mar 1988, celebrated her 27th birthday on 13 Mar 2015.

Oldest living parrot

Cookie, a Major Mitchell's cockatoo (*Cacatua leadbeateri*) at Brookfield Zoo in Illinois, USA, had surpassed an age of 80 years 107 days as of 15 Sep 2014. His estimated age on arrival in May 1924 was at least one year.

FACT

A tortoise's shell has nerve endings, so is sensitive to touch. The scales are called scutes and are made of keratin, as fingernails are. You can tell a tortoise's age from the growth rings around its scutes.

Most...

- **Keys removed from a keyring by a parrot in one minute:** On 9 Jan 2009, Smudge, a cockatoo owned by Mark Steiger (CHE), neatly removed 22 keys from a ring on the set of *Guinness World Records* in Madrid, Spain.
- **Socks removed by a dog in one minute:** Lilu, owned by Briana Messerschmidt (USA), slipped off 20 socks from a row of 10 volunteers on the set of *Guinness World Records Unleashed* in Los Angeles, California, USA, on 28 Jun 2013.
- **Knots undone by a dog in one minute:** Gustl, a terrier mix owned by Heidi Deml (DEU), untied 10 knots on the set of *Officially Amazing* in Attenkirchen, Germany, on 19 Dec 2012.

King of the track

GWR caught up with Marco Calzini, who, with his wife Janine (both UK, above), owns Adventure Valley, a family adventure park in Brasside, Durham, UK. The attraction is home to Bertie, the fastest tortoise (pictured below left), who reached a speed of 0.28 m/sec (0.92 ft/sec) on 9 Jul 2014.

Why did you try for this particular record?

Bertie has always been very active. Visitors to Adventure Valley would wonder just how fast he was. Having found a previous record for a tortoise named Charlie, I tested Bertie against it and he beat it every time. So we applied for the record.

What was the biggest challenge?

Building the track to the specifications in the guidelines. Also, sourcing an architect to verify the attempt. On the day, the local press were invited and I was worried that Bertie might not feel like it. But as soon as the timer started, I knew the record had been broken because of Bertie's pace.

What advice would you give to someone else attempting a record?

Don't give up. Have confidence and self-belief. If you don't manage it, there is always another day. Do your best.

What does Guinness World Records mean to you – and Bertie?

Since setting a new Guinness World Records title, Bertie has become quite a celebrity and very popular with visitors. He now lives in a luxury enclosure with his girlfriend Shelly and his Guinness World Records certificate proudly displayed on the wall.

I used to collect the *Guinness World Records* books – my first was the 1980 edition – and I fondly remember seeing them all in the shops. To be in the book is a dream come true, a massive achievement!

IN NUMBERS

50 km/h
Approximate top speed at which a cat can run (30 mph)

66%
Proportion of its life that a cat spends asleep

67.8
Decibel reading on 2 Apr 2015 for Merlin, the **loudest purring domestic cat**, who lives with Tracy Westwood at her home in Devon, UK

1 mile
Distance a hamster can cover in a day (1.6 km)

18 in
Approximate height a mouse can jump (47 cm)

3
Dogs that survived the sinking of the *Titanic*: two Pomeranians and one Pekingese

230 million
Scent receptors in a typical bloodhound's nose – around 40 times more than in a human nose

Most bottle caps removed by a parrot in one minute

On 1 Nov 2014, Gordon, supported by Julie Cardoza (USA), removed 12 caps from glass soda bottles in Los Altos, California, USA. Julie spent a year training her 13-year-old hyacinth macaw (*Anodorhynchus hyacinthinus*) to learn and perfect his technique.

This intelligent species is also the **longest parrot** and **largest flying parrot**, at up to 1 m (3 ft 3 in) long.

Tallest dog (female)

On 14 Nov 2014, Lizzy (USA) – a Great Dane aged seven years old – measured 37.96 in (99.41 cm) tall from floor to withers at the Verandah Pet Hospital in Fort Myers, Florida, USA. Vets used an approved measuring stick, incorporating a spirit level that rested on her shoulders. Lizzy lives with her owner Greg Sample in Alva, Florida, USA, and beat the previous record by 0.5 in (1.26 cm).

CONSTRUCTION

Largest model railway

The most extensive train set was assembled in Hamburg, Germany, and covers 1,300 m^2 (14,000 sq ft). More than 900 trains pull some 12,000 wagons along 13 km (8 mi) of track. This "wonderland", created by twin brothers Frederik and Gerrit Braun (pictured overleaf with their creation), mimics regions of Europe and the USA, and is populated by 200,000 figurines. Highlights (clockwise from top left) include Hamburg's Imtech Arena; a mini Las Vegas; St Wendelberg in the Alps; a sparkling night-time view; a rock festival with DJ BoBo. And the epic construction isn't finished yet...

CONTENTS

FACT

All the functions of the railway and its features are monitored from a control room with at least 40 computers. There are 50–60 "rail accidents" per day that need locating ASAP!

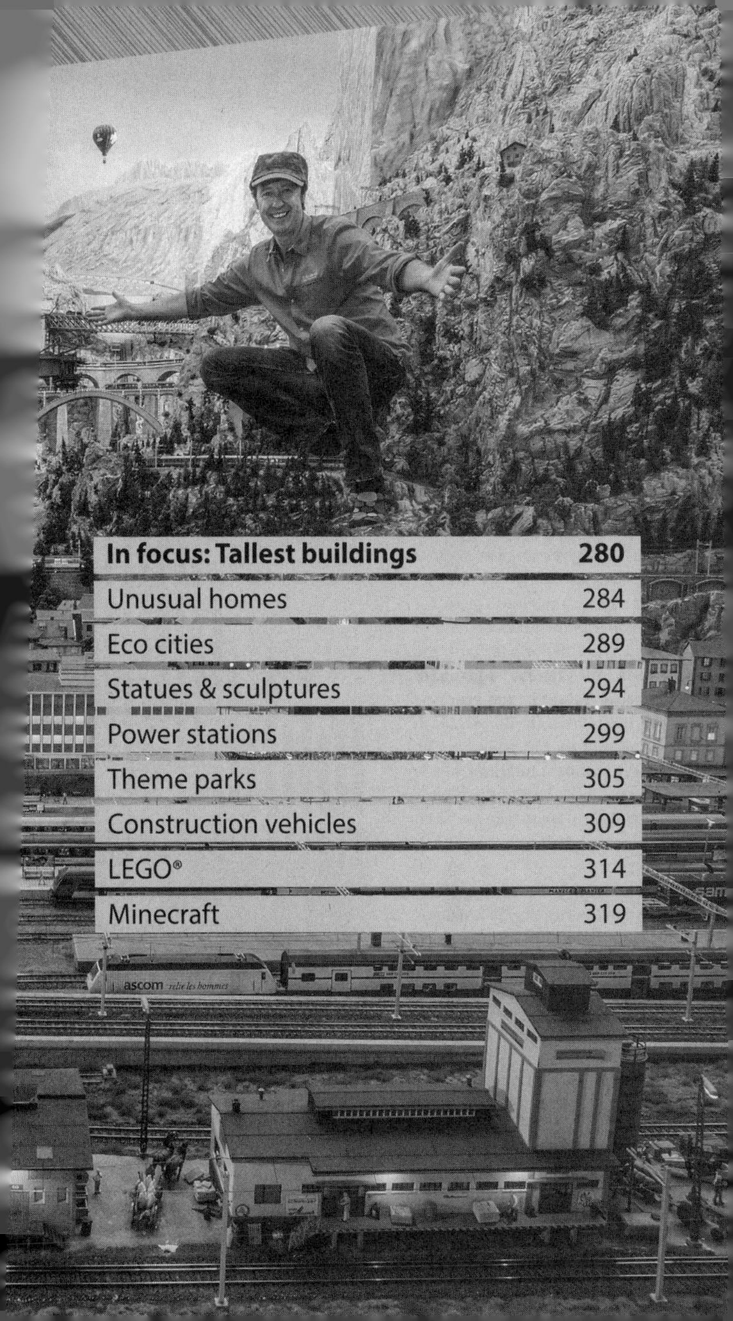
ascom

IN FOCUS

TALLEST BUILDINGS

From the top of **Willis Tower**, it's possible to **see four US states**: Illinois, Indiana, Wisconsin and Michigan

Could the ancient Egyptians ever have predicted that the 146.5-m-tall (481-ft) Great Pyramid of Giza, built c. 2560 BC, would remain the tallest man-made structure for nearly 4,000 years? To hold the record for so long seems alien today, with the race to build ever taller never more competitive.

From the awe-inspiring cathedrals of the Middle Ages via the **first skyscraper** – Chicago's Home Insurance Building built in 1885 – to today's "supertalls", our cities' skylines are growing constantly skyward.

And if 2014 is anything to go by, our vertical ambition shows no sign of slowing, with that year earning the accolade for **tallest aggregate skyscraper height in one year** (see graph, right). While the Burj Khalifa in Dubai, UAE, may be celebrating its fifth year as **tallest building**, a new kid on the block, the Kingdom Tower in Saudi Arabia, could take its crown once completed.

Keeping a close eye on all developments in this ever-shifting field is the Council on Tall Buildings and Urban Habitat (CTBUH), which publishes a comprehensive annual report of the architectural world's ups and downs. In the illustration on p.282–83 we take a closer look at the planet's top 10 tallest buildings, as completed by early 2015, highlighting some of their vital statistics as well as some of their record-breaking engineering.

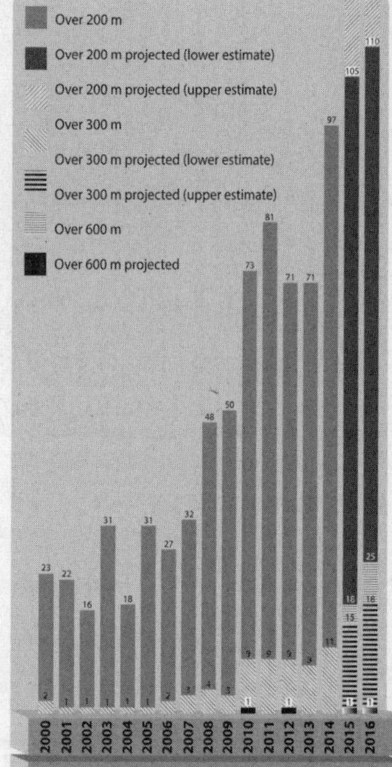

Supertalls on the up

As this graph from the CTBUH shows, the number of tall buildings (>200 m) and supertalls (>300 m) topped out in a year has seen a steady rise since the turn of the 21st century. While 2014 was a record-breaking year in terms of combined height (see p.323), the CTBUH predicts that 2015 and 2016 will surpass it, as well as seeing the arrival of two new "megatalls" (>600 m).

Not all about height...

Situated at the heart of the holy city of Mecca in Saudi Arabia, the Abraj Al-Bait Towers, aka Makkah Royal Clock Tower Hotel, is the **largest building by capacity,** with a gross floor area (GFA) of 1,575,815 m² (16,961,931 sq ft) – enough to accommodate 65,000 people.

The tallest central tower is a five-star hotel, but the complex also has a shopping mall, an Islamic museum, apartments and even a lunar observation centre.

Money matters

The tallest buildings aren't necessarily the costliest to build – in fact, only two of the top 10 feature in this round-up of the five most expensive projects completed to date. (Costs estimated by real-estate experts Emporis.)

One World Trade Center
(USA)
$3.9 bn
(£2.5 bn)

Palace of the Parliament
(ROM)
$3 bn
(£1.9 bn)

The Palazzo
(USA)
$1.9 bn
(£1.2 bn)

The Shard
(UK)
$1.9 bn
(£1.2 bn)

Taipei 101
(TPE)
$1.76 bn
(£1.14 bn)

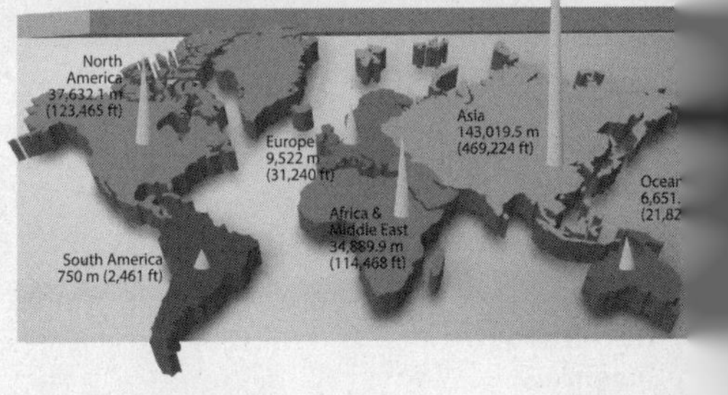

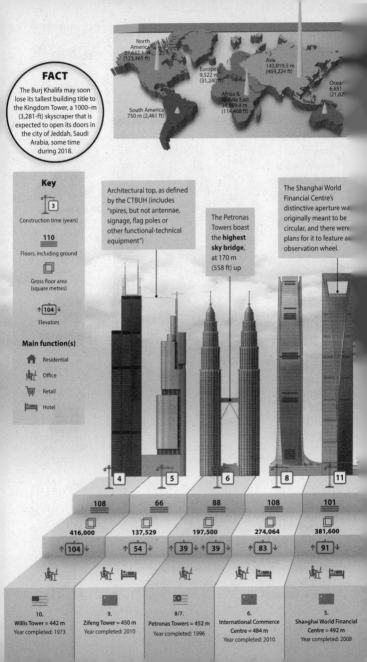

FACT

The Burj Khalifa may soon lose its tallest building title to the Kingdom Tower, a 1000–m (3,281-ft) skyscraper that is expected to open its doors in the city of Jeddah, Saudi Arabia, some time during 2018.

Key

3 Construction time (years)

110 Floors, including ground

Gross floor area (square metres)

104 Elevators

Main function(s)

Residential

Office

Retail

Hotel

Architectural top, as defined by the CTBUH (includes "spires, but not antennae, signage, flag poles or other functional-technical equipment")

The Petronas Towers boast the **highest sky bridge**, at 170 m (558 ft) up

The Shanghai World Financial Centre's distinctive aperture wa originally meant to be circular, and there were plans for it to feature a observation wheel.

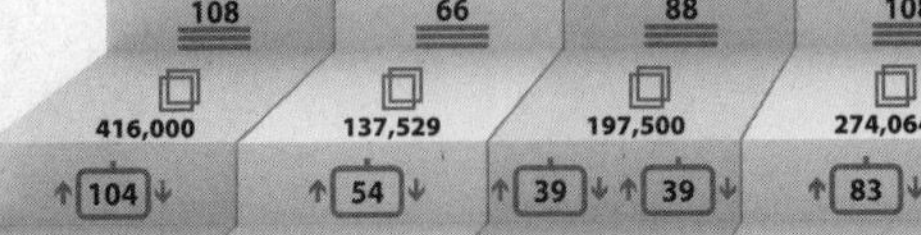

	10. Willis Tower	9. Zifeng Tower	8/7. Petronas Towers	6. International Commerce Centre	5. Shanghai World Financial Centre
Construction time (years)	4	5	6	8	11
Floors	108	66	88	108	101
Gross floor area	416,000	137,529	197,500	274,064	381,600
Elevators	104	54	39 / 39	83	91
Main function(s)	Office	Office, Hotel	Office	Office, Hotel	Office, Hotel

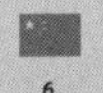

10. Willis Tower = 442 m
Year completed: 1973

9. Zifeng Tower = 450 m
Year completed: 2010

8/7. Petronas Towers = 452 m
Year completed: 1996

6. International Commerce Centre = 484 m
Year completed: 2010

5. Shanghai World Financial Centre = 492 m
Year completed: 2008

Tallest buildings by region

Illustrated left are the aggregate totals of all buildings 200 m (656 ft) or taller slated to be completed by the end of 2015. As you can see, Asia is the runaway leader, while South America lays claim to just three over this height.

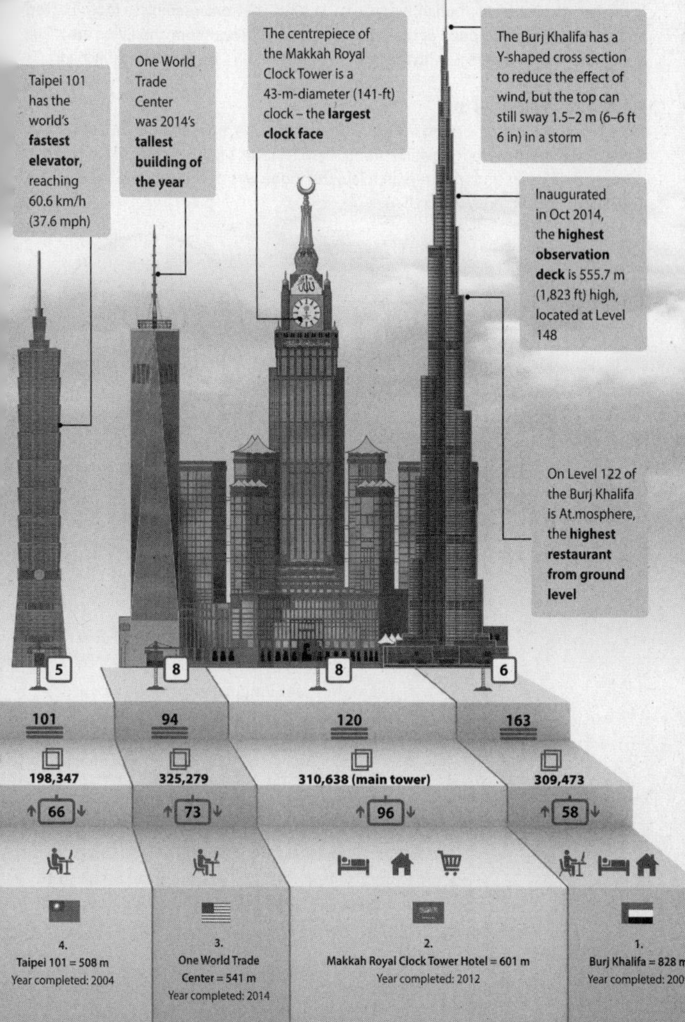

Taipei 101 has the world's **fastest elevator**, reaching 60.6 km/h (37.6 mph)
One World Trade Center was 2014's **tallest building of the year**
The centrepiece of the Makkah Royal Clock Tower is a 43-m-diameter (141-ft) clock – the **largest clock face**
The Burj Khalifa has a Y-shaped cross section to reduce the effect of wind, but the top can still sway 1.5–2 m (6–6 ft 6 in) in a storm
Inaugurated in Oct 2014, the **highest observation deck** is 555.7 m (1,823 ft) high, located at Level 148
On Level 122 of the Burj Khalifa is At.mosphere, the **highest restaurant from ground level**
5
8
8
6
101
94
120
163
198,347
325,279
310,638 (main tower)
309,473
66
73
96
58
4. Taipei 101 = 508 m
Year completed: 2004
3. One World Trade Center = 541 m
Year completed: 2014
2. Makkah Royal Clock Tower Hotel = 601 m
Year completed: 2012
1. Burj Khalifa = 828 m
Year completed: 2009

UNUSUAL HOMES

The **oldest houses**, built c. 7,500–5,700 BC, are at Çatalhöyük in modern-day Turkey

First house shaped like a crocodile

Artist Moussa Kalo and his apprentice Thierry Atta built a concrete crocodilian domicile in the Cocody district of Abidjan, Ivory Coast, in 2008. The front resembles a tooth-packed mouth, while the main body of the property serves as a bedroom and living area. The house is raised on four legs, with the main belly resting on a huge concrete lily pad.

First underwater hotel

Jules' Undersea Lodge, located in Key Largo, Florida, USA, opened in 1986. Guests dive down 30 ft (9 m) to the lodge, which sits on legs 5 ft (1.5 m) off the bottom of the Emerald Lagoon. Built as an undersea research lab, the lodge was developed as a hotel by Ian Koblick and Neil Monney (both USA).

FACT

Philipp Schuster's radical residence is tastefully decorated with vintage furniture, antiques and hunting trophies, recreating the look and feel of the original hunting lodge.

Largest home skateboard park

Twenty-eight-year-old pro skateboarder Philipp Schuster (AUT) dreamed of boarding at home, and in 2012, with the help of some friends and 8 tonnes (17,637 lb) of concrete, he transformed the ground floor of an old Austrian hunting lodge in Salzburg into an in-home skatepark. After creating banks, quarter pipes and bumps, Philipp can now skate up on to the walls, beneath the windows and over his fireplace.

Most transparent house

In all, 59% of the roof and walls of *House NA* (2011) in Tokyo, Japan, is made of glass or other transparent materials. Only the kitchen and bathroom have built-in fixtures, while the sparse furnishings make it feel even more transparent from the inside. The owners, a young professional couple, are clearly not worried about what their neighbours might say – or see. The steel-framed residence was designed by Japanese architects Sou Fujimoto.

Largest house shaped like a shoe

This five-storey, 7.6-m-high (24-ft 11.2-in), 15-m-long (49-ft 2.5-in) home in Pennsylvania, USA, was built in 1948 by a shoe manufacturer to advertise his wares. Its current residents are Carleen and Ronald Farabaugh.

Highest climbing-wall house

Between May and Aug 2009, Brazilian brothers Tiago and Gabriel Primo lived on a climbing wall, with furniture hung 10 m (32 ft 9 in) above the ground in Rio de Janeiro, Brazil. The two artists used climbing gear and their own skills to move between a bed, desk, sofa, chair, hammock and old-fashioned gramophone, all fixed to the wall. They slept, ate and worked for 12 hours a day in their "house" on the side of an art gallery, going inside only to use the bathroom.

Smallest temporary house

One-Sqm-House was designed by architect Van Bo Le-Mentzel (DEU) in 2012. Tilting the self-built wooden structure on its side lets its sole resident lie down to sleep, while four wheels allow the 40-kg (88-lb) microhouse to be relocated.

Tallest house shaped like a toilet

Sim Jae-duck (ex-mayor of Suwon in South Korea and self-styled "Mr Toilet") owned a 7.5-m-high (24-ft 7-in) loo-shaped home. Its name, Haewoojae, means "a place of sanctuary where one can solve one's worries". The 500-m² (5,382-sq-ft) floor area contains four high-tech toilets. Residents reach the roof balcony around the "rim" of the bowl via stairs in what would be the toilet's "drain".

Highest-altitude home

Orbiting an altitude of between 330 km (205 mi) and 410 km (255 mi) above Earth, the *International Space Station* (*ISS*) provides a place of residence for periods of several months or longer. First launched in 1998, the ISS normally accommodates six scientists and astronauts at any one time, and had been continuously inhabited for 14 years 82 days as of 21 Jan 2015.

Largest home in an airliner

It's missing its engines, but this Boeing 727 still has wings, landing gear and some seats. Owner Bruce Campbell (USA) uses the 99.04 m² (1,066 sq ft) of space frugally, sleeping on a futon and cooking with a microwave and toaster.

Largest house

The **largest**, **tallest** and **most expensive** house is *Antilia*, the 27-storey home of Mukesh Ambani (IND) in Mumbai, India. Finished in 2010 at a cost of around $2 bn (£1.3 bn), it has a living floor area of 37,000 m² (400,000 sq ft) and occupies a 4,532-m² (48,780-sq-ft) plot on Mumbai's elite Altamount Road. *Antilia* is 173 m (568 ft) high, but the triple-height spacing of the 27 floors make it as tall as a typical 60-storey office tower.

Largest house shaped like a Volkswagen Beetle

When Austrian architect/designer Markus Voglreiter and his wife Ursula bought a house near Salzburg, Austria, Markus opted to extend it with a 14-m-long (45-ft 11-in), 10-m-high (32-ft 9-in) wing shaped like a VW Beetle car. The three-storey, 900-sq-ft (83.61-m²) *Auto Residence* cost some $1.3 m (£750,000) to construct.

IN NUMBERS

1.2 m
Difference in height between the two ends of the Crooked House pub near Dudley, UK (4 ft)

9.7 m
Diameter of the **largest spherical house** (32 ft), Casa Bola in São Paulo, Brazil

90°
Angle through which the **first twisted skyscraper** turns – the HSB Turning Torso in Malmö, Sweden

360°
Angle through which Bohumil Lhota's home – in Prague, Czech Republic – can rotate. It can be moved up and down, too

65,000
Potential inhabitants of the Abraj Al Bait Towers in Mecca, Saudi Arabia, the **largest residential building by capacity**

Straight and narrow

Blink as you walk by and you might well miss it. Designed by Jakub Szczęsny of Polish architects Centrala, this super-slimline residence in Warsaw, Poland, has truly made the most of a (very small) gap in the housing market.

Completed in 2012, Keret House is, by a wide margin, the **narrowest house**. This tiny raised residence measures just 92 cm (3 ft) at its narrowest and 152 cm (5 ft) at its widest, with a total floor area of 14 m^2 (151 sq ft). Within its minuscule two-storey layout, it somehow squeezes in a bedroom with separate kitchen and bathroom, connected by a ladder instead of a conventional staircase.

The property is named after Israeli writer and film-maker Etgar Keret, who led the commission for the house and was its first resident. The steel frame structure is squeezed between two existing buildings at 22 Chłodna Street and 74 Żelazna Street, and is officially designated as an art installation because it does not meet local Warsaw building regulations.

"Although its dimensions are miniature, it can easily be used for living, as well as working," insists Szczęsny.

Residents have to make a lot of compromises, of course. The dining table only has room for two diners, the fridge can only hold two cans, and the windows cannot be opened. It's a fully functional living space, though: as well as a mini-bed and mini-bathroom, there is a mini-cesspool.

Etgar Keret was its patron as well as its first inhabitant, but the house has since served as a retreat for artists, writers and intellectuals. Presumably, none of them were claustrophobic...

Largest underground mining town

A South Australian opal mining town, Coober Pedy is home to around 2,000 residents in 1,500 "dug-outs". Each sits 2.4–6.7 m (8–22 ft) below ground with living rooms and bedrooms, and has air shafts for ventilation. All of this is in order to avoid scorching daytime temperatures that reach 51°C (125°F) in the shade.

ECO CITIES

In 1980, less than **20% of China's population** lived in cities; by 2030, an estimated **75% will be city dwellers**

Least polluted city

Pollution is measured in terms of the amount of fine particulate matter of 2.5 micrometres or less in diameter (PM2.5) that is present in the atmosphere. The World Health Organization's Outdoor Air Pollution Database 2014 showed that Powell River (above) in British Columbia, Canada, has an annual mean of just 3 micrograms of PM2.5 per m^3.

The Indian capital Delhi (inset right) has an annual mean of 153 micrograms of PM2.5 per m^3, making it the **most polluted city**.

Most environmentally friendly city (current)

As well as representing the **largest arcology project** (see p.291), Masdar City in Abu Dhabi, UAE, is the world's first city designed to be zero-carbon and zero-waste. All its power comes from renewable resources, and all waste material is recycled. Driverless vehicles replace cars, so the city's projected 50,000 citizens should leave no carbon footprint. A fascinating experiment, or an unachievable ideal? Either way, the project has provoked important debate on sustainable urban living.

First commercial vertical farm

The Earth's population is swelling by the second, and experts are concerned that there may come a day when there won't be enough land to farm in order to feed everyone. Vertical farming offers a novel solution, reducing the amount of land a farm takes up by putting the farm inside a high-rise building. In Oct 2012, the world's first ever commercial vertical farm opened in Singapore. The site, developed by Sky Greens, consists of 9-m-high (29-ft) aluminium towers, 120 in all, which can produce 500 kg (1,100 lb) of vegetables per day.

Densest cycle-lane network

The Finnish capital of Helsinki has the world's most concentrated cycle-lane network. A report by the Union Internationale des Transports Publics (UITP) published in Jan 2014 calculated that there are 4,678 km of bike lanes per 1,000 km^2 of city area – or 7,500 mi per 1,000 sq mi. The winters in Helsinki only last for around three months, which might contribute to the city's dedication to cycling infrastructure. In one six-month period in 2012, the 1.3-km (0.8 mi) Baana pathway alone was used by a total of 320,000 cyclists.

City with the highest percentage of bicycle trips

Approximately 50% of all trips in Groningen, Netherlands, are by bicycle, a number that rises to 60% in the city centre. Groningen has been known as the "World's Cycling City" for some time. In the 1970s, urban planners used the fact that there was very little sprawl to encourage non-automotive trips in the city centre by restricting vehicle movement there, which led residents to prefer cycling or walking to driving a car.

Largest green wall

The largest vertical garden, or green wall, was measured at 2,289 m^2 (24,638.59 sq ft) in Apr 2014. It was created by City Developments Limited (SGP), as part of the Tree House development in Singapore.

Aside from their aesthetic appeal, green walls help to improve air quality, protect buildings from temperature fluctuations (which helps with energy costs) and dampen noise pollution.

Highest percentage of journeys by public transport

Some 80% of all trips undertaken in Hong Kong, China, are made via public transit, with 11.3 million passenger boardings every day. Hong Kong is one of the world's most densely populated cities, with as many as 57,120 people per km^2 (147,940 people per sq mi). By contrast, the island of Manhattan, in New York City, USA, has 26,000 people per km^2 (67,340 people per sq mi).

Largest arcology project

An arcology is a concept city designed as an alternative to modern urban sprawl. First proposed by Italian-American architect Paolo Soleri in the 1960s, it is designed to be self-sufficient and have minimal environmental impact. The largest such project currently underway is Masdar City in Abu Dhabi. Initiated in 2006, the 6-km^2 (2.3-sq-mi) city is planned to host around 50,000 people and 1,500 businesses, and to be carbon-neutral.

CITY STATS FROM THE UNITED NATIONS

2 people per second
Rate of increase in the world's urban population

12%
Proportion of the world's population living in "mega" cities of 10 million people or more

28
Number of mega cities worldwide

54%
Proportion of the world's population that lives in urban areas; that figure is set to rise to 66% by 2050

5 million
Average monthly increase of residents in cities in the developing world

Largest car-free urban area

Automobiles are conspicuously absent from the Medina (old, walled part) of Fès el-Bali in the Moroccan city of Fès. While it is home to more than 156,000 people, none of them are allowed to drive cars within the city walls. Of course, it helps that the narrow design of the ancient streets – some no more than 2 ft (60 cm) wide – makes it virtually impossible for cars to get through.

Most bicycle-friendly city

The Copenhagenize Index rates cities by 13 bicycle-related categories, such as facilities and infrastructure for cyclists. In the 2013 Index, the Dutch city of Amsterdam topped the rankings. There are 881,000 bicycles in Amsterdam to 263,000 cars – a ratio of more than three to one.

Largest solar-powered stadium

The National Stadium in Kaohsiung, Chinese Taipei, is covered in 8,844 solar panels, which overlay 14,155 m^2 (152,363 sq ft) of the structure's exterior. This gives the arena the potential to generate 1.14 gigawatt-hours of electricity every year – enough to power 80% of its operating needs (including 3,300 lights and two giant video screens). This would prevent 660 tonnes (727 US tons) of carbon dioxide from being pumped into the atmosphere annually from conventional power stations.

Designed by architect Toyo Ito for the 2009 World Games, the horseshoe-shaped stadium – said to be based on the form of a curled dragon – can hold a total of 55,000 spectators. Its other eco-friendly features include reusable, domestically made materials.

Largest bus retrofit programme

The double-decker buses in London, UK, have become a symbol of the city's efforts to "green" its public transit fleet. In Jul 2014, the city's transit department Transport for London (TfL) completed the most extensive retrofit programme for older buses. Today, the exhaust systems on 1,015 buses (travelling on 50 different routes) are equipped with a Selective Catalytic Reduction (SCR) system to reduce their nitrogen oxide emissions. TfL is currently planning to increase the total of retrofitted buses to 1,800.

Most Blue Flag beaches in a municipality

The municipality with the greatest number of healthy beaches is Bodrum in Turkey. According to Blue Flag Beaches – an international voluntary programme that requires beaches to adhere to strict criteria regarding water quality, environmental management and education – 530 of Bodrum's beaches had been awarded with Blue Flags as of 2014.

Tianjin Eco-City

The ongoing rise in urban populations and expansion of cities and towns has inevitably been accompanied by greater levels of pollution and other environmental damage. Increasingly, however, city planners are turning their attention to creating more ecologically sustainable metropolises.

Located about 150 km (90 mi) south-east of Beijing in China, Tianjin Eco-City will be a 30-km² (11.5-sq-mi) community informed by the concept of green living.

The project is the result of a collaboration between the governments of Singapore and China and private investors. It has been estimated that once the work is completed, in 10–15 years, Tianjin Eco-City will have a population of 350,000, which will make it the largest eco-city by population. The site chosen for this ambitious project – currently costed at $24 bn (£15.8 bn) – was once a polluted wasteland about half the size of the island of Manhattan in New York City, USA.

A total of 20% of the city's energy usage will be from renewable energy sources – via solar panels or wind turbines, for example. "Passive" design features, such as orienting buildings to receive maximum light or natural ventilation, will further reduce energy demands.

Use of private vehicles will be discouraged and around 90% of the city's population are expected to travel by ecologically friendly transport such as electric or hybrid-fuel buses. What's more, many workplaces will be located within comfortable walking distance, or a bike ride, from home.

The **Statue of Liberty**, a gift to the USA from France, was shipped in 1885 in **350 pieces**

Smallest toothpick sculpture

Steven J Backman (USA) crafted a 19.86-mm-tall (0.782-in) Empire State Building from a single toothpick (right, actual size), as verified by the New York State Society of Professional Engineers in New York City, USA, on 18 Dec 2014.

LARGEST...

Traffic light sculpture

Pierre Vivant (FRA) used 75 sets of computer-controlled traffic lights in his 1998 *Traffic Light Tree*, which stands 8 m (26 ft 3 in) tall. The award-winning public artwork was moved in 2014 to a permanent plot at Canary Wharf in London, UK.

Another public piece, *Cadillac Ranch* in Amarillo, Texas, USA, includes the **most Cadillac cars in a sculpture**. In Jun 1974, San Francisco arts collective Ant Farm buried 10 Cadillacs nose-down in the ground, angled to mimic the Great Pyramid of Giza. The commission was for the eccentric Texas millionaire Stanley Marsh III.

Largest group of underwater life-size statues

In 2012, Jason deCaires Taylor (UK) completed *The Silent Evolution*, a group of 450 figures sitting 8 m (26 ft 3 in) below the surface at the National Marine Park off Mexico's Yucatán Peninsula. Based on a cross-section of local people and made from sand, cement, silicone and fibreglass, the sculptures help to promote the recovery of nearby natural reefs.

Largest monolithic sculpture

The Great Sphinx of Giza on the west bank of the Nile in Egypt is the largest sculpture hewn from a single piece of stone. It measures 72 ft 10 in (20.22 m) high, 241 ft 2 in (73.5 m) long and 63 ft 4 in (19.3 m) wide. Made around 2500 BC, it has the body of a lion and a man's face, with a small altar set between its front paws.

MONUMENTAL CONSTRUCTIONS

Here, in order of their total height, is a selection of record-breaking statues and sculptures. Superlatives are based on various factors – height, weight and overall size. Each numbered entry in this list corresponds to a picture in the graphic on pp.296–98.

1	**Largest solid gold statue**	*Golden Buddha*, Bangkok, Thailand	3 m
2	**Largest *caganer***	*Mare Magnum Caganer*, Barcelona, Spain	6 m
3	**Largest carved jade statue**	*Anshan Buddha*, Anshan City, Liaoning, China	7.95 m
4	**Tallest standing moai**	*Paro*, Easter Island	9.8 m
5	**Largest steel sculpture**	*The Fortune Bear*, Incheon, South Korea	23.57 m
6	**Tallest statue of Jesus**	*Christ the King*, Świebodzin, Poland	36 m
7	**Largest equestrian statue**	*Genghis Khan*, Tsonjin Boldog, Mongolia	40 m
8	**Heaviest statue**	*Statue of Liberty*, New York, USA	46.05 m
9	**Tallest totem pole**	*Kwakwaka'wakw Pole*, British Columbia, Canada	54.94 m
10	**Largest sword in a statue**	*The Motherland Calls*, Volgograd, Russia	87 m
11	**Tallest bronze Buddha**	*Ushiku Daibutsu*, Ushiku, Ibaraki, Japan	110 m
12	**Tallest Buddha**	*Spring Temple Buddha*, Lushan, Henan, China	127.68 m

LARGEST...

K'NEX sculpture

A full-sized reproduction of the *Bloodhound SSC* supersonic car was constructed from 350,000 K'NEX pieces at the Royal British Legion Industries in Aylesford, Kent, UK. The model, created by the BLOODHOUND SSC RBLI K'NEX Build Team (UK), measured 3.87 m (12 ft 8.3 in) high, 2.44 m (8 ft) wide and 13.38 m (43 ft 10.7 in) long when assessed on 26 Aug 2014.

Toy sculpture

To mark the opening of PopCorn Mall in Hong Kong, China, on 29 Jul 2012, five students added 9,800 small toys to an original tree shape of toy bricks. Shoppers then put more toys in place, bringing to fruition a tree standing 2.34 m (7 ft 8 in) high, 2.07 m (6 ft 9 in) wide and 1.2 m (3 ft 11 in) long.

The 29-m-long (95-ft) sword weighs 14 tonnes (30,864 lb)

The tallest totem pole represents numerous tribes of the Kwakwaka'wakw – an indigenous group from the Pacific Northwest coast

In the 1980s, *Liberty* was renovated and given a new copper torch plated with 24-karat gold

Viewing deck set in the horse's head

Total weight is 24,635.5 tonnes (27,156 US tons)

250-tonne (551,156 lb) statue clad in stainless steel

33-m body height equals Jesus's life span

10

9

8

7

6

5

4

3

2

1

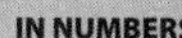

IN NUMBERS

14
Countries involved in the **largest land art sculpture**, *Rhythms of Life* by Andrew Rogers (AUS)

1,163,342
Buttons in the **largest 3D button sculpture**, replicating the Solar System

36 hr
Time it took Sarah Kaufmann (USA) to carve the **largest cheese sculpture**, on 14 Aug 2011

13 m
Length of each metallic petal in *Floralis Generica*, the **largest blooming flower sculpture** (42.6 ft)

50,000
Matches in David Mach's *Elvis Bust*, a portrait of singer Elvis Presley

FACT

Genghis Khan or "Universal Ruler" (1162–1227) led the Mongol tribes and conquered more than twice as much land as any other historical figure. All images of him were made after his lifetime.

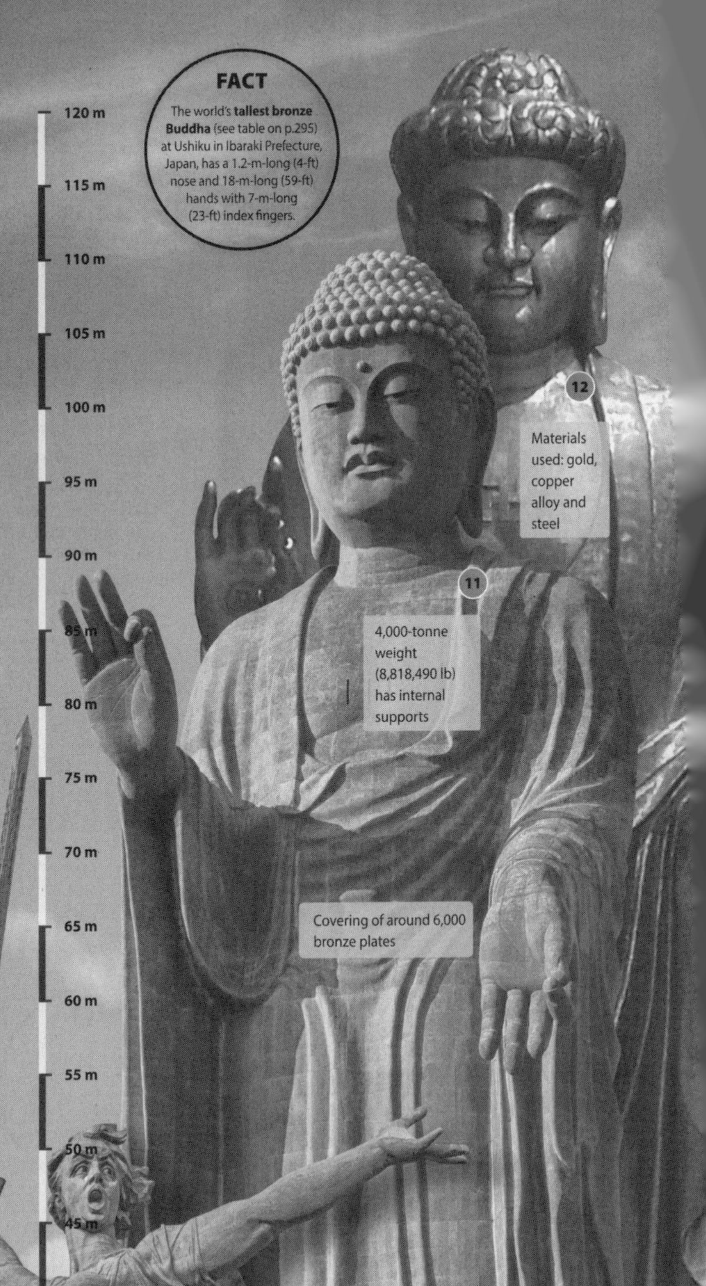
FACT
The world's **tallest bronze Buddha** (see table on p.295) at Ushiku in Ibaraki Prefecture, Japan, has a 1.2-m-long (4-ft) nose and 18-m-long (59-ft) hands with 7-m-long (23-ft) index fingers.
120 m
115 m
110 m
105 m
100 m
95 m
90 m
85 m
80 m
75 m
70 m
65 m
60 m
55 m
50 m
45 m
12
Materials used: gold, copper alloy and steel
11
4,000-tonne weight (8,818,490 lb) has internal supports
Covering of around 6,000 bronze plates

POWER STATIONS

Leonardo da Vinci proposed **solar power** to heat water in the late 15th century

Greatest geothermal power capacity

The USA's geothermal power industry reached a record capacity of 3,442 MW at the end of 2013.

Most powerful geothermal power-generation site

The Geysers geothermal field in the Mayacamas Mountains of California, USA, is the world's single-largest geothermal resource developed for electric generation. With 18 plants, The Geysers has a total installed capacity of some 1,500 MW – about enough to power a city the size of nearby San Francisco – but currently it's outputting around 900 MW. Today, 15 of the 18 geothermal power plants are owned and operated by the Calpine Corporation, with others operated by the Northern California Power Agency (NCPA) and US Renewables Group.

Largest power cut

On 31 Jul 2012, an estimated 620–710 million people in 20 of India's 28 states – half of the country's population and 9% of the global population – were left without power when three of the country's five power grids failed. The blame was initially placed on soaring demand and an over-drawing of power, although opposition parties pointed fingers at the government for not investing in the country's electricity infrastructure. Pictured is a Kolkata barber working by candlelight during the blackout.

Most powerful solar thermal power plant

Made fully operational in early 2014, the Ivanpah Solar Electric Generating System in the Mojave Desert, USA, has a maximum capacity of 392 MW. It uses 173,500 "heliostats" (movable mirrors) to reflect sunlight on to three towers and can power 140,000 homes.

FIRST...

Clean coal power station

Opened in Sep 2008, the Schwarze Pumpe power plant in Spremberg, Germany, uses coal, but with an eco-friendly twist. By burning the fossil fuel with pure oxygen, a technique called CCS (carbon capture and storage) is used to lock up the CO_2 emissions. Although not adding to global warming, it does produce a greater amount of CO_2.

Floating nuclear power station

Housed in a cargo ship stripped of its engines, the MH-1A came online in 1967, moored on Gatun Lake in the Panama Canal Zone (a US territory at the time). Its maximum output was 10 MW and it supplied electricity to the region for eight years.

Osmotic power station

In Nov 2009, a prototype power plant using osmosis was activated in Tofte, near Oslo, Norway. It works by filling two reservoirs – one with salt water and one with fresh water – divided by a porous membrane. As water molecules rush between the tanks to balance out salinity levels, their motion is used to turn an electricity-generating turbine.

MOST POWERFUL...

Biomass power station

Two units at the former coal-burning Ironbridge power plant, located in the Severn Gorge, UK, have run on wood pellets since 2013, with a total output of 740 MW. Despite running at half capacity since a fire in 2014, the facility still retains the record.

Tidal power station

Costing around $355 m (£217 m) to build and opened in 2011, the Sihwa Lake Tidal Power Station in South Korea boasts ten 25.4-MW underwater turbines, resulting in a total power rating of 254 MW. This beats the next most powerful tidal power station – La Rance Tidal Barrage in France – by 14 MW. La Rance is still noteworthy for being the **first tidal power station**.

Wave power station

Also harnessing the sea, the Land Installed Marine Powered Energy Transformer (LIMPET) on the island of Islay, UK, uses waves to compress and decompress an air-filled chamber, which drives a turbine. Its initial 500-kW capacity was reduced to 250 kW, but it still supplies power to the local grid.

Chicken manure power station

Switched on in 2008, BMC Moerdijk in the Netherlands is the most powerful facility to convert poultry waste into energy, combusting 440,000 tonnes (9.7 million lb) per year, with a 36.5-MW output.

Photovoltaic power plant

With a capacity of 550 MW, the Topaz Solar Farm in San Luis Obispo, California, USA, is capable of powering 160,000 homes. It is estimated that the solar plant, with its 9 million photovoltaic modules, saves 377,000 tonnes (8.3 million lb) of CO_2 per year – equivalent to taking 73,000 cars off the road.

Largest offshore wind farm

Spanning an area of 100 km^2 (38.6 sq mi) in the English Channel, the London Array wind farm consists of 175 Siemens turbines, each 147 m (482 ft) tall and with a 3.6-MW power output; this makes for a total capacity of 630 MW. With full operation reached on 8 Apr 2013, it's estimated that the facility powers 500,000 homes and saves 925,000 tonnes (2 billion lb) of CO_2 every year.

IN NUMBERS

73.3%
Proportion of nuclear power- generated energy in France in 2013, making it the country with the **highest percentage of nuclear power use**

1.7 million
People estimated to have been exposed to radiation after the accident at Chernobyl in the USSR in 1986, the **worst nuclear reactor disaster**

202 m
Height of the **tallest power station cooling towers** (662 ft) at India's Kalisindh Thermal Power Plant in Rajasthan

370 m
Height of the Damaoshan pylon in Zhejiang province, China – the **tallest electricity pylon** (1,213 ft)

100%
Proportion of Iceland's power generated by renewable sources (75% hydro and 25% geothermal)

4 million tonnes
Coal required to fuel a 1-GW, coal-fired power station for a year (8.81 billion lb)

Longest-running nuclear power station

First hooked up to the national grid on 26 Jun 1954, the APS-1 nuclear power station in Obninsk, USSR (now Russia) remained open until 29 Apr 2002 – a staggering 47-year span. The plant's reactor, known as *Atom Mirny* ("Peaceful Atom"), was a pioneering graphite-moderated, water-cooled design with a peak 6-MW electrical capacity.

Oldest nuclear power plant still in use

Russia may boast the **longest-running nuclear power station** (see above), but a contender is chasing its title. Beznau in Döttingen, Switzerland, first fired up on 24 Dec 1969. Despite originally having a 25-year life-span, the Beznau station received a full bill of health after a 2010 inspection. If it continues to operate until 2016, the plant will match the operational record of 47 years.

Most powerful natural gas station

Positioned on Dubai's coastline, the Jebel Ali Power and Desalination Plant in the UAE comprises six power stations with a total capacity of 7,801 MW. Annually, the complex generates 80% of the Dubai Electricity and Water Authority's electricity output.

FACT

According to Jan 2015 figures from the Nuclear Energy Institute, there are 437 nuclear reactors operational worldwide and a further 71 new nuclear plants under construction.

Glossary

Watt (W): Unit of power; measures how much energy is used per second. For example, a 60-W light bulb will deplete a battery faster than a 40-W light bulb if using the same type of battery. This is because the battery contains a finite amount of energy and the more powerful bulb will use more of that energy per second.

Kilowatt and megawatt (kW, MW): One thousand and one million watts, used to measure power in larger numbers for calculation convenience.

Hydro-powered home

Hydroelectricity may seem like a cutting-edge form of energy, but Cragside in Northumberland, UK (above), was using it as long ago as 1880, making it the first house powered by hydroelectricity.

The owner of Cragside was Victorian inventor and engineer William George Armstrong (UK). He first conceived of hydraulic power while fishing for trout, at the age of 24. As he would later explain: "I was lounging idly about, watching an old watermill, when it occurred to me what a small part of the power of the water was used in driving the wheel, and then I thought how great would be the force of even a small quantity of water if its energy were only concentrated in one column."

Armstrong grew rich selling hydraulic cranes, weapons and other mechanisms, which funded his ambitious designs for his home. Water was diverted from two nearby lakes via man-made falls (such as the one pictured left) to power a turbine-driven dynamo. Using this electricity, Cragside would also debut the **first incandescent light bulb** (below), invented by Joseph Swan (UK) in 1878.

Armstrong wanted to make Cragside into a "palace of a modern magician" and fit to receive important guests, who were to include the King of Siam, the Shah of Persia and the future king Edward VII.

THEME PARKS

Roller-coasters date back to **17th-century Russian slides** made of wood and **covered in ice**

MOST...

People down a waterslide in one hour

On 30 Jul 2014, 396 participants swooshed in strict relay down a 24-m (79-ft) indoor waterslide at the luxury year-round campsite Beerze Bulten in Overijssel, a rural area in the east of the Netherlands.

Vow renewals on a theme-park ride

On 9 Feb 2012, 41 couples renewed their wedding vows on the *Oblivion* ride at Alton Towers Resort in Staffordshire, UK, in an event organized by Signal 1 Radio.

Largest miniature world

The 48-ha (118.61-acre) Window of the World theme park in Shenzhen, Guangdong, China, features scale replicas of more than 130 world-famous buildings, landscapes and heritage sites, such as the Eiffel Tower, Niagara Falls and St Basil's Cathedral in Moscow, Russia (below).

FACT

The Window of the World park offers an encompassing view of five continents, with replicas built at ratios of 1:1, 1:5 and 1:15. If you walk quickly enough, you can travel across the world in a single day.

FIRST THEME PARK...

On a drug baron's estate

Hacienda Nápoles in Puerto Triunfo, Colombia, opened on 26 Dec 2007 on the 3,700-acre (1,497-ha) ranch of the notorious Pablo Escobar, a drug baron who died in 1993. Attractions include life-size dinosaur sculptures, a waterpark, plus a herd of hippos and other exotic species from Escobar's own zoo.

On the site of a nuclear power plant

Since 1995, Wunderland Kalkar, near Düsseldorf in Germany, has occupied the never-used SNR-300 nuclear power plant. Among its various attractions are a Ferris wheel and a roller-coaster, plus a 40-m-tall (131-ft 2-in) climbing wall in the former cooling tower.

Dedicated to the toilet

Opened in Suwon, South Korea, in Jul 2012, the Restroom Cultural Park is the creation of "Mr Toilet", aka Sim Jae-duck (KOR, see p.286). Lavatory designs from Roman times onwards captivate 10,000 visitors a month. Luckily, visitors don't have to spend a penny: entry to the park is free!

LARGEST...

Indoor theme park

Ferrari World Abu Dhabi on Yas Island, UAE, has a reported central area of 86,000 m^2 (925,696 sq ft) – larger than 10 soccer pitches. Its roller-coasters and other rides are themed on the luxury Italian sports car brand.

Largest transportable Ferris wheel

The R80 XL wheel, designed by Bussink Design GmbH (CHE), has a diameter of 69.8 m (229 ft) – a height of about 14 storeys tall. The first example produced, "Star of Puebla", was installed for the Puebla state government in Mexico on 15 Jul 2013. The wheel is transportable in that no changes to its structure are needed for its assembly or disassembly, and all of the pieces can fit into standard-sized shipping containers.

Longest marathon in a bumper car

On 14–15 Aug 2013, in an event organized by Free Radio at Drayton Manor Theme Park in Tamworth, Staffordshire, UK, local radio presenter Giuliano Casadei (UK) kept his bumper car moving for 26 hr 51 min 8 sec.

LARGEST...

Indoor water park

Tropical Islands in Krausnick, Germany, has a main hall estimated at 66,000 m^2 (710,400 sq ft) – a former airship hangar with an area equal to eight soccer pitches. Its height of 107 m (351 ft) makes it possible to take balloon rides inside the dome. Exotic areas include Tropical Sea, Bali Lagoon and Rainforest.

Political theme park

Opened on 26 Nov 1951, the Children's Republic, aka the City of Children, in La Plata Partido, Argentina, covers 52 ha (128.49 acres). Designed to explain and impart political ethics, it has child-size replicas of a parliament, church, court and other structures based on such landmark buildings as the Doge's Palace in Venice, Italy.

Largest drop on a wooden roller-coaster

Goliath opened on 19 Jun 2014 at Six Flags Great America in Gurnee, Illinois, USA. Its 180-ft (54.86-m) drop at an angle of 85.13° makes it the **steepest wooden roller-coaster.** With a top speed of 71.89 mph (115.7 km/h), it is also the **fastest wooden roller-coaster.**

Largest religious theme park

The Holy Land Experience is a 15-acre (6-ha) site in Orlando, Florida, USA, that opened on 5 Feb 2001. It recreates the holy city of Jerusalem from 1450 BC to AD 66. A daily average of 900 visitors come to see such attractions as the Jerusalem Street Market (above) and scenes from the life of Christ (inset).

Theme park in a nuclear bunker

Since Jan 2008, visitors have enjoyed a staging of the unscripted "1984 Survival Drama" at the Soviet Bunker in Naujasode, near Vilnius in Lithuania. Taken 5 m (16 ft 4 in) below ground to a 3,000-m^2 (32,291-sq-ft) nuclear bunker, they explore an immersive experience of 1980s Soviet life, complete with gas masks and KGB agents.

Largest theme-park operator

In 2013, 132,549,000 people – roughly the population of Japan – visited theme parks and attractions of the Walt Disney Company. The Magic Kingdom (left) at Walt Disney World in Lake Buena Vista, Florida, USA, is the **most visited theme park**, with 18,600,000 attendees in 2013.

IN NUMBERS

3,490
Roller-coasters in the world

51.38 m
Height of *Verrückt* at Schlitterbahn Waterpark in Kansas, USA – the **tallest waterslide** (168 ft 7 in)

8 min 45 sec
Longest scream by a crowd, achieved at Drayton Manor Theme Park in Staffordshire, UK, on 12 Apr 2014

50 hr
Longest marathon on a fairground attraction, by Sam Clauw (BEL) on 1 May 2014

1,509 m
Length of the "Factory of Terror" in Canton, Ohio, USA, the **longest walk-through horror house**, as of 17 Sep 2014 (4,951 ft)

A fantasy land

The Dwarf Empire – aka The World Eco Garden of Butterflies and the Dwarf Empire – near the city of Kunming in southern China, is the largest dwarf theme park. It was opened in 2009 by real-estate developer Chen Mingjing from Sichuan Province, and has, not surprisingly, attracted controversy.

The theme park is set up as a fantasy empire ruled by an emperor and his consort and is based on, and almost entirely staffed by, people with dwarfism.

The community comprises more than 100 dwarfs, each no more than 130 cm (4 ft 3.18 in) in height, and they entertain tourists twice a day with songs, dancing and other displays (above), including a version of *Swan Lake*. Performers are paid about $150 (£99) per month and provided with specially designed accommodation, although for the visitors they pretend to live in 33 small mushroom-shaped dwellings.

The Dwarf Empire has proved distasteful to some, who consider it exploitative and demeaning of people with dwarfism, while others see it as providing secure employment and friendship for the residents. One employee, Li Caixia, said she had found it very difficult to obtain a good job, and had been attracted to Dwarf Empire because the pay was double what she might obtain elsewhere.

Seen from left to right, below, entertainers Han Gui Lan, Liu Jin Jin, Han Zhen Yan and Yin Zheng Xiong pose in their costumes in front of their storybook village.

First official theme park based on a puzzle videogame

Särkänniemi Adventure Park in Tampere, Finland, is home to Angry Birds Land, which opened on 28 Apr 2012. Visitors can flock to the Lighthouse and Angry Birds Ride attractions, tackle an adventure course and munch on treats from Mighty Eagle Snacks and Red Bird Sweets.

Oldest continuously operating miniature world

Opened on 9 Aug 1929, Bekonscot Model Village & Railway in Beaconsfield, Buckinghamshire, UK, features six villages, hundreds of buildings, rivers, a racecourse and 10 mi (16 km) of miniature railway.

All the **JCB diggers** made in one year combined could shift **1.3 billion tonnes of material**

Most advanced space construction robot

When the world's space agencies were planning the Earth-orbiting *International Space Station*, it became clear that they required a construction vehicle with a difference. The solution was "Canadarm2" – a robotic arm with a reach of 17.6 m (57 ft 8 in) that could be used to slot new station modules into place. Part of the *ISS*'s Mobile Servicing System (MSS), the arm is double-ended, enabling it to crawl end-over-end across the station to position itself for each new assembly job. Since 2008, "Canadarm2" has been enhanced by a robot known as *Dextre*, which essentially serves as a more dexterous "hand".

Largest bulldozer ever

According to Off-Highway Research, the 336,000-lb (152.6-tonne) Komatsu D575A "Super Dozer" has a 24-ft 3-in x 10-ft 8-in (7.4 x 3.25-m) blade with a capacity of 2,437 cu ft (69 m³). The 38-ft 5-in-long (11.72-m) pusher is powered by an 858-kW (1,150-hp) turbo-charged diesel engine.

FACT

The "Super Dozer" blade alone weighs 20,000 lb (9,980 kg) and is 11 ft (3.3 m) long. One pass of that blade can clear away the equivalent of 720 wheelbarrows' worth of ground material.

First mechanical excavator

The earliest known example of a mechanized digger is the steam shovel, invented by US engineer William Smith Otis and patented by him in 1839. The device resembled a modern-day hydraulic excavator, with a wheeled chassis from which extended a digger arm and bucket. It was powered by a steam engine, heated from a boiler on the main chassis, and transferred its power to the shovel bucket by means of a system of pulleys.

Fastest tunnel boring

During construction of a 6.9-km (4.2-mi) underground route between Atocha and Chamartín stations in Madrid, Spain, in Aug 2008, a double-shield tunnel-boring machine recorded a speed of 92.8 m (304 ft 5 in) per day.

Heaviest weight lifted by a crane

On 18 Apr 2008, the "Taisun" crane at Yantai Raffles Shipyard in Yantai, China, lifted 20,133 tonnes (44.3 million lb) in the form of a barge ballasted with water.

Tallest mobile crane

The Demag CC 12600 built by Mannesmann Dematic (DEU) is 198 m (650 ft) high in its tallest configuration, which consists of a 120-m (394-ft) "fixed jib" attached to a 114-m (374-ft) near-vertical boom. It has a maximum lifting capacity of 1,600 tonnes (3.5 million lb) at a 22-m (72-ft) radius and is so large that it requires 100 trucks to transport all of its parts to a site.

Tallest telescopic crane

The Liebherr LTM 11200-9.1 telescopic crane has a maximum boom length of 100 m (328 ft). The boom consists of eight nested sections of steel tube that extend like a mariner's telescope – hence the name.

Largest tunnel-boring machine

In summer 2013, the colossal 57-ft 6-in-diameter (17.5-m) cutting head of "Bertha" the boring machine started drilling out the State Route 99 tunnel beneath Seattle, on the north-western coast of the USA. The cutter consists of a large steel face, into which are mounted 600 small cutting discs that grind away at the rock in its path. Manufactured by Japanese engineering firm Hitachi Zosen, the £50-m ($80-m) device is 300 ft (91 m) long and weighs 7,000 US tons (6,350 tonnes).

BUILDING THE CHANNEL TUNNEL IN NUMBERS

11
Number of boring machines used to create the Channel Tunnel; each was as long as a soccer pitch

1
Number of boring machines that remain buried in the Channel

13
Number of times you could fill London's Wembley Stadium with the material removed to create the Tunnel

250 ft
Distance dug per day (76.2 m)

1,100 tonnes
Weight of each boring drill (2.4 million lb)

£39,999
Amount that one boring machine sold for on eBay in Apr 2004 ($70,954)

Source: Eurotunnel.com

FACT

This JCB GT (right) is a supercharged, one-off mean machine. It's powered by a 572-cu-in (9.4-litre) "Big-Block" Chevrolet V8 engine, which is capable of producing 1,000 hp (745 kW).

Fastest backhoe loader

The highest speed achieved by a backhoe loader, or digger, is 116.82 km/h (72.59 mph), for a JCB GT driven by Matthew Lucas (UK) at Bathurst Airport in New South Wales, Australia, on 21 Oct 2014.

The 100-tonne (220,462-lb) boom is truck-mounted and is capable of lifting 1,200 tonnes (2.6 million lb), which also makes it the **most powerful telescopic crane**. It is powered by a six-cylinder, 240-kW (321-hp) engine – separate from the 500-kW (670-hp) engine powering the crane's 20-m (65-ft), nine-axle carrier vehicle.

Longest truck-mounted crane arm

Built by construction machinery maker Zoomlion Heavy Industry Science and Technology Co., Ltd. (China), the longest boom attached to a truck stretched 101.18 m (331 ft 11.46 in) when fully extended, as recorded in Changsha, Hunan, China, on 28 Sep 2012.

Zoomlion also manufactured the **longest tower crane arm**, which measured in at 110.68 m (363 ft 1.47 in) long on 28 Aug 2012.

LARGEST...

Land vehicle

According to Off-Highway Research, the largest vehicle capable of moving under its own power is the RB293 bucket-wheel excavator, an earth-moving machine manufactured by TAKRAF of Leipzig, Germany. Employed in an open-cast coal mine in the German state of North Rhine Westphalia, it measures 220 m (722 ft) in length and 94.5 m (310 ft) at its highest point. Requiring five people to operate, the 14,196-tonne (31.3 million-lb) RB293 is also the **heaviest land vehicle** and the **largest mobile industrial machine**. It is capable of shifting 240,000 m^3 (8.475 million cu ft) of earth per day.

Forklift truck

In 1991, Kalmar LMV (SWE) manufactured three counterbalanced forklift trucks capable of lifting loads up to 90 tonnes (198,400 lb) at a load centre of 2.4 m (7 ft 10 in). They were built to handle a huge man-made river project comprising two separate pipelines – one 998 km (620 mi) long, running from Sarir to the Gulf of Sirte, and the other running 897 km (557 mi) from Tazirbu to Benghazi in Libya.

Demolition shear

Used for dismantling large metal structures, a demolition shear is essentially a giant pair of powerful scissors mounted on a long arm. The biggest is the Rusch Triple 34-25 excavator with a Genesis 2500 Demolition Shear fitted to its excavator arm. With a reach of 34 m (111 ft), this monster was assembled by the Norwegian demolition contractor AF Decom in 2009 to raze disused oil platforms.

Mining monster

The Belaz 75710 is so big that it seems only fitting that it should hold more than one world record...

How big? Well, at 20.6 m (67 ft 7 in) long, it's about the same size as two double-decker buses placed end to end. And its empty weight of 360 tonnes (793,600 lb) makes it more than 1.5 times heavier than the Statue of Liberty! It is powered by a pair of 16-cylinder turbo-charged diesel engines, each with a power output of 2,300 hp (1,175 kW). It can reach a speed of 64 km/h (39.7 mph) – although you wouldn't want to be in the way when it does...

The Belaz 75710 is the **largest mining truck by volume**, at 645.4 m^3 (22,792 sq ft), and also by **payload capacity**, capable of shifting 450 tonnes (992,080 lb) of material at once.

This gargantuan vehicle was manufactured as part of the general trend within the mining industry for increasing the unit sizes of machinery. Larger trucks are capable of moving greater loads per haul cycle and so are therefore more time-efficient and economical.

The 75710 was measured, and its world records confirmed, at the Belaz (BLR) premises in Zhodino, Belarus, on 22 Jan 2014.

LEGO®

New York and London are **700 million LEGO studs** apart

FACT

When Danish toymaker Ole Kirk Christiansen first developed mini-bricks from natural plastic in 1949, wood was preferred for children's toys, and early sales of his plastic bricks were poor.

LARGEST...

Collection of interlocking plastic brick sets

As of 23 Jul 2011, Kyle Ugone of Yuma, Arizona, USA, had assembled 1,091 complete LEGO sets, the most in a private collection. Kyle, who is in the Marine Corps, began his collection as a young child, acquiring his first set in 1986.

Display of Star Wars Clone Troopers built with interlocking plastic bricks

On 27 Jun 2008, in Slough, Berkshire, UK, LEGO built a display of 35,210 Star Wars Clone Troopers. The serried ranks of menacing mini-figures, headed up by a lightsaber-wielding Darth Vader, took six-and-a-half hours to create.

Life-size house made from interlocking plastic bricks

On 17 Sep 2009, in Dorking, UK, 1,200 volunteers, together with James May (UK) for his TV series *James May's Toy Stories*, built a house measuring 4.69 m (15 ft 4 in) high, 9.39 m (30 ft 9 in) long and 5.75 m (18 ft 10 in) wide. It used 2,400,000 LEGO bricks and had two

Largest LEGO ship

In Nov 2014, at the BRICK event in London, UK, Bright Bricks (UK) displayed their 7.79-m-long (25-ft 7-in) model of the RMS *Queen Mary*. The real cruise ship, which at one time was the world's largest ocean liner, was operated from 1936 to 1967 by the Cunard Line and worked as a troop carrier during World War II. Built from c. 300,000 bricks, the LEGO reproduction took six people five months to make, and was constructed in eight sections.

Bright Bricks was founded by Duncan Titmarsh (UK), one of 14 LEGO Certified Professionals (LCPs) around the world – and the only one operating in the UK.

floors and four rooms. James spent one night in the house, only to find that it leaked when it rained.

Model of Hogwarts Castle made from plastic interlocking bricks

In 2012, Alice Finch of Seattle, USA, completed the 4-m-long (13-ft) replica of one of literature's most famous establishments for wizardry, from J K Rowling's *Harry Potter* series. Alice took 18 months to conjure up the project from around 400,000 LEGO bricks and more than 250 mini-figures. Details include recreations of floating candles in the Great Hall, and an old-fashioned slide projector in the Defense Against the Dark Arts classroom.

Fastest time to complete the LEGO Tower Bridge set (team of five)

On 30 Nov 2014, Team Brickish (UK), an Adult Fans of LEGO group, took 1 hr 30 min 38 sec to build the 4,287-piece bridge (set no.10214) at BRICK 2014, the LEGO event held at ExCeL in London, UK.

Fastest robot to solve a Rubik's cube

***CUBESTORMER 3*, an ARM-powered LEGO robot built by Mike Dobson (right) and David Gilday (both UK), solved a 3x3 cube in 3.253 sec at the Big Bang Fair at the Birmingham NEC in West Midlands, UK, on 15 Mar 2014. The cube had been scrambled using a computer-generated sequence.**

IN NUMBERS

915,103,765
Unique ways that six of the eight-studded bricks can be combined

62
LEGO bricks, on average, for every person on Earth

5,922
Pieces in the **largest commercially produced LEGO set**, the Taj Mahal

12
Age in years of the child who built a functional Braille printer from LEGO

28
LEGO sets sold every second at Christmas

18
Bricks per million that fail to meet LEGO standards

40 billion
Bricks needed to build a tower to reach the Moon

Largest drivable vehicle made from interlocking plastic bricks

On 11 Apr 2014, The Link Management Limited (HKG) used at least 200,000 bricks to make a drivable vehicle 12 ft 10 in (3.93 m) long, 4 ft 9 in (1.45 m) wide and 4 ft (1.22 m) high in celebration of the opening of Hong Kong International Hobby and Toy Museum in Kowloon. It ran non-stop for 42 ft 8 in (13 m), powered by a remote-control device.

Largest Great Ball Contraption

On 27 Nov 2014, at the BRICK event in London, UK, Maico Arts and Ben Jonkman (both NLD) erected an 88-module Great Ball Contraption (GBC) from LEGO Technics.

A GBC comprises an array of individual modules (inset) powered so that a small plastic ball can complete a circuit. This was the first GBC ratified by Guinness World Records.

First home-made LEGO prosthetic leg

On 12 Jun 2013, Christina Stephens (USA) uploaded a video to her YouTube channel, AmputeeOT, showing her creating a prosthetic made entirely from LEGO bricks. As of 19 Feb 2015, it had received 2,202,161 views.

Nathan Sawaya

New York-based artist Nathan Sawaya (USA, above) is best known for his colourful and witty creations from LEGO, and is recognized by the manufacturer as a LEGO Master Builder and Certified Professional.

Using millions of exactly the same bricks that children buy for themselves or receive as gifts, Nathan has built a global reputation as well as playful sculptures that grace museum and gallery spaces worldwide.

His trademark 3D portraits include such cultural icons as Elvis Presley, Superman and Lady Gaga, as well as his own concepts: for example, a skeleton, Mr Bones, captured in the act of draping a blue "skin" (of bricks, naturally) around his bones; and a Melting Man of transparent bricks.

The **largest skeleton built with interlocking plastic bricks** (left) is also Nathan's handiwork. At 6 m (20 ft) long and comprising 80,020 pieces, *Dinosaur Skeleton* is a *Tyrannosaurus rex* skeleton, meticulously built to scale. He built it over the summer of 2011 "in honour of the thousands of children who enjoy the art of LEGO building".

Longest span of a bridge made with interlocking plastic bricks in three minutes (team of eight)

On 14 Aug 2014, at the iCrossing team-building event in Brighton, UK, Kelly Sutherland, Joe New, Amy Fitter, Matt Allfrey, Lily Robertson, Andrew Cridland (all UK), Igor Lungo (ITA) and Oliver Hughes (FRA) built a bridge with a soaring arc of 1. 5 m (4 ft 11 in).

Most-viewed fan-made LEGO film based on a videogame

As of 19 Feb 2015, *LEGO: Black Ops* was the most popular LEGO videogame parody on YouTube, with 21,118,336 views. Created by veteran LEGO film-maker Keshen8, the *Call of Duty*-inspired clip was made with LEGO weapons by custom toymaker BrickArms.

Most expensive LEGO brick

On 3 Dec 2012, Brick Envy, Inc. (USA), a LEGO collector website founded by John Hughbanks and Mark Gallo (both USA), sold a 14-carat, 25.6-g (0.9-oz) gold brick for $12,500 (£7,752.42). These were made as gifts for long-serving members of the LEGO company from 1979 to 1981.

Tallest LEGO tower

On 25 May 2014, the LEGO Store in Budapest, Hungary, completed a 34.76-m (114-ft) obelisk in front of St Stephen's Basilica in Budapest. It took five days, some 450,000 bricks and the help of children and the public.

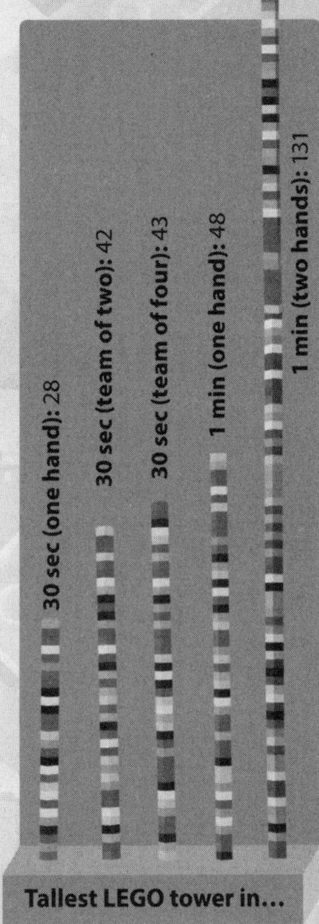

MINECRAFT

If each block is a 1-m cube, the playable area of the Minecraft world is about **eight times the surface area of Earth!**

FACT

In 2014, the Danish Geodata Agency created a 1:1-scale model of Denmark in *Minecraft*, making it the **first country modelled at full scale**. The project sought to help teach urban planning in schools.

Most popular videogame beta

With more than 10 million registered users by Jul 2011, *Minecraft* became the most successful game beta ever. It entered beta testing on 20 Dec 2010, with the first official version hitting the market in Nov 2011.

Largest playable area in an open-world videogame

In *Minecraft*, the map is theoretically infinite – the farther you travel across the blocky landscape, the more is generated. However, in reality, the game's physics only work effectively on blocks up to 32 million blocks away from the world centre, creating a total playable area of 4,096,000,000 km^2 (1,581,000,000 sq mi); this also gives *Minecraft* the **largest playable area in any videogame**.

Longest *Minecraft* journey

In Mar 2011, Kurt J Mac (USA) began an epic journey to the edge of *Minecraft*'s vast world in "Survival" mode, recording his voyage on his YouTube channel. He uses his annual checks of how far he's walked to raise money for charity. On 10 Apr 2015, four years into the trek, he had traversed 2,097.1 km (1,303 mi), or 2,097,152 blocks from his original spawn site.

Largest LEGO® Minecraft diorama

Measuring 17.1 m^2 (184 sq ft) in area, the largest diorama built using LEGO Minecraft was constructed at the Brick 2014 event held at the ExCeL Centre in London, UK, on 27–30 Nov 2014. Each visitor to the exhibition was given the opportunity to contribute to the diorama by building on a 16-stud-wide board. The completed boards were then assembled by LEGO Co-Creation Manager Julie Broberg and her team, and the final measurement was taken at the end of the four-day event. The 3D scene made up a fantasy landscape, with everything from buildings and statues to jungles and treehouses.

Gamer's Edition 2016

For more on *Minecraft* – in fact, an entire *Minecraft* section – unearth a copy of the new *Guinness World Records Gamer's Edition*. Find out more on pp.394–97.

Most snow golems made in one minute

Snow golems are a "mob" – any living, moving character in *Minecraft* – that players create to assist them. Consisting of two blocks of snow, topped with a pumpkin or jack-o'-lantern, they hurl snowballs at enemies. Brazilian gamer Nachtigall Vaz made his own personal army of 70 snow golems in just 60 sec on 7 Jan 2013.

Most downloaded texture pack

The LB Photo Realism Pack 256x256 Version, by "Scuttles", had had 2,195,836 downloads from fansite Planet Minecraft as of 17 Mar 2015. A texture pack is designed to alter the appearance of an in-game environment; in this case it makes the landscapes more life-like, spawning terrain-specific plants and adding reflectivity to water, for instance.

Most players simultaneously in one *Minecraft* world

Minecraft is not really designed to host hundreds of players in a world at once, but the popular gaming YouTube channel Yogscast managed to gather an impressive 2,622 players in a single world concurrently on 1 Aug 2011.

First *Minecraft* "mash-up" texture pack

Whether it's *The Legend of Zelda*, *Halo* or *Pokémon*, today it's hard to think of a gaming franchise that hasn't received the *Minecraft* treatment in special add-on packs. The first game officially imported into the blocky world, however, was sci-fi shooter *Mass Effect* in Sep 2013, when Mojang's indie hit launched its series of "mash-up" texture packs for the console edition. The downloadable add-on introduced 36 *Mass Effect* character skins, as well as transforming all of *Minecraft*'s blocks and items into their *Mass Effect* counterparts.

Strongest block in *Minecraft*

Every *Minecraft* block has its own qualities, but none is more robust than bedrock, which forms the foundation of all terrains. In standard settings, nothing can break it, which is just as well, as it's the only thing between you and the Void!

Largest real-world place created in *Minecraft*

In 2013, some 224,000 km² (88,745 sq mi) of Britain was recreated in *Minecraft* by map-makers Ordnance Survey, using 22 billion blocks. The second iteration of "Minecraft GB" was released in Sep 2014 and comprises 83 billion blocks. In addition to famous sites such as Stonehenge (above), there are rivers, forests and mountains, and you can even track down your own home!

Longest *Minecraft* tunnel

The longest tunnel built in *Minecraft* is 10,502 blocks, which equates to 10,502 m (34,455 ft). Dug by Lachlan Etherton (AUS) in 50 min at a games store in Greenwith, South Australia, on 3 Aug 2013, it beat the previous record by 500 m (1,640 ft). It took Etherton 10 min to walk through the final tunnel.

First *Minecraft* pack based on *Doctor Who*

The famous Time Lord came to *Minecraft* in Oct 2014, with the release of "*Doctor Who Skins* Volume I". Of the 54 characters included, there are several Doctors as well as notorious enemies such as the Daleks (above).

6
Years since *Minecraft* was first released

24 hr 10 min
Longest marathon on *Minecraft*, set by Martin Fornleitner (AUT) in Vienna, Austria, on 19–20 Aug 2011

93
Metacritic rating of the PC version

820 hr
Estimated time to walk to the edge of the map

535,542
Twitter followers

$322.4 m
Revenue made from *Minecraft* in 2013 – up 38% on 2012 (£195.4 m)

12.4 m
Sales on Xbox Live, according to Microsoft, making it the **best-selling Xbox Live Arcade game**

8
Versions released

$2.5 bn
Price Microsoft paid to buy out *Minecraft*-maker Mojang in Sep 2014 (£1.5 bn)

Top of the blocks

On 19–20 Aug 2011, Martin Fornleitner (AUT) played *Minecraft* for 24 hr 10 min, earning him the record for longest *Minecraft* marathon.

What drew you to this record?

It was part of another successful record attempt – the **longest marathon on a mobile phone game.** I chose to play *Minecraft* because it's a creative game. Someone once said that *Minecraft* is like LEGO for grown-ups – and that's so true.

Any tips for beginners?

There are two kinds of newcomer. Some people just want to build something with a relaxed gameplay; others want adventures. I like the "Adventure" mode as it's fun to fight Creepers and search for resources. Play the "Adventure" mode if you want more than digital LEGO.

Do you still play *Minecraft*? Looking to break any more records?

I really love *Minecraft* so I play it on my Mac, PS4 and iPhone. I like to build castles or any *Star Wars* stuff, like the *Millennium Falcon*. There are many records out there, but I've got a family so don't have much time to break another record. But who knows, maybe my kids will in a few years…

Most downloaded *Minecraft* project

The most downloaded user project from the Planet Minecraft website is *The Dropper*, by "Bigre", with 1,248,878 downloads as of 29 Jan 2015. In the project, players must fall through a series of structures and shapes, aiming to reach the bottom without hitting any obstructions.

The **most downloaded skin**, on the other hand, is *Ironman*, by "YoursCrafter", with 103,168 downloads to date.

Best-selling game on home computer formats

As of 17 Mar 2015, the official *Minecraft* website puts total PC and Mac sales of the title at 18,910,800 – that's an average sign-up rate of 13,507 people every day since its alpha launch on 17 May 2011.

Most watched gaming video on YouTube

Uploaded on 19 Aug 2011, a video called "Revenge – A *Minecraft* Parody of Usher's DJ Got Us Fallin' in Love…" had been viewed a staggering 156,076,698 times as of 20 Mar 2015. The parody was posted by "CaptainSparklez", aka Jordan Maron (USA).

Highest-rated movie-based *Minecraft* add-on

A galaxy far, far away has now come to the block-building phenomenon on Xbox Live and is the highest-rated *Minecraft* add-on as of 19 Mar 2015. Made by Disney, Microsoft and Lucasfilm, the "Star Wars Classic Skin Pack Trial" features iconic characters from the sci-fi movie series. Heroes include Yoda, Luke Skywalker, Chewbacca and the droids R2-D2 and C-3PO, while villains include Darth Vader and Emperor Palpatine.

SCIENCE & ENGINEERING

Tallest aggregate skyscraper height in one year

According to the Council on Tall Buildings and Urban Habitat, during 2014 there were more 200-m-plus (656 ft) buildings constructed than ever before. If all these new skyscrapers were stacked on top of one another, they would stand a staggering 23,333 m (76,551 ft 8.21 in) high, which would place the tip of this mega-building well into the stratosphere.

Making up 541.3 m (1,776 ft) of that total figure is the Freedom Tower, aka One World Trade Center, in New York City, New York, USA (pictured above and overleaf) – the **tallest building completed in 2014.** Erected on the site of the original Twin Towers of the World Trade Center, its 1,776-ft height is a nod to the year that America gained its independence.

CONTENTS

FACT

More than 200,000 cubic yards (152,910 m^3) of concrete were used to build One World Trade Center – enough to make a pavement from New York to Chicago! For more on this skyscraper, see pp.280–83.

IN FOCUS

LARGE HADRON COLLIDER

Particle accelerators have many uses, from **studying dark matter** to **drying paint on drinks cans**

A brief history of CERN

CERN grew out of Europe's need for a positive and collaborative scientific effort following the destructive consequences of World War II.

1949
Idea of a European lab is mooted by Louis de Broglie (FRA)

1954
Construction work begins near Meyrin, Switzerland

1957
The first accelerator, the Synchrocyclotron, begins research

1959
The Proton Synchrotron (PS) is switched on

1965
An antideuteron is seen for the first time

1971
First proton collisions take place in the PS

1974
Digging of the tunnel for the Super Proton Synchrotron (SPS) ends

1976
The SPS – fitted with 1,317 electromagnets – starts up

1981
Proton-antiproton collision research commences

1983
Never-before-seen W and Z particles are observed

1988
Large Electron-Positron collider (LEP) tunnel finished

1991
Tim Berners-Lee (UK) launches the **first website** at CERN

1997
ATLAS and CMS are approved, followed by ALICE (above) and LHC-b

1998
Construction of the four experiments' caverns starts

2008
The LHC is switched on and the first beam of protons is sent around

2012
The Higgs boson is recorded by the CMS and ATLAS

2015
The LHC starts its second run

Over its 61-year history, the European Organization for Nuclear Research (CERN) has made some of the most groundbreaking scientific discoveries of all time – so it's little wonder that it has gathered its fair share of Guinness World Records titles along the way.

Many of its records relate to a single piece of technology – the **largest scientific instrument** in the world, the Large Hadron Collider (LHC), which was completed in 2008. As well as being the **largest particle accelerator** today, it is also the **most powerful accelerator**, two attributes that enable scientists to study the fundamental components that make up matter in more depth than ever before.

One of its greatest coups to date came on 4 Jul 2012, when the LHC helped to unearth the **first proof of the Higgs boson** – a long-sought subatomic particle that is helping us to understand the basic building blocks of the universe. In 1964, three teams of physicists, one including Peter Higgs (UK), independently conceived of a field through which all fundamental particles gain mass. Later named the "Higgs field", the Higgs boson is the visible manifestation of this field, in much the same way as we perceive ocean currents by waves, or wind by moving clouds in the sky.

Although present everywhere, the Higgs boson proved very difficult to pin down, owing to its short-lived nature and sporadic decay pattern. But nearly 50 years later, thanks to the LHC, Higgs and François Englert (BEL) – a physicist from another of the teams – each received a Nobel prize for their pioneering research.

The LHC started its second run in 2015 after two years of renovation, which can only mean good things for record-breaking science. As CERN's director general, Rolf-Dieter Heuer (DEU), put it in Jun 2014: "Much work has been carried out on the LHC over the last 18 months or so, and it's effectively a new machine, poised to set us on the path to new discoveries."

In the diagram on the following pages, follow the epic journey that a proton takes through CERN's accelerator complex, until it collides at four key points around the LHC.

Too hot to handle *and* too cool for school

When two streams of particles moving at close-to-light-speed collide, a *lot* of heat is generated. In 2012, CERN's scientists recorded temperatures of 5.49 trillion Kelvin, which at about a million times hotter than the centre of the Sun is the **highest man-made temperature** ever achieved. The LHC is also the world's **largest fridge.** To maintain a stable magnetic field for the particles, liquid nitrogen is used to cool electromagnets to -193°C (-315.4°F), before liquid helium drops the temperature even further to -271.3°C (-456.3°F).

5.5 trillion °C
Quark-gluon plasma in the ALICE experiment

27 million °C
Sun's core

30,000°C
Air around a lightning bolt

5,600°C
Earth's core

1,400°C
Hottest part of a candle flame

100°C
Water boils

56.7°C
Highest recorded temperature on Earth in Death Valley, CA, USA

0°C
Water freezes

-60°C
Average temperature on Mars

-271.3°C
Lowest temperature at CERN

-273.15°C
Absolute zero

FACT

As of the end of 2013, CERN had just over 2,500 staff members; this total included 1,033 scientists and engineers, 885 technicians, 117 craftspeople and 21 apprentices.

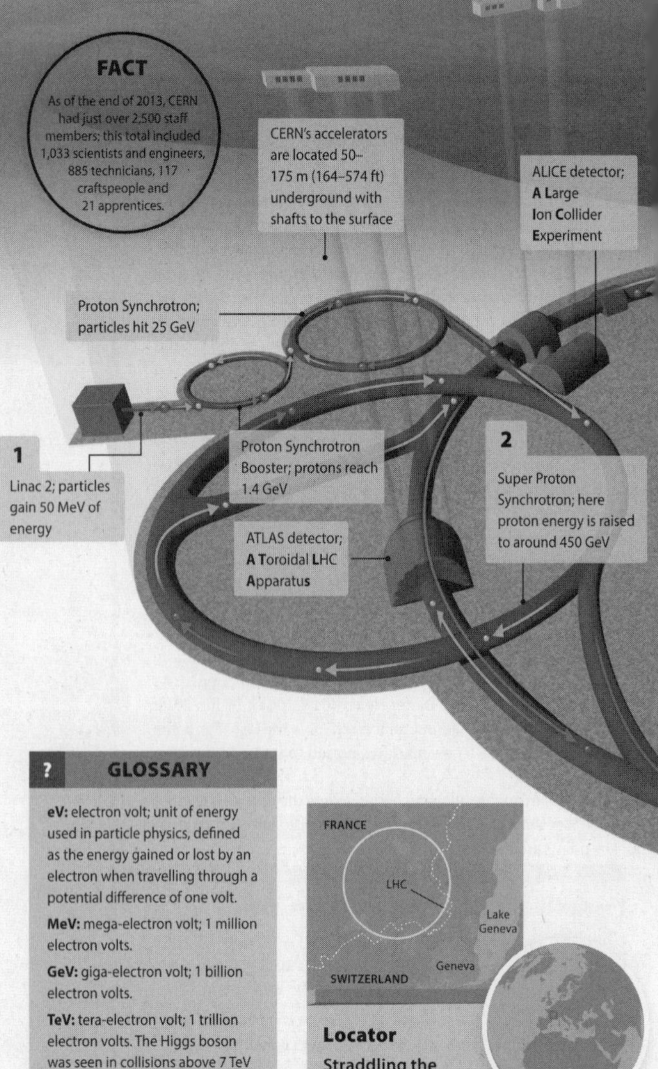

? GLOSSARY

eV: electron volt; unit of energy used in particle physics, defined as the energy gained or lost by an electron when travelling through a potential difference of one volt.

MeV: mega-electron volt; 1 million electron volts.

GeV: giga-electron volt; 1 billion electron volts.

TeV: tera-electron volt; 1 trillion electron volts. The Higgs boson was seen in collisions above 7 TeV (two beams colliding at ~3.5 TeV).

Boson: Also known as "force carriers", this distinct sub-family of particles are the medium through which matter particles interact.

Locator

Straddling the Franco-Swiss border, CERN sits between the towns of Saint-Genis-Pouilly and Meyrin.

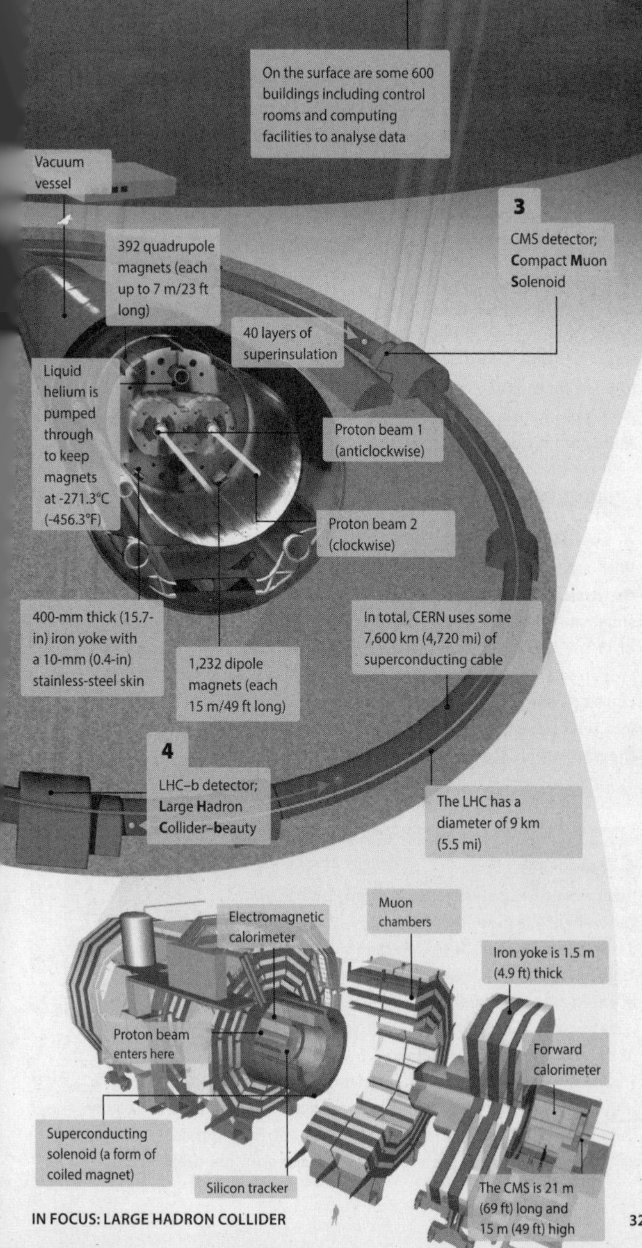
On the surface are some 600 buildings including control rooms and computing facilities to analyse data
Vacuum vessel
392 quadrupole magnets (each up to 7 m/23 ft long)
3
CMS detector; Compact Muon Solenoid
40 layers of superinsulation
Liquid helium is pumped through to keep magnets at -271.3°C (-456.3°F)
Proton beam 1 (anticlockwise)
Proton beam 2 (clockwise)
400-mm thick (15.7-in) iron yoke with a 10-mm (0.4-in) stainless-steel skin
1,232 dipole magnets (each 15 m/49 ft long)
In total, CERN uses some 7,600 km (4,720 mi) of superconducting cable
4
LHC–b detector; Large Hadron Collider–beauty
The LHC has a diameter of 9 km (5.5 mi)
Electromagnetic calorimeter
Muon chambers
Iron yoke is 1.5 m (4.9 ft) thick
Proton beam enters here
Forward calorimeter
Superconducting solenoid (a form of coiled magnet)
Silicon tracker
The CMS is 21 m (69 ft) long and 15 m (49 ft) high

1. Proton stripping

The process of smashing particles starts with a simple canister of hydrogen. Applying an electric field to the gas removes the atoms' electrons, so that only protons remain. The protons are then fed into the Linear Accelerator 2 (Linac 2), where they are pushed and pulled to increase their energy level.

2. Acceleration

Once at the required energy level (450 GeV), the protons enter the main accelerator: the Large Hadron Collider. Here, two streams of protons – released in "bunches" of 10,000 million or so – reach peak energy (6.5 TeV for the second run), accelerated by superconducting magnets. At this point, they are travelling around the 27-km (16.7-mi) ring at 11,000 times per sec.

3. Collision

Within 20 min, protons reach 99.9% light speed, when the streams are made to cross (1). As protons are so small, many travel past one another; at an energy of 13 TeV, there will only be about 40 collisions per crossing (2), though this still equates to 1 billion collisions per second. Those that do collide shatter into their basic components. Plotting their trails as they decay helps to identify them (3).

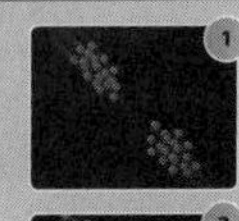

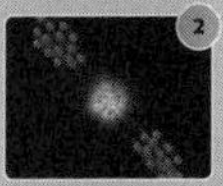

4. Detection

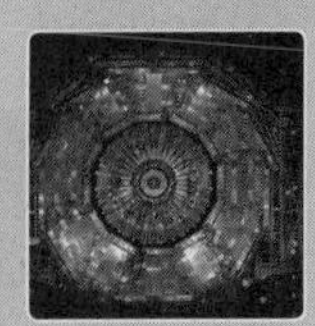

After a collision, sensitive instruments built into the walls of the detectors are ready to capture data. One of the key pieces of equipment used are "calorimeters", which measure minute changes in energy at an atomic level to identify various subatomic particles; for instance, a tell-tale sign of the Higgs boson is its mass of 125 GeV.

One of the detectors that helped find the Higgs boson, CMS (inset), is the **heaviest particle accelerator detector**, weighing 12,500 tonnes (27.5 million lb). The giant magnet found at the machine's core generates a magnetic field which is about 100,000 times stronger than Earth's.

Know your atoms

At school, we learn that atoms are made up of protons, neutrons and electrons, but for CERN's physicists, it's all about looking beyond that – at *subatomic particles* and how they behave. Here we explore the basic ingredients that make up everything.

Matter
Whether an apple or a human, all matter is made of millions of atoms.

Atom
A central nucleus is orbited by shells of negatively charged electrons.

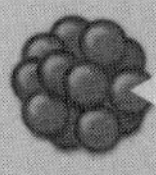

Nucleus
Nucleons (protons and neutrons) give an atom most of its mass.

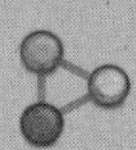

Subatomic particles
Inside nucleons are tight bundles of tiny quarks.

FORCE CARRIERS (GAUGE BOSONS)

LEPTONS

QUARKS

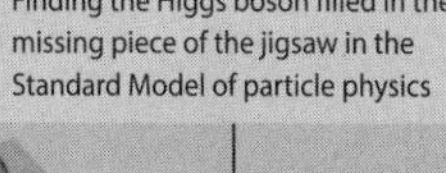

Finding the Higgs boson filled in the missing piece of the jigsaw in the Standard Model of particle physics

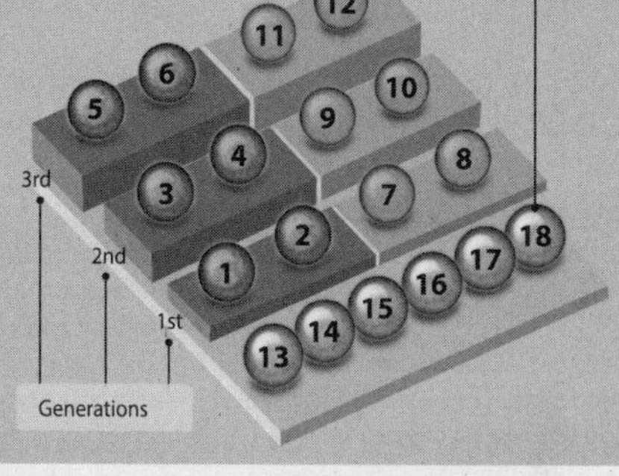

MEET THE SUBATOMIC PARTICLE FAMILY			
1	Electron	10	Charm
2	Electron neutrino	11	Bottom
3	Muon	12	Top
4	Muon neutrino	13	Photon
5	Tau	14	Z boson
6	Tau neutrino	15	W+ boson
7	Down	16	W- boson
8	Up	17	Gluon
9	Strange	18	Higgs boson

CUTTING-EDGE SCIENCE

In 2014, a **five-year-old girl** became the first child in the UK to receive a **3D-printed prosthetic hand**

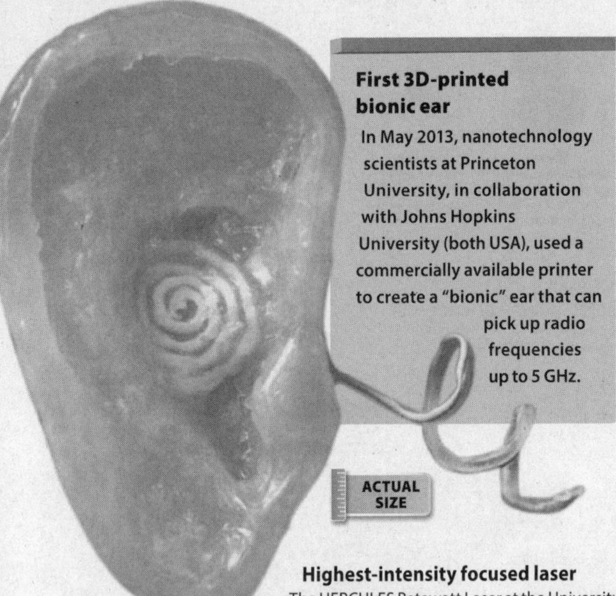

First 3D-printed bionic ear

In May 2013, nanotechnology scientists at Princeton University, in collaboration with Johns Hopkins University (both USA), used a commercially available printer to create a "bionic" ear that can pick up radio frequencies up to 5 GHz.

Highest-intensity focused laser

The HERCULES Petawatt Laser at the University of Michigan, USA, can produce a focused laser beam of $2\text{x}10^{22}$ W/cm^2 (20 billion trillion watts per sq cm). The laser pulse lasts just 30 million billionths of a second, and is equivalent to focusing all the sunlight that hits Earth on to a single grain of sand.

Highest-intensity atom beam

As published in the *New Journal of Physics* on 17 Feb 2014, the international Institute of Electronic Structure and Laser team at the Foundation for Research and Technology – Hellas (FORTH) in Crete, Greece, have built an "ultra-bright atom laser" that beams 40 million atoms per sec. An atom laser emits beams of matter instead of light. Researchers believe it could be used to test quantum theory, or to create "atomic holograms".

Highest-resolution optical microscope

On 1 Mar 2011, scientists at the University of Manchester, UK, revealed that they had created an optical microscope capable of imaging the inside of living cells. It uses microspheres (tiny particles) to amplify its optical power.

FACT

A 3D object is made by printing layer upon layer of material (e.g., plastic, ceramic or glass powders), following a digital 3D design. The layers are then fused together by heat or with a laser beam.

Most sensitive image sensor

In May 2013, a team at Nanyang Technological University (NTU) in Singapore demonstrated an image sensor 1,000 times more sensitive than those used in current cameras. It is made from graphene – the first time the super-strong-but-flexible carbon compound has been used for a broad-spectrum, highly photosensitive sensor.

Highly attuned to both visible and infra-red light, it could have applications for consumer cameras, professional instruments and even satellite imagers, and can record "starlit" scenes at 0.00001 lux (a candlelit room being 0.01 lux).

FASTEST...

2D camera

As reported in *Nature* on 4 Dec 2014, Professor Lihong Wang and a team at Washington University, USA, have created a camera that can capture images at 100 billion frames/sec. The camera's average image-capture rate is around 10 million frames/sec, allowing humans to see, at microscopic level, effects such as pulses of light. Professor Wang believes this can lead to new scientific discoveries and aid biomedical research.

First music tour to feature 3D-printed guitars

On their 2014 European tour, the indie trio Klaxons (UK) performed with white custom-made guitars, each printed in 15 hr. Bass guitarist Jamie Reynolds' Rickenbacker 4005-style model (right) and lead guitarist Simon Taylor-Davis' left-handed, Stratocaster-style instrument were designed and produced by Customuse in collaboration with 3DSystems (both UK).

FASTEST...

Computer

The supercomputer Tianhe-2, developed by China's National University of Defense Technology, performs at 33.86 petaflop/sec. Computational power is usually measured in how many floating point operations per sec (flops) a computer can complete: the more, the faster. One of Tianhe-2's core functions is high-order computational fluid dynamics simulations, for testing aero-dynamics and weather systems.

FIRST...

Bionic blood vessel implant

On 5 Jun 2013, a medical team at Duke University Hospital in North Carolina, USA, successfully transplanted a bioengineered blood vessel into the arm of a patient with end-stage kidney disease. The vein was grown in a solution of amino acids, vitamins and other nutrients. The walls of the vein were grown

First detection of gravitational waves from the Big Bang

On 17 Mar 2014, scientists at the South Pole working on the "Background Imaging of Cosmic Extragalactic Polarization 2" (BICEP2) experiment announced the discovery of gravity waves from the Big Bang. For three years, they had studied light patterns via the BICEP2 telescope (below; inset above with graduate student Justus Brevik). These revealed "primordial B-mode polarization" – a "curling" of light in the sky that dates back to 380,000 years after the Big Bang occurred. The team believed that this pattern could only be created by gravitational waves arising from the inflation of the universe soon after the Big Bang – strong evidence that the universe expanded rapidly after the huge explosion from which it was born.

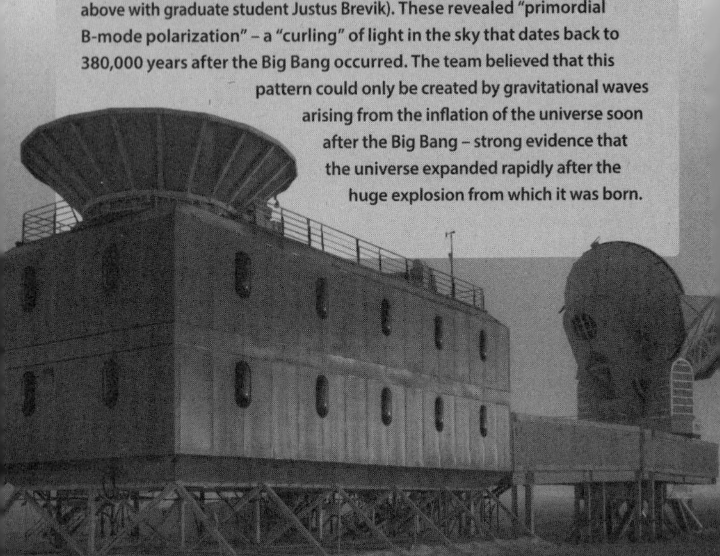

Fastest ultra-high-resolution 3D printer

A printer developed at the Vienna University of Technology in Austria can produce detailed 3D structures no bigger than a grain of sand – such as this microscopic model of a race car – at a speed 100 times that of similar devices. The printer builds shapes by depositing beads of liquid polymer at a linear speed of 5 m/sec (16 ft/sec); the polymer is then hardened by laser. On this basis, scientists hope the printer will have new applications in medical devices and implants.

from donated human cells and formed around a tubular mesh that shaped the cells into a blood vessel. Over a few months, the mesh gradually dissolved to leave the living vein. The scientists pumped nutrients through the vein in a pulse that mimicked the heartbeat so that it could build strength and resilience.

Longest neutrino beam

Neutrinos are one of the most difficult subatomic particles to detect. In an effort to find out more, and hopefully learn more about matter and the universe, an 810-km (503-mi) beam of neutrinos is being sent through the Earth at very nearly the speed of light (983,571,056 ft/sec; 299,792,458 m/sec), from Fermilab in Batavia, Illinois, to a detector in northern Minnesota (both USA). Fermilab announced that observations were underway on 6 Oct 2014. Called the NOvA experiment, the study is set to run for six years.

3D printing in orbit

On 25 Nov 2014, astronaut Barry Wilmore (USA), commander on the *International Space Station*, printed an extruded plate with "Made in Space" and the NASA logo on it. He used a 3D printer that is part of a microgravity experimental installation to trial the printing of items that astronauts need, so avoiding the wait for their delivery by supply rockets.

IN NUMBERS

2,400 m
Depth of the China Jinping Underground Laboratory, the **deepest underground lab** and the **most shielded lab for studying high-energy cosmic rays** (7,900 ft)

1 mm
Length of *Caenorhabditis elegans*, a 959-cell worm that is the **first animal to be genetically sequenced** (0.03 in)

400 km
Width of the **largest impact zone made by a meteorite** (250 mi), in Australia, reported by geophysicists on 7 Mar 2015

75+
Number of CubeSats, just 10 cm (4 in) wide, launched into space in 2014 to observe deforestation, river patterns and urban development on Earth

1,000
Number of robots, the size of US quarter coins, programmed to work together without human supervision in a 2014 US research project

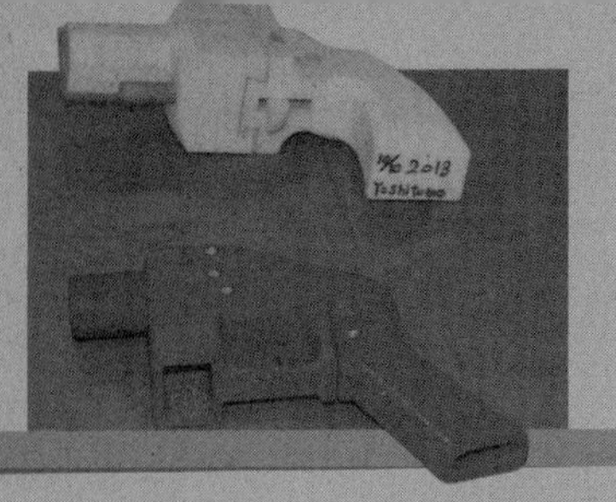

3D printing

On 21 Oct 2014, Yoshitomo Imura (JPN, below), received the first jail sentence for 3D printing – a two-year term for creating a 3D-printed, six-shot revolver (above).

Imura was arrested in May 2013 for reportedly printing five plastic "Zig-Zag" revolvers, two of which could fire bullets. (The name refers to the zig-zag grooves in the barrel.) He then posted several videos on YouTube, including a tutorial with design data and a test of the gun firing blank bullets.

Japan has very strict gun laws, and the ruling judge, Koji Inaba at Yokohama District Court, gave Imura a custodial sentence for creating a deadly firearm, describing his videos as "vicious". The case flagged up the safety risks of one aspect of 3D technology that was already of widespread concern.

Most 3D printing, however, offers a game-changing, even revolutionary, method for making items in plastic, concrete, glass, textiles and even biological material. It's a handy way to view new designs, from buildings to pairs of shoes, and it's already used to produce everything from car and fighter-jet components to complete dinosaur skeletons. In 2014, a team at the University of Southern California, USA, even developed a printer capable of printing out a whole house, in concrete, in a day!

Food and drugs are thought to be likely candidates for 3D printing. Medical researchers are experimenting with 3D bioprinting to create living human tissue of the skin, bone and heart. And in forensic investigation, it can reconstruct evidence ranging from a fingerprint to an entire crime scene.

Carbon nanotube computer

Developed at Stanford University in California, USA, "Cedric" may only have the capability of today's programmable calculators, but it is the first working example of the future of computer technology.

Transistors built with molecule-sized carbon nanotubes are faster and more energy-efficient than any silicon counterpart currently in operation. The technology is likely to take some years to mature because of cost, but their potential makes carbon nanotube computers attractive for the large, power-hungry servers of today.

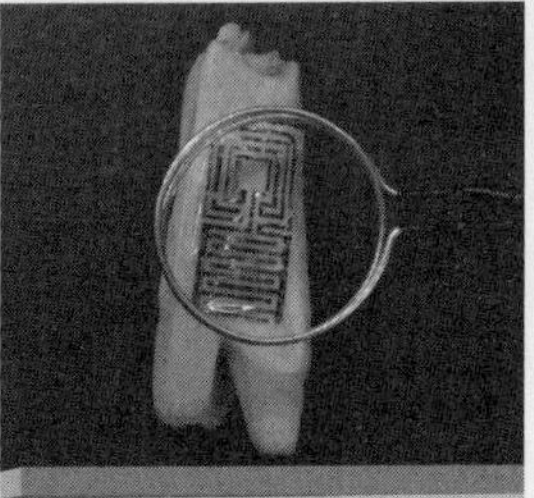

First biomedical tooth "tattoo"

In May 2012, scientists at Princeton University, USA, announced the development of a tiny graphene sensor that can attach to tooth enamel. It has minuscule electrodes and a wireless coil so that it can be powered by – and transmit information to – a remote device. The "tattoo" senses bacteria that cause tooth decay and infections, then alerts its wearer to a problem.

3D printers can now print in **metal**, **glass** and even **chocolate**

Fastest single-core fibre-optic cable

In Apr 2011, NEC Laboratories in Princeton, New Jersey, USA, demonstrated a data-sending rate of 101.7 terabits per second through 165 km (102 mi) of single-core fibre-optic cable. This is the equivalent of 250 Blu-ray discs sent every second.

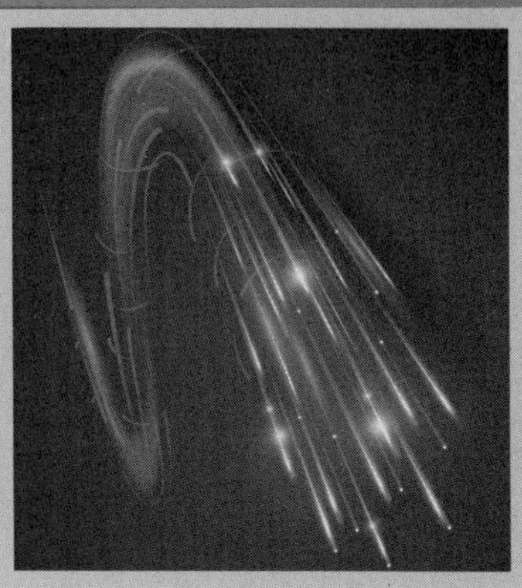

Newest chemical element

In May 2014, researchers confirmed the existence of an element first synthesized in 2010 by US and Russian scientists at the GSI Helmholtz Centre in Darmstadt, Germany. Named "element 117" (and, temporarily, ununseptium), it was made by launching calcium-48 ions into a berkelium target.

As its name suggests, it has the atomic number 117; the term "atomic number" refers to the quantity of protons in an atom's nucleus. "Heavy" elements are those with atomic numbers above 92, making element 117 the **heaviest element** verified so far.

First self-repairing concrete

In 2012, scientists at the Delft University of Technology (NLD) created a concrete mixture capable of repairing cracks in itself when set. Activated by water, bacteria in the concrete ingest "food" provided in the mixture to combine calcium with oxygen and carbon dioxide and form a type of limestone. The built-in bacteria only activate if water permeates a crack.

Most widely used plastic

By 2014, approximately 272 million tonnes (300 million US tons) of plastic were consumed worldwide. Of this total, polyethylene accounted for around 80 million tonnes (88 million US tons). For comparison, in 2012 the weight of the world's adult population was estimated at 287 million tonnes (316 million US tons).

Hardest substance

An aggregated diamond nanorod (ADNR) – or collection of nano-scale diamonds – is the hardest substance known to science. It was first created in 2005 by researchers at the Bayerisches Geoinstitut in Bayreuth, Germany. ADNR is also 11% less compressible than diamond.

First man-made plastic

Parkesine was invented by Alexander Parkes (UK) and unveiled at the Great International Exhibition in London, UK, in 1862. Derived from plant cellulose, this first-manufactured plastic could be moulded when heated, but kept its shape once cooled.

Largest ship built from carbon fibre

The first of five new Swedish *Visby*-class corvettes came into service in 2009. The vessel is the largest ship to be made of carbon fibre – an extremely hard, lightweight plastic. It is faster and lighter than a conventional ship, attributes that, with its angular shape, make it an effective stealth craft.

The *Visby* is 73 m (239 ft) long, weighs 600 tonnes (661 US tons) and has a crew of 43 sailors. It is designed mainly for anti-submarine work and can reach 35 knots (64 km/h; 40.2 mph). The vessel costs $184 m (£115 m).

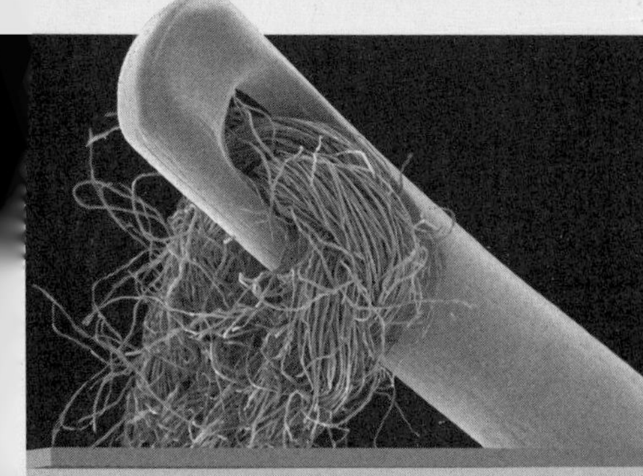

First textile fibre

In the form of linen, the wetland plant flax (*Linum usitatissimum*) is considered to be the world's oldest textile fibre. In 1983, linen fabric remnants dating from c. 7000 BC were found in the cave of Nahal Hemar in Israel's Judaean Desert. Linen has many useful properties: it becomes stronger when it is wet and does not feel damp to the touch until it has absorbed 20% of its own weight.

First transparent metal

In Jul 2009, scientists at the University of Oxford, UK, revealed that subjecting aluminium to soft (low-energy) X-rays made it transparent, albeit for just 40 femtosec. (A femtosec is one-quadrillionth of a second.) The Oxford team used the FLASH X-ray generator at the University of Hamburg in Germany to remove an electron from each atom in an aluminium sheet. The resultant material showed near-perfect transparency in the ultra-violet end of the spectrum. Scientists describe it as a new state of matter.

IN NUMBERS

1 atom
Thickness of graphene, the **thinnest man-made material**

2.3%
Proportion of light that graphene absorbs, making the material virtually transparent

20%
Additional proportion of its length to which graphene can be stretched

€1,000
Approximate cost of the amount of graphene to cover the head of a pin (£800; $1,360)

3 million
Sheets of graphene stacked on top of each other needed to reach a height of just 1 mm (0.04 in)

Most chemical- resistant material

In 1938, while working for Kinetic Chemicals in New Jersey, USA, Roy Plunkett (USA) accidentally created polymerized perfluoroethylene, or polytetrafluoroethylene (PTFE). Today, it has many uses, from weatherproof clothing (it is integral to Gore-Tex) to non-stick frying pans. Kinetic Chemicals trademarked the material as "Teflon" in 1945.

Strongest fibre

Spider silk, one of the strongest natural fibres, combines two types of proteins. In 2011, scientists from Hanyang University in South Korea mimicked this natural fibre by combining a polyvinyl alcohol (PVA) polymer with sheets of reduced graphene oxide flakes (RGOFs) and carbon nanotubes (CNTs). The resulting yarns produce fibres that can be sewn like threads and may be useful in the manufacture of body armour and engineering materials.

Most waterproof material

In 2013, a team from the Brookhaven National Laboratory in New York, USA, created an unprecedentedly waterproof substance. Conventional waterproof fabrics still become "wet" to some degree, but the surface of this material is engineered with thin, microscopic cone structures that force water to ball up and roll away – as demonstrated here by Brookhaven physicist Antonio Checco.

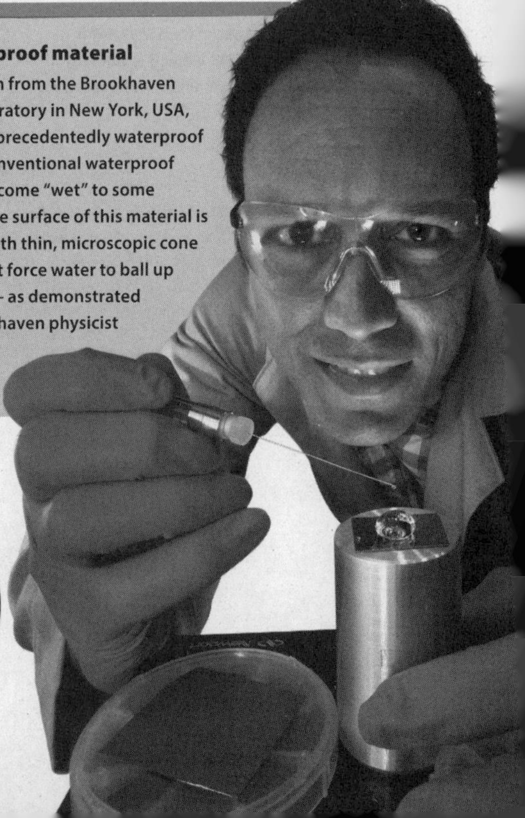

FACT

As water droplets carry dirt, surfaces coated in this new waterproof material would both repel water and stay cleaner. This could make it useful in the manufacture of windscreens for cars or planes.

First mass-produced plastic chair

The Bofinger Chair (BA 1171), designed by architect and designer Helmut Bätzner (DEU) in 1964, went into mass production in 1966. The now-ubiquitous stacking plastic chair was a one-piece item made of through-dyed, fibreglass-reinforced polyester and created in a single press over a steel mould.

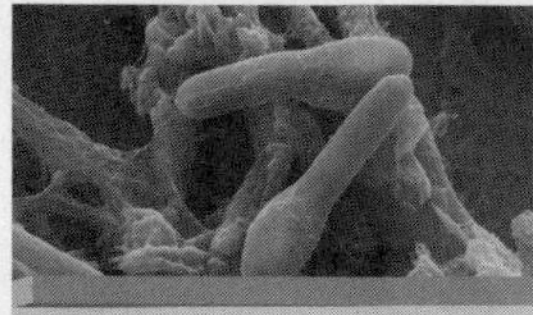

Most toxic substance used in cosmetics

Anti-wrinkle treatment Botox is made using a diluted form of botulinum toxin, produced by the bacterium *Clostridium botulinum* – the **deadliest known toxin**. This toxin is so deadly that an amount equal to a grain of salt is enough to kill a 90-kg (200-lb) adult.

The new black

Imagine something so dark that you can't see anything on its surface. To the naked eye, it would appear simply as a void, like a deep black hole. That's what you'd see if you were looking at the darkest man-made substance: Vantablack.

Created by Surrey NanoSystems (UK) and unveiled in Jul 2014, Vantablack is so dark that the human eye cannot discern any shapes or features on its surface. It absorbs 99.96% of all light – even types of light that fall outside the visible range, such as ultraviolet and infrared – as well as microwave radiation and radio waves.

Vantablack is made from carbon nanotubes, a fast-growing substance some 10,000 times thinner than the average human hair. "We grow the tubes like a field of carbon grass," explains Ben Jensen, NanoSystems' chief technical officer. When light particles hit Vantablack, they bounce between the nanotubes, which are spaced apart, and are then absorbed. Or as Ben puts it, "Light goes in, but it can't get back out." The word "vanta" refers to the structure of the substance – it stands for "vertically aligned carbon nanotube arrays".

So far, so sci-fi – but how would you use it? Well, as light has virtually no impact on Vantablack, it could be very useful in improving the sensitivity of astronomical cameras and infrared scanners. It could boost the sensitivity of telescopes so that they could see stars farther away than is currently possible. Its facility for absorbing light would also make it valuable for "stealth" military equipment.

FORENSICS

It's almost **impossible** to distinguish the **DNA of identical siblings**, although police are hoping to introduce a new test soon

c. 800,000 BC: Oldest non-human DNA

In Jul 2007, scientists announced that they had discovered DNA dating back as far as 800,000 years within ice cores taken from Greenland's ice sheet. The DNA reveals that moths and butterflies were abundant among the spruce and pine forests that existed on Greenland during this much warmer period of its history.

The **oldest extracted human DNA** found and analysed ("sequenced") was taken from the thigh bone of a 400,000-year-old human-like species whose remains were found in a cave called Sima de los Huesos ("Pit of Bones") in the Spanish province of Burgos. The results of the study by scientists at the Max Planck Institute for Evolutionary

Largest forensic-science training scheme

The most thorough training programme for forensic crime-scene investigation is that offered at the University of Tennessee's National Forensic Academy in Knoxville, USA. Competition for the 16 places on the 10-week course is tough, and only candidates already employed by a law-enforcement agency can apply. Since 2001, a total of 609 people have graduated. Above is Law Enforcement Innovation Center Program Manager Donna Kelley showing off crime collectables donated to the University by the author Patricia Cornwell; inset left, students examine a "body" in the burnt-out remnants of a car.

Anthropology in Leipzig, Germany, with co-authors in Spain and China, were published in the journal *Nature* on 4 Dec 2013.

c. 250 BC: First lie detector test

The Ancient Greek physician Erasistratus of Ceos discovered that pulse rates increase when people tell lies. This stemmed from his comprehensive studies of the heart and circulatory system, among other key works on the nervous system and bodily functions. It is said that he used this technique to know when his patients were telling lies about their symptoms and whether or not they were faithfully following his prescribed treatments.

221–206 BC: First identification of individuals using fingerprints

Clerics of the Chinese Qin Dynasty (221–206 BC) used fingerprints as a means of identification. The earliest known description of the forensic use of fingerprints comes from a Chinese document, the title of which translates as "The Volume of Crime Scene Investigation: Burglary". It describes how handprints were used as evidence in trials of the time.

1248: First use of forensic entomology

According to renowned forensic biologist Mark Benecke (DEU), the study of insects recovered from crime scenes and corpses can be traced back to a 55-volume medico-legal text book entitled *Hsi Yuan Lu* ("The Washing Away of Wrongs"). Its author, Sung Tz'u, was a Chinese lawyer and forensic expert. When called upon to investigate a fatal stabbing in a rice field, Sung Tz'u asked workers to lay down their sickles; soon, blow flies gravitated to one particular sickle covered in invisible traces of blood, forcing its owner to confess. It is now known that certain blow flies such as *Calliphora vomitoria* prefer to lay their eggs in fresh blood.

Hsi Yuan Lu also included descriptions of how to distinguish drowning from strangulation. This is the **first recorded use of medical knowledge to solve crimes**. Sung T'zu's methodology included investigating the damage to throat cartilage to solve murder cases involving strangulation.

1302: First forensic autopsy

Italian physician Bartolomeo da Varignana performed the first medico-legal autopsy in 1302, as part of an investigation into the suspected murder of a nobleman. Bartolomeo was later involved in a number of other legally required autopsies prior to his death in 1321.

1477: First use of teeth to identify a corpse

Charles the Bold, Duke of Burgundy, planned to create an independent state between France and Germany in the 15th century. This gave rise to considerable political tension. Armed conflict ensued and Charles was killed at the Battle of Nancy on 5 Jan 1477. His body was badly mutilated and lay on the field of battle for three days, but his page was able to identify Charles from his dentition – he had lost some teeth in a fall some years before.

1784: First person convicted using forensic material matching

In 1784, John Toms of Lancaster, UK, was tried and convicted for murdering Edward Culshaw with a pistol. During the examination of Culshaw's body, a pistol wad (crushed paper used to secure powder and balls in the muzzle) was found in the victim's head wound. It perfectly matched torn newspaper found in Toms's pocket and was used as the primary evidence leading to his conviction.

1835: First forensic bullet comparison

In 1835, a woman known as Mrs Maxwell from Southampton, UK, was shot and killed in her home. Her butler, Joseph Randall, claimed that an exchange of gunfire with burglars had taken place. However, when Henry Goddard (UK) – of early British police force the Bow Street Runners – examined Randall's gun and ammunition, he identified an identical pimple on all the bullets found at the scene, including the ones that killed Mrs Maxwell and which Randall alleged were fired at him. Goddard found a corresponding pinhead-sized hole in the mould from which the bullets had been made, proving that the murder had been committed by Randall himself.

FACT

Fingerprints provide a more accurate method of identification than DNA testing – even identical siblings have different fingerprints. Our prints stay the same for life, but can wear down.

Forensic diversity

The term "forensic" simply means "suitable for a court of law", and is applied to various criminal cases. "Forensic accounting" refers to the in-depth investigation of financial improprieties such as fraud or embezzlement. "Cyberforensics" is the detailed analysis of computer technology. "Forensic psychiatry" is the study of offenders who are mentally unstable, while the scope of "forensic linguistics" ranges from close analysis of oral or written statements to identifying an author or establishing legal meaning.

c. 250 BC – First lie detector test

1248 – First use of forensic entomology

1302 – First forensic autopsy

First use of DNA profiling

Sir Alec Jeffreys (UK, above) invented the technique of deoxyribonucleic acid (DNA) fingerprinting at Leicester University, UK, and first published a paper on its potential in *Nature* (vol. 314, pp.67–73; 7 Mar 1985). He first demonstrated its practical use during the spring of 1985 by determining the paternity of a child who was involved in an immigration debate.

IN NUMBERS

93%
Remains at crime scenes that are identified using dental records

1987
Year of the **first use of DNA profiling in a criminal conviction**

100
Bodies donated to the **longest-running body farm** in Knoxville, Tennessee, USA. The facility was set up to enable scientists to study decaying corpses

6
Age in months by which a human foetus has fully developed fingerprints

1477

First use of teeth to identify a corpse

1883

First forensic facial reconstruction

1896

First system of fingerprints

Forensic artistry

Since 1982, Lois Gibson (USA) has been using her artistic abilities to help bring criminals to justice. In fact, she's been so successful that she has earned her own Guinness World Records title, for the **most criminals positively identified owing to the composites of one artist**. To date, the detailed composites drawn by this talented forensic artist have helped to bring more than 1,000 offenders to justice in the US state of Texas.

Lois currently works for the police department in Houston, Texas. Her remarkable career started in the most dramatic fashion possible: she suffered a brutal, life-threatening assault. The shocking experience inspired the former street artist to move to Houston and offer her services to the city's police department. The first two sketches that she produced had no impact, but the third one helped to secure a conviction. Since then, she's never looked back.

Lois's job requires not only artistic talent but also great patience. "It's getting [victims] to remember the last thing they want to remember," she observes.

The photograph right is that of Donald Eugene Dutton, an escaped convict who shot a police officer named Deason several times and then drove over him, dragging him 17 m (55 ft). Sitting by the semi-conscious officer's hospital bedside, Lois asked him to describe his assailant and produced the sketch seen here.

A few days later, Dutton was caught shoplifting and his resemblance to Lois's sketch was noted. At a line-up staged in Officer Deason's hospital room, the policeman picked out Dutton as his attacker.

1883: First forensic facial reconstruction

In 1883, anatomist and anthropologist Hermann Welcker (DEU) demonstrated that the form of muscles and soft tissue on a person's face could be characterized and superimposed on a skull to create an impression of what that person originally looked like. The process forms the basis of both criminal and anthropological forensic face reconstruction today.

1896: First system of fingerprints

The earliest effective system of identification by fingerprints – known as the science of dactylography – was instituted in 1896 by Edward Henry, Inspector-General of Police in British India, who went on to become Commissioner of Metropolitan Police in London, UK.

FACT

All humans share 99.9% of their DNA. It's only that last 0.1% that distinguishes us from each other. In fact, we share around 98% of our DNA with chimpanzees – and around 70% with slugs!

Hieroglyphs may be written **left to right, right to left** or **top to bottom**

FIRST...

Ancient Egyptian site discovered by satellite remote sensing

In 1996, Japanese researchers from Tokai University and the Waseda Institute for Advanced Study examined the west bank of the River Nile using satellite sensing. They detected an unusual feature that, when excavated, proved to be a mud-brick tomb from the time of Tutankhamun. Named "Dahshur North", it is the first ancient Egyptian site to be discovered from space.

App giving access to national archaeological sites

On 7 Nov 2013, Wales launched an app that catalogued and allowed interactive access to the nation's archaeological data. *Archwilio* ("to examine") was commissioned by all four Welsh archaeological trusts to provide public access to more than 100,000 sites across the country.

Hieroglyphs

These sacred carved letters were engraved on monuments by ancient Egyptians to communicate their religious beliefs. The oldest known examples date back to 3400–3200 BC. They were found in 1999 in Abydos, Egypt.

By contrast, the **last hieroglyphs** unearthed are those at Hadrian's Gate in the Temple of Philae, on an island in the Nile, Egypt. They date back to 24 Aug AD 394.

Highest archaeological site

In 1999, Dr Johan Reinhard (USA) and a team sponsored by the National Geographic Society found the remains of three frozen Inca mummies at an altitude of 22,000 ft (6,706 m) on the peak of Llullaillaco, a volcano in Salta, Argentina. The mummies (two of whom can be seen above, on the ground in front of the group) were perfectly preserved, with organs intact and blood in their lungs and hearts.

The mummified bodies were those of children who had been sacrificed about 500 years ago. Their frozen state had helped to preserve their bodies, to the extent that experts believe they are the best-preserved mummies in the world.

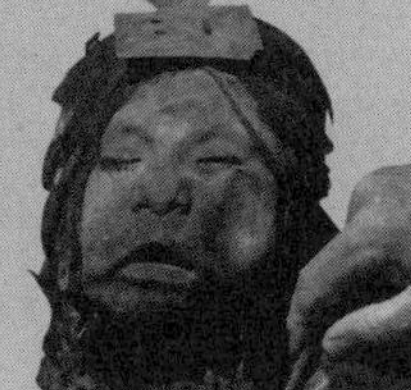

Largest archaeological archive

Part of the UK's Museum of London, the London Archaeological Archive and Research Centre houses material from more than 8,500 excavations made in London since 1830. It includes material from Shakespeare's Rose theatre and the city's Roman amphitheatre.

OLDEST SURVIVING...

Board game

Archaeologists have found games of Senet ("Passing") dating to 3500 BC and 3100 BC in Pre-dynastic and First Dynasty tombs at Abydos and Saqqara in modern-day Egypt. The game, representing the journey to reunite with the Sun god, involved two players moving their group of up to seven pieces along a board comprising three rows of 10 squares. The player who moved their pieces past those of their opponent and off the board first was the winner.

First confirmed gladiators' graveyard

In 1993, a team from the University of Vienna in Austria who were working at Ephesus in Turkey (Roman ruins pictured above) found a 20-m^2 (215.28-sq-ft) area filled with human bones and tomb reliefs depicting gladiators. Sixty-eight individuals were identified, all bearing trauma wounds consistent with a career in the arena. Analysis proved the injuries matched the types of weapons used by gladiators and their manner of fighting.

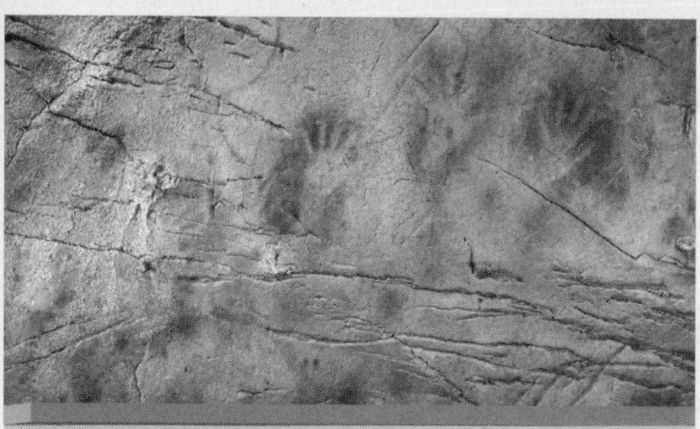

First discovered cave art

Discovered in the 1870s, paintings of animals and handprints from the El Castillo cave in Puente Viesgo in the province of Cantabria, Spain, have been proved to be at least 40,800 years old. This makes them not only the oldest cave art, but the **oldest paintings** of any kind.

Depiction of armed forces

The earliest armies emerged c. 3000 BC, notably in the Sumerian culture of Mesopotamia (largely modern-day Iraq). The oldest images of an organized force that could be termed an army appear on the Royal Standard of Ur. This wooden box, decorated with wartime and peacetime scenes, was excavated in the 1920s by archaeologist Sir Leonard Woolley from a Sumerian city-state. It shows light infantry with javelins and battleaxes and heavy, helmeted infantry with longer spears.

IN NUMBERS

18 mi
Length of excavations begun in Jul 2014 on the former wartime Belgian frontline from Ypres to Passchendaele – the **largest excavation of a World War I battlefield** (28.9 km)

4,000
Metalwork items dated to c. 7th century AD discovered by Terry Herbert (UK) on 5 Jul 2009 in Staffordshire, UK – **the largest hoard of Anglo-Saxon metal**

8,000+
Life-size statues in the "Terracotta Army" within the tomb of Chinese emperor Qin Shi Huang (see p.350)

11,000 years
Period that people have lived in the city of Jericho, in the Palestinian territories (the **oldest continuously inhabited city**)

OLDEST SURVIVING...

Footwear (dated directly)

In 1938, Luther Cressman (USA) of the University of Oregon uncovered dozens of ancient sandals at Fort Rock Cave in Oregon, USA. Made of sagebrush, they were most likely worn by native North Americans. Ten of the sandals were carbon-dated to 9,300–10,500 years old, making them the oldest samples of footwear to have been precisely dated from the items themselves rather than from sediments or objects around them.

Human faecal matter

A paper published in science journal *PLOS ONE* (Public Library of Science) on 25 Jun 2014 dated the earliest known human excrement to c. 50,000 years ago. Found at a Neanderthal campsite at El Salt near Alicante, Spain, the samples were analysed using gas chromatography at the USA's Massachusetts Institute of Technology. The evidence also lends support to the theory that Neanderthal man was omnivorous and consumed meat as well as vegetable matter.

Homo sapiens bones

The oldest known bones of *Homo sapiens* – our own species – were discovered at Kibish in Ethiopia in 1967. In 2005, Frank Brown (of the University of Utah, USA), Ian McDougall (Australian National University in Canberra) and John Fleagle (Stony Brook University in New York, USA) re-analysed the mineral deposits and volcanic debris surrounding the bones. They concluded that the artefacts were 195,000 years old.

Man-made place of worship

In 1994, a team directed by Klaus Schmidt (DEU) of the University of Heidelberg in Germany began to excavate the site of Göbekli Tepe in south-eastern Turkey. Six stone circles were uncovered, built with 9-ft (2.7-m) megaliths, surrounded by stone walls and including T-shaped pillars carved with animals found sacrificed on the site. No signs of human habitation were found, making Göbekli Tepe a purely ritual site. The circles were

Largest tomb of a known individual

The final resting place of Qin Shi Huang, the first emperor of a unified China, lies within a grave mound measuring 355 x 345 m (1,164 ft x 1,131 ft), just under one quarter the size of the Forbidden City in Beijing, China. The three-storey mausoleum is a miniature version of the emperor's palace in his capital of Xianyang. It is one of the three largest tombs in the world, and the only one that can be attributed with certainty to a specific person. The tomb is guarded by the 8,000+ life-sized figures of the Terracotta Army (below).

Neolithic, dating to 10,000 BC – some 7,000 years before the construction of Stonehenge in Wiltshire, UK.

Reading glasses

A pair of spectacles found in 1981 by archaeologists in the City of London, UK, date from the 15th century. Designed to be clipped on the nose, the frames were made of bull horn. When uncovered, the lenses were missing.

Shipwreck

Peter Throckmorton (USA) of the Hellenic Institute of Marine Archaeology discovered a wreck off the Greek island of Dokos in the Aegean Sea on 23 Aug 1975. It was identified by a large pile of pottery 20 m (65 ft) below the sea, believed to be cargo. Archaeologist George Papathanasopoulos (GRE) dated the wreck to 2200 BC, making it 4,215 years old as of 2015.

Viking boats

Two Viking ships were found on the island of Saaremaa in Estonia in 2008 and 2010. The wood of the hulls had rotted away, but iron rivets allowed archaeologists to trace their outlines. These light, fast warships were filled with artefacts that identified them as Scandinavian in origin. Radiocarbon dating has dated them to AD 700–750, predating the accepted advent of the age of the Vikings by 50–100 years.

FACT

Willard F Libby developed carbon dating in the late 1940s. The method measures the number of carbon-14 atoms in an object. These atoms decay over time, so the fewer atoms present, the older the object.

Best before 5000 BC

What might a meal of record-breaking archaeological finds consist of?

We might start with the **oldest bowl of noodles** (above), uncovered in Oct 2005 at the Lajia archaeological site in north-western China. The thin yellow noodles, made from millet, were preserved under an upturned bowl 3 m (10 ft) below the surface and are around 4,000 years old.

To go with it, you could try the **oldest wine**... but you'd have to lick it off pottery shards. Physical evidence of wine dating from as far back as c. 5000 BC was detected in remains of an ancient jar (left) found in 1968 at Hajii Firuz Tepe, Iran. The yellowish residue contained two of the hallmarks of wine, one of which was tartaric acid, a chemical naturally abundant in grapes.

The **oldest beer** can be dated to about the same time. Written references to the drink from c. 5000 BC have been found in Mesopotamia. In 1973, an expedition from Canada's Royal Ontario Museum detected physical evidence of beer dating to c. 3500 BC in the remains of a jug at Godin Tepe, Iran.

We're on safer ground with the **oldest cake** (below). The 11-cm-diameter (4.25-in) delicacy has sesame on it, honey inside and may have been made with milk. It was sealed and vacuum-packed in the grave of an individual named Pepionkh, who lived in ancient Egypt c. 2200 BC.

To round it off, perhaps a taste of the **oldest chocolate**? In 2007, a group from Cornell University in the USA found cocoa in pottery samples dating back to 1150 BC. They were uncovered at sites near Puerto Escondido in Honduras, Central America.

REMOTE-CONTROL TECH

In 1997, ***Sojourner***, on the Mars Pathfinder mission, became the **first remote-controlled vehicle to roam another planet**

Fastest internal-combustion-engine-powered, radio-controlled (RC) model car

Controlled by Jason Bradbury (UK), a model car fitted with an internal combustion engine raced to 137.86 km/h (85.66 mph) on the set of *The Gadget Show* in Stratford-upon-Avon, UK, on 29 Oct 2008.

Greatest distance by an RC model boat in 24 hours

On 4–5 May 2002, a 1:32-scale model of the Type 42 destroyer HMS *Gloucester*, built by Francis Macnaughton and piloted by Mike Watts and Paul Ellison (all UK), travelled 121.59 mi (195.68 km) at Bude Model Boat Festival in Cornwall, UK.

On 20 Apr 2013, David Stevens (AUS) drove his 1:10-scale Formula One (F1) model car at the Templestowe Flat Track Racing Club in Templestowe, Victoria, Australia, for 38.28 km (23.79 mi), or 374 oval laps. This is the **greatest distance by an RC model car on one set of batteries**. The attempt was to promote RC F1 racing.

Longest remote-controlled model multicopter flight (duration)

On 22 Aug 2014, Forrest Frantz, with members of the Frantz family (all USA), flew a self-built model multicopter (a drone with two-plus rotors) for 1 hr 39 min 23 sec in Parkdale, Oregon, USA.

Longest flight by a UAV (duration)

The carbon-fibre, High-Altitude Long-Endurance (HALE) spy plane *Zephyr* was launched at 6:41 a.m. on 9 Jul 2010 at the US Army's Yuma Proving Ground in Arizona, USA. It remained continuously airborne for 336 hr 22 min 8 sec – just over two weeks – landing on 23 Jul. Its flight also recorded the **highest altitude for a solar-powered UAV** to date: 70,740 ft (21,561 m).

FACT

Developed by the UK company QinetiQ, *Zephyr* is entirely solar-powered by day and at night uses lithium-sulphur batteries that have been recharged during the day by solar power.

Most RC model helicopters airborne simultaneously

On 8 Sep 2013, at an event organized by the Radio Controlled Helicopter Association (RCHA, UK), 98 helicopters flew for one minute at Prestwold Hall airfield in Leicestershire, UK. On the same day, the RCHA achieved the **most inverted RC model helicopters airborne simultaneously**, when 53 flipped over and flew upside down for one minute.

FIRST...

Unmanned aerial vehicle (UAV) to cross the Pacific Ocean

On 23 Apr 2001, a Northrop Grumman RQ-4 Global Hawk UAV flew non-stop for 22 hr, taking off from Edwards Air Force Base in California, USA, and landing at the Royal Australian Air Force Base in Edinburgh, Adelaide, Australia. The same flight set a record for the **greatest distance flown by a UAV**: 13,219.86 km (8,214.44 mi).

Phone-controlled aerial drone

The AR.Drone, introduced in 2010 by wireless tech developer Parrot (FRA), is a hovering, rotor-powered device for playing augmented-reality games. The four-rotored quadricopter can be controlled by iOS and Android devices via Wi-Fi.

An on-board camera allows the player to see the landscape from the device's point of view, making it easier to target virtual enemies. The drone can fly for 12 min on a 90-min charge and reach a height of 50 m (164 ft), although the limit for stable flight is 6 m (20 ft).

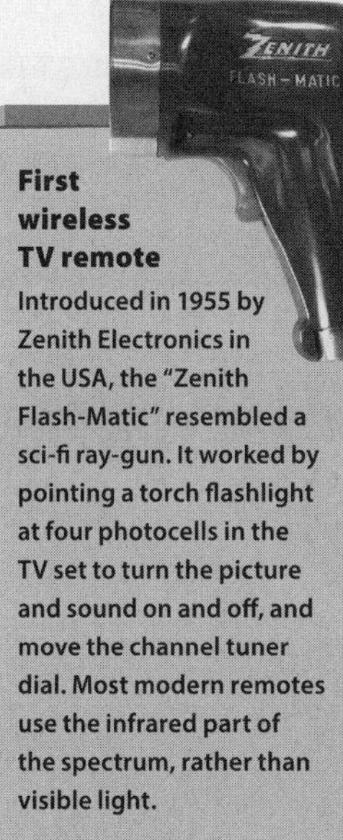

First wireless TV remote

Introduced in 1955 by Zenith Electronics in the USA, the "Zenith Flash-Matic" resembled a sci-fi ray-gun. It worked by pointing a torch flashlight at four photocells in the TV set to turn the picture and sound on and off, and move the channel tuner dial. Most modern remotes use the infrared part of the spectrum, rather than visible light.

Deepest dive by a remote-controlled device

The **deepest point in the oceans** is the Challenger Deep in the Mariana Trench, near the island of Guam in the western Pacific (see p.29). On 24 Mar 1995, Japanese research craft *Kaikō* became the first remote-controlled craft to visit this extremity, 10,911.4 m (35,799 ft) below sea level. Until 2003, it made more than 250 dives, collecting marine species and bacteria, the latter being of high potential value in medical research.

Most expensive UAV

The Northrop Grumman RQ-4 Global Hawk has a unit cost of $222 m (£146 m), according to a US General Accountability Office Report in Mar 2013. The Hawk can fly at 65,000 ft (19,800 m) on 30-hr flights and is equipped with a powerful suite of radar, optical and IR sensors, enabling it to survey an area the size of the state of Illinois, USA. In Sep 2014, *AV1* – the first ever completed Global Hawk – made its 100th flight.

FIRST...

Remote-controlled hormone implant

MicroCHIPS (USA) has invented a new type of contraceptive in the form of a chip to be implanted under the skin. At 20 x 20 x 7 mm (0.79 x 0.79 x 0.28 in), it is designed to last up to 16 years, delivering a daily dose of 30 mcg of the hormone levonorgestrel. A remote control turns the chip off, and back on again as needed. Clinical trials begin in 2016 with a view to sales starting in 2018. The chip could also release any drug on demand, or to a pre-programmed schedule.

Remote-controlled arm in space

Launched on 12 Nov 1981, the Canada-built Shuttle Remote Manipulator System (SRMS), aka *Canadarm 1*, was a multipurpose, remote-controlled arm attached to the US Space Shuttle cargo bay.

First used on the *Columbia* shuttle mission STS-2, it could deploy or retrieve payloads of up to 332.5 kg (733 lb) in space. It was later developed into a larger-capacity system for the *International Space Station*.

Satellite remote control for truck immobilization

In Oct 2003, engineers at Satellite Security Systems Inc. (USA) used the Motorola satellite data network to relay a "stop" message to a receiver in the dashboard of a gasoline truck 850 km (528 mi) away. Using a small square satellite antenna, the truck was remotely brought to a gradual stop over a period of 40 sec.

FACT

Two Global Hawk aircraft conduct high-altitude science missions for NASA. They can fly 12,600 mi (20,370 km) while satellite links enable ground-based researchers to view and evaluate data in real time.

IN NUMBERS

10 sec
Duration of the **first flight of the first RC helicopter**, invented by Arthur M Young (USA) in c. 1931

74.5 mi
Longest flight for a micro UAV (120 km), by the *Pterosoar*, a joint project by Oklahoma State University and California State University (both USA)

36.9 m
Longest ramp jump by an RC model car (121 ft 0.75 in), a Carson Specter 6S guided by Thomas Strobel (DEU)

8 g
Weight of the smallest RC model helicopter (0.28 oz): the PicooZ MX-1 by Silverlit Toys Manufactory Ltd (CHN)

100 mph
Speed that the fastest nitro-fuelled RC cars can reach (160 km/h)

Century of invention

Remote-controlled technology has been with us for over 100 years...

1898: Serbian-American inventor Nikola Tesla presents the **first radio-controlled device**, a boat called the "teleautomaton"

1903: Engineer Leonardo Torres Quevedo (ESP) demonstrates his RC robot *Telekino* at the Paris Academy of Sciences

1931: Britain's *Fairey Queen* becomes the **first RC aircraft**

1939: Philco (USA) markets the Mystery Control, the **first wireless radio control**, for Philco radios and radio-phones

1954: Don Brown (USA) introduces the *Galloping Ghost* system of proportional control, still the basic principle underlying radio control today

1956: Zenith Electronics (USA, see p.353) launches the **first ultrasound remote control for TV sets**, the "Space Command"

1987: Apple inventor Steve Wozniak (USA) introduces a remote control that can learn signals from other remotes. The Controller of Remote Equipment (CORE) becomes the **first universal remote control**

2000 onwards: Intense proliferation of remote control from phones, computers and other programmable devices

2014: *Philae*, the robotic European Space Agency lander, leaves the *Rosetta* spacecraft in the **first unmanned landing on a comet** (see p.366)

The technology was developed fo hazardous vehicles and trucks that could be used in terrorist activities, and to allow police to stop a stolen vehicle.

SMALLEST RC MODEL...

Car

In 2002, in Tokyo, Japan, Michihiro Hino (JPN) developed a 25-mm-long (0.98-in) model Mercedes-Benz Smart car to a perfect scale of 1:90. When fully charged, it could run for around 15 min.

Sailing boat

A boat built by Claudio Diolaiti (ITA) measured 5 in (15.2 cm) long and 2 in (6.3 cm) wide, with a height – including mast, keel and bulb – of 1 ft 2 in (38 cm), when tested in Nice, France, on 14 Nov 2007. Claudio made his craft from fibreglass and other materials used to manufacture full-sized boats.

Aircraft

John Wakefield (UK) created an RC aircraft with a wing-span of 69 mm (2.72 in) in Lancaster, UK, as recognized on 27 Oct 2010.

Helicopter

The Nano Falcon created by Silverlit Toys Manufactory Ltd (CHN) in Hong Kong measures 5.85 cm (2.30 in) long, 4.55 cm (1.79 in) high, 1.73 cm (0.68 in) wide and has a rotor size of 5.91 cm (2.33 in). It first went on sale in Japan on 5 Dec 2014.

MILITARY TECH

Leonardo da Vinci designed a **prototype of a tank** in 1487, and a **parachute** in c. 1485

FIRST...

Naval airstrikes

On Christmas Day 1914, German aircraft attacked a British naval presence – the Harwich Force – in the Heligoland Bight. No damage occurred on this occasion, however. The **first successful naval airstrike launched from a ship** against targets on land took place on 19 Jul 1918, when the British ship HMS *Furious* launched seven Sopwith 2F.1 Camels, in two separate flights, against the Zeppelin facility at Tondern in Schleswig-Holstein, Germany. The first wave of Camels destroyed Zeppelins L.54 and L.60.

Tank

"No.1 Lincoln" was produced by William Foster & Co Ltd (UK) and later modified and renamed "Little Willie". It first ran on 6 Sep 1915. Tanks first saw action with the Heavy Section of the Machine Gun Corps, later the Tank Corps, at the Battle of Flers-Courcelette in France on 15 Sep 1916.

On 24 Apr 1918, the **first tank-versus-tank battle** took place at Villers-Bretonneux

First supersonic unmanned combat demonstrator aircraft

Built by the UK defence manufacturer BAE Systems, the Taranis made its first test flight on 10 Aug 2013 at the Woomera Test Range in Australia. A highly classified stealth aircraft, it is designed to show that an unmanned aircraft is capable of complex multi-tasking in the roles of intelligence gathering, surveillance, targeting and combat strikes.

First ducted-fan UAV

Developed by Tactical Robotics Ltd, based in Yavne, Israel, the AirMule is a vertical-take-off-and-landing UAV. It is the first and only such UAV with no exposed rotors. The lift fan is internal and two ducted fans at the rear of the UAV provide propulsion. The AirMule can fly into a 40-m² (430-sq-ft) space; any helicopter attempting to do so would risk damaging its rotors.

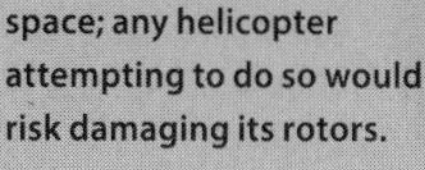

Longest- serving variable swing-wing fighter

The Russian MiG-23 fighter aircraft (NATO name "Flogger") was first introduced into service in 1970. As of 2015, it is still operated by a number of nations, including North Korea, Syria and Cuba. The term "swing-wing" denotes that the MiG's wings can be repositioned to improve aerodynamic performance.

in France between three British Mark IV tanks and three German A7V Sturmpanzerwagen. Two British tanks were damaged and withdrew but the third, armed with a six-pounder gun, halted to give the gunner a stable platform for a shot. The German A7V keeled over and was counted as the first tank kill. It later transpired, however, that the German tank had simply run down a steep bank and overturned.

Aircraft in a naval battle

The Battle of Jutland on 31 May 1916 saw an aircraft involved in a naval battle for the first time. After contact had been made between British and German cruisers, Flight

First crowdsourced military vehicle design

Built by Local Motors and DARPA, the XC2V FLYPMode used design ideas from more than 150 people. Built to replace the Humvee, the prototype was presented to President Obama at the end of Jun 2011, less than three-and-a-half months after the original design was completed.

Lieutenant F J Rutland took off in Seaplane No.8359 at 15:08 p.m. from HMS *Engadine* for reconnaissance. He and his observer reported a number of course changes by an enemy cruiser before a broken carburettor pipe curtailed their sortie.

Airship to carry its own defensive fighter

On 3 Nov 1918, a British Vickers R-23 airship first flew with, and released, an unmanned Sopwith Camel biplane over Pulham air station, near Norwich, UK. It glided safely to the ground with its controls locked. On 6 Nov that year, Lieutenant R E Keys undertook the first manned flight in a Sopwith Camel, launching from the R-23 at an altitude of 914 m (3,000 ft), having started the engine on the ground, and landing at Pulham.

Modern-day stealth aircraft used in combat

Stealth aircraft that could not be seen by enemy radar brought a new dimension to weapon delivery. The first such fighter to be used in action was the American F-117 Nighthawk, made by Lockheed Martin. It first flew in 1981 and remained classified until Nov 1988; in all, 64 aircraft were built. The aircraft was first used operationally in the US invasion of Panama in Dec 1989, when it bombed the Río Hato airfield.

Attack by an unmanned aerial vehicle (UAV)

On 3 Nov 2002, an AGM-114 Hellfire missile was fired from a CIA-operated General Atomics RQ-1 Predator at six alleged Al-Qaeda operatives in a car in Yemen.

Military "spider-man"

On 5 Jun 2014, the US Defense Advanced Research Projects Agency (DARPA) announced that its Z-Man project had successfully demonstrated hand-held suction pads that enable a soldier to climb vertical surfaces – even when carrying a 50-lb (22.68-kg) load. The pads are based on the adhesive on a gecko's toes and can stick and detach quite easily. The technology will ultimately replace ropes and ladders for scaling.

Demonstration of naval robotic attack craft

Small vessels can attack large naval craft in narrow waterways, where they are less manoeuvrable. To counter this threat, and also allow small craft to swarm around a threat vessel and neutralize it, the US Navy's Office of Naval Research (ONR) has developed equipment that can be fitted to nearly any vessel, transforming it into an unmanned surface attack craft. Named Control Architecture for Robotic Agent Command and Sensing (CARACaS) technology, it was first used in a demonstration on the James River in Virginia, USA, in Aug 2014.

IN NUMBERS

51.10 mph
Speed of the **fastest tank** (82.23 km/h), the UK's S 2000 Scorpion Peacekeeper LC

230 mph
Speed of the **fastest operational torpedo** (370 km/h), Russia's Shkval, or "Squall", developed by the Moscow Aviation Institute

140
Beats per minute of the fastest marching speed maintained by light infantry and rifle regiments

Mach 7.0
Speed of projectiles leaving the muzzle of an electro-magnetic test gun

2,110 mph
Speed of the **fastest combat jet** (3,395 km/h), Russia's Mikoyan-Gurevich MiG-25 fighter, NATO code name "Foxbat"

Most common fighter aircraft (active)

According to Flight Global's World Air Forces 2014, the US F-16 Fighting Falcon, manufactured by General Dynamics/Lockheed Martin, is the most common active combat aircraft, with 2,281 examples, representing 15% of the world's combat aircraft. It first flew on 20 Jan 1974.

FACT

The *Gerald R Ford* has a length of 1,092 ft (332.8 m) and a beam of 134 ft (40.8 m). Shown here is the christening ceremony for the ship's launch on 9 Nov 2013 in Newport News, Virginia, USA.

USS *Gerald R Ford*

Given its gargantuan size and advanced technology, it's perhaps appropriate that the USS *Gerald R Ford* (CVN-78) has already accumulated its fair share of Guinness World Records titles.

The ship is both the **largest aircraft carrier** (see left) and the **largest nuclear aircraft carrier**. In the picture above, government officials and family members of Gerald Ford (the former US president) salute a model of the ship at a naming ceremony in Washington, USA, in Jan 2007.

The USS *Gerald R Ford* is also the **first aircraft carrier designed using a full-scale 3D product model**, called CATIA (Computer Aided Three-Dimensional Interactive Application) V5 release 8. This is a 3D Product Lifecycle Management software suite developed by Dassault Systèmes (FRA). CATIA helps with the whole "life cycle" of a product's creation, from initial concept to design, engineering and final manufacture. This software suite also helps to improve weapon-handling procedures and thereby increase the number of sorties possible in a given time.

When launching from a carrier, aircraft must be accelerated to flying speed very quickly, as the length of available deck is relatively short. The *Gerald R Ford*-class carriers will be equipped with the Electro-Magnetic Aircraft Launch System (EMALS), the **most advanced launch catapult for aircraft carriers**. A new generation of catapult, EMALS is being developed using an electromagnetic rail gun, to enable a smoother and more controlled launch than current systems allow. EMALS will require a large amount of space but will not need as many sailors to operate it, nor require dangerous steam pipes running through the ship, so it will be safer and far more efficient.

All that technology doesn't come cheap, of course. At a cost of $13 bn (£8.1 bn), the USS *Gerald R Ford* will be the **most expensive carrier ever built**.

Largest aircraft carrier

The USA's *Gerald R Ford*-class aircraft carriers will replace the Nimitz-class carriers. At the time of going to press, the first of the new class, the USS *Gerald R Ford*, was being fitted out and was due to enter full service in 2016. It will have a fully loaded displacement of approximately 101,000 tonnes (223 million lb).

There is an age difference of **52 years** between the **oldest** and **youngest astronauts**

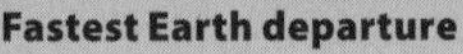

Fastest Earth departure

The fastest speed at which a spacecraft has ever taken off from our planet is 36,250 mph (58,338 km/h). It was achieved by NASA's *New Horizons* spacecraft (see graphic opposite, bottom), which launched from Cape Canaveral, Florida, USA, on board an Atlas V rocket on 19 Jan 2006, embarking on its nine-year flight to study the dwarf planet Pluto and its moons. It was *New Horizons*' third attempt at launching after the first two were called off because of high winds.

FIRST...

"Selfie" on another planet

Although planetary landers have imaged parts of themselves before the first selfie showing the whole lander is a mosaic of NASA's *Curiosity* rover shot on 31 Oct 2012.

The **first human selfie in space** was captured by Michael Collins (USA) on board the *Gemini 10* capsule on 19 Jul 1966.

Food grown in space

On 10 Oct 1995, the US Space Shuttle *Columbia* blasted off with an important cargo on board: five potato leaves. During the course of *Columbia*'s 16-day mission in orbit around Earth, these leaves were encouraged to grow in the Astroculture plant growth facility – a plant incubator in which levels of water, nutrients and UV light can be carefully controlled. By the mission's end, the leaves had begun to sprout tubers.

Find out more: *New Horizons* now

On 6 Dec 2014, *New Horizons*' mission control on Earth instructed the spacecraft to wake up from its hibernation. With the probe now operational, it is due to perform a long-range survey of Kuiper belt object VNH0004 before beginning observations of Pluto and its moons in Jul 2015. This will be the first in-depth study of the make-up and evolution of bodies in the Solar System's icy outer region.

Largest manned space capsule

Launched into space by a Delta IV Heavy rocket on 5 Dec 2014, the *Orion* capsule has a diameter of 5 m (16 ft) and an internal habitable volume of 8.95 m^3 (316 cu ft). Previous NASA capsules, as well as current Chinese and Russian models, were designed for a maximum crew of three. *Orion* can carry four astronauts on deep-space missions, or as many as six for low-Earth-orbit missions.

The New Horizons Probe

LORRI: **Lo**ng **R**ange **R**econnaissance **I**mager, for mapping the topology and geology of Pluto and its moons

REX: **R**adio Science **Ex**periment, for studying atmospheric composition and temperature

SWAP: **S**olar **W**ind **A**round **P**luto, for analysing the effects of solar wind in this distant region

High-gain antenna

Thruster

Radioisotope thermoelectric generator (RTG) – the nuclear battery

Star trackers

FIRST...

Companion robot in space

Kirobo, the first talking robot sent into space, arrived at the *International Space Station* (*ISS*) on 9 Aug 2013. Its primary objective was to serve as a companion to astronaut Koichi Wakata (JPN). Inspired by the cartoon character "Astro Boy", *Kirobo* was programmed to communicate in Japanese and keep records of its conversations with Wakata.

LONGEST...

Spacewalk

Jim Voss and Susan Helms (both USA) spent 8 hr 56 min on an extravehicular activity (EVA) on 11 Mar 2001. Their job was to make room on the *ISS* for the Italian cargo module *Leonardo*, which was carrying supplies and equipment.

Orbital survey of an outer planet

The *Cassini* spacecraft had been in orbit around Saturn for 10 years 249 days, as of 5 Mar 2015. *Cassini*'s original mission was to orbit Saturn for just four years, but extra funding has allowed for an extension until at least 2017.

First Mercury orbiter

Only the second probe to visit Mercury, NASA's *MESSENGER* spacecraft (**M**ercury **S**urface, **S**pace **En**vironment, **Ge**ochemistry and **R**anging; launch capsule pictured above) entered orbit around the Solar System's smallest planet in 2011 (artist's rendering, above left).

Among its key discoveries is that of water ice in craters at the north pole and a high quantity of sulphur on the surface, which may hint at a volcanic past.

LARGEST...

Menu in space

The Russian crew of the *ISS* have a choice of more than 300 different food dishes on board the space station. A daily menu for a Russian cosmonaut can include everything from mashed potato, apple quince chip sticks, borsch, goulash, rice with meat, broccoli with cheese, peaches and nuts.

If they care to dine with a view, they can head to the *Cupola* module on the *ISS*. Comprised of seven clear panels in a dome shape, with an overall diameter of 2.95 m (9 ft 8.1 in), the *Cupola* is the **largest window in space**.

Recorded lunar impact

On 11 Sep 2013, astronomers at the University of Huelva in Spain detected a bright flash on the Moon. It was caused by an impactor estimated to have been around 400 kg (880 lb) in mass travelling at 61,000 km/h (37,900 mph). On striking, the rock's collision released the equivalent of some 15 tonnes (33,000 lb) of TNT.

Longest surviving rover on Mars

NASA's *Opportunity* rover had been active on the surface of Mars for 11 years 24 days, or 4,042 days, as of 18 Feb 2015. *Opportunity* and its twin, *Spirit*, touched down on the Red Planet in 2004. On 22 Mar 2010, NASA lost contact with *Spirit* and declared the mission over in 2011, but *Opportunity* is still going strong, having travelled more than 26 mi (41 km) since it landed.

IN NUMBERS

1,890
Exoplanets confirmed by The Extrasolar Planets Encyclopaedia, as of Feb 2015

12
Number of people who have walked on the Moon

17 km/h
Land-speed record on the Moon (10.5 mph), achieved in a Lunar Roving Vehicle on separate occasions by NASA's John Young and Eugene Cernan (both USA)

108 min
Duration of the **first manned spaceflight** by Yuri Gagarin (USSR, now RUS), achieved in 1961

4 billion km
Distance that *New Horizons* (see pp.362–63) has travelled (2.9 billion mi)

Landing on a comet

On 12 Nov 2014, space exploration history was made when *Philae* became the first spacecraft to land on a comet, but the mission didn't all go to plan...

Back in 2004, the European Space Agency (ESA) launched the *Rosetta* spacecraft, carrying the *Philae* soft lander. On 6 Aug 2014, it arrived at its target – a comet called 67P/Churyumov–Gerasimenko. Having placed *Rosetta* into orbit around the comet, by November the ESA was ready to deploy *Philae*.

The lander touched down at 15:34 UTC after a journey of just under seven hours. Everyone at ESA mission control (below) was happy with progress, up to then...

Owing to the comet's weak gravity, harpoons (inset right) were meant to fire into the surface to keep it anchored. A thruster was also supposed to counter any bounce from the landing. However, none of these landing systems functioned correctly and *Philae* bounced back up, reaching around 1 km (0.6 mi).

At 17:25 UTC, *Philae* landed once more and bounced before coming to rest in shadow, away from its planned landing site. It had just enough time to take some samples before contact was lost on 15 Nov owing to failing batteries. But the ESA still considers the mission a success, as all the primary objectives were fulfilled.

LARGEST...

Space funeral

The ashes of 24 space pioneers, including *Star Trek* creator Gene Roddenberry (USA) and rocket scientist Krafft Ehricke (DEU), were sent into orbit on 21 Apr 1997 on board the USA's Pegasus rocket.

MOST...

Active spacecraft orbiting another planet

As of Dec 2014, there were five operational spacecraft orbiting Mars. In order of arrival, they were: *Mars Odyssey* (NASA, 2002), *Mars Express* (ESA, 2003), *Mars Reconnaissance Orbiter* (NASA, 2006), *MAVEN* (NASA, 2014) and India's first probe, *Mars Orbiter Mission* (aka *Mangalyaan*, 2014).

Remote man-made object

Launched on 5 Sep 1977, NASA's *Voyager 1* probe had ventured 19.569 billion km (12.160 billion mi) from Earth as of 10 Feb 2015.

While *Voyager 1* has travelled farther, its sister craft, *Voyager 2*, has recorded the **most planets visited**, having stopped by all four of the outer gas giants – Jupiter, Saturn, Uranus and Neptune.

Time spent in space

Sergei Krikalev (RUS) has clocked up 803 days 9 hr 39 min in space over six flights. His last mission was as Commander of the ISS in 2005.

ON THE MOVE

At 13.62 m, the **largest motorized model car** is more than 20 times longer than the **smallest roadworthy car**

Tallest rideable bicycle

Built and ridden by Richie Trimble (USA), *Stoopidtall* was measured at 6.15 m (20 ft 2.5 in) in Los Angeles, California, USA, on 26 Dec 2013.

In this category, the measurement is taken from the ground to the handlebars, and the bicycle must be able to travel a distance of at least 100 m (328 ft) without using stabilizers.

Fastest 3,000-m climb in an electric aircraft

Chip Yates (USA) soared to an altitude of 9,840 ft (3,000 m) in just 5 min 32 sec over Inyokern in California, USA, on 24 Nov 2013. For more of Chip's electrifying records, see p.370.

Longest motorcycle

Some people go to enormous lengths to make it into *GWR*. Take Bharatsinh Parmar (IND), for example. Bharatsinh has created a 26.29-m (86-ft 3-in) extended motorcycle, which was measured at Lakhota Lake in Jamnagar, Gujarat, India, on 22 Jan 2014. Bharatsinh's bike is more than 4 m (13 ft) longer than the previous record holder's.

FACT

To ensure that his super-stretched motorcycle would be able to perform like a conventional motorbike, Bharatsinh rode it along a road for 100 m (328 ft) without putting his feet down.

Tallest rideable unicycle

On 28 Sep 2013, Mushegh Khachatryan (ARM) rode a 3.08-m-tall (10-ft 1.26-in) unicycle for 25.19 m (82 ft 7.7 in) in Yerevan, Armenia. He started unicycling aged 12, as part of Yerevan's Circus Studio.

Hairiest car

Maria Lucia Mugno and Valentino Stassano (both ITA) have covered their Fiat 500 with 120 kg (264 lb 8 oz) of human hair. The hirsute vehicle was weighed at a public weighbridge in Padula Scalo, Salerno, Italy, on 15 Mar 2014.

Longest monster truck

Russ Mann's (USA) mega monster truck measured 32 ft (9.8 m) long at Last Stop in White Hills, Arizona, USA, on 10 Jul 2014.

Smallest helicopter

In terms of rotor length, the smallest helicopter is the GEN H-4 made by Gen Corporation (JPN), with a rotor length of just 4 m (13 ft), a weight of only 70 kg (154 lb), and consisting of one seat, one landing gear and one power unit. Unlike more traditional helicopters, it has two sets of coaxial contra-rotating rotors, which eliminate the need for a tail to act as a balance.

Longest bicycle

The longest true bicycle – that is, one with only two wheels and no stabilizers – is 35.79 m (117 ft 5 in) long and was built by members of the Mijl van Mares Werkploeg (NLD) in Maarheeze, Netherlands, on 5 Aug 2011. Brothers Twan (front) and Ruud Meulendijk (back, both NLD) are shown here giving it a road test. Longing to find out more? See the panel on the right.

Smallest roadworthy car

Austin Coulson (USA) presented a pint-sized car that measured 63.5 cm (2 ft 1 in) high, 65.41 cm (2 ft 1.75 in) wide and 126.47 cm (4 ft 1.75 in) long in Carrollton, Texas, USA, on 7 Sep 2012. The vehicle is licensed to be driven on public roads that have a speed limit of 25 mph (40 km/h).

FASTEST MODIFIED...

Golf cart

Driving a Plum Quick Motors golf cart, Robby Steen (USA) reached 166.81 km/h (103.65 mph) at Darlington Dragway in Hartsville, South Carolina, USA, on 4 Oct 2013. Robby completed a 0.25-mi (0.40-km) course in the cart in 14.183 sec.

Lawnmower

Honda and Team Dynamics (both UK) constructed and raced a lawnmower that achieved a speed of 187.61 km/h (116.57 mph) at the IDIADA Proving Ground in Tarragona, Spain, on 8 Mar 2014.

FACT

Several aluminium trusses (the kind used for lighting rigs at concerts) were used to link the ends of the **longest bicycle**. If the team had used only one truss for such a huge length, it would have sagged.

Stretching it

Frank Pelt is the team leader of the group that built the longest bicycle. We caught up with him while GWR's film and picture crew were in the Netherlands.

Why did you attempt this record?
It was the 50th anniversary of a cycle competition that we organize. We wanted to break the record to mark it.

What was the biggest challenge of the record attempt?
Making it work properly at that size and length was very difficult. Then we had to ride it!

How did you build the bike?
We got together a team of people. Each one understood about specific parts of a bike – such as the front, the back, the chain and the gearing.

How easy is it to ride?
With the right gearing, it's easy to ride. And because it is so heavy and long, it only needs small gearing. [As with a conventional bicycle, this record-breaking vehicle is pedalled from the rear and steered from the front.]

How do people typically react when they see you on the bike?
They ask questions about what I'm doing, how long the bike is and why I made it. I tell them it was a challenge to get into *Guinness World Records*!

How far could you ride your bicycle?
You can go as far as you like along a straight road – just don't turn any corners!

What advice would you give anyone else trying to break this record?
I have no advice for anyone else attempting such a record. We figured it out, so anyone can!

EDD CHINA IN NUMBERS

5
"Fast furniture" records held by Edd China (UK)

68 km/h
Fastest toilet (42.2 mph): *Bog Standard*, a motorcycle and sidecar under a bathroom set of bathtub, sink and laundry bin

92 km/h
Fastest mobile gaming rig (57 mph): driven in London, UK, as its three passengers played home consoles

94 km/h
Fastest garden shed (58.4 mph): *Gone to Speed*, in Milan, Italy, on 1 Apr 2011

111 km/h
Fastest bed (69 mph): timed on a private road in London, UK, on 7 Nov 2008

140 km/h
Fastest office (87 mph): a roadworthy desk with computer, monitor and potted plant, in London, UK, on 9 Nov 2006

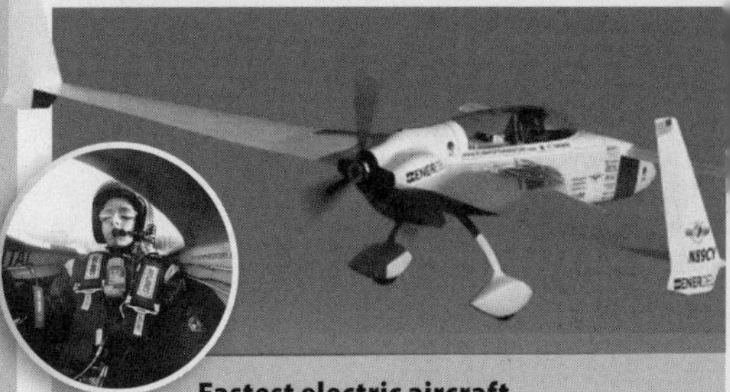

Fastest electric aircraft

Chip Yates (USA) reached a speed of 324.02 km/h (201.34 mph) in a modified Rutan Long E-Z aircraft in Inyokern, California, USA, on 23 Nov 2013. The figure was an average taken over a 3-km (1.8-mi) course.

Chip also holds the record for the **fastest electric motorcycle**, having ridden his SWIGZ Electric Superbike Prototype at 316.899 km/h (196.912 mph) on 30 Aug 2011.

FASTEST MODIFIED...

Milk float

Weetabix on the Go Breakfast Drinks built a super-fast float that Rob Gill (UK) drove at 136.081 km/h (84.556 mph) in Bruntingthorpe, Leicestershire, UK, on 25 Jun 2014.

Motorhome (RV)

On 21 Oct 2014, Simon Robins (UK) raced a motorhome at 227.35 km/h (141.3 mph) at Elvington airfield in North Yorkshire, UK.

Motorized chariot

On 10 Aug 2013, Jack Wallace Jr and Mark Dawson (both USA) sped into the record books on their motorized chariot. The duo achieved a speed of 98.79 km/h (61.39 mph) at the Willow Springs Raceway in Rosamond, California, USA.

Shopping trolley

On 18 Aug 2013, Matt McKeown (UK) drove his super-fast motorized supermarket trolley at a speed of 70.4 mph (113.2 km/h) at Elvington airfield in North Yorkshire, UK.

Sofa

Glenn Suter (AUS) reached 163.117 km/h (101.36 mph) while driving a motorized sofa at an event organized by The Monkeys for Ice Break (AUS). The successful attempt took place at Camden Airport in New South Wales, Australia, on 26 Sep 2011.

MEDIA & LEISURE

Highest box-office gross by a science-fiction film series

Star Wars made its big-screen debut on 25 May 1977. Later retitled *Star Wars: Episode IV – A New Hope*, the film – along with its sequels and prequels – has earned more than $4.4 bn (£2.8 bn) in global ticket sales.

And the legend lives on. *A New Hope* grossed $35,906,661 (£21,903,063) in US cinemas on the weekend of 31 Jan to 2 Feb 1997, making it the **most profitable opening weekend for a re-released film**. With the long-awaited *Episode VII: The Force Awakens* set for Dec 2015 release, the stellar success of the *Star Wars* franchise shows no signs of abating. The movie's trailer shows a mixture of new faces, such as the newly resdesigned stormtroopers (above), and old favourites like the *Millenium Falcon* (overleaf).

CONTENTS

FACT

This image is from the upcoming *Star Wars* sequel, *The Force Awakens*. Released on 28 Nov 2014, a teaser clip became one of the most viewed movie trailers ever, with 58.2 million views in five days.

IN FOCUS
THE INTERNET

Each **Google query has to travel** an average **1,500 mi** (2,415 km) and back before returning an answer

500 million tweets are sent per day; 80% of Twitter's active users access the site by mobile

FACT

All of the website logos represented here are shown to scale, in terms of their popularity. In other words, their size reflects the number of visitors they attract each month, relative to each other.

In 2014, Amazon's net revenue was $88.99 bn (£59.13 bn)

In 2014, 76% of LinkedIn users voted "Who's Viewed Your Profile" as their favourite feature

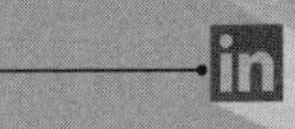

Google Japan

In Dec 2014, there were an average 890 million active Facebookers

3,125,000 "likes" on Facebook per minute

By 2014, there were more than 4.7 million English Wiki articles

Baidu claims an estimated 79% of China's total search-engine market

"World Cup 2014" was 2014's most-searched request on Google
There are 2,848,328 searches per minute on Google.com, according to Internet Live Stats
Daily visitors to Weibo spend an average 8 min 41 sec on the website
Of Yahoo.com's total visitors, most hail from the USA (29.9%), followed by India (7.9%)
You Tube
5,745,350 YouTube videos viewed per minute, according to Internet Live Stats
Yahoo! Japan
Google India
sina
SINA, which also owns Weibo.com, reported a net revenue of $768.2 m (£515.5 m) in 2014
eBay had 155.2 million active users, as of 2014
淘
Owner of both Tmall and Taobao, Alibaba receives an estimated 12.7 billion orders per year, equating to around 86% of China's eCommerce

Internet lovers should highlight 6 Aug 2016 in their diaries, as this date marks 25 years since the very **first website** launched, created by Tim Berners-Lee (UK).

It is one of a long line of major milestones for the internet in recent years. In 2015, the 3-billion user threshold was surpassed. Up from just over 2 billion in 2010, it's now well on the way to equalling half of the global population.

Meanwhile, in 2014, the number of websites reached 1 billion – a figure that rose to 1.23 billion by Mar 2015. Many sites are destined for obscurity, but not all. Certain ubiquitous names dominate the online market, drawing in millions of people daily, along with the lucrative advertising revenue that high traffic attracts.

No web presence is more dominant right now than Google (see graphic on pp.374–75). With records including **largest internet advertiser (brand)**, **largest search engine** and **largest map online**, the company's empire is constantly expanding.

As well as proliferation online with sub-sites such as Google Earth and buy-outs of other mega-brands such as YouTube, Google is also partnering with powerful players in other sectors such as Android, AOL and NASA. If you "Google" Google in 2015, you'll get links to everything from wind farms to driverless cars.

It's hard to imagine life without the internet today. How big will it be in another 25 years? We'll just have to watch this cyberspace.

Need for speed

The internet has come a long way since the days of dial-up. In 2015, scientists at the University of Surrey, UK, are reportedly working on a 5G data connection up to 65,000 times faster than the current 4G. Here, see which five countries are ahead in the connection speed race, according to cloud specialist Akamai's 2014 report.

Fastest connection speeds (Mbps)

South Korea 25.6
Japan 14.6
Hong Kong 13.3
Switzerland 12.7
Netherlands 12.4

147,388,472
Emails sent (67% of which were spam)

1,545,051 GB
of internet traffic

2,062
megawatt hours of electricity – enough to power 189 US homes for a year

2,450 tons
of CO_2 emissions generated by the internet (2,222 tonnes)

712
new websites created

34
websites hacked

2,623
blog posts written

Internet in a minute...

Set up by a global group of web analysts and developers, InternetLiveStats.com uses real-time counters and icons to visually represent the ever-shifting online landscape, focusing on some of the biggest websites. All the stats in this column were collated from InternetLiveStats.com over 60 sec on 12 Feb 2015.

TOP 20 WEBSITES (REACH/MONTH)

There are several ways to measure website popularity. Here we rank them by monthly reach of total internet users (this stood at 3,075,000,000 in Feb 2015)

Website	Visitors	Website	Visitors
Google.com	1.46 bn	Live.com	199.9 m
Facebook.com	1.23 bn	Google.co.in	178.4 m
YouTube.com	956.3 m	Sina.com.cn	175.3 m
Yahoo.com	461.3 m	LinkedIn.com	172.2 m
Baidu.com	449.0 m	Weibo.com	150.7 m
Wikipedia.org	418.2 m	Blogspot.com	135.3 m
Amazon.com	292.1 m	Tmall.com	126.1 m
Twitter.com	289.1 m	Yahoo.co.jp	107.6 m
QQ.com	267.5 m	Google.co.jp	= 95.3 m
Taobao.com	224.5 m	Ebay.com	= 95.3 m

Internet on the map

According to Internet Live Stats, these 10 nations had the most people with internet access in 2014

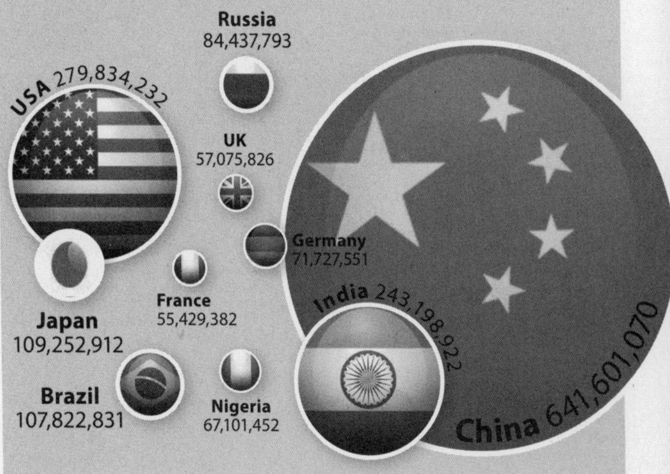

Internet milestones

What we know as the internet today took decades of research and technology development, culminating in the World Wide Web, which went live on 30 Apr 1993.

1957

The USSR launches *Sputnik*, the **first satellite**, into orbit

1958

Bell Labs (USA) invents the **first modem**

1961

Leonard Kleinrock (USA) of MIT publishes a paper on "packet switching"

1965

The first wide area network (WAN) is successfully tested

1969

The **first operational packet switching network** and internet forerunner, ARPANET, goes live

1971

Ray Tomlinson (USA) sends the **first email**. He can't recall what it said

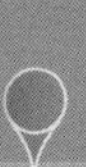

1974

Americans Vint Cerf and Robert Kahn coin the term "internet"

1978

The **first electronic spam** is sent by Gary Thuerk (USA)

1989

Tim Berners-Lee (UK) starts to develop the World Wide Web at CERN

1997

Google is registered by Larry Page (USA) and Sergey Brin (RUS)

2001

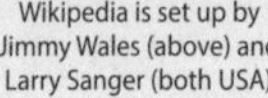

Wikipedia is set up by Jimmy Wales (above) and Larry Sanger (both USA)

2004

Facebook is launched by five students from Harvard University, USA

2005

Jawed Karim (DEU/BGD) uploads the **first YouTube video**, shot at a zoo

2015

Internet users surpass the 3-billion mark

FACT

Scholar and writer Archbishop Isidore of Seville (ESP, c. 560–636) was declared the patron saint of the internet in 1997, owing to his encyclopaedic works about popular culture.

Where does all the data go?

As the internet continues to grow and our lives become ever-more digital, we need infrastructure to store and process all that data. That's where data centres come in. These huge facilities are the physical locations of the "cloud", home to the servers that drive the internet.

Currently, the largest data centre (single building) is the Lakeside Technology Center in Chicago, Illinois, USA (above), with a floor area of 1.1 million sq ft (102,193 m2). The largest data centre complex is the Switch SUPERNAP in Las Vegas, Nevada, USA (right), with a floor area of 2.2 million sq ft (204,386 m2), spread over several buildings across the city.

MOVIES

After more than **70 years** of trying to adapt Hans Christian Andersen's ***The Snow Queen***, Disney finally released ***Frozen*** in 2013

Longest continuous production for a movie

Writer/director Richard Linklater (USA) began principal photography for his film *Boyhood*, starring a then seven-year-old Ellar Coltrane (USA), on 15 Jul 2002. Shot intermittently over the next 11 years, it follows Coltrane's character as he grows up in real time. The movie premiered in Jan 2014, marking 11 years 86 days in production.

This is some way behind the **longest production time for an animated movie**, though, which took 31 years. Released in 1995, *The Thief and The Cobbler*, aka *Arabian Knight*, dates back to 1964, when animator Richard Williams (CAN) initially began working on the film.

Fastest film production

The 75-min-long *Just Drive: A Namibian Story* was produced in 10 days 4 hr 47 min by CamelEye Productions (NAM) at Warehouse Theatre in Windhoek, Namibia, on 16–26 Mar 2014.

Highest-grossing dinosaur franchise

The three films released in the *Jurassic Park* series (in 1993, 1997 and 2001) have grossed $2.2 bn (£1.4 bn) worldwide. The franchise will surely take another big bite of revenue with 2015's fourth instalment, *Jurassic World*.

Highest-grossing IMAX (Image MAXimum) film

With more than 1 hr of footage recorded using IMAX cameras, no movie has been more extensively shot in this high-res format than *Interstellar*, which had taken $665.4 m (£452.5 m) by Jan 2015.

The thriller, starring Matthew McConaughey and Anne Hathaway as astronauts who venture into a black hole in search of a new planet fit for colonization, was released in 760 IMAX theatres in Nov 2014, making it the **largest IMAX opening.**

HIGHEST-GROSSING...

Film composer

The 90 movies scored by Hans Zimmer (DEU) – including *Interstellar* (2014, see opposite, bottom) – have earned $24.7 bn (£16.5 bn).

John Williams (USA) has scored 106 movies for film and television, although full financial data is only available for 72 of them. The average box-office gross for those 72 movies is $279.4 m (£177.8 m), which makes Williams the **highest-grossing composer per film** for composers with 20 or more movies in their filmography.

Female action star

Jennifer Lawrence's (USA) portfolio of action franchises – *The Hunger Games* (in which she stars as Katniss Everdeen) and *X-Men* (Raven/Mystique) – had grossed $3.3 bn (£2.24 bn) as of Jan 2015.

Fastest movie to gross $1 bn

The high-octane crime thriller *Furious 7* grossed $1 bn (£650 m) at the global box office in just 17 days from its release on 1 Apr 2015. The latest in the *Fast & Furious* franchise, it stars the late Paul Walker (above), who died in a car crash on 30 Nov 2013; CGI and body doubles were used to complete the film.

Highest film gross by a female director

Frozen (2013), which Jennifer Lee (inset) co-directed with Chris Buck (both USA), has earned $1.27 bn (£841 m) in cinemas worldwide. This also makes *Frozen* the **first film by a female director to gross $1 bn** as well as the **highest-grossing animation.** Lee and Buck teamed up again to direct a spin-off short animation called *Frozen Fever*, which was released in Mar 2015.

HIGHEST-GROSSING...

Sci-fi film

Directed by James Cameron (USA), the sci-fi actioner *Avatar* (2009), set on the verdant planet of Pandora, had box-office sales of $2.78 bn (£1.72 bn) as of 12 Aug 2010.

Bollywood film

Comedy movie *PK*, starring Aamir Khan (IND), swiftly became the most successful Indian film of all time after its release in Dec 2014, with a total worldwide gross of 6.22 bn Indian rupees ($101.2 m; £67.4 m) by Jan 2015.

Zombie film

World War Z (2013), starring Brad Pitt (USA) – the **most bankable Hollywood star**, according to The Numbers (see profile box p.384) – attracted hordes to the cinema, amassing a total of $540 m (£335.8 m).

Vampire film

The final instalment in teen vampire series *The Twilight Saga: Breaking Dawn – Part 2* (2012) had accumulated in excess of $832 m (£557 m) in global ticket sales over 113 days after its release.

Sports film

The highest-grossing sports movie of all time is the Academy Award-nominated *The Blind Side* (2009), which had grossed $305 m (£210 m) at the worldwide box office as of 1 Jun 2010. This narrowly beats the previous record holder, *Rocky IV* (1985), which had taken $300 m (£234 m) worldwide by 1 Mar 1986. If adjusted for inflation, however, *Rocky IV*'s take would be valued today at $638 m (£386 m), compared with *The Blind Side*'s $331 m (£200 m).

Most sequels released in a calendar year

Of the top 100 most widely released films of 2014, an unprecedented 29 of them were sequels, spin-offs or franchise entries, narrowly beating the previous record of 27 franchise films released in 2011.

The list featured some of 2014's biggest blockbusters, including (pictured top to bottom) *The Hobbit: The Battle of the Five Armies*, *The Amazing Spider-Man 2* and *Night at the Museum: Secret of the Tomb*.

Hotly anticipated sequels set to shake up 2015 include the new Bond film, *Spectre*, *Jurassic World* and the long-awaited seventh *Star Wars* movie, *The Force Awakens*.

Most successful animation studio

In terms of global box-office sales, DreamWorks Animation SKG, Inc (USA) is No.1, with a worldwide gross of $12.19 bn (£8.14 bn) from 29 movies, as of 15 Oct 2014. Its biggest hit of 2014 was *How to Train Your Dragon 2* (above), released in June, with takings of $616.1 m (£413.1 m) by Mar 2015.

Most successful superhero actor

As of 24 Mar 2015, the four films starring Robert Downey Jr (USA) as Tony Stark, aka Iron Man, had earned $3.89 bn (£2.65 bn) worldwide.

With *Avengers: Age of Ultron* released in Apr 2015, it looks set to be another successful year for Downey Jr, who was 2014's **highest-earning actor**, taking home an estimated $75 m (£46.6 m) – see p.232.

The first film in the series, *The Avengers* (2012), remains the **highest-grossing superhero movie**, having taken $1.51 bn (£938 m) at the worldwide box office.

IN NUMBERS

$1.5 m
Amount paid to US author Michael Crichton (1942–2008) in 1990 for the rights to turn *Jurassic Park* into a movie (£778,000)

$1.03 bn
Estimated worldwide gross for *Jurassic Park*, according to The-Numbers.com (£706.51 m)

868
Expletives in *Swearnet* (2014) – the **most swearing in a movie**

87
Academy Awards ceremonies staged since the Oscars started in 1929

$5,702,153
Amount raised via Kickstarter for *Veronica Mars* (2014; £3,708,480) – the **most crowdfunded film**

7 min
Length of *Frozen* spin-off *Frozen Fever* (2015), co-directed by Jennifer Lee

800 TB
Final data count of *Interstellar* (2014), owing to extensive effects

Hollywood Highs

The Numbers Bankability Index gauges the monetary value that Hollywood figures bring to the movie industry each year, based on lifetime box-office takings and performance over the last decade. In Feb 2015, producer/director Steven Spielberg (USA, above) ranked No.1 with an annual contribution estimated at $27,674,059 (£18,379,574). Joining Spielberg in the top 10 are:

2. Brad Pitt (USA)
Actor
Movies/year: 2.4
$23,672,569 (£15,725,641)

3. Johnny Depp (USA)
Actor
Movies/year: 3.1
$22,989,298 (£15,274,824)

4. Samuel L Jackson (USA)
Actor
Movies/year: 4.6
$22,561,208 (£15,018,898)

5. Hans Zimmer (DEU)
Composer
Movies/year: 4.2
$22,475,688 (£14,962,098)

6. Tom Cruise (USA)
Actor
Movies/year: 1.2
$22,292,617 (£14,850,077)

7. Tom Hanks (USA)
Actor
Movies/year: 2.4
$21,829,081 (£14,543,542)

8. Adam Sandler (USA)
Actor
Movies/year: 2.2
$20,211,897 (£13,462,181)

9. Leonardo DiCaprio (USA)
Actor
Movies/year: 1.9
$20,041,463 (£13,344,396)

10. Morgan Freeman (USA)
Actor
Movies/year: 3.7
$19,713,643 (£13,126,121)

All movies made in the USA unless otherwise stated

Highest annual earnings for an actress

Sandra Bullock (USA) earned an estimated $51 m (£30.4 m) in the year ending Jun 2014. The biggest hit for Bullock during this period was Alfonso Cuaron's sci-fi blockbuster *Gravity* (2013), which grossed $716 m (£487 m) worldwide.

STAR WARS

The actors who played the original **Darth Vader** – David Prowse (the body) and James Earl Jones (the voice) – have **never met**

MOVIES

Largest personal fortune made from a film franchise

Famously, George Lucas (USA) turned down his director's fee for the first *Star Wars* film in 1977 in exchange for rights to all future merchandising and sequels.

Lucas made $500 m (£215 m) between 1977 and 1980 from merchandise sales alone, having set up Lucasfilm Ltd in 1971 before founding special-effects company Industrial Light & Magic.

In Mar 2015, Forbes estimated Lucas's net worth at $5 bn (£3.3 bn), contributed to by the 2012 sale of Lucasfilm to Disney for $4 bn (£2.5 bn). He is nevertheless serving as creative consultant on *Star Wars Episode VII: The Force Awakens*.

Most Oscar-nominated living person

With 49 acknowledgements (and five wins), John Williams (USA) has composed scores for 101 feature films across his career, each earning a record average of $279.4 m (£177.8 m) at the box office (see p.381). This figure is helped by his work on high earners such as the first six *Star Wars* films and several entries in the *Harry Potter* film series. It was confirmed in 2013 that he would be providing the score for *The Force Awakens*.

Highest-grossing...

• **Sci-fi movie (adjusted for inflation):** Based on its domestic gross adjusted for ticket-price inflation, *Star Wars Episode IV: A New Hope* is the most successful sci-fi movie of all time. According to box-office

IN NUMBERS

1138
An "Easter egg" number often featuring in *Star Wars*, referring to another George Lucas sci-fi film, *THX 1138* (1971)

314
Largest voice cast in an MMO game, in *Star Wars: The Old Republic* (Electronic Arts/ LucasArts, 2011)

10
Academy Award nominations in 1978 for the first *Star Wars* movie; it won six, plus a Special Achievement Award

Largest collection of *Star Wars* LEGO® sets

Jon Jessesen of Vika, Norway, owned a most impressive 378 *Star Wars* LEGO sets as of 1 Jan 2015. The sets – containing 151,428 individual pieces – are all complete and unopened. Jessesen is also the proud owner of all 646 LEGO *Star Wars* mini-figures released between 1999 and 2012.

Largest *Star Wars* sculpture

The 11th Brigade of the Japan Ground Self-Defense Force in Hokkaido spent almost a month crafting 3,175 tonnes (7 million lb) of snow into Snow *Star Wars* for the 66th Sapporo Snow Festival, held in Feb 2015. The Lucasfilm-approved sculpture measured 15 m tall by 23 m wide (49 ft by 75 ft) and featured Darth Vader, three Stormtroopers, Vader's TIE Advanced fighter and the Death Star.

intelligence service The Numbers, the movie's debut in 1977 plus its various re-releases (in 1978, 1979, 1981, 1982 and 1997) earned $1.33 bn (£825 m) in North America alone, surpassing the adjusted grosses for *ET: The Extra-Terrestrial* (1982) and *Avatar* (2009).

By comparison, the **highest-grossing sci-fi movie (non-adjusted)** is *Avatar*, with a domestic gross of $760 m (£478 m) as of 18 Nov 2010. *Avatar* is also the **highest-grossing movie at the global box office**, taking a non-adjusted $2.78 bn (£1.74 bn).

• ***Star Wars* movie:** In terms of global non-adjusted box-office takings, the most successful film in the *Star Wars* franchise is *Star Wars Episode I: The Phantom Menace* (1999), which had earned $1.007 bn (£612.7 m) as of 18 May 2012. (See below for the box-office figures across the six-film series.)

STAR WARS EPISODE I THE PHANTOM MENACE	STAR WARS EPISODE II ATTACK OF THE CLONES	STAR WARS EPISODE III REVENGE OF THE SITH
1999, 2012	**2002**	**2005**
$1,007,044,677	**$656,695,615**	**$848,998,892**
(£612,744,000)	**(£451,120,000)**	**(£442,487,000)**

Years refer to release and re-release dates. Source: The Numbers

• **Re-released movie:** On its return to US cinemas in 1997, after some $10 m (£6 m) was spent on extensive digital remastering, *Star Wars Episode IV: A New Hope* pulled in $138 m (£83 m) at the domestic box office and $257 m (£155 m) worldwide.

SPIN-OFFS

Most critically acclaimed videogame based on a toy

LEGO Star Wars II: The Original Trilogy (Traveller's Tales, 2006) for PC held an 86.83% review score on gamerankings.com across 21 reviews, as of 6 Mar 2015.

Star Wars is also the **most prolific videogame series based on a licensed property**. As of 2013, 296 *Star Wars*-themed games had been released for 44 platforms.

First *Star Wars* videogame

Based on the second film, *The Empire Strikes Back* (Parker Brothers) was released in 1982 for the Atari 2600 and Intellivision consoles.

The **first videogame to contain lightsaber action** was *Star Wars: Jedi Arena* (Parker Brothers, 1983) on the Atari 2600. While duelling wasn't possible, it did allow the player to kill enemies by deflecting laser bolts.

STAR WARS EPISODE IV A NEW HOPE	STAR WARS EPISODE V THE EMPIRE STRIKES BACK	STAR WARS EPISODE VI RETURN OF THE JEDI
1977, 1978, 1979, 1981, 1982, 1997	1980, 1981, 1982, 1997	1983, 1985, 1997
$786,598,007 (£487,208,000)	$534,171,960 (£330,859,000)	$572,700,000 (£354,726,000)

Star Wars super-fan

Steve Sansweet (USA) was Director of Content Management and Head of Fan Relations at Lucasfilm before retiring in 2011 and dedicating himself to amassing the largest collection of *Star Wars* memorabilia. As of 4 May 2015, "only" 93,260 items of his collection – on display at Rancho Obi-Wan in Petaluma, California, USA – had been audited, but this was already sufficient to surpass the previous record by a factor of four.

What first drew you to *Star Wars*?
I got interested in *Star Wars* as a result of loving science-fiction growing up. I read all of the classic science-fiction novels, saw all the cheesy movies and TV shows. [For a while], there wasn't much sci-fi in the media, but then *Star Wars* came out. I was hooked from the very beginning.

How is the inventory progressing?
We started to do an inventory about [eight] years ago and there have been some interruptions. The count is now up to more than 92,000, but we think that is less than one-third – there's an estimated 300,000 individual pieces in total.

What are the most popular exhibits?
Visitors love the life-size pieces. We have the four members of the Cantina Band, and they're audio-animatronic, so you can dance to them!

We've got a full-size battle droid made for toy store FAO Schwarz, and the only two full-size LEGO figures ever produced for sale: a Darth Vader and a Boba Fett.

There's an arcade room with almost every *Star Wars* videogame and pinball game made. If I turned that room on before the tour ended I'd lose everybody, so we wait until the end now.

Most successful book series based on a film series

Lucas Licensing has recorded at least 100 million sales of *Star Wars* books across more than 850 movie novelizations, original novels, reference and children's books, including 80 *New York Times* best-sellers.

Most successful action-figure range

In their first 30 years on sale, the *Star Wars* toy lines operated by Kenner/Hasbro had accounted for over $9 bn (£4.5 bn) in sales. Kenner's first range of figures sold more than 40 million units in 1978, and *Star Wars* remained the best-selling boys' toy licence in the USA between 2007 and 2010, netting $510 m (£321.3 m) in 2010 alone.

Best-selling Star Wars app

Rovio's *Angry Birds Star Wars* (2012) is the highest-ranked *Star Wars* app for the iOS platform, as of Mar 2015, ranking 90th overall for the most-downloaded paid-for app in Apple's iTunes store.

THEATRE

Rather than clapping, **ancient Greek** theatre audiences **stamped their feet**

Shortest run for a West End musical

Oscar, a musical biopic of the writer Oscar Wilde with musics, lyrics and book by Mike Read (UK), closed after its opening night at the Shaw Theatre in London, UK, on 22 Oct 2004. Read, better known as a TV and radio presenter in the UK, also produced, directed and starred in the ill-fated show.

Highest-grossing year for Broadway theatres

According to the League of American Theatres and Producers, the highest-grossing year for theatres on Broadway in New York City, USA, was 2014, with $1.36 bn (£876.54 m) in ticket sales from the week ending 5 Jan 2014 to the week ending 28 Dec 2014. Attendance figures reached 13.13 million, up 13% on 2013.

Most successful stage adaptation of a film

Disney's *The Lion King* is the most profitable screen-to-stage adaptation ever. The theatrical version of the 1994 film has generated more than $5.4 bn (£3.9 bn) worldwide since it premiered in 1997 – at least five times the total amount grossed by the film in cinemas.

Longest career as theatre producer for the same production

Vado Souza (BRA) produced his one-man show "O Navio Negreiro" for 40 years 7 months, from 23 Oct 1971 to May 2012. A GWR certificate was presented to Vado after a special performance at Churrascaria Vento Haragano in São Paulo, Brazil, on 17 May 2012.

Most Tony Awards won by an actress

Audra McDonald (USA) has secured six Tonys since 1994. She is shown above on 12 Jan 2012 at the opening night of *Porgy and Bess*, a show that earned her the Tony for Best Performance by an Actress in a Leading Role in a Musical.

AWARDS

Most Tony Awards won by an individual

As of the 68th Tony Awards on 8 Jun 2014, Harold Prince (USA, b. 30 Jan 1928) had won 21 Tony Awards, including eight for directing, eight for producing, two as producer of the year's Best Musical, and three special Tony Awards. Prince received his 21st award in Jun 2006, for Lifetime Achievement in the Theatre.

First solo female to win the Tony Award for Best Original Score

Cyndi Lauper (b. Cynthia Ann Stephanie Lauper, USA) is the only female to solely win the Tony Award for Best Score. She took home the trophy in 2013 for the music and lyrics for *Kinky Boots*. The show is based on the true story of the strait-laced owner of a men's shoe factory who turns to stitching outrageous footwear for drag queens in order to overcome a dip in business.

Most Tony Award nominations for a musical without a win

The 2010 musical *The Scottsboro Boys*, by David Thompson (book), John Kander (music) and Fred Ebb (lyrics), recounted the true story of a 1930s race-related miscarriage of justice. It ran on Broadway for just two months and received 12 Tony Award nominations but did not win a single award.

FACT

Known as "The Glums" to the theatre community, *Les Mis* has been seen by more than 70 million people in 43 countries and 22 languages.

Longest theatrical run for a musical in the West End

Les Misérables – by France's Claude-Michel Schönberg (music) and Alain Boublil (lyrics) – celebrates the 30th anniversary of its West End debut on 4 Dec 2015. The show, which opened in 1985, was inspired by the French Revolution-era novel by Victor Hugo.

Highest single-week box-office gross on Broadway

Wicked, the musical prequel to *The Wizard of Oz*, grossed $3,201,333 (£2,113,790) on Broadway in nine performances during the week ending 29 Dec 2013. According to the Broadway League, the musical – now in its 12th year – broke its own box-office record, set the same week the previous year, when it took $2,947,172 (£1,822,840).

Longest theatrical run for a show on Broadway

The Andrew Lloyd Webber (UK) musical *The Phantom of the Opera* saw its 10,000th Broadway performance at the Majestic Theatre in New York City, USA, on 11 Feb 2012. As of 22 Feb 2015, it had run to 11,263 performances according to the Internet Broadway Database.

IN NUMBERS

40
"Broadway" theatres – but only four are on the road Broadway itself

150+
Wigs used in the musical *Hairspray; Les Misérables* uses just 85

232+
Puppets in the stage show of *The Lion King*

$2,057,354
Raised for charity Broadway Cares/ Equity Fights AIDS by screen- and stage-star Hugh Jackman (AUS), the **highest weekly gross for a one-man show on Broadway** (£1,323,380)

Highest-grossing original show on Broadway

The Book of Mormon stage musical takes its name from a sacred text of the Latter Day Saint movement, but it is an original creation with book, lyrics and music by Trey Parker, Matt Stone and Robert Lopez (all USA). Since previewing at the Eugene O'Neill Theatre on 24 Feb 2011, the show has grossed $316,574,288 (£208,580,000), making it the 10th highest-grossing show in Broadway history.

Indiscretions, a translation by Jeremy Sams (UK) of Jean Cocteau's 1938 play *Les Parents Terribles*, did not pick up a single Tony Award despite receiving nine nominations – the **most Tony nominations for a play without a win**. The Paris-set drama opened at the Ethel Barrymore Theatre on 3 Apr 1995 and closed on 4 Nov, after 28 previews and 220 performances. Its cast included Kathleen Turner, Cynthia Nixon and Jude Law.

Highest-grossing Broadway show

Since opening on Broadway in Oct 1997, Disney's *The Lion King* had taken $1.12 bn (£742.8 m) as of Jan 2015. In all, 12,091,055 seats have been sold for the musical across 7,170 performances. Only three other Broadway shows have run for longer.

Most Laurence Olivier Awards won

The Curious Incident of the Dog in the Night-Time won a total of seven Olivier awards on 29 Apr 2013. The National Theatre production equalled the record set by the Royal Shakespeare Company's *Matilda the Musical* in 2012.

On 15 April 2012, Eleanor Worthington-Cox (UK) became the **youngest winner of a Laurence Olivier Award**: aged 10, she played Matilda in *Matilda the Musical*. She is the youngest of four girls who shared the part, the others being Cleo Demetriou, 10 (just a few weeks older than Eleanor), Kerry Ingram and Sophia Kiely, both 12. All are younger than any previous Laurence Olivier Award winner.

Most Laurence Olivier Award nominations for a show

The 2008 musical *Hairspray* received a total of 11 Laurence Olivier Award nominations from 10 categories. Based on the 1988 John Waters film of the same name, the comedy won four gongs, including Best New Musical.

The 2001 revival of Cole Porter's (USA) *Kiss Me, Kate* garnered nine Laurence Olivier Award nominations at the 2002 ceremony but won none, the **most Laurence Olivier Award nominations for a show without a win**.

Stephen Sondheim

The acclaimed Broadway composer-lyricist – who turned 85 on 22 Mar 2015 – holds the record for the most Tony Awards won by a composer, taking home eight statuettes (1971–2008).

The Tony Awards – aka the Antoinette Perry Awards for Excellence in Theatre – are the Oscars of the theatre world, and Stephen Sondheim has been recognized more than any other composer, living or dead. For his 1971 show, *Company*, he won twice, for Best Music and Best Lyrics (two categories that were later merged), and then won Best Score for *Follies* (1972), *A Little Night Music* (1973), *Sweeney Todd* (1979), *Into the Woods* (1988) and *Passion* (1994). He was also recognized in 2008 with a Special Tony Award for Lifetime Achievement in the Theatre.

For an actor, securing a role in a Sondheim show can be a career-defining event. The role of Mama Rose from the stage musical *Gypsy* (for which Sondheim provided the lyrics), for example, has resulted in the **most Tony Award nominations for a character**, with five actresses being recognized for playing the part: Ethel Merman (1960), Angela Lansbury (1975, winner), Tyne Daly (1990, winner), Bernadette Peters (2003) and Patti LuPone (2008, winner). This also represents the **most Tony Award wins for a character**, a record shared by Pseudolus from Sondheim's *A Funny Thing Happened on the Way to the Forum*, with wins for Zero Mostel (1963), Phil Silvers (1972) and Nathan Lane (1996).

It was also in a Sondheim role – that of The Witch from the 2014 movie version of *Into the Woods* – that Meryl Streep (below) earned her 19th Oscar nomination (the **most Oscar nominations for an actress**).

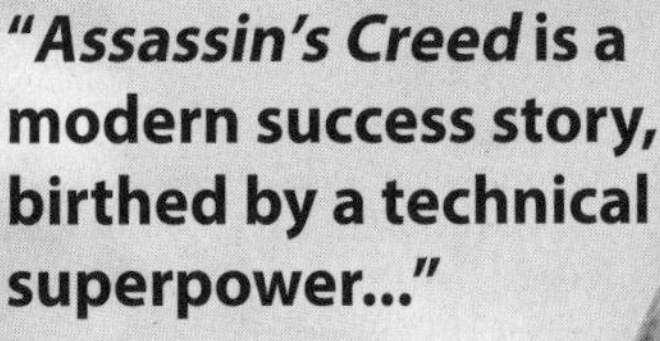

"*Assassin's Creed* is a modern success story, birthed by a technical superpower..."

HardcoreGamer.com

Greatest aggregate time playing *Assassin's Creed* (all players)

As of 22 May 2014, a staggering combined-platform total of 451 centuries 62 years 131 days 19 hr had been clocked up globally on *Assassin's Creed IV: Black Flag* (Ubisoft, 2013). This beat *Assassin's Creed III*'s impressive total by at least 100 centuries. Gamers had collected 964,721,963,817 animus fragments, found 980,305,303,180 treasure chests, destroyed 5,372,737,156 ships and harpooned 1,295,005,143,470 sea creatures.

Highest-earning *Call of Duty* player

As of 30 Apr 2015, professional *Call of Duty* player Damon "Karma" Barlow (CAN) had accrued a total of $241,411 (£156,937) in career earnings, according to eSportsEarnings.com. Barlow won the *Call of Duty* Championship in 2013 as a member of team Impact and again in 2014 as a member of team compLexity.

FACT

18th-century pirates who patrolled the Caribbean were well-armed and made themselves rich from plundering the ships of colonial empires such as England and the Netherlands.

D.Y.K.?

To enforce player stealth in *Assassin's Creed IV*, fights were made harder, enemies attacked faster and more effectively, and a player died after two shots.

Fastest completion of *Call of Duty: Ghosts – Extinction*

On 10 Jul 2014, gamer "Jon The Chief" completed the alien-killing survival mode o Activision's videogame in 39 min 53 sec – a remarkable achievement since it is designe for four players.

Longest marathon playing a real-time strategy game

"The Hiveminders", aka Jeff Nation and J J Locke (both USA), played *StarCraft II: Heart of the Swarm* (Blizzard, 2013) for 44 hr on 5–7 May 2014 in Bozeman, Montana, USA.

Greatest aggregate time playing *Battlefield 3*

As of 18 Jun 2013, gamer "mihmei" had spent 4,945 hr 3 min playing *Battlefield 3* (EA DICE, 2011) multiplayer – equivalent to 206 real-world days of *Battlefield 3* action.

As of 23 Mar 2015, an Austrian known as "DIEMEXO" had achieved the **highest score on *Battlefield 4*** (EA DICE, 2013): 272,066,776 points on the PC version of the game.

Most successful *DotA 2* hero

According to the *DotA* Academy, Intelligence hero "Leshrac" had racked up the highest number of wins in *DotA 2* pro matches, as of 20 Jun 2013. All in all, the disco pony has helped crush 690 of his opponents' Ancients.

Tips 'n' Tricks

An easy way to gain studs in *LEGO Batman: The Videogame* (see below) is to complete a level with The Joker, which should put him in prison. Go to the experiment room and zap the Joker Henchmen as they walk in. Be sure to zap the villain that follows you now and again. Every time he is zapped, the Henchmen will yield an increasing number of studs after they are killed.

Power brick locations include:

- **You Can Bank On Batman: on the left side of the cage that Clayface stands on**
- **Two-Face Chase: at the final stage of the fight, in the top left corner of the park on the left...**

Best-selling superhero game

As of 5 Mar 2015, *LEGO® Batman: The Videogame* (Traveller's Tales, 2008) had sold 13.10 million units according to VGChartz. It is the first LEGO game to feature licensed characters in an original story. Players control a character in various environments, collecting the game's currency of LEGO studs.

Most "likes" for a game on Facebook

As of 26 Feb 2015, 70,859,985 people had "liked" *Texas HoldEm Poker* (Zynga, 2007) – making it more popular than the pages of superstars such as Katy Perry.

Meanwhile, the **highest-rated Facebook game**, *Criminal Case* (Pretty Simple Games, 2012), won an average rating of 4.4, with 1,114,724 people awarding it a maximum five stars as of 18 Jun 2013.

D.Y.K.?

Skylanders: Spyro's Adventure was written by two authors of the original *Toy Story* film. Each toy has a chip that activates it for play, and it can be used in other players' games.

Best-selling interactive gaming toys

According to *Forbes* and *Fortune*, more than 240 million *Skylanders* figures and playsets have been sold. Trigger Happy (above) is one of 32 standard characters and belongs to the game's Tech element. Since Activision launched *Spyro's Adventure* in 2011, the *Skylanders* series has earned more than $3 billion (£1.9 billion).

No secret, big success

On 18–21 Jul 2014, the five members of "NewBee" (CHN) won the greatest prize money in a videogame competition by a team: $5,028,121 (£3,251,103) at The International *DotA 2* Championships held at the KeyArena in Seattle, Washington, USA.

Why did NewBee do so well in the finals?
We thirsted for the championship and knew our rivals well. In preparation, we carried out closed-door training and many exercises with domestic teams. We have no secret for success – just faith in our team-mates and ourselves.

Did winning come as a surprise?
It was a great surprise for us. At the group stage, we were on the verge of elimination, but our team spirit tells us "never give up". In the play-offs we beat six rivals in a row and ultimately became world champions.

Is gaming becoming a spectator sport?
eSports not only have the same sense of competition and strict rules as traditional sports, but also contain dazzlingly cool magic skills, making it highly enjoyable to watch.

Any advice on earning a living as a gamer?
One should never choose this path to escape reality, but plan for a career, avoid addiction, find methods for self-improvement, practise diligently and persevere. Generally, it is not recommended to make a living playing eSports: innate aptitude is so important and there's a low probability of turning professional.

COMICS & MANGA

Some **2 billion manga publications** are sold each year, generating **$10 bn (£6.5 bn)**

Best-selling videogame based on a comic

As of 6 Feb 2015, *Batman: Arkham City* (Rocksteady, 2011) had sold more than 10.57 million copies according to VGChartz.

Largest comic strip

Adidas Japan and the Sky Comic project team created a comic strip that measured 3,785.35 m^2 (40,745.16 sq ft) in Ota-ku, Tokyo, Japan, on 25 May 2010. Each of its 13 frames depicted a player in Japan's World Cup soccer squad.

Largest comics festival

Comiket is a three-day festival of *dōjinshi* – self-published manga comics. It is currently held at the Tokyo Big Sight convention centre in Odaiba, Koto, Tokyo, twice a year. The highest attendance for this event was 590,000 visitors, at Comiket 84 in the summer of 2013.

Largest comic book

Chapter one of the graphic novel *CruZader™: Agent of the Vatican*, by Omar Morales (USA), measured 2 ft x 3 ft 1 in (60.9 x 94.4 cm) in Fremont, California, USA, on 30 Aug 2014. The full-colour 28-page work was printed in a run of 105 copies. It sold for $300 (£185) and $200 (£123) in the international and US markets respectively.

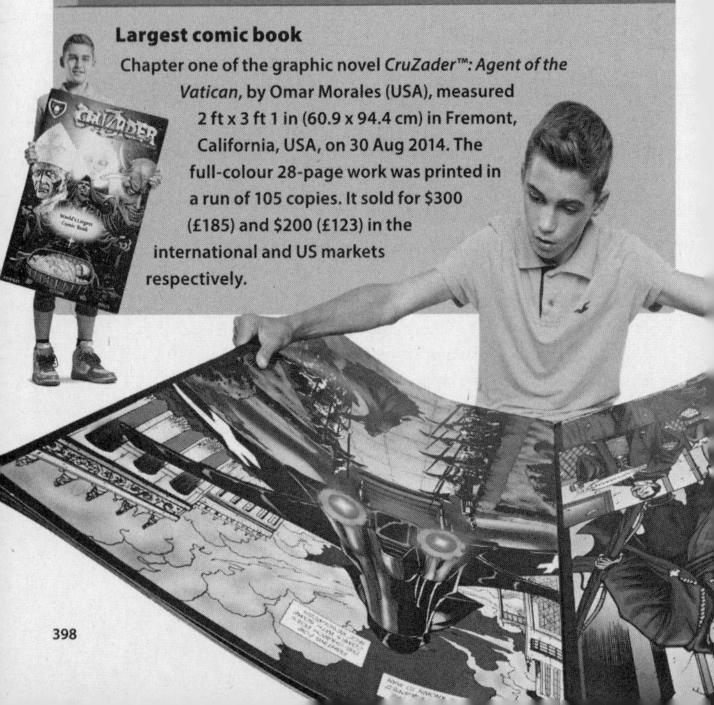

Largest annual circulation for a manga magazine

Based on figures from the Japanese Magazine Publishers Association for the 12 months to Sep 2014, the most popular manga magazine is Shueisha's *Weekly Shonen Jump*, with a circulation of 2.7 million copies. "Shonen" manga is aimed at a broadly teenage, primarily male audience.

Longest-running...

- **Monthly comic:** *Detective Comics* has been printed by DC Comics in the USA since issue #1 in Mar 1937. As of Vol. 2 Issue 39 (cover dated Apr 2015), a total of 927 issues had been published, in two volumes (1937–2011; 2011–present). Batman debuted in issue #27 (May 1939).
- **Weekly comic:** British humour comic *The Beano* debuted on 30 Jul 1938 and has been published ever since, except for a period during World War II. As of 27 Jan 2015, *The Beano* had run to 3,768 issues.
- **Comic based on a videogame:** The US comic *Sonic the Hedgehog*, published by Archie Comics, first appeared in Jul 1993. Its 268th edition was printed in Jan 2015.
- **Comic strip still syndicated:** Newspaper strip *The Katzenjammer Kids*, by Rudolph Dirks (USA), saw its 117th anniversary on 12 Dec 2014. First published in the *New York Journal* on 12 Dec 1897, it is syndicated to 50 newspapers.
- **Yonkoma manga:** Yonkoma ("four frame") manga are Japan's equivalent of Western newspaper strips. *Sennin Buraku* ("Hermit Village"), by Kō Kojima (JPN), ran in the adult magazine *Weekly Asahi Geinō* from Oct 1956 to Aug 2014. That's 58 years and 2,861 issues.

Most movies from the work of a comic-book creator

As of 5 Mar 2015, the creations of Marvel's Stan Lee (USA) had been made into 21 movies

Most popular digital comics service

As of 13 Jan 2014, comiXology, a cloud-based delivery platform for comics and graphic novels, had provided more than 6 million pages of comics, according to the App Store. Available via comixology.com as well as iOS, Android, Windows 8 and Kindle apps, it had provided 200-million-plus downloads as of Sep 2013.

Most wins of the Shogakukan Manga Award

First held in 1956, the Shogakukan Manga Awards are manga's Oscars. Mangaka Naoki Urasawa (JPN) has won in the "general" category three times, for *Yawara!* (1989), *Monster* (2000) and *20th Century Boys* (2002).

FIRST...

Comic-book lawsuit

Not long after Superman's debut, (see opposite), Detective Comics took Bruns Publications, the publishers of *Wonder Comics* #1, to court for copyright infringement. Detective Comics alleged that Bruns' Wonder Man copied Superman. Heard on 6–7 Apr 1939, the case was decided in favour of Detective Comics.

FACT

Rich Burlew's Kickstarter scheme clearly struck a chord with comic fans. His modest goal was $57,750 (£36,400), but Rich's 14,952 backers donated nearly 22 times that amount.

Most money pledged for a Kickstarter comic project

Seeking to re-issue the out-of-print *The Order of the Stick* books, Rich Burlew (USA) launched a Kickstarter project. "The Order of the Stick Reprint Drive" was successfully funded on 21 Feb 2012 to the tune of $1,254,120 (£790,570).

Most contributors to a published comic book

Ninety-four artists from 17 countries contributed to *Pieces Project – Pieces Book 1*, published on 30 Oct 2013 by Jakub Mazerant (POL), founder of IllustrateYourLIFE in Sydney, New South Wales, Australia. The book starts with a panel depicting a group of characters in a given setting, and each successive "piece", by a different artist, develops the plot.

Most expensive comic

A copy of *Action Comics* #1 sold for $3,207,852 (£2,014,450) to Metropolis Collectibles (USA) during an online eBay auction on 24 Aug 2014. Featuring the debut appearance of Superman, the comic was first published in Jun 1938 and originally sold for 10 cents. Pictured below are comic dealer Vincent Zurzolo (left) and Stephen Fishler of Metropolis Collectibles.

FACT

Writer Jerry Siegel and artist Joe Shuster came up with Superman in 1933. Five years later, they sold the character to Detective Comics, later to become DC Comics.

IN NUMBERS

€312,500

Most expensive page of comic-book art sold: a hand-drawn page from the 1963 Tintin book *The Castafiore Emerald by* Belgian cartoonist Hergé (£279,875; $461,503)

€1.3 m

Most expensive comic-book cover: special edition of *Tintin in America* sold in 2012 (£1m; $1.6 m)

€2.5 m

Most expensive comic endpapers: 34 drawings of Tintin and his dog Snowy (£2 m; $3.4 m)

Word magician

Alan Moore (UK, above) is the globally renowned writer and graphic novelist whose work has earned him two personal Guinness World Records titles: the most Eisner comic awards for best graphic album (5) and best writer (9). He also conceived the 76-m-long (250-ft) comic strip *The Worm*, which was pivotal to setting the record for the most professional contributors to a graphic novel (133). GWR asked Alan about his pioneering work.

You hold these extraordinary records, but of which works are you the proudest and why?

Early in my career I decided that awards were meaningless. Initially, I discreetly threw them away, until my sentimental mother asked to keep them. This lasted until she gored herself on my Hugo [award for *Watchmen*]. As regards my own pride in my work, since I don't actually own two-thirds of it, I'm afraid I've had to disown it.

The works I'm proudest of would be pieces like my novels *Voice of the Fire* and *Jerusalem*, or *Lost Girls*, *From Hell* and *The League of Extraordinary Gentlemen* (right), which I co-own with the artists concerned – I am still more than happy to attach my name to it.

What do you look for in your artistic collaborators?

These days I seek authentic friendship and loyalty.

Any advice for the next generation of writers?

If your talent isn't continually breaking new ground and moving forward, then, as with the shark, it's probably dying. Be original and be sufficient to your times.

Oldest comic artist

Kenneth "Ken" Bald (USA, b. 1 Aug 1920) has drawn comics, comic strips and movie posters for more than 83 years. As of 4 Mar 2015, aged 94 years 215 days, he was still doing commissioned sketches of superheroes for fans.

Superhero team

The founding members of the Justice Society of America, or JSA, were the Atom, Doctor Fate, the Flash, Green Lantern, Hawkman, Hourman (then "Hour-Man"), the Sandman and the Spectre. They first appeared together on the cover of *All Star Comics* #3, dated for the winter of 1940.

Superhero videogame to tie into a comic storyline

The Death and Return of Superman (Blizzard Entertainment) was released for the SNES and Mega Drive/Genesis in 1994–95. It was the earliest superhero videogame to tie in with a comic-book storyline that was being published at the same time.

BROADCASTING

British citizens were required to have a **licence to listen to radio** from 1922 to 1971

Longest-running network broadcast

The first episode of *Music and the Spoken Word* (USA)– a 30-min radio and TV programme consisting of classical music, hymns and spoken verse – was broadcast on 15 Jul 1929. It has been transmitted every week since, for eight-and-a-half decades. As of 11 Jan 2015, a total of 4,452 episodes had been aired.

Most popular music-streaming service

In 2014, Pandora had 200 million users, compared with "just" 40 million for closest rival Spotify. Even the number of Pandora accounts that are actively used each month – more than 70 million – trumps Spotify's user base.

Most radio interviews conducted in 24 hours

"Gilly", aka John Gillmore (UK), hosted 293 interviews on BBC Radio Lancashire in Blackburn, UK, on 13 Nov 2014 as part of Guinness World Records Day.

Longest career as a broadcaster

As of Oct 2014, Bob Wolff (USA) had worked in US radio and television for 75 years. He started on 23 Oct 1939, with WDNC in Durham, North Carolina, USA, and has since served as the play-by-play commentator for eight different professional teams in five separate sports. Bob is shown above with GWR's Mike Janela and basketball legend Walt "Clyde" Frazier.

First internet radio show

Developed by Carl Malamud (left) and produced by Internet Talk Radio (both USA), the earliest internet radio show was *Geek of the Week*. It was first broadcast on 1 Apr 1993.

Most people singing live on a radio broadcast

In all, 3,885 singers were officially counted at The Biggest Band (UK) at Wembley Arena in London, UK, on 8 Jul 2011. The ensemble sang East 17's "It's Alright" on Resonance FM. The track was released two days later, with download proceeds going to Save the Children.

Most radio stations

According to the CIA World Factbook, the country with the greatest number of FM, AM and shortwave radio broadcast stations is the USA, with 13,769.

UNESCO has compared data on the typical number of radio receivers owned by members of the general public from different countries. It found that the USA has the

Highest annual earnings for a radio host

Compiled by *Forbes* magazine, the annual list of highest-earning celebrities places radio DJ Howard Stern (USA) at position number 62, with an income of $95 m (£55.7 m) for the year ending Jun 2014. At least $15 m (£8.7 m) of Stern's earnings were made from his appearance as a judge on TV reality show *America's Got Talent*, but this is dwarfed by his contract with US satellite broadcasting company Sirius XM.

Longest underwater live radio broadcast (unsupported)

Richard Hatch (UK), presenter at British Forces Broadcasting Service (BFBS) Radio, hosted a live show for 4 hr 43 min 54 sec at the Underwater Studio in Essex, UK, on 24 Nov 2011. The show, dubbed the "BFBS Pool Party", was broadcast live to British troops. The term "unsupported" indicates that only SCUBA gear may be used for this record; a diving bell is not allowed.

most radio receivers per capita, at an average of 2.11 receivers per member of the population.

Oldest public-service broadcasting organization

On 14 Nov 1922, two news bulletins became the first transmissions to be made by the British Broadcasting Corporation (BBC), from Marconi House in London, UK. That was 93 years ago, and the corporation is still going strong, making it the oldest broadcaster whose primary purpose is to benefit the public rather than to make a profit.

FIRST...

Telephone news service

Before the emergence of radio, a Hungarian inventor named Tivadar Puskás perfected a system whereby broadcasts could be made over a telephone exchange. The first "telephone news service", called Telefon Hírmondó, went live in Budapest, Hungary, in 1893.

Public radio broadcast

The first-ever public radio broadcast was transmitted from the Metropolitan Opera House in New York City, USA, on 13 Jan 1910. American inventor Lee de Forest had rigged up microphones around

IN NUMBERS

59%
Proportion of US population that radio reaches daily

49%
Proportion of US population that the internet reaches daily

21.4 hr
Average time per week that UK citizens spend listening to radio, as of late 2014, according to Statista.com

60
Most radio DJs presenting one show simultaneously, by Bradford Community Broadcasting (UK) on 31 Mar 2012

198 hr
Longest radio DJ marathon, by Giel Beelen (NLD) on the *GIEL! Breakfast Show* on 3FM Radio, from 12 to 20 May 2014

51,000+
Radio stations worldwide, according to UNESCO

the auditorium and connected these to a transmitter that could beam the evening's entertainment – a rendition by operatic tenor Enrico Caruso – around the city.

Podcast

The earliest podcast consisted of an interview conducted by TV and radio broadcaster Christopher Lydon with software developer Dave Winer (both USA). Winer was one of the first people to maintain a blog on the internet, and helped develop much of the associated technology. Using Winer's distribution system, Lydon released the audio interview to his blog in Jul 2003, making it the first podcast.

LONGEST...

Career as a radio DJ/presenter (male)

Herbert "The Cool Gent" Rogers Kent (USA, b. 5 Oct 1928) has been on the radio since 1944. As of 2015, he still hosts a weekend show on WVAZ radio (or "V103", as locals know it) in Chicago, Illinois, USA.

Maruja Venegas Salinas (PER, b. 3 Jul 1915) has enjoyed the **longest career as a radio presenter/DJ (female)**. She has presented the radio programme *Radio Club Infantil* on Radio Santa Rosa in Lima, Peru, since 18 Dec 1944. As of 2 Jul 2014, her career had spanned 69 years 196 days. At the age of 99, Ms Salinas declared that she had no plans to retire from her long-running programme.

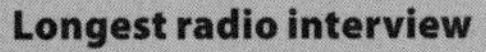

Longest radio interview

Radio host/writer Richard Glover (right) interviewed writer/sports star Peter FitzSimons (left, both AUS) on 702 ABC Sydney for exactly 24 hr. The attempt took place in a pop-up studio staged in the window of an ABC shop in Sydney, Australia, from 10 a.m. on 11 Dec 2011 to 10 a.m. the following day.

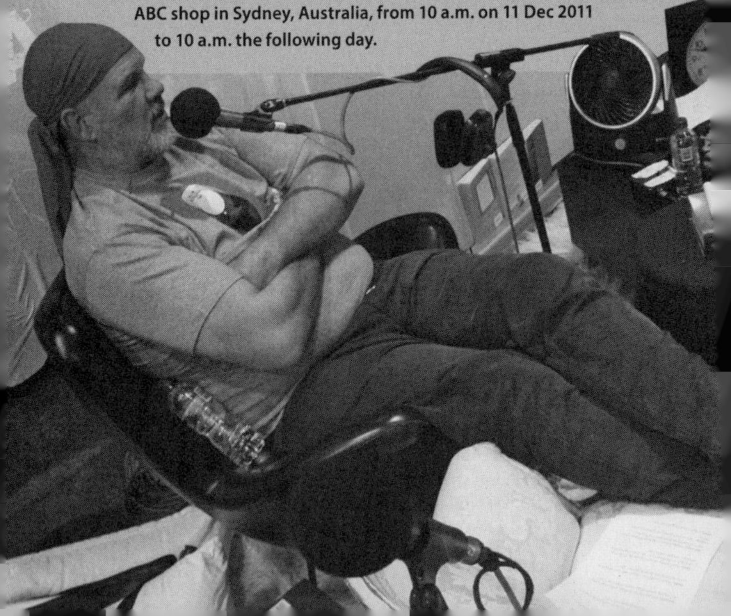

Radio play broadcast continuously

Nissan A, Abe Reiji aired non-stop for 8 hr 23 min 31 sec on 22 Dec 2013, to mark the 400th show in the radio series of the same name. The attempt was carried out by actors from the series, supported by Nissan Motor Co., Tokyo FM Broadcasting Co. and Kamaishi Saigai FM (all JPN) in Yokohama, Kanagawa, Japan.

FACT

The term "podcast" was coined in Feb 2004, by writer Ben Hammersley (UK). It mixes the words "pod", from Apple's then new iPod portable audio player, and "cast", from the term "broadcast".

The Archers

Created by Godfrey Baseley (UK) and first broadcast on 1 Jan 1951, *The Archers* is an institution of British radio. Indeed, its 64-year-plus run has made it the longest-running radio drama.

For 59 years 177 days of that period, Norman Painting (UK, b. 23 Apr 1924, d. 29 Oct 2009) starred as Philip Archer. (The photograph above shows the cast gathered for the 50th-anniversary episode in 2001. Norman is the white-bearded gentleman in the middle.) He debuted in the first pilot episode on 29 May 1950, and his last episode came just two days before his death and was broadcast posthumously on 22 Nov 2009. That extraordinary run gives him the **longest career for a radio actor in the same role (male)**.

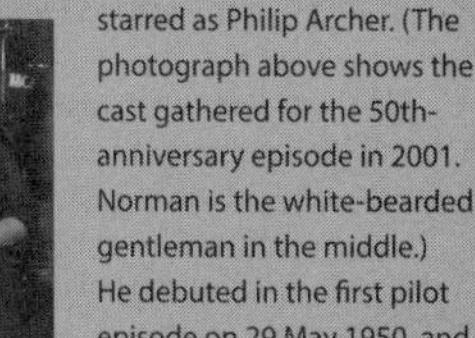

The show was partly inspired by tough times. Post-war Britain endured rationing until 1954 – the year the photo above left, showing Bob Arnold (who played Tom Forrest) and Courtney Hope (who played Widow Turvey), was taken. The British government was keen to encourage farmers to boost production, hence the show's original billing – "an everyday story of country folk" – and the agricultural themes that dotted the show.

The Archers is often seen as a cosy celebration of English middle-class life and values, but today's storylines carefully incorporate contemporary social issues. And there's definitely no sign of its popularity waning: by Oct 2014, the *Archers* podcast, which launched in 2007, had been downloaded 63.4 million times.

TV

By **2020, 965 million TV sets** will be web-enabled

First Emmy award-winner

Ventriloquist Shirley Dinsdale (USA) delighted early TV audiences with her dummy, Judy Splinters, on the show of the same name. She won the award for Most Outstanding Television Personality in 1949.

Most-tweeted TV series in one minute

According to the Nielsen "Tops of 2014: Social TV" report, the TV series with the most tweets in 60 sec was *The Voice* (NBC), with 310,000 tweets sent in the USA at 8:59 p.m. EST on 13 May 2014. Reality TV is the most tweeted-about TV show category, accounting for up to 70% of live TV-series tweeting.

Highest annual earnings for a television actress in a current series

In 2014, for the third year running, *Modern Family* star Sofía Vergara (COL) was television's highest-paid actress, with an annual income estimated by Forbes to be $37 m (£21.7 m) from Jun 2013 to Jun 2014. Once again she has earned more than her male counterpart Ashton Kutcher (USA), the **highest-paid actor** (with $26 m; £15.25 m).

Greatest prize money won on a TV game show

On 23 May 2009, appearing on the popular German Pro 7 show *Schlag den Raab* ("Beat the Host"), Nino Haase (DEU) did exactly that. By defeating host Stefan Raab, he won €3,000,000 (£2,559,122; $4,183,594).

Most Primetime Emmy awards for Outstanding Comedy Series

At the Primetime Emmys on 25 Aug 2014, *Modern Family* (ABC, USA, 2009–present) picked up its fifth consecutive Emmy for Outstanding Comedy Series, drawing the show level with *Frasier* (NBC, USA, 1993–2004). Its creators Steven Levitan and Christopher Lloyd were executive producers on *Frasier*.

FACT

Each episode of *Game of Thrones* costs an average of $6 m (£3.8 m) to make. That's a big budget, but each episode of the last season of *Friends* – made in 2003 – cost $1 m (£634,700) more.

Highest-rated TV series (current)

HBO's *Game of Thrones: Season 5*, which premiered in the USA on 12 Apr 2015, scored 91 out of 100 on review aggregator site Metacritic. It currently shares the record with Louis C K's (USA) FX comedy series *Louie*, also in its fifth season.

Game of Thrones went on to break the record for the **largest simultaneous broadcast of a TV drama**: starting with episode two of season five on 20 Apr 2015, the series was simulcast to 173 different countries and territories. Pictured is Maisie Williams (UK), who plays Arya Stark, accepting a GWR certificate on behalf of the show.

Most series broadcast for a TV game show

Broadcast by Channel 4 and produced by ITV Studios, *Countdown* began its 72nd series on 5 Jan 2015. It has been broadcast in the UK since 1982.

Most TV quiz appearances by a contestant

As of 15 Jul 2014, David St John (UK) had appeared 34 times as a contestant on TV quiz shows between 1982 and 2013.

LONGEST...

Career as a television news broadcaster

As of 22 May 2014, Alfonso Espinosa de los Monteros (ECU) had anchored television news shows for the Ecuavisa station since 1 Mar 1967, a total of 47 years 83 days. The only significant break in his career was in 1970, during the dictatorship of Velasco Ibarra, when the station decided to go off air for a period of three months.

IN NUMBERS

$9
Cost of 20 sec of TV airtime in the USA in 1941 (£11.70)

$1.8 m
Cost of 20 sec of advertising time paid by Pepsi-Cola during Super Bowl XXXVI in 2002, the **most expensive TV advertising campaign** (£1.2 m)

57.4 million
Subscribers to Netflix as of Jan 2015, according to Forbes.com

114 million
Worldwide subscribers to US cable and satellite TV network HBO

317.01 million
Estimated number of global households with analogue TV in 2014, according to Statista.com; in 2010 the figure had been 531.85 million

Most Primetime Creative Arts Emmy wins for a made-for-TV movie

Behind the Candelabra (HBO, USA, 2013), a biopic about pianist Liberace, secured 11 Emmys. The film won the award for Outstanding Miniseries or Movie, and there were wins for Michael Douglas and Steven Soderbergh (both USA) as lead actor and director, respectively.

LONGEST...

Live television shot for a drama series

A 23-min 25-sec live TV camera shot featured in the 1,000th episode of the Tamil-language television serial *Nadhaṣwaram* on 5 Mar 2014. It is credited to Sun TV Network Limited and TV series director Thirumurugan Muniyandi (both IND) and was filmed in Karaikudi, Tamil Nadu State, India.

Uninterrupted broadcast of a TV franchise

FXX broadcast *The Simpsons* for 12 days in Los Angeles, USA, between 21 Aug and 1 Sep 2014. It ran for 200 hr 50 min 4 sec, commercials aside, and included every episode of *The Simpsons* as well as shorts and the full-length movie, all shown in order of release.

The Simpsons has received the **most Emmys for an animated TV series**, with 31 wins as of 2014 and 78 Emmy nominations in all.

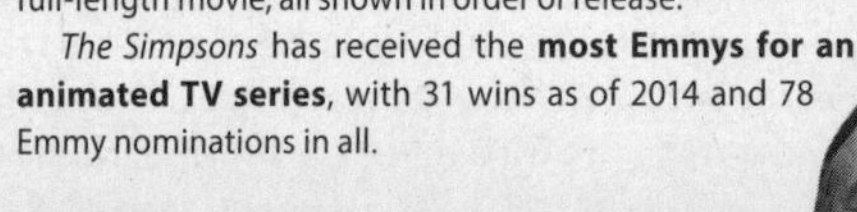

Uninterrupted transmission of a TV series

Crime drama *NCIS* was broadcast on Japan's FOX International Channels for 234 hr in all, from 29 Dec 2013 to 8 Jan 2014.

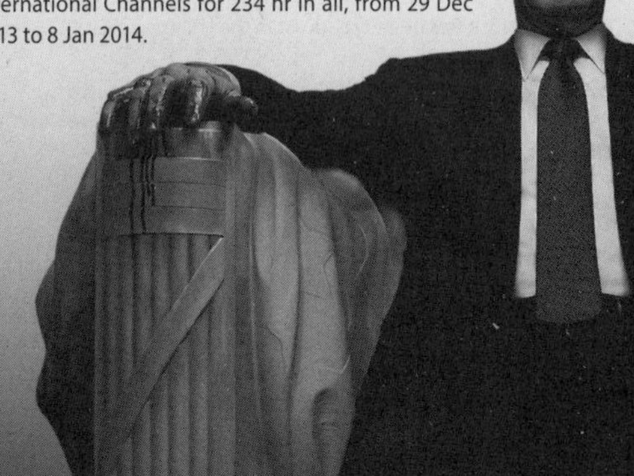

Most Emmy nominations for best comedy actress

In 2014, Julia Louis-Dreyfus (USA) earned a 15th Primetime Emmy nomination for her comedy acting. Her four wins for Lead Actress in a Comedy Series (in *The New Adventures of Old Christine and Veep*) see her tied with Helen Hunt (*Mad About You*).

Mary Tyler Moore and Candice Bergen (both USA) are tied for the **most Lead Actress in a Comedy Series wins**, with five each.

NETFLIX

A turning point for TV?

Offering on-demand streaming online, Netflix provides the chance to see major new TV series when viewers choose. With *House of Cards* (USA, 2013–present), it produced a real game-changer.

Established in 1997, Netflix initially offered a mail-order DVD rental service, then diversified into online video on demand. In 2011, however, Netflix also began commissioning original content that subscribers could stream online. *House of Cards* – an acclaimed drama about power politics starring Kevin Spacey (below left) as Frank Underwood and Robin Wright as his wife Claire – became the **first major series to premiere on an online streaming service**. Swiftly garnering acclaim, *House of Cards* proved that Netflix could compete with rival HBO (home to *The Sopranos*, *The Wire*, and *Game of Thrones*, among others) when it came to producing TV series with the scope and quality of the best movies.

House of Cards had nine nominations at 2013's Emmys (of a total 14 nominations for Netflix shows). Based on the earlier UK TV series of the same name, it became the **first online streaming show to be nominated for a major Primetime Emmy**, in the categories of Outstanding Directing for a Drama Series, Outstanding Lead Actor and Outstanding Lead Actress.

House of Cards is also the **first web-only series to win an Emmy** award (making Netflix itself the **first streaming video service to win an Emmy**). The show picked up three Emmys, including the coveted Outstanding Directing for a Drama Series, awarded to David Fincher for helming the first episode of the first season.

With such a promising start, it looks like Frank Underwood's dark deeds will be available to stream on a screen near you for some time to come.

Most-watched sporting events

The New England Patriots' defeat of the Seattle Seahawks in 2015's Super Bowl XLIX was seen by an average US audience of 114.4 million (peaking at 120.8 million) – the **largest TV audience for a domestic sports broadcast.**

The 2010 World Cup final between Spain and the Netherlands on 11 Jul 2010 drew a global audience of 329 million, the **largest audience for a TV broadcast of a soccer match** (inset). FIFA estimates that the 2014 World Cup final between Germany and Argentina was viewed by as many as 1 billion, but this figure is yet to be verified.

LONGEST...

TV commercial

Arby's (USA) produced a 13-hr 5-min 11-sec TV commercial to promote the Smokehouse Brisket sandwich. It was aired on My 9 KBJR-TV in Duluth, Minnesota, USA, from 24 to 25 May 2014.

LONGEST-RUNNING...

Live TV variety show on the same channel (episodes)

Waratte Iitomo! (Fuji Television Network Inc.) aired in Japan from 4 Oct 1982 to 31 Mar 2014, for a total of 8,054 episodes.

Children's TV programme (non-consecutive years)

The glove puppet Sooty has appeared on TV since 1952, when puppeteer Harry Corbett (UK) debuted with him on BBC TV's (UK) *Talent Night*. He continues to appear in his own show, *Sooty*, on the CITV channel (ITV). He appeared on television in consecutive years from 1952 to 2004, returning to TV screens in 2011. Barring the hiatus, Sooty has been on air for 63 years as of 2015.

Educational TV show

Costa Rica's *Teleclub* was first broadcast on 8 Feb 1963. As of 24 Mar 2015, it was still on the air, from Monday to Friday every week, after 52 years continuous transmission.

300 hours of video are uploaded to YouTube **every minute**

FACT

Established in Dec 2009, VEVO is a music-video-hosting service run by Universal Music Group, Google, Sony Music Entertainment and Abu Dhabi Media. It can be accessed in 200 countries.

Most "liked" video online

"Gangnam Style", the 2012 smash hit by South Korean pop/rap star PSY (aka Park Jae-sang, see p.414), had been "liked" 9,371,381 times on YouTube as of 3 May 2015. It also had 1,256,756 "dislikes".

Most concurrent views for a live event on YouTube

Skydiver Felix Baumgartner (AUT) made a record-breaking freefall from a balloon at an altitude of 38,969.4 m (127,852 ft) above eastern New Mexico, USA, on 14 Oct 2012 (see p.467). The event attracted more than 8 million concurrent views on YouTube, as reported by Google UK.

Highest-earning *Minecraft* contributor to YouTube

As of Feb 2015, YouTube statistics expert Social Blade estimated that the highest-earning YouTuber focusing on the open-world game *Minecraft* is "PopularMMOs", with annual earnings of \$750,900–\$12 m (£486,700–£7.7 m). This results in an average of \$6.37 m (£4.12 m). The *Minecraft* videos, which feature unusual missions and fun in-game mods, had in excess of 2.4 billion views from Popular MMOs' 4,255,285 subscribers as of 3 May 2015. For more information about the inherent challenges involved in calculating the earnings of YouTube stars, see p.416.

Most viewed VEVO video in 24 hours

Nicki Minaj's (USA) "Anaconda" video was viewed 19.6 million times on VEVO on 19–20 Aug 2014, beating Miley Cyrus's 19.3 million views for "Wrecking Ball" on 9–10 Sep 2013.

Most viewed online videogame walkthrough

"New Super Mario Bros Walkthrough Part 22" was uploaded by "cesaritox09" on 8 Jun 2009. As of 3 May 2015, the guide for the Nintendo DS platform game *New Super Mario Bros.* (Nintendo, 2006) had been watched 30,221,835 times.

Most viewed official movie trailer

The trailer for *Avengers: Age of Ultron* had received 73,761,359 views as of 3 May 2015. According to Digital Spy, it was viewed 26.2 million times on YouTube within the first 24 hr of its release on 22 Oct 2014.

MOST VIEWED...

Music video online (female artist)

Released on 20 Feb 2014, Katy Perry's (USA) song "Dark Horse", featuring American rapper Juicy J, had been viewed on YouTube 931,194,248 times as of 3 May 2015. Perry also boasts the second-most-watched music video by a female artist: "Roar", with 902,750,117 views as of 3 May 2015.

Sci-fi movie trailer

With 67,645,982 views as of 3 May 2015, the most watched sci-fi movie trailer on YouTube is "*Star Wars: Episode VII – The Force Awakens* Official Teaser Trailer #1", for the long-awaited seventh film in the *Star Wars* series, due to hit screens in Dec 2015.

First video to receive 1 billion views

PSY's "Gangnam Style" was the first video of any kind to receive 1 billion views online, with 1,000,382,639 hits on YouTube as of 21 Dec 2012. It was first posted online in Jul 2012.

App trailer

As of 3 May 2015, the trailer for the *My Talking Tom* app had been viewed 133,193,235 times on YouTube. The app centres on a kitten called Tom, which players can nurture to adulthood and guide through a variety of games. Created by app developer Outfit7, *My Talking Tom* inspired a series of spin-offs, including *Talking Angela*, *Talking Pierre* and even *Talking Santa*.

Online word-game video

"Scramble with Friends Match (2700 points, 1 Round)" was uploaded by YouTube user "thedotnetkid" on 3 Apr 2012. As of 3 May 2015, its view total stood at 348,027.

Most consecutive daily personal video blogs posted

As of 7 May 2015, Charles Trippy (USA) had posted 2,200 vlogs, without missing a day, on his YouTube channel Internet Killed Television.

IN NUMBERS

18 sec
Length of the first-ever YouTube video, "Me at the zoo", showing YouTube co-founder Jawed Karim at San Diego Zoo in California, USA, uploaded on 23 Apr 2005

50%
Proportion of YouTube views on mobile devices

60%+
Proportion of internet users who use YouTube

600+
Tweets per minute that carry a YouTube link

$4 bn
YouTube's revenue in 2014, according to *The Wall Street Journal* (£2.5 bn)

Most viewed independent music act on YouTube

Brothers Alejandro, Daniel and Fabian Manzano (all USA) make up Boyce Avenue. As of 3 May 2015, the band had more than 1.87 billion views and 7 million subscribers to their YouTube channels ("boyceavenue" and "BoyceAvenueExtras") – more views than the official channels of P!nk, Adele and Coldplay have received.

MOST YOUTUBE SUBSCRIBERS FOR A...

Band

As of 3 May 2015, the VEVO channel for British pop group One Direction had 15,812,273 subscribers. VEVO is one of YouTube's partners.

Highest-earning YouTube contributor

As of Feb 2015, YouTube stats expert Social Blade estimated that DisneyCollectorBR (aka "FunToyzCollector") was earning between $1.5 m (£900,000) and $23.4 m (£15.1 m) per year. The anonymous female poster uploads videos of toys and shows how they work. As of 3 May 2015, DisneyCollectorBR had 4,398,113 subscribers and 6,316,071,933 views.

FACT

Why such a broad range in YouTube earnings estimates? Social Blade says it's because the CPTs [cost per thousand views] for channels vary so widely. The figures also don't factor in Google's cut.

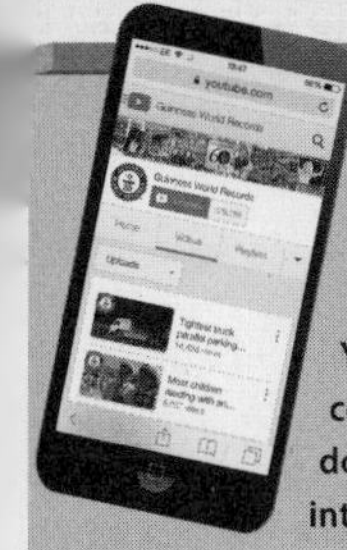

Largest video-sharing website

YouTube continues to dominate the internet as the principal source of videos, with more than 6 billion hours of video watched and more than 1 billion unique users visiting the site each month. As of Jan 2015, the number of daily subscriptions was up more than four times on 2014.

Comedy channel

VEVO channel "HolaSoyGerman.", published by Chilean comedian/entertainer Germán Alejandro Garmendia Aranis, had racked up 22,026,825 subscribers by 3 May 2015. This is some way ahead of the second-most-subscribed-to comedy channel: duo Smosh had 20,310,103 subscribers as of the same date.

Musician

The VEVO channel for US rapper Eminem (b. Marshall Bruce Mathers III) had 15,273,154 subscribers as of 3 May 2015.

It's PewDiePie!

If you're a gamer, chances are you're already very familiar with this man.

As of Feb 2015, Social Blade estimates that the **highest-earning gaming contributor to YouTube** is games reviewer "PewDiePie" – aka Felix Arvid Ulf Kjellberg (SWE). He enjoys annual earnings of $1.2 m–$18.9 m (£777,800–£12.2 m), a mean average of $10.05 m (£6.51 m).

For any non-gamers… "PewDiePie" has become famous for his over-the-top games commentaries – often indie efforts such as *McPixel* (2012) and *Goat Simulator* (2014) – made while he's playing them. As of 3 May 2015, he had more than 8.6 billion views and 36,376,634 subscribers – the **most subscribers on YouTube**. It's a mark of his skyrocketing popularity that back in 2013, when he received his GWR certificate, it was for a "mere" 12,115,082 subscribers.

"PewDiePie"'s rise may be indicative of a general trend among teens – at least in the USA, according to entertainment trade magazine *Variety*. In Jul 2014, *Variety* carried out a survey among 13–18-year-olds, 1,500 of whom were asked about who they regarded as the most influential celebrities. The resulting top five were all YouTube stars: Smosh came in first, with "PewDiePie" taking third place, ahead of "mainstream" celebs such as Jennifer Lawrence and Johnny Depp.

The YouTube sensation is shown below in 2013 on the red carpet at the Social Star Awards in Singapore, for movers and shakers in the world of social media.

There had been more than **75 billion app and game downloads** from Apple's App Store by Jun 2014

Most expensive App Store videogame

As of 5 Jan 2015, *BallAHolic HD* (A Local Chaos Project, 2011) was retailing for $349.99 (£228.29), making it the priciest game in Apple's App Store, according to InsiderMonkey.com. Players have to control a character called Uberhero, navigating around the perilous 3D surfaces of a series of balls.

Most expensive in-app purchase

Peter Molyneux's experimental game *Curiosity – What's Inside the Cube?* (22Cans, 2012) invited players to chip away at a big block, each layer unveiling something new and the promise of a life-changing experience for the person who unlocked the secret at its centre. Players could increase their tapping power by a factor of 100,000 by purchasing a Diamond Chisel for 3 billion in-game coins, costing an eye-watering £47,000 ($75,000) in real-world money.

Most international No.1s by an App Store game

Angry Birds (Rovio, 2009) hit the No.1 spot in 67 countries on Apple's App Store.

FACT

Clash of Clans is a "freemium" app. The app itself is free to download, but features within it (e.g. extra levels, characters or abilities) cost money to unlock, creating a stream of revenue for the publisher as the app is used.

Highest-grossing iOS gaming app by daily revenue

As of Feb 2015, multiplayer online strategy game *Clash of Clans* was generating $1,639,220 (£1,050,120) per day for its publisher Supercell in the USA – nearly $500,000 (£324,084) per day ahead of its closest rival, Machine Zone's fellow-MMO *Game of War: Fire Age* at $1,145,999 (£742,800).

Most popular App Store category

According to online quantitative data portal Statista.com, as of Sep 2014 games represented 20.38% of all available apps on Apple's online store.

Most YouTube views for a gaming app TV commercial

Increasing numbers of app publishers are looking to TV "app-vertising" to promote their products to a mass audience. A gaming app TV commercial for *Clash of Clans*, first broadcast on 23 Dec 2013, had been viewed 27,664,097 times as of 5 Mar 2015.

First Android app to reach 1 billion downloads

On 14 May 2014, Google announced that its Gmail application had achieved 1 billion downloads from the Google Play app store. That's almost one copy of the software downloaded for every seven human beings on Earth.

FIRST...

App in MoMA

In Jun 2014, *Biophilia* (2011) by Icelandic singer-songwriter Björk was acquired by the Museum of Modern Art (MoMA) in New York City, USA. *Biophilia* is a hybrid of an app and an album, whereby the music is enhanced with graphics and animations. Users can interact with both the visual and musical aspects of the app to create their own compositions, so that listening to the album becomes more of a participatory experience rather than a passive one, as is usually the case.

IN NUMBERS

1 in 5
People who own a smartphone, according to Businessinsider.com

1 in 5
Apps that are used only once after downloading, according to Localytics.com

11.11 billion
Statista.com's estimate of paid-for apps downloaded in 2014 alone

127.7 billion
Statista.com's estimate of free apps downloaded in 2014

35 days
Time for *Angry Birds* (Rovio, 2009) to reach 50 million users; it took radio 38 years to reach the same audience

275
Consecutive days *Angry Birds* topped the US Apple App Store chart, the **most days as the best-selling app in the iTunes Store**

Get flappy

Software developer Dong Nguyen was born in 1985 in Hanoi, Vietnam. He's best known today as the man behind the phenomenally successful mobile app *Flappy Bird*.

Although Dong's parents weren't wealthy, they were able to buy him a Nintendo Game Boy when he was young. He played it almost obsessively; aged 16, Dong was writing his own programs. Aged 19, he was studying computer science at university and had completed an internship at Punch Entertainment – a Vietnamese games company.

He conceived of *Flappy Bird* (.GEARS, 2013) as a game that could be played easily on the move – such as by busy commuters standing on a train with only one hand free.

The game proved highly successful, netting Dong $50,000 a day in advertising revenue at its peak. But he soon became disturbed with how hooked on the game players were becoming. "*Flappy Bird* was designed to play in a few minutes when you are relaxed. But it happened to become an addictive product. I think it has become a problem," he admitted.

So much so that on 10 Feb 2014, Dong removed the game from the Apple App Store, making it the **first app to be withdrawn after topping the Apple App Store chart**. After Dong Tweeted a warning about removing the app, *Flappy Bird* received 10 million downloads in the last 22 hours of its life. Since its demise, mobile phones pre-loaded with the game have sold for thousands on eBay. Dong continues to run .GEARS, the independent game developer that he founded in 2005.

Youngest mobile-game app developer

Aged seven years old, Zora Ball (USA) wrote a game that involves a ballerina searching for a jewel in a nail salon while trying to avoid a vampire. It was created in an open-source programming language called Racket and launched in Feb 2013.

FIRST...

Gaming app to earn $1 bn

Candy Crush Saga and *Clash of Clans* (see below left) may be more familiar to Western gamers, but neither can lay claim to being the first mobile gaming app to earn $1 bn. That honour goes to the Japanese free-to-play mobile title *Puzzle & Dragons* (known as *Pazudora* in Japan), released on iOS in Feb 2012. Its developer, GungHo Online Entertainment, revealed that 91% of its $1.5-bn (£0.9-bn) revenues in 2013 was down to this game, which earned $650 m (£394 m) via Apple's App Store and $775 m (£470 m) via Google Play. *Puzzle & Dragons* is a fantasy-themed puzzle game with role-playing elements.

Mobile game app developer to run a global TV advertising campaign

King Digital Entertainment (UK)was the first mobile game app developer to run its own global TV advertising campaign,

Most successful App Store publisher ever

The list of the top 25 paid iPhone apps Apple released in May 2013 featured five titles published by Electronic Arts (EA) – more than any other company. The games included *Plants vs. Zombies* and *The Sims 3*, along with classic board game spin-offs *Scrabble*, *Monopoly* and *The Game of Life* (all released in 2010).

Most apps available for download (marketplace)

According to app-analytics firm App Annie, the Google Play app store overtook Apple's App Store in the number of available apps to download in 2014. Google Play had over 1.6 million available apps, compared with just over 1.3 million for Apple's App Store.

initially to promote *Candy Crush Saga* in the USA, UK and Japan, but later including other popular titles in its stable such as *Bubble Witch Saga* (2012), *Farm Heroes Saga* (2014) and *Pet Rescue Saga* (2014). The move most notably paid dividends in Japan, where *Candy Crush Saga* leapt up the iOS chart from outside the top 100 most downloaded iPhone games to No.1 in five days.

Videogame pizza delivery system

In Feb 2005, Sony Online Entertainment added a pizza delivery system to *EverQuest II* (2004). By typing "/pizza", players would be linked to the Pizza Hut ordering site. This was the first time that a massively multiplayer online role-playing game (MMORPG) could accept orders for real-world items.

Eight years later came the **first shopping app for a games console**, and once again Pizza Hut played a pivotal role. On 23 Apr 2013, Microsoft released *Pizza Hut for Xbox*, an app for the Xbox 360 that enables players to order anything from Pizza Hut's online menu and have it delivered without having to leave their games consoles.

Most popular Facebook music app

As of Feb 2015, there were 39.83 million monthly active users of music-streaming service Spotify's (SWE) Facebook application, according to website Statista.com.

In autumn 2014, female artists held every spot in the ***Billboard* Hot 100 Top 5** for **seven weeks in a row**

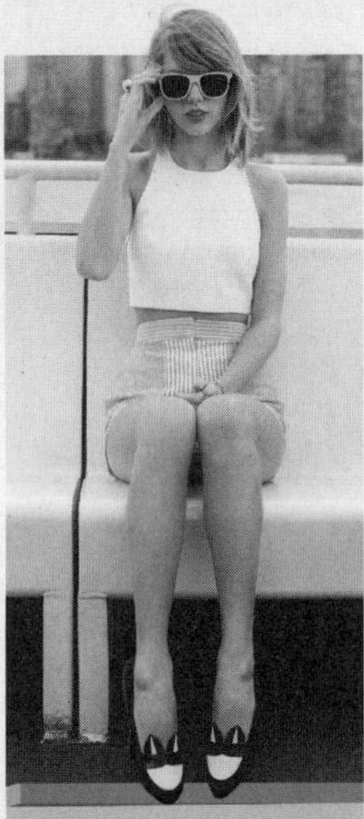

Most million-selling weeks on US albums chart

Taylor Swift (USA) is the only act to have had three million-selling weeks on the *Billboard* 200 albums chart since Nielsen SoundScan started tracking sales in 1991. The "Shake It Off" star achieved the feat with first-week sales of her third, fourth and fifth studio albums.

Most Grammy Awards won by a female artist

Alison Krauss (USA) has won 28 Grammys since her first award in 1990. Her haul includes two coveted Album of the Year awards – for *O Brother, Where Art Thou?* in 2001 and *Raising Sand* in 2008, the latter recorded with ex-Led Zeppelin vocalist Robert Plant.

The **most Grammy nominations for a female artist** is 53 for Beyoncé Knowles (USA), who received six nominations ahead of the 57th Awards in Feb 2015, extending her lead over Dolly Parton (46 nominations).

Highest-ranked female in Forbes' "Celebrity 100"

It was a good year for Beyoncé: in the 12-month period to 1 Jun 2014, she earned an estimated $115 m (£68.6 m), enough to top Forbes' list of the "most powerful celebrities". The star played 95 concerts on her "The Mrs Carter Show World Tour" in this tracking period, with each show raking in an average of $2.4 m (£1.7 m). In Dec 2013, she released her self-titled "visual album", which shifted 828,773 copies worldwide in three days of availability as a digital download, becoming the **fastest-selling iTunes album**.

Highest-grossing music tour by a female

Madonna's (USA) "Sticky & Sweet Tour" grossed $408 m (£251.1 m). The 85-date trek, in support of the *Hard Candy* album, visited 32 countries between 23 Aug 2008 and 2 Sep 2009 and attracted 3.54 million fans, who paid an average of $186 (£115) per ticket.

Since her debut set in 1983, Madonna has sold more than 300 million albums, making her the **best-selling female recording artist**.

Best-selling studio album by a female solo artist

Come On Over by Shania Twain (CAN) has sold in excess of 40 million copies worldwide since it was released on 4 Nov 1997.

Fastest-selling album in one country

American-born singer-songwriter Hikaru Utada (JPN) released her third studio album, *Distance*, on 28 Mar 2001. By the end of its first week on sale, the album had shifted 3,002,720 copies in Japan. Utada would later be named the most influential artist of the 2000s by *The Japan Times*.

Best-selling digital artist in the USA

Katy Perry (USA, b. Katheryn Hudson) had certified sales of 72 million digital singles Stateside as of 31 Oct 2014. Her biggest tracks include the nine-time-platinum "Firework" (2010), and "California Gurls" (2010) and "E.T." (2011) – both seven-time-platinum. She is seen here in the video for her 2013 hit "Dark Horse", a six-time-platinum smash.

As of 5 Feb 2015, Perry had 64,630,666 followers on Twitter, the **most Twitter followers.** The second most-followed female musician was Taylor Swift (USA), who had 51,939,930 followers as of the same date.

FACT

Perry's Egyptian-themed video proved to be a massive hit with YouTube viewers. It attracted more than 700 million views in 2014, making it the most-viewed music video on YouTube that year.

First song to reach the UK Top 40 on streams alone
On the UK's Official Singles Chart dated 4 Oct 2014, "All About that Bass" by Meghan Trainor (USA) climbed into the Top 40 on the strength of 1.17 million audio streams, with 100 streams equal to one download.

Biggest-selling *X Factor* contestant

Leona Lewis (UK) has sold more than 30 million records worldwide since appearing in the third UK series (2006) of *The X Factor*. Her debut album *Spirit* (2007) has sold more than 8 million copies.

Lewis was also the **first solo female to top the UK singles and albums charts simultaneously**. Single "Bleeding Love" and parent album *Spirit* were jointly top on 24 Nov 2007.

Most simultaneous UK Top 40 albums by a female

On the UK albums chart dated 6 Sep 2014, Kate Bush (UK) had eight Top 40 entries. They were: *The Whole Story* (1986, No.6), *Hounds of Love* (1985, No.9), *50 Words for Snow* (2011, No.20), *The Kick Inside* (1978, No.24), *The Sensual World* (1989, No.26), *The Dreaming* (1982, No.37), *Never for Ever* (1980, No.38) and *Lionheart* (1978, No.40). Bush's chart spike coincided with the start of her 22-night "Before the Dawn" residency at the Hammersmith Apollo in London, UK, her first live shows in 35 years.

Most consecutive weeks in the UK Top 20 (female)

Starting with her debut single "Heartbeat", Ruby Murray (UK, 1935–96) had at least one single in the UK Top 20 for 52 weeks in a row between 3 Dec 1954 and 25 Nov 1955.

Most languages featured on a single (multiple singers)

A 25-language version of "Let It Go", the award-winning song from Disney's *Frozen* (USA, 2013; the **highest-grossing animated film**, see p.381), became available to download in Jan 2014.

Accompanied by a YouTube video of the track as sung by Princess Elsa (voiced by Idina Menzel, see panel overleaf) in the movie, the dubbed version features 22 different female vocalists. The lyrics are performed in English, French, German, Dutch, Mandarin, Swedish, Japanese, Latin American Spanish, Polish, Hungarian, Castilian Spanish, Catalan, Italian, Korean, Serbian, Cantonese, Portuguese, Bahasa Malaysia, Russian, Danish, Bulgarian, Norwegian, Thai, Canadian French and Flemish.

IN NUMBERS

6
Most consecutive decades with a US No.1 album, achieved by Barbra Streisand (USA)

11
Consecutive weeks that *21* (2011) by Adele (UK) topped the UK albums chart, the **longest-running UK No.1 album in the 21st century**

50 min
Time it took Taylor Swift's (USA) "We Are Never Ever Getting Back Together" to top the iTunes singles chart – the **fastest-selling digital single**

106
Dolly Parton's (USA) record for the **most hits on the US Hot Country Songs chart by a female artist**

Idina Menzel

Since the tail-end of 2013, native New Yorker Idina Menzel has been all over the world's media. The award-winning Broadway actress, singer, songwriter and film and TV star provided the adult voice of Elsa, Queen of Arendelle, in Disney's animated blockbuster *Frozen* (USA, 2013). It was then that an icy blast of power pop propelled her into the Top 10.

Born Idina Mentzel on 30 May 1971, the entertainer mapped out her career at New York's Tisch School of the Arts, financing her studies by belting out tunes at bar mitzvahs while seeking fame and fortune on a grander stage. In 1996, she made her Broadway debut playing performance artist Maureen Johnson in Jonathan Larson's rock musical *Rent* (a role she reprised in a 2005 movie version), before seizing the opportunity to launch a pop career with her debut album *Still I Can't Be Still* (1998).

At the 58th Tony Awards (2004), Menzel took home the prize for Best Performance by a Leading Actress in a Musical in recognition of her starring role as Elphaba Thropp in the 2003 Broadway adaptation of *Wicked: The Untold Story of the Witches of Oz*. She reached a wider audience by playing Vocal Adrenaline coach Shelby Corcoran in the hit TV series *Glee* (Fox, USA) after a fan-driven campaign to cast her as the mother of Rachel Berry (played by Menzel "lookalike" Lea Michele). The duo's rendition of "I Dreamed a Dream" was a Season 1 highlight.

Menzel hit a new career peak with the release of *Frozen* and its mega-selling soundtrack, featuring "For the First Time in Forever" (a duet with Kristen Bell) and "Let It Go", complete with lyrics and a melody that are now ingrained on the minds of Disney fans worldwide. With a No.5 chart peak and more than 3.5 million copies sold in the USA alone, 60+ weeks on the UK singles chart, an Academy Award for Best Original Song and a 2015 Grammy for Best Song Written for Visual Media, "Let It Go" (see p.425) has been an overwhelming success.

First celebrity to attract 100 million "likes" on Facebook

The Colombian vocalist Shakira (b. Shakira Mebarak Ripoll) received her 100 millionth Facebook "like" on 18 Jul 2014. As of 8 May 2015, the "Hips Don't Lie" star, whose page is regularly updated with videos, news, photos and promotional material, had 100,247,580 "likes".

FACT

After Shakira reached the 100-million landmark, it was reported that 1 in 13 of all Facebook users had "liked" her; 3 out of 10 of her Facebook fans were called Maria and 4,642 were called Shakira!

MUSIC

"**None of us could read music**. None of us can write it." – John Lennon on **The Beatles**

First gig on a floating iceberg

Industrial metal band The Defiled (UK) braved sub-zero temperatures to perform a 30-min gig on a floating iceberg in the middle of the Greenland Sea, near the settlement of Kulusuk, on 15 Oct 2014. The audience watched the concert – the latest challenge in Jägermeister's Ice Cold Gig series – from fishing boats (inset).

FACT

Defiled members Stitch D, Vincent Hyde, The AvD and Needles explored the hostile environment for two days before locating an iceberg large – and thick – enough to host the gig.

Best-selling solo artist

Jan 2016 marks the 60th anniversary of the release of "Heartbreak Hotel", which would become the first No.1 pop single by the "King" of rock 'n' roll, Elvis Presley (USA, 1935–77). Presley has achieved worldwide record sales (vinyl, cassettes, CDs and downloads) of more than 1 billion units, and holds further records for the **most hit albums on the UK** and **US albums charts** (129 on both charts) and the **most cumulative weeks at No.1 on the UK** (80) and **US singles charts** (79).

Highest earnings ever for a musician

According to Forbes, hip-hop musician/producer Dr Dre (USA, b. Andre Young) raked i estimated pre-tax earnings of $620 m (£378 m) in the 12 months to Jun 2014. Despite no releasing an album of new material since 1999, the veteran rapper cashed in on the $3-br (£1.8-bn) sale of Beats Electronics – the headphone-manufacturing company which he founded with Jimmy Iovine – to Apple in May 2014, enabling him to smash the $125 m (then £76.2 m) earned by Michael Jackson (USA) in 1989.

Highest-grossing tour by a solo artist

Comprising 219 shows across six legs and three years (2010–13), Roger Waters' (UK) *The Wall Live* tour grossed a record $458.6 m (£286 m). The trek – witnessed by 4.1 million people worldwide and reportedly costing $60 m (£37.4 m) to stage – saw the Pink Floyd co-founder performing the band's classic 1979 album *The Wall* in its entirety.

Most US Hot 100 entries by a solo artist

As of 15 Nov 2014, US rapper Lil Wayne (b. Dwayne Carter Jr) had placed 124 singles on the *Billboard* Hot 100.

Most valuable album

A single copy of hip-hop collective Wu-Tang Clan's (USA) album *Once Upon a Time in Shaolin…* was made at a cost of c. $3 m (£1.9 m) and offered exclusively to one buyer. The double album – housed "in a box within a box within a box" at the Royal Mansour hotel in Marrakesh, Morocco – has reportedly attracted bids of up to $5 m (£3.1 m).

Most consecutive weeks in UK Top 40 (one single)

"Happy", written, produced and performed by Pharrell Williams (USA), made its debut in the UK's Official Singles Chart Top 40 on 14 Dec 2013 and spent its 49th and final week in the Top 40 on 15 Nov 2014. The track – which spent four non-consecutive weeks at No.1 and 20 weeks inside the Top 10 – has sold more than 1.6 million copies in the UK alone.

Longest climb to No.1 on UK singles chart

Ed Sheeran's (UK) 2014 ballad "Thinking out Loud" took 19 weeks to reach the top of the UK's Official Singles Chart. The third single from Sheeran's album *x* ("multiply") debuted at No.26 on the chart dated 5 Jul 2014 and peaked at No.1 on 8 Nov 2014. The track spent all 19 weeks inside the Top 30 and climbed to No.1 after the singer-songwriter had performed it live on the TV talent show *The X Factor* in the UK.

Most consecutive days writing a song

As of 16 Nov 2014, Jonathan Mann (USA) had written one song every day for 2,146 days in a row. He embarked on his "Song-a-Day" project on 1 Jan 2009, with each song videoed and posted to his self-titled YouTube channel, which has attracted more than 15 million views. Mann's songs include "Duet with Siri" (a collaboration with iPhone's virtual assistant), "Non-Existent Cat", "The Charlie Sheen Quotes Song" and "iOS Autocomplete Song" (with lyrics provided by the mobile operating system's autocomplete function).

Youngest club DJ

Dextrous One, aka Brandan Duke (CAN, b. 10 Nov 2006), made his professional debut as a DJ at the Kool Haus club in the Guvernment entertainment complex in Toronto, Ontario, Canada, on 15 Jun 2013 aged 6 years 217 days. "I made the crowd go crazy!" said Brandan, who first took to his father's decks at the age of three and who still needs a riser to reach the turntables.

IN NUMBERS

$250 million
Value of the **most lucrative recording contract**, signed between Sony and the estate of Michael Jackson, nine months after the singer's death

185,224,749
Streams of Eminem and Rihanna's "The Monster" on Spotify, as of 2 Dec 2014

13
Most debuts at No.1 on the US albums chart, by US rapper Jay Z

9 min 38 sec
Length of "All Around the World" by Oasis, the **longest No.1 single on the UK chart**

900
Weeks *The Dark Side of the Moon* spent on the US *Billboard* 200, as of 11 Apr 2015

3.7 million
Sales of *Noël* by Josh Groban in 2007/08, the **most successful Christmas album on the US chart**

One Direction

They may have finished third in the 2010 series of the UK talent show *The X Factor*, but former five-piece One Direction proved themselves to be the ultimate winners, releasing a string of hit albums, conquering the USA and earning themselves numerous world records:

First UK group to debut at No.1 in USA with a debut album: On 31 Mar 2012, *Up All Night* debuted at No.1 on the US *Billboard* 200 albums chart with first-week sales of 176,000. This betters the US chart starts of both The Beatles (1964) and the Spice Girls (1997).

Highest debut by a UK group on the US singles chart: On 20 Oct 2012, they debuted at No.3 on the US singles chart with "Live While We're Young", amassing first-week digital sales of 341,000 and eclipsing the Spice Girls and their No.5 debut with "Say You'll Be There" (1997).

First group to debut at No.1 in the US with their first four albums: 1D's unprecedented run of success on the US *Billboard* 200 albums chart began with *Up All Night* in 2012, and their debut album was followed to the top by *Take Me Home* (2012), *Midnight Memories* (2013) and the appropriately titled *Four* (2014), which entered at No.1 with first-week sales of 387,000 on 6 Dec 2014.

Most followers on Twitter for a music group: As of 28 Apr 2015, @OneDirection had 23,393,106 followers on Twitter.

Most popular dance-game track: As of 28 Apr 2015, the video of "What Makes You Beautiful" from Ubisoft's *Just Dance 4* had 40,351,368 views on YouTube.

Largest album launch

Backed by a PR campaign from Apple valued at $100 m (£61.8 m), *Songs of Innocence* by U2 (IRL) was gifted to 500 million iTunes customers – 7% of the world's population – on 9 Sep 2014. It was reported one month later that 81 million iTunes customers in 119 countries had "experienced" the album, whose delivery met with mixed reactions. "Only" 26 million people downloaded the set in its entirety.

ADVENTURERS

First ice-climb of Niagara Falls

On 27 Jan 2015, aged 47, veteran extreme adventurer Will Gadd (CAN) climbed Niagara's semi-frozen Horseshoe Falls in Ontario, Canada. Describing the sensation of scaling one of the world's most powerful waterfalls, he said: "It vibrates your intestines and makes you feel very, very small." Gadd is not new to this difficult activity, having picked up three golds in the sport in 1998–99, the most X Games medals for ice-climbing. Shortly after, Gadd was followed up Horseshoe Falls by Sarah Hueniken (CAN), achieving the first ice-climb of Niagara Falls (female).

CONTENTS

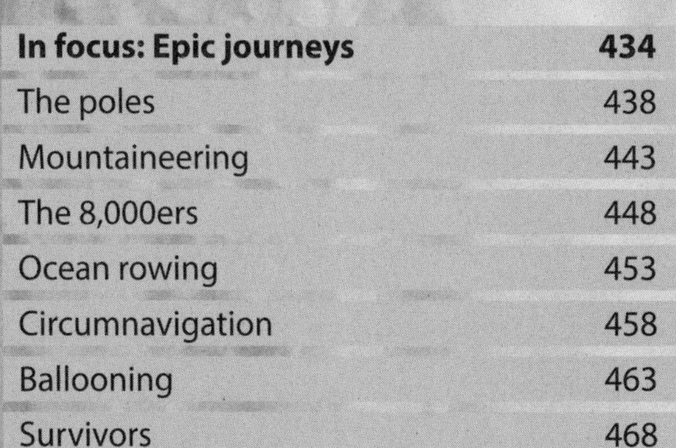

FACT

Despite appearances, Niagara Falls never freezes completely, with water continuing to pass beneath the ice. Only once, in 1848, did water stop flowing altogether, but this was the result of an "ice jam" farther upriver.

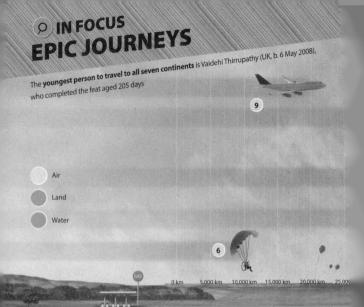

IN FOCUS
EPIC JOURNEYS

The **youngest person to travel to all seven continents** is Vaidehi Thirrupathy (UK, b. 6 May 2008), who completed the feat aged 205 days

Air

Land

Water

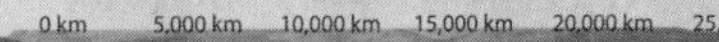

1. Air boat
- William Fadeley Jr and Eugene Hajtovik (both USA)
- 1,770 km (1,099 mi)
- Jacksonville, Florida, to New York City, New York, USA (1986)

2. *Minecraft*
- Kurt J Mac (USA)
- 2,097 km (1,303 mi)
- From original in-game spawn point towards Far Lands (2011–)

3. Open-water swimming
- Martin Strel (SVN)
- 5,268 km (3,273 mi)
- Swam the length of the Amazon River, from Peru to Brazil (2007)

4. Hovercraft
- David Smithers (UK)
- 8,000 km (4,970 mi)
- Passed through eight countries in western and equatorial Africa (1970)

5. Windsurfing
- Flávio Jardim and Diogo Guerreiro (both BRA)
- 8,120 km (5,045 mi)
- Chuí to Oiapoque along the Brazilian coast (2004–05)

6. Powered paraglider
- Miroslav Oros (CZE)
- 9,132 km (5,674 mi)
- Travelled throughout the Czech Republic, beginning at Sazená and finishing at Lipová-lázně (2011)

7. Skateboard
- Rob Thomson (NZ)
- 12,159 km (7,555 mi)
- Leysin, Switzerland, to Shanghai, China (2007–08)

8. Jet-ski
- Adriaan Marais and Marinus du Plessis (both ZAF)
- 17,266 km (10,728 mi)
- Alaska, USA, to Panama City, Panama (2006)

9. Commercial aircraft
- Boeing 777-200LR Worldliner
- 21,601 km (13,422 mi)
- Hong Kong, China, to London, UK (2005)

10. Lawnmower
- Gary Hatter (USA)
- 23,487 km (14,594 mi)
- Portland, Maine, to Daytona Beach, Florida, via 48 US states, Canada and Mexico (2001)

In it for the long haul? Take a look at other awe-inspiring around-the-world journeys on pp.458–62

11

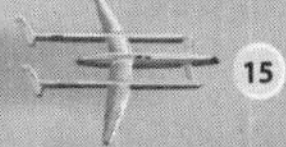

km 40,000 km 45,000 km 50,000 km 55,000 km 60,000 km 65,000 km 70,000 km

17 20 MOON 18 13

Earth's circumference

16

11. Hot-air balloon (solo)	13. Wheelchair	15. Non-stop flight by any aircraft	17. Fire engine	19. Solar-powered boat
• Steve Fossett (USA) • 33,195 km (20,626 mi) • Northam, Western Australia, to Queensland, Australia, around the world (2002)	• Rick Hansen (CAN) • 40,075 km (24,901 mi) • Vancouver, British Columbia, Canada, and back, around the world (1985–87)	• Steve Fossett (USA) • 42,469 km (26,389 mi) • Florida, USA, to Bournemouth, Dorset, UK (2006)	• Stephen Moore, supported by his crew (all UK) • 50,957 km (31,663 mi) • London, UK, and back, around the world (2010–11)	• Christian Ochsenbein, Raphaël Domjan (both CHE) and Jens Langwasser (DEU) • 60,023 km (37,296 mi) • Monaco and back, around the world (2010–12)
12. Tandem bicycle	**14. Hot-air balloon**	**16. Canoe (with portages)**	**18. Quad bike/ATV**	**20. Taxi**
• Phil and Louise Shambrook (both UK) • 38,143 km (23,701 mi) • Brigg, Lincolnshire, UK, and back, around the world (1994–97)	• Bertrand Piccard (CHE) and Brian Jones (UK) • 40,814 km (25,360 mi) • Château-d'Oex, Switzerland, to the Egyptian desert (1999)	• Verlen Kruger and Steven Landick (both USA) • 45,129 km (28,041 mi) • Montana to Michigan, USA, via Canada (1980–83)	• Valerio De Simoni, Kristopher Davant and James Kenyon (all AUS) • 56,239 km (34,945 mi) • Istanbul, Turkey, to Sydney, Australia (2010–11)	• Leigh Purnell, Paul Archer and Johno Ellison (all UK) • 69,716 km (43,319 mi) • London, UK, and back, around the world (2011–12)

11
Huskies that returned with Roald Amundsen (NOR) after his South Pole expedition in 1911–12; he had set out with 52

17
Sailors who returned from Ferdinand Magellan's (PRT) around-the-world trip; a total of 239 departed

24
Years that Marco Polo (ITA) spent away from Venice – 17 of them in China. He only intended his trip to last a few years

157°–337°
Last-known position of aviator Amelia Earhart (USA) before she disappeared over the Pacific in 1937

50%
Success rate of Christopher Columbus (ITA); two of his four voyages resulted in his flagship being wrecked

15.2 cm
Thickness of the windows (6 in) in the bathyscaphe *Trieste*, which made the **deepest manned descent**; one cracked, but the 1960 dive was still a success (see p.29)

Best-laid plans...

As far as records go, those that involve travelling for thousands of kilometres require more dedication than most. That said, with today's cutting-edge technology and range of vehicles suited to all conditions, we've arguably never been better equipped to take on a long-haul trip.

If you're in any doubt, have a look at these stats from past voyages that didn't quite go to plan...

A journey of a thousand miles begins with one step, or so the saying goes. The ancient Chinese philosopher Lao Tzu's aphorism is an apt introduction to the subject of record-breaking trips, although to earn a GWR title, you really have to go that extra mile.

We humans are a restless bunch, and have always taken great risks in the name of exploration. In the past, the rewards – riches, power and fame – typically outweighed the dangers, and if asked to name an explorer, you would likely think of historical explorers such as Christopher Columbus and Marco Polo (both ITA), or adventurers such as Amelia Earhart (USA) and Robert Scott (UK). But don't assume that the age of exploration has been and gone. As the selection of travellers shown on pp.434–35 attests, the urge to go on an epic voyage is as strong as ever.

That's not to downplay the feats achieved by early pioneers. When Ferdinand Magellan (PRT) set off from Spain in 1519, nobody had ever travelled all the way around the world. Three years later, the expedition landed back in Spain with less than 10% of the crew that departed; Magellan himself was hacked to pieces en route by a Filipino tribe. Nevertheless, the voyage still takes credit for being the **first circumnavigation**.

While our options for getting from A to B today have diversified, the spirit of adventure remains a driving force. Whether it's relying on engine power, natural forces, your own steam – or even actions in a virtual world – every trip offers its own unique rewards and challenges, yet every epic journey has to begin with that first step.

FACT

Based on a moderately active person walking 7,500 steps per day, in an average lifetime (70.5 years) that equates to a distance of some 161,000 km (100,000 mi) – four times around the world!

EXTRA-EPIC JOURNEYS

Some travellers truly go to amazing lengths in their pursuit of a record-breaking voyage. Here we round up some of the longest trips ever undertaken…

Name(s)	Transport	Distance	Duration
Emilio Scotto (ARG; below left)	Motorcycle	735,000 km	1985–95
Emil & Liliana Schmid (both CHE)	4WD	692,227 km	1984–
Walter Stolle (UK)	Bicycle	646,960 km	1959–76
Harry Coleman & Peggy Larson (USA; below right)	Camper van	231,288 km	1976–78
Hughie Thompson, John Weston & Richard Steel (all UK)	Bus	87,367 km	1988–89
Ben Carlin (AUS)	Amphibious vehicle	78,215 km	1950–58

Out-of-this-world odyssey

While all of these incredible journeys are extreme in their own ways, they all pale in comparison to the **most remote man-made object**: the *Voyager 1* satellite. Since departing Earth in 1977, the spacecraft has notched up 19.569 billion km (12.160 billion mi), as of 10 Feb 2015. In Aug 2012, it became the **first probe to leave the Solar System** and it is now travelling through interstellar space – the barren region between stars. Amazingly, *Voyager 1* is still transmitting data, so who knows what deep-space discoveries it may yet uncover on its epic journey into the cosmos?

THE POLES

The **ancient Greeks** named the **south polar region**, which they had never seen, **"Antarktos"** – the opposite of the "Arktos" or Arctic

First person to reach the North Pole solo

On 14 May 1986, Dr Jean-Louis Etienne (FRA) reached the Geographic North Pole after 63 days on skis and pulling a sled from Ward Hunt Island in Canada. He covered more than 1,000 km (620 mi), skiing eight hours a day non-stop, and was resupplied several times.

First people to trek (ski) to the North Pole

Leaving Henrietta Island near the Bering Strait on 16 Mar 1979, a seven-man Soviet team, led by explorer Dmitry Shparo, reached the North Pole on 31 May after a 1,500-km (900-mi) trek of 77 days.

In 1988, Shparo led a Soviet-Canadian ski expedition of 12 people in the **first traverse of the Arctic Ocean**, from Russia via the Geographic North Pole to Canada. During this crossing, they used dog-sleds and resupplies.

On 22 Dec 2007 – the winter solstice – Shparo's son, Matvey Shparo, and Boris Smolin (both RUS) began the **earliest winter expedition to the North Pole**, from Komsomolets Island in the Arctic Ocean. They reached the Pole on 14 Mar 2008, eight days before the start of the "polar day".

Fastest aggregate time to complete a marathon on each continent and the North Pole

From 8 Apr 2013 to 27 Jul 2014, Fiona Oakes (UK) ran eight marathons in a cumulative time of 28 hr 20 min 50 sec. She came first in three: the North Pole, Isle of Man and Antarctic Ice marathons.

First person to trek to both Poles solo (unsupported and unassisted)

Polish-born Marek Kamiński (USA) reached the North Pole from Cape Columbia in Canada on 23 May 1995, a 70-day journey of 770 km (478 mi), and the South Pole from Berkner Island in Antarctica on 27 Dec 1995, a 53-day trek of 1,300 km (807.78 mi).

Fastest marathons on the North and South Poles by a married couple (aggregate)

Uma and Krishna Chigurupati (both IND) ran the Antarctic Ice Marathon on 15 Dec 2010 and the North Pole Marathon on 8 Apr 2011 in a total time of 35 hr 6 min 28 sec. Uma finished the Antarctic race in 8 hr 16 min 22 sec, and Krishna in 8 hr 27 min 26 sec. They both ran the Arctic race in 9 hr 11 min 20 sec.

Most polar expeditions by an individual

Richard Weber (CAN) reached the Geographic North Pole from the coast six times between 2 May 1986 and 14 Apr 2010, and the Geographic South Pole from the coast twice, on 7 Jan 2009 and 29 Dec 2011. In his last trip to the North Pole, his son Tessum was part of the team.

Longest polar trek

On 7 Feb 2014, Ben Saunders and Tarka L'Herpiniere (both UK) completed a 2,890-km (1,795-mi) journey to the South Pole and back, on skis and hauling sleds that at the start weighed almost 200 kg (440 lb) apiece. Their epic 105-day trek also made them the **first to complete Captain Scott's Terra Nova Expedition** of 1912.

FACT

It took Manon and her team of mechanics and guides 16 days 8 hr 35 min to reach the South Pole – a journey of 2,309 km (1,434 mi). There, they rested for 24 hours before the return trip.

First expedition to the South Pole in a wheeled tractor

On 22 Nov 2014 at 18:55 (UTC), Manon Ossevoort (NLD) left Novo Runway in Antarctica in a Massey Ferguson 5610 tractor. She went on to complete a 4,638-km (2,881.91-mi) round trip to the South Pole that would last 27 days 19 hr 25 min. The Antarctica 2 expedition arrived back at Novo Runway on 20 Dec 2014, having clocked 438 hr 17 min of driving time.

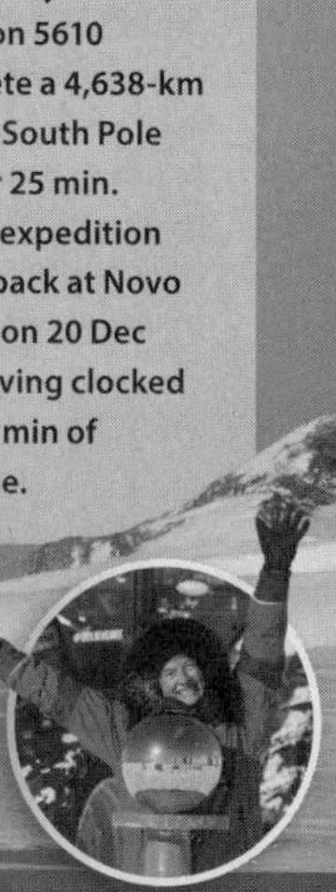

FACT

In 1911, Roald Amundsen (NOR) launched the **first successful expedition to the South Pole**, from the Bay of Whales. His ship, the *Fram*, had a rounded hull that allowed it to slide over ice floes.

Most southerly navigation

On 27 Jan 2014, *Arctic P*, an 87.6-m (287.4-ft) motor yacht owned by the Packer family and commanded by Captain Russell Pugh (both AUS), reached 78°43.0336'S 163°42.1317'W – in the Bay of Whales in the Ross Sea of Antarctica – the farthest south recorded for a ship.

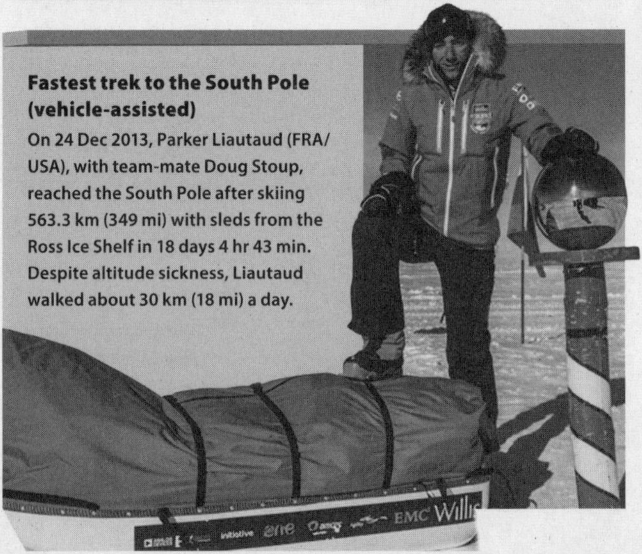

Fastest trek to the South Pole (vehicle-assisted)

On 24 Dec 2013, Parker Liautaud (FRA/USA), with team-mate Doug Stoup, reached the South Pole after skiing 563.3 km (349 mi) with sleds from the Ross Ice Shelf in 18 days 4 hr 43 min. Despite altitude sickness, Liautaud walked about 30 km (18 mi) a day.

Youngest person to trek to the South Pole

Lewis Clarke (UK, b. 18 Nov 1997) was 16 years 61 days old when he reached the Geographic South Pole on 18 Jan 2014. He and polar guide Carl Alvey, of Adventure Network International, left the Hercules Inlet on the Ronne Ice Shelf on 2 Dec 2013 and skied 1,123.61 km (698.18 mi) unsupported, although medical and food resupplies were used.

Fastest bicycle ride to the South Pole

On 17 Jan 2014, Spain's Juan Menéndez Granados (below) reached the South Pole solo on his "fatbike" – a wide-tyred bicycle adapted for riding on snow and varied terrain – after travelling 700 mi (1,130 km) from the Hercules Inlet in 46 days. He was unsupported and unassisted but skied and pulled his bike on his sled when unable to progress by bike.

Daniel Burton (USA, inset below right) completed the same route on a fatbike a few days later, on 21 Jan, after 51 days of cycling (and pushing his bike), with four resupplies.

The **first person to cycle to the South Pole** (assisted by a support team) was Maria Leijerstam (UK), who arrived on 27 Dec 2013 on a recumbent tricycle.

IN NUMBERS

20,000
Number of years ago that the first humans visited the north polar region, crossing from north-eastern Asia via the frozen Bering land bridge

24
Time zones covered by the Arctic, which occupies one-sixth of Earth's land mass

6 months
Duration of the Arctic winter, from early Oct to early Mar, when there is continuous darkness

3,223 m
Height above sea level of the eastern Antarctic Plateau, the **coldest**, **driest**, **highest** and **largest desert** (10,574 ft)

99%+
Proportion of Antarctica that is covered in ice; it is around the same distance across as the USA

Sir Ranulph Fiennes

On 29 Aug 1982, Ranulph Fiennes (above) and Charles Burton (both UK) completed the first surface circumnavigation of the world via both Poles: 35,000 mi (56,327 km) in all.

Tell us about your circumnavigation… Beforehand, we spent seven years working non-stop to get sponsorship. We trained and did a trial in the Arctic, and went to Greenland to get to know the crevasses of the Antarctic. We chose two people out of 800 applicants to join us – neither had ever been on an expedition. We were in Antarctica for 18 months, four of us 600 mi (965 km) from anywhere in a cardboard house under the snow.

After reaching the North Pole, we were very weak. We had become the **first humans to reach both Poles** but the last 1,800 mi (2,900 km) from the North Pole were lethal. Of course, we had no sat nav, no GPS. We had to float on an ice floe, hoping to get to Siberia. Bears were coming across it, and it was breaking up. It would have been very difficult to get a rescue – and if we had, 11 years of our lives would have been wasted right at the last minute…

What does it mean to hold a GWR title?
I am really, really proud to have held GWR records over the last 40 years. GWR is the greatest place for collecting world records with total honesty, checking out every fact. It has also helped us get vital sponsorship – without media coverage for breaking records, you can't do that.

Which sections of the book are you particularly interested in?
The latest records. It took me 17 years to cross both ice caps and climb Everest – and meanwhile I was always looking in that section to make sure no one did it first.

Fastest time to reach the South Pole by a married couple (unassisted, unsupported)

Chris and Marty Fagan (USA) reached the South Pole from the Ronne Ice Shelf in 48 days, leaving on 2 Dec 2013 and arriving on 18 Jan 2014. They covered 980 km (609 mi), at an average of 20.4 km (12.6 mi) per day.

Most expeditions to the South Pole

Between 4 Nov 2004 and 9 Jan 2013, Hannah McKeand (UK) trekked six times to the Pole. On the second trip, from 19 Nov to 28 Dec 2006, she skied alone and made the **fastest solo journey to the South Pole by a woman (unsupported, unassisted)**: 39 days 9 hr 33 min.

MOUNTAINEERING

Tectonic plate movements cause **Everest** to rise by **4 mm each year**

Highest-altitude concert on land

Oz Bayldon (UK) played a concert at 6,476 m (21,246 ft) on Mera Peak in Nepal on 16 May 2012. The performer, musicians and audience were representing Music4Children, a London-based charity that raises money for under-privileged children in Nepal. The aim was to fund the building of a self-sustainable orphanage near Kathmandu.

Most 6,000-m Andean mountains climbed

Maximo Kausch (UK) is attempting to climb all of the 6,000-m-high (19,685-ft) mountains in the Andes. On 1 Sep 2014, he summitted Uturunco (aka Uturunku, 6,015 m; 19,734 ft), his 58th successful climb, which is more than any other mountaineer to date.

There are an estimated 99 to 106 mountains of 6,000 m or more in the Andes, which are second only to High Asia in altitude. The Andes are the world's **longest mountain complex**, spanning 7,600 km (4,720 mi) across seven countries – Argentina, Bolivia, Chile, Colombia, Ecuador, Peru and Venezuela – and measuring up to 300 km (186 mi) in width. The **first person to climb the 12 highest Andean mountains** – all of them above 6,600 m (21,653 ft) – is Argentina's Darío Bracali. The pioneering climber, who disappeared in May 2008 while attempting a solo ascent of Dhaulagiri I in Nepal, conquered this Andean challenge in 2004.

Fastest time to climb the North Face of the Eiger solo (unassisted)

Ueli Steck (CHE) took just 2 hr 47 min 33 sec to scale the North Face of the Eiger in Switzerland's Bernese Alps on 13 Feb 2008.

On 20 Apr 2011, fellow Swiss Dani Arnold soloed the Eiger in 2 hr 28 min. This broke Steck's record by 19 min, but Arnold used fixed ropes on the Hinterstoisser Traverse section. This represents the **fastest time to climb the North Face of the Eiger solo (assisted)**.

Oldest person to climb Everest

Yuichiro Miura (JPN, b. 12 Oct 1932; above left) made his third ascent of Everest (8,848 m; 29,029 ft) on 23 May 2013 aged 80 years 223 days. On his descent, he was helicoptered from Camp 2 to Kathmandu.

Junko Tabei (JPN, b. 22 Sep 1939; above right) reached the summit on 16 May 1975, making her the **first woman to ascend Everest**. Since then, Tabei has gone on to conquer more than 70 other major mountains around the world. For more on Tabei's ascents, see p.446.

Oldest person to climb the Seven Summits (Carstensz list)

Climbers who choose to ascend the highest points on each continent can choose from two lists, depending on how the continent of Oceania is defined: the Kosciuszko (Australia) or Carstensz (Indonesia) list.

High achiever

Mountaineering is fraught with danger, and for this reason, Guinness World Records will not accept applications from climbers under the age of 16. However, this didn't stop Jordan Romero (USA) completing a climb of all Seven Summits by the age of 15 years 165 days. He conquered his first Seven Summits peak, Kilimanjaro in Tanzania, aged 10, and finished on 24 Dec 2011 with an ascent of Vinson Massif in Antarctica. He is also the youngest person to climb an "8,000er" (see p.453–57), ascending Everest on 22 May 2010 at the age of 13 years 314 days.

FACT

In 2010, Jordan climbed Everest, which sits on the Nepal-China border. Nepal insists that any climbers attempting Everest be aged 16 or older. China, however, has no such rule.

Werner Berger (ZAF/CAN, b. 16 Jul 1937) completed his ascent of the more taxing Carstensz list by 21 Nov 2013, at the age of 76 years 128 days. He achieved the record when he successfully climbed Carstensz, aka Puncak Jaya – at 4,884 m (16,024 ft), the **highest island peak**. He had completed the Kosciuszko list six years earlier, on 22 May 2007.

The **oldest person to climb the Seven Summits (Kosciuszko list)** is Ramón Blanco (ESP, b. 30 Apr 1933), who was aged 70 years 243 days on his final climb, of Kosciuszko, on 29 Dec 2003.

For the youngest person to climb both lists of the Seven Summits, see "High achiever", opposite.

Most people in a mountain ascent (single mountain)

On 3 Sep 2011, a total of 972 employees of the Norwegian IT firm Atea scaled Galdhøpiggen (2,469 m; 8,100 ft) in Norway's Jotunheimen National Park.

The **most people to take part in a mountain ascent across multiple mountains** occurred during the Atunas Formosa 100 Hiking event on 2 Oct 2011. A total of 6,136 people simultaneously climbed 10 different mountains located across Taiwan.

Highest mountain unclimbed

At 7,570 m (24,835 ft), Kangkar Pünzum in Bhutan/China is the world's 40th-highest mountain, and the highest yet to be climbed. Unsuccessful attempts were made to summit the peak in the 1980s; subsequently, in 1994, a partial ban of mountaineering in the country – for religious reasons – was declared. Since 2003, all climbing in Bhutan has been outlawed, so Kangkar Pünzum may remain unclimbed for many years to come.

The current **highest mountain unclimbed in winter** is K2, at 8,611 m (28,251 ft) the world's second-highest

First person to climb the "Triple Seven Summits"

Christian Stangl (AUT) climbed the first-, second- and third-highest mountains on all seven continents – known as the "Triple Seven Summits" – by 23 Aug 2013, when he reached the top of Shkhara (5,193 m; 17,040 ft) on the Georgia-Russia border. Stangl also became the **first person to climb the "Second Seven Summits"** (by 15 Jan 2013) and the **"Third Seven Summits"** (by 23 Aug 2013).

IN NUMBERS

25%
Proportion of the Earth's surface covered in mountains, according to the United Nations

12%
Proportion of the world's population who live on mountains, according to the United Nations

64%
Proportion of Nepal's territory occupied by mountains

33%
Proportion of oxygen available at the top of Mount Everest compared with the oxygen available at sea level

80%
Proportion of the first 10 climbers to attempt the North Face of the Eiger who died

mountain. It is unclimbed in both the calendar winter (20 Dec–20 Mar) and the meteorological winter (1 Dec–28 Feb). So far, there have been only three unsuccessful attempts to climb K2 in this season.

Fastest time to reach the peaks of Everest and Lhotse

On 15 May 2012, with the benefit of bottled oxygen, Michael Horst (USA) became the first person to cross from the top of Everest – the world's **tallest mountain** – along the South Col pass, to the top of Lhotse (8,516 m; 27,939 ft), the fourth-highest mountain. This is also the first time that two 8,000-m mountains were summitted in a 24-hr period.

FIRST...

Ascent of Everest

At 11:30 a.m. on 29 May 1953, Edmund Percival Hillary (NZ) and Tenzing Norgay (IND/Tibet) became the first people to conquer Everest. The expedition was led by Colonel Henry Cecil John Hunt. Hillary was knighted and Norgay awarded the George Medal.

Ascent of the Seven Summits

Richard "Dick" Bass (USA) completed the Kosciuszko version of the Seven Summits on 30 Apr 1985. The **first ascent of the Seven Summits (Carstensz list)** was by Patrick Morrow (CAN), who completed this more taxing list on 5 Aug 1986.

Junko Tabei (JPN) became the **first female to climb the Seven Summits** when she topped Elbrus in Russia on 28 Jul 1992. This ascent completed her climb of both the Kosciuszko and Carstensz lists.

Ascent of Saser Kangri II

On 7 Sep 1985, a Japanese-Indian expedition summitted Saser Kangri II's north-west peak (c. 7,500 m; 24,600 ft), but its highest south-east peak (7,518 m; 24,665 ft) was not conquered until 24 Aug 2011, when it was reached by Mark Richey, Steve Swenson and Freddie Wilkinson (all USA). Until then, it was the world's second-highest unclimbed mountain after Kangkar Pünzum (see p.445), and the **highest mountain unclimbed where climbing is not prohibited** – a record now held by an unnamed mountain in the Lapche Kang range in southern Tibet, at c. 7,250 m (23,786 ft).

Fastest time to climb the highest points in all 50 US states

Between 3 Jun and 16 Jul 2010, Mike Moniz (USA) scaled the highest peak in each of the 50 US states, taking just 43 days 3 hr 51 min. Mike was accompanied by his son, Mike Jr, who was ineligible for Guinness World Records recognition owing to him being under the age of 16 years (see "High achiever", p.444).

Ascent of Everest from both sides in a season

David Liaño González (MEX) climbed Everest from Nepal on the south side on 11 May 2013 and returned to the peak on 19 May, climbing from Tibet on the north side. This is the first time that any climber has scaled Everest from both sides in a single season.

Twins to climb Everest

On 23 May 2010, Argentina-born Damián and Willie Benegas (USA) became the first twin brothers to climb Everest. They did so from the South Col.

Tashi and Nungshi Malik (IND) are the **first twin sisters to climb Everest**, doing so on 19 May 2013. They reached the peak along with Samina Baig, the first Pakistani woman to successfully complete the climb. The following year, on 16 Dec 2014, they also became the **first twins** (and **first siblings**) **to complete the Seven Summits**.

Astronaut to climb Everest

On 20 May 2009, former NASA astronaut Scott Parazynski (USA) scaled Everest, becoming the first person to travel in space and climb Earth's highest mountain. Once at the top of Everest, he left a small Moon rock that had been collected by the crew of Apollo 11.

Earthquake in Nepal

Just before midday on Saturday, 25 Apr 2015, an enormous earthquake struck the continent of Asia. With a magnitude of 7.8 on the Richter scale, the tremor caused widespread devastation and loss of life throughout China and India. Its epicentre was about 80 km (50 mi) north of Kathmandu in Nepal.

By 28 Apr, an estimated 5,000 people were confirmed to have died in the quake. Authorities were already anticipating a total of nearer 10,000, however, as rescue teams struggled to reach the less accessible mountain regions in the west of the country: some 6.6 million people live in the regions affected, according to the United Nations. Approximately 6,500 people were injured and residential areas were damaged or destroyed, leading to widespread homelessness. Many historical monuments were also lost.

The colossal quake brought about avalanches on Everest – some 220 km (137 mi) east of the epicentre – causing a massive slab of ice to shear off and plough through Base Camp. At least 19 people died in the resulting devastation. There may have been in excess of 1,000 people on the mountain when the quake struck. Around 60 climbers were injured, but in the confusion surrounding the immediate aftermath of the disaster, dozens of climbers were still missing. Many remained marooned in the higher reaches of Everest. Fortunately, around 200 individuals who had been on the mountain were saved.

Whatever the final figures, this grim day in the history of mountaineering will certainly result in the greatest number of deaths on Everest in one day. Guinness World Records extends its condolences and sympathy to everyone affected by this unprecedented and shocking event.

THE 8,000ERS

The "8,000ers" are the **14 mountains** that extend **beyond 8,000m (26,246 ft)** above sea level

First person to climb all 8,000-m mountains

Reinhold Messner (ITA) became the first person to climb the 14 mountains over 8,000 m (see full list below) when he summitted Lhotse on the Nepal/Tibet border on 16 Oct 1986. He began with Nanga Parbat in Jun 1970. As of 31 Mar 2015, only 34 people had matched his feat.

The **first woman to climb all 8,000ers** is Oh Eun-sun (KOR), although her climb of Kangchenjunga was disputed. The first female to achieve this milestone without dispute is Edurne Pasaban (ESP), who began by summitting Everest on 23 May 2001 and finished on Shisha Pangma on 17 May 2010.

The **first woman to climb all 8,000ers without bottled oxygen** is Gerlinde Kaltenbrunner (AUT). The "Queen of the Death Zone", as she is known, achieved the record after climbing K2 on 23 Aug 2011 – her seventh attempt at the second-highest mountain on Earth. In doing so, she earned her place in a small group of elite climbers who have conquered the 8,000ers without supplementary oxygen.

The **first female to summit an 8,000er in winter** is Switzerland's Marianne Chapuisat, who topped Cho Oyu on the border of China and Nepal, on 10 Feb 1993.

Most climbs over 8,000 m by siblings

Basque brothers Alberto and Félix Iñurrategi (ESP) ascended twelve 8,000ers together. During the descent of their 12th climb – Gasherbrum II on 28 Jul 2000 – Félix died after his rope snapped; over the next 22 months, Alberto went on to complete the fourteen 8,000ers, finishing with an ascent of Annapurna I on 16 May 2002.

Most climbs over 8,000 m

Phurba Tashi Sherpa (NPL, above) has completed 32 ascents of the 14 mountains taller than 8,000 m (26,246 ft). His 32nd conquest came on 25 Sep 2014 with his fifth climb of Manaslu.

The 44-year-old has also made the **most ascents of Everest**, with 21 successful attempts as of 23 May 2013. He shares this record with Apa Sherpa (NPL, see p.452), who scaled Everest for the 21st time on 11 May 2011.

First Explorers' Grand Slam

This feat involves reaching the North and South poles on foot, climbing the highest mountains on all seven continents (the "Seven Summits") and all the 8,000ers. Park Young-seok (KOR) became the first person to do so when he reached the North Pole by foot on 30 Apr 2005. His quest had begun when he summitted Everest on 16 May 1993.

Oldest to climb Kangchenjunga

On 18 May 2014, Carlos Soria (ESP, b. 5 Feb 1939) topped Kangchenjunga from the south side. He was 75 years 102 days old at the time. The **oldest to climb Kangchenjunga without bottled oxygen** was Òscar Cadiach (ESP, b. 22 Oct 1952) on 20 May 2013, aged 60 years 210 days.

The Iñurrategi brothers also set the record for the **fastest time to climb the top five 8,000ers**, taking 4 years 219 days to climb Makalu, Everest, K2, Lhotse and Kangchenjunga (between 30 Sep 1991 and 6 May 1996). Significantly, they did these climbs without the use of supplementary (bottled) oxygen.

The **most siblings on an 8,000er** is three: sisters Lakpa and Mingkipa and brother Mingma Gelu Sherpa (NPL) climbed Everest together on 22 May 2003.

Oldest person to climb an 8,000-m mountain without bottled oxygen

As of Apr 2014, only five people older than 65 have summitted an 8,000er without the use of bottled oxygen. The undisputed record goes to Carlos Soria (ESP, b. 5 Feb 1939, see above), who summitted Manaslu on 1 Oct 2010, aged 71 years 238 days. Boris Korshunov (RUS, b. 31 Aug 1935) has stated that he climbed Cho Oyu on 2 Oct 2007, aged 72 years 32 days, but some alpinists dispute this claim.

Youngest person to climb Everest without bottled oxygen

Tenzing Sherpa (b. 7 Mar 1992) of Sanam, Nepal, climbed Everest on 18 May 2012 without supplementary oxygen at the age of 20 years 72 days. He was accompanied by Swiss climber Ueli Steck (see p.443).

Most ascents of K2 in a day

On 26 Jul 2014, a total of 33 people climbed to the peak of K2, the world's second-tallest mountain. This surpassed the previous record of 28 on 31 Jul 2012.

First 8,000er ascents without oxygen

Only seven of the fourteen 8,000ers were first ascended without the use of supplementary oxygen:

Mountain	Date	Climber
Manaslu	25 Apr 1972	Reinhold Messner (ITA)
Gasherbrum I	10 Aug 1975	Peter Habeler (AUT), Reinhold Messner
Makalu	6 Oct 1975	Marjan Manfreda (SVN)
Lhotse	11 May 1977	Michel Dacher (DEU)
Everest	8 May 1978	Peter Habeler, Reinhold Messner
K2	6 Sep 1978	Louis F Reichardt (USA)
Kangchenjunga	16 May 1979	Doug Scott, Peter Boardman, Joe Tasker (all UK)

Fastest ascent of Manaslu

On 25 Sep 2014, Polish mountaineer Andrzej Bargiel scaled the eighth-highest point in the world – Manaslu in Nepal – in just 14 hr 5 min. He descended in slightly less than half that time.

Most ascents of Manaslu

On 3 Oct 2014, Phura (Phurba) Chhiri Sherpa (NPL) successfully climbed Manaslu for the seventh time in his mountaineering career.

Most climbs over 8,000 m by a married couple

Nives Meroi and Romano Benet (both ITA) – who were married in 1989 – climbed twelve 8,000ers together, without bottled oxygen, between 20 Jul 1998 (Nanga Parbat) and 18 May 2014 (Kangchenjunga).

First climb of Shisha Pangma in winter

Simone Moro (ITA, below) and Piotr Morawski (POL) climbed Shisha Pangma on 14 Jan 2005, the first summit of the mountain in the calendar winter, when conditions are more treacherous.

The **most 8,000ers climbed in winter** is four, by Jerzy Kukuczka (POL): Dhaulagiri I and Cho Oyu in 1985, Kangchenjunga in 1986 and Annapurna I in 1987.

IN NUMBERS

10+

Multiples of the **tallest building** – the Burj Khalifa (828 m; 2,716 ft) in Dubai, UAE – it would take to match the height of Everest

3

Multiples of Everest it would take to match the height of Olympus Mons on Mars – at 25 km (15 mi), the **tallest mountain in the Solar System**

16 years 271 days

Average age of a team of students from the Lawrence School Sanawar in Himachal Pradesh, India, who ascended Everest in 2013; as one climber was under 16, the team was ineligible for Guinness World Records ratification

52

Successful ascents of K2 by 45 Nepalese climbers – the **most ascents of K2 by a single nation**; of these, four climbed without bottled oxygen

Apa Sherpa

As of Apr 2015, the record for the **most conquests of Everest** is shared by two climbers – see p.449 – and the first to reach this milestone, Apa Sherpa, spoke with GWR about his achievements.

How did your climbing career begin?
I became a porter when I was 12, then a tracking guide. I climbed two or three 8,000-m peaks such as Annapurna I first. Then I climbed Everest, aged 28.

What was the first ascent of Everest like?
It was in 1990, we were a big international group – I was so proud to climb with Rob Hall (NZ) and Peter Hillary [son of Sir Edmund Hillary, see p.446]. It wasn't easy, but we were a great group. When I got to the top I was so excited! You feel like you've got to heaven. I'm most proud of that climb, because it was my first time to the top of Everest.

What are the biggest differences between then and now?
Climate change is one – Everest is more rocky now. Technology has made a big, big difference too. It makes it much easier for the climber. In 1999, I sent a hand-written letter to my family from the Tibet side of Everest. It took a month to get home. In 2010, I called my family from the top!

Why did you stop climbing?
I retired in 2011 because my family worried about me. Now I can spend more time with them. I also work raising money for the Foundation. [The Apa Sherpa Foundation assists the local Nepalese community.] But yes, I miss climbing!

Youngest person to climb all 8,000ers

Mingma Sherpa (NPL, b. 16 Jun 1978) climbed all 8,000ers between 12 May 2000 and 20 May 2010, finishing aged 31 years 338 days.

His brother Chhang Dawa Sherpa (NPL, b. 30 Jul 1982) reportedly climbed all 8,000ers between 14 May 2001 (Makalu) and 30 Apr 2013 (Shisha Pangma), completing the set at the age of 30 years 274 days. However, this claim is disputed, as Chhang Dawa may not have reached the highest point of Annapurna I on 20 Apr 2012. If it can be confirmed that Chhang Dawa Sherpa had indeed reached the top of Annapurna I, not only would there be a new holder for this title, but the two brothers would be the first set of brothers to summit all 14 of the 8,000-m mountains, although not together.

Fastest ascent of all mountains over 8,000 m

Kim Chang-ho (KOR) climbed the 8,000ers in 7 years 310 days between 2005 (Nanga Parbat) and 2013 (Everest). He achieved this feat without the use of supplementary oxygen.

FACT

The "calendar winter" extends from 21 Dec to 20 Mar, while the "meteorological winter" extends from 1 Dec to 28 Feb. Because of the extreme conditions, winter ascents are much more taxing.

OCEAN ROWING

In 1896, Norwegian-born Frank Samuelsen and George Harbo completed the **first ocean row ever,** across the Atlantic

Oldest person to row across any ocean

Tony Short (UK) was 67 years 252 days old when he began rowing the Atlantic Ocean east to west, from La Gomera to Barbados, as part of a team of four, in *Spirit of Corinth*. The row lasted from 5 Dec 2011 to 22 Jan 2012 – a total time of 48 days 8 hr 3 min.

Oldest team to row the Atlantic west to east

Chris "Darby" Walters (UK, b. 2 May 1958) and Elliott Dale (UK, b. 30 Jun 1959) had a combined age of 111 years 13 days when they set out to row from New York City, USA, to the Scilly Isles, UK, between 7 Jun and 6 Aug 2014. Their crossing of 60 days 1 hr 6 min recorded the fastest row of the Atlantic from the New York area west to east by a team of two in an open-class boat.

Youngest person to complete two solo ocean rows

Sarah Outen (UK, b. 26 May 1985) was 27 years 336 days at the start of her second solo row, the Mid-Pacific route from Chōshi in Japan to off Adak in Alaska, from 27 Apr to 23 Sep 2013. She had successfully completed the solo Indian Ocean row between 1 Apr and 3 Aug 2009, aged 23 years 310 days at the start.

Longest-distance ocean row in 24 hours

Simon Chalk, Roland Burr, John Farndale, Stephen Harpin, Oliver Waite, Jeremy Webb (all UK) and Noel Watkins (NZ) travelled 192.4 km (119.55 mi) on the Atlantic Ocean "Trade Winds I" route, from 4 a.m. on 2 Jan to 4 a.m. on 3 Jan 2015. With this crossing, Simon added to his record for **most ocean rows:** nine – two on the Indian Ocean and seven on the Atlantic.

Youngest female to row the Mid-Pacific

Susannah Cass (UK, b. 11 Jun 1998) was 25 years 363 days old at the start of her row in a team of four, travelling from Monterey in California, USA, to off-O'ahu, Hawaii, from 9 Jun to 5 Aug 2014.

Fastest row of the Mid-Pacific east to west by a pair in an open-class boat

Between 18 Jun and 2 Aug 2014, Sami Inkinen (FIN) and Meredith Loring (USA) rowed from Monterey in California, USA, to Honolulu in Hawaii, USA, in 45 days 3 hr 43 min on board *Roosevelt*.

Fastest solo row across the Atlantic east to west in an open-class boat

From 6 Feb to 13 Mar 2013, Charlie Pitcher (UK) rowed his 6.5-m (21-ft) carbon-fibre boat, *Soma of Essex*, from La Gomera in the Canary Islands to Barbados in the Caribbean in 35 days 33 min.

FIRST...

Female to row three different oceans

Roz Savage (UK) rowed the Atlantic in 2005–06, the Pacific in 2008–10, and the Indian Ocean from Perth in Australia to Mauritius in 2011 – all east to west. Roz spent 510 days at sea and covered more than 15,000 mi (24,100 km).

Team to row the Mid-Pacific east to west

Between 21 May and 20 Jul 2014, Angela Madsen (USA, see panel on p.457) and Tara Remington (NZ) rowed from Long Beach in California, USA, to Honolulu in Hawaii, USA, in 60 days 5 hr 5 min, on board *Spirit of Orlando*.

Their feat was followed soon after by the **first team of four to row a Pacific route**. Craig Hackett (NZ), Andre Kiers (NLD), Junho Choi (KOR) and Caspar Zafer (UK) rowed the same route in 43 days 7 hr 39 min from 9 Jun to 23 Jul 2014. This also establishes the record for the **fastest row of the Mid-Pacific east to west by a team of four**.

Fastest solo row of the Indian Ocean in an open-class boat

Between 30 Nov 2013 and 25 Jan 2014, Emmanuel Coindre (FRA) rowed 5,960 km (3,700 mi) on board *Long-Cours* from Carnarvon in Western Australia to Port West on the island of Réunion, 700 km (435 mi) east of Madagascar, in 56 days 7 hr 29 min 11 sec. He rowed on average 18 hr per day and en route even crossed the path of Tropical Cyclone Colin.

First female crew of four to row the Mid-Pacific east to west

Between 19 Jun and 8 Aug 2014, Emily Blagden, Amanda Challans (both UK), Ingrid Kvale (USA) and Aoife Ni Mhaoileoin (IRL) rowed one of the two Mid-Pacific routes, from Monterey in California, USA, to Honolulu in Hawaii, USA. They took 50 days 8 hr 14 min to cover the 2,400-mi (3,860-km) distance on board *Black Oyster*.

Rowing routes

- **Pacific west–east**: Japan/Russia to the USA/Canada
- **Pacific east–west**: North America/Peru/Chile to Papua New Guinea/Australia
- **Mid-Pacific east–west**: South America to a mid-Pacific island; or the USA to Hawaii
- **Atlantic east–west**: Canary Islands to the Caribbean/ northern South America ("Trade Winds I"); or Senegal/Cape Verde to the Caribbean/northern South America ("Trade Winds II")
- **Atlantic west–east**: North America to the British Isles/ Europe
- **Indian Ocean**: Western Australia to Mauritius/Madagascar/ Seychelles

Male team to row the Mid-Pacific

From 9 Jun to 23 Aug 2014, Clément Héliot and Christophe Papillon (both FRA) rowed from Monterey in California, USA, to Honolulu in Hawaii, USA, in 75 days 9 hr 25 min.

Person to row the Atlantic both ways non-stop

On 9 Jul 2012, Charles Hedrich (FRA) set off from Saint Pierre and Miquelon (French territory off Newfoundland, Canada) on *Respectons la Terre* and landed in Martinique in the Caribbean on 2 Dec 2012. The non-stop voyage via European and African coasts took him 145 days 10 hr 57 min.

IN NUMBERS

48,806 km
Farthest total distance rowed on the ocean (30,327 mi), by Erden Eruç (TUR), totalling 876 days at sea in 2006–12

85 days 2 hr 5 min
Fastest tandem row across the Indian Ocean, by Laurence Grand-Clément and Laurence De Rancourt (both FRA), 19 Apr–13 Jul 2012

187 years 247 days
Combined age of the crew of the *HM & S Twiggy* – Graham Witham, Jason Howard-Ady, Aldo Diana and Ken Maynard (all UK) – who rowed the Atlantic east to west from Gran Canaria to Barbados between 14 Dec 2011 and 17 Feb 2012: the **oldest row across any ocean by a team of four**

730
Number of people who have rowed an ocean, by individuals from 45 countries, as of Mar 2015

FIRST...

Crossing of the Atlantic from mainland Africa to mainland North America

Between 30 Dec 2013 and 20 Jun 2014, Riaan Manser and Vasti Geldenhuys (both ZAF) rowed from Agadir in Morocco to New York City in the USA, via The Bahamas and Miami in Florida, in 172 days 8 hr. The crossing, on board *Spirit of Madiba*, required an estimated 1,800,000 strokes.

Person to sail and row the Indian and Atlantic oceans

From 8 Jan to 13 Feb 2005, Captain James Kayll (UK) sailed across the Indian Ocean from Thailand to Djibouti in east Africa. From 21 Apr to 6 Jul 2011, he skippered a four-man rowing team from Geraldton in Western Australia to the island of Mauritius, off the African coast.

Kayll's Atlantic adventure began with sailing from Gran Canaria in the Canary Islands to St Lucia in the Caribbean, from 19 Nov to 6 Dec 2000. He capped this as skipper of a four-man team (including two military amputees) rowing from La Gomera in the Canary Islands to Antigua in the Caribbean, between 4 Dec 2013 and 21 Jan 2014.

FACT

Open-class boats are built to individual specifications for shape, length, height and number of hulls. Their differenc from classic boats, which are slower, is such that the two types do not compete.

Person to row solo from Europe across both the Atlantic and the Caribbean Sea to North America

Between 21 Oct 2014 and 14 Mar 2015, Abraham Levy (MEX) rowed from Huelva in Spain to Cancún in Mexico, via La Gomera in the Canary Islands and Antigua in the Caribbean, in 144 days 1 hr 32 min.

First solo row mainland to mainland non-stop across the Pacific east to west

Departing from Concón in Chile on 22 Dec 2013 on board the lightweight, fibreglass *Tourgoyak*, Fedor Konyukhov (RUS) rowed 11,898 km (7,393 mi) to land at Mooloolaba in Queensland, Australia, on 31 May 2014. He took just 159 days 16 hr 58 min, achieving the **fastest solo row across the South Pacific east to west**.

Fastest row across the Indian Ocean by a team

From 11 Jun to 7 Aug 2014, Tim Spiteri, Shane Usher (both AUS), skipper Leven Brown, Jamie Douglas-Hamilton, Heather Rees-Gaunt (all UK), Fiann Paul (ISL) and Cameron Bellamy (ZAF) rowed from Geraldton in Western Australia to Mahé in the Seychelles in 57 days 10 hr 58 min. It was also the **longest row of the Indian Ocean by a team:** 6,772 km (4,208 mi).

Angela Madsen

Former US Marine and top-level basketball player Angela Madsen (b. 10 May 1960) is a medal-winning Paralympic athlete, adaptive (disabled) rower and winner of numerous records.

Madsen's athleticism and willpower helped her to overcome her disability (paraplegia resulting from back surgery), so that, by 1997, she was participating in the Veterans Wheelchair Games, and within three years had qualified for the US national adaptive rowing team. In 2008, she won the Mixed Double Sculls with Scott Brown at the Beijing Paralympics (below). But the ocean was already beckoning, and Madsen went on to achieve many records at sea:

- **first females to row the Indian Ocean**, set with Helen Taylor (UK), as part of a team of eight rowing east to west from Geraldton, Western Australia, to Port Louis, Mauritius, on 28 Apr–25 Jun 2009.
- **most ocean rows by a female**, with four rows including crossing the Atlantic east to west as skipper of the 16-man catamaran *Big Blue* on 15 Jan–4 Mar 2011 (the **largest team to row an ocean**), and more recently being part of the **first team to row the Mid-Pacific east to west** (see p.455).
- **oldest woman to row around the British mainland**, 1 Jun–23 Jul 2010, aged 50 years 21 days at the start of her row, as part of the **first all-female team to row around the British mainland**.

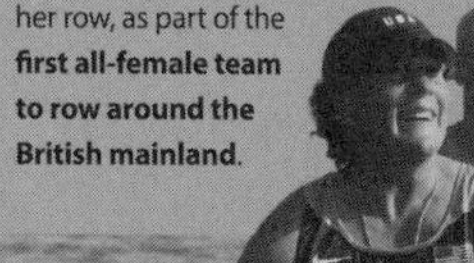

CIRCUMNAVIGATION

David Kunst wore out **21 pairs of shoes** on his **walk around the world**

Longest journey by solar-powered boat

MS *Tûranor PlanetSolar* (CHE) returned to Monaco on 4 May 2012 after 1 year 220 days at sea, having covered 32,410 nautical mi (60,023 km; 37,296 mi). It had left the principality on 27 Sep 2010, circling the world in a westward direction. The crew included founder and expedition leader Raphaël Domjan, engineer Christian Ochsenbein (both CHE), bosun Jens Langwasser (DEU) and captains Patrick Marchesseau and Erwann Le Rouzic (both FRA).

On land, the **longest journey by solar electric vehicle** is 29,753 km (18,487 mi), by the SolarCar Project Hochschule Bochum (DEU). The team left Australia from Adelaide on 26 Oct 2011 and arrived back, at Mount Barker, on 15 Dec 2012.

Fastest circumnavigation by bicycle (female)

Juliana Buhring (DEU, below) cycled 29,069 km (18,063 mi) in 152 days 1 hr, starting and finishing at Piazza del Plebiscito in Naples, Italy, from 23 Jul to 22 Dec 2012.

The fastest circumnavigation by bicycle, by Alan Bate (UK), took 125 days 21 hr 45 min. He cycled 29,467.91 km (18,310.47 mi) from 31 Mar to 4 Aug 2010, starting and ending at the Grand Palace in Bangkok, Thailand.

FASTEST CIRCUMNAVIGATION...

By car

The record for the first and fastest man and woman to have circumnavigated the Earth by car covering six continents under the rules applicable in 1989 and 1991 embracing more than an equator's length of driving (24,901 road miles; 40,075 km), is held by Saloo Choudhury and his wife Neena Choudhury (both India). The journey took 69 days 19 hours 5 minutes from 9 September to 17 November 1989. The couple drove a 1989 Hindustan "Contessa Classic" starting and finishing in Delhi, India.

Fastest circumnavigation by helicopter (female)

Jennifer Murray (UK) piloted her Robinson R44 helicopter around the world solo in 99 days, crossing 30 countries from 31 May to 6 Sep 2000. She was 60 at the time of the attempt.

By helicopter

According to the Fédération Aéronautique Internationale (FAI), the fastest helicopter flight around the world was achieved by Edward Kasprowicz and his crewman Stephen Sheik (both USA). The flight was completed on 18 Aug 2008 in 11 days 7 hr 5 min and involved more than 70 refuelling stops. They flew eastbound for 12 to 13 hours a day in an AgustaWestland Grand helicopter, at an average speed of 136.7 km/h (84.9 mph). The duo started and finished in New York, USA, travelling via Greenland, the UK, Italy, Russia and Canada.

By microlight

Colin Bodill (UK) flew around the globe in his Mainair Blade 912 Flexwing microlight aircraft in 99 days, from 31 May to 6 Sep 2000, starting and landing in Weybridge, Surrey, UK. He was accompanying Jennifer Murray on her solo circumnavigation (see above). The pair covered 35,000 km (21,750 mi).

By sail around Great Britain and Ireland

Sidney Gavignet (FRA) and the six-strong crew of the trimaran *Musandam-Oman Sail* circled the British mainland and Ireland in a time of 3 days 3 hr 32 min 36 sec, finishing their journey on 14 Aug 2014. They covered the 1,773-nautical-mi (3,283-km; 2,040-mi) route at an average of 23.48 knots (43.48 km/h; 27 mph).

First inland circumnavigation of the Greenland ice cap

Eric McNair-Landry (CAN, left) and Dixie Dansercoer (BEL, right) circled the Greenland ice cap from 10 Apr to 4 Jun 2014. The 4,044.9-km (2,513.38-mi) kite-supported and unassisted expedition started and finished at 66°02771'N, 39°26409'W on the world's **largest island** and second-largest ice body. Their kite is seen in action, below right.

Fastest circumnavigation by powered boat

On 26 Jun 2009, *Earthrace* (NZ) was granted the Union Internationale Motonautique (UIM) record for the fastest circumnavigation by powered boat. The journey took 60 days 23 hr 49 min, beginning in Sagunto, Spain, on 27 Apr 2008 and finishing on 27 Jun 2008.

FIRST CIRCUMNAVIGATION...

By aircraft

The first flight around the world was by two US Army Douglas World Cruiser seaplanes in 57 "hops" between 6 Apr and 28 Sep 1924, beginning and ending in Seattle, Washington, USA. The *Chicago* was piloted by Lieutenants Lowell H Smith and Leslie P Arnold, and the *New Orleans* by Lieutenants Erik H Nelson and John Harding (all USA). Their flying time for the 42,398-km (26,345-mi) trip was 371 hr 11 min.

Captain Elgen M Long (USA) carried out the **first aircraft circumnavigation via both poles**, flying a twin-engined Piper PA-31 Navajo between 5 Nov and 3 Dec 1971. He covered a distance of 62,597 km (38,896 mi) in 215 flying hours.

By car

Racing driver Clärenore Stinnes (DEU), accompanied by film-maker Carl-Axel Söderström (SWE), embarked upon what is considered to be the first round-the-world drive on 25 May 1927. They set off from Frankfurt in Germany and finished in Berlin on 24 Jun 1929, a distance of 46,063 km (28,622 mi). The pair drove a three-speed, 50-hp Adler Standard 6 automobile. The trip took 2 years 30 days.

By foot

The first person reputed to have walked round the world is George Matthew Schilling (USA), between 1897 and 1904. The first verified such feat, however, was by David Kunst (USA), who walked 23,250 km (14,450 mi) through four continents from 20 Jun 1970 to 5 Oct 1974.

By sail around the Americas, non-stop solo

Matt Rutherford (USA) sailed his 27-ft-long (8.2-m) ship *St Brendan* single-handedly on a non-stop circumnavigation of North and South America. His 43,576-km (27,077-mi) journey started on 13 Jun 2011 at Annapolis City Dock in Chesapeake Bay, Maryland, USA, and finished there 310 days later on 18 Apr 2012.

During the trip, Rutherford also set the record for the **smallest boat to negotiate the Northwest Passage**, a notoriously dangerous Arctic Ocean route.

IN NUMBERS

14 days 19 hr 50 min

Longest duration flown by a balloon solo, by Steve Fossett (USA) in *Bud Light Spirit of Freedom* from 19 Jun to 4 Jul 2002 (for more outstanding ballooning feats by Fossett, see p.465)

57 days 13 hr 34 min 6 sec

Fastest solo circumnavigation by sail, achieved by Francis Joyon (FRA) from 23 Nov 2007 to 20 Jan 2008

4 years 31 days

Fastest time to visit all countries using public surface transport, by Graham Hughes (UK); he passed through 197 countries from 1 Jan 2009 to 31 Jan 2013

Matt Guthmiller

Aged 19 years 227 days, Matt Guthmiller (USA, b. 29 Nov 1994) became the youngest person to circumnavigate the world solo by aircraft, flying a 1981 Beech A36 Bonanza from 31 May to 14 Jul 2014, starting and completing his journey in El Cajon, California, USA.

When did you get the idea for flying solo round the world?
On 3 May 2013. I read an article about a 20-year-old from California [Jack Wiegand] who was going to attempt to set the record, and I figured I could do that, too, and hopefully inspire other people to think the same way in the process.

What were the most exciting moments?
If I had to pick one single moment, it'd probably be flying into Cairo and looking down and realizing I was flying over the Pyramids. That was pretty surreal.

And the scariest?
There were a couple of times when I ended up in clouds with heavy rain and turbulence. That gets a bit nerve-wracking until you find a way back to clear air… and then a way around the storm, which often takes a couple of hours.

What is in store next for you?
I'm studying electrical engineering and computer science [at Massachusetts Institute of Technology], and I've always thought starting the next Apple could be fun. But I found out test pilots make more money than software engineers, so I guess we'll just see what happens! Ultimately, I'll just keep aiming high and hoping I land somewhere good.

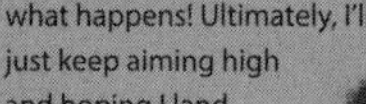

Oldest person to sail solo and non-stop around the world

Minoru Saitō (JPN, b. 7 Jan 1934) was aged 71 years 150 days when he completed a 233-day solo circumnavigation by yacht on 6 Jun 2005.

The **oldest woman to sail solo around the world** is Jeanne Socrates (UK, b. 17 Aug 1942, inset), who was 70 years 325 days by the end of her trip on 8 Jul 2013, after more than 258 days at sea.

BALLOONING

The **first balloon passengers** were a **sheep, rooster and duck** in 1783

If party balloons are more your thing, pop over to pp.204–08.

Highest flight by a hot-air balloon

Dr Vijaypat Singhania (IND) reached 68,986 ft (21,027 m) in a Cameron Z-1600 balloon over Mumbai, India, on 26 Nov 2005.

Oldest person to fly in a hot-air balloon

Dr Emma Carrol (USA, b. 18 May 1895) took a flight in Ottumwa, Iowa, USA, on 27 Jul 2004 at the age of 109 years 70 days.

Largest balloon

Manufactured by Winzen Engineering, Inc (USA), the SF3-579.49-035-NSC-01 balloon had an inflatable volume of 2,003,192 m³ (70,742,058 cu ft). The unmanned balloon was launched from the National Scientific Balloon facility in Palestine, Texas, USA, on 1 Oct 1975, but the flight was aborted owing to technical issues.

The largest manned balloon, meanwhile, was used on the Red Bull Stratos mission on 14 Oct 2012, carrying Felix Baumgartner (AUT) in a capsule to an altitude of 38,969.4 m (127,852 ft). The balloon – as tall as the Statue of Liberty when fully inflated – had a capacity of approximately 850,000 m³ (30 million cu ft).

Fastest walk between two balloons

On 4 Oct 2014, Freddy Nock (CHE) crossed 18 m (59 ft) in 7.49 sec for *CCTV-Guinness World Records Special* in Nanjing, China. Appropriately enough, Nock's motto is "The sky is the limit" – a belief that no doubt helped him secure seven highwire and tightrope records in seven days in 2011. He has been honing his balancing skills since his youth, first taking to the tightrope at just four years old.

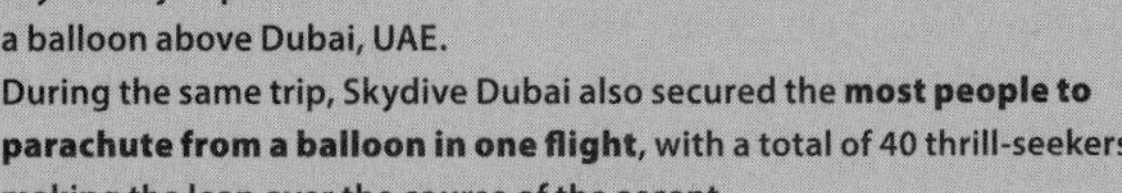

Most people to parachute from a balloon simultaneously

On 10 Feb 2013, a total of 25 skydivers jumped at once from a balloon above Dubai, UAE.

During the same trip, Skydive Dubai also secured the **most people to parachute from a balloon in one flight**, with a total of 40 thrill-seekers making the leap over the course of the ascent.

FIRST...

Balloon flight

Constructed by Father Bartolomeu de Gusmão (PRT), an unmanned hot-air balloon was first flown indoors in Terreiro do Paço, Portugal, on 8 Aug 1709.

Manned balloon flight

Frenchman Jean-François Pilâtre de Rozier is widely regarded as the first person ever to have flown. On 15 Oct 1783, he rose 26 m (84 ft) in a tethered hot-air balloon designed by Joseph and Jacques Montgolfier (both FRA).

The following month, on 21 Nov, De Rozier would achieve the **first free manned flight** (untethered), on a 25-min trip accompanied by the Marquis d'Arlandes (FRA).

War balloon

In Jun 1794, an aerostat balloon known as *L'Entreprenant* ("The Enterprising One") was used by the French Aerostatic Corps as a military reconnaissance vehicle at the Battle of Fleurus (present-day Belgium). The silk balloon, filled with hydrogen, was employed to track the movements of the Coalition Army troops, and played a key role in the French Republic's victory.

Aerial wedding

With an audience of 50,000 spectators at the Cincinnati Hippodrome in Ohio, USA, Mary Walsh and Charles Colton (both USA) were married in a balloon on 19 Oct 1874. The balloon was named *P T Barnum*, in honour of their employer, who paid for the ceremony.

Oddly, the **first balloon honeymoon** took place nine years *before* the first aerial wedding. Dr John Boynton and his fiancée Mary West Jenkins (both USA) took a 20-km (12.4-mi) balloon trip after exchanging their vows, travelling across New York, USA, from Manhattan to Mount Vernon on 8 Nov 1865. The pair had wanted to get married in the balloon too, but the priest refused to perform the ceremony while aloft.

Woman in the stratosphere

Accompanied by her Swiss husband Jean Félix Piccard – of the famed explorer family – and their pet turtle, Jeannette Ridlon Piccard (USA) piloted the *Century of Progress* to an altitude of 17,550 m (57,580 ft) on 23 Oct 1934.

The **longest gas balloon flight by an all-female team** lasted 69 hr 22 min 9 sec, achieved by Dr Ann Rich and Dr Janet Folkes (both UK) from 5 to 8 Sep 2009.

Fastest circumnavigation by balloon (solo)

Taking off and landing in Australia, the late adventurer Steve Fossett (USA, below) circled the world in 13 days 8 hr 33 min in *Bud Light Spirit of Freedom* from 19 Jun to 2 Jul 2002 – also the **first solo balloon circumnavigation.**

This beat the **first non-stop circumnavigation in a balloon**, completed by Bertrand Piccard (CHE) and Brian Jones (UK) in 1999 (see p.467), by more than 150 hr.

IN NUMBERS

322.25 km/h
Top speed reached by Steve Fossett (USA) in the *Bud Light Spirit of Freedom* – the **fastest speed by a manned balloon** (200.23 mph)

19
Fatalities from an accident over Luxor, Egypt, in 2013: the **worst hot-air balloon disaster**

4,632 m
Highest bungee jump from a hot-air balloon (15,200 ft), by Curtis Rivers (UK) on 5 May 2002

4 min 30 sec
Estimated time it took Alan Eustace (USA) to free-fall to Earth from 41,420 m (125,892 ft) – see p.466

58
Editions of the Gordon Bennett Cup, as of 2014 – the **oldest aviation race**; the first was in 1906

19 days 21 hr 47 min
Longest time flying a balloon, held by Bertrand Piccard (CHE) and Brian Jones (UK) – see p.467

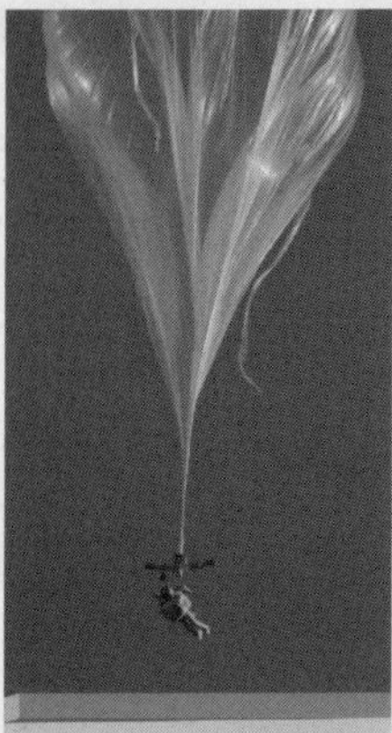

Highest free-fall parachute jump

As verified by the FAI, the governing body for air sports, Google executive Alan Eustace (USA, below) fell to Earth from 41,422 m (135,898 ft) on 24 Oct 2014. This beat Felix Baumgartner's Oct 2012 record by an incredible 2,453 m (8,046 ft).

Greatest mass balloon ascent

A total of 408 hot-air balloons launched within an hour at the Lorraine Mondial Air Ballons event (FRA) held in Lorraine, France, on 31 Jul 2013, beating the previous mark by 63. Started in 1989, the ballooning festival, aka "BallonVille", takes place at a former NATO air base every other year.

A real high-flyer

Along with pilot Per Lindstrand (SWE, pictured bottom right), Richard Branson (UK) shares the records for first hot-air balloon journey across the Atlantic and Pacific. Here he tells us how his transatlantic voyage played out…

What was the inspiration behind your Atlantic crossing?
I'd just started Virgin Atlantic, so we had to come up with fun ways of promoting the airline. Having succeeded in setting a new time for transatlantic crossing by boat, I got a knock on my door and Per Lindstrand said, "You've done it in a boat, I think we can do it in a balloon."

Tell us about your relationship with record-breaking…
I love adventure. I love trying to achieve things that haven't been achieved before. My first GWR attempt was flying across the Atlantic in a hot-air balloon. The farthest anyone had been then was about 600 mi [965 km], and the Atlantic's 3,000 mi [4,830 km]. It was a long, eventful flight, but somehow we survived.

Why are balloon records so iconic?
Before we did the Atlantic crossing, seven people had attempted it; six had died – so it was pretty perilous. At the end of the trip, Per jumped into the sea and I was [briefly] left flying the biggest balloon ever built; I'd only just learned to fly a balloon so it was a very hairy ending! I think those "man against the elements" challenges are few and far between.

Farthest distance flown in a hot-air balloon

Although they lost the title for fastest circumnavigation, Bertrand Piccard (CHE, inset, right) and Brian Jones's (UK, inset, left) voyage in the *Breitling Orbiter 3* (above) from 1 to 21 Mar 1999 still holds the non-stop distance record, covering a staggering 40,814 km (25,361 mi).

SURVIVORS

We can last for c. **30 days** without food, but only around **five days** without water

Longest time without a pulse

On 14 Aug 1998, Julie Mills (UK) was at the point of death from severe heart failure and viral myocarditis. Surgeons at the John Radcliffe Hospital in Oxford, UK, opted to use a non-pulsatile blood pump (AB180) to support her for one week, during which time her heart recovered.

Most bee stings removed

A total of 2,443 bee stings were removed from Johannes Relleke (ZWE) at the Kamativi tin mine at Gwaii River in Wankie, Zimbabwe (then Rhodesia), on 28 Jan 1962. One sting delivers c. 50 micrograms of venom, and 1,000 stings is sufficient to kill an average, healthy and non-allergic adult human.

Longest skid mark

On 15 Oct 1964, while decelerating after an attempt at the land speed record at the Bonneville Salt Flats in Utah, USA, driver Craig Breedlove (USA) lost control of the jet-powered *Spirit of America*. With a malfunctioning parachute, the car sped across the desert, leaving skid marks nearly 6 mi (10 km) long, before clipping telegraph poles and crashing into a salt pond (inset). Incredibly, Breedlove walked away unharmed.

Another land-speed driver to experience a lucky escape at Bonneville was Donald Campbell (UK). In Sep 1960, he crashed his car *Bluebird* at 360 mph (579 km/h). The car flipped and Campbell fractured his skull, setting the record for **fastest car crash survived**.

FACT

Craig Breedlove is thought to have slowed down to "just" 300 mph (480 km/h) by the time he lost control of his car. His (unofficial) timed runs before the crash averaged 526 mph (846 km/h)!

Highest percentage of burns to the body survived

Tony Yarijanian (USA) survived 90% burns to his body after an explosion caused by a gas leak in California, USA, on 15 Feb 2004.

Highest blood alcohol level

The greatest blood alcohol content (BAC) recorded in a human being who lived to tell the tale is 1.374, equivalent to 13.74 g of pure alcohol per litre of blood. To put that in context, the UK drink-driving limit corresponds to a BAC of 0.08; anything above 0.4 may result in death. The individual concerned, an unnamed 40-year-old Polish man, was found unconscious by the roadside in the village of Tarnowskiej Woli, in south-east Poland, in Jul 2013.

First person to survive two nuclear attacks

Tsutomu Yamaguchi (JPN, 1916–2010) was in Hiroshima, Japan, on 6 Aug 1945 when a US B-29 dropped the "Little Boy" atomic bomb on the city, killing 140,000 people. Suffering burns to his upper body, Tsutomu went home to Nagasaki on 8 Aug. The next day, the US Army dropped the "Fat Man" atomic bomb on that city. Around 73,000 people died, but Tsutomu had only minor injuries. In both cases, he was within 3 km (1.8 mi) of ground zero.

Fastest motorcycle crash survived

In 2008, Jason McVicar (USA) was travelling at 391 km/h (243 mph) when he lost control of his bike at the Bonneville Salt Flats in Utah, USA, during the annual Bonneville Speed Week event. It's thought that the crash was caused when debris on the track punctured his rear tyre. He was taken to hospital with a broken kneecap and friction burns, sustained through his leathers from sliding across the salt at such speed. He was discharged the same day, but the crash wrecked his Suzuki Hayabusa 1300, the fastest production motorcycle at the time.

Highest altitude survived in an aircraft wheel well

On 14 Nov 1986, Gabriel Pacheco (CUB) was discovered in the nose-wheel well of an Air Panama Boeing 707 cargo plane when it landed in Miami after a 2.5-hour flight from Panama. The aircraft had reached an altitude of 39,000 ft (11,900 m). Temperatures at this altitude reach as low as -63°C (-81.4°F), but heat from the plane's electronic equipment may have helped him survive.

Farthest distance survived in a tornado

On 12 Mar 2006, 19-year-old Matt Suter (USA) was engulfed by a tornado while inside a mobile home near Fordland, Missouri, USA. He was knocked unconscious and awoke 398 m (1,307 ft) away in a nearby field, having suffered only slight injuries.

Longest time adrift at sea

Japanese Captain Oguri Jukichi and one of his sailors, named Otokichi, were in a ship that was damaged in a storm off the Japanese coast on 26 Nov 1813. The pair drifted in the Pacific for 484 days before being rescued by an American ship off California, USA, on 24 Mar 1815.

The **longest recorded survival alone on a raft** is 133 days, by Second Steward Poon Lim (b. HKG) of the UK Merchant Navy. His ship, the SS *Ben Lomond*, was torpedoed in the Atlantic 910 km (565 mi) west of St Paul Rocks in Lat. 00°30'N, Long. 38°45'W at 11:45 a.m. on 23 Nov 1942. He was picked up by a Brazilian fishing boat off Salinópolis, Brazil, on 5 Apr 1943 and was able to walk ashore.

First person to survive a drop over Niagara Falls

On 24 Oct 1901, American schoolteacher Annie Edson Taylor became the first person to survive the 51-m (167-ft) drop over New York's Niagara Falls when she plummeted over Horseshoe Falls – the largest of the three Niagara waterfalls – in a barrel. A crowd watched from the foot of the falls, many convinced that she was facing certain death. However, although battered and bruised, she made it. The feat was made all the more impressive by the fact that it took place on her 63rd birthday.

Between 1901 and 1955, a total of 15 people tried to mimic Annie's daredevilry. Five of them perished.

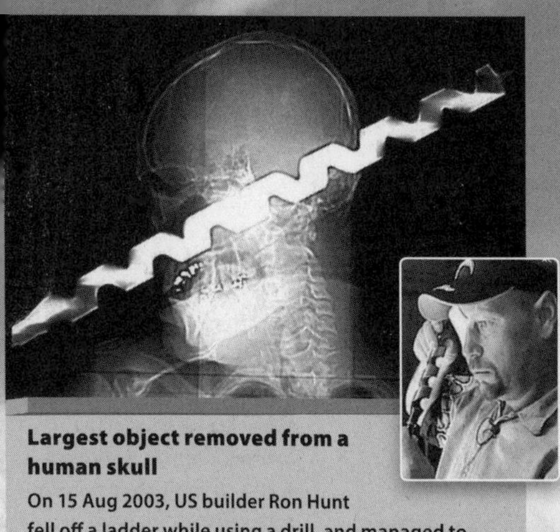

Largest object removed from a human skull

On 15 Aug 2003, US builder Ron Hunt fell off a ladder while using a drill, and managed to fall face-first on to the 18-in (46-cm) drill bit, which was still revolving. It passed through his right eye and exited through his skull above his right ear. Surgeons at Washoe Medical Center in Nevada, USA, found that it had pushed his brain aside rather than penetrating it, saving his life.

IN NUMBERS

96%
Survival rate for victims of plane crashes

10,160 m
Distance of the **highest fall survived with no parachute** (33,333 ft)

10%
People struck by lightning who die

1/3
Proportion of babies born in the UK in 2012 who are expected to reach 100 years

43%
Brain matter lost by British soldier Robert Lawrence in a sniper attack in 1982; remarkably, he survived

23
Storeys that Stuart Jones (NZ) fell in the **highest fall survived down a lift shaft**, a distance of 70 m (229 ft)

Dogged by calamity

The next time you're having a bad day, spare a thought for Dosha the dog. On 15 Apr 2003, this mixed-breed canine experienced enough bad luck to last several lifetimes.

It all started innocently enough. Louetta Mallard, Dosha's owner, released the 10-month-old pit-bull cross to play in her yard in Clearlake, California, USA. Dosha promptly vaulted over a fence and was run over by a car. "She wasn't moving and was glassy-eyed," revealed neighbour Rolf Biegiela afterwards. "I said to myself, 'That's a dead dog.'"

The police officers who arrived at the scene couldn't help but agree with Mr Biegiela. After surveying Dosha's injuries they concluded that she had little chance of surviving. Wanting to spare the luckless hound any further pain, they shot her in the head. The officers sealed Dosha's body in a bag and placed it in the freezer at an animal centre to await disposal. But that wasn't the end of the matter. Remarkably, staff discovered her sitting bolt upright two hours later.

Apparently, the bullet, which had entered Dosha's head just below her right eye, had travelled along her skull and come to rest in the skin beneath her jaw, just fractionally missing her brain. The poor pooch had also proved resilient enough to survive the hypothermia she had endured from being prematurely placed in the freezer. And even more extraordinarily, she had incurred no broken bones at all from the collision with the car that had started off this bewildering chain of events. She had survived three potentially fatal experiences in less than 24 hours.

At least Dosha earned herself a Guinness World Records title from the day, for being the **hardiest dog**!

Greatest radioactive contamination survived

In 1976, at the Hanford Nuclear Reservation in Washington State, USA, Harold McCluskey (USA) was accidentally exposed to 500 times the safe lifetime dose of radioactive material. For a period, he was so radioactive that he could set off a Geiger counter at a distance of 15 m (50 ft).

FACT

US Olympian and World War II airman Louis Zamperini, the subject of the book and movie *Unbroken* (USA, 2014), survived with fellow airman Russell Phillips at sea on an inflatable dingy for 47 days.

SPORTS

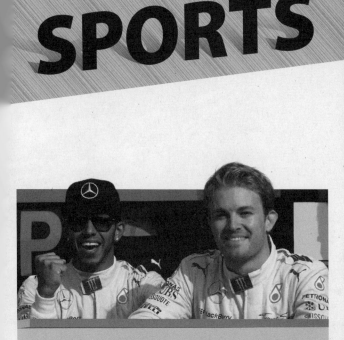

Most wins by a constructor in a Formula One season

Mercedes (DEU) recorded 16 victories during the 2014 Formula One season. Their two drivers, Lewis Hamilton (UK, above left) and Nico Rosberg (DEU, above right), won 16 of the 19 races staged between 16 March and 23 November. Hamilton won 11 races while Rosberg won five, with the former also winning the Drivers' World Championship.

In the same season, Mercedes enjoyed eight Hamilton-Rosberg one-two finishes (in Malaysia, Bahrain, China, Spain, Italy, Japan, Russia and USA) along with three Rosberg-Hamilton one-two finishes (in Monaco, Austria and Brazil). This is the **most one-two finishes by a constructor in an F1 season.** The picture overleaf shows Lewis Hamilton (at rear) passing Nico Rosberg to take the lead in the 2014 Italian Grand Prix.

Mercedes' total of 701 points in 2014 also represents the **most points by a constructor in an F1 season.**

CONTENTS

FACT

The temperature in a Formula One car can top 50°C (122°F). A driver's blood pressure may rise by 50%, their heart rate can double to 200 beats per minute and they may lose 3 litres (101 US fl oz) of fluid.

IN FOCUS

BACKLIFTING

The **hercules beetle** (*Dynastes hercules*) can lift 42 kg (92 lb) – equivalent to a human lifting **four double-decker buses**!

Heaviest ship pulled by teeth
Omar Hanapiev (RUS) pulled the 576-tonne (1,269,861-lb) tanker *Gunib* a distance of 15 m (49 ft 2.4 in)

Heaviest aircraft pulled by a man
Kevin Fast (CAN) hauled a CC-177 Globemaster III of 188.8 tonnes (416,233 lb) a distance of 8.8 m (28 ft 10.46 in)

Farthest washing machine throw
Strongman Žydrūnas Savickas (LTU) hurled a washing machine 4.13 m (13 ft 6.60 in) in 2014

Heaviest tyre deadlift
Žydrūnas Savickas also holds this title, lifting eight Hummer tyres with a total weight of 524 kg (1,155 lb 3.55 oz) in 2014

Most overhead lifts of a quad bike in one minute
Žydrūnas strikes again, raising a 140-kg (308-lb 10.3-oz) ATV 14 times in 60 sec

Throughout history and cultures, lifting heavy objects has epitomized human power, but ancient Greece is credited for turning it into a sport.

Of course, the things we lift and the ways in which we lift them differ hugely today, and many historical claims are now being scrutinized and debated.

As far as disciplines go, the backlift has seen more ups and downs than most. This technique enables us to bear more weight than any other lift. Typically, it involves the athlete crouching beneath a loaded platform before straightening the arms and legs to push the platform up.

Until now, virtually every backlift has used bespoke apparatus, made from varying materials and using everything from safes to livestock as the load. Such inconsistency has made the sport notoriously difficult to monitor.

But that's set to change with the formation of the Committee for the Study of Human Strength by former powerlifters and strength-sport academics Jan and Terry Todd. The international body aims to rigorously vet this controversial discipline, so valid feats of strength get the recognition they deserve. Their mission will be aided greatly by a new backlifting machine, developed by Rogue Fitness (USA; see main illustration on p. 478-479).

Lifting methods and technology continue to evolve, but at its heart this sport is the same iconic display of power that it has always been and always will be.

Strong but strange

While some GWR strength records use traditional weightlifting equipment in a gym setting, others are a little more "imaginative"... Whether it's planes, ships or washing machines, there's always an alternative to pumping iron.

FACT

A typical breakfast for strongwoman "Minerva" consisted of rare beef, oatmeal, French fries, tomatoes and two cups of coffee. On the dinner menu were French soup, squabs, game and veg.

*I'll be back*lifting

Arnold Schwarzenegger (AUT/USA, above left) may be better known for his movies, but his roots lie in weightlifting. This passion led him to set up the Arnold Sports Festival with Jim Lorimer (USA, inset below right, with Terry Todd) in 1989. Here Schwarzenegger and Lorimer exclusively share their thoughts on resurrecting the backlift.

"Over a hundred years ago, during the golden age of professional strongmen and strongwomen, one of the most important feats was the backlift, in which someone could lift more weight at one time than in any other way. It's the ultimate brute strength feat and many called it the 'King of Lifts'.

"The top men in this lift often used it to publicize that they were the world's strongest people. Naturally, the importance of the backlift meant that many would exaggerate their lifts, sparking controversy.

"But now we have a way to accurately measure what someone can backlift, thanks to Rogue Fitness, which makes most of the heavy-duty equipment we use in our strongman contests. What Rogue Fitness has done is to make an adjustable and safe backlift platform that will fit a man or woman of almost any size. Standing nearly 10 ft [3 m] tall, it was on display at this year's festival, held in March. Fully loaded to Ernst's record 5,340 lb [2,422.18 kg] (see p.481), it drew a lot of people.

"Our plan is to organize a backlifting contest in 2016 as a way to let people see and use this fantastic platform. We believe that it won't be long before Ernst's record is broken, and we'd like to see it happen at the Arnold Sports Festival."

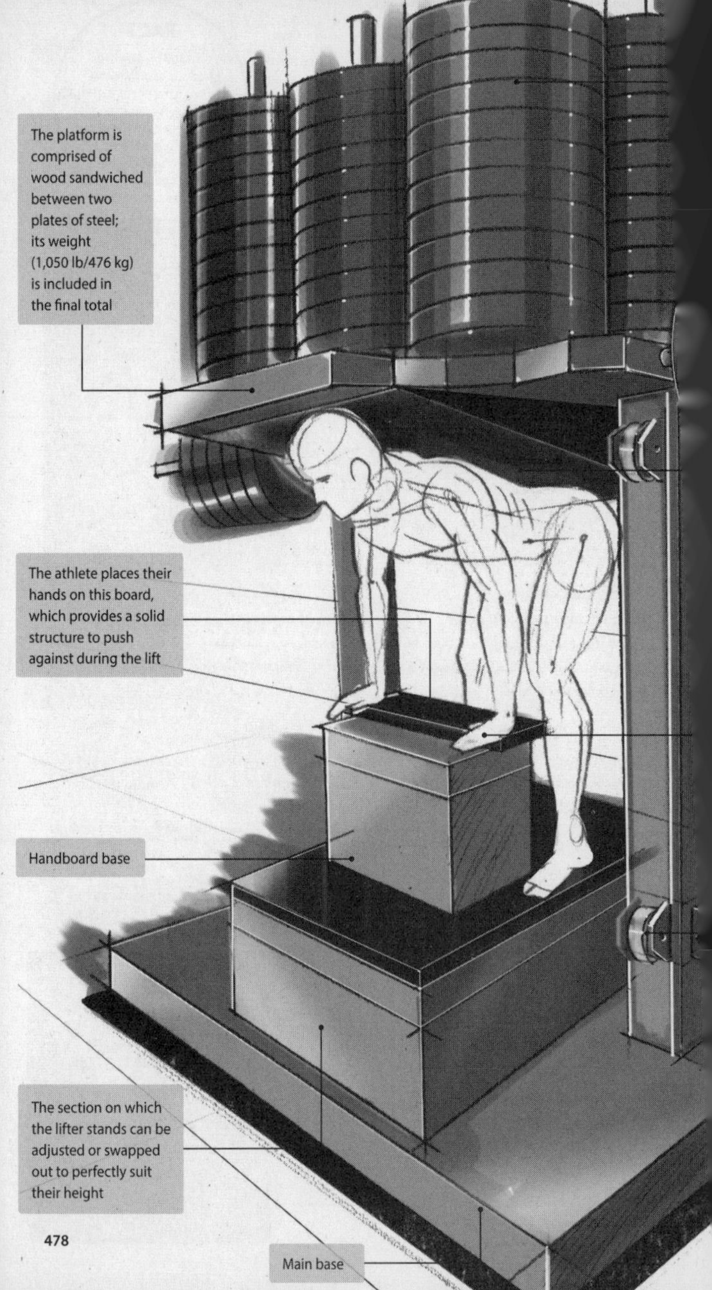
The platform is comprised of wood sandwiched between two plates of steel; its weight (1,050 lb/476 kg) is included in the final total
The athlete places their hands on this board, which provides a solid structure to push against during the lift
Handboard base
The section on which the lifter stands can be adjusted or swapped out to perfectly suit their height
Main base

Weights can be distributed evenly across the platform via a series of high-tensile steel bars: six on the top and two on each side

See p.158–60 for other amazing feats of strength

The hinged backplate is also adjustable to suit the lifter. Ernst used an inclined backplate for his record lift, but other backlifters have preferred the plate to be parallel to the floor

Two 66-in-tall (167.6-cm) square, steel uprights support the platform

Rogue Fitness collaborated with Gregg Ernst and other lifting experts such as Terry Todd when designing the new platform to ensure it was both safe and accurate

Hands should be perpendicular to the shoulders, so that the pushing force is directly upwards

Hard caster wheels in the uprights allow the platform to slide smoothly up and down when force is applied from below

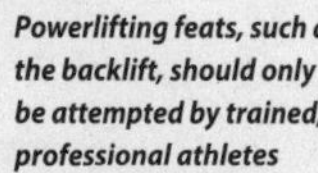

Powerlifting feats, such as the backlift, should only be attempted by trained, professional athletes

Iconic lifters of the 19th/20th centuries

Josephine Blatt

"Minerva", aka Josephine Blatt (DEU/USA, c.1865–1923), is one of the most famous strongwomen of all time. She once said she "took a fancy for lifting" at the age of seven. Her most famous feat – a hip-and-harness lift in 1895 at the Bijou Theatre in New Jersey, USA – is contested, with estimates ranging from 3,564 lb (1,616 kg) to as low as 3,000 lb (1,360 kg). Whatever the precise weight, there's no denying that "Minerva" was one of history's strongest women.

Louis Cyr

Growing up on a farm in Quebec, Canada, Louis Cyr (1863–1912) demonstrated his immense strength from a young age. He entered his first strongman contest aged 18, lifting a huge stone clean off the ground. Another time he reportedly withstood the pull of four draught horses (two on each side of his body). Again, exact figures for his top backlift record are debated, but early editions of *GWR* put his 1896 effort at 4,133 lb (1,874 kg).

Paul Anderson

Raised in Georgia, USA, Paul Anderson (1932–94) was a world and Olympic champion weightlifter. He claimed to have backlifted 6,270 lb (2,844 kg) in 1957, which GWR recognized as the **heaviest weight lifted by a human**. But after a conflict in evidence arose, GWR decided to no longer list the claim. Even if it is never fully documented, nothing can take away from the role he played in bringing back strength feats to the mainstream.

Gregg Ernst

While historical lifting records are often dogged by conflicting reports, in 2014 Canadian strongman Gregg Ernst (right) was confirmed to have lifted the **heaviest weight lifted by a human**, in 1993. He did this by backlifting a wooden platform with two Ford Festiva cars, plus their drivers (inset below left) – a total of 5,340 lb (2,422.18 kg).

Asked how his strength has helped him, Ernst told us: "In farming, blacksmithing and life, many times my strength has been a major asset. Lifting cars out of ditches, moving pianos, putting a hammerlock on an unruly cow. It saved my life once, but that is a long story…"

Don't just put your back into it!

The backlift enables us to bear more weight than any other lift, principally as it spreads the load across numerous muscle groups in the body. Here are some of the key muscles that take the strain…

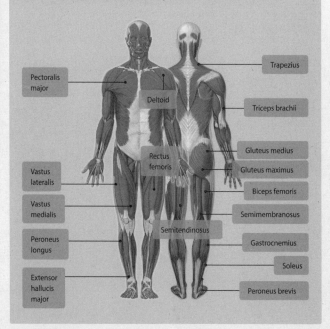

AMERICAN FOOTBALL

Americans **eat more on Super Bowl Sunday** than any day except Thanksgiving

Fastest time to reach 10,000 receiving yards in an NFL career
Calvin Johnson reached the milestone of 10,000 receiving yards in 115 games during the 2014 season. He has played for the Detroit Lions since 2007.

Largest NFL comeback win by a visiting team
The Cleveland Browns overcame a 28–3 deficit at Tennessee to beat the Titans 29–28 on 5 Oct 2014, the largest such win in National Football League (NFL) history.

Most-watched NFL championship game
According to NBC, an average audience of 114.4 million watched the New England Patriots beat the Seattle Seahawks in the Super Bowl on 1 Feb 2015.

First person to play in the Super Bowl and World Series
Deion Sanders played for the Atlanta Braves in the 1992 Baseball World Series. He was also on a Super Bowl-winning team on two occasions, in 1995 (with the San Francisco 49ers) and 1996 (with the Dallas Cowboys).

In 1989, "Neon Deion" became the **first person to both hit an MLB home run and score an NFL touchdown in the same week.** On 5 Sep 1989, he hit a homer for the New York Yankees against the Seattle Mariners. Five days later, he touched down for the Atlanta Falcons vs the Los Angeles Rams.

Longest kick-off return for a touchdown

The Minnesota Vikings' Cordarrelle Patterson (below, holding ball) made a 109-yd kick-off return for a touchdown against the Green Bay Packers on 27 Oct 2013. The same feat sees him share the record for the **longest play,** with Antonio Cromartie, who covered the same distance on a return of a missed field goal for the San Diego Chargers against the Minnesota Vikings on 4 Nov 2007.

FACT

Both Patterson and Cromartie were behind the goalposts, and within a yard of the back line, when they received the ball. The distance that they ran is the greatest possible distance an NFL play can be.

Youngest player to achieve a 200-yd receiving game

At the age of 21 years 87 days, Mike Evans (b. 21 Aug 1993) of the Tampa Bay Buccaneers caught seven passes for 209 yd and two touchdowns in a 27–7 victory over the Washington Redskins on 16 Nov 2014.

MOST...

Consecutive field goals to start an NFL career

Rookie Chandler Catanzaro converted 17 attempts for the Arizona Cardinals in 2014.

Three-hundred-yd passing games in an NFL season

Drew Brees achieved this feat 13 times while playing quarter-back for the New Orleans Saints in 2011. The **most consecutive 300-yd passing games by a quarterback**, meanwhile, was also achieved by Brees, who played nine 300-yd passing games in a row for the New Orleans Saints in the 2011 and 2012 seasons. Brees also had the **most consecutive 4,000-yd passing seasons by an NFL quarterback** (nine), for the Saints in 2006–14.

Five-hundred-yd passing NFL games

Ben Roethlisberger is the first player to enjoy two 500-yd passing games. Playing quarterback for the Pittsburgh Steelers, he threw for 503 yd against the Green Bay Packers on 20 Dec 2009 and 522 yd against the Indianapolis Colts on 26 Oct 2014.

In weeks eight and nine of the 2014 season, Roethlisberger also threw 12 touchdown passes – the **most touchdown passes over a two-game span** – surpassing the 11 thrown by Tom Flores in 1963 and by Tom Brady in 2007.

Consecutive 100-yd rushing games to start an NFL season

From 7 Sep to 27 Oct 2014, DeMarco Murray of the Dallas Cowboys became the first player in NFL history to rush for at least 100 yd in his team's first eight games of the season.

First player with 300 yd passing and 100 yd rushing in a game

Russell Wilson of the Seattle Seahawks passed for 313 yd and added 106 yd rushing in a 28–26 loss to the St Louis Rams on 19 Oct 2014. With Peyton Manning, he also shares the record for **most touchdowns thrown by a first-year player**: 26.

Point-after-touchdowns converted in an NFL season

Matt Prater of the Denver Broncos kicked 75 points following touchdowns in 2013.

Points scored in an NFL season by a rookie

First-year player Cody Parkey scored 150 points as place-kicker for the Philadelphia Eagles in 2014.

Touchdown passes in an NFL career

Peyton Manning has made 530 touchdown passes for the Indianapolis Colts (1998 to 2011) and the Denver Broncos (2012 to present).

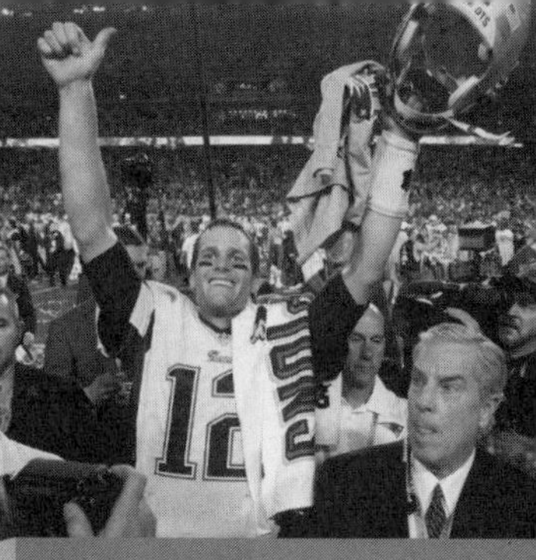

Tom Brady

On 9 Sep 2010, Tom Brady of the New England Patriots signed a four-year, $72-m (£47-m) contract extension. This made him the highest-paid player in the NFL, with a salary of $18 m (£12 m).

By leading the Patriots through the playoffs en route to a 28–24 victory over the Seahawks at Super Bowl XLIX, Brady further cemented his legacy as one of the greatest quarterbacks of all time, with the records to prove it.

He has played in the **most postseason games in NFL history** (29); thrown the **most touchdown passes** (53); thrown the **most yards** (7,345); completed the **most passes** (683); and won the **most games for a starting quarterback** (21). With a rotating cast of receivers, running backs and linemen over his 13 seasons as a full starter (15 in total), Brady has been the one constant of the Patriots' offense and he has led the team to an unprecedented nine conference championship games.

At the Super Bowl, meanwhile, Brady's achievements include the **most touchdown passes** (13); the **most passing yards** (1,605); and the **most passes completed** (164).

As we were going to press, Brady had been handed a four-game suspension by the NFL for a "lack of co-operation" with an investigation into the use of deflated balls during the AFC Championship Game. He is appealing the decision.

IN NUMBERS

6
Most touchdown passes in a Super Bowl game, by Steve Young of the San Francisco 49ers in 1995

13
Most touchdown passes in a Super Bowl career, by Tom Brady for the New England Patriots in 2001, 2003–04, 2007, 2011 and 2014

12 sec
Fastest time for a team to score in a Super Bowl game, by the Seattle Seahawks vs the Denver Broncos on 2 Feb 2014

48
Most points in a Super Bowl career, by Jerry Rice in 1989–2003, for the San Francisco 49ers and the Oakland Raiders

42 years 11 days
Age of the **oldest player to score in the Super Bowl**: Matt Stover struck a 38-yd field goal for the Indianapolis Colts vs the New Orleans Saints on 7 Feb 2010

Most passes received and completed in a Super Bowl game

Demaryius Thomas (above, holding ball) received a total of 13 passes for the Denver Broncos at Super Bowl XLVIII against the Seattle Seahawks on 2 Feb 2014, at the MetLife Stadium in East Rutherford, New Jersey, USA.

The **most passes completed in a Super Bowl game** is 37 by Tom Brady, for the New England Patriots in their 28–24 victory over the Seattle Seahawks on 1 Feb 2015.

Most times as the NFL's single-season passing yardage leader

The New Orleans Saints' Drew Brees has been the single-season passing yardage leader on five occasions, equalling the all-time record set by Dan Marino of the Miami Dolphins and Sonny Jurgensen of the Philadelphia Eagles and the Washington Redskins.

BASEBALL

In 1963, **Jimmy Piersall** (USA) celebrated his 100th home run by **running the bases backwards**

First MLB franchise to hit 15,000 home runs

On 21 Sep 2014, the New York Yankees (USA) hit the mark when Brett Gardner connected off Drew Hutchison in New York's 5–2 victory over the Toronto Blue Jays (CAN) at Yankee Stadium.

Longest MLB postseason game

On 4 Oct 2014, in a game lasting 6 hr 23 min, the San Francisco Giants defeated the Washington Nationals (both USA) 2–1 in Game 2 of their National League Division Series. Its duration of 18 innings also made it the **longest MLB postseason game by innings**.

Fewest errors by a team in an MLB season

In 2013, the Baltimore Orioles (USA) achieved just 54 errors in a 162-game season. At the same time, their fielding percentage of .991% brought them the **highest fielding percentage in an MLB season by one team**.

First player in the College World Series and MLB World Series in the same year

In 2014, Brandon Finnegan (USA) pitched for Texas Christian University in the College World Series, and then was selected by the Kansas City Royals in the MLB draft, later appearing in two games of the World Series for the Royals.

Most consecutive seasons leading Major League Baseball in earned run average

While pitching for the Los Angeles Dodgers, Clayton Kershaw (USA) posted the lowest earned run average in Major League Baseball (MLB) in each of four consecutive seasons from 2011 to 2014. The previous mark was three, by Greg Maddux and Robert "Lefty" Grove (both USA).

MOST HOME RUNS HIT IN AN MLB CAREER

A home run is a hit in which the batter scores by circling all bases and reaching home plate (base) in one play.

Rank	Name	Career span	Home runs
1	**Barry Bonds**	**1986–2007**	**762**
2	Hank Aaron	1954–76	755
3	"Babe" Ruth	1914–35	714
4	Willie Mays	1951–73	660
5	**Alex Rodriguez**	**1994–**	**654**
6	Ken Griffey Jr	1989–2010	630
7	Jim Thome	1991–2012	612
8	Sammy Sosa	1989–2007	609
9	Frank Robinson	1956–76	586
10	Mark McGwire	1986–2001	583

All nationalities USA. Source: MLB.com; correct as of Feb 2015

Largest MLB contract for a baseball player

On 18 Nov 2014, Giancarlo Stanton (USA) of the Miami Marlins signed a 13-year contract for $325 m (£209 m). This is considered the largest deal in US sporting history and its duration makes it likely to be the largest in any sport, surpassing even the best-paid soccer players and Formula One drivers.

Stanton made his debut in 2010 and hit 154 home runs in the first five years of his career. A two-time All-Star (2012 and 2014), he was the National League home run champion in 2014 with 37 home runs.

MOST...

Saves by a pitcher in a postseason

While pitching for the Kansas City Royals in the 2014 postseason, Greg Holland (USA) made seven saves. He shares that record with five others, latterly Koji Uehara (JPN) of the Boston Red Sox in 2013.

On 30 Sep 2014, the Royals (USA) achieved the **most stolen bases by a team in an MLB postseason innings**: four. They accomplished this in the eighth innings of their American League Wild Card game against the Oakland Athletics, which the Royals won 9–8.

The 2014 postseason continued in glorious style for the Royals, as they won their next seven games – the **most consecutive wins to start a postseason by an MLB team** (8) – and achieved the **most stolen bases by a team in an MLB postseason game** (7).

Batters consecutively retired by an MLB pitcher

In 2014, Yusmeiro Petit (VEN) for the San Francisco Giants retired 46 batters in a row over an eight-game stretch.

Players used by a team in an MLB season

The Texas Rangers (USA) used 64 players in 2014, breaking the previous mark of 59 players used by the Cleveland Indians in 2002 and the San Diego Padres in 2002 and 2008. Also in 2014, the Rangers set a record for **most pitchers used by a team in an MLB season**: 40.

Highest strikeouts-to-hits ratio by a pitcher in a season

In the 2014 MLB season, Aroldis Chapman (CUB) of the Cincinnati Reds achieved a ratio of 5.05-to-1 strikeouts-to-hits.

In the same season, Chapman notched up the **most consecutive MLB games with a strikeout by a relief pitcher** (49); the **most strikeouts per nine innings by a pitcher** (17.67); and the **highest percentage of batters struck out by a pitcher** (52.5%). In 2010, he also threw the **fastest baseball pitch** (105.1 mph; 169.14 km/h).

IN NUMBERS

3,465
Most hits by a shortstop in an MLB career, by Derek Jeter (USA)

363
Career wins by pitcher Warren Spahn (USA); coincidentally, also his career number of hits

2
Teams for whom Joel Youngblood (USA) played in two cities on the same day

24
Most games pitched in the World Series, by Mariano Rivera (PAN)

10
Seasons in the career of pitcher Jim Abbott (USA), who had no right hand

7
Number of baseballs that Johnny Bench (USA) could hold in one hand

.342
Batting average of star player George Herman "Babe" Ruth Jr (USA)

Most hits in a single MLB postseason

Pablo Sandoval (VEN), aka "Kung Fu Panda", made 26 hits for the San Francisco Giants during the 2014 postseason. He broke the previous record of 25 in Game 7 of the World Series, which the Giants won 3–2 against the Kansas City Royals.

Strikeouts in an MLB season (all teams)

During the 2014 regular season, would-be MLB batters struck out 37,441 times. Meanwhile, pitchers for the Cleveland Indians (USA) struck out 1,450 batters, the **most strikeouts by a pitching staff in an MLB season**. And on 15 Sep 2014, Jacob deGrom (USA) matched the **most strikeouts by a pitcher to start an MLB game**: eight for the New York Mets, a feat only achieved twice before by Jim Deshaies (USA).

Most innings pitched in a single MLB postseason

During the 2014 postseason, Madison Bumgarner (USA) threw 52.2 innings for the San Francisco Giants. The **first player to pitch more than 50 innings**, he won the 2014 World Series and was also voted its Most Valuable Player (MVP).

The left-handed pitcher also posted the **lowest-earned run average in a World Series career** (with at least 20 innings pitched): 0.25 in the 2010, 2012 and 2014 World Series.

Most games in a postseason career

Derek Jeter (USA) played in 158 postseason MLB games with the New York Yankees between 1995 and 2014. In this period, he also achieved the **most**:

- **hits** (200)
- **runs scored** (111)
- **plate appearances** (734)
- **total bases** (302)
- **at bats** (650)
- **doubles** (32)
- **triples** (5) – shared with Rafael Furcal (DOM) and George Brett (USA).

Calvin Ripken Jr

From 30 May 1982 to 19 Sep 1998, Cal Ripken Jr (USA) proved his dedication to baseball by playing in 2,632 games without a break – the most consecutive games played by an MLB player.

Over this period, Ripken would win one World Series, two American League MVP awards, two Gold Gloves and eight Silver Sluggers, all playing for the Baltimore Orioles.

By the end of his record stretch, the shortstop/third baseman had justifiably earned the title of "Iron Man".

What made this Hall of Famer's streak even more impressive is that he also set the MLB record for **most consecutive games played without missing an innings**: 903 from 5 Jun 1982 to 14 Sep 1987. Ripken's historic run finally ended by choice, as he decided to sit out the team's final home game of the 1998 season. He went on to play through to the 2001 season and finished his career with 3,184 hits and 431 home runs.

In 2014, as part of Guinness World Records' 60th anniversary celebrations, Ripken was awarded a special medal and certificate (above) to recognize his skills. His records look set to remain unchallenged for years to come: the longest current active streak heading into the 2015 season is 383 games, held by the San Francisco Giants' Hunter Pence.

BASKETBALL

LeBron James (USA) of the Cleveland Cavaliers is the **highest-earning basketball player**, netting $72 m (£42 m) in the 12 months to Jun 2014

Most regular season games refereed in a career

Dick Bavetta (USA) officiated 2,635 National Basketball Association (NBA) games in a row over his 39-year career, from 1974–75 to his retirement after the 2013–14 season.

WNBA

Most assists in a career

From 1998 to 2012, Ticha Penicheiro (PRT) notched up 2,599 assists over 454 games (also the **most assists per game** at 5.7), playing for the Sacramento Monarchs, LA Sparks and Chicago Sky.

Most points scored in a WNBA All-Star Game

Shoni Schimmel (USA) scored 29 points as the East pulled out a 125–124 win over the West in the first WNBA All-Star Game to go into overtime, played in Phoenix, Arizona, USA, on 19 Jul 2014.

While playing in the Finals for the Phoenix Mercury in 2007, 2009 and 2014, Diana Taurasi (USA) scored 262 points – the **most points in a WNBA Finals career**. She surpassed Deanna Nolan's (USA) previous career record by four points.

Largest margin of victory in a Finals game

With a score of 97–68 in their Game 2 win over the Chicago Sky, the Phoenix Mercury (USA) stormed to a 29-point win on 9 Sep 2014.

It was truly a boundary-pushing year for the Arizona team. With 29 victories in 2014, they secured the **most wins by a WNBA team in a season**. Phoenix's record of 29–5 beat the previous mark of 28 achieved by the Seattle Storm in 2010 and the Los Angeles Sparks in 2000 and 2001.

Most blocks in a game

Success continued on an individual level when Phoenix Mercury centre Brittney Griner (USA) kept out 11 shots by the Tulsa Shock on 29 Jun 2014.

Overall top spot for dashing shooters' dreams goes to Margo Dydek (POL). Over 323 games, she racked up 877 blocks – the **most blocks in a WNBA career**.

NBA

Most field goals in a career

Playing for the Milwaukee Bucks and the Los Angeles Lakers over a period of two decades, Kareem Abdul-Jabbar (USA) scored a staggering 15,837 field goals. His 20-year career also qualifies Abdul-Jabbar for the **most NBA minutes played**: 57,446.

In contrast, the **most missed field goals in a career** is 13,766, by Kobe Bryant (USA) for the LA Lakers between 1996 and 2015.

FACT

In a 2005 US survey on sports injuries, basketball was number one with 512,213. Cycling was second with 485,669 and American football third with 418,260 injuries reported.

Most Championship titles

The Boston Celtics' (USA) trophy cabinet must be bursting, with the team taking first place 17 times: in 1957, 1959, 1960–66, 1968–69, 1974, 1976, 1981, 1984, 1986 and 2008.

The team with the **most WNBA Championship titles** is the Houston Comets (USA), winning four times between 1997 and 2000.

Highest percentage shooting in one half of a Finals match

The San Antonio Spurs (USA) achieved 75.8% in the first half of their battle against the Miami Heat in Game 3 of the 2014 NBA Finals on 10 Jun 2014. In this match, the Spurs also set a record for **highest shooting percentage in one quarter**, with 86.7%. Victory went to the Spurs with a final score of 111–92.

TOP 5 ALL-TIME SCORERS (NBA & WNBA)

Successful shots taken outside the three-point line are awarded three points, two points are given for shots made within the line, and one point for free throws

Name	Career	Points
1 Kareem Abdul-Jabbar	**1969–89**	**38,387**
2 Karl Malone	1985–2004	36,928
3 Kobe Bryant	1996–	32,482
4 Michael Jordan	1984–2003	32,292
5 Wilt Chamberlain	1959–73	31,419
1 Tina Thompson	**1997–2013**	**7,488**
2 Diana Taurasi	2004–	6,722
3 Tamika Catchings	2002–	6,554
4 Katie Smith	1999–2013	6,452
5 Lisa Leslie	1997–2009	6,263

All nationalities USA. Sources: NBA.com, WNBA.com

Most three-point field goals in an NBA season

Stephen Curry (USA) scored 286 three-point field goals for the Golden State Warriors from 29 Oct 2014 to 15 Apr 2015.

Curry also achieved the **most consecutive seasons leading the NBA three-point field goal charts**, with three: 2012–13, 2013–14 and 2014–15.

Most team appearances in the Finals

As of 12 Feb 2014, the LA Lakers (USA) had made it to the Finals on 31 occasions: 1949–50, 1952–54, 1959, 1962–63, 1965–66, 1968–70, 1972–73, 1980, 1982–85, 1987–89, 1991, 2000–02, 2004, 2008–10. The Lakers also hold the record for **most consecutive wins**, with 33 victories in 1971–72.

FACT

Invented in 1891 by PE teacher Dr James Naismith (CAN), basketball is thought to have been inspired by a game called "duck on a rock", which involved knocking a smaller rock off a boulder.

Fewest points scored by both teams in an NBA quarter

The New York Knicks and the Orlando Magic (both USA) managed just 15 points between them during the second quarter of their regular-season game at the Amway Center in Orlando, Florida, USA, on 11 Apr 2015.

Fewest rebounds in a game

The Brooklyn Nets (USA) won just 17 rebounds against the Oklahoma City Thunder on 31 Jan 2014.

Most steals in a WNBA career

Proving her formidable defensive skills, Tamika Catchings (USA) of the Indiana Fever has made 957 steals since 2002.

The **most steals in an NBA career** is 3,265 by John Stockton (USA), playing for the Utah Jazz from 1984 to 2003.

The late basketball great Wilt Chamberlain (USA, 1936–99) rarely missed a chance to capitalize on an off-target shot. He achieved 23,924 rebounds – the **most rebounds in a career**.

Most three-point field goals scored by an individual in a game half

Chandler Parsons (USA), of the Houston Rockets, notched up 10 three-pointers in the second half of a game against the Memphis Grizzlies on 24 Jan 2014. Despite this impressive performance, the Rockets went on to lose by 88–87.

Parsons surpassed the mark of nine three-pointers set by Deron Williams (USA) in 2013.

IN NUMBERS

501
Number of games by which Dick Bavetta beat the previous referee record (see p.492)

18 in
Diameter of a basketball hoop (45.7 cm)

10 ft
Height of hoop above floor (3.05 m)

8 psi
Pressure of a regulation basketball (0.56 kg/cm²)

48.4%
Highest team field goal percentage in a WNBA season, achieved by the Phoenix Mercury in 2014

2.45 m
Height of Suleiman Ali Nashnush (LBY, 1943–91) – the **tallest basketball player ever** (8 ft 0.25 in)

6
Most underhanded half-court shots scored in one minute, by Buckets Blakes (USA) of the Harlem Globetrotters on 3 Nov 2014

108,713
Fans watching an All-Star Game on 14 Feb 2010 – the **largest attendance for a basketball game**

Klay Thompson

To score 37 points in one game is impressive. To score that many points in one half is improbable. To score that many points in one quarter is impossible… isn't it?

On 23 Jan 2015, Klay Thompson (USA) of the Golden State Warriors did the unthinkable when he broke the NBA record for **most points scored in one quarter** by dropping 37 points against the Sacramento Kings.

Few players in NBA history have had a night like Thompson's against the Kings. During the third quarter, he was a perfect 13-for-13 from the field, 9-for-9 from beyond the three-point line and 2-2 from the free-throw line. His nine field goals from behind the arc also broke the NBA record for **most three-point baskets in a single quarter**.

The Warriors ended up running away with the game and won 126–101, thanks to Thompson's shooting. Despite the blow-out win, the game was actually tied at 58 before Thompson scored his first points of his record-breaking quarter. At one point in the third quarter he scored 19 consecutive points, and went on to out-score all other players on both teams, 37–26.

With Golden State well ahead in the fourth quarter by 30 points, the shooting guard exited the game with 9:27 remaining and 52 points in 33 min. On the bench for the remainder of the game, Thompson was denied the chance of scoring more than 59 points to break Wilt Chamberlain's record for **most points in a single half** from 1962.

Most three-point field goals converted by an individual in an NBA playoff career

Ray Allen (USA) has converted 385 three-pointers in his playoff career since 1996. In that time, Allen has also achieved the **most attempted three-point field goals**, with 959 goal shots taken from behind the three-point line.

CRICKET

The **turf at Melbourne Cricket Ground** is cut daily in summer to precisely **11 mm**

First Test cricketer to reach 100 years old

Right-arm pace bowler Norman Gordon (ZAF, b. 6 Aug 1911, d. 2 Sep 2014) played in South Africa's five-match home series against England in 1938–39. He took 20 wickets and averaged 40.35 runs per wicket. His career was cut short by the outbreak of World War II.

Oldest living Test cricketer

England bowler Eileen Whelan (b. 30 Oct 1911) was 103 years 111 days old as of 18 Feb 2015. In 1937–49, Whelan played seven Test matches against Australia, taking 10 wickets for 230 runs. She is also the **first female Test cricketer to reach 100 years old**.

Oldest player to score a century in an ODI

Left-handed captain Khurram Khan (UAE) was 43 years 162 days old when he plundered 132 not out in a One-Day International (ODI) against Afghanistan at ICC Academy in Dubai, UAE, on 30 Nov 2014.

First player to score a century and take 10 wickets in a Test match

On 3–7 Nov 2014, Shakib Al Hasan of Bangladesh matched the double feat first achieved by England's Ian Botham, playing India at Wankhede Stadium in Bombay (now Mumbai), India, on 15–18 Feb 1980.

Fastest century in international cricket

On 18 Jan 2015, South African captain A B de Villiers smashed a 31-ball hundred in an ODI against the West Indies at New Wanderers Stadium in Johannesburg, South Africa. The record-shattering knock featured eight fours and 11 sixes.

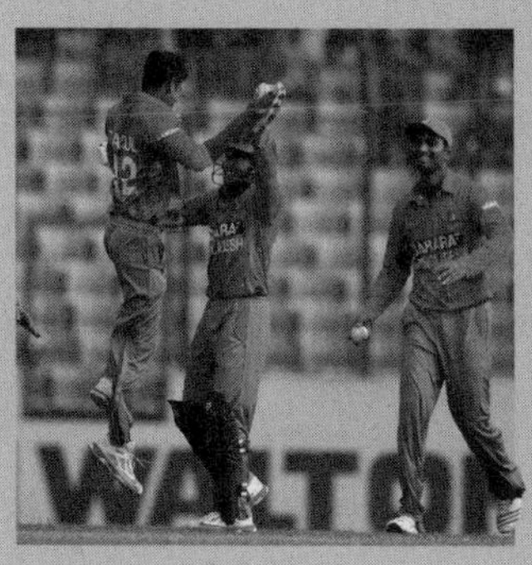

First bowler to take a hat-trick on an ODI debut

On 1 Dec 2014, left-arm spinner Taijul Islam (BGD, far left) claimed three wickets in consecutive balls in a day/night match against Zimbabwe at Shere Bangla National Stadium in Mirpur, Bangladesh. This reduced the beleaguered tourists from 120 for 6 to 124 for 9.

MOST WINS OF DOMESTIC FIRST-CLASS COMPETITIONS

Competition	Team	Titles
Sheffield Shield (AUS)	New South Wales	46
Ranji Trophy (IND)	Bombay/Mumbai	40
County Championship (ENG/WAL)	Yorkshire	32 (1 shared)
Premier Trophy (LKA)	Sinhalese Sports Club	31 (3 shared)
Sunfoil Series (ZAF)	Transvaal/Gauteng	29 (4 shared)
Plunket Shield (NZ)	Auckland/Auckland Aces	26
Regional Four Day Competition (West Indies)	Barbados	22 (1 shared)
Quaid-i-Azam Trophy (PAK)	Karachi Blues	10
Logan Cup (ZWE)	Mashonaland	9
National Cricket League (BGD)	Rajshahi Division Dhaka Division	5 5

Figures correct as of 23 Mar 2015

First player to score three hundreds in their first three Test innings as captain

Virat Kohli (IND) made 115 and 141 in the First Test against Australia in Adelaide on 11 and 13 Dec 2014, and 147 in the Fourth Test's first innings in Sydney on 8–9 Jan 2015.

Highest Test match 10th-wicket partnership

Joe Root and James Anderson (both England), batting at numbers 5 and 11, scored 198 runs for the 10th wicket during the First Test between England and India at Trent Bridge, UK, on 11–12 Jul 2014.

Overall, the series yielded the **most runs for the 10th wicket in a Test series**: 499 runs from 14 partnerships, including 111 by Bhuvneshwar Kumar and Mohammed Shami (both IND).

Most international runs in a calendar year

In 2014, Kumar Sangakkara (LKA, see profile panel p.411) amassed 2,868 runs in 48 matches: 1,493 in Tests, 1,256 in ODIs and 119 in T20 Internationals. He also achieved eight hundreds in 57 innings.

Best bowling by a left-hander in a Test match innings

Sri Lanka's Rangana Herath took nine wickets for 127 runs in 33.1 overs against Pakistan at Sinhalese Sports Club Ground in Colombo, Sri Lanka, on 15–16 Aug 2014. A record 29 of the match's 40 wickets went to left-handers.

Youngest player to score a century in a Test match (both innings)

At 20 years 98 days, batsman Phillip Hughes (AUS, 1988–2014) hit 115 in the first innings and 160 in the second during the Second Test against South Africa at Kingsmead in Durban on 6 and 8–9 Mar 2009.

Most runs in an international career

Between 16 Nov 1989 and 15 Nov 2013, Sachin Tendulkar (IND) made 34,357 runs. The total comprised 18,426 in ODIs, 15,921 in Tests and 10 in a single T20 International.

Tendulkar also notched up a total of 2,278 runs in 44 innings at six Cricket World Cup tournaments between 22 Feb 1992 and 2 Apr 2011, to achieve the **most runs in an ICC World Cup career**.

Highest successful run chase in a Twenty20 International match

On 11 Jan 2015, the West Indies chased down South Africa's 231 for 7 to win a Twenty20 (T20) International by four wickets at New Wanderers Stadium in Johannesburg. Thanks to 90 in 41 balls from Chris Gayle (JAM) and 20 not out from captain Darren Sammy (LCA, above right), who hit the winning runs, it was also the **highest winning chase by a team in any professional Twenty20 match.**

IN NUMBERS

8,463
Runs scored by former English Test cricketer Alec Stewart, coincidentally born on 8 Apr 1963 (8.4.63)

18 balls
Deliveries it took for Brendon McCullum (NZ) to score the **fastest 50 in an ICC World Cup match**, against England on 20 Feb 2015

199
Centuries scored in first-class cricket by early master Sir Jack Hobbs (UK, 1882–1963); he also scored 61,760 first-class runs

465,000
Largest attendance at a five-day Test match, between India and Pakistan in Calcutta on 16–20 Feb 1982

100,024
Spectator capacity of the **largest cricket ground**: Melbourne Cricket Ground in Australia

Most runs by a player in an ODI

Opener Rohit Sharma, playing for India against Sri Lanka, scored 264 in a day/night match at Eden Gardens in Kolkata, India, on 13 Nov 2014.

Most runs by a player in a T20 International

Female: Meg Lanning (AUS) scored 126 runs off 65 balls in a Women's World T20 group match against Ireland in Sylhet, Bangladesh, on 27 Mar 2014.
Male: Aaron Finch (AUS) made 156 runs against England at the Ageas Bowl in Southampton, UK, on 29 Aug 2013.

Most runs scored by a player in an ICC World Cup match

On 21 Mar 2015, Martin Guptill (NZ) scored 237 not out in a quarter-final match against the West Indies at Westpac Stadium in Wellington, New Zealand – the second-highest innings ever in a One-Day International. The opener's explosive knock featured 24 fours and 11 sixes, and eclipsed opponent Chris Gayle's 215 against Zimbabwe, set 25 days previously.

FACT

Guptill's 237 not out was made off 163 balls in 223 min. Only Rohit Sharma, with 42 (33 fours, nine sixes) in his ODI record 264 (see above), has hit more boundaries than the 35 in Guptill's innings.

Fastest Test match hundred

On 2 Nov 2014, Pakistan captain Misbah-ul-Haq scored 100 from 56 balls in the Second Test against Australia at Sheikh Zayed Stadium in Abu Dhabi, UAE – equalling the 1986 record of Viv Richards (West Indies). As Misbah's second century of the match, it made him, at the age of 40 years 158 days, the oldest player to score two hundreds in a match.

Kumar Sangakkara

As of 18 Feb 2015, Kumar Sangakkara (LKA) was the world's top-ranked Test batsman. Besides his diverse records (see p.498), on 3–4 Jan 2015 he scored the 11th double hundred of his Test career. Only Don Bradman (AUS) achieved more in his career, with 12.

Born in Matale, Sri Lanka, on 27 Oct 1977, Kumar Chokshanada Sangakkara was raised in the city of Kandy. He first played cricket at the age of seven, and made his first-class debut for Colombo's Nondescripts Cricket Club in 1997–98. The following season, Sangakkara graduated to international cricket with Sri Lanka A before stepping up to the senior team in a One-Day International against Pakistan on 5 Jul 2000.

Sangakkara is perhaps most fondly remembered for a Test match in Jul 2006 against South Africa in Colombo, when he and team-mate Mahela Jayawardene racked up an astonishing 624 runs together: the **highest partnership in Test match cricket**. In his 224th innings at the start of 2015, Sangakkara also recorded the **fastest time to reach 12,000 Test runs** – only the fifth man to do so.

When not smashing cricket balls to, and over, the boundary rope, Sangakkara will often be found keeping wicket. As of 18 Mar 2015, he had the **most dismissals by a wicket-keeper in an ODI career** (482 in 404 matches/353 innings) and the **most stumpings in an ODI career** (99). In all international cricket (Tests, ODIs and T20 Internationals), Sangakkara had made a record 139 stumpings, as of the same date.

Turning 38 years old in Oct 2015, Sangakkara has already retired from T20 Internationals and was expected to bow out of ODIs after the 2015 World Cup, where he hit four tons, the **most successive ODI centuries**, on 26 Feb–11 Mar.

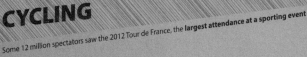

Some 12 million spectators saw the 2012 Tour de France, the **largest attendance at a sporting event**

Most race wins on the UCI World Tour

Philippe Gilbert (BEL) won 10 races on the Union Cycliste Internationale (UCI) World Tour from 17 Oct 2009 to 14 Oct 2014.

First person to win the cycling Triple Crown

The first winner of cycling's Triple Crown is Eddy Merckx (BEL), who won the Tour de France, Giro d'Italia (Tour of Italy) and UCI Road World Cycling Championships in 1974. The only other person to have achieved this feat is Stephen Roche (IRL) in 1987.

Fastest crossing of the USA by bicycle

Christoph Strasser (AUT) finished the Race Across America (RAAM, see opposite) in 7 days 15 hr 56 min, from 10 to 18 Jun 2014. In the 2013 edition of the race, he became the first person to cycle across the USA in under eight days, with a time of 7 days 22 hr 11 min. His average 2014 speed of 16.42 mph (26.43 km/h) is also a US-crossing record in terms of **fastest average speed** – his 2013 average was 15.6 mph (25.1 km/h).

FACT

The route of the Race Across America varies from year to year. The course was 26.7 mi (42.9 km) shorter in 2013 than in 2014, which makes Strasser's record ride in 2014 all the more impressive.

Most consecutive wins of the Race Across the Alps

Maurizio Vandelli (ITA) was the first rider to record three consecutive wins of cycling's Race Across the Alps (RATA), from 2008 to 2010. The feat was equalled by Daniel Rubisoier (AUT), from 2012 to 2014.

RAAM 2014

The 3,000-mi (4,828-km) route for the 2014 Race Across America began in Oceanside, California, and ended in Annapolis, Maryland. But the original race held in 1982 – an informal contest between four riders – ran between Santa Monica Pier in Los Angeles, California, and the Empire State Building in New York City.

GRAND TOURS

Most consecutive finishes

The Tour de France, Giro d'Italia and Vuelta a España (Tour of Spain) are regarded as cycling's three Grand Tours. Between 13 Jun 1954 and 19 Jul 1958, the Spanish rider Bernardo Ruiz achieved 12 Grand Tour finishes in a row.

Fastest average speed in a Tour de France stage (team)

Australia's Orica-GreenEDGE team set an average speed of 57.7 km/h (35.85 mph) on stage four of the 2013 edition of the Tour de France in Nice, France, on 2 Jul 2013.

Most podium finishes in the Giro d'Italia (female)

Edita Pučinskaitė (LTU) scored six top-three finishes in the women's Tour of Italy (aka the Giro d'Italia Femminile, or Giro Rosa). Her achievement was equalled by Fabiana Luperini (ITA) from 1995 to 2008 and Nicole Brändli (CHE) between 2001 and 2009.

The **most wins of the Giro d'Italia (female)** is five, by Fabiana Luperini, from 1995 to 1998 and in 2008.

Men's one-hour unpaced standing start

The greatest distance covered by a male cyclist in one hour is 52.491 km (32.616 mi) by Rohan Dennis (AUS, right) at Velodrome Suisse in Grenchen, Switzerland, on 8 Feb 2015. The record was first set by Henri Desgrange (FRA), who covered 35.325 km (21.949 mi) on 11 May 1893.

The **most wins of the Giro d'Italia (male)** is also five. Three riders share this record: Alfredo Binda (ITA, in 1925, 1927–29 and 1933), Fausto Coppi (ITA, in 1940, 1947, 1949 and 1952–53) and Eddy Merckx (BEL, in 1968, 1970 and 1972–74).

UCI WORLD CHAMPIONSHIPS

Most wins of the road race at the UCI Road World Championships (male)

Alfredo Binda (ITA) won three championships, in 1927, 1930 and 1932. His feat was matched by Rik van Steenbergen in 1949 and 1956–57, Eddy Merckx (both BEL) in 1967, 1971 and 1974, and Óscar Freire (ESP) in 1999, 2001 and 2004.

The **most wins of the road race at the UCI Road World Championships (female)** is five, by Jeannie Longo-Ciprelli (FRA) in 1985–87, 1989 and 1995.

Most UCI track cycling team pursuit gold medals

Men: 10, by Australia in 1993–2014.
Women: six, by Great Britain between 2008 and 2014.

Most UCI para-track cycling gold medals (men)

Great Britain secured 24 elite gold medals in this discipline between 2007 and 2014. The nearest rival to Great Britain is Australia, with eight.

TRACK CYCLING – ABSOLUTE					
Men	**Start**	**Time/ Distance**	**Name & Nationality**	**Place**	**Date**
200 m	Flying	00:09.347	François Pervis (FRA)	Aguascalientes, Mexico	6 Dec 2013
500 m	Flying	00:24.758	Chris Hoy (UK)	La Paz, Bolivia	13 May 2007
1 km	Standing	00:56.303	François Pervis (FRA)	Aguascalientes, Mexico	7 Dec 2013
4 km	Standing	04:10.534	Jack Bobridge (AUS)	Sydney, Australia	2 Feb 2011
Team 4 km	Standing	03:51.659	Great Britain (S Burke, E Clancy, P Kennaugh and G Thomas)	London, UK	3 Aug 2012
Women	**Start**	**Time/ Distance**	**Name & Nationality**	**Place**	**Date**
200 m	Flying	00:10.384	Kristina Vogel (DEU)	Aguascalientes, Mexico	7 Dec 2013
500 m	Flying	00:29.234	Olga Streltsova (RUS)	Moscow, Russia	30 May 2014
3 km	Standing	03:22.269	Sarah Hammer (USA)	Aguascalientes, Mexico	11 May 2010
1 hour	Standing	46.065 km	Leontien Zijlaard-van Moorsel (NLD)	Mexico City, Mexico	26 Oct 1996
Statistics correct as of 13 Jan 2015					

Oldest winner of the UCI World Tour

In the UCI World Tour (instituted 2009), riders earn points from 29 races, including the three Grand Tours, during the calendar year. Alejandro Valverde (ESP, b. 25 Apr 1980) won the 2014 UCI World Tour on 14 Oct 2014 aged 34 years 172 days.

He is pictured (inset) having won the 2014 La Flèche Wallonne, one of the Tour's races, which is held in Belgium.

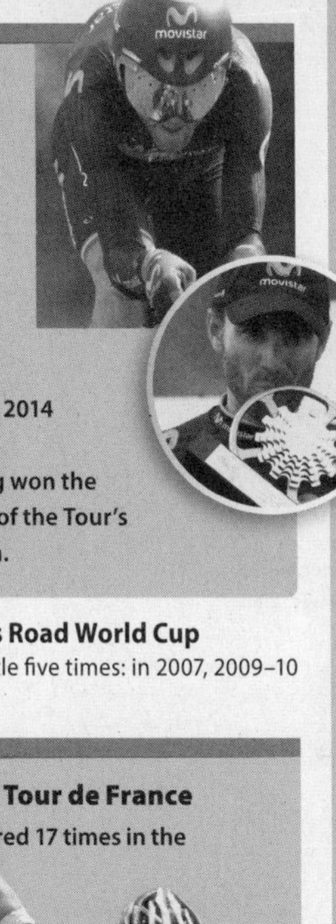

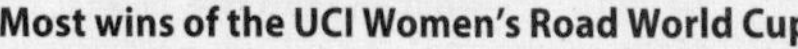

Most wins of the UCI Women's Road World Cup

Marianne Vos (NLD) has won this title five times: in 2007, 2009–10 and 2012–13.

Most appearances in the Tour de France

Three riders have each appeared 17 times in the Tour de France: George Hincapie (USA) between 1996 and 2012; Stuart O'Grady (AUS) from 1997 to 2013; and Jens Voigt (DEU, right), with consecutive appearances from 1998 to 2014 (his last Tour de France).

Voigt finished 14 of the 17 editions of the Tour he entered, falling just short of the record for the **most Tour de France races completed**. Hendrik "Joop" Zoetemelk (NLD) finished 16 races (in 1970–73 and 1975–86), with a win in 1980 and six second-place finishes.

IN NUMBERS

3,663.5 km
Distance covered in the 2014 Tour de France (2,276.3 mi)

11 sec
Time between the winner and runner-up in the **closest-run Giro d'Italia**, in 1948

4
Riders who have died during the Tour de France

6–7,000 calories
Daily intake required by Grand Tour cyclists

198
Riders in the 2014 Tour de France, divided into 22 teams of nine cyclists

Anna Meares

She started cycling at the age of 11. By her own admission, her diminutive size and slight frame made her a less-than-stellar athlete for many years. But her sheer enjoyment of the sport – along with never-say-die dedication and hours of rigorous training – helped turn Anna Meares (AUS) into a modern-day track-cycling legend.

Today, Anna holds the record for the **most Olympic track cycling medals (female)**, with five. Her earliest podium finishes came in Athens, Greece, in 2004, when she won gold in the 500 m time trial (becoming Australia's first ever track-cycling gold medallist) and bronze in the individual sprint. She followed that four years later with silver in the individual sprint in Beijing, China. Finally, she picked up gold in the individual sprint at the 2012 London Games, along with a bronze in the team sprint, shared with fellow Australian Kaarle McCulloch.

That silver at Beijing (Australia's sole cycling medal at that Games) must have felt special. Seven months earlier, Anna broke her neck in a crash at a World Cup race in Los Angeles, USA. She came home in a wheelchair and wearing a neck brace.

On 6 Dec 2013, she broke the record for the **500 m unpaced standing start (female)** at the UCI World Cup meet in Aguascalientes, Mexico, with a phenomenal time of 32.836 sec. In fact, Anna had originally taken this record back in 2004 at the Olympic Games in Athens, when she became the first woman to register a time of less than 34 seconds in the event. With her 2013 victory, Anna also became the first female rider to complete the course in under 33 seconds.

Relentless training has helped keep Anna at the peak of her profession, and she still dedicates six days a week to it, putting in hours at the gym and on static cycles as well as track and road work. But over the years, it has more than paid off. As of Jan 2015, her medal tally from all competitions stood at 110 gold, 54 silver and 29 bronze. And we're pretty sure she's not quite finished yet…

Most wins of the Tour of Spain

Tour of Spain organizers recognize three cyclists to have won the race three times each: Tony Rominger (CHE) won the Tour consecutively from 1992 to 1994. His record was equalled by Roberto Heras (ESP) in 2000 and 2003–04 and by Alberto Contador (ESP, above) in 2008, 2012 and 2014.

FACT

Of cycling's three Grand Tours, the Tour de France is the oldest – the first edition was staged back in 1903. The Giro d'Italia debuted in 1909, while the Vuelta a España dates back to 1935.

Banzai skydiving: a parachute is thrown from a plane. A 'chute-less skydiver follows and tries to catch, strap on and deploy the parachute before it's too late

Largest street hockey tournament

The sports festival "Hockey Night in Canada's Play On!" held between May and Sep 2013 featured a street hockey tournament in which 35,970 players were divided into 5,360 teams. The event was staged across 21 cities in Canada.

Most wins of the freestyle scooter ISA World Championships

The International Scooter Association (ISA) World Championships began in 2012, and Dakota Schuetz (USA) has won all three tournaments held to date. In 2014, Schuetz finished with 87 points, marginally ahead of Dylan Morrison (AUS) with 86.7 points.

Longest dirt-to-dirt motorcycle ramp jump

On 6 Jul 2013, Alex Harvill (USA) achieved a 90.69-m (297-ft 6-in) dirt-to-dirt ramp jump at the Horn Rapids Motorsports Complex in West Richland, Washington, USA.

Fastest speed by a speed skydiver

Marco Wiederkehr (CHE) reached a speed of 531.42 km/h (330.21 mph) at the first International Speed Skydiving Association (ISSA) World Series event at Dropzone Günzburg in Germany on 11 May 2013.

Most gold medals won at the Winter X Games (female)

Lindsey Jacobellis (USA, left) has won nine gold medals at various Winter X Games staged in Aspen, Colorado, USA, between Jan 2003 and Jan 2015. All of her wins came in the Snowboarder X event.

The **fastest speed by a female speed skydiver** is 442.73 km/h (275.09 mph), by Clare Murphy (UK) during a competition in Utti, Finland, at the World Cup staged from 15 to 17 Jun 2007.

Longest-duration wingsuit flight

Jhonathan Florez (COL) maintained an unbroken flight of 9 min 6 sec in a wingsuit above La Guajira in Colombia on 20 Apr 2012.

The next day, at the same site, the fearless Florez made the **highest-altitude wingsuit jump**, from a height of 37,265 ft (11,358 m).

The **greatest absolute distance flown in a wingsuit** is 17.83 mi (28.70 km), by Shinichi Ito (JPN) above Yolo County in California, USA, on 26 May 2012.

Farthest flight by a paraglider (male)

The greatest straight distance covered in a paraglider is 502.9 km (312.5 mi), by Nevil Hulett (ZAF) at Copperton in South Africa on 14 Dec 2008.

Seiko Fukuoka-Naville (JPN) recorded the **farthest flight by a paraglider (female)**, with a distance of 336 km (208.7 mi) in a 10-hr flight from Quixadá, Brazil, on 20 Nov 2012.

Most medals won by an individual at the Summer X Games

Brazilian-born US skateboarder Bob Burnquist picked up an unprecedented 27 Summer X Games medals between 1997 and Jun 2014. Burnquist has won 12 gold medals, seven silver and eight bronze in a range of disciplines, including Vert, Big Air and Vert Best Trick. However, he said, "I still have plenty of stuff I want to do."

FACT

It's fair to say that Bob likes his extreme sports. In 2006, at the Grand Canyon in Nevada, USA, he skated down a ramp leading to a rail grind and then a BASE jump into the canyon itself.

Highest BASE jump from a building

A BASE jump is a leap from a fixed object such as a bridge or cliff. On 21 Apr 2014, Fred Fugen and Vince Reffet (both FRA) jointly performed a BASE jump from a height of 828 m (2,716 ft 6 in). They plunged from the top of the Burj Khalifa tower in Dubai, UAE, the **tallest man-made structure ever built on land**. An unnamed cameraman, also visible right, recorded their death-defying jump.

Most wins of the Red Bull Cliff Diving World Series

The Red Bull Cliff Diving World Series is a high-diving contest that began in 2009. To date, the most successful diver has been Gary Hunt (UK), who won the series four times, in 2010–12 and 2014. The 2014 series was staged at seven different sites, or "stops", on three continents.

IN NUMBERS

268,390
Visitors to the ESPN Summer X Games Five, held in San Francisco, California, USA, in 1999 – the **largest attendance at an action-sports event**

10
Skydivers in the **largest simultaneous indoor BASE jump**, at the Tropical Islands resort near Berlin in Germany on 31 Jan 2005

30
Skydivers in the **largest simultaneous outdoor BASE jump**, from the Ostankino television and radio tower in Moscow, Russia, on 3 Jul 2004

68
Participants in the **largest wingsuit skydive formation**, over Lake Elsinore, California, USA, on 11 Nov 2009

138
Participants in the **largest head-down vertical skydiving formation**, on 3 Aug 2012 at a skydiving festival near Chicago in Illinois, USA

Fastest ice climber

On 9 Feb 2013, Russia's Pavel Batushev climbed a 15-m-high (49-ft) vertical ice wall in 7.77 sec at the 2013 UIAA Ice Climbing World Tour in Buşteni, Romania. In 2014, the sport was demonstrated at the Winter Olympics in Sochi, Russia.

X GAMES

Most appearances at the Summer X Games

Bob Burnquist (BRA/USA), Andy Macdonald, Brian Deegan (both USA) and Rune Glifberg (DNK) each made 23 Summer X Games appearances from 1995 to 2014.

The **most Winter X Games appearances** is 17, by snowboarder Kelly Clark (USA) in 1999–2015.

Longest skateboard ramp jump

Danny Way (USA) performed a 79-ft (24-m) 360 air from a mega ramp at X Games X in Los Angeles, California, USA, on 8 Aug 2004.

Most BMX Freestyle medals at the Summer X Games

Dave Mirra (USA) secured 23 BMX Freestyle medals in 1995–2011.

Most skateboard medals at the Summer X Games

From 1996 to 2013, Andy Macdonald (USA) picked up 23 Summer X Games medals in skateboarding. He won eight gold medals, seven silver medals and eight bronze medals.

LEADING X GAMES MEDALLISTS		
Most medals at the Summer Games	27	Bob Burnquist (BRA/USA)
Most medals at the Summer Games (female)	8	Cara-Beth Burnside (USA)
Most medals at the Winter Games	18	Shaun White (USA)
Most medals at the Winter Games (female)	13	Kelly Clark (USA)
Most gold medals at the Winter and Summer Games combined	15	Shaun White (USA)
Most gold medals at the Summer Games	14	Dave Mirra (USA)
Most gold medals at the Summer Games (female)	7	Fabiola da Silva (BRA)
Most gold medals at the Winter Games	13	Shaun White (USA)
Most gold medals at the Winter Games (female)	9	Lindsey Jacobellis (USA)

Statistics correct as of 30 Mar 2015

First double backflip on a motorcycle

Travis Pastrana (USA) debuted this daredevil trick at ESPN X Games 12 in Los Angeles, California, USA, on 4 Aug 2006.

Highest snowboard air on a superpipe

On 30 Jan 2010, Shaun White (USA) performed a 23-ft (7-m) air on a superpipe at Winter X Games 14 in Aspen, Colorado, USA.

Highest Moto X Step Up jump

The greatest height ever attained in the Moto X Step Up is 47 ft (14.33 m), by Ronnie Renner (USA) at X Games 18 in Los Angeles, California, USA, on 29 Jun 2012.

Most gold medals in Snowmobile SnoCross at the Winter X Games

Tucker Hibbert (USA) has chalked up nine gold medals in the Winter X Games Snowmobile SnoCross event, in 2000, 2007–11 and 2013–15.

BMX-stasy

Takahiro Ikeda (JPN, above right and below) holds three GWR records, including the most BMX Time Machines in one minute (83) – in which he stands on his bike and spins it through 360°.

Why did you choose to try this record?
To show as many people as possible what a great skill the "Time Machine" is – and to be the best at it.

What was the biggest challenge in attempting the record?
Keeping the spin going for a whole minute. Normally, the technique is demonstrated for a much shorter time.

What hurts the most?
All the muscles start to hurt, but the thigh is under the most strain.

Have you had any bad accidents?
Lots! I guess the worst injury was a badly twisted ankle.

Where do you practise?
I often practise in public parks – and I am always surprised when I look up and see a huge crowd of children cheering me on – or just staring!

What advice would you give to someone else attempting a record?
Everyone who can gather enough self-confidence should try for a record. Gaining the record made me much more confident and it has very positively changed my life.

What does Guinness World Records mean to you?
I used to read the book in the library of my elementary school and became very interested in all types of records. My life has definitely changed for the better because of my Guinness World Records titles.

GOLF

A golf ball has 300–500 **dimples**. Why? They help to increase the **distance** it travels

Largest one-day golf tournament

The Mission Hills Golf World Record Challenge, organized by the Mission Hills Golf Club in Shenzhen, China, on 18 Jun 2014, attracted a record 1,987 participants.

Most debutants at a US Masters

A total of 24 golfers made their debut in the US Masters held at Augusta National Golf Club in Georgia, USA, between 10 and 13 Apr 2014.

Lowest score in a single round at a Major

On 11 Sep 2014, in the first round of the 2014 Évian Championship at Évian-les-Bains, France, Kim Hyo-joo (KOR) scored a low of 61 (10 under par). Kim, a 19-year-old student at the time, hit 10 birdies and went on to win the event, her first tournament win on the LPGA tour. Her score of 61 is the lowest in any men's or ladies' Major: the **lowest single-round score at a Major (male)** is 63, achieved 26 times by 24 different golfers.

FACT

A golf "round" usually comprises 18 holes. By playing one full round on a standard golf course, carrying your own clubs, you would walk some 6.4 km (4 mi) and burn off around 1,500 kilocalories.

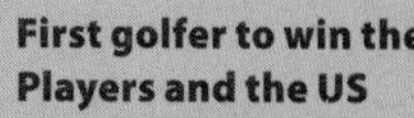

First golfer to win the Players and the US Open in the same year

Germany's Martin Kaymer won the Players at TPC Sawgrass in Ponte Vedra Beach, Florida, USA, on 11 May 2014 (main image) and the US Open at Pinehurst Resort in Pinehurst, California, USA, on 15 Jun 2014 (inset). Kaymer was the first player from mainland Europe to win the US Open. From 12 to 13 Jun 2014, he also recorded the **lowest total score for the first 36 holes at the US Open:** 130 (65-65).

Youngest golfer ranked world number one

Lydia Ko (NZ, b. KOR, 24 Apr 1997) topped the world rankings aged 17 years 284 days on 2 Feb 2015.

She is also the **youngest LPGA Tour winner**, having won an event aged 15 years 122 days in 2012.

Most successful Ryder Cup captain

Walter Hagen (USA) captained the US team to victory four times, in 1927, 1931, 1935 and 1937.

Most northerly Ryder Cup

The Gleneagles Hotel, at 56.2858°N, 3.7475°W in Perthshire, Scotland, UK, hosted the Ryder Cup from 26 to 28 Sep 2014.

Lowest score below par in a PGA Tour event (72 holes)

South Africa's Ernie "The Big Easy" Els scored -31 (31 under par) after 72 holes at the Mercedes Championships in Maui, Hawaii, USA, from 9 to 12 Jan 2003.

The **lowest score below par in an LPGA Tour event (72 holes)** is 258 and was first achieved by Karen Stupples (UK), who shot 63-66-66-63 at the Welch's/Fry's Championship at Dell Urich Golf Course in Tucson, Arizona, USA, on 14 Mar 2004. This feat was equalled by Angela Stanford (USA) and Park Hee-young (KOR), who hit 63-67-64-64 and 65-67-61-65 respectively at the Manulife Classic at Grey Silo Golf Course in Waterloo, Ontario, Canada, on 14 Jul 2013.

Oldest golfer to break par at the US Masters

Tom Watson (USA, b. 4 Sep 1949) was aged 65 years 219 days when he carded 71 (1 under par) in the first round in Augusta, Georgia, USA, on 9 Apr 2015 – achieving the feat against opponents who were two generations younger.

Most consecutive golf Majors won in a year (female)

In 2013, Inbee Park (KOR), aged just 24 years old, won the first three Majors of the season: the Kraft Nabisco Championship, the LPGA Championship and the US Women's Open. Her feat equalled that of the multi-talented athlete Mildred Ella "Babe" Didrikson Zaharias (USA) in 1950, who won all three golf Majors on offer in the opening season of the LPGA.

Highest career earnings on the European Tour

Ernie Els (ZAF) won €30,314,819 (£23,958,578; $38,643,029) on the European Tour in 1989–2014. Other highest-earnings records include:

- **US PGA Tour:** $109,612,414 (£68,403,781), by Tiger Woods (USA) as of 26 Oct 2014.
- **US LPGA Tour:** $22,573,192 (£17,292,700), by Annika Sörenstam (SWE) in 1993–2009.
- **Champions Tour:** $26,587,272 (£16,759,900), by Hale Irwin (USA) in 1995–2012.
- **Asian Tour:** $4,458,796 (£2,816,717), by Thongchai Jaidee (THA) in 1999–2012.

Youngest winner of the PGA Tour Rookie of the Year award

Jordan Spieth (USA, b. 27 Jul 1993) was 20 years 62 days old when he won the award on 27 Sep 2013. Tiger Woods (USA) is the only previous 20-year-old winner. Just over 18 months later, on 9–12 April 2015, Spieth won his first Major at the Masters in Augusta, Georgia, USA, to become the second-youngest winner after Woods. At this event, he also achieved the:

- **most birdies in the US Masters**: 28
- **lowest total score (72 holes)**: 270, equalling Tiger Woods' record
- **lowest total score for the first two rounds (36 holes)**: 130
- **lowest total score for the first three rounds (54 holes)**: 200

FACT

In Jul 2013, two weeks before he turned 20, Spieth won the John Deere Classic, making him the first teenager to win a PGA Tour event in 82 years. He credited his success to the "luckiest shot I've ever hit".

The **most golf balls hit over 300 yd**? Find out on p.180.

Youngest winner of a World Golf Championships (WGC) event

Patrick Reed (USA, b. 5 Aug 1990) was aged 23 years 216 days when he won the 2014 WGC-Cadillac Championship by one shot playing on the Blue Monster Course in Doral, Florida, USA, on 9 Mar 2014.

The **youngest golfer to win a women's Major golf championships** is Morgan Pressel (USA, b. 23 May 1988). She was just 18 years 313 days old when she triumphed at the Kraft Nabisco Championship at Mission Hills Country Club in Rancho Mirage, California, USA, on 1 Apr 2007.

MOST WINS		
British Open	6	Harry Vardon (UK)
US Open	4	Willie Anderson (UK) Bobby Jones Jr (USA) Ben Hogan (USA) Jack Nicklaus (USA)
US Women's Open	4	"Betsy" Rawls (USA) Mickey Wright (USA)
US PGA	5	Walter Hagen (USA) Jack Nicklaus (USA)
LPGA	4	Mickey Wright (USA)
US Masters	6	Jack Nicklaus (USA)

Statistics correct as of 15 Apr 2015

IN NUMBERS

600
Years since golf was first played at Scotland's St Andrews Links

160 mph
Average speed at which a golf ball leaves the tee (257 km/h)

2
Golf balls on the Moon. They were struck and left there during the Apollo 14 mission in 1971

100,000
Golf balls found in Loch Ness in 2009

12,500:1
Approximate chances of an amateur golfer hitting a hole-in-one

2.06 m
Tallest pro golfer; Marcel Pickel (DEU) (6 ft 9 in)

4.25 in
Diameter of golf holes (10.8 cm), as standardized in 1891

Rory McIlroy

Northern Ireland's Rory McIlroy, MBE (b. 4 May 1989) showed golfing prowess from early on. At two years old, he struck his first 40-yd (120-ft; 36.5-m) drive. "Rors" went on to achieve the:

- **lowest score in a round at the British Open** (63, a joint record), in 2010
- **lowest score to par at the US Open**, with 16 under par, and the **lowest total score (72 holes)**, with 268 strokes, in Bethesda, Maryland, USA, from 16 to 19 Jun 2011 – his first career Major win
- **greatest winning margin in the PGA Championship** (eight strokes), from 9 to 12 Aug 2012 at Kiawah Island in South Carolina, USA
- **youngest winner of the PGA Championship in the strokeplay era** (since 1958), aged 23 years 100 days

What – or who – was your inspiration?
My Dad. He took me to Holywood Golf Club [in Co. Down, Northern Ireland]… and I was given a plastic club and a few air balls – my favourite toys. I was six or seven when I began to take golf very seriously. I was thinking how I could improve and work on weaker parts of my game – which were many, as a seven-year-old…

What do you feel is your greatest tournament to date?
The 2014 PGA at Valhalla [in Kentucky, USA]. On the last day, it was so close and finding that extra something is what really made the victory memorable.

Who are your heroes?
Anybody in sport who has achieved against the odds. My golfing heroes are the likes of Arnold Palmer and Jack Nicklaus, the trailblazers of their day. Today's equivalent is Tiger [Woods]. Almost 20 years after he broke on to the scene, we're all still chasing his records and trying to match his imagination on the course.

How does it feel to be a record-breaker?
It feels really great – but it's also a little funny seeing my name there among all the sportsmen and sportswomen I've always admired. It's sort of inspirational, too… it makes me want to keep trying to set new targets and goals.

Longest golf drive on the European Tour

Nicolas Colsaerts (BEL, above) notched up a 447-yd (408-m) drive at the Wales Open on the Twenty-Ten Course at Celtic Manor in Newport, UK, on 18 Sep 2014.

The **longest golf drive on the PGA Tour** since records began in 1992 is 498 yd (455 m) by Tiger Woods (USA). He achieved his epic drive on the 18th hole of the Plantation Course in the Kapalua Resort, Hawaii, USA, during the 2002 Mercedes Championships.

In 1930, goalie Abie Goldberry **caught fire** in a game when a puck struck a **matchbox** in his pocket

First NHL team to score the season's first goal with a penalty shot

Chris Kelly of the Boston Bruins (USA) scored the first Bruins goal of the season with a penalty against the Tampa Bay Lightning on 3 Oct 2013.

Highest attendance in an NHL season (all teams)

In all, 21,758,902 fans filled NHL arenas during the 2013/14 season, exceeding the previous high of 21,475,223 set in 2008/09.

Longest winning streak by an NHL goaltender

Canadian goaltender Gilles Gilbert won 17 games consecutively while playing for the Boston Bruins from 26 Dec 1975 to 29 Feb 1976.

Most consecutive wins by a rookie goaltender to start an NHL career

Martin Jones (CAN) won the first eight games he started as a rookie for the Los Angeles Kings during the 2013/14 season. This equalled the record set by Bob Froese (CAN) for the Philadelphia Flyers in the 1982/83 season.

Most game-winning goals in an NHL career

Jaromír Jágr (CZE) had 124 goals through 20 seasons and, as of Feb 2015, was adding to his record in his 21st year in the league.

Fastest time to score in an NHL period

James van Riemsdyk (USA) of the Toronto Maple Leafs scored just 4 sec into the second period of a game against the Philadelphia Flyers on 28 Mar 2014. This equalled the National Hockey League (NHL) record first set by Claude Provost of the Montreal Canadiens on 9 Nov 1957 and matched by Denis Savard (both CAN) on 12 Jan 1986.

Most consecutive Game 7 wins in an NHL career

Henrik Lundqvist (SWE) won six Game 7s in a row for the New York Rangers. Since joining them, he has recorded the **most consecutive 30-win seasons to start an NHL goaltender career** too, a run of 30, 37, 37, 38, 35, 36 and 39 wins between the 2005/06 and 2011/12 seasons.

Largest deficit overcome by an NHL team in a postseason series

Four NHL teams have overcome a 3–0 series deficit, winning four straight games to make the ultimate comeback in the best-of-seven-game series. They are: the Toronto Maple Leafs (CAN) over the Detroit Red Wings in 1942; the New York Islanders (USA) over the Pittsburgh Penguins in 1975; the Philadelphia Flyers (USA) over the Boston Bruins in 2010; and, most recently, the Los Angeles Kings (USA, pictured below) over the San Jose Sharks in 2014.

Martin Brodeur: super saver

Goaltending legend Martin Brodeur (CAN) – who retired on 29 Jan 2015 – netted a whole heap of GWR records since his NHL debut for the New Jersey Devils in 1992.

Back in 2003, he achieved the **most shutouts in an NHL playoff season by a goaltender** (7). The following year, Brodeur became the **youngest person to win 400 career matches in the NHL as a goaltender**, aged 31 years 322 days. By Jan 2015, he held NHL goaltending career records for **most saves** (28,928), **most matches won** (691), **most regular-season games played** (1,266) and **most regular-season minutes played** (74,439).

Most game-winning goals in an NHL season

Two players share this record, with 16 each: Phil Esposito (CAN) for the Boston Bruins in the 1970/71 and 1971/72 seasons and Michel Goulet (CAN) of the Quebec Nordiques in 1983/84.

Most shootout goals in an NHL career

A shootout occurs when the score in a game remains tied after an overtime period. Brad Boyes (CAN) and Zach Parise (USA) had each scored 37 shootout goals as of the end of the 2013/14 season.

IN NUMBERS

7 in
Height of the first Stanley Cup (17.7 cm); today's Cup is five times taller

3 in
Diameter of an ice-hockey puck (7.6 cm)

200 ft
Length of regulation North American ice-hockey rinks (61 m)

0.75 in
Depth of ice on a pro ice-hockey rink (2 cm)

-9°C
Temperature of ice on a pro ice-hockey rink (15.8°F)

5–10 lb
Weight a player loses in a game – mostly as sweat (2.25–4.5 kg)

NATIONAL HOCKEY LEAGUE

Most Stanley Cup wins	24	Montreal Canadiens (CAN), 1916–93
Most Stanley Cup Finals appearances	34	Montreal Canadiens, 1916–93
Most games in a career	1,767	Gordie Howe (CAN), from 1946/47 season to 1979/80 season
Longest team winning streak	17	Pittsburgh Penguins (USA), between 9 Mar and 10 Apr 1993
Longest undefeated run	35	Philadelphia Flyers (USA), from 14 Oct 1979 to 6 Jan 1980 (25 wins, 10 ties)
Most goals scored	894	Wayne Gretzky (CAN), from 1979/80 season to 1998/99 season
Most goals in a game (player)	7	Joe Malone (CAN), for Quebec Bulldogs vs Toronto St Patricks on 31 Jan 1920
Most goals in a game (team)	16	Montreal Canadiens, in a 16–3 win vs Quebec Bulldogs on 3 Mar 1920

All statistics correct as of 21 Jan 2015

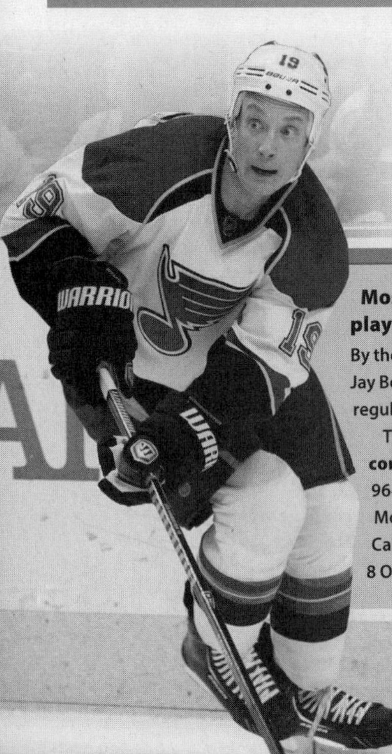

FACT

Since his NHL debut in 2002, Bouwmeester has played for three teams: the Florida Panthers (2002/03–2008/09), Calgary Flames (2009/10–2012/13) and St Louis Blues (2013/14–present).

Most consecutive games played by an NHL defenceman

By the end of the 2013/14 season, Jay Bouwmeester (CAN) had played 717 regular-season games in a row.

The outright record for the **most consecutive NHL games played** is 964, by Doug Jarvis (CAN) for the Montreal Canadiens, Washington Capitals and Hartford Whalers from 8 Oct 1975 to 10 Oct 1987.

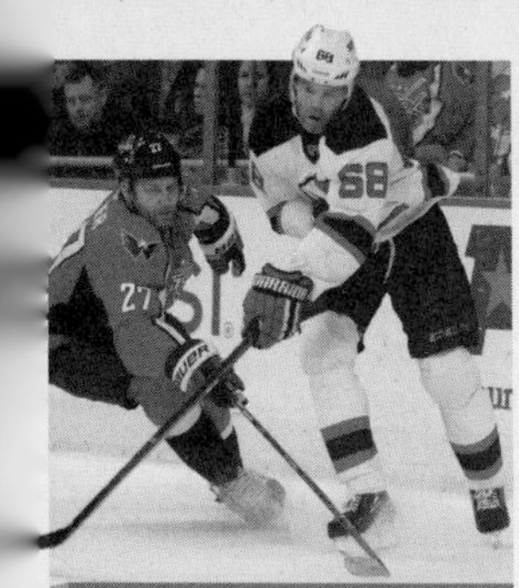

Oldest NHL hattrick scorer

Jaromír Jágr (CZE, above right, b. 15 Feb 1972) was aged 42 years 322 days when he netted three goals for the New Jersey Devils versus the Philadelphia Flyers at the Prudential Center in Newark, New Jersey, USA, on 3 Jan 2015. New Jersey won the game 5–2.

? **GLOSSARY**

Best of seven: The format of the Stanley Cup. Each team plays a series of up to seven matches; four victories win the series and the Cup.

Game 7: The last game in a best-of seven-game series.

Postseason: After the end of a regular NHL season, a group of 16 teams compete in playoffs. The winner is awarded the Stanley Cup.

Shutout: A game in which the goaltender has not conceded a goal.

Nathan MacKinnon

Nathan MacKinnon (CAN, b. 1 Sep 1995) is the youngest winner of the NHL Rookie of the Year award, which he received at the age of 18 years 296 days.

During the 1990s and early 2000s, the Colorado Avalanche were consistently among the NHL's best teams, winning two Stanley Cup titles in a six-year span. But their championship in 2001 was followed by a trophy drought. The Avalanche earned the No.1 pick in the 2013 draft and used it to select Nathan MacKinnon (above and below left), with hopes that the young centre would return the team to relevance in the NHL. He has delivered in a big way, winning the Calder Memorial Trophy for the league's top rookie (first-year player) on 24 Jun 2014.

The young Canadian was a near-unanimous winner, with 130 first-place votes out of a possible 137. MacKinnon finished first among all rookies in points (63), goals (24) and assists (39). By scoring a point in 13 consecutive games, he also achieved the longest single-season points streak by a player aged 18 or younger, surpassing the total of 12 set by Canadian legend Wayne Gretzky.

In his record-breaking rookie season, MacKinnon helped lead the once-dominant franchise back to the playoffs and finished with 10 points in seven playoff games. The future looks bright once again for the Avalanche.

MARATHONS

The first **New York City Marathon** in 1970 attracted 127 runners – **55 finished**

FACT

The ITU (International Triathlon Union) World Triathlon Series comprises eig triathlon events held annual around the world. The athle who wins the most points overall is declared champion.

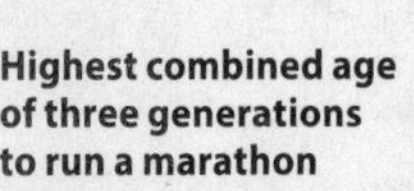

Highest combined age of three generations to run a marathon

Shigetsugu Anan, aged 90 years 51 days, Yasuko Nakatake, aged 54 years 192 days, and Suguru Nakatake, aged 28 years 285 days (all Japan), ran the Tokyo Marathon in Tokyo, Japan, on 22 Feb 2015, with a combined age of 173 years 163 days.

First athletes to win all 4 Deserts races in a calendar year

Vicente Garcia Beneito (ESP) and Anne-Marie Flammersfeld (DEU) won every race of the 2012 edition of the 4 Deserts Race Series in the male and female categories. The four seven-day, 250-km (155-mi) races comprise the Atacama Crossing in Chile, the Gobi March in China, the Sahara Race in Egypt and The Last Desert in Antarctica – some of the driest, windiest, hottest and coldest places on Earth.

Most wins of ITU World Triathlon Series events (male)

Alistair Brownlee (UK) has won 18 events at the annual series organized by the International Triathlon Union (ITU). His first win came in Madrid, Spain, in 2009, and his most recent was achieved in Cape Town, South Africa, on 26 Apr 2015.

Largest ultramarathon

The 89 km (56 mi) Comrades Marathon in South Africa usually attracts around 20,000 entrants. The number for the 2015 marathon was capped at 23,000.

Fastest time to complete...

- **A marathon by a linked team:** 2 hr 54 min 17 sec, by Team Legati De Cauza Hospice (ROM) in Bucharest, Romania, on 6 Oct 2013.
- **A marathon by a relay team (male):** 2 hr 4 min 32 sec, by Al Wafa Marathon (UAE) in Al Ain, UAE, on 26 Mar 2014.
- **A marathon by a relay team (female):** 3 hr 9 min 2 sec, by the Piemonte Dream Team (ITA) at the Turin Ring Marathon in Turin, Italy, on 26 Feb 2012.
- **An ironman triathlon (male):** 7 hr 45 min 58 sec, by Marino Vanhoenacker (BEL) at Ironman Austria in Klagenfurt, Austria, on 3 Jul 2011.
- **The London Wheelchair Marathon (male):** 1 hr 28 min 57 sec, by Kurt Fearnley (AUS) on 26 Apr 2009.

First person to win the Berlin, New York and London marathons

Wilson Kipsang (KEN) won the 2014 New York City Marathon in New York, USA, on 2 Nov 2014, following victories at the London Marathon in the UK (2012 and 2014) and the Berlin Marathon in 2013 – three of the six World Marathon Majors.

Most ITU World Triathlon Series wins (male)

The 2014 Series saw Javier Gómez (ESP) become champion for the fourth time, having won in 2008, 2010 and 2013 – a record previously set by Simon Lessing (UK). Gómez has also won the **most medals in the ITU World Triathlon Series**: eight, from 2007 to 2014.

- **The London Wheelchair Marathon (female):** 1 hr 45 min 12 sec, by Tatyana McFadden (USA) in London, UK, on 13 Apr 2014.
- **The Berlin Inline Skating Marathon (male):** 58 min 10 sec, by Bart Swings (BEL).
- **The Berlin Inline Skating Marathon (female):** 1 hr 7 min 44 sec, by Manon Kamminga (NLD). Both records were set in Berlin, Germany, on 27 Sep 2014.

IN NUMBERS

40,600
Most runners to finish the Chicago Marathon, in Illinois, USA, on 12 Oct 2014

500 m
Depth below sea level of the **deepest marathon** (1,640 ft), held at an old salt mine in Thuringia, Germany

13
Most medals won at the IAAF World Half Marathon Championships (male), by Zersenay Tadese (ERI) in 2006–14

163.785 km
Farthest distance run in 12 hours on a track (101.771 mi), by Zach Bitter (USA) in Phoenix, Arizona, USA, on 14 Dec 2013

5,164
Number of steps climbed in the Great Wall Marathon in China

7
Marathons completed by Sir Ranulph Fiennes (UK) in 2003, on seven continents in seven days

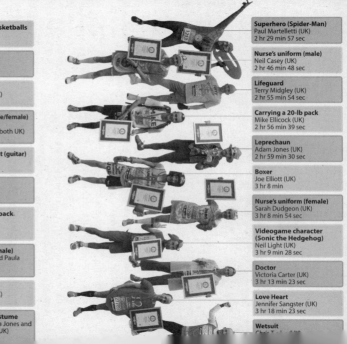

Superhero (Spider-Man)
Paul Martelletti (UK)
2 hr 29 min 57 sec

Nurse's uniform (male)
Neil Casey (UK)
2 hr 46 min 48 sec

Lifeguard
Terry Midgley (UK)
2 hr 55 min 54 sec

Carrying a 20-lb pack
Mike Ellicock (UK)
2 hr 56 min 39 sec

Leprechaun
Adam Jones (UK)
2 hr 59 min 30 sec

Boxer
Joe Elliott (UK)
3 hr 8 min

Nurse's uniform (female)
Sarah Dudgeon (UK)
3 hr 8 min 54 sec

Videogame character (Sonic the Hedgehog)
Neil Light (UK)
3 hr 9 min 28 sec

Doctor
Victoria Carter (UK)
3 hr 13 min 23 sec

Love Heart
Jennifer Sangster (UK)
3 hr 18 min 23 sec

Wetsuit

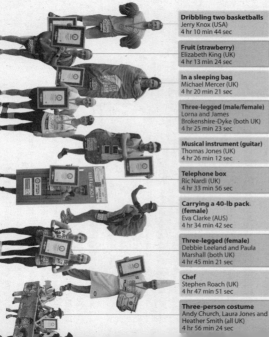

Dribbling two basketballs
Jerry Knox (USA)
4 hr 10 min 44 sec

Fruit (strawberry)
Elizabeth King (UK)
4 hr 13 min 24 sec

In a sleeping bag
Michael Mercer (UK)
4 hr 20 min 21 sec

Three-legged (male/female)
Lorna and James Brokenshire-Dyke (both UK)
4 hr 25 min 23 sec

Musical instrument (guitar)
Thomas Jones (UK)
4 hr 26 min 12 sec

Telephone box
Ric Nardi (UK)
4 hr 33 min 56 sec

Carrying a 40-lb pack (female)
Eva Clarke (AUS)
4 hr 34 min 42 sec

Three-legged (female)
Debbie Leeland and Paula Marshall (both UK)
4 hr 45 min 21 sec

Chef
Stephen Roach (UK)
4 hr 47 min 51 sec

Three-person costume
Andy Church, Laura Jones and Heather Smith (all UK)
4 hr 56 min 24 sec

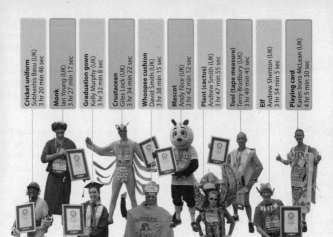

Cricket uniform
Subhashis Basu (UK)
3 hr 20 min 46 sec

Monk
Ian Young (UK)
3 hr 27 min 17 sec

Graduation gown
Kelly Murphy (UK)
3 hr 32 min 8 sec

Crustacean
Giles Lock (UK)
3 hr 34 min 22 sec

Whoopee cushion
David Smith (UK)
3 hr 38 min 15 sec

Mascot
Andy Nice (UK)
3 hr 42 min 12 sec

Plant (cactus)
Andrew Smith (UK)
3 hr 47 min 55 sec

Tool (tape measure)
Terry Bradbury (UK)
3 hr 49 min 45 sec

Elf
Andrew Shenton (UK)
3 hr 54 min 5 sec

Playing card
Karen Irons-McLean (UK)
4 hr 5 min 30 sec

3D bird
Bob Johnson (UK)
5 hr 50 min 8 sec

Carrying an 80-lb pack
Marc Jenner (UK)
5 hr 53 min 20 sec

Bomb disposal suit
Iain Church (UK)
6 hr 28 min 6 sec

2015 Virgin Money London Marathon: new records

Marathon running is a serious business for elite athletes, but for others it is a great excuse to have fun and raise money for charity at the world's premier marathon event: the London Marathon. Here are some of this year's colourful characters, in order of their running times.

Dennis Kimetto

In 2014, for the third time in four years, a new record was set for marathon running. And for the third time in four years, it was achieved by a Kenyan at the Berlin Marathon.

At 30 years old, Dennis Kimetto earned his place in history on 28 Sep 2014, in perfect running conditions, by completing the Berlin Marathon in 2 hr 2 min 57 sec (below) – the **fastest marathon**. It was 26 sec less than the previous record of 2 hr 3 min 23 sec, achieved by Wilson Kipsang at the 2013 Berlin Marathon (see p.523). Previously, the honours had gone to Patrick Makau, who ran a time of 2 hr 3 min 38 sec in 2011, also in Berlin.

The one recent year in which no record was set was 2012, when Kimetto made his marathon debut. That year, he finished in second place, losing by just 1 sec to his team-mate Geoffrey Mutai. In fact, Kimetto only began serious training in 2010, after a chance encounter with Mutai, who trained athletes in Kenya. Fast-forward to 2014, and both Kimetto and another Kenyan, Emmanuel Mutai, broke Kipsang's marathon record – Kimetto finishing 16 sec faster than Mutai.

The record for **fastest marathon** has now been broken six times in an 11-year period, all at the Berlin Marathon. That's a huge tribute to contemporary athletes' fitness, but the course does offer certain advantages to runners. It has a flat terrain with relatively few corners to negotiate, for example, and is staged at a time of year when temperatures are usually mild.

Fastest half-marathon...

- **On crutches:** 2 hr 31 min 59 sec, by Larry Chloupek II (USA) in Washington DC, USA, on 15 Mar 2014.
- **Running backwards (male):** 1 hr 40 min 29 sec, by Achim Aretz (DEU) at the 19th TUSEM August Blumensaat in Essen, North Rhine-Westphalia, Germany, on 28 Nov 2009.
- **In a two-person pantomime costume:** 2 hr 3 min 20 sec, by Stephen McAdam and Nathan Saber (both AUS) in Geelong, Victoria, Australia, on 15 Apr 2012.
- **In superhero costume (male):** 1 hr 17 min 30 sec, by Stephane Hetherington (CAN) in Toronto, Canada, on 19 Oct 2014.

Most wins of ITU World Triathlon Series events (female)

From 19 Apr 2013 to 4 Sep 2014, Gwen Jorgensen (USA) won eight events: three in the 2013 series and five in 2014. These more recent five wins represent the **most wins of ITU World Triathlon Series events in a single season (female).**

ROAD RACING

Race	Men	Name/Nationality	Date	Women	Name/ Nationality	Date
10 km	0:26:44	Leonard Komon (KEN)	26 Sep 2010	0:30:21	Paula Radcliffe (UK)	23 Feb 2003
15 km	0:41:13	Leonard Komon (KEN)	21 Nov 2010	0:46:14	Florence Kiplagat (KEN)	15 Feb 2015
20 km	0:55:21	Zersenay Tadese (ERI)	21 Mar 2010	1:01:54	Florence Kiplagat (KEN)	15 Feb 2015
Half-marathon	0:58:23	Zersenay Tadese (ERI)	21 Mar 2010	1:05:09	Florence Kiplagat (KEN)	15 Feb 2015
25 km	1:11:18	Dennis Kimetto (KEN)	6 May 2012	1:19:53	Mary Keitany (KEN)	9 May 2010
30 km	1:27:37	Geoffrey Kamworor (KEN)	28 Sep 2014	1:38:29	Deena Kastor (USA)	9 Oct 2005
30 km	1:27:37	Abera Kuma (ETH)	28 Sep 2014	-	n/a	-
30 km	1:27:37	Emmanuel Mutai (KEN)	28 Sep 2014	-	n/a	-
Marathon	2:02:57	Dennis Kimetto (KEN)	28 Sep 2014	2:15:25	Paula Radcliffe (UK)	13 Apr 2003
100 km	6:13:33	Takahiro Sunada (JPN)	21 Jun 1998	6:33:11	Tomoe Abe (JPN)	25 Jun 2000

Statistics correct as of 8 Apr 2015

Most runners in a marathon

A record total of 50,564 out of 50,869 starters completed the New York City Marathon in New York, USA, on 2 Nov 2014. There were 30,144 male and 20,420 female finishers from 130 countries and all 50 US states. Mary Keitany (KEN) won the women's race, while the men's race was won by Wilson Kipsang (KEN, see p.523)

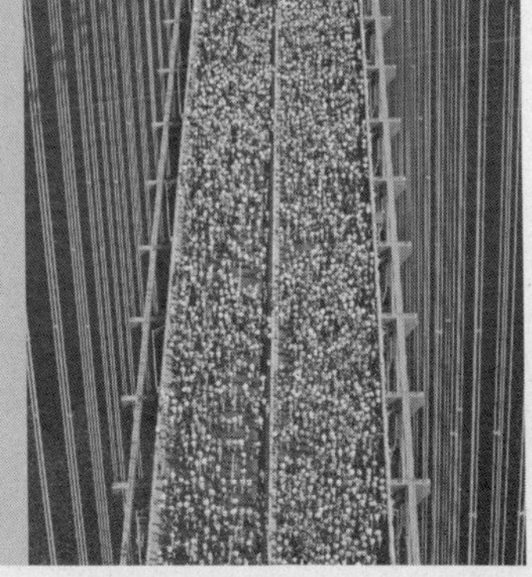

Formula One **car engines** last for just **two hours** of racing

CARS

Most Formula One Grand Prix career wins by a driver

Michael Schumacher (DEU) won 91 Grands Prix between 30 Aug 1992 and 1 Oct 2006. The **most points scored in a Formula One (F1) career** is 1,767, by Fernando Alonso (ESP) between the 2003 and 2014 seasons.

Germany's Sebastian Vettel picked up 397 points in 2013, the **most points scored by a driver in an F1 season**.

Most consecutive F1 Grand Prix finishes from debut

Racing for Marussia, Max Chilton (UK) had 25 F1 Grand Prix (GP) finishes from his debut on 17 Mar 2013 to 25 May 2014.

Most consecutive F1 GP points finishes

Kimi Räikkönen (FIN) achieved 27 consecutive finishes in the top 10 between the Bahrain Grand Prix on 22 Apr 2012 and the Hungarian GP on 28 Jul 2013. His streak ended, with tyre failure during the Belgian GP on 25 Aug.

The **most consecutive F1 finishes** is 41 by Nick Heidfeld (DEU), logged between the 2007 French GP and the 2009 Italian GP.

FACT

Formula One is the premier class of single-seater motor racing. The word "formula" refers to the regulations to which all teams and vehicles must adhere. The "one" simply means it is the top class.

Most consecutive seasons to win a Formula One Grand Prix from debut

The 2008 and 2014 world champion Lewis Hamilton (UK, below) made his F1 Grand Prix debut in 2007 with his first win on 10 Jun of that year, driving for McLaren. Hamilton went on to win at least one Grand Prix in the eight successive seasons up to and including his victory in a Mercedes at the Grand Prix in Sepang, Malaysia, on 30 Mar 2014.

Most wins in the modern NASCAR era (1972–present)

Jeff Gordon (USA) won his 92nd race in the AAA 400 at Dover International Speedway in Dover, Delaware, USA, on 28 Sep 2014.

Longest active NASCAR team

As of 2014, Wood Brothers Racing (USA) had competed regularly in NASCAR since they were formed in 1950 – a total of 64 years.

Most IndyCar Series race winners in a single season

There were 11 different IndyCar Series winners in 2000 and 2001, a feat most recently matched in 2014.

Most NHRA Top Fuel Drag Racing Championships

Tony Schumacher (USA) has eight titles: 1999, 2004–09 and 2014. He has driven for the US Army Drag Racing team since 2000.

Most IndyCar Series race wins in a career

Scott Dixon (NZ) enjoyed 34 race wins from 2 Mar 2003 to 24 Aug 2014. Since the inception of the IndyCar Series in 1996, no other driver has won 30 races. His closest rival at the end of the 2014 Series was Brazil's Hélio Castroneves, with 23 wins.

First all-electric car championship

The first racing series featuring only electric vehicles is the Formula E Championship. Approved by the Fédération Internationale de l'Automobile (FIA), it began in Beijing, China, on 13 Sep 2014 and comprised nine rounds staged on four continents. Former Formula One drivers including Nelson Piquet Jr and Nick Heidfeld participated in the inaugural season, which lasted until 27 Jun 2015.

CARS

Most wins in an NHRA drag racing career

From 1990 to 3 Aug 2014, John Force (USA) won 141 Funny Car races.

BIKES

Most MotoGP championships won

Italy's Valentino Rossi won a total of six MotoGP championships, in 2002–05 and 2008–09.

The **most MotoGP championships won by a constructor** is eight, achieved by Honda (JPN) in 2002–04, 2006 and 2011–14.

Most MotoGP wins in a season by an individual

Marc Márquez (ESP) won his 13th race of the 2014 MotoGP season in Valencia, Spain, on 9 Nov 2014.

Fastest Isle of Man TT Superbike race

On 2 Jun 2013, Michael Dunlop (UK) completed the six laps of the Isle of Man TT Superbike race in Douglas on the Isle of Man, UK, in 1 hr 45 min 29.98 sec on a 1,000-cc TT Legends Honda.

FACT

For some turns, MotoGP riders lean their bikes at an angle of around 60°. Depending on conditions, their tyres can reach temperatures of 200–240°F (93.3–115.5°C) during a race.

Most consecutive MotoGP wins in a season by an individual

Giacomo Agostini (ITA) won 10 consecutive MotoGP races in 1968, 1969 and 1970. His record was equalled by Australia's Mick Doohan in 1997 and by Marc Márquez (ESP, left) from 23 Mar to 10 Aug 2014.

On 10 Nov 2013, Márquez (b. 17 Feb 1993) had become the **youngest MotoGP world champion**, aged 20 years 266 days.

Most wins of the Brickyard 400 NASCAR Sprint Cup race

The Brickyard 400 is a 400-mi (643-km) race held at the Indianapolis Motor Speedway in Indiana, USA, and is currently the NASCAR race that offers the second-highest purse, behind the Daytona 500. Jeff Gordon (USA) has won the race five times altogether, driving for Hendrick Motorsports, in 1994, 1998, 2001, 2004 and 2014.

The **fastest lap by a rider at the Isle of Man TT in the Superbike class** is 17 min 6.68 sec, by Bruce Anstey (NZ) riding a Honda CBR1000RR in Douglas on 31 May 2014.

The **most events won in one year at the Isle of Man TT** is five (Senior, Superbike, Superstock and Supersport 1 and 2), by Ian Hutchinson (UK) in Jun 2010. This memorable achievement also represents the **most consecutive wins at the Isle of Man TT**.

Youngest person to start the Le Mans 24-hour race

On 14 Jun 2014, Matthew McMurry (USA, b. 24 Nov 1997) began the Le Mans 24-hour race in France, driving for Caterham Racing, aged 16 years 202 days. The next day, he became the **youngest person to finish the Le Mans 24-hour race**, aged 16 years 203 days.

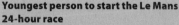

IN NUMBERS

0.8 sec
Time it takes for an NHRA dragster to accelerate from 0 to 100 mph (160 km/h)

2.05 sec
Fastest F1 pit stop, by Infiniti Red Bull Racing (AUT) at the Malaysian Grand Prix on 24 Mar 2013

8
Number of times the length of the Le Mans 24-hour circuit has changed; it is currently 8.45 mi (13.59 km)

10
Flags used in F1 races

37.73 mi
Length of the Isle of Man TT course (60.72 km), the **longest motorcycle race circuit** (see p.532)

264
Number of corners on the Isle of Man TT course

43
Maximum number of cars in a NASCAR race

Isle of Man TT

Racing on public roads was banned in Britain by an act of Parliament, and in 1903 a speed limit of 20 mph (32 km/h) became law. But authorities on the Isle of Man (located in the Irish Sea, UK) proved more flexible...

In 1904, racing cars took to the roads of the Isle of Man, and on 28 May 1907 came the first Isle of Man Tourist Trophy (TT) race for motorbikes. The Snaefell Mountain Course was added in 1911, though at first vehicles struggled with the circuit. It was little more than a dirt track in places and included gates between fields. The lead rider opened them; the last rider closed them again.

With circuit and vehicle improvements, lap speeds increased. By 1920, the course record was 52.62 mph (84.68 km/h); by 1939 it was 90 mph (144 km/h), and in 1957 Bob McIntyre (UK) recorded the first official 100-mph (160-km/h) lap.

For many, the TT's golden years were the late 1950s and early 1960s, with legends such as the UK's Mike Hailwood (a 14-time TT winner) and Italy's Giacomo Agostini (10 wins, 1966–72). The year 1977 saw the first win for Joey Dunlop (UK, below), who claimed six consecutive TT titles during the 1980s and set a new lap record of more than 115 mph (185 km/h) in 1980. By 2000, he had the **most TT races career wins**: 26.

Carl Fogarty and Steve Hislop (both UK) lit up the 1990s, but since 2000, John McGuinness (UK, above) has led the field with 21 wins – his most recent victory being the 2014 TT Zero on 4 Jun 2014.

Competitors need world-record bravery too. The twisting course, partly hemmed in by buildings and walls, has seen the deaths of nearly 250 riders since 1911.

Youngest driver to claim an F1 World Championship point

Max Verstappen (NLD, b. 30 Sep 1997) was aged 17 years 180 days when he finished seventh in the Malaysian Grand Prix, driving for Toro Rosso-Renault on 29 Mar 2015.

Most Sidecarcross World Championships by a driver

Also known as the Sidecar Motocross World Championships, this annual event dates back to 1980 and is run by the Fédération Internationale de Motocyclisme (FIM). Daniël Willemsen (NLD) has won 10 times, racing with passengers including Marcel Willemsen (1999), Kaspars Stupelis (2003–04), Sven Verbrugge (2005–06 and 2011), Reto Grütter (2007–08), Gertie Eggink (2010) and Kenny Van Gaalen (2012).

The Rio 2016 Games with be the **31st** modern Summer Olympiad

Most individual Olympic medals

Larisa Latynina (USSR/now UKR) won 14 medals in individual events at the Olympic Games between 1956 and 1964. She won a further four medals in team events.

To the right, Latynina is seen at the 1956 Summer Olympics in Melbourne, Victoria, Australia. Below, she is seen competing at the 1964 Tokyo Games on the uneven bars, in the Women's Artistic Gymnastics Individual All-Around event.

Largest attendance at an Olympic Games

A total of 8.3 million tickets were sold for the 1996 Games in Atlanta, Georgia, USA – often referred to as the "Centennial Olympics". This equates to more than half a million spectators watching on each day of the two-week event. Approximately 11 million tickets were sold for the London 2012 Olympics and Paralympics. An estimated 7.5 million tickets will be made available for Rio 2016, of which around 3.8 million will cost less than $30 (£19).

Most countries at a Summer Olympic Games

A total of 204 National Olympic Committees (NOCs) were represented at the 2008 Summer Olympics, which were staged in Beijing, China.

Three countries – Montenegro, the Marshall Islands and Tuvalu – took part in the Games for the first time that year after being recognized as NOCs in 2008, 2006 and 2008 respectively.

Longest distance travelled during the Olympic torch relay

The torch relay for the XXIX Olympic Summer Games in Beijing, China, covered 137,000 km (85,000 mi). The relay began in Athens, Greece, on 24 Mar 2008, visited 21 countries and reached Beijing National Stadium for the opening ceremony on 8 Aug 2008. This picture shows climbers bearing Olympic torches on top of Mount Everest.

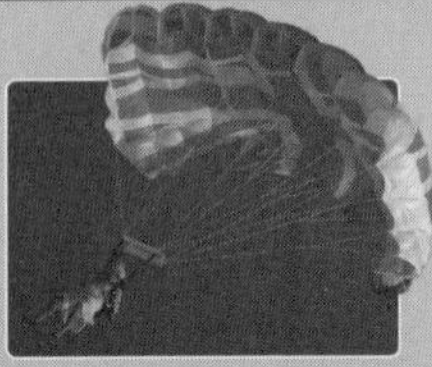

Most Summer Olympic Games opened by an individual

HM Queen Elizabeth II opened the 1976 Montreal Games (below inset) and 36 years later, on 27 Jul 2012, inaugurated the 2012 Games in London, UK (main picture). The photo left shows stuntman Gary Connery as the Queen, parachuting into the Olympic Stadium in Stratford, London, for the 2012 opening ceremony.

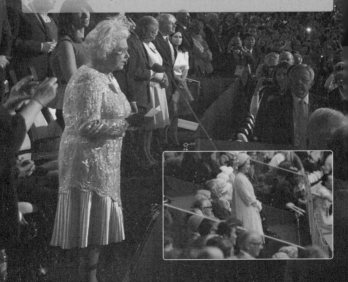

SUMMER OLYMPICS HALL OF FAME

The most successful Olympians in the Summer Games by total medals won

	Name	Date	Medals	G	S	B
1	Michael Phelps (USA)	2004–12	22	18	2	2
2	Larisa Latynina (USSR/now UKR)	1956–64	18	9	5	4
3	Nikolay Andrianov (USSR/RUS)	1972–80	15	7	5	3
4	Boris Shakhlin (USSR/UKR)	1956–64	13	7	4	2
	Edoardo Mangiarotti (ITA)	1936–60	13	6	5	2
	Takashi Ono (JPN)	1952–64	13	5	4	4
7	Paavo Nurmi (FIN)	1920–28	12	9	3	0
	Birgit Fischer (GDR/DEU)	1980–2004	12	8	4	0
	Sawao Kato (JPN)	1968–76	12	8	3	1
	Jenny Thompson (USA)	1992–2004	12	8	3	1
	Dara Torres (USA)	1984–2008	12	4	4	4
	Alexei Nemov (RUS)	1996–2000	12	4	2	6
	Natalie Coughlin (USA)	2004–12	12	3	4	5

Source: olympic.org

Most appearances by an Olympian

Canadian equestrian Ian Millar, aka "Captain Canada", made his 10th Olympic appearance when he rode for his country's show-jumping team at the London 2012 Games on 4 Aug, aged 65. Millar's first taste of the Olympics came in 1972, aged 25 (inset). He went on to appear at eight consecutive Games from 1984 to 2012.

IN NUMBERS

1984
First year that China won an Olympic medal

386
Olympic medals won by China

4
Times the USA has hosted the Summer Games – **the most by any country**

13
Nations who competed at the first modern Games in 1896 in Athens, Greece

204
Nations who competed at the 2008 Games in Beijing, China

0
Female athletes allowed to compete in the 1896 Games

4,847
Female athletes who competed at the London 2012 Olympics

Altogether, 166 National Paralympic Committees (NPCs) sent athletes to the 201 Paralympic Games in London, UK, the **most countries at a Summer Paralympic Games** Fifteen countries – including eight from Africa – were competing at a Summer Paralympic Games for the first time: Antigua & Barbuda, Brunei, Cameroon, Comoros, Djibouti, the Democratic Republic of the Congo, Gambia, Guinea-Bissau, Liberia, Malawi, Mozambique North Korea, San Marino, the Solomon Islands and the US Virgin Islands.

Both these records look set to be broken at Rio 2016: 205 countries are scheduled to participate in the Olympics, with 176 scheduled for the Paralympics.

In all, 2.7 million tickets were bought for the 2012 Paralympic Games in London, UK, the **most tickets sold for a Paralympic Games** and the first sell-out in the 52-year history of the event. The original allocation of 2.5 million tickets sold out during the Games but seating plans were fine-tuned and another 200,000 tickets were subsequently made available.

The **most medals won at the Summer Paralympics by a country** is 2,067, achieved by the USA from 1960 to 2012.

Most events at an Olympics

According to the official Rio 2016 website, 306 medal events are scheduled for the XXXI Olympiad in Rio de Janeiro, Brazil.

First return to an Olympic city

Hosting the Olympics in 1900 and 1924, Paris became the first city to hold the Games twice. In 1924, France also held the inaugural Winter Olympics, in Chamonix in the French Alps, becoming the **first nation to host both the Summer and Winter Games in the same year**. The feat was matched by the USA in 1932 and by Germany in 1936.

Most Olympic golds won at a Games

Between 9 and 17 Aug 2008 at the Beijing Games, Michael Phelps (USA) won gold in eight swimming disciplines: 400 m individual medley, 100 m freestyle relay, 200 m freestyle, 200 m butterfly, 200 m freestyle relay, 200 m individual medley, 100 m butterfly and 100 m medley relay. His overall haul of 13 medals at three Games also represents the **most individual Olympic medals (male).**

FACT

Phelps's four golds at London 2012 outstripped the total gold hauls of – among others – Spain, Brazil and South Africa (with three each) and Denmark, Poland and Norway (with two each).

Oldest Summer Olympic Games gold medallist (female)

Sybil "Queenie" Newall (UK, b. 17 Oct 1854) won a gold medal in the Double National Round discipline in the archery event at the 1908 Olympic Games at White City in London, UK, on 18 Jul 1908. She was aged 53 years 275 days at the time.

Newall's victory marked the last time a female British archer would win an Olympic medal until Alison Williamson secured bronze in 2004.

The road to Rio 2016

Having staged a memorable FIFA World Cup in 2014, Rio de Janeiro turns its attention to the small matter of hosting the Olympic Games (5 to 21 Aug 2016), followed by the Paralympics (7 to 18 Sep). It's the first time that the Olympics and Paralympics have been held in South America, and official mascots Vinicius (left, representing Brazil's fauna) and Tom (right, representing its flora) seem delighted at the prospect...

During the 17 days of the Olympics, Rio will host 10,500 athletes from 205 countries, who will compete in 42 sports. Some 1.8 million tickets will be made available for the Paralympics, which will see 4,350 athletes from 176 nations compete in 528 medal events.

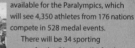

There will be 34 sporting venues for the Olympics (21 for the Paralympics), mostly in four different areas of Rio. Additional venues located in four other Brazilian cities will help to stage the Olympic soccer matches.

Rio 2016 also marks the return of two sports to the Olympics: rugby (after a 92-year break) and golf (last contested by Olympians 112 years ago). Meanwhile, the Paralympics welcome two entirely new sports: paracanoe and paratriathlon.

Of course, such a sporting extravaganza doesn't come cheap. By Apr 2014, the cost of the Games was estimated at 36.7 bn reais ($16.3 bn; £9.7 bn).

The whistle first used by **Welsh referee Gil Evans** in 1905 is blown to **kick off** every Rugby World Cup tournament

First Rugby World Cup try

Michael Jones (NZ), playing for the All Blacks against Italy, was the first player to score a World Cup try, in Auckland, New Zealand, on 22 May 1987.

First English Premiership rugby union final decided in extra time

The 2013–14 final between Northampton Saints and Saracens at Twickenham in London, UK, on 31 May 2014, ran to 100 min. In the very last minute, the Saints secured their first ever Premiership win (24–20).

Tallest active English Premiership rugby union player

Will Carrick-Smith (UK, below, holding ball) measures 2.11 m (6 ft 11 in) in height and plays for the Exeter Chiefs as of the 2014–15 season. Like nearly all the tallest players in rugby union, he plays as a lock in the second row.

The **tallest international rugby union player ever** is Richard Metcalfe (UK), at 2.13 m (7 ft) in height. He played nine Tests for Scotland in 2000–01.

FACT

The first rugby balls were made from pigs' bladders encased in leather, then inflated by blowing through a clay tube – a smelly and potentially hazardous job if the bladder was diseased.

Most appearances by a team in the Women's Rugby World Cup final

Since the first "unofficial" Women's World Cup in Wales in 1991, England have been in every final except in 1998, making a total of six appearances. They have won the trophy twice: in 1994, beating the USA 38–23, and in 2014, beating Canada 21–9. New Zealand have won the **most Women's Rugby World Cup titles:** four (1998–2010).

First season in the National Rugby League (NRL) with no sendings-off

The 2014 season of the NRL in Australia was the first with no dismissals in the league's 106-year history. The competition in its current format began in 1998, when there were 17 sendings-off.

MOST...

Australian National Rugby League titles won by a team

From the inaugural 1908–09 season, when the competition was known as the New South Wales Rugby League, the South Sydney Rabbitohs had won 21 titles up to 2014.

Rugby league World Club Challenge wins

A total of three wins was first achieved by Wigan (UK) in 1987, 1991 and 1994, and equalled by the Bradford Bulls (UK) in 2002, 2004 and 2006, and by their neighbours the Leeds Rhinos in 2005, 2008 and 2012. Most recently, the Sydney Roosters (AUS) matched it in 1976, 2003 and 2014.

MOST...

Points scored in a rugby league Challenge Cup match (individual)

On 6 Mar 2011, in the third round of the 2011 Challenge Cup at Huntington Stadium in York, UK, Chris Thorman (UK) scored 54 points, helping the York City Knights to beat Northumbria University 132–0. This result brought the Knights the **highest score in a rugby league Challenge Cup match (team)**.

Tries scored in a Super League career

Half-back Danny McGuire (UK) scored 215 tries for Leeds Rhinos from 22 Jun 2002 to 12 Sep 2014. In 2005 alone, he scored 23 tries in 27 appearances. His total broke the record

Most appearances in a rugby union Super Rugby career

On 7 Mar 2015, Keven Mealamu (NZ) led out the Blues against the Lions in his 163rd Super Rugby game, surpassing Nathan Sharpe (AUS) by one match. Mealamu has also made the **most Super Rugby appearances for a team:** 152 for Auckland's Blues.

FACT

When Mealamu was first called up to start for the Blues in 2000, he was so excited that he left his boots at the hotel. Fortunately, he was able to borrow a spare pair from one of his team-mates.

First player sent off in a Super League final

On 11 Oct 2014, Ben Flower (UK), playing for Wigan Warriors against St Helens at Old Trafford in Manchester, UK, was sent off after just 3 min for punching Kiwi opponent Lance Hohaia as he lay on the ground. With one player short, Wigan went on to lose the match 14–6.

Most tries in a rugby league World Club Challenge match by an individual

Michael Jennings (AUS), playing for the Sydney Roosters against Wigan Warriors, scored a hat-trick at Sydney Football Stadium in Australia on 22 Feb 2014. Jennings' performance helped his team to win a third title.

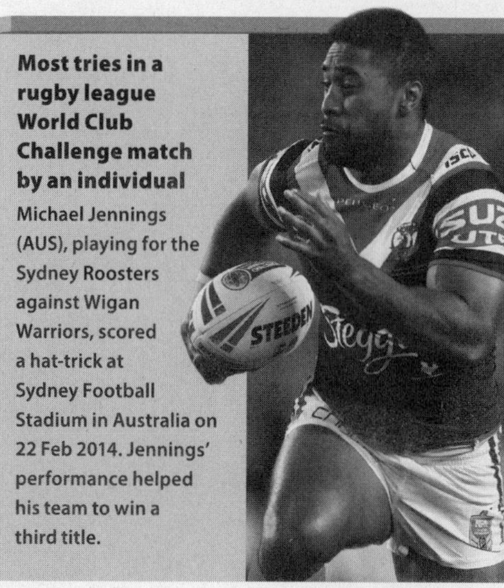

IN NUMBERS

61,823
Largest attendance at a rugby union Super Rugby match: the 2014 final between the Waratahs (AUS) and the Crusaders (NZ) in Sydney, Australia

39
Highest margin of victory in a rugby league World Club Challenge match, when South Sydney Rabbitohs (AUS) beat St Helens (UK) 39–0 on 22 Feb 2015

3
Number of countries whose national sport is rugby: New Zealand, Wales and Madagascar

4
Olympic Games at which rugby has been contested: in 1900, 1908, 1920 and 1924

58
Most penalty goals kicked at the Rugby World Cup, by Jonny Wilkinson (UK)

40 years 26 days
Age of the **oldest player to appear in a Rugby World Cup match**: Diego Ormaechea (URY), versus South Africa on 15 Oct 1999

of former team-mate Keith Senior, who had scored 199 tries as of 2011.

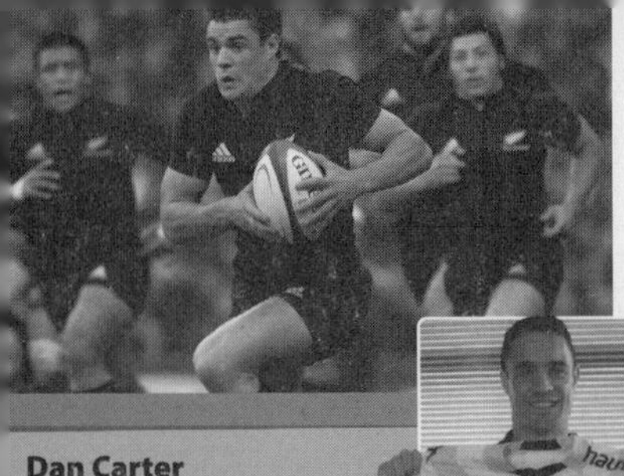

Dan Carter

The Kiwi fly-half will become the highest-paid rugby union player ever when he joins Top 14 club Racing Metro in Paris, France, in Oct 2015. He has signed a three-year contract and will reportedly earn a salary of 1,500,000 euros (£790,000; $1,670,570).

Going into 2015, Carter had achieved the **most conversions** (260), the **most penalties** (258) and the **most points in an international rugby union career** (1,457), which for him spanned 12 years and brought him 102 caps. His speed and tactical awareness make him much more than just an outstanding kicker, and at present the 33-year-old has a fantastic 88.72% win rate in international rugby. Carter has won the World Cup once, in 2011, and also scored the **most points in The Rugby Championship (formerly Tri Nations)** – 531 – playing in 11 of those tournaments.

At club level, he has won four Super Rugby championships with the Canterbury-based Crusaders, the **most successful team in the competition's history**, with seven titles. Carter is one of just nine players to have appeared for the club on more than 100 occasions. He will now hope to set even more records in France with Racing Metro.

Games unbeaten in international rugby union in a calendar year

In the 2013 season, the All Blacks (NZ), aided not least by key player Dan Carter (see left), were undefeated in all 14 games, the first time this has happened since international rugby began. The clinching victory, by a slender two-point margin (24–22), came against Ireland at the Aviva Stadium in Dublin on 24 Nov 2013.

Most appearances in the Super League Grand Final

In 1999–2014, Paul Wellens (UK, below) played with St Helens 10 times to win five titles. And in 2001–12, Jamie Peacock (UK) won eight titles in 10 games with Bradford Bulls and Leeds Rhinos.

CLUB SOCCER

Legendary Brazilian player **Pelé** was the first to call soccer **"the beautiful game"** – "o jogo bonito"

Most Champions League goals

As of 6 May 2015, Lionel Messi (ARG) had scored 77 goals for Barcelona in UEFA Champions League matches, one more than Cristiano Ronaldo (PRT), formerly of Manchester United and now of Real Madrid. Messi scored five goals in a single game, a joint record (see p.545), and a decisive double against Bayern Munich in the semi-final.

Most away goals scored in an English Premier League season by a club

On 5 May 2014, Liverpool scored three times against Crystal Palace to bring them 48 away goals in the 2013–14 season. They scored three or more goals in 10 of their 19 away games, overtaking Manchester United's 2001–02 record by a single goal.

Fastest English Premier League goal by a substitute from kick-off

On 11 Feb 2015, Manchester United's Chris Smalling (UK) headed a record-breaking goal just 5 min 9 sec into a match against Burnley, (having come on as a substitute 22 sec earlier). The game took place at Old Trafford in Manchester, UK. He scored again before half-time, achieving the **most goals in the first half of an English Premier League match by a sub**.

Highest total spend in a single transfer window (same division)

A reported sum of £835 m ($1.34 bn) was splashed out collectively by the English Premier League in the summer transfer window from 1 Jul to 1 Sep 2014. The amount smashed the previous record, also held by the Premier League, of £603 m ($901 m) and easily out-spent the other major European leagues. Manchester United spent the most: around £150 m ($221 m), with half of that sum reported to have gone towards Argentine winger Ángel Di María.

Most wins in a single Ligue 1 season by a team

During the 2013–14 season, Paris Saint-Germain (FRA) won 27 games. The only team they failed to beat was AS Monaco. They drew eight games, lost three and earned the **most points in a single Ligue 1 season by a team** (89).

Most European Cups/Champions Leagues won by a football manager

The highly respected Carlo Ancelotti (ITA) has achieved three wins, with AC Milan (ITA) in 2003 and 2007, and Real Madrid (ESP) in 2014. The record is shared with Bob Paisley (UK) as manager of Liverpool (UK) in 1977–78 and 1981.

Most appearances in the Italian Serie A by a foreign player

From 27 Aug 1995 to 18 May 2014, Javier Zanetti (ARG) made 615 appearances for Inte Milan. In that period, he won the Serie A five times and the Coppa Italia four times, along with the UEFA Cup, the Champions League and the Club World Cup. As of 2014, he had also played the most games for the Argentina national team.

Fastest time to be sent off in a Copa Libertadores match

On 11 Mar 2014, while playing for Atlético Nacional against Nacional de Uruguay in Medellín, Colombia, Alejandro Bernal (COL) was shown the red card after 27 sec.

MOST GOALS...

In a La Liga career

Between 1 May 2005 and 14 Mar 2015, striker Lionel Messi claimed yet another record (see more on p.543) when he scored his 275th goal for Barcelona in Spain's national top division, La Liga.

Lampard's scoring genius

During his 13 years wearing a Chelsea shirt, Lampard became the club's top scorer, with 211 goals in all competitions. His record-setting strike (see below) for Manchester City was scored against Chelsea – his former club. This late equalizer brought the 36-year-old midfielder his 172nd Premier League goal. It also saved City from a second successive home defeat and halted a run of Chelsea wins.

Most different teams scored against in the English Premier League

Midfielder Frank Lampard (UK) scored against 39 out of 46 clubs while playing for West Ham United, Chelsea and Manchester City between 1995 and 2015. He scored against his 39th club, Chelsea, at the Etihad Stadium in Manchester, UK, on 21 Sep 2014.

Longest goal scored in a competitive match

On 2 Nov 2013, goalkeeper Asmir Begović (BIH), playing for Stoke City against Southampton in the English Premier League, scored from 91.9 m (301 ft 6 in) at Stoke's Britannia Stadium, UK. On receiving his GWR certificate, Begović said, "I feel amazing to be honoured in this way… [it] will certainly take pride of place on the wall at home!"

Most goals in a Champions League match

On 21 Oct 2014, Luiz Adriano (BRA), playing for Shakhtar Donetsk in Ukraine, scored five goals against BATE Borisov at the Borisov Arena in Barysaw, Belarus. This matched Lionel Messi's feat against Germany's Bayer Leverkusen on 7 Mar 2012.

IN NUMBERS

6
Most appearances in the FIFA Club World Cup by a team: Auckland City (NZ), 2006–14

38 years 59 days
Age of the **oldest player to score a goal in the UEFA Champions League**: Francesco Totti (ITA) for Roma on 25 Nov 2014

124
Most goals scored by a goalkeeper: Rogério Ceni (BRA) for São Paulo, 1998–2015; he also won the **most matches for the same club**: 606, as of 1 Apr 2015

2
Most consecutive wins of the UEFA Women's Champions League, shared by Umeå IK (SWE), Olympique Lyonnais Féminin (FRA) and VfL Wolfsburg (DEU)

2 min 56 sec
Fastest hat-trick in the English Premier League, scored by Southampton winger Sadio Mané (SEN) against Aston Villa on 16 May 2015

Youngest coach to win the Copa Sudamericana

Marcelo Gallardo (ARG, b. 18 Jan 1976) was 38 years 326 days old when he guided Argentine club River Plate to victory over Atlético Nacional in Buenos Aires, Argentina, on 10 Dec 2014.

MOST GOALS...

In the Copa Libertadores

Playing for Peñarol and Barcelona SC from 19 Apr 1960 to 22 Mar 1972, Alberto Spencer (ECU) put away 54 goals in the Copa Libertadores, the most prestigious club tournament in South America.

In the FIFA Club World Cup

Argentine winger César Delgado, representing Monterrey, has scored a total of five goals in FIFA's Club World Cup. He netted three in the 2012 tournament and two in the 2013 fifth-place play-off.

In a Major League Soccer career

In 2001–14, Landon Donovan (USA), playing for the San Jose Earthquakes and Los Angeles Galaxy, scored 144 goals. In 2014, his last season before retirement, he scored 10 during the regular season, as LA Galaxy cruised into the play-offs to win a record fifth MLS Cup. Donovan also made 136 assists, scored 41 game-winning goals and won six MLS Cups.

Longest unbeaten streak in the German Bundesliga by an individual

Defender Jérôme Boateng (DEU), playing for Bayern Munich from 3 Nov 2012 to 19 Dec 2014, enjoyed an unbeaten run of 56 games. Boateng played in neither of Bayern's two league defeats (by Augsburg and Borussia Dortmund) since his record run began.

Most hat-tricks in a La Liga career

Cristiano Ronaldo (PRT) scored 25 hat-tricks for Real Madrid between 5 May 2010 and 2 May 2015, including one scored in just 8 min during an epic match against Granada that ended 9–1. He achieved his 25th hat-trick against Sevilla on 2 May 2015 to take the record outright.

FACT

On 2 June 2010, in South Africa, Jérôme (Germany) and Kevin-Prince Boateng (Ghana) became the **first brothers to play against each other in a FIFA World Cup**.

José Mourinho

José Mário dos Santos Mourinho Félix (PRT, b. 26 Jan 1963), manager of Chelsea (UK) for the second time from 2013, has won 20 trophies and broken a host of records in his 15-year coaching career.

In 2004, the 41-year-old Mourinho was then the youngest coach to win the Champions League, with Porto, having won the UEFA Cup the previous year. Such success in Europe saw him snapped up by Chelsea under the ownership of Russian billionaire Roman Abramovich.

In May 2005, he became the **highest-paid soccer manager**, with a contract extension worth £5.2 m ($9.8 m) a year. This followed a record-breaking season in which Chelsea won the **most points in a Premier League season** (95), along with the **fewest goals conceded in a Premier League season** (15 in 38 matches).

During Mourinho's two-year stint at Inter Milan, the Italian giants won a rare treble in 2010. It included the Champions League, which, with his 2004 win with Porto, saw Mourinho equal the record for the **most Champions League titles won by a manager with different clubs**. In 2012, while manager of Real Madrid, he became the **youngest manager to reach 100 games in the Champions League**, aged 49 years 312 days.

In his second spell at Chelsea, Mourinho finally lost a home game, ending his stunning record of the **most games unbeaten at home in the Premier League** (77).

INTERNATIONAL SOCCER

A **black-and-white ball** was first used in the **1970 World Cup**, to make it stand out on black-and-white televisions

Most consecutive wins of the African Player of the Year award

Yaya Touré (CIV, below) is the first to win the award in four successive years: 2011–14. He debuted with the Côte d'Ivoire national team, aka "The Elephants", in 2004, replacing Didier Drogba as captain in 2014. Touré has represented the Ivorians six times in the Africa Cup of Nations, a title that they won on 8 Feb 2015 for the first time in 23 years under his helmsmanship. The African Player of the Year award has been in place since 1970, and Samuel Eto'o (inset left) has also won four times, but not successively: in 2003–05 and 2010.

FACT

Since 2010, midfielder Touré has played for Manchester City in the English Premier League. On 1 Mar 2015, he faced his brother Kolo, a Liverpool defender, for the first time in a competitive match.

Youngest player in a UEFA European Championships match

On 13 Oct 2014, Martin Ødegaard (NOR, b. 17 Dec 1998) came on as a substitute for Norway versus Bulgaria, in Oslo, Norway, aged 15 years 300 days. The midfielder helped to set up a goal to give his team a 2–1 win. Ødegaard has since moved to Spain, joining Real Madrid's B team.

Most international matches managed by a coach

Between 15 Mar 1983 and 20 Jun 2009, Bora Milutinović (SRB) managed eight national teams: Mexico (104 games), Costa Rica (9), USA (96), Nigeria (11), China (46), Honduras (10), Jamaica (7) and Iraq (4), making a grand total of 287 games.

Most consecutive wins in international soccer

From 26 Jun 2008 to 20 Jun 2009, Spain notched up 15 wins, first beating Russia 3–0 in the semi-finals of the 2008 European Championships. Their 15th successive win came with a 2–0 victory over South Africa in their final group game in the 2009 Confederations Cup.

Most goals scored in international matches by an individual

As of 6 Mar 2015, American striker Abby Wambach (USA) had 178 goals to her name, scored since 9 Sep 2001. She surpassed her former team-mate Mia Hamm's record of 158 on 20 Jun 2013, with four goals against South Korea.

The **most goals scored in international matches (male)** is 109, by Ali Daei (IRN) in 1993–2006. Daei played a key role in such victories as Iran's 19–0 defeat of Guam during the qualification rounds for the 2002 FIFA World Cup.

Most FIFA World Cup tournaments played in by an individual

Lothar Matthäus (DEU) is a veteran of five World Cups (1982, 1986, 1990, 1994 and 1998), a record shared with Antonio Carbajal (MEX), but the German has played the **most World Cup games** (25). Matthäus called his GWR award "a special tribute, and one that I am very proud of".

FACT

Scored in the 113th minute by Mario Götze (near right), the winning goal of the 2014 World Cup final made Germany the first European team to win a World Cup in the Americas.

argest tournament (female)

.opa Telmex 2013, sponsored by undación Telmex (MEX), consisted f 33,534 players and 1,863 teams laying matches throughout Mexico rom 2 Jan to 15 Dec 2013.

Longest-running international competition for national teams

The South American Championship (Copa América since 1975) dates from 1916. It first took place in Argentina, the record holder for the **most times a country has hosted the Copa América** (9) – in 1916, 1921, 1925, 1929, 1937, 1946, 1959, 1987 and, most recently, 2011.

The most **appearances in Copa América tournaments by a player** is eight, achieved by Álex Aguinaga (ECU) in 1987, 1989, 1991, 1993, 1995, 1999, 2001 and 2004. He equalled the record of Ángel Romano (URG) in 1916–26.

Germany

The German national team have been a major force in international soccer since their first World Cup victory – as West Germany – in 1954 (below).

At the most recent edition of soccer's biggest prize, in Brazil, Germany won their fourth world championship (above and below left). This left them one short of the record for **most FIFA World Cups won** (held by Brazil), but they have plenty of others to their name. It was their eighth World Cup final, surpassing Brazil's seven, and the clinching goal by Mario Götze was the **first winning goal by a substitute in a World Cup final**. It was also the team's 224th goal in the competition – the **most goals in the FIFA World Cup**.

In the semi-final, they inflicted a 7–1 defeat on Brazil, the **heaviest defeat suffered by a host nation at the World Cup**. The game saw veteran striker Miroslav Klose (shown above, with trophy) score his 16th World Cup goal – the **most World Cup finals goals by an individual**.

The triumph in Brazil was the result of a new youth-development strategy implemented after the disappointment of exiting Euro 2000 at the group stage, a competition that Germany has traditionally dominated. They hold the record for the **most matches played in the UEFA European Championships** (43), as well as the **most wins** (23). In 2016, Germany will hope to continue their recent success and regain the record, recently matched by Spain, for the **most UEFA European Championships titles**, both sides having three trophies apiece.

IN NUMBERS

171
Most goals in a single FIFA World Cup, scored in France in 1998 and Brazil in 2014

3.5 billion
Estimated number of fans of association football, making it the **most popular spectator sport**, according to *The Economist*

17 years 249 days
Age of the **youngest winner of the World Cup**: Brazil's Pelé on 29 Jun 1958

0
Number of matches lost by Brazil when Pelé and Garrincha (a dazzling dribbler) played together

6
Number of times the host country has won the World Cup (out of 20 tournaments)

Most wins of the Africa Cup of Nations by a player

Ahmed Hassan played in eight tournaments for Egypt between 1996 and 2010, and has been on the winning side four times: in 1998, 2006, 2008 and 2010.

Samuel Eto'o (CMR, see p.548), playing for Cameroon between 1996 and 2010, has scored the **most goals in the Africa Cup of Nations by an individual**: 18.

Most goals in an Asian Cup match by an individual

On 16 Jan 2015, Hamza Al-Dardour (JOR) scored four goals against Palestine in Melbourne, Australia. This record, first set by Behtash Fariba on 22 Sep 1980, was equalled by Ali Daei (both IRN) on 16 Dec 1996 and Ismail Abdullatif (BHR) on 14 Jan 2011. There have been 16 hat-tricks to date, including the four by these record holders.

On 15 Jan 2015, while playing against Bahrain in Canberra, Australia, Ali Mabkhout (UAE) scored after just 14 sec, the **fastest goal in an Asian Cup match**. UAE won the game 2–1.

Most siblings to score in an OFC Nations Cup match

On 1 Jun 2012, three brothers – Jonathan Tehau, the eldest, and twins Lorenzo and Alvin – scored eight goals for Tahiti against Samoa in the 2012 OFC (Oceania Football Confederation) Nations Cup at the Lawson Tama Stadium in Honiara, Solomon Islands. Jonathan scored twice, Lorenzo four times and Alvin twice, while their cousin Teaonui Tehau was also on the scoresheet, contributing one goal to the overall victory of 10–1.

The Tehaus also scored in subsequent matches against New Caledonia, Vanuatu and the Solomon Islands. Tahiti went on to win the tournament, the first time that a team other than Australia or New Zealand has done so.

Most wins of the OFC Women's Nations Cup

In the 10th edition of the tournament, on 25–29 Oct 2014, New Zealand racked up their fifth victory. They had previously won in 1983, 1991, 2007 and 2010.

Most goals scored in the UEFA European Championships, including qualifying matches

From 12 Jun 2004 to 14 Nov 2014, Portugal's Cristiano Ronaldo scored 23 goals in 37 games: 17 in qualifying matches and six in the European Championships. He surpassed the record of 22, held by Jon Dahl Tomasson (DNK) and Hakan Şükür (TUR), with his game-winning goal against Armenia in the Euro 2016 Group I qualifier.

Most consecutive international match losses

Between 4 Sep 2004 and 14 Oct 2014, San Marino recorded 61 defeats. They were on a high in Aug 2004, having won their only international victory ever, beating Liechtenstein 1–0. A subsequent

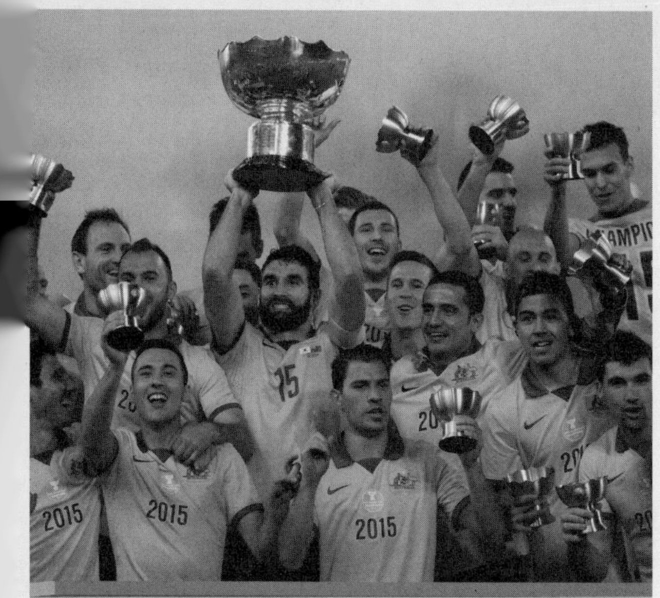

First team to win a continental title on different continents
On 31 Jan 2015, Australia became the first national team to win two continental trophies, triumphing 2–1 over South Korea in the 2015 AFC Asian Cup final in Sydney, Australia. They had previously won the OFC (Oceania Football Confederation) Nations Cup four times, in 1980–2004. The 2015 Asian Cup drew an aggregate audience of 650,000.

run of losses finally ended on 15 Nov 2014, when they drew 0–0 against Estonia in a European Championships qualifier – their first ever point in the qualifiers.

Most matches won in the UEFA European Championships by a team

Between 1960, when the UEFA European Championships was founded, and 2012, Germany (see panel on p.551) won 23 matches.

Most tweets per minute during a sporting event

On 13 Jul 2014, a total of 618,725 tweets per min were sent during the FIFA World Cup final in Rio de Janeiro, Brazil, between Germany and Argentina: a record third time that the two sides had met in the final. The tweet rate reached its peak the moment that Germany won the game.

SWIMMING & WATERSPORTS

Water polo originated as a form of **"water rugby"**, played in rivers and lakes in the UK using a **pig's stomach** for a ball

First brothers to make up a relay team

On 15 Dec 2010, the four Al Jasmi brothers – Obaid, Saeed, Bakheet and Faisal (all UAE) – took part in the 4 x 100 m freestyle relay at the Fédération Internationale de Natation (FINA) World Swimming Championships (25 m) in Dubai, UAE. They finished 14th in the heats, with a time of 3 min 35.72 sec. It was the first time four brothers had competed in the same event at the FINA Championships.

Fastest canoe/kayak 200 m flatwater (female)

Lisa Carrington (NZ) finished in 37.898 sec at the ICF Canoe Sprint World Championships in Moscow, Russia, on 10 Aug 2014, just hours after collecting silver in the 500 m event. This was her third win at the World Championships for the 200 m sprint, for which she also won an Olympic gold in 2012.

MOST MEDALS AT THE...

FINA World Swimming Championships (25 m)

From 7 Oct 2004 to 7 Dec 2014, Ryan Lochte (USA; see panel, p.558) racked up 38 medals at the short-course World Championships: 21 gold, 10 silver and seven bronze. Included in this tally is a record eight that he collected at a single championships, in Istanbul, Turkey, in 2012, a feat that he matched in 2014 in Doha, Qatar.

FINA Men's Water Polo World Cup

Hungary have achieved nine World Cup medals overall, with golds awarded in the 1979, 1995 and 1999 events. In 2014, they won their fourth silver medal, having also come second in 1993, 2002 and 2006. In 1989 and 1997, they took home bronze medals.

FINA Synchronized Swimming World Cup (team)

Canada and Japan have competed in every World Cup since its inception in 1979, each winning 31 medals up to 2014.

2014 SWIMMING RECORDS

Swimming championships held around the world in 2014 – from Perth and Gold Coast in Australia to Dubai, UAE, and Irvine in California, USA – threw up new records in men's, women's and mixed short- and long-course events.

Fastest...	Name/Country	Time (min:sec)
Long-course 400 m freestyle (women)	Katie Ledecky (USA)	3:58.86
Long-course 1,500 m freestyle (women)*	Katie Ledecky (USA)	15:28.36
Long-course relay 4 x 100 m freestyle (women)	Australia	3:30.98
Long-course relay 4 x 100 m freestyle (mixed)	Australia	3:23.29
Long-course relay 4 x 100 m medley (mixed)	Australia	3:46.52
Short-course 1,500 m freestyle (women)	Lauren Boyle (NZ)	15:22.68
Short-course 200 m breaststroke (men)	Dániel Gyurta (HUN)	2:00.48
Short-course 50 m backstroke (men)*	Florent Manaudou (FRA)	22.22
Short-course 100 m butterfly (men)*	Chad le Clos (ZAF)	48.44
Short-course 100 m individual medley (men)*	Markus Deibler (DEU)	50.66

**FINA pending*

Most Diving World Series 3 m springboard wins

Female: He Zi (CHN, above) dived to victory 19 times between 2009 and 4 May 2014. She won an incredible five out of six individual events in 2013, continuing her excellent form with three victories in 2014.
Male: He Chong (CHN) achieved 12 wins between Sep 2007 and Jun 2014; he won four of the six events in the 2014 World Series.

WINDSURFING

Most Formula Windsurfing World Championship wins

Male: A windsurfer since the age of five, Antoine Albeau (FRA) has won four times, in 2005, 2007, 2010 and 2011, in Australia, Brazil, Argentina and Puerto Rico, respectively.
Female: Dorota Staszewska (POL) recorded four wins, in 2000–02 and 2004.

Longest time windsurfing a wave

Camille Juban (FRA) rode a crest for 7 min 3 sec at Chicama, Ascope, Peru, on 19 Aug 2013.

Fastest speed-sailing (female)

On 17 Nov 2012, windsurfer Zara Davis (UK) achieved 45.83 knots using a Mistral 41 board and Simmer Sail 5.5 SCR in Lüderitz, Namibia. She set a new female record for the highest speed reached under sail on water by any craft over a 500-m timed run.

Most medals won in individual events at a single FINA World Championships (25 m)

From 3 to 7 Dec 2014, Katinka Hosszú (HUN) secured eight medals at the 12th FINA World Championships held in Doha, Qatar. She won gold medals in the 100 m backstroke, 200 m backstroke, 100 m individual medley and 200 m individual medley. She also picked up silver in the 400 m individual medley, 200 m freestyle and 200 m butterfly, and a solitary bronze in the 50 m backstroke.

Most wins of the ICF Canoe Polo Men's World Championships

Canoe polo was inaugurated by the International Canoe Federation (ICF) in Sheffield, UK, in 1994. Australia was the first team to achieve three wins, in 1994, 1996 and 1998, followed by the Netherlands in 2004, 2008 and 2012. Most recently, France won three times, in 2006, 2010 and 2014.

Most gold medals won at the ICF Canoe Slalom World Championships

After winning four gold medals out of a possible eight at the first World Championships in 1949, the French returned to the top of the medals table in 2014 by taking gold four times. They became the only nation to surpass the 50-gold-medal mark, winning 52 between 30 Aug 1949 and 21 Sep 2014.

Most participants in an IDBF Club Crew World Championships

The International Dragon Boat Federation event from 3 to 7 Sep 2014 in Ravenna, Italy, drew 5,400 participants in 338 races. The Chinese-style boats are rowed by 20 athletes each. Clubs from Iran, Israel and Spain took part for the first time, while two clubs from Canada came first and second respectively in the medals table.

Fastest long-course 50 m butterfly (female)

On 5 Jul 2014, Sarah Sjöström (SWE) achieved a lightning 24.43 sec in Borås, Sweden, at the Swedish National Championships.

The 21-year-old broke the previous record of 25.07 sec, held for almost five years. She then swam a 55.73-sec split (section) in the women's 400 m medley relay, in which her team came second.

IN NUMBERS

100 km/h
Speed at which some players can throw the ball in water polo (62 mph)

700,000
Gallons contained in an Olympic swimming pool (3,182,260 litres)

14 hr 31 min
Time it took Gertrude Erdele (USA) to swim the English Channel in 1926 – faster than any previous swimmer, male or female

600
Calories per hour burned by a water polo player in a game

102
Age at which diver Viola Cady Krahn (USA) was inducted into the International Masters Swimming Hall of Fame on 26 Jan 2004

Ryan Lochte

"The Lochtenator" – three-time FINA Swimmer of the Year and twice voted American Swimmer of the Year by *Swimming World Magazine* – is a record-breaker with an eye on Rio 2016…

The 31-year-old American has been a dominant force in the medley, freestyle and backstroke disciplines at the 100, 200 and 400 m distances for over 10 years. He won the first of his five Olympic gold medals in Athens in 2004 as part of the US men's 4 x 200 m freestyle team that included Michael Phelps, and his first individual triumph in the Olympic pool was in the 200 m backstroke in Beijing, where he posted a world-record time to beat countryman Aaron Peirsol.

Going into 2015, Lochte held four individual world records: in **long-course 200 m medley** and in **short-course 100 m, 200 m** and **400 m medley**. He was also part of the **4 x 200 m freestyle** quartet that swam under 7 min in Rome in 2009.

Lochte's ability to swim in multiple disciplines and over multiple distances has earned him a host of medals at World Championships, especially in the 25-m pool, where his speed underwater counts for so much. No surprise, then, that he holds the record for the **most medals won at the short course FINA World Swimming Championships** (see p.555).

His achievements have not gone unnoticed by the swimming community: he has been named FINA Male Swimmer of the Year three times (2010, 2011 and 2013) since the award was inaugurated in 2010, more than any other athlete.

Fastest short-course 200 m butterfly

Female: Mireia Belmonte's (ESP, above) time of 1 min 59.61 sec at the FINA World Championships in Doha, Qatar, on 3 Dec 2014 marked the first time that a female swimmer had finished this race in under 2 min.

Male: Chad le Clos (ZAF) finished in 1 min 48.56 sec at the FINA Swimming World Cup in Singapore on 4 Nov 2013.

Most consecutive FINA Men's Water Polo World Cup wins

A run of three victories was achieved by Serbia in 2006, 2010 and in Almaty, Kazakhstan, on 24 Aug 2014 after a penalty shoot-out. Serbia also won the European Water Polo Championship and the Water Polo World League the same year.

King Charles VIII (FRA) died after hitting his head **entering his tennis court** in 1498

Most wheelchair singles matches won in a row

Female: With a fourth title at the London 2012 Paralympics, Esther Vergeer (NLD) claimed her 470th consecutive victory on 7 Sep 2012.

Male: Between 23 Jan 2008 and 20 Nov 2010, Japanese player Shingo Kunieda triumphed in 106 singles matches in a row.

First international team-based tennis tournament

The inaugural International Premier Tennis League (IPTL) tournament ran from 28 Nov to 13 Dec 2014. It featured 21 Grand Slam champions and 14 current or former world No.1s doing battle for one of four Asian-based franchises: Indian Aces, Manila Mavericks, Singapore Slammers and UAE Royals. The Indian Aces – featuring the likes of Roger Federer (CHE), Pete Sampras (USA) and Ana Ivanovic (SRB) – took the first title, netting $1 m (£636,000).

Largest attendance at an ATP World Tour Finals

The 2014 ATP (Association of Tennis Professionals) World Tour Finals held in London, UK, on 9–16 Nov attracted 263,560 spectators. The event features the tour's highest-ranked men's singles and doubles players and was a sell-out for nine of the 15 sessions.

Most tournament singles wins

Female: Martina Navratilova (USA) won 1,442 matches in her pro career (1975–2004).

Male: Jimmy Connors (USA, above) won 1,253 singles matches from 1972 to 1996, including 109 title victories – also the **most tournament titles** won.

GRAND SLAMS

Largest fine

Serena Williams (USA) may be the top earner in women's tennis (see p.560), but she's also received the biggest fine at a Grand Slam. She had to pay $82,500 (£53,000) for aggravated behaviour against a line judge at the 2009 US Open semi-final on 12 Sep 2009.

Most tournament doubles titles won

After claiming victory at Florida's Delray Beach Open on 22 Feb 2015, American twins Bob and Mike Bryan's tally of doubles titles stood at 104.

On 12 Oct 2014, they became the **first doubles team to achieve a "Career Golden Masters"** – winning at least one title at every ATP World Tour Masters 1000 event – when they went all the way at China's Shanghai Masters.

Highest earnings in a tennis career (female)

As of 9 Mar 2015, 19-time Grand Slam champion Serena Williams (USA) had accumulated $66,211,528 (£44,782,600) since turning pro in 1995. This is almost double that of the second-wealthiest female player, Maria Sharapova (RUS), with $34,094,202 (£22,656,100).

With 17 Grand Slam singles titles to his name, Roger Federer (CHE) had the **highest earnings in a tennis career (male)**, with $89,280,550 (£59,328,100) as of the same date.

Fastest serve

Female: Sabine Lisicki (DEU, left) clocked 210.8 km/h (131 mph) at the Bank of the West Classic in California, USA, on 29 Jul 2014. Even at the time, Lisicki could tell that it was special: "I knew that it was big," she told GWR. "I had been serving well all week." But she admits that although "my serve is a big part of my game… I didn't think about breaking the record. I thought at some point, it may happen."
Male: Samuel Groth (AUS) hit a serve at 263 km/h (163.4 mph) during an ATP event in Busan, South Korea, on 9 May 2012.

IN NUMBERS

8 mm
Height to which the grass is cut on Wimbledon courts (0.3 in)

AUS$40 m
Largest prize for a Grand Slam (£21.6 m; $32.5 m), at the 2015 Australian Open

50,970
Strokes in the **longest rally**, between father and son Frank and Dennis Fuhrmann (both DEU)

198 cm
Height of the **tallest player to win a Grand Slam** (6 ft 6 in), a record shared by Juan Martín del Potro (ARG, 2009) and Marin Čilić (HRV, 2014)

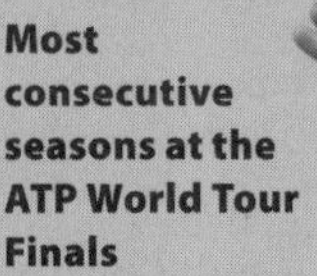

Most consecutive seasons at the ATP World Tour Finals

In 2014, Roger Federer (CHE) made his 13th appearance at the ATP World Tour Finals, surpassing Ivan Lendl's (CZE/USA) 12-year run (1980–91). Federer also boasts the most singles titles at the ATP World Tour Finals, with six.

First "golden set"

At 2012's Wimbledon tournament, Yaroslava Shvedova (KAZ) won a set against Sara Errani (ITA) without conceding a single point. This was the first time in Grand Slam history that the feat, known as a "golden set", had been achieved.

Longest duration singles tennis match

At the 2010 Wimbledon Championships, John Isner (USA) and Nicolas Mahut (FRA) began playing at 6.13 p.m. on 22 Jun, only for the first-round match to be stopped owing to fading light. The next day, they continued on to a fifth set when play was suspended again because of the light. The match ended at 4.48 p.m. on 24 Jun, after a total of 11 hr 5 min.

Most five-set matches

As of 22 Jan 2015, Lleyton Hewitt (AUS) had played 43 five-setters at Grand Slam tournaments, with a win-loss ratio of 26–17. In 2014, he equalled and then surpassed Andre Agassi's (USA) 41 five-set Grand Slam matches.

Youngest person to win a wheelchair tennis calendar Grand Slam (female)

Aged 20 years 135 days, Yui Kamiji (JPN, b. 24 Apr 1994) won the 2014 US Open women's doubles with partner Jordanne Whiley (UK) in New York, USA, on 6 Sep 2014.

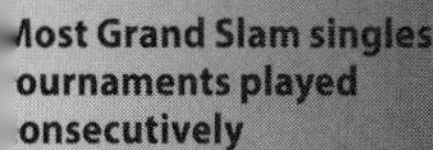

Most Grand Slam singles tournaments played consecutively

Ai Sugiyama (JPN) played 62 consecutive Grand Slam singles tournaments, from Wimbledon in 1994 to the US Open in 2009. As of Mar 2015, Sugiyama's feat of endurance was coming under threat from Roger Federer (61 consecutive Grand Slams) and Francesca Schiavone (ITA, 58 consecutive Grand Slams), who both extended their sequences at the 2015 Australian Open.

FACT

Novak Djokovic is the only player to have beaten Roger Federer in all four Grand Slam tournaments. Likewise, Federer is the only player to have beaten Djokovic in these same four Majors.

Novak Djokovic

With 49 singles titles – including eight Grand Slams – to his name as of Feb 2015, world No.1 Novak Djokovic (SRB) is currently the ace in the pack on the ATP circuit. Below, we celebrate some of his career highlights.

Melbourne Park in Australia on 1 Feb 2015 was the scene of Djokovic's latest Grand Slam triumph (at the time of writing): a four-set defeat of Andy Murray (UK) on a sun-drenched Rod Laver Arena.

This not only gave the Serbian a fifth Australian Open title, but also extended his remarkable run of Grand Slam results "Down Under" to 32 wins in 33 matches. Djokovic's three consecutive Australian victories from 2011 to 2013 also made him the **first player to win three successive Australian Open titles (open era)**.

In 2014, the ATP Player of the Year earned $14,250,527 (£9,173,650), surpassing his previous top annual earnings by more than $1.5 m (£1 m).

He won seven ATP titles in 2014, including Wimbledon for a second time and the ATP World Tour Finals for the third year in a row, and became only the 23rd man in the open era to reach the landmark of 600 career wins. But perhaps his proudest moments came off court, where he exchanged vows with childhood sweetheart Jelena Ristic and became a father.

At 2012's Australian Open, Djokovic earned another record with opponent Rafael Nadal (ESP). Their 5-hr 53-min battle on 28 Jan 2012 stands as the **longest Grand Slam final**. Djokovic eventually won 5–7, 6–4, 6–2, 6–7, 7–5.

It's his tally of eight Grand Slam wins – equalling the number won by open-era legends Jimmy Connors (USA), Ivan Lendl (CZE/USA) and Andre Agassi (USA) – allied with his fighting spirit and athleticism, which have already marked him down as an all-time great. Game, set and match, Djokovic.

In the original **Olympic Games** in ancient Greece, **javelin throwers** competed on **horseback**

IAAF INDOOR WORLD CHAMPIONSHIPS

Most medals won

Female: Running the 800 m, Maria Mutola (MOZ) took nine medals from 1993 to 2008. This was equalled by Natalya Nazarova (RUS) in the 400 m and 4 x 400 m relay between 1999 and 2010.

Male: Cuban high-jumper Javier Sotomayor leapt his way to six medals between 1985 and 1999.

Country: The most successful nation is the USA, with a haul of 214 medals from 1985 to 2014.

Oldest medallist

Female: Russian runner Yekaterina Podkopayeva took gold in the 1,500 m in Paris, France, aged 44 years 271 days on 9 Mar 1997.

Male: Bernard Lagat (USA, b. KEN) won a silver medal in the 3,000 m at the age of 39 years 87 days in Sopot, Poland, on 9 Mar 2014.

Fastest 4 x 400 m relay indoors

Kind Butler III, David Verburg, Calvin Smith and Kyle Clemons (all USA, left to right) ran a time of 3:02.13 at the 2014 IAAF World Indoor Championships in Sopot, Poland, on 9 Mar 2014. The previous record of 3:03.01, held by Poland, had stood for 15 years.

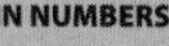

Most Diamond Race titles

Pole-vaulter Renaud Lavillenie (FRA, above) has won five times at the Diamond League, an annual track-and-field contest organized by the International Association of Athletics Federations (IAAF). The female title is tied at four between runner Milcah Chemos Cheywa (KEN), shot-putter Valerie Adams (NZ) and hurdler Kaliese Spencer (JAM).

OLYMPICS & PARALYMPICS

Fastest 100 m (T11)

Male: Running in the T11 category, which is for athletes with a visual impairment, Paralympian David Brown (USA) ran a time of 10.92 sec on 18 Apr 2014, improving on the existing record by 0.11 sec.
Female: Terezinha Guilhermina and her sighted guide Guilherme Santana (both BRA) ran 100 m in 12.01 sec at the London Paralympic Games on 5 Sep 2012.

IN NUMBERS

13,471
Maximum points available in a decathlon

9,971
Maximum points available in a heptathlon

16 lb
Weight of a shot put for male IAAF athletes (7.26 kg)

2.3 m
Maximum length of a javelin for female IAAF athletes (7 ft 6 in)

85 mm
Diameter of the medals at the 2012 Games – the **largest Summer Olympics medals** (3.3 in)

213
IAAF member federations, as of Feb 2015

126
Most points scored in a Diamond League career, set by Valerie Adams (NZ) between 2010 and 2014

3 hr 32 min 33 sec
Fastest 50 km road walk, set by Yohann Diniz (FRA) in Zurich, Switzerland, on 15 Aug 2014

OUTDOOR TRACK EVENTS (MALE)

Event	Time	Name (nationality)	Date
100 m	9.58	Usain Bolt (JAM, pictured)	16 Aug 2009
200 m	19.19	Usain Bolt (JAM)	20 Aug 2009
400 m	43.18	Michael Johnson (USA)	26 Aug 1999
800 m	1:40.91	David Rudisha (KEN)	9 Aug 2012
1,000 m	2:11.96	Noah Ngeny (KEN)	5 Sep 1999
1,500 m	3:26.00	Hicham El Guerrouj (MAR)	14 Jul 1998
1 mile	3:43.13	Hicham El Guerrouj (MAR)	7 Jul 1999
2,000 m	4:44.79	Hicham El Guerrouj (MAR)	7 Sep 1999
3,000 m	7:20.67	Daniel Komen (KEN)	1 Sep 1996
5,000 m	12:37.35	Kenenisa Bekele (ETH)	31 May 2004
10,000 m	26:17.53	Kenenisa Bekele (ETH)	26 Aug 2005
20,000 m	56:26.00	Haile Gebrselassie (ETH)	27 Jun 2007
25,000 m	1:12:25.4	Moses Cheruiyot Mosop (KEN)	3 Jun 2011
30,000 m	1:26:47.4	Moses Cheruiyot Mosop (KEN)	3 Jun 2011
3,000 m steeplechase	7:53.63	Saif Saaeed Shaheen (QAT)	3 Sep 2004
110 m hurdles	12.80	Aries Merritt (USA)	7 Sep 2012
400 m hurdles	46.78	Kevin Young (USA)	6 Aug 1992
4 x 100 m relay	36.84	Jamaica	11 Aug 2012
4 x 200 m relay	1:18.63	Jamaica	24 May 2014
4 x 400 m relay	2:54.29	USA	22 Aug 1993
4 x 800 m relay	7:02.43	Kenya	25 Aug 2006
4 x 1,500 m relay	14:22.22	Kenya	25 May 2014

OUTDOOR FIELD EVENTS (MALE)

Event	Metres	Name (nationality)	Date
High jump	2.45	Javier Sotomayor (CUB)	27 Jul 1993
Pole vault	6.14	Sergey Bubka (UKR)	31 Jul 1994
Long jump	8.95	Mike Powell (USA)	30 Aug 1991
Triple jump	18.29	Jonathan Edwards (UK)	7 Aug 1995
Shot put	23.12	Randy Barnes (USA)	20 May 1990
Discus	74.08	Jürgen Schult (GDR)	6 Jun 1986
Hammer	86.74	Yuriy Sedykh (USSR)	30 Aug 1986
Javelin	98.48	Jan Železný (CZE)	25 May 1996
Event	**Points**	**Name (nationality)**	**Date**
Decathlon	9,039	Ashton Eaton (USA)	23 Jun 2012

Statistics correct as of 17 Feb 2015

OUTDOOR TRACK EVENTS (FEMALE)

Event	Time	Name (nationality)	Date
100 m	10.49	Florence Griffith-Joyner (USA)	16 Jul 1988
200 m	21.34	Florence Griffith-Joyner (USA)	29 Sep 1988
400 m	47.60	Marita Koch (GDR)	6 Oct 1985
800 m	1:53.28	Jarmila Kratochvílová (TCH)	26 Jul 1983
1,000 m	2:28.98	Svetlana Masterkova (RUS)	23 Aug 1996
1,500 m	3:50.46	Qu Yunxia (CHN)	11 Sep 1993
1 mile	4:12.56	Svetlana Masterkova (RUS)	14 Aug 1996
2,000 m	5:25.36	Sonia O'Sullivan (IRL)	8 Jul 1994
3,000 m	8:06.11	Wang Junxia (CHN)	13 Sep 1993
5,000 m	14:11.15	Tirunesh Dibaba (ETH)	6 Jun 2008
10,000 m	29:31.78	Wang Junxia (CHN)	8 Sep 1993
20,000 m	1:05:26.6	Tegla Loroupe (KEN)	3 Sep 2000
25,000 m	1:27:05.9	Tegla Loroupe (KEN)	21 Sep 2002
30,000 m	1:45:50.0	Tegla Loroupe (KEN)	6 Jun 2003
3,000 m steeplechase	8:58.81	Gulnara Galkina (RUS)	17 Aug 2008
100 m hurdles	12.21	Yordanka Donkova (BGR)	20 Aug 1988
400 m hurdles	52.34	Yuliya Pechenkina (RUS)	8 Aug 2003
4 x 100 m relay	40.82	USA	10 Aug 2012
4 x 200 m relay	1:27.46	USA "Blue"	29 Apr 2000
4 x 400 m relay	3:15.17	USSR	1 Oct 1988
4 x 800 m relay	7:50.17	USSR	5 Aug 1984
4 x 1,500 m relay	16:33.58	Kenya	24 May 2014

OUTDOOR FIELD EVENTS (FEMALE)

Event	Metres	Name (nationality)	Date
High jump	2.09	Stefka Kostadinova (BGR)	30 Aug 1987
Pole vault	5.06	Elena Isinbayeva (RUS)	28 Aug 2009
Long jump	7.52	Galina Chistyakova (USSR)	11 Jun 1988
Triple jump	15.50	Inessa Kravets (UKR)	10 Aug 1995
Shot put	22.63	Natalya Lisovskaya (USSR)	7 Jun 1987
Discus	76.80	Gabriele Reinsch (GDR)	9 Jul 1988
Hammer	79.58	Anita Włodarczyk (POL)	31 Aug 2014
Javelin	72.28	Barbora Špotáková (CZE)	13 Sep 2008
Event	**Points**	**Name (nationality)**	**Date**
Heptathlon	7,291	Jackie Joyner-Kersee (USA)	24 Sep 1988
Decathlon	8,358	Austra Skujytė (LTU)	15 Apr 2005

Statistics correct as of 17 Feb 2015

Usain Bolt

Every sport has its heroes, but few reach the level of fame attained by sprinter Usain St Leo Bolt (JAM). Not only holder of the 100 m and 200 m records (see table p.556), he is also the first athlete to win the 100 m and 200 m at successive Olympic Games. But how did the fastest man become an athletics superstar?

Usain Bolt was often accused of being hyperactive when growing up. In his early teens, he turned to sport as a way of putting this excess energy to good use.

Bolt's first passion was cricket, but on noting his speed, his parents encouraged him to focus on track and field. His first medal – a bronze – was achieved at his high school at the age of 13. Although it was for 80 m hurdles, this early win served to galvanize his athletics ambitions.

In 2002, he made his global debut at the IAAF World Junior T&F Championships in Kingston, Jamaica. Running the 200 m in 20.61 sec, he earned his country's only individual gold at the event, aged just 15.

Despite a period of illness, Bolt came back fighting at the 2008 Beijing Olympics, breaking records for the **100 m**, **200 m** and **4 x 100 m relay** – all of which he beat again in subsequent competitions.

Asked how he felt about receiving a medal during GWR's 60th anniversary (above), Bolt told us: "When one thinks of Guinness World Records, automatically, extraordinary and remarkable comes to mind. So for me to be included, I am truly honoured and delighted."

OLYMPICS & PARALYMPICS

Most Paralympic gold medals for athletics

Female: Chantal Petitclerc (CAN) picked up 14 gold medals between 1996 and 2008, for a range of racing events in the T53 and T54 classifications dedicated to athletes with spinal cord injuries.

Male: Between 1980 and 2000, Franz Nietlispach (CHE) also won 14 golds, for wheelchair racing.

Fastest 20 km walk (female)

Elena Lashmanova (RUS) clocked 1 hr 25 min 2 sec at the London Summer Games on 11 Aug 2012.

Most Olympic medals won for athletics

Male: Finnish runner Paavo Nurmi earned a staggering 12 medals during his athletics career (nine gold and three silver) in the Games of 1920, 1924 and 1928. He gained five of his golds at the 1924 Paris Summer Olympics alone, which to this day is the **most golds for athletics at a single Games**.

Female: Jamaican sprinter Merlene Ottey won nine Olympic 100 m and 200 m medals – three silver and six bronze – between the 1980 Games in Moscow, Russia, and the 2000 Games in Sydney, Australia.

Ottey also comes top among female athletes for **most athletics medals won at the IAAF World Championships**, achieving a total of 14 medals from 1983 to 1997.

Farthest hammer throw (female)

Anita Włodarczyk (POL) threw the hammer 79.58 m (261 ft 1 in) at the Olympiastadion in Berlin, Germany, on 31 Aug 2014 during the IAAF World Challenge. Włodarczyk had previously set the record in 2009 and 2010.

Most Diamond League appearances

Multi-discipline athlete Blessing Okagbare from Nigeria participated at 38 Diamond League events between 3 Jul 2010 and 5 Sep 2014. Okagbare's specialities are the 100 m and 200 m sprints and the long jump (pictured right).

KIDS' CONTEST

Guinness World Records partnered with By Kids For Kids, Co. (BKFK) in the fall of 2014 to create the "60 Years/60 Words Challenge!"

BKFK is a leader in creating educational programmes and competitions that challenge youths to be innovative and creative while offering teachers, youth groups and parents free turn-key resources and activities.

The BKFK-powered challenge asked kids aged 7–12 to select a favourite Guinness World Records title and describe it in a poem, song, rap, poster or video using EXACTLY 60 words – no more, no less! Here we meet the winner of the competition and find out more about some of the records that inspired such great 60-word masterpieces!

CONGRATULATIONS BRETT!

PRIZE-WINNER

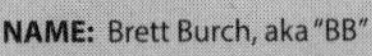

NAME: Brett Burch, aka "BB"
AGE: 10 **SCHOOL:** BASIS Washington DC
LIKES: Gymnastics and Taekwondo

Who is your role model and why?
Gymnast and Olympian John Orozco (below) because he's a tough competitor and winner in my favourite sport.

What was the inspiration behind your idea?
When I saw the record for the **largest bubblegum bubble**, I thought it was cool because most kids like bubblegum and like to blow bubbles. I want to be a rapper when I grow up, so I decided to rap about the record.

Is there a world record you'd like to break?
Ronnie Renner's record for the **highest dirt bike jump** [pictured right].

What piece of advice would you like to pass on to other young kids?
Be responsible and be awesome.

THE SEMI-FINALISTS

Alina
9, Austin, TX
Likes: Dance and Piano
"My advice to other children is to be creative and think outside the box."

Liam
10, New Windsor, MD
Likes: Soccer and Photography
"My dad is my role model because he's really smart and learns something new every day."

Grace
9, Mukwonago, WI
Likes: Volleyball and Theatre
"I thought that the **shortest living woman** was so cool and it was good to hear she now feels she fits in better."

Parker
11, South Lyon, MI
Likes: Chess and Theatre
"I would like to break the record for the **largest box-office opening**, with me as the lead actor!"

Brett's entry, a 60-word rap about the **largest bubblegum bubble blown**, won him and his school a $500 scholarship. See his winning entry at: *www. guinnessworldrecords.com/ schoolscontest*

NOW IT'S YOUR TURN TO BE A WINNER!

Go to ***www.guinnessworldrecords.com/schoolscontest*** to enter the latest Guinness World Records-themed contest for the 2015 school year!

Brett (WINNER):
Largest bubblegum bubble
On 24 Apr 2004, at Double Springs High School (now Winston County High School) in Alabama, USA, Chad Fell (USA) blew up a bubblegum bubble with a diameter of 20 in (50.8 cm) – without using his hands to steady or stretch the bubble. He used the combined strength of three pieces of Dubble Bubble gum to create his pink balloon.

Alexandria
10, Mukwonago, WI
Likes: Dance and Softball
"The inspiration for my idea was my cat, Angel, and the fact that I LOVE cats!"

Blain
10, Mukwonago, WI
Likes: Baseball and Orchestra
"The record I would most like to break is **most rushing yards in a football season**."

Amelia
9, Austin, TX
Likes: Piano and Writing
"My role model is my mother, who is hard-working, loving and nice, and my sister because she is funny!"

William
9, Austin, TX
Likes: Table tennis and Maths
"My advice for other children is to write a poem, because it's not as hard as you might think."

Semi-finalists' chosen records

Here are the records that inspired our eight semi-finalists' competition entries...

Amelia: Youngest female to ski to the North Pole

On 25 Apr 2010, Amelia Darley (née Russell, UK, b. 29 Aug 1982) reached the Geographic North Pole at the age of 27 years 239 days. Her 485-mi (780-km) trek from Ward Hunt Island in Canada, with her husband Dan Darley, received no external support or assistance – the team carried all their own food and supplies.

Alex: Longest fur on a cat

A black-and-white cat called Sophie Smith, owned by Jami Smith (USA), has luxurious fur that measured 10.11 in (25.68 cm) in Oceanside, California, USA, on 9 Nov 2013.

Alina: Longest career as an ice-cream man

Allan Ganz (USA, b. 13 Jul 1937) has been selling ice-cream since 1947, when he was just 10 years old. He achieved the record in 2014, in Peabody, Massachusetts, USA, at the age of 76.

Parker: Longest duration living with scorpions

Kanchana Ketkaew (THA) lived in a 130-sq-ft (12-m^2) glass room seething with 5,320 scorpions at the Royal Garden Plaza hotel in Pattaya, Thailand, from 22 Dec 2008 to 24 Jan 2009. During the 33 days and nights, Kanchana was stung 13 times.

William and Blain: Longest successful basketball shot

On 11 Nov 2013, Corey "Thunder" Law of the Harlem Globetrotters threw a basketball 109 ft 9 in (33.45 m) into the net (see p.161). His record-breaking basket occurred at the US Airways Center in Phoenix, Arizona, USA, on GWR Day 2013.

Liam: Heaviest aircraft pulled by a man

Reverend Kevin Fast (CAN) pulled a Boeing CC-177 Globemaster III a distance of 28 ft 10 in (8.8 m) at Canadian Forces Base in Trenton, Ontario, Canada, on 17 Sep 2009. The massive military transport aircraft weighed 416,299 lb (188.83 tonnes). Among Kevin's other records (see p.163) is the **heaviest vehicle pulled with an arm-wrestling move** – a 24,380-lb (11,060-kg) truck – achieved in Cobourg, Ontario, on 26 Apr 2013.

Grace: Shortest living woman

On 16 Dec 2011, her 18th birthday, Jyoti Amge (IND) measured 2 ft 0.7 in (62.8 cm) in Nagpur, India. On receiving the title, Jyoti, formerly the **shortest living teenager**, said, "Getting this record has made me feel better about myself. I feel popular, special and important."

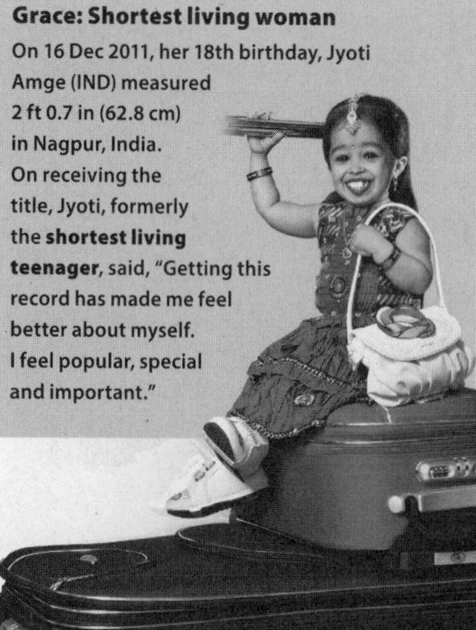

SUPER BOWL 50

Why the **Roman numerals**? Because Super Bowls **cross calendar years**

It's not just a game...

The Super Bowl is a national event – an unofficial US holiday to the millions who tune in annually to watch the best two teams in football compete for the Vince Lombardi Trophy. As the NFL gears up for Super Bowl 50, aka the "Golden Super Bowl", GWR looks at how the game has evolved, starting below with a comparison between the very first final on 15 Jan 1967 and the most recent on 1 Feb 2015.

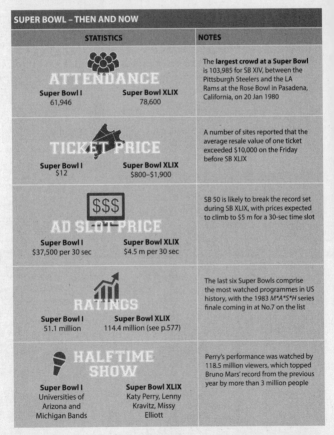

SUPER BOWL – THEN AND NOW

STATISTICS			NOTES
ATTENDANCE	**Super Bowl I** 61,946	**Super Bowl XLIX** 78,600	The **largest crowd at a Super Bowl** is 103,985 for SB XIV, between the Pittsburgh Steelers and the LA Rams at the Rose Bowl in Pasadena, California, on 20 Jan 1980
TICKET PRICE	**Super Bowl I** $12	**Super Bowl XLIX** $800–$1,900	A number of sites reported that the average resale value of one ticket exceeded $10,000 on the Friday before SB XLIX
$$$ AD SLOT PRICE	**Super Bowl I** $37,500 per 30 sec	**Super Bowl XLIX** $4.5 m per 30 sec	SB 50 is likely to break the record set during SB XLIX, with prices expected to climb to $5 m for a 30-sec time slot
RATINGS	**Super Bowl I** 51.1 million	**Super Bowl XLIX** 114.4 million (see p.577)	The last six Super Bowls comprise the most watched programmes in US history, with the 1983 *M*A*S*H* series finale coming in at No.7 on the list
HALFTIME SHOW	**Super Bowl I** Universities of Arizona and Michigan Bands	**Super Bowl XLIX** Katy Perry, Lenny Kravitz, Missy Elliott	Perry's performance was watched by 118.5 million viewers, which topped Bruno Mars' record from the previous year by more than 3 million people

Look at the starting quarterbacks for the first 10 Super Bowl winners: Bart Starr, Joe Namath, Len Dawson, Johnny Unitas, Roger Staubach, Bob Griese and Terry Bradshaw – seven of the greatest signal callers of all time, and all in the Hall of Fame. But some of the longest-lasting Super Bowl records centre on low-scoring games and dominating defences:

SB VI: **Fewest points allowed**: three, by Dallas, who beat Miami 24–3 in 1972. *Above: the Cowboys' Chuck Howley is seen in action at SB VI. Below: the Dolphins' Bob Griese turns to hand the ball off to a running back in the game.*

SB VII: **Longest time to hold a team scoreless**: 57 min 53 sec, by Miami, who beat Washington 14–7 in 1973.

SB IX: **Fewest total yards allowed**: 119, by Pittsburgh, who beat Minnesota 16–6 in 1975.

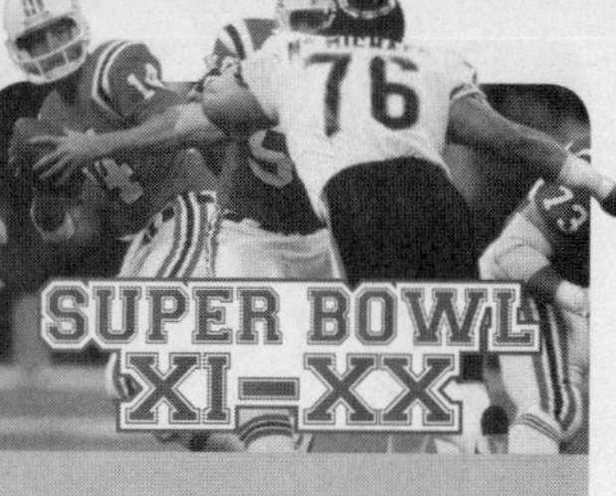

Scoring drastically increased between Super Bowls XI and XX compared with the first 10 years of the event, with the winning team averaging 10 more points per game. In the first 10 Super Bowls, only twice did a team score more than 25 points (Super Bowls I and II); during the next 10, every winner eclipsed that total. Again, however, defensive performances by the likes of the Steel Curtain and '85 Bears truly defined this era.

SB XII: **Fewest passing yards allowed**: 35, by Dallas, who defeated Denver 27–10 in 1978.

SB XVII: **Fewest pass completions allowed**: four, by Washington, who beat Miami 27–17 in 1983.

SB XX: **Fewest rushing yards allowed**: seven, by Chicago, who beat New England 46–10 in 1986.

Above: Tony Eason of New England Patriots prepares to pass at SB XX. Below: Oakland Raiders' linebacker Rod Martin celebrates victory over Philadelphia Eagles at SB XV in 1981.

Thanks to record-breaking offenses, this was the era of the NFC dynasty. Winning teams averaged more than 37 points per game, which is the highest of any era, and the margin of victory peaked at nearly a 20-point differential. Every team that won in this era would go on to win a second: the 49ers won three, while the Giants, Redskins and Cowboys won two apiece. The AFC went a woeful 0–10 during this span, with the Bills losing four in a row.

SB XXII: **Most total yards gained**: 602, by Washington, who beat Denver 42–10 in 1988. *Above: the Redskins' Doug Williams in play.*

SB XXIV: **Most points scored**: 55, by San Francisco, who beat Denver 55–10 in 1990. *Below: the 49ers' Roger Craig breaks away in the second quarter of the game.*

While the previous era featured a number of blowouts, this period brought a heightened level of drama to the Super Bowl. In its first 30 years, seven games had been decided by one touchdown or less, but this decade saw five of those nail-biting victories, including three by the Tom Brady-led Patriots in a four-year span. With games becoming closer and closer, and teams more evenly matched, fewer records were set. *Above: Denver Broncos' Terrell Davis, who set a record at SB XXXII.*

SB XXXIV: **Fewest rushing yards by a winning team**: 29, by St Louis, who beat Tennessee 23–16 in 2000. *Below: Titans safety Blaine Bishop tackles Kurt Warner of the Rams during the game.*

SB XXXVII: **Most team interceptions**: five, by Tampa Bay in 2003 vs Oakland, returning them 172 yards for three touchdowns.

SUPER BOWL XLI–XLIX

The most recent Super Bowl era has seen the greatest parity in the 49 years of the game. Eight teams have won in the past nine years, the Giants being the only team to repeat. The scoring gap has been the lowest in Super Bowl history: this is the only era in which the differential has been less than 10 points. Six of the last nine games have hinged on less than a touchdown. *Above: New England Patriots' quarterback Tom Brady holds the Vince Lombardi Trophy after the Patriots beat the Seahawks at SB XLIX in 2015.*

SB XLIX attracted the **largest TV audience for a domestic sports broadcast** (peaking at 120.8 million). *Below: Pittsburgh's Santonio Holmes, star of SB XLIII.*

SB XLIII: **Most Super Bowl wins**: six, by Pittsburgh, who most recently beat Arizona 27–23 in 2009.

SB XLVIII: **Most Super Bowl defeats**: five, by Denver, who were most recently beaten 43–8 by Seattle in 2014.

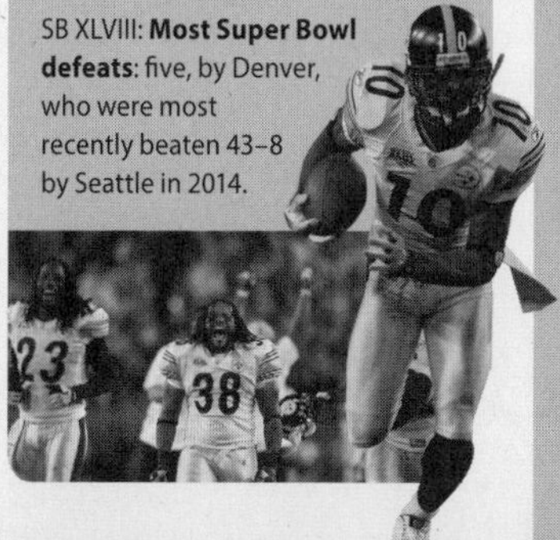

THE WINNING TEAMS

Every team here is a Super Bowl champion (see dates). Each also has at least one GWR title to its name.

NEW ENGLAND PATRIOTS
XXXVI, XXXVIII, XXXIX, XLIX
The **most consecutive pass completions in a game** is 16, by Tom Brady at SB XLVI in 2012.

SEATTLE SEAHAWKS
XLVIII
The **most tackles in a Super Bowl career** is 22, by Bobby Wagner during Super Bowls XLVIII and XLIX.

BALTIMORE RAVENS
XXXV, XLVII
The **longest touchdown in a Super Bowl** is by Jacoby Jones, with a 108-yard kick-off return for a touchdown in 2013's SB XLVII.

NEW YORK GIANTS
XXI, XXV, XLII, XLVI
The **highest passer rating by a quarterback in a game** is 150.92, by Phil Simms at SB XXI in 1987.

GREEN BAY PACKERS
I, II, XXXI, XLV
The **most punt return yards in a game** is 90 yards, by Desmond Howard at SB XXXI in 1997.

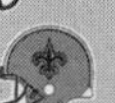

NEW ORLEANS SAINTS
XLIV
The **most 40-plus-yard field goals in a game** is three, by Garrett Hartley in 2010 at SB XLIV.

PITTSBURGH STEELERS
IX, X, XIII, XIV, XL, XLIII
The **youngest coach to win a Super Bowl** is Mike Tomlin (b. 15 Mar 1972), aged 36 years 323 days at SB XLIII in 2009

BALTIMORE/INDIANAPOLIS COLTS
V, XLI
The **most tackles in a Super Bowl game** is 13, by Gary Brackett at SB XLIV in 2010.

TAMPA BAY BUCCANEERS
XXXVII
The **most interceptions returned for a touchdown in a game** is two, by Dwight Smith at SB XXXVII in 2003.

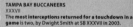

ST LOUIS RAMS
XXXIV
The **most passing yards in a game** is 414 yards, by Kurt Warner at SB XXXIV in 2000.

DENVER BRONCOS
XXXII, XXXIII
The **most rushing touchdowns in a game** is three, by Terrell Davis at SB XXXII in 1998.

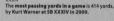

DALLAS COWBOYS
VI, XII, XXVII, XXVIII, XXX
The **most rushing touchdowns in a career** is five, by Emmitt Smith at SB XXVII, XXVIII and XXX.

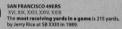

SAN FRANCISCO 49ERS
XVI, XIX, XXIII, XXIV, XXIX
The **most receiving yards in a game** is 215 yards, by Jerry Rice at SB XXIII in 1989.

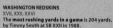

WASHINGTON REDSKINS
XVII, XXII, XXVI
The **most rushing yards in a game** is 204 yards, by Timmy Smith at SB XXII in 1988.

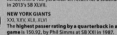

CHICAGO BEARS
XX
The **farthest opening kick-off return** is 92 yards, by Devin Hester at SB XLI in 2007.

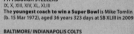

LOS ANGELES/OAKLAND RAIDERS
XI, XV, XVIII
The **most interceptions in a game** is three, by Rod Martin at SB XV in 1981.

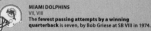

MIAMI DOLPHINS
VII, VIII
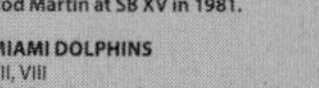
The **fewest passing attempts by a winning quarterback** is seven, by Bob Griese at SB VIII in 1974.

KANSAS CITY CHIEFS
IV
The **highest punting average in a career with at least 10 punts** is 46.5 yards, by Jerrel Wilson at SB I and IV.

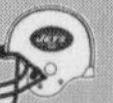

NEW YORK JETS
III
The **fewest passing touchdowns by a Super Bowl MVP-winning quarterback** is 0, by Joe Namath.

CONTRIBUTORS

Hans Åkerstedt

Hans's interest in flight began with a book he received as a childhood present: *Sergeant Bigglesworth CID*. His enthusiasm for aviation subsequently led him to earn his gliding licence. Hans joined the Swedish Air Force in 1962, gained his pilot wings in 1963 and worked as an airline pilot from 1969 to his retirement in 2002. Among his other achievements, Hans was also the Swedish delegate for the Fédération Aéronautique Internationale (FAI) Ballooning Commission from 1974 and a member of the FAI Astronautical Commission from 2010.

Dr Mark Aston

FRAS; CPhys; MInstP; DSc in Optical Physics; BSc (Hons) in Physics and Astrophysics

Mark is a technologist and physicist with more than 20 years' experience in academia and industry. From building telescope instrumentation to probing the mysteries of space and designing high-visibility traffic lights, he possesses a wide range of experience in science and technology. Mark has worked with GWR for more than five years.

Professor Iain Borden

BA; MA; MSc; PhD; Hon FRIBA

Iain is Professor of Architecture and Urban Culture and Vice-Dean of Communications at The Bartlett faculty at University College London. He is the author of more than 100 books and articles on everything from architecture and cities to automobile driving, film and skateboarding.

Rob Cave

BA (Hons) English with Media; CELTA

Rob began his publishing career working on wildlife encyclopedias and magazines about electrical engineering before writing and editing books on his twin passions: comics and videogames. He has worked on BleedingCool.com, *500 Essential Graphic Novels* (2008) and *1001 Comics You Must Read Before You Die* (2011). He has served as GWR consultant on comics, manga and graphic novels and also works on the *Gamer's Edition*.

Creative Urban Projects Inc.

Creative Urban Projects Inc. (CUP) is a boutique urban planning shop that specializes in cable cars (aka ropeways). CUP uses state-of-the-art applied and adaptive research methods, combined with an interdisciplinary thought process, to create new ideas and help cities solve the unique challenges they face.

Dick Fiddy
Dick is a writer/researcher specializing in the field of archive and contemporary television. Having worked for some time as a television comedy scriptwriter, he has subsequently served as a consultant to organizations such as the BBC and the British Film Institute (BFI).

David Fischer
David has written numerous books on sports, most recently *Derek Jeter: Thanks for the Memories* and *Facing Mariano Rivera* (both 2014). He has written for *The New York Times* and *Sports Illustrated for Kids*, and has worked for *Sports Illustrated, NBC Sports* and *The National Sports Daily*. David has been senior US sports consultant for Guinness World Records since 2006.

Mike Flynn
Mike is the author of a number of best-selling books, award-winning websites and groundbreaking exhibitions. A former curator at the Science Museum in London, he has published widely in the fields of science, technology, mathematics, history, popular culture and music.

Justin Garvanovic
Having co-founded The Roller Coaster Club of Great Britain in 1988, Justin went on to create the magazine *First Drop* for roller-coaster fans. In 1996, he founded The European Coaster Club. Justin has been involved in the designs for a number of roller-coasters and takes photographs of coasters for several parks and ride manufacturers.

The H J Lutcher Stark Center for Physical Culture & Sports
Based at the University of Texas in Austin, USA, the Stark Center is directed by Professors Terry and Jan Todd and houses the world's foremost collection dedicated to physical culture. The Todds have held world records in powerlifting and Jan was featured in GWR for more than 10 years. They publish the journal *Iron Game History* and sit on the Committee for the Study of Human Strength, which is striving to regulate strength sports.

Ben Haggar
Born into a family of cinema lovers – his great-great-grandfather was a pioneer of silent film in Wales – Ben's own love of film began after watching *The Jungle Book* in his father's cinema at the age of three. Three decades later, he still dedicates as much time as possible to researching, writing about and, most importantly, watching movies.

Ralph Hannah

BA (Hons) in History

A passionate sports fan with an eye for statistics, Ralph has worked for Guinness World Records for eight years. He currently lives in Luque, Paraguay, where he helps locate new world records in the region. As an Arsenal fan, his favourite record is the **longest unbeaten run in the Premier League**.

Dave Hawksett

Dave has been GWR's principal science consultant and contributor for 15 years. He has a background in astrophysics and planetary science and is passionate about communicating scientific issues to wide audiences. He has also worked in television, education, government policy and the commercial space sector and is founder of the UK Planetary Forum.

Bruce Nash

Bruce is President of Nash Information Services, LLC, the premier provider of movie industry data and research services. The company operates three major services: The Numbers (www.the-numbers.com), a site providing box office and video sales tracking; the OpusData movie data service; and research services for some of the biggest, and some of the smallest, film studios and production companies.

Eberhard Jurgalski

Eberhard has been fascinated by mountains since early childhood, and in 1981 he began formally chronicling the high mountains of Asia. He has developed the system of "Elevation Equality", a universal method to classify mountain ranges and peaks, and his website, 8000ers.com, has become the main source of statistics for altitude in the Himalayas and Karakorum ranges. He is also co-author of *Herausforderung 8000er*, the definitive guide to the world's 14 mountains over 8,000 m.

The Ocean Rowing Society International (ORS Int.)

The Ocean Rowing Society was established in 1983 by Kenneth F Crutchlow and Peter Bird, later joined by Tom Lynch and Tatiana Rezvaya-Crutchlow. It keeps a record of all attempts to row the oceans and major bodies of water such as the Tasman Sea and Caribbean Sea, as well as rowing expeditions around Great Britain. The society also classifies, verifies and adjudicates ocean-rowing achievements.

Glen O'Hara

MA in Modern History; MSc in Economic History; PhD

Glen is Professor of Modern and Contemporary History at Oxford Brookes University and previously taught at the University of Bristol and the University of Oxford. He is the author of a series of books on modern Britain, including *Britain and the Sea Since 1600* (2010) and *Governing Post-War Britain: The Paradoxes of Progress, 1951–1973* (2012).

Dr Paul Parsons

DPhil in Theoretical Cosmology

After training as a research scientist, Paul Parsons became editor of the BBC science and technology magazine Focus and is also the author of *The Science of Doctor Who*. He currently works for a leading UK bookmaker, building mathematical models of sports.

Dr Clara Piccirillo

PhD in Materials Science

Clara Piccirillo has been working in materials science and microbiology research for almost 20 years and is interested in the communication of science to the general public. She writes online articles about scientific research and discoveries and their practical applications in everyday life (see www.decodedscience.com/author/clara-piccirillo).

Dr Nancy L Segal

BA in Psychology and English; MA in Social Science; PhD in Behavioural Science. Post-Doctoral Fellow and Research Associate, University of Minnesota (1982–91)

Dr Segal is Professor of Psychology and Director at the Twin Studies Center in California State University, Fullerton, USA. She has authored more than 200 publications and several books on twins. *Born Together – Reared Apart: The Landmark Minnesota Twin Study* (2012) won the 2013 William James Book Award from the American Psychological Association. She also received the James Shields Award for Lifetime Contributions to Twin Research from the International Society for Twin Studies in 2005.

Natasha Sheldon

BA (Hons) in Ancient History and Archaeology; MA in Ancient History and Historiography

Natasha researches and writes on the subjects of ancient history and archaeology. Her articles have been published by Italianvisits.com, TravelThruHistory.com and DecodedPast.com. Natasha's books include *Discovering Pompeii* (2013), *Not a Guide to Leicester* (2013) and *Leicester in 100 Dates* (2014). Her website is www.ancienthistoryarchaeology.com.

Dr Karl P N Shuker

BSc (Hons) in Zoology; PhD in Zoology and Comparative Physiology; Scientific Fellow of the Zoological Society of London; Fellow of the Royal Entomological Society; Member of the Society of Authors

Karl is a freelance zoologist, media consultant and the author of 21 books and many hundreds of articles covering all aspects of natural history. His work has a particular emphasis upon the subject of anomalous animals, including new, rediscovered and unrecognized species, superlative (record-breaking) animals, and beasts of mythology, folklore and legend.

Matthew White

"Matt the Stat" served as proof-reader and researcher on the last four editions of the "Bible of Pop", *British Hit Singles & Albums* (2002–06), and was also editor of an online version of the book. He has been proof-reader for *Guinness World Records* since 2008 and the *Gamer's Edition* since 2009 and is GWR's music, cricket and tennis consultant. Matthew's knowledge of popular music has been put to good use on books such as *Top 40 Charts* (2009) and the *Rock Atlas* series (2011–present) and projects for the likes of EMI and the Official Charts Company.

Group Captain Stephen Wrigley RAF (Retd)

After graduating from the RAF College Cranwell as a pilot, Stephen flew transport aircraft. He served as an exchange pilot with the German Air Force and later commanded 47 Squadron (Hercules). Subsequently, he operated in the intelligence and military liaison worlds and worked as a defence attaché. For the past 15 years, he has been a defence consultant. Stephen is also a linguist.

Robert D Young

MA in Gerontology; MA in History

Robert is GWR's senior consultant for gerontology. He has maintained lists of the world's oldest people for the Gerontology Research Group (GRG) since 1999, and has worked with the Max Planck Institute for Demographic Research and the International Database on Longevity. He became Director of the Supercentenarians Department for the Gerontology Research Group in 2015. Robert is the author of *African-American Longevity Advantage: Myth or Reality?* (2009).

Country codes

ABW	Aruba
AFG	Afghanistan
AGO	Angola
AIA	Anguilla
ALB	Albania
AND	Andorra
ANT	Netherlands Antilles
ARG	Argentina
ARM	Armenia
ASM	American Samoa
ATA	Antarctica
ATF	French Southern Territories
ATG	Antigua and Barbuda
AUS	Australia
AUT	Austria
AZE	Azerbaijan
BDI	Burundi
BEL	Belgium
BEN	Benin
BFA	Burkina Faso
BGD	Bangladesh
BGR	Bulgaria
BHR	Bahrain
BHS	The Bahamas
BIH	Bosnia and Herzegovina
BLR	Belarus
BLZ	Belize
BMU	Bermuda
BOL	Bolivia
BRA	Brazil
BRB	Barbados
BRN	Brunei Darussalam
BTN	Bhutan
BVT	Bouvet Island
BWA	Botswana
CAF	Central African Republic
CAN	Canada
CCK	Cocos (Keeling) Islands
CHE	Switzerland
CHL	Chile
CHN	China
CIV	Côte d'Ivoire
CMR	Cameroon
COD	Congo, DR of the
COG	Congo
COK	Cook Islands
COL	Colombia
COM	Comoros
CPV	Cape Verde
CRI	Costa Rica
CUB	Cuba
CXR	Christmas Island
CYM	Cayman Islands
CYP	Cyprus
CZE	Czech Republic
DEU	Germany
DJI	Djibouti
DMA	Dominica
DNK	Denmark
DOM	Dominican Republic
DZA	Algeria
ECU	Ecuador
EGY	Egypt
ERI	Eritrea
ESH	Western Sahara
ESP	Spain
EST	Estonia
ETH	Ethiopia
FIN	Finland
FJI	Fiji
FLK	Falkland Islands (Malvinas)
FRA	France
FRG	West Germany
FRO	Faroe Islands
FSM	Micronesia, Federated States of
FXX	France, Metropolitan
GAB	Gabon
GEO	Georgia
GHA	Ghana
GIB	Gibraltar
GIN	Guinea
GLP	Guadeloupe
GMB	Gambia
GNB	Guinea-Bissau
GNQ	Equatorial Guinea
GRC	Greece
GRD	Grenada
GRL	Greenland
GTM	Guatemala

GUF French Guiana
GUM Guam
GUY Guyana
HKG Hong Kong
HMD Heard and McDonald Islands
HND Honduras
HRV Croatia (Hrvatska)
HTI Haiti
HUN Hungary
IDN Indonesia
IND India
IOT British Indian Ocean Territory
IRL Ireland
IRN Iran
IRQ Iraq
ISL Iceland
ISR Israel
ITA Italy
JAM Jamaica
JOR Jordan
JPN Japan
KAZ Kazakhstan
KEN Kenya
KGZ Kyrgyzstan
KHM Cambodia
KIR Kiribati
KNA Saint Kitts and Nevis
KOR Korea, Republic of
KWT Kuwait
LAO Laos
LBN Lebanon
LBR Liberia
LBY Libyan Arab Jamahiriya
LCA Saint Lucia
LIE Liechtenstein
LKA Sri Lanka
LSO Lesotho
LTU Lithuania
LUX Luxembourg
LVA Latvia
MAC Macau
MAR Morocco
MCO Monaco
MDA Moldova
MDG Madagascar
MDV Maldives
MEX Mexico
MHL Marshall Islands
MKD Macedonia
MLI Mali
MLT Malta
MMR Myanmar (Burma)
MNE Montenegro
MNG Mongolia
MNP Northern Mariana Islands
MOZ Mozambique
MRT Mauritania
MSR Montserrat
MTQ Martinique
MUS Mauritius
MWI Malawi
MYS Malaysia
MYT Mayotte
NAM Namibia
NCL New Caledonia
NER Niger
NFK Norfolk Island
NGA Nigeria
NIC Nicaragua
NIU Niue
NLD Netherlands
NOR Norway
NPL Nepal
NRU Nauru
NZ New Zealand
OMN Oman
PAK Pakistan
PAN Panama
PCN Pitcairn Islands
PER Peru
PHL Philippines
PLW Palau
PNG Papua New Guinea
POL Poland
PRI Puerto Rico
PRK Korea, DPRO
PRT Portugal
PRY Paraguay
PYF French Polynesia
QAT Qatar
REU Réunion
ROM Romania
RUS Russian Federation
RWA Rwanda
SAU Saudi Arabia
SDN Sudan
SEN Senegal
SGP Singapore
SGS South Georgia and South SS
SHN Saint Helena
SJM Svalbard and Jan Mayen Islands
SLB Solomon Islands
SLE Sierra Leone
SLV El Salvador
SMR San Marino
SOM Somalia
SPM Saint Pierre and Miquelon
SRB Serbia
SSD South Sudan
STP São Tomé and Príncipe
SUR Suriname
SVK Slovakia
SVN Slovenia
SWE Sweden
SWZ Swaziland
SYC Seychelles
SYR Syrian Arab Republic
TCA Turks and Caicos Islands
TCD Chad
TGO Togo
THA Thailand
TJK Tajikistan
TKL Tokelau
TKM Turkmenistan
TMP East Timor
TON Tonga
TPE Chinese Taipei
TTO Trinidad and Tobago
TUN Tunisia
TUR Turkey
TUV Tuvalu
TZA Tanzania
UAE United Arab Emirates
UGA Uganda
UK United Kingdom
UKR Ukraine
UMI US Minor Islands
URY Uruguay
USA United States of America
UZB Uzbekistan
VAT Holy See (Vatican City)
VCT Saint Vincent and the Grenadines
VEN Venezuela
VGB Virgin Islands (British)
VIR Virgin Islands (US)
VNM Vietnam
VUT Vanuatu
WLF Wallis and Futuna Islands
WSM Samoa
YEM Yemen
ZAF South Africa
ZMB Zambia
ZWE Zimbabwe

ACKNOWLEDGEMENTS

Editor-in-Chief
Craig Glenday

Senior Managing Editor
Stephen Fall

Layout Editors
Rob Dimery, Alice Peebles

Project Editors
Adam Millward, Ben Hollingum

Gaming Editor
Stephen Daultrey

Proofreader
Matthew White

Indexer
Marie Lorimer

Picture Editor
Michael Whitty

Deputy Picture Editor
Fran Morales

Picture Researchers
Saffron Fradley, Laura Nieberg

Talent Researcher
Jenny Langridge

VP Publishing
Jenny Heller

Director of Procurement
Patricia Magill

Publishing Manager
Jane Boatfield

Production Assistant
Thomas McCurdy

Production Consultant
Roger Hawkins

Printing & Binding
GGP Media GmbH, Germany

Design
Jon Addison, Nick Clark, Neal Cobourne, Nick Evans, Jane McKenna, Rebecca Buchanan Smith, Nigel Wright (XAB), Dan Prescott (Couper Street Type Co.)

Illustration
Tim Brown, William Donohoe, Valesca Ferrari, Tim Starkey

Original Photography
Cristian Barnett, Richard Bradbury, Daniel Deme, James Ellerker, Paul Michael Hughes, Shinsuke Kamioka, Ranald Mackechnie, Gil Montano, Kevin Scott Ramos, Ryan Schude, Walter Succu

CORPORATE OFFICE
Global President:
Alistair Richards

PROFESSIONAL SERVICES
Chief Financial Officer:
Alison Ozanne
Financial Controller:
Zuzana Reid
Account Receivable Manager:
Lisa Gibbs
Assistant Accountant:
Jess Blake
Accounts Payable Manager:
Victoria Aweh
Management Accountants:
Shabana Zaffar, Daniel Ralph
Trading Analysis Manager:
Andrew Wood
Head of Legal & Business Affairs: Raymond Marshall
Solicitor: Terence Tsang
Legal & Business Affairs Executive: Xiangyun Rablen
Office Manager: Jackie Angus
Director of IT: Rob Howe
Desktop Administrator:
Ainul Ahmed
Developer: Cenk Selim
Junior Developer: Lewis Ayers

GLOBAL BRAND STRATEGY
SVP Global Brand Strategy:
Samantha Fay

GLOBAL PRODUCT MARKETING
VP Global Product Marketing:
Katie Forde
B2B Product Marketing Manager: Tanya Batra
Digital Product Marketing Manager: Veronica Irons
Online Editor: Kevin Lynch
Community Manager:
Dan Thorne
Digital Video Producer:
Matt Musson
Designer: Jon Addison
Junior Designer:
Rebecca Buchanan Smith
Product Marketing Assistant:
Victor Fenes

TV & PROGRAMMING
Director of Global TV Content & Sales: Rob Molloy
Senior TV Distribution Manager: Denise Carter-Steel/ Caroline Percy
Senior TV Content Executive:
Jonathon Whitton

RECORDS MANAGEMENT TEAM
SVP Records: Marco Frigatti
Head of RMT Operations:
Jacqui Sherlock
Records Managers:
Sam Golin, Sam Mason, Victoria Tweedy, Chris Lynch, Corinne Burns, Mark McKinley
Database & Research Manager:
Carim Valerio
Adjudications Manager:
Ben Backhouse
Specialist Records Manager:
Anatole Baboukhian
Customer Service Managers:
Louise McLaren/Janet Craffey
Senior Project Manager:
Alan Pixsley
Program Manager – Attractions: Louise Toms
Project Manager:
Shantha Chinniah
Records Consultants:
Aleksandr Vypirailenko, Sophie Molloy
Official Adjudicators:
Eva Norroy, Lorenzo Veltri, Pravin Patel, Anna Orford,

Jack Brockbank, Fortuna Burke, Lucia Sinigagliesi, Şeyda Subaşı Gemici, Chris Sheedy, Sofia Greenacre, Evelyn Carrera, Michael Empric, Philip Robertson, Mai McMillan, Glenn Pollard, Justin Patterson, John Garland, Brittany Dunn

EMEA & APAC
SVP EMEA & APAC: Nadine Causey
VP Creative: Paul O'Neill
PR Director: Amarilis Whitty
PR Manager: Doug Male
Senior Publicist: Madalyn Bielfeld
UK & International Press Officer: Jamie Clarke
B2C Marketing Manager: Justine Tommey
B2C Marketing Executive: Christelle BeTrong
B2B Marketing Manager: Mawa Rodriguez
Head of Publishing Sales: John Pilley
Sales & Distribution Manager: Richard Stenning
Licensing Manager, Publishing: Emma Davies
Head of Commercial Sales: Sam Prosser
Commercial Account Managers: Lucie Pessereau, Roman Sosnovsky, Jessica Rae
Commercial Account Executive: Sadie Smith
Commercial Representative, India: Nikhil Shukla
Country Manager, MENA: Talal Omar
Project Manager: Samer Khallouf
B2B Marketing Manager: Leila Issa
Commercial Account Manager: Muhsen Jalal

AMERICAS
SVP Americas: Peter Harper
Publishing Sales & Product Director: Jennifer Gilmour
Head of Client Services: Amanda Mochan
Director of RMT – Latin America: Carlos Martinez
Head of RMT – North America: Kimberly Partrick
Account Managers: Nicole Pando, Alex Angert, Ralph Hannah
Commercial Representative, Latin America: Ralph Hannah
Junior Account Manager: Hanna Kubat
PR Manager: Kristen Ott
B2B Marketing Executive: Tavia Levy
Project Manager: Casey DeSantis
Records Manager: Annie Nguyen
HR & Office Manager: Kellie Ferrick

JAPAN
VP Japan: Erika Ogawa
Office Manager: Fumiko Kitagawa
Director of RMT: Kaoru Ishikawa
Project Manager: Aya McMillan
Records Managers: Mariko Koike, Gulnaz Ukassova
Designer: Momoko Cunneen
PR & Sales Promotion Manager: Kazami Kamioka
Digital & Publishing Content Manager: Takafumi Suzuki
Commercial Sales & Marketing Director: Vihag Kulshrestha
Marketing Executive: Asumi Funatsu
Account Manager: Takuro Maruyama
Senior Account Executive: Daisuke Katayama
Account Executive: Minami Ito

GREATER CHINA
President: Rowan Simons
HR & Office Manager: Tina Shi
Office Assistant: Kate Wang
Marketing Director: Sharon Yang
Digital Manager: Jacky Yuan
PR Assistant: Leila Wang
B2B Marketing Manager: Iris Hou
Marketing Executive: Tracy Cui
Head of RMT: Charles Wharton
Records Manager: Lisa Hoffman
Records Manager/ Project Co-ordinator: Fay Jiang
Content Director: Angela Wu
Commercial Director: Blythe Fitzwilliam
Senior Account Manager: Dong Cheng
Account Manager: Catherine Gao

ACKNOWLEDGEMENTS

British Library
Cataloguing-in-publication data: a catalogue record for this book is available from the British Library

1-910561-15-0
978-1-910561-15-7

Records are made to be broken – indeed, it is one of the key criteria for a record category – so if you find a record that you think you can beat, tell us about it by making a record claim. Find out how on pp.vii–xi. Always contact us before making a record attempt.

Check the official website – **www.guinnessworldrecords.com** – regularly for record-breaking news, plus video footage of record attempts. You can also join and interact with the Guinness World Records online community.

Sustainability
The paper used for this edition is derived from forestry responsibly managed by Holmen Paper (Sweden). Holmen work in accordance with certified management systems.

Guinness World Records Limited has a very thorough accreditation system for records verification. However, while every effort is made to ensure accuracy, Guinness World Records Limited cannot be held responsible for any errors contained in this work. Feedback from our readers on any point of accuracy is always welcomed.

Guinness World Records Limited uses both metric and imperial measurements. The sole exceptions are for some scientific data where metric measurements only are universally accepted, and for some sports data. Where a specific date is given, the exchange rate is calculated according to the currency values that were in operation at the time. Where only a year date is given, the exchange rate is calculated from 31 Dec of that year. "One billion" is taken to mean one thousand million.

Appropriate advice should always be taken when attempting to break or set records. Participants undertake records entirely at their own risk. Guinness World Records Limited has complete discretion over whether or not to include any particular record attempts in any of its publications. Being a Guinness World Records record holder does not guarantee you a place in any Guinness World Records publication.

OFFICIALLY AMAZING

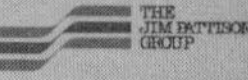

Guinness World Records would like to thank the following for their help in compiling this edition:

James Acraman; Roger Acraman; Alexa; Carmen Alfonzo de Hannah; Jamie Antoniou; Tarik "Cilvaringz" Azzougarh; Andrea Bánfi; Anthony Barbieri-Low (UCSB); API Laminates Ltd; Oliver Beatson; Theresa Bebbington; Bergsteigerschule Pontresina (Gian and Jan Peer); Brian Birch; Luke Boatfield; Joseph Boatfield; Ryan Boatfield; Brandon Boatfield; Betty Bond; Brighouse High School; Joe Brown; Saul Browne; Cartoon Museum, London; Ren and Una Cave; CERN (Frédérick Bordry, André David, Heather Gray, Rolf-Dieter Heuer, Joanna Iwanska, Kate Kahle, Abha Eli Phoboo); Frank Chambers; Martyn Chapman; Stuart Claxton; Clod Magazine; Adam and Carey Cloke; Collaboration Inc. (Mr Suzuki, Miho, Kyoto and all their colleagues); Connection Cars (Rob and Tracey Dunkerley); Grace Coryell (ESPN X Games); Cosplay Sky; Fiona Craven (Bluehat Group); David Crystal; Martyn Davis; Fernando Delgado; Denmaur Independent Papers Limited (Julian Townsend); Mrs M E Dimery; Amy S Dimstail; Christian Duarte; Warren Elsmore (BRICK); Europroduzione (Stefano and Orsetta); Europroduzione srl (Renato, Paola, Alessio, Gabriela, Marcy); Amelia and Toby Ewen; Benjamin Fall; Rebecca Fall; Jonathan Fargher; Jonathan de Ferranti; FJT Logistics Ltd (Ray Harper, Gavin Hennessy); Formulation Inc. (Yuko Hirai, Mr Suzuki, Kyoko, Miyabi); Forncett St Peter CEVA Primary School; Bob Fox; Marshall Gerometta; Martha Gifford; Damien Gildea; Global Eagle Entertainment; Paul Gravett; Great Pumpkin Commonwealth (Ian Paton, Dave Stelts); Victoria Grimsell; H J Lutcher Stark Center for Physical Culture & Sports; Quinton Hamel; Hampshire Sports and Prestige Cars; Amy Cecilia Hannah; Sophie Alexia Hannah; Bob Headland; Johanna Hessling; The Himalayan Database; HoloLens Technology Co., Ltd; Marsha K Hoover; Hotel Cour du Corbeau, Strasbourg; Colin Hughes; Icebar by Icehotel Stockholm; ICM (Michael, Greg and Greg); Integrated Colour Editions Europe (Roger Hawkins, Susie Hawkins, Clare Merryfield); International Committee for the Study of Human Strength (ICSHS); Rich Johnson (Bleeding Cool); Enid Jones; Michael Jungbluth; Res Kahraman; Richard Kebabjian (www.planecrashinfo.com); John Kendall (www.rubymurray.org); Harry Kikstra; Rex Lane; Orla Langton; Thea Langton; David Lardi; Lionsgate (Bianca Boey, Emma Micklewright); Frederick Horace Lazell; Kuo-Yu Liang (Diamond Comic Distributors); Lion Television (Simon, Jeremy, Nick, Kirsty, Sarah, Millie, Susan, Tom, Ruth); Rüdiger Lorenz; Jason Mander (Global Web Index); Jonathan Mann; Kez Margrie; Christian de Marliave; Dr Niki Mavropoulou; Dave McAleer; Helen McCarthy; Mercedes-Benz Hanover; Sevim Mollova; Harriet Molloy; Sophie, Joshua, Florence and Amara Molloy; Colin Monteath; Alan Moore; Leah Moore; Dan Mudford; Oakleigh Park School of Swimming; Victoria (Tori) Oakley; Percy Inc; Olly Pike; Abhishek Ponia (International Premier Tennis League); James Pratt; Dr Robert Pullar (University of Aveiro); Harro Ranter (Aviation Safety Network – www.aviation-safety.net); Brandon Reed; John Reed (World Sailing Speed Record Council); Martyn Richards; Joe Rodriguez; the Rogers; Royal Museums Greenwich (Emma Gough, Rory McEvoy, Sheryl Twigg); Edward and Thomas Rushmere; RZA (aka Robert Diggs); Dr Michael Delle Selve (FEVE – the European Glass Container Federation); Michael Serra (São Paulo FC); Ben Shires; Shotokan Karate, Barnet; Dr Marios Skarvelakis (D-Waste); Mr Pedro Sousa (Quercus); Spectratek Technologies, Inc. (Terry Conway, Mike Foster); Glenn Speer; Bill Spindler; St Chad's CEVA Primary School; Samantha Stacey; Peter Stanbury; Chris Staros (IDW/Top Shelf Productions); David Stelts; Ray Stevenson; Kay Sugihara; Amy Swanson; Sebastian Sylvester; TG4; Holly, Daisy and Charlie Taylor; Simon Thompson; Ellan Tibbs; Terry and Janice "Jan" Todd; Martyn Tovey; UPM Plattling, Germany; Visual Data (Anita and Amy); Sierra Voss; Jonah Weiland (Comic Book Resources); Wensum Junior School; Sevgi and Lara White; William, Charlie, Sally and Poppy Whelton; the Whittons; Beverly Williams (Production Suite); Mr Jim Wood (American Iron & Steel Institute); Daniel Woods; Fraser Wright (IMG Tennis); Nigel Wright (XAB Design); WSSA; Madeleine Wuschech; Freddie and Stanley Wynne; Matthew D Zolnowski (J A Green & Company)

Picture credits

i: Ranald Mackechnie/GWR **iv–vii**: Reuters, Paul Michael Hughes/GWR, Alamy, Ranald Mackechnie/GWR, Daniel Deme/GWR, Supercell, Getty **vii–xi**: Paul Michael Hughes/GWR, Europroducciones, CCTV, Ranald Mackechnie/GWR, Diana Santamaria **xii–xix**: Alamy, Matt Groening **xx–xxiv**: Alamy **1–3**: Alamy, Thinkstock **4–9**: Tim Brown, Map Resources, William Donohoe, TopFoto, Alamy, Bridgeman **10–14**: Alamy, AP/PA, Cabinet Magazine **15–19**: Alamy, Paulina Holmgren, Reuters, Bethel Area Chamber of Commerce **20–24**: Corbis, Alistair McMillan, iStock, Shutterstock, Aurora Photos **25–29**: Getty, Alamy, Rex AP/PA **30–34**: Shutterstock, Alamy, Getty, Reuters, PA **35–40**: AFP, Euronav, Zhong & Huang, Corbis, Reuters **41–43**: Amanda Brewer **44–49**: Tim Brown, Matthew H Adjemian, William Donohoe, Alamy, Shutterstock **50–54**: Alamy, Rex, FLPA, Getty, Corbis, Getty **55–59**: Fotolia, Alamy, FLPA, Reuters, SuperStock **60–65**: Nature PL, Getty, Photoshot, Alamy **66–70**: Ronai Rocha, Alamy, SuperStock, Science Photo Library, Nature PL, Steve Woodhall, Manchester Museum, **71–75**: Alamy, Ardea, iStock, US Navy, Plymouth University **76–80**: Reuters, FLPA, iStock, Alamy, Getty **81–86**: Alamy, cowyeouw/Flickr, Nature PL, NHPA **87–92**: Alamy, Blair Hedges, Rex, Discover Fossils **93–98**: Getty, FLPA, Alamy, Science Photo Library, SuperStock, Mandy Lowder, Reuters **99–101**: Paul Michael Hughes/GWR **102–107**: Shutterstock, Alamy **108–112**: Reuters, Alamy, Jessica McGowan/GWR **113–117**: Paul Michael Hughes/GWR, Ranald Mackechnie/GWR, Prakash Mathema/GWR **118–122**: Gil Montano/GWR, Ranald Mackechnie/GWR **123–127**: Abraham Joffe/Diimex, Walter Succu/GWR, Dermablend, Jorge Silva/Reuters, Cristian Barnett/GWR **128–132**: Alamy, Mirrorpix, AP/PA, Mary Ellen Stumpfl, Getty, AP/PA, NASA **133–137**: Memory Sports, Paul Michael Hughes/GWR **137–139**: Roger Baer, Alamy **146–148**: Richard Bradbury/GWR **149–151**: Andi Southam/Sky **155–157**: Getty, Paul Michael Hughes/GWR **158–160**: Fitness Sutra, Paul Michael Hughes/GWR **161–163**: Paul Michael Hughes/GWR **164–166**: Erik Svensson, Christian Horn **167–169**: Ryan Schude/GWR, Andreas Lander, Paul Michael Hughes/GWR **170–172**: Paul Michael Hughes/GWR **173–175**: ESPN, Paul Michael Hughes/GWR, Sandro Zangrando **176–180**: Paul Michael Hughes/GWR, Matt Crossick, Ranald Mackechnie/GWR, Ryan Schude/GWR **181–183**: Kevin Scott Ramos/GWR **184–189**: William Donohoe, Nigel Andrews, Alamy **190–193**: Ranald Mackechnie/GWR, Richard Bradbury/GWR, Paul Michael Hughes/GWR, Philip Robertson/GWR **199–203**: Alamy, Ranald Mackechnie/GWR, Getty, Kevin Scott Ramos/GWR **204–208**: National Geographic, Getty **209–213**: Steve Zylius, Alamy, Andres Allain **214–218**: Michel Bega, Ranald Mackechnie/GWR **219–223**: Kevin Scott Ramos/GWR, Ranald Mackechnie/GWR, Cindy Goodman/North Shore News, AP/PA, Paul Michael Hughes/GWR **224–228**: Shropshire Star, Reuters **229–231**: Reuters, Alamy **232–236**: Getty, Alamy, Disney/Rex, New Line Cinema, Marvel/Rex **237–241**: Getty, iStock, Erik Kabik, Reuters, Alamy **242–246**: Richard Bradbury/GWR, Costa Coffee, Matt Writtle **247–251**: Walt Disney Pictures, US Navy, Getty, Jean Leon Gerome Ferris **252–256**: Reuters, Columbia Pictures, Alamy, Getty **257–261**: USAF, Alamy, AP/PA, PA **116**: Caters, Reuters, Omar Almarrie, Alamy, Lindsey Hoshaw, NOAA **267–271**: James Ellerker/GWR, Kevin Scott Ramos/GWR, Ranald Mackechnie/GWR **272–276**: James Ellerker/GWR, Shinsuke Kamioka/GWR, Paul Michael Hughes/GWR **277–279**: Richard Bradbury/GWR **280–283**: Tim Brown, Getty, Alamy **284–288**: NASA, Iwan Baan, Red Bull, Reuters, Visit PA Dutch Country, Camera Press, Rex Features, Alamy **289–293**: Alamy, Getty **294–298**: Fotolia, Alamy **299–303**: Alamy, Brightsource, AP/PA, Getty, PA **304–308**: Alamy, Getty, Corbis **309–313**: PA **314–318**: Daniel Deme/GWR, Paul Michael Hughes/GWR, Cristian Barnett/GWR **319–322**: Daniel Deme/GWR, Alamy, Paul Michael Hughes/GWR **323–325**: Corbis **326–331**: Tim Brown, Alamy, William Donohoe **332–336**: Michael McAlpine/Princeton University, Getty, Frank Wojciechowski, Steffen Richter **337–341**: Alamy, Rex, Science Photo Library **342–346**: AP/PA, Getty, Bridgeman, Science Photo Library, US National Library of Medicine, Institute For Forensic Art, Alamy **347–352**: Johan Reinhard, Getty, Museum of London, Alamy **352–356**: AP/PA, IBM Research, USAF, Alamy **357–361**: USAF, Alamy, Reuters **362–366**: Getty, NASA, Reuters, Science Photo Library, Alamy **367–370**: Ranald Mackechnie/GWR, Richard Bradbury/GWR **371–373**: Lucasfilm **374–379**: Alamy, Andrew Jameson **380–384**: Universal Pictures, New Line Cinema, Marvel Enterprises, Twentieth Century Fox, DreamWorks Animation, Paramount Pictures, Alamy, Marvel Studios, Reuters **385–388**: LEGO, Alamy, Zoltán Simon (SimonZ), Ryan Schude/

GWR **389–393**: Alamy, Getty, Reuters, Reuters, Walt Disney Pictures **398–402**: Paul Michael Hughes/GWR, Alamy **403–407**: George Kalinsky, Getty, Joi Ito, PA, Alamy **408–412**: Paul Michael Hughes/GWR, Reuters, Getty, Rex, HBO **413–417**: Reuters, Matt Crossick, Marvel Entertainment, Alamy **418–421**: Harambee Institute of Science & Technology, Getty **422–430**: Sony Music, Disney, Reuters, Getty, Tom McShane, Rex **188**: Red Bull **434–437**: Tim Brown, NASA **438–442**: Sarah McNair-Landry, Simon Foster, Tim Soper, South Pole Epic, Ranald Mackechnie/GWR, PA **443–447**: Shinsuke Kamioka/GWR, Alamy, Rex, Paul Michael Hughes/GWR, Getty, Reuters **448–453**: Marcin Kin/Source, The North Face **453–457**: Ellen Hoke, Richard Rossiter, Greg Roberts, Corbis, Getty **458–462**: Reuters, Scuttlebutt Sailing News **463–467**: AP/PA, Paul Michael Hughes/GWR, Rex **468–472**: Corbis, The Seattle Times, Robert Carp, AP, Alamy **473–475**: Reuters, Alamy **476–481**: Tim Starkey, AP/PA, Terry Todd/Rouge Fitness, Alamy **482–486**: Getty, Alamy, Reuters **487–491**: Reuters **214**: AP/PA, Getty, Alamy, Reuters **497–501**: Reuters, Getty, AP/PA, **502–506**: Alamy, Lupi Spuma, William Donohoe, Getty, Reuters **507–511**: ESPN, Red Bull, Dreamstime, Paul Michael Hughes/GWR **512–516**: Alamy, Reuters, Getty, AP/PA **517–521**: Reuters, Alamy, Getty **522–528**: Reuters, Alamy, Getty, Trevor Adams/GWR **528–532**: Reuters, Alamy, Getty, John Brooks, AP/PA **533–537**: Getty, Reuters, Topham, **538–542**: Getty, Rex, Alamy, **543–553**: Alamy, Phil Greig, Reuters, AP/PA, Getty, Alamy **554–558**: Alamy, Giorgio Scala, AP/PA, Joel Marklund/Bildbyrån, Russell McKinnon, Reuters **559–563**: Getty, Reuters, Philip Robertson/GWR, Alamy, **564–569**: Getty, Alamy, Reuters **570–573**: Alamy, Red Bull, Ranald Mackechnie/GWR, Richard Bradbury/GWR, Barry Gossage, Paul Michael Hughes/GWR **254**: Shutterstock, Getty, Reuters, Alamy

INDEX

Bold entries in the index indicate a main entry on a topic; **BOLD CAPITALS** indicate an entire chapter.

B

C

E

F

G

H

J

K

L

M

N

O

P

S

U

V

W

X

Y

Z

Q&As

SENSE OF SCALE

Scoping out the scale of the universe, from the smallest to the largest

0.00000000000000000000000000000000001 m Size at which space "boils" into a frothy "quantum foam", according to quantum mechanics theories

0.00000000000000000000001 m Neutrino, the **lightest known particle**, weighing a maximum of 0.000000000000000000000000000000000000018 kg

0.00000000000005 m Diameter of the negatively charged electron

0.000000000000015 m Nuclear diameter of uranium (U), the **heaviest naturally occurring element**

0.000000000025 m Atomic radius of helium (He), the first of the noble gases and the **most inert element**

0.0000000005 m Median wavelength of X-rays, at the higher-frequency/lower-wavelength end of the electromagnetic spectrum

0.000000003 m Width of a single DNA molecule; unravelled, all of the DNA in your body would stretch from Earth to the Sun many times

0.00000013 m Diameter of the influenza (flu) virus; the **worst influenza epidemic** killed at least 30–50 million people worldwide in 1918–19

0.0000015 m Length of the Y chromosome in humans; its presence or absence determines whether you develop into a male or a female

0.000007 m Diameter of an erythrocyte, aka red blood cell; these round cells transport oxygen and carbon dioxide around the body

0.0001 m Thickness of a human hair

0.00011 m Thickness of a US dollar bill

0.00075 m Width of *Thiomargarita namibiensis* (sulphur pearl of Namibia), the **largest bacterium**; it is visible to the naked eye

0.0015 m Diameter of a typical raindrop; the **largest raindrops recorded** measured 0.0086 m – or 8.6 mm (0.338 in) – wide, in Sep 1995 in Brazil and Jul 1999 in the Marshall Islands

0.005 m Length of a grain of rice

0.0096 m Height of a single LEGO® brick

0.024 m Diameter of the human eye

0.045 m Length of a Savi's pygmy shrew (*Suncus etruscus*), the **smallest land mammal** – about the size of your thumb

0.05 m Length of the wingless queen of the fulvous driver ant (*Dorylus fulvus*), the **largest ant species**

0.0604 m Diameter of a 12-US-fl-oz (355-ml) drinks can

0.15 m	Height of an ostrich egg, the **largest bird egg**; despite this, it is also the **smallest egg compared with body weight**, at just 1.4–1.5% of the adult bird's weight
0.228 m	Maximum diameter of a FIFA-approved size 5 soccer ball (circumference must be between 0.68 m and 0.70 m)
0.5 m	Median height of a full-term baby born in a Western country
0.628 m	Height of Jyoti Kisanji Amge (IND), the **shortest living woman**
1.118 m	Zeus the Great Dane (USA, 2008–14), the **tallest dog ever**
1.65 m	Height of the average human female
2.51 m	Height of Sultan Kösen (TUR), the **tallest living person**
2.75 m	Wing-span of a swan
4.16 m	Height to the shoulder of the **largest land mammal** specimen: a bull elephant shot in Mucusso, Angola, on 7 Nov 1974; it was estimated to have weighed 12.24 tonnes (26,984 lb)
5.33 m	**Longest beard ever**, grown by Hans N Langseth (NOR, 1846–1927); now housed in the Smithsonian Institution (USA)
9.14 m	Length of a London Routemaster double-decker bus
10 m	Length of the **longest snake** – a reticulated python (*Python reticulatus*) shot in Celebes (Sulawesi), Indonesia, in 1912
20.22 m	Height of the Great Sphinx of Giza in Egypt – the **largest monolithic sculpture** (see p.295)
50 m	Height of the Christ the Redeemer statue in Rio de Janeiro, Brazil
50 m	Length of an Olympic swimming pool
51 m	Height of Niagara Falls, on the border of the USA and Canada; with 22.5 million tourists annually, it's the world's **most-visited waterfall**
70.4 m	Length of a Boeing 747 jumbo jet
93 m	Height of the Statue of Liberty including the base (from the ground to tip of torch)
109 m	Length of the *International Space Station*; it is the **largest space station** ever built, with a mass of 419,455 kg
110.6 m	Height, including the module, of *Saturn V*: the **largest rocket**

115.54 m	Height (in 2006) of Hyperion, the **tallest living tree**; the coast redwood (*Sequoia sempervirens*) is located i Redwood National Park in California, USA
146.7 m	Original height of the Pyramid of Khufu (aka Great Pyramid) at Giza in Egypt, the **tallest pyramid**; erosion and vandalism have reduced its height to 137.5 m (451 ft) today
269 m	Length of RMS *Titanic*
381 m	Architectural height of the Empire State Building in New York, USA; with its pinnacle (spire), it attains a total height of 443.2 m
399 m	Length of the Mærsk Triple E class, the **longest container ships**; the lead vessel is the MV *Mærsk Mc-Kinney Møller*, which launched in Feb 2013
541.3 m	Height of One World Trade Center, aka the "Freedom Tower", in Lower Manhattan, New York City, USA – the **tallest building completed in 2014** (see pp.323–25)
828 m	Height of the **tallest building** (and **tallest man-made structure on land**), the Burj Khalifa, in Dubai, UAE
1,600 m	Average depth of the Grand Canyon, the **largest land gorge**; it extends 446 km (277 mi) across north-central Arizona, USA
4,807 m	Height of Mont Blanc on the border of France and Italy: the highest point in the Alps and the highest point in Western Europe
8,848 m	Height of Everest (aka Sagarmāthā or Chomolungma), Earth's **highest mountain**; it is located in the Himalayas
10,911 m	Depth of "Challenger Deep" – the **deepest point in the sea**, located in the Pacific Ocean's Mariana Trench
24,000 m	Typical diameter of a neutron star, the **smallest type of star**; incredibly dense, a piece of neutron star material the size of a grain of sand would have the mass of a skyscraper
42,195 m	Distance run in an official marathon; instituted by the IAAF in 1921, it is based on the length of the course at the 1908 Summer Olympics in London, UK
100,000 m	Altitude of the Kármán Line, the official boundary between Earth and space, according to the Fédération Aéronautique Internationale (FAI)
342,000 m	Straight-line distance between London and Paris
354,000 m	Average altitude of the *International Space Station*; at a cost of c. \$100 bn (£66.7 bn), the *ISS* is the **most expensive man-made object**
446,000 m	Length of the Grand Canyon, the world's **largest land gorge**; it extends from Marble Gorge to the Grand Wash Cliffs in north-central Arizona, USA

507,000 m	Length of the Hudson River, which flows through New York, USA, and drains into the Atlantic
1,030,000 m	Length of the Caspian Sea, the world's **largest lake**
2,324,000 m	Diameter of the dwarf planet Pluto – about two-thirds the size of the Moon
2,600,000 m	Length of the Great Barrier Reef off Queensland, north-eastern Australia, the world's **longest reef**
3,460,000 m	Main-line length of the Great Wall of China, the world's **longest wall**; it has a further 3,530 km (2,193 mi) of branches and spurs
3,477,000 m	Diameter of Earth's moon; at c. 0.27 times the diameter of Earth, it is the **largest moon compared with its planet**
3,932,000 m	Distance between New York and Los Angeles in the USA
6,670,000 m	Length of the Nile, the **longest river**; it passes through 11 countries in North Africa before emptying into the Mediterranean Sea
6,779,000 m	Diameter of Mars, the planet in our Solar System with the **most similar environment to Earth**
12,756,000 m	Diameter of the Earth
40,000,000 m	Diameter of the Great Red Spot on the planet Jupiter, the **largest anticyclone in the Solar System**, which is rapidly shrinking
49,244,000 m	Diameter of Neptune, at 4.5 billion km (2.8 billion mi) from the Sun, the **farthest planet in the Solar System**
139,822,000 m	Mean diameter of Jupiter, the **largest planet in the Solar System**
201,695,000 m	Diameter of the red dwarf Proxima Centauri; excluding our Sun, it is the **closest star to Earth**
384,000,000 m	Distance between the Earth and the Moon
1,391,684,000 m	Diameter of the Sun
97,000,000,000 m	Total length of the road network in the USA
40,000,000,000 m	Diameter of Polaris (North Star)
3,000,000,000,000 m	Diameter of the red supergiant VY Canis Majoris, the **largest star**; it is more than 2,000 times larger than our own Sun
9,460,730,472,580,800 m	One light year: the distance that light travels in a vacuum in one year (a measure of distance, not time)
1,140,000,000,000,000,000,000 m	Maximum diameter of the Milky Way, the barred spiral galaxy that is home to our Solar System
53,000,000,000,000,000,000,000 m	Diameter of the supergiant elliptical galaxy IC 1101, the **largest known galaxy**, with c. 100 trillion stars
879,850,000,000,000,000,000,000,000 m	Diameter of the observable universe

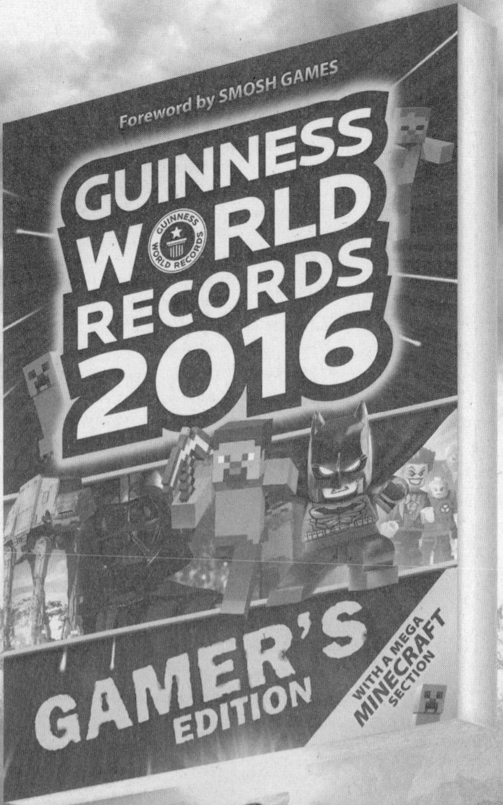

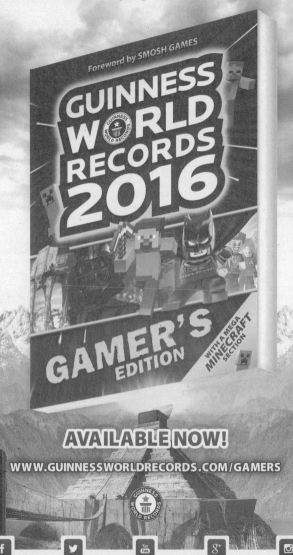